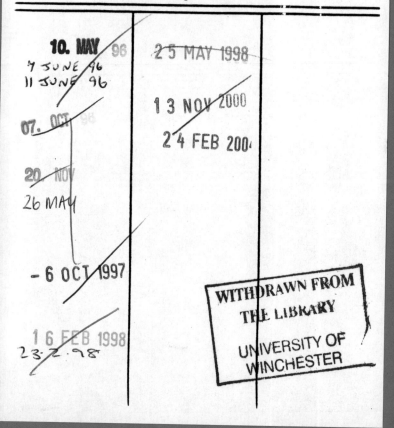

WILLIAM MORRIS

WILLIAM MORRIS

A Life for Our Time

◆

FIONA MacCARTHY

faber and faber

First published in 1994
by Faber and Faber Limited
3 Queen Square London WC1N 3AU

Photoset in Linotype Imprint by Parker Typesetting Service, Leicester
Printed in England by Clays Ltd, St Ives plc

© Fiona MacCarthy, 1994

Fiona MacCarthy is hereby identified as author of this work
in accordance with Section 77 of the Copyright, Designs and
Patents Act 1988

A CIP record for this book
is available from the British Library

ISBN 0–571–14250–8

Title page: Wood engraving by William Morris, probably from a Burne-Jones
illustration, used for the title page of *The Earthly Paradise*.

2 4 6 8 10 9 7 5 3

Contents

Introduction

When Morris was dying one of his physicians diagnosed his disease as 'simply being William Morris, and having done more work than most ten men'. Morris was one of the best-known and most prolific Victorian poets. He was the greatest artist-craftsman of his period. He ran a successful decorating and manufacturing business and he kept a high-profile central London retail shop. Morris was also a passionate social reformer, an early environmentalist, an educationalist and would-be feminist; at the age of fifty he crossed the 'river of fire' to become a revolutionary Socialist. There is something almost suspect in this sheer range of activity. In an age of ever-narrowing specialization Morris's versatility is difficult to grasp.

Over the past five years of research on this biography my aim has been to reclaim Morris in the detail of his idiosyncrasy and *strangeness* as he appeared to his contemporaries and to argue that his highly original, painfully heroic progress through life impinges on us still, from old Socialists to new conservationists. His largeness of vision is the key to it. Morris was his own emblem of wholeness. He wanted to integrate the city with the country, the present with the past, the public and the personal moralities. Most of all he was concerned with proper human occupation, whether going under the name of work or play. In the late twentieth century throughout the West this is our urgent problem. Technological advance has made ordinary skill and modest pride in work redundant. But redundancy of people brings the threat of disconnection from life.

Morris knew a great deal but stayed peculiarly innocent. People noted how even in old age he looked like a large child. If my book dwells on Morris's childhood this is conscious, since the memories of childhood permeate his later visions, creeping through his letters, edging out into his poetry. His Utopian novel, *News from Nowhere*, is a shimmeringly hopeful and a very childlike book. Morris kept his mind open to a different *sort* of future. His oddness, and importance, lies in this disengagement from contemporary structures. Like the child on the beach he could knock down the whole sandcastle, envisaging a finer one erected in its place.

Even to his contemporaries Morris seemed peculiar. Victorian memoirs overflow with references to his 'rum and indescribable deportment', his 'tempestuous and exacting company', his disconcerting habit of pacing up and down a room like a caged lion to work off his superabundant energy. 'Beg Pardon, Sir, were you ever Captain of the *Sea Swallow*?' asked a fireman, accosting him in a street in Kensington. 'I was not,' replied Morris. But in his robust blue seaman's jacket, with his rollicking gait, he could quite well have been.

Recent books about Morris have tended to take specialist views of him. We have had the Marxist Morris, the Jungian Morris, the Freudian Morris. He has now been appropriated by the Greens. The layers of theory have obscured his 'whole' personality. I hope to reverse this process, to unwrap him and describe him and, if possible, to penetrate a little of his mystery in a way that no one has attempted since J. W. Mackail, Morris's first biographer, whose fine two-volume *Life of William Morris* was published in 1899. If I have not managed to recapture Morris's strange vigour, his talent for bracing 'the nerves of the flaccid', his extraordinary veerings from Nordic stoicism to an almost female tenderness, his ebbs and flows from rampageousness to sweetness, then this book will be no good.

Morris had a sense of place so acute as to be almost a disability. Places clung to him. When one of his places was endangered, in the sense of being demolished or crassly redeveloped, he felt it as a human grief. Much of the research for this biography has taken the form of voyages around the places where Morris lived and worked and travelled. Readers may find it eccentric that I have listed places in my sources, but I have found them as crucial as literary sources, often more so. There is no real way of understanding Morris until you can see, almost with his eyes, the particular pattern of a landscape, the relationship of buildings, the precise lie of the land. Without tramping around Kelmscott, finding the hidden churches that so delighted Morris, the glimpses of the river, the mediaeval barns, it would be difficult to comprehend the hold that

Kelmscott had on him. Without retracing his journeys around Northern France and Iceland it would be hardly possible to see how the places he returned to, in his imagination, lasted all his life.

Morris had a deep attachment to *things*, and a huge reservoir of knowledge of their history. The Bodleian Library in Oxford as well as the then South Kensington Museum deferred to his judgement. He was in the great tradition of the Victorian connoisseur. But unlike most connoisseurs he was himself a maker. With an almost manic industriousness Morris set out to rediscover lost techniques for fabricating, in succession: embroidery; stained glass; illumination and calligraphy; textile dyeing, printing and weaving; high-warp tapestry. The last few years of his life were spent in reviving hand-printing at his own Kelmscott Press. Morris's objects, like his places, have loomed large in my sources. I have tried to steep myself in his own sense of tangibility, scrutinizing, stroking – when permitted by their owners – the things that Morris made. I began by imagining, as most people imagine, his wallpapers and chintzes as the peak of his achievement, together with the most spectacular of the Kelmscott Press editions. After searching out his less accessible artefacts (my notebooks bulge with details of over a hundred visits) I believe the glorious sequence of Morris & Co. stained-glass windows surpasses the rest. It is the logical development of Pre-Raphaelite painting, vividly pictorial, art beyond the easel, telling stories, conveying information even to the Victorian illiterate.

Words too poured out of Morris. There was a neurotic basis to his fluency. On a good day he could write 1,000 lines of verse. (Most serious writers are content with 1,000 *words* of *prose*.) After his death his work was assembled into twenty-four volumes, an act of devotion by his second daughter May. He is seldom read these days, outside anthologies. I believe this is mistaken. I would not press the claims of Morris's own favourite *Sigurd the Volsung*; it is too large, too chant-like. Volsungs are out of fashion. *Sigurd* sounds as if composed in transit, and may well have been; Morris frequently wrote verse on trains between engagements or on the swaying seat of a London omnibus. But there is much to reward the modern reader in Morris's early poems, *The Defence of Guenevere*, short, spare, edgy narratives of violence and loss. And most of all his 1890s' novels repay reading. *The Wood beyond the World* (1894); *The Water of the Wondrous Isles* (1895); *The Well at the World's End* (written in 1896, the year of Morris's death): these are fantasy stories, early science fiction, written in a curiously archaic language. James Joyce, who admired Morris, used it as a thesaurus. Morris's magic stories are dream-sequences, symbolist and surrealist. It is time they were reprinted. They are as modernist as Morris ever comes.

In the century since his death there has been a long battle for the emotional ownership of Morris. Perhaps more than any other Victorian celebrity he has been the victim of the keepers of the flame, people anxious to play down – or even up – his revolutionary Socialism. Foremost among these were the Burne-Jones family, the widow and descendants of Morris's close friend since Oxford, the painter Sir Edward Burne-Jones. In 1934, at the opening of Morris's centenary exhibition at the Victoria and Albert Museum, Lady Burne-Jones's nephew, Stanley Baldwin, a former – and future – Conservative prime minister, succeeded in making a speech that did not mention Morris's political activities at all.

It was with family support that the commission to write the authorized biography of Morris went to J. W. Mackail, Burne-Jones's son-in-law, an academic and civil servant, translator of the *Aeneid* and author of *Select Epigrams from the Greek Anthology*. Mackail was at the time employed in the Education Department, where he was an assistant secretary from 1903 to 1919. He was also Professor of Poetry at Oxford from 1906 to 1911. His biography, in many ways sensitive and generous, is understandably cagey on the politics. Mackail was the originator of the view, widely accepted over the next few decades, that Morris's membership of, first, the revolutionary Democratic Federation, then the Socialist League, were aberrations from which he soon recovered to enjoy a golden twilight of renewed artistic and literary activity. Mackail produced the happy ending where Morris, in old age, became himself again.

Abetting the Burne-Jones faction, in what amounted to a conspiracy of memory, was Sydney Cockerell, Director of the Fitzwilliam Museum in Cambridge from 1908 to 1937. Cockerell was knighted in 1934. The first step in his remarkably successful journey upwards had been his appointment in 1894, then an eager but unqualified young man, as Morris's secretary at the Kelmscott Press. Cockerell was self-appointed chief of Morris's literary executors. A small proportion of the hundred or so Socialist lectures had been published. Cockerell discouraged May Morris from including any more of them in her edition of the *Collected Works*, using a typically unctuous argument:

My view about these volumes is that much of your father's writing in his later years was hasty and was intended to be ephemeral and that the three existing volumes of lectures contained the greater part of what he wished to stand as his message on art and socialism.

May Morris did include some of the lectures, in defiance. In her later 1936 collection *William Morris, Artist, Writer, Socialist* she printed more of them. This is the volume with the brilliantly mischievous preface, 'William Morris as I Knew Him', by Bernard Shaw.

There is still no full edition of Morris's lectures, though these contain some of the most splendid of his writings as he grapples with ideas and formulates a policy, pushed to the limits of his clarity and passion by the prospect of addressing by no means captive audiences, some of them virtually uneducated. Even more disgracefully there is no complete published collection of his enormous output of editorials, articles, propaganda playlets, his jobbing journalism for the Socialist cause. To read these, one has to thumb through the yellowing copies of *Commonweal* and *Justice* in the socialist libraries of Clerkenwell and Manchester and Amsterdam. They are uneven, often careless, vehement, exhilarating, revealing an unknown, unbuttoned, unselfconscious Morris. Raymond Williams once described him as a 'generalized swearer'. These political diatribes show what an accomplished and resourceful swearer he actually was.

We do at least have easy access to his letters, in the comprehensive and meticulous edition Professor Norman Kelvin of New York City College and University has been amassing since 1965. I am, I think, the first biographer of Morris to have made full use of this resource. Indeed I often wonder how I could have embarked on this enterprise without it, since the letters give the key to Morris's inner feelings, often so well hidden, and resound with his oddities and quirkiness of language. Through the letters we arrive at Morris's authentic voice. They finally disprove the Mackail/Burne-Jones confection that Morris's Socialism was a temporary madness. Read through in their long sequence, they show convincingly that, far from being an aberration, Morris's progression from the heart of the mercantile establishment (his father was a bill broker) to the forefront of late Victorian Socialist agitation in Britain had a grand inevitability.

The conspiracy of silence has extended to William Morris's marriage. Morris married Jane Burden, the daughter of an Oxford stablehand, in

xi

1859 when he was twenty-five. Mackail was, not surprisingly, circum-spect about it. Marital troubles were not the subject matter of official biographies of the 1890s. Janey Morris was living when he wrote his book on Morris, and she did not die until 1914. He was faced with an additional family complication: how far Morris did, or did not, turn for consolation to Mackail's own mother-in-law, Georgiana Burne-Jones. As Mackail discovered more and more unpublishable details about the past *amours* of the older generation he alternated between fascination and frustration: 'How extraordinarily interesting one could make the story, if one were going to die the day before it was published.'

In the circumstances it is indeed surprising that he nevertheless gives us some impression that William and Janey's marriage was an anguished one, suggesting diplomatically that his readers should look for an account of it in the more melancholy of Morris's poems. The full extent of his unhappiness, and his fortitude and generosity in facing it, is only now being revealed, bit by bit and gradually, as the national libraries yield up their collections of confidential papers, under the fifty-year embargo rule.

In 1964 the British Museum's collection of letters from Dante Gabriel Rossetti to Jane Morris became available for consultation. The sealed collection of Wilfrid Scawen Blunt's papers at the Fitzwilliam Museum in Cambridge was first opened in 1972. As these papers indicate, Rossetti and Blunt had been, in succession, Janey's lovers in Morris's lifetime. Morris's most recent biographer, Jack Lindsay, would in theory have had access to both caches of material. But in his biography, published in 1975, he is obviously unaware of Janey's exact relationship with Blunt.

In his personal relations Morris was very reticent. He was the inar-ticulate Englishman personified. There is something horribly ironic about Janey's need to turn to two of the most notoriously honey-tongued philanderers of the age. Reading her correspondence with Rossetti and with Blunt it becomes obvious that their male bravado and sexual attentiveness gave Janey a self-confidence that Morris, with his shyness and his multitude of energetic preoccupations, patently did not. With her lovers Janey blossoms, becomes tender, even witty. The failure of his marriage caused Morris considerable pain. What we do not know is how exactly he arrived at his ideas of the non-possessiveness of sexual relationships: by natural progression of his thought? Or by bitter force of circumstance? In 1886 Morris wrote a famous letter on sexual relations, in which he insists that copulation is 'worse than beastly' unless it is the outcome of natural desires and kindliness, in effect abrogating the legally enforceable Victorian male insistence on marital rights. His friend and publisher F. S. Ellis suggested in the 1880s that Morris's opinions on the relations of the sexes had altered. His views in the old days were by no means 'the same as he professes to hold now'.

The Morris family's health has been another taboo subject. Physical debilities were not within the remit of the Victorian biographer. Despite the effect they had on Morris's day-to-day domestic life, Mackail did not feel it would be proper to investigate either Morris's intermittent rages and trances, or the epileptic attacks which dramatically affected his elder daughter Jenny from her mid-teens onwards, virtually incapacitating her. As Mackail maintained to Cockerell, assuming full agreement:

The fluctuations of illness are certainly no matter for permanent record, either in his own case or in that of others; one of the sources of embarrassment in his more intimate letters is the perpetual recurrence of Jenny's state of health from day to day.

The first public intimation that Morris's legendary rages were in fact eclampsia, a form of epilepsy, was given only in 1949, in a review in *The Observer* by Bernard Shaw who went on to suggest that Morris's desperation over Jenny's illness was caused by his conviction that she had inherited it. He felt himself to blame.

There remains the mystery of the ill health of Mrs Morris, who took to the sofa in 1869, at the age of twenty-nine, and never really left it. The details of her treatment at the German spa town of Bad Ems suggest her problems were gynaecological in origin. But the ease with which Janey could spring back into normal activity, with Rossetti or with Blunt, able suddenly to walk for many miles across the countryside, suggests her illnesses were psychological as well.

The effects of his invalid household upon Morris were complex and far-reaching. Undoubtedly it deepened his poetic imagination and his capacity for sympathy; it is plausible to argue that his domestic troubles sharpened his awareness of the unfortunate in general, helping to propel him into political activity. But at the same time his household of the ailing put obvious constraints on his own freedom of manoeuvre. He remained the capitalist father of the family, riding out the inevitable charges of political inconsistency, and one's admiration for his sheer productivity is redoubled in the light of these domestic handicaps.

The most interesting and in some ways enigmatic of Morris's three women was his second daughter May. As a girl May had been a famous beauty. She appears in the centre of Burne-Jones's lascivious assemblage of dream women in his large oil painting *The Golden Stairs*. May followed her father into Socialism, acting as his factotum, his adjutant. The full extent of her involvement is made clear in the hoard of so far unpublished material in the Socialist League papers in the International Institute of Socialist History in Amsterdam. May married a Comrade, the young, untalented and impecunious Henry Halliday Sparling. The marriage was a failure. It failed partly because of the cynical intrusion of Bernard Shaw into the Sparlings' household. It also failed, I suggest, because no Comrade could replace May's father. May eventually found emotional security in a female friendship assumed by those who knew her to be lesbian. In the years between the wars she and Miss Lobb, an ex-land girl, retired to Kelmscott Manor. May became, in her own right, a superb embroiderer and did much to advance the status of British craftswomen. William Morris's Comrade daughter has a significant role in this book.

Because he so consciously cultivated manliness Morris has consistently been put over as impervious to women. This view is incorrect. It is not that I underestimate his male entourages. He had a deep emotional need for these gatherings of cronies: Morris's formations and renewals of male brotherhoods are the recurring pattern of his life. Nor would I deny the closeness of his male friendships, though I have my reservations about his supposedly exclusive fondness for Edward Burne-Jones. Surely this was a figment of the Burne-Jones mythology. Morris had other friends as intimate, especially Philip Webb. But I have come to realize that Morris, more than most Victorians, was aware of women's unfulfilled potential. As early as 1880 he was speaking in public on women's rights and his work in the Socialist circles of that decade brought him into contact, as his equals in the struggle, in committees, demonstrations, on the Socialist platforms, with such formidable women as Eleanor Marx, Annie Besant and Charlotte Wilson. It was C. S. Lewis who first noted the pervasive eroticism of William Morris's writing and it is noticeable that, as Morris becomes older, in his years of devotion to the Socialist cause, his most desired women get more positive and active, sunburnt, comradely, resplendent (the opposite of pale and slender Janey, languid on her sofa). One of the revelations of William Morris's letters is that only to two female correspondents – Georgiana Burne-Jones and Aglaia Coronio – is he able to open his heart.

Morris is often viewed as the high priest of the countryside. Reasonably so, since no one has written or spoken more persuasively about the special rural qualities of England. Part of the reason for the lasting popularity of Morris's wallpapers and textiles with the urban middle classes is their fecundity of rural imagery: they put us back in touch with our lost imagined landscapes. You can see the rabbits lollop and hear the blackbirds sing. But the image of Morris as exclusively the ruralist is mistaken, sentimental. After his years at Red House in the early 1860s he never spent the bulk of his time in the country. Kelmscott Manor was a house he only visited occasionally, for long weekends and holidays. He did not even own it. Most of his adult life was taken up in the town and not just in any town but in London, 'the Great Wen' whose Victorian expansiveness alternately stimulated Morris – it provided the basis for his business – and drove him to a terrible despair. Morris was indeed involved in the formation, in the late 1870s, of the Commons Preservation Society. But at the same period he was also a prime mover in the Society for the Protection of Ancient Buildings and the Kyrle Society, whose remits were much broader, embattled against environmental carelessness, ugliness and squalor generally. Here in Sheffield, where I write surrounded by industrial wasteland of the middle 1990s, Morris's worst fears for the city ring hideously true.

Those who, through the years, have denigrated Morris have taken their cue from his *Times* obituary of 1896 which, in preposterously condescending terms, wrote down his politics to a general woolly-mindedness, an excess of eccentric optimism in Morris's opinions:

if they led him, as they have led other generous men before him, towards Socialism, the world can afford to judge him indulgently, as not apprehending much danger from his rhetoric.

I hope, if nothing else, that this book refutes all charges of the woolliness of Morris. His importance surely lies in the reverse: in his precision. He knew *exactly* what the bourgeois motivation was, since he was 'one of us'. He understood the workings of commerce; he belonged to it. As a person who made things he understood completely the essential disciplines of materials and techniques. As a writer he was up against the nuances of language. Morris allowed himself few self-deceptions. He was steely and straight, also ruthless in facing his own failure. He was accurate and dangerous enough to know that the things he most valued *would* go under in the end.

Some heroic images of the Victorian rebel: Morris arrested in Lime-house for disorderly conduct. Morris mounting the trolley to address what seemed a sea of striking miners in Northumberland in 1887. Morris speaking from the Socialist wagon to the workers in Clerkenwell on 'Bloody Sunday' before marching in the ill-fated columns of protesters towards Trafalgar Square. Morris acting as pall-bearer in the funeral procession for Alfred Linnell, crying out over the coffin 'Let us feel he *is* our brother', with a 'fearful earnestness' in his voice. As a Victorian protester he belongs with Carlyle, Ruskin, Kingsley, Angela Burdett-Coutts, Octavia Hill, Elizabeth Fry, men and women of another century. What is special about Morris is the way in which his ideas and personality have outlasted events and issues of the time into our own aspirations and concerns. Like Sigmund Freud he has settled in our consciousness. As the late E. P. Thompson so marvellously put it, 'he is one of those men whom history will never overtake'.

At Morris's death there seemed very little future for the indigenous socialism he invented. Of the two main organizations with which he had been associated, the Socialist League had exploded into anarchy; the Social-Democratic Federation continued, but was dispirited, depleted and as riven by dissension as it had always been. The initiative in socialist reforms by now belonged to the Fabian Society and the Independent Labour Party, both in their ways anathema to Morris who distrusted what he termed 'gas and water' socialism, the Fabians' emphasis on material improvement at the expense of the politics of vision, and who had a deep-rooted dislike of the institution of Parliament itself.

Keir Hardie had been elected the first Independent Labour Party member of Parliament in 1892. There was a lull for the next decade. Morris was disregarded, no longer considered a serious political force. Then, remarkably quickly, his ideas can be seen resurfacing as the passionate socialism that he stood for was seized upon by young idealists as the antidote to Edwardian complacency. G. D. H. Cole, the twentieth-century's leading socialist theoretician, writing in 1959, looked back on his conversion:

I became a Socialist more than fifty years ago when I read *News from Nowhere* as a schoolboy and realised quite suddenly that William Morris had shown one the vision of a society in which it would be a fine and fortunate experience to live.

Morris was an early influence on R. H. Tawney, the great Socialist historian and teacher, who in the early 1900s was entreating his sister to read William Morris's books. Tawney's radical Utopian vision of a socialist ideology not handed down by intellectuals but rising from within the working classes is rooted in Morris's imaginative, iconoclastic views.

Harold Laski, the political theorist and teacher who dominated the London School of Economics, wrote to May Morris in the early 1930s: 'You can be very sure that among at least the Socialists of my generation your father remains a constant and abiding inspiration'.

Graham Wallas, Laski's contemporary, the political psychologist, wrote to tell May of a conference at which he had just spoken: 'I argued that a body of men who ask to be made a government (as the Fabians have done for the last thirty years) must try to see life as a whole, as your father did, and not from the simple economic angle.' He told her he was trying to put these ideas into a book, presumably *Social Judgment*, published posthumously in 1934.

To me the most poignant of these affidavits of the 1930s is that of Barbara Castle, one of the most enduring of Labour politicians in the second half of the twentieth century, coming home from Oxford to West Yorkshire in the bleak years of the Depression, walking the lonely moors with her lover, looking down on the smoky industrial valleys below and reading Morris's revolutionary poem 'The Message of the March Wind':

> But lo, the old inn, and the lights, and the fire,
> And the fiddler's old tune and the shuffling of feet;
> Soon for us shall be quiet and rest and desire,
> And tomorrow's uprising to deeds shall be sweet.

This poem, she says, taught her that Socialism was not merely about struggle but was about sensual fulfilment, and it gave her hope.

Morris's aspirations were still very much alive in the reconstruction and reform of post-war Britain by the 1945 Labour government. Clement Attlee, then prime minister, was another of the young men whose Socialist vision had been formed by reading Morris's works. He represented Limehouse, where William Morris had once had a spot of bother with the police. Attlee was familiar with the detail of William Morris's lectures and political journalism: 'How we Live and How we Might Live'; 'A Factory as It Might Be'; 'Useful Work *versus* Useless Toil'. It is fascinating, and in a way ironic, to see Morris's precepts percolating through to inspire an institution he would certainly have been dubious about: the Welfare State of the early 1950s. Attlee was steeped in *News from Nowhere*. He quoted avidly from Morris's *A Dream of John Ball*, with its messages of brotherhood: 'Forsooth, brothers, fellowship is heaven and lack of fellowship is hell.' In 1953 (after Labour had lost office) he wrote to Sydney Cockerell, full of memories of Morris: 'I was telling a group of foreign socialists the other day how much more Morris meant to us than Karl Marx.'

The following year Attlee, handicapped by his famous brevity and clearly very nervous, went through the ordeal of his first major television interview. The interviewer was the young Kenneth Harris, soon to become an early media star. Harris, desperate to elicit some sort of credo, asked what the Labour party had to offer to the voters of mid-twentieth-century Britain. Attlee reached out for William Morris with a touching confidence:

ATTLEE: Well, you know there's nothing better than the motto that we have in this Borough, by our greatest citizen, William Morris – 'Fellowship is Life' – we believe in the kind of society where we've fellowship for all. You can't get that while there's grave inequalities in wealth. That is the hope of the world, and we offer fellowship with all other countries.
HARRIS: Do you find it then apt, Mr Attlee, that we should be meeting tonight in the Borough of Walthamstow, which is the town of William Morris?
ATTLEE: I think that's absolutely right.

It has always been quite easy to pick holes in William Morris. As with all great visionaries there are flaws in his arguments, for those who choose to find them. His practice did not by any means bear out his theories. His own factory was not 'A Factory as It Might Be'. There is a kind of wilful blindness in his attitude to population growth and the new technologies. But the quarrel with Morris on such individual issues has been used by his detractors as a distraction from the vigour and to many the *terror* of his underlying message, which was the abandonment of capitalism itself and its replacement by more equitable, humane social structures. It is to this generous, immense and sweeping challenge that the left in Britain has returned, with a curious compulsion, throughout the century. William Morris has provided a voice of inner conscience. In his purity and passion he has been the pivotal figure, connecting socialist collectivism in Britain to its origins in early nineteenth-century Romantic libertarianism. Morris has, uniquely, married the tradition of socialism as a critique of political economy with the tradition of Romantic anti-industrialism.

If you are finally going to say to an increasing number of people that they are simply surplus to requirements, that they are not really necessary in this society, at that point the basic question returns, of what people need to produce and how they need to produce it and how, over and above all this, they relate to each other while they are producing it.

This was Raymond Williams, speaking on Morris's relevance to the economic crisis of the 1980s. And his hopes and fears seem even more prophetic in the industrial north of England ten years further on.

A William Morris arrives only once or twice each century, in the sense of someone of their time and yet beyond it. Morris is a time-traveller. He does it in his writing, in those oddly hypnotic futuristic novels. He does it in his politics and his polemic. It is part of his magic that we know what his response is to events he did not survive long enough to see. We can feel quite certain that the world collapse of Marxism would have overjoyed him. Morris called himself a communist, but Communism as developed in the Soviet Union and in Eastern Europe would never have been what he envisaged. Unlike Shaw and the Webbs, he would have seen through Lenin and Stalin and their political economy instantly. We can also feel confident that he would have looked on the Thatcher years in the Britain of the last two decades of this century as amongst the worst he could imagine in terms of human destructiveness and capitalist greed.

Electronic addiction? Drug culture? Inner city planning? Bottom line banking? Political correctness? Post-Modernist architecture? Theme parks? Niche retailing? Bargain breaks? Time-share homes? Spaghetti junctions? Shopping malls? Leisure centres? Tele-cottages? Health farms? Saturation advertising? Freebie magazines? Junk mail? Fast food? Course modules? Heritage trails? Craft Fayres? Business parks? Garden centres? Sound bites? Opinion polls? Chat shows? Designer clothes? Executive phones? Pulp literature? Video porn? Corporate sponsorship? Market-orientated society? . . .

'Damn'd pigs! Damn'd fools!' You can hear Morris expostulate, robust, fidgety, tremendous, pulling out the hairs (singly) from his great prophetic beard.

CHAPTER ONE

Walthamstow
1834–48

'To this day', said William Morris, getting aged, 'when I smell a may tree I think of going to bed by daylight.' Scents could always trigger off a surge of recollections, stretching right back to his childhood. The sweet pungent smell of balm brought back with sharp immediacy very early days in the kitchen garden of the Morris home at Woodford, 'and the large blue plums which grew on the wall beyond the sweet-herb patch'. Scents for Morris had a potency that verged on the erotic. Look at Clara, charming suntanned unselfconscious heroine of his abandoned novel, posthumously published as *The Novel on Blue Paper*, making for the river on a blazing summer day, her feet 'bruising scent from the great horse-mint as she picked her way between the willow stems', with wafting aromas of the marshland hay and clover, humming of the bees and the tinkle of sheep bells.

William Morris was born on 24 March 1834 into what he later described as 'the ordinary bourgeois style of comfort'. It was not a visually sensitive household. Discussing whether the love of beauty was natural or acquired Morris said his own love of beauty must have been inborn since neither his father or his mother nor any of his relations had the least idea of it. His father, also William, who was thirty-six at the time of his son's birth, was by then a financier, making a small fortune as senior partner in a bill-broking business with an office in Lombard Street, in the commercial centre of the City. His mother Emma, whose maiden name was Shelton, had been a neighbour of the Morrises in earlier years, when their two families had lived in Worcester. There had already been some connection by marriage. The families were also intertwined in their tastes and expectations. The degree to which the marriage of his parents was an arranged marriage may have weighed with William, whose own marriage was to be so relatively reckless. The family kept up its connections with Worcester and Morris referred to being taken there on visits in the days when he 'sucked at a bottle' and cried for his 'bamper'. He remembered Prince Arthur's Chantry and the mediaeval tombs in the cathedral from a single later visit in the 1850s, when he went to see his aunts.

William was the third of his parents' surviving children, and the first to be born at Elm House in Walthamstow. After they were married his parents set up house in Lombard Street, in rooms above the office. It was a convention in City firms in those days that a member of the firm should reside on the premises. They also had a cottage in Sydenham, for holidays and weekends. Their first child, born in Lombard Street in August 1827, was Charles Stanley who only lived four days. Then there were two sisters, Emma and Henrietta, born in 1829 and 1833 respectively. They were the close companions of William Morris's childhood, and maybe this encouraged his later quasi-mystical belief in the significance of trios: he was always attuned to doing things in threes. After William came Stanley, born in 1837; Rendall in 1839; Arthur in 1840; Isabella in 1842; Edgar in 1844; and Alice who was born in 1846 and died in Tunbridge Wells as late as 1942. William's brothers pursued the conventional professions, Rendall and Arthur becoming army officers and Stanley a prosperous gentleman farmer, breeding Jersey and Guernsey cows. Of all the Morris children it was only Isabella, leading light in the Anglican deaconess movement of the 1880s, who had any of her brother's contrariness and zeal.

The Morrises developed substantial figures. Though the early engagement pictures of his parents show a relatively slight and even wistful couple, his mother with small corkscrew curls curtaining her forehead, the children acquired a certain weightiness, seemingly in keeping with their rising status in the world. In their photographs they stand well-upholstered and commanding with the square jowl that was even more pronounced in Morris's sisters than his brothers. William escaped it: in the early portraits his face looks almost heart-shaped. But people used to comment on the heavy jowl-line of his daughters Jenny and May.

Morris believed in fate and, as he grew older and immersed himself in sagas, he came to espouse a particularly Nordic version of fate that he referred to as the 'Weird'. The idea of grand inevitability enthralled him: 'I am in the hands of Weird, to wend as she will have me,' cries

Osberne setting out on his heroic travels in *The Sundering Flood*, Morris's last Nordic story. The Weird is inescapable, the thing ordained for you, a theme also explored in *The Earthly Paradise* with its six fairy ladies delivering their rulings over the cradle of Ogier the Dane. It was Morris's own Weird to be born into a family so redolent of early Victorian bourgeois values: industrious; acquisitive; uncritical; incurious. Morris was himself industrious: his energy was legendary. In some precise respects he too remained the bourgeois. But it is also true that his upbringing within that narrow setting of commercial endeavour fed his later actions when he came to embrace the Socialist cause with the passion of the lover, in his own description. He attacked the middle classes, conscious he belonged to them, instinctively aware of what they were about.

'I am a boor, and a son of a boor,' William Morris stormed across the table at a London dinner party in the 1860s, his eyes set and his fist clenched. And indeed the Morris dynasty did have a certain ruggedness. His paternal ancestors on both sides were Welsh. His father's father was apparently the first of this family of Morrises to drop the Welsh 'Ap' ('son of') from the surname. Morris's grandfather had come to Worcester from a remote valley of the upper Severn in the late eighteenth century, setting up his business and transforming himself into a city burgess praised in contemporary records as the epitome of probity 'and very religious'. His wife Elizabeth, the daughter of a retired naval surgeon from Nottingham, was a tall and stately woman who in her senility became part of the extended Morris family at Woodford Hall in Essex, offering William a trip to her home town if he was 'a *very* good boy'.

Like Frank Lloyd Wright, William Morris was intrigued by his roots in wild Wales and its 'lovely ancient literature', though he never acquired more than a few words of the Welsh language, which he described as 'difficult but beautiful'. He attributed his natural empathy with the Tristram sagas to Wales: 'All my literary life', he wrote, 'I have been deeply moved by that Cycle of Romance, as indeed I ought to be, being myself Welsh of kin'. He blamed the Cymry for his dark hair and for his melancholy streak. When the chance came in the middle 1870s Morris was off eagerly to look at his lost 'Fatherland'. He loved its dreariness and mystery. He went as far as Towyn, 'a little queer grey Welsh town by the sea-shore on the flats under the mountains in the most Welsh part of Wales'.

William's birthplace was an early nineteenth-century house with a large garden in what was then the Essex countryside. Commuterland loomed already. William Morris Senior travelled every day by stage coach to his office. Elm House was not a grand house: the Morrises got grander. But it was emphatically a gentleman's residence, standing prominently on Clay Hill, rising ground which allowed vistas north-east across the valley of the River Lea towards Epping Forest, two miles or so away. J. W. Mackail, William Morris's first biographer, was just in time to see Elm House before its demolition in 1898 and described 'a plain roomy building' with the garden front facing south on to a large lawn surrounded by shrubberies and kitchen gardens, and a great mulberry tree leaning across the grass. Morris's old Oxford friend Cormell Price, who accompanied Mackail on a sentimental journey

1 *Elm House, Walthamstow*, William Morris's birthplace. Drawing, 1898, by E. H. New for J. W. Mackail's *The Life of William Morris*.

around William Morris's haunts, made the comment that the windows were set wide apart, so much so that the rooms tended to look dark. However, he added, 'by making a clean sweep of all the houses around under 40 years of age you can conceive it was a very pleasant spot'.

Morris himself, with his intense consciousness of the political over-tones of buildings, would later have dismissed Elm House as dull and bourgeois: he would have preferred to have been born in the little whitewashed cottage or the mediaeval hall. But the use he made years later of Elm House as the basis of Parson Risley's rectory, in *The Novel on Blue Paper*, shows in how much detail it had lingered in his mind, and with what sense of ambiguity. The white panelled hall, with its stuffed tiger and its trophies of the hunting field; the wide carved staircase; the open glass door leading from the drawing-room out into the old-fashioned flower garden with its mulberry tree and straight-cut flower borders, and the great row of full-foliaged elms: the rectory is partly a place of loneliness, oppressiveness, and partly a place of decor-ous delight. It is wonderfully typical of Morris that he should use his birthplace as the background of a fable on the moral power of beauty to transform – and disconcert. Risley is a Morris villain, sexually crass and lamentably indolent, but as he wanders around his lovely garden in the evening, while the yellow sun is sinking, he is shot through with a pang 'compounded of the memory of hopes and fears, pleasures and pains of many past years'.

Morris was a cosseted child, fed on calves' foot jelly and beef tea. This may have been an overreaction of his mother's after the loss of her firstborn. But William's later rugged strength and tempestuous energy could be misleading: he was never as robust as he appeared to be. Indeed there was a history of ill health in the family. His father, always nervous, became gouty; his mother was prone to partial seizures, an epileptic tendency that intensified down the Morris line. Treated as a little invalid, housebound and quiet, Morris read: 'Ever since I could remember,' he told Andreas Scheu in the 1880s, 'I was a great devourer of books'. He could not recall ever being taught to read; nor could he envisage a time when he did not. This was perhaps the first example of Morris's peculiar process of osmosis, his ability to soak up knowledge without trying, the knack that was later to mystify his friends and worry his opponents. At the age of four the infant William Morris was deep in the Waverley novels, and he claimed that by the time he was seven he had read the entire *œuvre* of Walter Scott. What did he find in Scott?

5

Small figures in spare landscapes of the mountains and the deserts; bright colours, strong emotions, mystic rituals, fierce crowd scenes; the cult of the outlaw; the dwelling upon violence, 'the clang of the scourge and the groans of the penitent'; the idealized woman, intense love unconsummated; the concept of manliness and chivalric self-sacrifice seized upon by Morris as a kind of battle-cry: 'And it is good to do one thing, and then die.' William Morris was always decisive in his tastes. Once he had discovered a thing he loved, he stuck to it: this was in one sense his great strength, in another sense his flaw. He went on and on reading Walter Scott for ever. Scott, he used to say, meant more to him than Shakespeare. Intimate Scott allusions turn up in his letters, providing a consistent reference point, an anchor. His only other comparable hero would be Dickens. Books to Morris had a magic. They were realler than the real.

At Elm House Morris learned words; and he first comprehended *things*, the emotional meanings of appearances and textures. As a small child he kept two pieces of flannel in his bed: one was for sucking, the other one for washing. He particularly loved a toy lamb that squeaked and a model of a Dutch town he could spread out on the carpet like a Floor Game, the educational building bricks designed by H. G. Wells. William was a watchful child, describing later how he spied on some Bluecoat schoolboys eating off their wooden trenchers, traditional flat boards without a rim or gravy channel: he 'noticed their devices (with much interest) for banking up a little soup with a potato toft'. From this very early age things were not just a delight to him in all their quirks and beauties. They were also a necessity, a method of orientation. Things were Morris's means of getting his bearings in the world. Later on he was accused of preferring things to people and there was something in it. In the middle 1880s he was saying that he knew from experience 'what a comfortable life one might lead if one could be careful not to concern oneself with *persons* but with *things*; or persons in the light of things'. By 1888 his vision of the future entailed de-government, a total dismantling of the parliamentary system, which he came to see as merely perpetuating class antagonisms, and the replacement of a government of *persons* by 'an administration of *things*'.

William was six when the family moved eastward from Elm House to Woodford Hall, an imposing Georgian mansion, sub-Palladian in style, and right next to Epping Forest. There was only a fence between the

6

forest and the Morrises' fifty-acre park. This high bourgeois idyll was the sign and symbol of the burgeoning commercial successes of William Morris's father. He was still with the City firm of bill (or discount) brokers he joined twenty years before, when he had first arrived in London, making use of his family connection with Joseph and Robert Harris, two of the partners in the firm then known as Harris, Sanderson & Harris. The firm had since then moved from Lombard Street to King William Street. The banking crisis of 1825, which had led to the collapse of many broking firms, in fact had strengthened Harris, Sanderson & Harris and opened out new areas of operation. William Morris Senior became a partner in 1826, at the age of twenty-eight. The Harris brothers had by then retired. The firm continued trading as Sanderson & Co. By the early 1840s, when the Morris family installed itself at Woodford, it was one of the only four discount houses in the City of any real significance. Its prosperity can be gauged by the fact that Morris's father was able to pay £600 a year in rent for Woodford Hall. He had chosen a house of little architectural subtlety. But Woodford Hall had bulk. It had good views and great amenities besides the kind of grandiose serenity that no doubt recommended it to Mrs Gladstone, wife of the prime minister, who eventually took it over as a convalescent home for the East London poor.

Woodford Hall operated as a world within a world. The charms of feudal life there were to be described by Morris with the exactness of the natural observer, sharpened by his guilt at what he called 'the good luck only of being born prosperous and rich'. To a large extent the estate was self-sufficient, with its gardens and orchards, its horses and cows, its poultry and pigs. The butter, cream, beer and bread were home produced. Shop-bought food was purchased only from specialist merchants who understood their customers' personal predilections. William Morris's mother would sometimes stop her lumbering carriage horses in the City and make her discreet purchases from small dark arcane shops there. The family knew the rarefied luxuries of home-made wines, wine-jellies and syllabubs, sweet cured hams, filberts from their own nut-walks, fine desserts of peaches plucked from red-brick garden walls. Morris liked to describe a peach as 'pinch-ripe'. A stop-gap meal was served at Woodford Hall in the middle of the morning, between breakfast and dinner, in the mediaeval manner, when the children were given cake and cheese with a glass of home-brewed small beer. The cake, said Morris, was 'nicer than anything of the kind he ever tasted since'.

The estate at Woodford Hall extended far beyond the park. A further hundred acres of farmland sloped down to a small river, the Roding. Here William and his brothers used to fish. Morris always enjoyed fishing, developing into 'a greedy fisher, and proud of his cunning'. He divided the world into fishers and non-fishers, implying that non-fishers could never quite be trusted. Fishing was the only sport he ever really liked. When they grew older he and his brothers would also go out shooting. William apparently conceived the ambition of shooting wood-pigeons with a bow and arrow. This he did not manage. But the boys with their shotguns would kill redwings, fieldfares, rabbits. They were then allowed to roast the birds for supper.

Although in many ways so stratified and stultified, the life of the Victorian country house had secret fluencies. Children in particular could find room for manoeuvre, exchanging the allotted roles and crossing the set boundaries between the family quarters and the servants', and sometimes establishing a rapport with the servants more affectionate and comforting than that with their own parents. This evidently happened to some extent at Woodford, affecting in profound ways Morris's vision of community, in more practical ways his attitude to kitchens. Morris felt at home in kitchens, coming to define them as cosy, unpretentious, functional, *productive* places. With all the contradictions of the man whose income was to come from decorating drawing-rooms, he considered the kitchen the best room in the house.

The small boy had his own garden, first of many. All his gardens were beautiful, wrote the old friend who had seen most of them. William Morris's early interest in individual flower forms is not so surprising in the person who became the most floral of designers. At Woodford Hall he studied the family copy of John Gerard's *Herball* (1597), an encyclopaedic study with meticulous drawings of plant forms. As a child he was already developing his sense of floral colours, textures, scents, structures and life cycles. Growing up when he did, he was poised between the Romantic and the Darwinian: this underlaid his clarity and gave him his robust curiosity. Looking at him looking at flowers, one is conscious of the Victorian spirit of botanical inquiry being transfigured by a sensuous delight, an onrush of accumulated memory and meaning. In the 1890s Morris was describing a particularly beautiful full-blown pink and blue *hepatica*, remembering that this was the flower he used to love so much when he was 'quite a little boy'.

He had deep appreciation of a garden's possibilities. Gardening was another of those esoteric subjects his friends perceived he knew about almost as if by instinct. He was not the great practitioner, he did not wield the spade; but the making and nurturing of gardens satisfied his organizing powers and his most private urges. The gardens he created were a strange and lovely mixture of formality and wildness, reflecting quite uncannily the tension between the conservative and radical in Morris's own temperament. In so much of his writing, both poetry and prose, a garden is set right at the emotional centre, the place of discovery, the end of the long journey, where lovers meet and linger, on a carved primaeval bench, by a swiftly flowing fountain, by a mediaeval trellis. There are always scents and blossoms. It becomes almost a formula. Even the peripheral buildings, summer houses, huts and tool sheds, are drawn into the emotional landscape, invested with the sharpness of a desperate nostalgia. In *The Novel on Blue Paper* John, the highly strung young hero, just before a disconcerting encounter with his father, runs out into the tool shed and 'in after days he could never smell the mixed scent of a tool-house, with its bast mats and earthy roots and herbs, in a hot summer evening, without that evening, with every word spoken and gesture made, coming up clear into his memory'. Outside, the sweet-smelling abundant kitchen garden; the musky smell of promise exuding from the melon beds, where the melon globes are swelling so absurdly in their dung-heaps; the fullness of the bush from which John with such impatience strips the first of the white currants: these are images of things known well in Morris's childhood, intimations of remembered garden landscapes of desire.

From Morris's later descriptions, his childhood was in many ways idyllic. He was 'the happy child on a sunny holiday', when he had 'everything that he could think of'. In its old-fashioned way it was a reassuring household, generous and solid, with gregarious rituals: a full-blown Christmas and an even more lavish celebration of Twelfth Night when the Masque of St George was performed and the children were given half a tumbler of rum punch. William, the eldest son, was evidently petted and indulged. He was allowed to play with his sisters' precious miniature tea set and dinner set, including an early Georgian silver tea urn and teaspoons: his indoctrination into that traditionally female world of household objects. His father took the small boy on expeditions: one was to the Chiswick Horticultural Gardens; another to the Isle of Wight, where Black Gang Chine enthralled him. He was told that it had been inhabited by pirates. He was given a miniature suit of armour and rode around the park on his Shetland pony wearing it. Bernard Shaw, a protégé of later years, attributed Morris's bouts of petulance to this early history of pampering, the way he was treated almost as a little prince.

But even as a small child William was prone to terrors. There was often a black cloud, like the one Guest, the narrator, encounters at the end of the novel *News from Nowhere*, rolling down the village street to envelop him inexorably, like a nightmare of his childish days. Morris was always haunted by his childhood image of the stocks at Woodford, still in the 1840s standing on the wayside green in the middle of the village:

beside them stood the *Cage*, a small shanty some 12 ft sq.: and as it was built of brown brick roofed with blue slate, I suppose it had been quite recently in use, since its *style* was not earlier than the days of Fat George. I remember that I used to look at these two threats of law (and) order with considerable terror, and decidedly preferred to walk on the other side of the road.

That description, in a letter to his daughter written in the 1880s, shows with what immense exactness the details of the structure, the dimensions, materials, had been stored up in his mind. Morris became almost a connoisseur of prisons. Many of his early poems dwell on physical imprisonment, and even as a child there is a sense he was aware of other sorts of prisons, the confinements of the heart.

William Morris's relations with his mother were peculiarly tortuous. Emma Morris's family, in the bourgeois hierarchy of Worcester, was socially and culturally above her husband's. The Sheltons could trace back their origins to Henry Shelton, mercer, of Birmingham in Henry VII's reign. They were prosperous merchants and small landowners with a particular bias towards music: two of Emma's uncles became singing canons of Worcester Cathedral and Westminster Abbey; a third, Joseph, was more visually orientated and became an art teacher in Worcester. There was much in her background to have made her sympathetic to the inner compulsions of the creative life. She was small and fair and sweet looking. Her granddaughters adored the picture in her bedroom showing her as a young woman, slightly smiling, with her fair hair dressed in loops and bows, her slim arms enveloped in a careless blue scarf, her hands almost hidden under the long sleeves secured at the wrists with golden bracelets. The dress, as described by May Morris, was 'beautifully blue'. Blue was William Morris's own favourite colour. The picture of his mother sounds like one of his dream portraits of decorous yet slightly *décolleté* young women. Yet, although he loved her, she would disappoint him subtly and dismayingly the whole of her long life.

Throughout his childhood, his mother was often pregnant. Morris tended to be unsympathetic to the pregnant. In his socialist polemic it was the fact of childbirth that prevented him allowing that women could be equals of men in the economy of labour. There was perhaps an element of fear in his view of pregnancy: 'the babe 'neath thy girdle that groweth unseen'. Pregnant women belong to Morris's gallery of shape changers, the damsels into swans, queens into old crones, ladies into fork-tongued sea dragons that populate his stories. Morris sensed his mother's curious apartness, superficially vivacious, intellectually inert: not unlike the mother in *The Novel on Blue Paper*, 'whose sweet and kindly feelings hardly included passions, as her dreamy and vague mind hardly included reason'. Emma Morris was good natured, but she did not like disturbances. She was one of nature's compulsive glossers over; and the sense of loss so deep and sharp in Morris's writing is not just a matter of his marital despairs but also derives from a complex knowledge of the hazards of real communication between sons and their mothers. In *The Pilgrims of Hope*, Morris's romantic poem of the Commune, the mother holds her baby son in a bitter-sweet embrace:

'and yet 'twixt thee and me
Shall rise that wall of distance, that round each one doth grow,
And maketh it hard and bitter each other's thought to know.'

'I used to dread Sunday when I was a little chap.' For Morris, Woodford Sundays had *longueurs* identical to those he would complain about when drawing from a model: a similar feeling of doing the unnatural, and the same resentment at having to keep still, an agony to anyone so naturally restless. The Morrises were narrowly Evangelical. William later referred bitterly to the 'rich establishment puritanism' of his upbringing. He had been baptized on 25 July 1834, four months after his birth, at the church of St Mary's, Walthamstow. The Morris children were forbidden to play with Nonconformists, being taught that Dissenters were undesirable and Unitarians beyond the pale completely. However, an exception was made for Quakers. Sanderson & Co. was a firm with Quaker leanings and indeed the Quakers were in dominant positions in many London banking and bill-broking cliques. It seems probable that Morris's father owed his own employment to distant family connections with the Quakers. So religion underpinned the Morris family prosperity. At Woodford the hall was close to the church, with a private doorway leading through into the churchyard. Henrietta, in her plaid skirt and trim jacket, was empowered to keep the younger children in order through the service, and seems to have been particularly strict with William. 'O Willie, you *naughty* boy!' was her refrain. It is tempting to see her as the first of the succession of those sadistic women, eyes glittering, whips lashing, the overwrought she-demons of Morris's fairytales.

The religion of his childhood was a literal piety: a child's picture-book view of hell and of damnation, with the directness of personal devotion to Jesus Christ, the saviour and friend. What effect would this have had on Morris's perceptions? Edward Burne-Jones, his partner and co-designer, used to claim that the child brought up on the Last Judgement was enriched: 'though it did fill our childhood with terrors, it was an incitement to our imaginations, and there's no telling what good there is in that.' Certainly the stained-glass windows made by Morris, Marshall, Faulkner & Co. from the 1860s onwards, several thousand of them, reflect a very intimate knowledge of the Bible. 'Abraham's Sacrifice'; 'Enoch and the Angel'; 'Noah Building the Ark'; 'Daniel in the Lion's Den'; 'Christ Walking on the Water'; 'Christ Healing the Woman with an Issue of Blood': the depiction of these stories has a matter-of-fact quality. They are not outlandish, they are part of a known landscape. It is this immediacy, this sense of domesticity, that sets them apart from almost all the other stained-glass windows of their time. The dove that descends to Mary in William Morris's 'Annunciation' window is not a rarefied bird, but ragged, rather homely; paschal lambs are white and woolly like the lambs of rural England; in the Morris & Co. window in the chancel of St Michael and St Mary Magdalene in Easthampstead the dead push their way up through the flagstones towards Heaven as if they were ascending literally through the pavement of a mid-Victorian city. And talking of 'Last Judgements', the immense blue, green and scarlet Burne-Jones window made in the 1890s for Birmingham Cathedral is the pictorial masterpiece of the Victorian age.

Morris tended to view children as detached, mysterious people, figures from another tribe. He notes strange little encounters with children in his letters: the thirteen-year-old bell-boy in Scotland, so self-confident; the children who loom up out of the mist on the lonely strand in Iceland, offering him fish. You find similarly self-sufficient children in his stories. Children happily camping in the reclaimed wood of Kensington appear in *News from Nowhere*, Morris's novel of the future; they hang about the little tents pitched on the greensward. Some of the children have fires burning with cooking pots suspended above them, 'gipsy fashion'. In *The Novel on Blue Paper* John meets 'a little brown-faced girl with a basket and a solemn stumped-tailed mongrel of a dog'. He is cheered up by the sight of her. The odd subdued contentment of such not quite adult people with their own preoccupations seems to be a sign of hope.

Morris in his own childhood became adept at pursuing his own interests. He soon began to wander and discovered in the landscape his own stimulus and solace. The flat, marshy Essex countryside he roamed through on his pony is often in the background of his poetry and stories. 'I was always a lover of the sad Lowland Country' says Frank in 'Frank's Sealed Letter', an early Morris story, launching into a defence of the recherché beauties of 'that spreading of the broad marsh lands round the river Lea'. In one of the most famous passages in *News from Nowhere* Morris's prophetic vision of the England of the future is focused on that landscape:

Past the Docks eastward and landwards it is all flat pasture, once marsh, except for a few gardens, and there are very few permanent dwellings there: scarcely anything but a few sheds and cots for the men who come to look after the great herds of cattle pasturing there. But however what with the beasts and the men, and the scattered red-tiled roofs and the big hayricks, it does not make a bad holiday to get a quiet pony and ride about there on a sunny afternoon of autumn, and look over the river and the craft passing up and down, and on to Shooter's Hill and the Kentish uplands, and then turn round to the wide green sea of the Essex marshland, with the great domed line of the sky, and the sun shining down in one flood of peaceful light over the long distance.

Morris, child of the Romantic age, had sensed himself the outcast. The households of his childhood, solid, kindly, were constricting. He depended on long distances, complex unnerving vistas, surprises in the setting of the buildings in the landscape. He looked for ecstasy, 'that delightful quickening of perception by which everything gets emphasized and brightened, and the commonest landscape looks lovely'. He could find it almost anywhere: in Iceland, in Great Yarmouth. That early Essex countryside had taught him what it was.

Morris understood the movement of the water through the country, how rivers change their character, broadening, then narrowing within their tall reed walls. He appreciated the detail of the river: the speckled small fish, the water under the willow boughs, from which the tiny flies they fed on fell in myriads; the great chub splashing at a late moth in the morning. These sights and sounds would bring back the rivers of his childhood. At Woodford he had his first glimpses of the tributaries of the Thames making desultory progress through the marshes and the cornfields. On these waters there were boats with white and red-brown sails. The Thames was to become William Morris's river, regarded almost as his personal possession, traversed from end to end, grumbled at, protected, defended vehemently from the threats of the so-called Thames Conservancy Board. The river was for him a spiritual investment, an essential human link back to antiquity and history. One of his fiercest protests was made in the 1870s to the Metropolitan Board of Works. The Board's proposal to raise and open up the Water Gate of York House in the Strand seemed to him like sacrilege: 'in its present position', wrote Morris, 'the Gate serves to mark the ancient course of the Thames'.

As a child he saw the river as escape and as adventure. Even in middle age the mere sight of calm, clear water near the church at Inglesham made him long for an expedition. Wilfrid Blunt once commented that Morris, on the river, underwent a kind of change of personality, becoming playful, charming. Water for Morris was a lure, a titillation, often used as a starting point in his romances when his heroines are apt to disrobe and tiptoe down through gilded gates to hidden waterways where little boats lie waiting to speed them up the river. Waters held a sexual promise. In *The Sundering Flood* we are not far from consummation in 'the dark green deeps and fierce downlong swirl of the stream'.

The boy had set off into the depths of Epping Forest like a small-scale version of one of his own heroes. Like Lionel the wood child in 'Golden Wings', equipped with magic armour by his mother, the witchwoman; like Thiodolph in *The House of the Wolfings* walking steadily onwards away from his familiar tribal dwelling place into a wood so dense that little of the heavens could be seen 'save the crown of them, because of the tall tree-tops'. In Morris's iconography of nature a forest was the

14

place where you both lost yourself and found yourself. A forest is monotonous but also very complex with its thicknesses and clearings, its dryness and its marshiness, its sameness and yet total versatility of colour: the amassing of what seems like almost every shade of green.

William Morris's ideal forests were enormous: 'I don't care much about a wood unless it is a very big one,' Morris once wrote to Georgiana Burne-Jones, pouring scorn on Buscot wood for being a mere coppice. Epping Forest, an area much larger then than now, was defined by Morris as 'certainly the biggest hornbeam wood in these islands, and I suppose in the world'. When young he knew it 'yard by yard' from Wanstead to the Theydons, and from Hale End to the Fairlop Oak. In the course of his campaign in the 1890s to save Epping Forest from the greed of the developers Morris recollected the effect the forest had on him. 'In those days,' he wrote bitterly, 'it had no more foes than the gravel stealer and the rolling fence maker and was always interesting and always beautiful.'

It was part of Morris's argument that Epping, of all forests, was magnificently idiosyncratic: its special character came from the strangeness of the hornbeam, 'a tree not common save in Essex and Herts'. The hornbeams were regularly lopped and pollarded, a practice that increased their natural tendency to knobbliness. These were majestically grotesque trees, interspersed with lower-lying shiny, spiky holly thickets. The result, said Morris, was 'a very curious and characteristic wood, such as can be seen nowhere else'. There was the added oddness of two earthworks in the forest: Loughton Camp, an early Iron Age encampment on a spur of the land, roughly oval in shape with its single rampart and forty-five-feet-wide ditch; and Ambresbury Banks, an Iron Age hill-fort, rectangular in plan, enclosing twelve acres, the walls broken by two entrances, one of them mediaeval. Morris, child and adult, was extremely keen on earthworks. He always saw his role as the defender of the mystery: 'we want a thicket, not a park, in Epping Forest.' He believed there was a certain morality in wildness, a recuperative value. In the Socialist days, no doubt with his encouragement, Epping was the site of a Socialist League picnic. May Morris remembered it: 'I have a sudden vision of a long train of loaded pleasure-vans with red flags waving, threading their way through the narrow streets of the City eastwards to Epping Forest.' A few of the Socialists wandered away quietly into the bracken with Morris who showed them the great hornbeams and talked of his childhood days there.

Morris learned about birds in the garden and the forest. He could identify them easily. He knew a lot about them. In later years in London Cormell Price wrote in his diary that Morris could 'go on for hours about their habits: but especially about their form'. The birds in William Morris's tapestries and chintzes show his delight in their colours and their plumage. Both he and Burne-Jones especially loved feathers: not just birds' feathers but the divine feathers in their angels' wings. As a boy at Woodford William Morris used to birds'-nest and when he proposed later, in a letter to a client, to paint her boudoir woodwork 'a light blue green colour like a starling's egg' he spoke from exact knowledge of the real thing.

He responded to the drama of the isolated building: the cottage in the clearing; the tower on the hillside. Again this was a part of his Romantic sensibility. As a boy he had discovered Queen Elizabeth's Hunting Lodge at Chingford. This was a strange erection in the middle of the forest, originally built as a 'Greate Standinge' or grandstand from which Henry VIII could watch the hunt on Chingford Plain. The King was by then too portly to ride after the deer. The lodge's upper floors were originally open, making spectators' balconies, but by Morris's day the space had been filled in and the original timberwork enclosed in lath and plaster. The picturesque lodge standing so four-square in the landscape was not in fact unknown: by the early nineteenth century it had its local tourists. Pictures of the 1830s show picnickers in groups around the lawn. But Morris, in describing the first visit of his childhood, endued the lodge with things he always hoped to find in buildings: solid structure; quirky detail; the sense of the organic, the accretion of past history; and a certain loneliness.

He had evidently made his way in through the ground-floor kitchen, hung with the tenant farmer's flitches of bacon, and on up the large wide stairway which Queen Elizabeth reputedly ascended on her horse. The upper floor was then at least partially finished, being used for local Manor Court proceedings. From this vantage point Morris looked outward on to the forest with its oddness of texture: huge gnarled trees with the ground beneath reduced to smoothness by grazing sheep. Looking inward Morris saw the sort of room he loved immediately and always sought to emulate in one way or another. The bareness of its outline and the richness of the detail; space, strength and masculinity; the overtones of chivalry. Morris's ideal interiors are here. Much later in his lecture 'The Lesser Arts of Life' he tried to explain the impact of the upper room at Chingford 'hung with faded greenery, and the impression of romance it always made on him'. Things worked on Morris's imagination just as words did: as a child he was absorbing the visual and verbal with the same degree of intensity. He compared his own responses to the Tudor room at Chingford to the feeling that came over him whenever he read, and re-read, the very literary description of the Green Room at Monkbarns in Sir Walter Scott's *The Antiquary*: 'yes, that was more than upholstery, believe me'.

The faded greenery Morris recollected was in fact a succession of figurative tapestries hung around the room in the mediaeval manner. They apparently depicted mythological and rural scenes, not unlike the hangings at Ruddywell Court in *The Novel on Blue Paper*, tapestries 'in which knights and ladies were walking and playing amid a faded grey garden, populous with pheasants and rabbits'. The tapestries at Chingford were part of the general mustiness and dustiness of ambience that Morris enjoyed in the battered-about building. But he also appreciated something more specific: his susceptibility to embroideries and carvings was already unusually sharp. A particular picture of Abraham and Isaac worked in brown worsted was a long-remembered object; he had also observed carefully 'a carved ivory junk with painted and gilded puppets in it in a glass case'. As a child he showed no interest in paintings or in drawings: given ordinary pictures he could not understand them. What he liked was the three-dimensional, the tactile. Here already were the seeds of the revival by Morris and Burne-Jones from the 1880s onwards of the art of large-scale tapestry, the art Burne-Jones described as 'half way between painting and ornament'. He added: 'I know nothing that's so deliciously half way.'

This was the beginning of the age of gazing. The Pre-Raphaelites were soon to rediscover what they saw as a lost innocence of vision, scrutinizing with an almost manic intensity the blades of the grass, the veins of the leaves, the bumps on the pebbles. Holman Hunt's poor sheep and goats were subjected to scrutiny for days. The Anglo-Catholic church architects, with a similar extremism, studied the genuine mediaeval architecture, sketching, measuring it up, and looking at it fervently. G. F. Bodley, the church architect, an early patron of Morris, Marshall, Faulkner & Co., arrived at his extraordinary knowledge of Early French Gothic by a long process of gazing; the style entered his bloodstream so that people sometimes wondered if his buildings were old or new. Exploring the country around Woodford, stopping and examining the ruins and the churches, William Morris too was on a training course in observation. He, of all people, learned to articulate his gazing. No one described better 'that exhilarating sense of space and freedom which satisfactory architecture always gives to an unanxious man who is in the habit of using his eyes'.

Some of the Essex churches were obscure, small, queer ones. As a boy Morris took in the touching details of each building: the monuments and brasses that related the church to its community, locality. It seems that more than anything the wall paintings excited him, launching him into little visionary passages: in one unfinished story Kilian, drinking from the fountain, sees men and women thronging 'clad in albes of white and sky colour, and rosy red, and fresh greens like to the angels painted on the walls about the high altar in the church of St James by the Water'. In *The Well at the World's End* Ralph appears just like 'the angel painted on the choir of the church'. A church's large assemblage of oddities inspired him. His architect friend Philip Webb would vouch for the effect on Morris's later attitude to buildings of the 'peculiar' Essex churches of his childhood roamings. Morris was the pioneer of the irreligious visit, the forerunner of twentieth-century Pevsnerians. He tended to treat a church like a museum, milking it for what it could tell him of the meaning of his country. Already William Morris had a cognizance of England as not grandiose and savage but mobile and domestic. As he came to describe it:

all is measured, mingled, varied, gliding easily one thing into another: little rivers, little plains, swelling, speedily-changing uplands, all beset with handsome orderly trees; little hills, little mountains, netted over with the walls of sheep walks: all is little; yet not foolish and blank, but serious rather, and abundant of meaning for such as choose to seek it: it is neither prison nor palace, but a decent home.

As well as little churches, huge cathedrals were a part of it. When he was about eight Morris's father took him to Canterbury Cathedral. At the time Chingford church was the only substantial Gothic building he had seen. Morris later described in terms of awe the impact that Canterbury made on him when he first stood in it as a little boy. He told Wilfrid Blunt he felt the gates of Heaven had been opened to him. Blunt, after such an accolade, went on his own visit but he was disappointed. This was 1896, the year of Morris's death, and tremendous restoration work was under way.

From his first sight of Canterbury a cathedral became Morris's dream building. Quite literally so: his own dreams were filled with buildings, and cathedrals are the setting for several of Morris's dream narratives. The grand out-of-scale stone structures loom over his town-scapes as they do in the strange etchings of that later mediaevalist and devotee of Morris's, the Chipping Campden artist F. L. Griggs. With emotions so strong as to be almost insane, Morris identified himself with the cathedral. He had only to look at a cathedral such as Peter-borough to feel he had himself been one of its own builders. This is why he responded as if personally threatened when he felt a cathedral was being despoiled. Peterborough was another of the churches of his childhood. His accumulated feeling for its wonders would pour out of him in one of the most spectacular passages in *The Earthly Paradise*, the Wanderer's description of the west front of Peterborough under construction:

> I, who have seen
> So many lands, and midst such marvels been,
> Clearer than those abodes of outland men,
> Can see above the green and unburnt fen
> The little houses of an English town,
> Cross-timbered, thatched with fen-reeds coarse and brown,
> And high o'er these, three gables, great and fair,
> That slender rods of columns do upbear
> Over the minster doors, and imagery
> Of kings, and flowers no summer field doth see,
> Wrought on these gables. Yea, I heard withal,
> In the fresh morning air, the trowels fall
> Upon the stone, a thin noise far away;
> For high up wrought the masons on that day,
> Since to the monks that house seemed scarcely well
> Till they had set a spire or pinnacle
> Each side the great porch.

Sydney Cockerell, Morris's secretary, once suggested a cathedral game. Ford Madox Brown was Peterborough, Philip Webb was Dur-ham, Edward Burne-Jones was Wells. He hit problems with Rossetti, so emphatically of the passionate south: 'Is Monreale the nearest we can get to him?' Morris was definitely to be Lincoln. This would have pleased him. He admired Lincoln's great quality, its 'kind of careful delicacy of beauty'. No other English minster he ever saw came up to it: he called it 'in short a miracle of art'.

Morris came to feel that his first pleasures, the things he claimed to have discovered for himself, were stronger than anything else he had in life. On the holiday on which he first saw Canterbury Cathedral he also saw the minster in Thanet. Fifty years later Morris managed to describe it from memory precisely, although he had not been there in the intervening years. On the same eventful journey Morris saw his first illuminated manuscript. It gave him the same twinges of rapture he had had on his first sight of the cathedral: a precocious reaction for a child. Morris was revealing his peculiar ability for finding his pleasures in the recondite and, through his energies in pursuing these enthusiasms, for transforming obscure subjects into common currency. He was right about the lasting strength of those first pleasures. He was not perhaps quite honest about their derivation. It was after all his father who had brought him within reach of them: it was under his aegis that the child had seen the marvels of the churches and the manuscripts. But in later years when he rejected with such vigour, even with such cruelty, the values of his father this was not a provenance he would have wanted to admit.

When he was nine William Morris was sent off to a preparatory school, the Misses Arundale's Academy for Young Gentlemen. It was two miles away from Woodford Hall and he rode there on his pony. This was his first formal place of education. Up till then he had been taught in a haphazard way at home by his sisters and their governesses. He was ten before he was taught to write; but in two months he learned to write competently. He remembered the pains of being taught to spell, forced to stand on a chair with his shoes off as a punishment for making so many mistakes. Morris was never a good speller. He was cavalier about it. He was a notoriously careless proof-reader later in his life.

A year or two later the school moved to George Lane in Woodford, much nearer Woodford Hall. Morris continued there, first as a day boy. This period of his schooldays is confusingly recorded. Mackail maintains that Morris later boarded with the Misses Arundale; May Morris reports that her father was a boarder briefly at a school of Dr Greg's. What does seem certain, and significant, is that Morris was a boarder at a school only a few hundred yards from his own home. May describes how he used to see his family at church on Sundays but was not allowed to speak to them. The sudden enforced isolation, so near and yet so far from his familiar childhood setting, may partly account for the vituperative tone of his later account of his tribulations as the child of the conventional rich: 'my parents', wrote Morris, 'did as all right people do, shook off the responsibility of my education as soon as they could; handing me over first to nurses, then to grooms and gardeners, and then to a school – a boy farm I should say. In one way or another I learned chiefly one thing from all these – rebellion to wit.' He added that if his parents had been poorer and had had more character they would have tried to educate him. The consequences might have been even more traumatic. In the century before the 1960s' child uprisings and the *Little Red Book*'s demands for juvenile autonomy, Morris came to the conclusion that children have as much need for revolutions as the proletarians have.

Morris's life can be seen as a whole sequence of awakenings, widening out like the ripples on the mill pond until his opposition to prevailing custom and practice brought him to the outer edge of possibility. The first of the awakenings came in these early schooldays. Morris had been brought up in a mainly female household. He was closest in age to his two sisters: there was less than a year between him and Henrietta. There was then a three-year gap between William and his brothers. Stanley, Rendall and Arthur, following in quick succession, tended to band together. These were tougher children, united in their embryonic masculine pursuits. The day-to-day administration of the household was done by Morris's mother. This was a large task at which she was efficient. Morris did not underestimate the value of good housekeeping. Was he thinking of his mother when he wrote in *News from Nowhere*, 'don't you know that it is a great pleasure to a clever woman to manage a house skilfully, and to do it so that all the house-mates about her look pleased and are grateful to her?' As the delicate child at the centre of that household he developed an affinity with female occupations: cooking, sewing, overseeing garden flowers, garden produce, decoration of the house, the family festivities. There was a certain softness in his background, natural affiliations to quiet household things. All this was swept away when Morris first went to the boy farm, with a decisiveness that had the force of a whole culture shock: for the first time he was aware of the routines and the assumptions that marked the route to a separate male world.

In that world Morris's father was by now a figure of swaggering success. In 1843, the year that Morris went to school, William Morris Senior was granted a coat of arms from the Herald's College: 'Azure, a horse's head erased argent between three horseshoes or, and for crest, on a wreath of the colours, a horse's head couped argent, charged with three horseshoes in chevron sable'. For Morris, whose love of heraldry and the ritual of chivalry was combined with deep distrust of commercial practice, this coat of arms posed problems he would never totally resolve. In the early 1840s Morris's father began to speculate in the booming share market. In this he joined his brothers: Thomas, the coal merchant who lived in Camberwell, with interests in South Wales, and Francis, who lived in Denmark Hill, and was a member of the Coal Exchange. Their involvement in the financing of West Country copper mining was inherently risky but potentially lucrative. William Morris Senior and his brother Thomas formed a consortium with the family stockbroking firm of P. W. Thomas & Sons to put up the finance to begin prospecting in Blanchdown Woods on the Devon bank of the Tamar, the Duke of Bedford's land. The Devonshire Great Consolidated Copper Mining Co., later to be known as Devon Great Consols, was registered as a joint stock company in 1845. Of 1,024 shares the Morris brothers between them held 304, Thomas becoming the resident director, in control of the company from day to day. Their triumphant speculation was to provide the basis of the Morrises' 1840s' fortunes: they were what would now be called seriously rich. Shared risk-taking and shared affluence united still more closely the family already temperamentally so clannish. A copper mine was named Wheal Emma after Morris's mother when it was opened up in 1848.

Sometimes William Morris's father would take him to the City. He watched several Lord Mayor's Shows from the upper storeys of the office at King William Street. Brought up for the day, and left there until called for, he would entertain himself watching the tea dealers opposite making up interesting packets of tea and coffee. Morris always liked small traders. He enjoyed their skills and deftness and tended to treat shopkeeping as an oasis of relative innocence in the retrograde commercial world. In *News from Nowhere* it is children who are shopkeepers, plying their trade with the usual demureness of Morris's fictional children, packing up tobacco in a red morocco bag as nicely as the shopkeepers he used to watch in King William Street. But there is a difference: in Morris's Utopia necessities, even desired objects, are all free.

Morris had deeply divided feelings about cities: the city and the country; urban squalor, wealth of culture; the power of a city to create and to destroy. The sense of those bleak contrasts, which he knew because he lived them, made him one of the acutest and most troubling commentators on the city in the whole Victorian period. His perceptions of cities, in particular his long love-hate relationship with London, began early, back in those childhood days. He already saw London as a place of vast uncertainty, viewed from a distance:

> Hark, the wind in the elm boughs! From London it bloweth
> And telling of gold, and of hope and unrest.

Morris built his later critique of the city on the alienation factor, the ability of cities to turn people to automatons and deaden human passions. He was one of the prime poets of the city as the nightmare: 'a crowd that swept o'er us in measureless streams'. But Morris could also see his cities as resplendent, goals and havens where morality will always reassert itself. This is the double vision that makes him so resourceful and so credible a prophet. In so many of his stories the city takes its role as the place of ratification, recognition, where the rightful king is crowned and the lovers are united with banners, feasts and joustings and elaborate processions. In Morris's vivid visual imagination, scarlet and yellow cities are where his stories end.

What exactly was his father *doing* in the City? With his fearsome child's acuity it dawned on him his father was doing very little; or anyway not following the sort of occupation Morris in his later days would regard as manly. To Morris the idea of work became equated with creative vigour and directness: mental and manual effort that resulted in the actual production of a carpet, a story, a translation of *The Iliad*. His father's form of business activity, in contrast, was abstract and complicated to the point of being arcane. His primary occupation of bill broking was a middleman activity *par excellence*, involving the raising of bills of exchange, much used in the days before the banks offered their customers loan or overdraft facilities. These were orders to pay a particular sum by a specified date. The purchaser could claim the full amount when it was due or sell it on, at a discount, to a further buyer. The younger William Morris was caustic about bill broking. He once said that if he had gone into it he would have broken the bills into very small bits. His father's subsequent and yet more profitable ventures into West

23

Country copper mines were even remoter and in a way more shameful, involving cynical exploitation of labour and large-scale despoliation, with the Duke's co-operation, of the Devon countryside. In the valley of the Tamar near Tavistock the buildings and the slag heaps of those mines can still be seen.

A savage little squib, 'The Boy Farms at Fault', appears in *Commonweal*, the Socialist journal edited by Morris, for 30 July 1887. Using the dialogue method he developed to grab the attention of his largely working-class readers Morris mounts a comic confrontation between the rich businessman father and his son returning home for the school holidays. The father attacks his son for holiday lethargy, pointing out how hard he himself works as the provider of food, clothes, a fine home and an expensive schooling. The son turns on his father and says, 'What do you do, Pa, when you're *not* having a holiday?' He reminds him of the day he spent with his father in his City office the Christmas before: his father's so-called work consisted of reading the paper, chastising the clerks (who did what work there was to do), writing a letter and having a luxurious lunch with a client before going home:

'Come, Pa, turn to and make me wiser now by telling me how it is that you can't stand me doing nothing and boring people through the holidays, and you keep me gratis all the while; and there you are all the while doing the same thing, and being kept gratis; and you would be very much surprised if they were to send you off to a man-farm and try to get something out of you in the way of work – a big strong chap like you.'

The father's parting sally is a wonderful example of Morris's ability to play with his past and use the past to feed the present. 'I wonder what will happen to that boy. Suppose he should turn Socialist when he grows up!!'

What he hated in his father was the lack of self-awareness. He explained this, in remarkably public context, in a letter to the *Manchester Guardian* in 1884, referring sardonically to the rich men of Manchester:

I wonder if any of them remember an old story, that was taught me when I was a boy, about a beggar and a rich man. I was naive enough then, and it used to make me feel very uncomfortable, I remember, though I don't think it had the same effect on my father, who was a city man and very 'religious'.

Even as a boy he found his father an embarrassment. There is all the force of recollected agony in the passage in *The Novel on Blue Paper* in which Arthur, home from school, enters the inn at Hamington and feels 'quite queer' at seeing some strange farmers there in case they should begin to talk about his father. One of the most passionate underlying arguments of William Morris's attacks on capitalist wealth was the human one that wealth involved a change of personality. The action of making oneself rich was itself damaging: 'rich men are most commonly damned stingy'; 'I've never known a man who hasn't been spoilt by the accession of wealth'. He had watched the aggrandizement of his own father. Did William Morris Senior deserve all this opprobrium? An interesting comment has survived from a little local newssheet of the 1840s:

We advise the far-famed auctioneer, W. Morris of Woodford Hall, not to be so uncharitable as to try to prevent your peoples from getting water, this severe weather, from off his premises – his worthy predecessor did not act in this manner. Look out, old boy, for all the world knows what you are and what you have been.

The tone is sharp, if jocular; it seems the squire of Woodford Hall behaved with the arrogance of the *nouveau riche*.

Woodford Hall seems to have been a pocket of immunity in the social upheavals of the period. The 'condition of England' question was obsessing, and dividing, more liberally inclined professional families by the middle 1840s. Political debates passed the Morris household by. At Woodford Hall, Carlyle was not a name to conjure with. The family prosperity depended upon financial speculation and, at a further remove, on the employment of labour in the Devon copper mines in less than humane conditions. But what were the responsibilities of the employers? There is no sign that the Morrises were even aware of the weight of contemporary arguments against an economy in which the cash payment was the sole basis of the relationship between the master and the employee. The facts were available. The Morrises were literate. They could have read Dickens. They could have read Disraeli's 'condition of England' trilogy: *Coningsby* (1844), *Sybil* (1845) and *Tancred* (1847). Elizabeth Gaskell's *Mary Barton*, published in 1848, was an accessible and blistering indictment of class disparity and the plight of the urban industrial poor. There is no sign that Morris family apathy was lifted even when the Great Chartist demonstration in London in 1848 brought social disturbances close to home.

The Morrises could not connect. The family psychology was ruefully and truthfully described by May Morris, William Morris's second daughter, who in the 1930s subjected her own family to an almost sociological assessment, finding 'amiable people of limited experience' for whom the poor were always elsewhere. 'If these kind harmless people', wrote May,

were told that they were shutting their eyes in the face of great dangers, that they were shirking responsibilities and ignoring suffering, they would have been puzzled. They were sufficient to themselves; they gave in charity; they observed the Sabbaths; they treated their dependents well, even with affection in many cases.

Indeed the little nursemaid who used to put the infant William to bed stayed in the family for fifty years. For Morris such kindly inertia was baffling. Whereas he might have managed to excuse class prejudice, definable, opposable, what he could not forgive was his family's sheer dullness. The incriminating dullness of the British middle classes was to surface as one of his most constant, bitter themes. Morris came to believe in the morality of action, like the hero of his story who had found within himself 'the strongest will for good and evil'. No regrets for the impossible: Morris was a realist. But he later on arrived at *'fierce determination'* to do everything he could.

The father and son image was one of the most potent of the period, and especially forceful in the banking fraternities of William Morris's father. Morris told Wilfrid Blunt he had been groomed for the succession, as a matter of course. He gave Blunt a vivid picture of the agony entailed. There in the tensely autobiographical *Novel on Blue Paper* is the lingering remembrance of his fear of such a future: the son resists a posting to the Russian finance house. This same fear lay behind the terrifying picture, the most sharply imagined in any Morris story: the dream of the father on horseback, screaming, riding in pursuit of his son. The boy turned round to see his father 'and his face was all aflame'.

In 1847, quite unexpectedly, Morris's father died. He was only fifty. In the autobiographical account Morris supplied for Socialist propaganda in the 1880s he described the event curtly: 'My father died in 1847 a few months before I went to Marlborough; but as he had engaged in a fortunate mining speculation before his death, we were left very well off, rich in fact.'

Morris evades completely the element of drama that surrounded his father's death. Seven days later Sanderson & Co. suspended business. Their total liabilities amounted to over £2 million (about £200 million at current rates). That collapse caused consternation in the City, although it could perhaps have been predicted in the context of the national commercial and political crisis of 1847–48. Discount houses were put at particular risk by the inconsistent policies of the Bank of England which, after the Bank Act of 1844, began to lend money and to discount freely, in direct competition with the discount houses. In 1847, frightened by falling reserves, it reversed policy, and the London discount market effectively snarled up. It seems possible that business anxieties had caused or anyway accelerated the hyperactive William Morris Senior's death. Sanderson's itself made a partial recovery and the firm recommenced trading as Sanderson, Sandeman & Co. But the blow to Morris family finances was irreparable. It was not just a matter of the loss of the regular income of the former managing partner of the business. There was also the loss of his share of the partnership capital which Emma Morris could have withdrawn and reinvested, had not Sanderson's itself got into difficulties. It seems possible that Mrs Morris was compelled to liquidate some personal assets to pay off Sanderson's creditors. The family was now entirely dependent for its income on the interest from their shares in Devon Great Consols and these too had been falling in value. The decision was made to give up Woodford Hall and to move to a smaller house in the vicinity. The family was still by normal standards rich but a great deal less rich than before. At least some of these stresses must have devolved on William; as he once so rightly commented, children have a knack of absorbing information, even when too young to understand it absolutely. As the eldest son he was the pivot in that crisis. But of the year of financial turmoil that followed his father's death he gave no hint.

The effect of that death should not be underestimated. As the years went by, the figure of his father became the more entrenched in William Morris's mind as the capitalist villain, the symbol of hypocrisy. He became the prize example of the richness that in its reality was extreme poverty, in Morris's great diatribes on richness versus wealth. Perhaps this was an example of absence breeding hatred: William Morris's mother, after all, was physically *there* for most of her son's life, to be visited and humoured and up to a point loved. It is easier for the dead and half-forgotten to acquire the status of the ogre in the mind.

Fixation on the father as the figure of anathema was an especially Victorian and Evangelical phenomenon. It was rife in Morris's own Socialist-artistic milieu. C. R. Ashbee, the architect and Morris's disciple, would cringe when he considered H. S. Ashbee's background in finance and commodities and his scholarly relish for pornography. But Morris's denunciation of his forebears has a desperate grandeur, an apocalyptic fury:

how often it consoles me to think of barbarism once more flooding the world, and real feelings and passions, however rudimentary, taking the place of our wretched hypocrisies. With this thought in my mind all the history of the past is lighted up and lives again to me.

Morris knew in his heart he was not so unlike his father. This was the cause of his self-castigation. It was one of the main reasons why the conscience of the rich arose in him in so extreme a form. His father was ambitious, resourceful and farsighted; Morris himself had these same Victorian virtues. In his involvement in West Country copper mining William Morris Senior showed his acumen and his financial nerve: Devon Consols were one of the successes of their period, imaginative, thorough. Morris's own business, though more idealistic, was commercial innovation, highly conscious of its markets. No less than his father William Morris was the successful Victorian entrepreneur. Even his domestic life, in some respects so unconventional, had its built-in decorums. He was never a bohemian. He too was the Victorian paterfamilias. May Morris wrote fondly of the family's 'sheer faith' in his doings; she and her sister Jenny would talk about their father with a loyalty and rapture that made their schoolfriends smile.

In denying his father Morris perpetuated the sense of his own loss. There are little intimations of this all though his writings. The father as the person of undisclosed potential, the father with the unsuspected hidden streak of sympathy: the sadness that these things could not now ever be pursued. In Morris's late fairytale, the uncompleted 'Kilian of the Closes', the true nature of the father is the source of speculation. There was the suggestion that beneath the bluff exterior lay accretions of sorrow and remembrance of disaster; 'and it was this picture of the latter days as they really were that touched Kilian's heart to the quick at last, and he felt as if he had verily shared in the life of his father who was gone and who was indeed a part of him.'

This was the closest Morris came to an admission that in a profound sense he was his father's son.

CHAPTER TWO

Marlborough
1848–52

William Morris went to Marlborough College in February 1848 and acquired the nickname Crab. His father had bought the nomination to Marlborough, which was then a new school, not long before he died. Here Morris was remembered as the dark, thickset, rather solitary schoolboy sitting making nets for catching fish and birds hour after hour in the big schoolroom: he would fasten the net to a desk and work at it compulsively. Another image was of Morris the Marlborough madman, teased for eccentricity, 'in reply to which he would rush roaring – but only half angry – with his head down and his arms whirling wildly, at his tormentors'. Perhaps this ferocious clawing action was the reason for his nickname. From this period at Marlborough the physical descriptions of Morris, one of the most-described Victorians, begin accumulating: there was something about him that riveted spectators, a sense of pent-up energy, his alternating stillness and eruptiveness. At school he first discovered the uses of collusion, helping in the manufacture of his erratic image. At Marlborough he developed the first instincts that made him such a powerful and provocative de-schooler, an educational anarchist in the tradition of Godwin, Kropotkin and Goodman, arguing with all his subversive common sense that children's education was a matter too important to be settled by their parents. He saw Marlborough as boy farm on a colossal scale, as it remained for the following century, to judge from the memories of the literate.

The school had been opened only five years earlier, following the move westwards of the railway. The prospectus stressed its proximity to Swindon, 'which is to be the great point of junction of the chief lines of railway in the kingdom'. This was a school with strong religious bias, founded by a group of clergymen, country gentlemen and lawyers, intended as the main Church of England school for the south of England, with a discount in fees for the sons of clergymen. Of the early intake, sons of clergy accounted for at least two thirds. (Later, the dominant influence was military.) When Morris arrived there were still signs of the chaos of the opening days in 1843 when the first 199 boys, some arriving by train, some in their fathers' coaches, had converged on a school unfinished, underfunded, with no structure and no rules. The boys had run mad in the wilderness and stormed up and down the Mound, the ancient earthwork near the main school buildings, massacring frogs.

MARLBOROUGH COLLEGIATE SCHOOL.

2 The original buildings of Marlborough College, founded in 1843, five years before Morris arrived there as a pupil.

The intake increased fast. The school in that sense was successful. In 1848 Morris was one of 109 new boys, recorded in the register as 'Morris, William, son of Mrs. Morris, Woodford Hall, Essex, aged 14' (he was actually thirteen). Above him appears Money, below him appears Nicholls, respectively aged ten and eleven, both clergymen's sons. By this time the number of boys at Marlborough had already risen above the total stipulated by the Council. There were over 500 boys in the school. But the mechanism was not geared to such expansion, resulting in an unusual regime of terror, surpassing even Winchester, which in those days was notoriously rough. A Marlborough history describes the years 1848 to 1852, the exact period Morris was a pupil, as the 'gloomiest' in the whole history of the school.

Marlborough is a red-brick school on the outskirts of the town, centred on an early eighteenth-century brick mansion originally built for the Duke of Somerset. This self-confident classical colonnaded building, originally crowned by a cupola, came to represent many of the things in architecture Morris most detested: this was power building, impressive and oppressive. Before being taken over by the school, it had already fallen from glory and become the Castle Inn. Around this *ersatz* mansion, the C-House of the school, arose a quick succession of new houses, the dining-hall and chapel. Building work was still in progress when Morris got to Marlborough. The architect was Edward Blore, a fashionable Gothicist and antiquarian scholar with an all-important reputation for economy. He had been called in to work at Buckingham Palace when Nash was dismissed for exceeding the budget. For Marlborough Blore chose a style, William and Mary, that was unusual in the mid-nineteenth century but which set a minor trend in educational building: Wellington College is similar in feeling. For Morris at Marlborough Blore's meretricious buildings, with their disconcerting mixture of pomposity and cheeseparing, gave him an early insight into architectural shiftiness, a subject he returned to again and again with such tremendous scorn and vigour. The phrase he used for classicists like Blore was the Arabian one: these were architects of 'the ignorance'.

Morris's own house at Marlborough was A-house, recently completed. Outside it looked demure: one visitor described it as 'like an Italian town palace'. Inside it was more brutal, an enormous cage or prison, a three-storey iron structure with a great well in the centre, rising to a skylight, the only source of daylight. It was almost a model for Bentham's *Panopticon*, his scheme for improving prison discipline. This was an interior designed for public surveillance: privacy was non-existent. Again like a prison, the structure encouraged secret terrorizations, bullyings, cabals. Rugby's ritual torture of the tossing in the blanket or toasting by the fire has haunted the English liberal conscience ever since Thomas Hughes's *Tom Brown's Schooldays*; Marlborough had an equivalent, the suspension of small boys in sheets over the upper banisters of A-house. Those who underwent it would sometimes be unable to speak at all of Marlborough after forty years, like victims from the concentration camps. Small boys' ears were also bored with pins or pocket knives. Morris's memories of A-house surface dourly in a letter to Philip Burne-Jones, at Marlborough in the 1870s. When he returned to look at it he thought his old room there 'such a dismal place'. He added:

31

'a troublous life I led of it there for two years after which I became a dignified person comparatively and was Captain of the room.'

Torture by boys was one thing. The diary of Morris's friend and contemporary Robert Nunns records countless minor incidents of stealing, smashing, whacking, fighting as well as more specific bodily assaults: 'Hughes and Glennie filled my mouth with dust'; 'Hughes, Sidebottom and Hickman put me on the raft without oars and splashed me. Very wet all over'. But more insidious was the torture by the masters. In the late 1840s Marlborough was understaffed, most of the masters being men in holy orders. The school was badly organized, and staff morale was low. Teaching was carried out in two large draughty schoolrooms: Lower School and the new Upper School, in which the boys of nine forms spent their entire indoor lives. The only obvious way of keeping discipline was caning. Public and often indiscriminate caning was not at the time peculiar to Marlborough; but there it was apparently particularly vicious. Sometimes two masters would be caning simultaneously in the large schoolroom with a rhythm that seemed to a fascinated witness like that of two blacksmiths hammering on an anvil.

The ultimate punishment at Marlborough was flogging by the birch. The culprit was marched off between two prefects to the inner sanctum of the headmaster's study from which emanated the familiar noises of the swish of the rod and the outstretched victim's yells. The headmaster carried out this fearsome ceremony with a certain desperation: Dr Wilkinson of Marlborough was not a Dr Arnold of Rugby. He was inexperienced, pale, short, chinless and lacked *gravitas*. Under his headmastership the new school lurched disastrously beyond control. A boy of Morris's generation described graphically 'the crushing repressions which the new boy of artistic or intellectual taste encounters'. He himself arrived at school with a good knowledge of French and a strong taste for music. Over the next four years, in the struggle for existence, these tastes were 'simply crushed out'.

How did Morris, then, a child of abnormal sensitivity, survive his years at Marlborough? It was partly that he learned to keep his distance. Indeed he regretted later that he had not done more fighting, since in his few fights he had come out quite successfully. Morris added:

for the rest I had a hardish time of it, as chaps who have brains and feelings generally do at school, or say in the world even, whose griefs are not much shared in by the hard and stupid: nor its joys either, happily so that we may be well content to be alive and eager, and to bear pain sometimes rather than to grow like rotting cabbages and not to mind it.

Morris has an extraordinary gift for transformation, for extracting possibilities from painful situations: here are the first signs of what one might describe as his creative stoicism.

As a small child William Morris had had a very random form of home-based education, reading with his sisters, pursuing what interested him in his surroundings. This remained in a way his ideal of education: 'children', he would often say, 'bring each other up'. At the Misses Arundale's school he had experienced for the first time an educational framework of school rules and school curricula. That had been a shock, but not on the scale of Marlborough. The Misses Arundale's was a less formal school, nearer home and, like most small boys' schools of the time, was run by women. Both at school and at home, until he went to Marlborough, women in fact were Morris's chief figures of authority. At Marlborough he found himself in a community where the maleness was unfamiliar and alarming and where the attempted rigid discipline was no less onerous for being ineffective. There was a daily timetable, beginning with prayers at seven forty-five a.m., followed by lessons from eight to nine, from ten to twelve, from two to five. Although in those days Marlborough had no fixed uniform there were definite conventions about clothes and appearance and details of behaviour enforced with all the dogmatism of enclosed, inbred communities. A spoof letter in the school magazine of Morris's period tells the sad story of the new boy's Sunday cap: 'Tom said that the braiding on the top of it was like an open tart, and some of the boys have pulled it off.'

Morris at Marlborough was desperately homesick. He poured out his feelings a little shamefacedly to his sister Emma, in a letter written in his second term at Marlborough, asking her for seven postage stamps and describing the isolated misery of the dark late October days, when the school gates shut at five o'clock and the lamps were lit simultaneously. 'I am sure you must think me a great fool to be always thinking about home always, but I really can't help it I don't think it is my fault for there are such a lot of things I want to do and say, and see.' This is the earliest of Morris's extant letters. It is characteristic in its sweetness and confidingness: Morris wrote vivid letters, completely unselfconscious and rambling like his talk. What makes this letter so poignant is the fact that it was sent at the time the Morris family moved from Woodford Hall to Water House in Walthamstow. No one seems to have told him precisely which the new house was. Morris, with his deep need for rootedness, sounds anguished. Have they moved to the house that was once a Mrs Clarke's house? 'Or is it the one next to it where whenever I passed there were sure to come up to the street gate a whole legion of greyhounds Scotch, English, and Italian, do you know the one I mean?'

As a boy Morris had trained himself in rapid observation and mental spontaneity. At Marlborough he found himself in a foreign land of learning by rote: catechisms, translations, repetitions. He told Emma, 'Today being a Saints day I am one to be chatechized [*sic*] in Evening Service today as I was also catechized last Sunday.' He used to fulminate against his Marlborough education, saying that he learned nothing because nothing was taught. This was not entirely accurate. In some respects the teaching he received was a bombardment. But it was not what Morris meant by education. 'We have begun the epistle of Dido to Aeneas,' wrote a new boy of Morris's period to his sister. 'We do ten lines at a time and also 12 lines of the Vth book of Caesar. We also do a good deal of Greek or Latin grammar.' Here at Marlborough in the late 1840s was a regime that was an almost exact counterpart of teaching at Rugby in the early 1830s, described in graphic detail in Hughes's *Tom Brown's Schooldays*. This was a deadly system that relied on correct answers and edged out of real thinking: a life of living by the crib.

Morris entered the school in the Fourth Form 1st Remove; he left three years later from the Fifth Form 2nd Remove. The teaching he received was based on the Classics. In the classical set Morris learned Greek and Latin, History and Divinity. The forms were subdivided into different divisions for Maths and French, the set for French being notoriously noisy. A Mr Fleuss is listed in the records for that period as teaching German and Drawing. It is not clear whether or not Morris was taught drawing, although his housemaster, the Rev. E. R. Pitman, was a competent artist in pen-and-ink. Morris does not refer to this at all. What he did record later, in the 1890s, was his boredom with his masters and their narrowness of vision. He put this in the context of his burgeoning contrariness: 'I was educated at Marlborough under clerical masters, and I naturally rebelled against them. Had they been advanced men, my spirit of rebellion would have probably led me to conservatism merely as a protest. One naturally defies authority.'

There was certainly no question of the lessons being beyond him. This was after all the man who would intimidate his friends with his range and depth of knowledge: Wilfrid Blunt went so far as to describe him as 'the strongest intellect I have had the good fortune to come into close contact with during my life'. He was never to be in the strictest sense a scholar but he had a very strenuous, retentive, clearcut intellect: the grand apotheosis of the magpie mind. At Marlborough his mediocre marks around the middle level of the class lists suggest a definite resistance to the system in which one could achieve success through a mere glibness. Morris loathed the spurious. He always found out fudgers. He had ways of telling instantly a guess from a known fact. The basis of his whole critique of education was his belief that there was a true and a false knowledge. Marlborough seemed to him, like Eton, a place equipped for teaching 'rich men's sons to know nothing'. The most they learned was to acquire a knowing suavity. When Morris actually went to Eton in the 1880s to lecture about Socialism his reception even by the boys was hostile. The master who invited him was embarrassed to remember the contrast between spruce, correct Etonians, dressed for the evening event in their white ties, and Morris himself, 'the sturdy figure in the rough pilot coat and blue shirt and his curly solid head.'

Morris tended to exaggerate his failures as a schoolboy. He told Blunt he was always bottom in arithmetic: school records show his very worst placing as twelfth out of sixteen. At his best he rose to sixth. But certainly his cast of mind was never mathematical. He claimed he never knew a mathematician who could reason, and the study of mathematics was low on the agenda when he came to formulate his ideal curriculum. For Morris it was history that was the be-all and end-all. He saw history as solemn, deep and absolutely central: he accepted other subjects only in as far as they threw light on history. Despite Marlborough teaching, he approved of Greek and Latin, adding Sanskrit or Persian and one modern language, preferably German. French should be learned, but solely for its literature: Morris dismissed French and English as not strictly speaking languages, because they lacked the proper syntax. English grammar would be banned unless it was arrived at through a course of philological readings beginning at the fourteenth century. As Morris himself grew older the ideal curriculum became more and more elastic. By the 1890s it included 'politics and Socialism of course – and many other things'.

By the time he came to write *News from Nowhere* he had formed an ideal of education that was the absolute antithesis of Marlborough and which strikes one now as uncannily prophetic of the ethos of British twentieth-century progressive schools. Morris's active suntanned children, boys and girls together, in their tents in the forest, learning by doing, noticing wild creatures, swimming, cooking, thatching, mowing, making rough-hewn timber furniture in an atmosphere of intellectual freedom and sexual liberation: this could be a summer camp at Summerhill or Dartington in the years between the wars. He arrived at a large, generous view of education, seeing it as inevitably a life-long process. Morris is the prophet of the Third Age movement. When Guest in *News from Nowhere* suggests that education is for young people only, his guide around Utopian England turns and snubs him: 'Why not old people also?' In Morris's idealistic vision of the future he denies the sort of cramming that had deadened him at Marlborough, arguing for a scheme of voluntary information: information that stays in the mind because you need it. In that community, leisured because not greedy, everyone can afford to give themselves the time to grow.

Morris had a kind of genius for seeing what he wanted by rejecting the alternative. He was the man of instinct in the scientific age. W. B. Yeats, who knew Morris from the 1880s and admired him, explained wonderfully well his prophetic quality, the bound of the imagination he could take to envisage new conditions of making and doing. As Yeats put it:

in the teeth of those scientific generalizations that cowed my boyhood I can see some like imagining in every great change, and believe that the first flying fish first leaped, not because it sought 'adaptation' to the air, but out of horror of the sea.

Morris said he had learned almost everything he knew of architecture and mediaeval things running around the country near Marlborough when he was a schoolboy. In some ways the laxity of those early years of Marlborough suited him ideally. There was no regular regime of organized games as at public schools later. Morris avoided easily the small amount of cricket and football that was played. Out of school hours supervision was minimal. The wilder of the boys raged around the neighbourhood in gangs, 'with knobbed sticks and squalars, with jackets buttoned tight up to their throat, and a look of pluck and determination on their faces'. The squalar was a ferocious home-made weapon consisting of a piece of lead the size and shape of a pear with an eighteen-inch cane handle. Its prime target was the squirrel, but rabbits, hares and deer were killed with it and some of the boys became expert at deer skinning. Morris must have drawn on memories of Marlborough when he came to write his novels of the warring of the tribes.

His own pleasures were gentler. Marlborough, he wrote, is 'in a very beautiful country, thickly scattered over with prehistoric monuments, and I set myself eagerly to studying these and everything else that had any history in it, and so perhaps learned a good deal.' Right at hand, in the school grounds, was the mysterious Mound, sixty feet high, the only surviving sign of the Norman royal castle previously on the site. In the early eighteenth century the Mound had been transformed into a show-piece of the picturesque, equipped with a cascade and a grotto: it was described as both newer and 'prettier than Twickenham', where Alexander Pope's fashionable garden also contained a grotto and a mound. The Mound quickly became a part of Marlborough College folklore. John Betjeman, at school there in the 1920s, mounted a campaign for its proper conservation. To Morris too it had its charms, not least its charm of form, like an upturned pudding basin. In his early years he had little of his later feeling for mountains: that came after Iceland. But mounds, domestic, comely, humorous, appealed to him. In one of his tales there is the curiously typical apparition in the distance of two castles on twin mounds.

Sheep have often grazed on the top plateau of a mound beside which the Mound at Marlborough seems child-size. This is Silbury Hill, the tallest prehistoric structure in Europe, visited by Morris innumerable times in his rambles around Wiltshire. What delighted Morris were the things that had intrigued those earlier enthusiasts, John Aubrey in the seventeenth century and William Stukeley in the eighteenth: the incongruities and the strong sense of ancient days in a landscape so replete with banks and ditches, hillocks, tumuli, long barrows, suggestive shapes erupting in the quiet English fields. Morris described to Emma a visit to Silbury in April of his second year at school. He calls it 'an artificial hill made by the Britons'. He comments that 'it must have taken an immense long time to have got it together': already practicalities concern him. The mysteries surrounding the enormous earthen mound were exciting to him too. Was it a giant burial mound?

In fact no evidence of burial has ever been discovered. The Duke of Northumberland employed Cornish miners to sink a shaft down into the mound in 1777 but without result. Is it, as has more recently been claimed, the central edifice of the Stone Age cult of the Great Goddess? Are the hill and its moat *actually* the Great Goddess? This is speculation Morris would have much enjoyed.

At the time he discovered it the hill was covered by a blanket of wild flowers of many different species. In 1857 it was the site of a botanical survey; more recent botanical investigations listed eighty-five species of flowering plants growing in the grass. Morris as a schoolboy had climbed the hill attentively. He said to Emma, 'I brought away a little white snail as a memento of the place and have got it in my pocket book.'

On that same expedition Morris went to Avebury. He was puzzled at first by the peculiar formation of this vast prehistoric earthwork set with sarsens. He went back to Marlborough to find out more about it and returned again to Avebury next day. On that second visit he could understand much better how the sarsens had been fixed, sending Emma a technical description of the biggest stone he saw. Its height above the ground was about sixteen feet; it was roughly ten feet thick and twelve feet broad. Near the Avebury stones he saw a very old church: 'the tower was very pretty indeed it had four little spires on it of the decorated order and there was a little Porch and inside the porch a beautiful Norman doorway loaded with mouldings the chancel was new and was paved with tesselated pavement this I saw through the window for I did not know where the sexton's house was, so of course I could not get the key.' Morris, only just fifteen, was already showing the expertise of the practised church visitor and he was beginning to record his observations with the mixture of succinctness and deep feeling that made him so exceptional a writer about landscape. Jenny Morris used to say her father could make you see a place exactly in just half a dozen words.

What he loved and understood was the rhythm of the landscape: the way that, at Avebury, the 'pretty little Parsonage house' was built beside the church and this proximity was sharpened by the rugged and surrealistic outlines of the sarsens; the way that textures changed from grassiness to mud lanes to water fields to water meadows. William Morris's attempt to explain to Emma, distant in Walthamstow, the nature of a Wiltshire water meadow results in a description that is partly childlike in its physical exuberance and partly very adult in its accurate perception of the way in which things function:

So for your edification, I will tell you what a delectable affair a water meadow is to go through; in the first place you must fancy a field cut through with an infinity of small streams say about four feet wide each the people to whom the meadow belongs can turn these streams on and off when they like and at this time of year they are on just before they put the fields up for mowing the grass being very long you cannot see the water till you are in the water and floundering in it.

Luckily, he says, the water was not boggy when they went through it: 'else we should have been up to our middles in mud'.

William Morris's relation to landscape was already, in his Marlborough days, a physical experience of sensual intensity. He appreciated both the depths and heights of it. He wrote about the marshes and the marigolds, deep ditches, muddy furrows with the enthusiasm of an early Seamus Heaney. Years later, when revisiting the country around Pewsey, 'a little scrubby town', he could easily recapture his extreme exhilaration at the great expanse of downland: 'it was all very fine and characteristic country especially where we had to climb the Marlborough downs at a place that I remembered coming on as a boy with wonder and pleasure: Oare Hill they call it.' The downs had had a mesmeric effect with their vast stretches: 'no end to them almost'. And then there would be a sudden group of yew and scotch-fir growing on fine turf. Morris clung to the landscape, absorbed it and defended it, maintaining that there was no square mile of the earth's surface that was not beautiful in its way. His childhood experience of two such different Englands – Essex domesticity, the sweep and surge of Wiltshire – was always to be drawn upon by Morris in his vision of unsullied variegated countryside. This was a vision so vital and so intimate it could only be experienced in terms of the erotic: 'intense and overweening love of the very skin and surface of the earth on which man dwells, such as a lover has in the fair flesh of the woman he loves'.

He had his own link with that prehistoric landscape. His father's coat of arms was the horse's head with horseshoes. Morris loved the graphic qualities of heraldry. His poems and his tales are full of decorative banners bearing strongly outlined symbols. The image of the bear, of the dragon, of the raven: a militant and primitive corporate identity, the recognition symbols of the tribes. In some romantic way Morris liked to imagine he was himself a tribesman of the white horse. The giant horse cut out of chalk in the Berkshire downs at Uffington near Lambourn aroused strong emotions in him. When he lived at Kelmscott he would make an annual pilgrimage. He even went to see it, by then in flagging health, in the year before his death. Such signs of ancient life had a peculiar effect on him. He could summon up past scenes, repeople empty landscape, with an almost lunatic exactness: 'Not seldom I please myself', wrote Morris,

with trying to realize the face of mediaeval England; the many chases and great woods, the stretches of common tillage and common pasture quite unenclosed; the rough husbandry of the tilled parts, the unimproved breeds of cattle, sheep and swine, especially the latter, so lank and long and lathy, looking so strange to us; the strings of packhorses along the bridle-roads, the scantiness of the wheel-roads, scarce any except those left by the Romans, and those made from monastery to monastery; the scarcity of bridges, and people using ferries instead, or fords where they could; the little towns well bechurched, often walled; the villages just where they are now (except for those that have nothing but the church left to tell of them), but better and more populous; their churches, some big and handsome, some small and curious, but all crowded with altars and furniture, and gay with pictures and ornament; the many religious houses, with their glorious architecture; the beautiful manor-houses, some of them castles once, or survivals from an earlier period; some new and elegant; some out of all proportion small for the importance of their lords.

This was Morris's sort of history: a detailed picture history, a sensitive time traveller's reclaiming of the past. It is essentially a cinematic vision. Had he lived a little later he might have been an Eisenstein. Morris in full flood is grandiloquent, persuasive: 'How strange it would be to us if we could be landed in fourteenth century England'. Strange but curiously real.

Near the school was William Morris's other forest, Savernake. This was very different in character from Epping, chalky, lighter, more domestic, the trees less gnarled and lowering. Here in Savernake they were mainly beech and oak. It had been a royal forest since the Conquest. By the late 1840s Savernake was peculiar in being the only English forest privately administered; the Marquesses of Ailesbury were its 'hereditary wardens'. The Ailesbury family, before they were ennobled, had owned the red-brick building taken over to form the core of Marlborough College. The links between Savernake and Marlborough continued, in that the boys tended to look upon the forest as a kind of extended playground of the school. Morris's friend Robert Nunns, for instance, enters in his diary: 'In afternoon went with Tomkins into Forest and got a very large quantity of crabs.'

Morris was on intimate terms with a great forest which because of its past history was more selfconsciously romantic than Epping. The first Earl of Ailesbury, in the eighteenth century, had made the land partly agricultural, partly commercial woodland. His son married the sister of Lord Burlington, the amateur architect. The second earl started the planting of beech avenues, culminating in the Grand Avenue. As a forest Savernake by this time was not so much a thicket, more a series of beautifully interconnected sylvan glades. But Morris would have seen layers of history and oddity. Knowle Farm, within the Forest, was an important Stone Age site which yielded up huge quantities of Acheulean flint hand-axes, many of them with a peculiar surface gloss. And just behind the farm there is a problematic chapel, a rectangular stone building said to date from the late thirteenth century. The Chapel of St Martin, with its air of desolation, seems straight out of a novel by Sir Walter Scott.

In the back of Morris's mind was a third forest, the New Forest. As a child he was an avid reader of the stories of Captain Maryatt. Maryatt's most famous book, *The Children of the New Forest*, was published the year before Morris entered Marlborough. This was an emotional story of the Civil War. Morris would have identified easily with the family of orphans, two boys and two girls, brought up by the old retainer in the forest: Edward, the eldest, was exactly his own age. The retainer raised the children as if they were his grandchildren, teaching the boys all he knew of forestry. They became his inseparable companions in the wood. Their life of happy isolation possibly encouraged William Morris's own intermittent longing for the simple life in a cottage in deep country, spending his time translating Homer and amusing himself taking tremendously long walks.

In the end it is revealed that the children are not cottagers but the scions of the noble house of Beverly and they are returned to the bosom of the royalists. It is interesting and not coincidental that Morris's own stories often have the same momentum: they often concern children who are brought up in the wilderness not knowing their true parentage. Morris's noble savages are literally noble. These narratives explore the effect of a childhood spent outside society on people pre-selected by their birth to be its leaders. At the end of a long story true nobility will out.

Morris stressed the fact that his wanderings at Marlborough were fuelled by his reading. First to know and then to look, and by looking transform knowledge: this was a *modus operandi* based on continued and systematic reading. He was grateful that there was a good library at Marlborough to which he 'sometimes' had access. This was Adderley Library, installed not long after Morris entered the school. An article of 1849 described the new library, 'with good oak fittings', formed by throwing together two large rooms of the old mansion. Already it had acquired a thousand volumes from 'a liberal member of the council'. This collection was being added to and was available, under certain regulations, to 'the trustworthy boys'.

The implication is that Morris had been one of the chosen. He never had much problem of access to libraries. It was normally assumed he was one of nature's library users, perhaps because he came to behave as if he owned them. H. M. Hyndman, then his colleague in the Democratic Federation, remembered the morning he went with William Morris to the Bodleian Library in Oxford. To his astonishment, the head librarian insisted Morris come and identify the contents of a large parcel of illuminated missals. They went into an inner room where the missals were arrayed on the table. Morris sat down beside them and 'taking them up one by one, looked very quickly but very closely and carefully at each in turn, pushing it aside after inspections with "Monastery so and so, date such and such", "Abbey this in such a year", until he had finished the whole number'. To Hyndman there seemed not the slightest doubt in the librarian's mind that Morris's judgement was correct and final. Perhaps at Marlborough he gave out that same aura of careful confidence.

There is evidence that Morris acquired, perhaps encouraged, a reputation as a literary oddity. He was the boy who was expert at evading rituals he disliked; amongst these was fagging out, doing jobs and running errands for the older boys at school. He would wander away to the forest or the river. 'Even then he mooned and talked to himself and was considered "an ass",' wrote a contemporary, D. R. Fearon. At first he and Morris used to go for walks together, Morris telling endless stories of knights and fairies, in which one adventure overlapped into another. Fearon got tired of these stories very soon. At one stage the captain of Morris's dormitory began to cultivate him. The captain had a craving for tales of romance. Here we see Morris already in the tricky role of tale-teller, boring some, enchanting others. His *Marlburian* obituary shows him as an oddball, a large lad with thick dark curly hair and pronounced forehead, with his slightly suspect repertoire of stories. His check waistcoat is partly a 'warm blue'.

Marlborough did not extinguish Morris's imagination. Maybe in perverse ways it actually fed it. Perhaps one should see Morris, like those later poets and Marlburians John Betjeman and Louis MacNeice, as part of that strange seam of the exotic that has always flourished even at the most philistine of English public schools. But Morris was never a performer of the mainstream like the intellectual schoolboys of those later generations. He seemed then a rather taciturn and introverted figure, remarkable mainly for his sudden bursts of temper. He does not seem ever to have won the prize for the best English essay, the subject of which, in 1850, was 'A garden is the purest of human pleasures'. Nor does he appear to have contributed to any of the contemporary issues of *The Marlborough Magazine*, though this literary venture included many of the sorts of subjects that Morris later turned to: folk tales; the story of 'The Old Oak Chest'; a poem on 'an ancient Druidical Monument near Marlborough'. The most striking similarities are in 'The Allegory' of 1848, a romantic schoolboy tale of adventure and enchantment, in which the dream framework prefigures the dream landscapes that became almost the William Morris hallmark, and in which the lady on the sofa in the castle already has something of Pre-Raphaelite seductiveness: 'She was most beautifully, though somewhat voluptuously attired, in a loose and flowing robe.'

No one at Marlborough got William Morris's measure. But there was a sense in which he did not allow it. Already he was set in his persona of the outcast. His later blossomings were unexpected. 'When tidings came how elaborate were his rooms, and how he had become a celebrity at Oxford, surprise was manifested in the school.'

In March 1849 Morris was confirmed by the Bishop of Salisbury in Marlborough College chapel. This ceremony took place early on a Saturday. The boys went into chapel at eight a.m., the candidates for confirmation sitting together in pews near the altar. They stood for the bishop to confirm them, the service taking about twenty minutes. Morris told his sister Emma that the bishop, Edward Denison, was very tall and thin. He did not look old, although he was bald at the top of his head. Morris also commented that he was of a high family. The next day Morris received his first Holy Communion: 'it is here', he told Emma, 'administered to every one singly.' The school was strong on ritual. The effeminate figure of Dr Wilkinson, who wore a cummerbund or scarf around his cassock, confirmed the general impression that Marlborough was a *cache* of Anglo-Catholics.

The chapel was new. Like the rest of the school buildings of that period it had been commissioned from Edward Blore. It was another cut-price building. *The Ecclesiologist* was highly critical of the ethics of the architect who undertook to build 'a cathedral' for the sum of £5,000, castigating the chapel for having 'just that amount of sham and unreality which no artist, who reverenced his profession, or his immediate work, would have been guilty of'. This critic's chief scorn was directed to the altar, 'of a most preposterous size', perhaps as much as nine foot long, fitted with a strange recess compounded of a fireplace and Easter sepulchre: 'consequently the sideboard aspect predominates.' But no fault was found in the religious ceremonial: 'Twice every day is the whole school assembled at the morning and evening prayers of the church. The punctual attendance of all the masters, the voluntary presence of so many of the household officers, the reverent behaviour of the boys, makes this a sight which few who witnessed it can forget.'

There are all the signs that Morris entered into the religious life of Marlborough with enthusiasm. This may partly have been because Morris, like John Betjeman, appreciated the apartness of the chapel: it was the one school building where he could be *alone*. It was also a building which was, in its form, familiar. Morris, having read widely in a library so rich in books on ecclesiastical architecture, had a precocious knowledge of historic styles of building: he claimed he knew most of what there was to know about English Gothic before he left school. Blore's chapel was Middle Pointed in character, eight bays long with four angle turrets and a bell-turret. It had its shortcomings: the bell was so puny it could not be heard even within the college. But this was a building with which Morris could feel an immediate emotional rapport. He could respond to the music in the chapel from his own family knowledge of cathedral musicology. The music at Marlborough, compared with other schools, was unusually good with an energetic choir composed of boys and masters. Morris, aged fifteen, reported to his sister:

We here had the same anthem on Monday and Tuesday as on Sunday it was the three first verses of the 72nd Psalm . . . a gentleman (one of the boy's fathers) said on the whole our choir sang better than at Salisbury Cathedral; Anyhow I thought it very beautiful. The first verse was sung by the whole the second begun by one treble voice till at last the base took it up again gradually getting deeper and deeper then again the treble voice again then the base the third verse was sung entirely by base, not very loud but with that kind of emphasis which you would think befitting to such a subject. I almost think I liked it better than either of the other two the only fault in the anthem seemed to me that it was too short.

This was the religion of sensuous extremes. Morris would have been aware of Pugin's treatise *The True Principles of Pointed or Christian Architecture* published in 1841 and, still more relevant, his *Apology for the Revival of Christian Architecture in England* of 1843. He would have seen the illustrations of Catholic and Anglo-Catholic interiors which transformed religion into a quasi-theatrical experience by the use of vivid colour, lavish gilding, glinting silver, ornate vestments sometimes supplied by theatrical costumiers, expert manipulation of light and shade. From a relatively open and brightly lit nave emotions were channelled down the church towards the darkness and richness and mystery of the chancel, the mystery accentuated by the rood screen and the rood itself, suspended from the dark recesses of the chancel arch. Puginesque architecture has a histrionic quality. Its literary counterparts are Walter Scott and even Mrs Radcliffe, pioneer of shudderscape.

The Anglo-Catholic movement and the Romantic movement of the early nineteenth century were related: the one had fed upon the other. They were closely intertwined in Morris's mind. Ideals of renunciation, overlaid by the shadowy attractions of the celibate life, influenced Morris towards a decision that was as much aesthetic as intellectual. It was settled during his time at Marlborough that he would be entering the Church.

Perhaps it was of the essence of rich establishment puritanism that it should breed the opposite. Morris's oldest sister Emma, as one sees from the confident tone of his school letters, obviously shared his own religious predilections. Emma was soon to marry Joseph Oldham, a young clergyman, formerly curate at Walthamstow: he too was very High Church in his views. William Morris's second sister Henrietta was converted to Roman Catholicism, in Rome itself, in early middle age and was photographed soon after in a pious black mantilla with a pendant crucifix. Another of his sisters, Isabella Gilmore, the South London deaconess, rejected the puritan practice of her childhood in favour of the richly sacramental form of Anglicanism that sustained her in her work in the Battersea slums. Morris flung himself into the religious life at Marlborough with an extremism that was both opposed to and inherent in his family and which was to resurface in his passionate adherence to the other religion of the Socialist cause.

In November 1851 Marlborough College erupted into what was always described as 'The Rebellion'. Morris's own part in it seems to have been minimal although he regaled his own children with accounts of it. The Marlborough Rebellion was Dr Wilkinson's débâcle, the disastrous culmination of a headmastership that had been becoming increasingly distraught. Through that autumn the tension at the school had been accelerating. Three boys had been reported for tormenting an old miller travelling locally along the lanes by donkey: they had seized the donkey from him and driven it into the river. A mass curfew had resulted from the failure of the culprits to confess. An attack on the lodge of the gate sergeant of the College, who had made himself unpopular by flogging a number of boys caught dancing by moonlight on the roof of C-house, had caused a new commotion. The ringleader was expelled. Early in November the boys began amassing fireworks, forbidden on the premises. They collected a grand total of some eighty dozen squibs and crackers, plus 'heavier artillery'. Five o'clock on Guy Fawkes' night was zero hour. 'Punctually at that hour', wrote an enthralled spectator, 'we saw a rocket shoot up into the sky from the centre of the court, and knew that the revolution had begun.'

Fireworks were let off in all the houses and the schoolrooms. A great many windows were broken in the chapel. Dr Wilkinson himself was attacked with fire crackers when he tried to address the boys in Upper School. He and several of the masters were standing near the fire when a bottle of gunpowder was thrown into the flames where it exploded 'with a fearful bang'. The explosions and riots went on for many days. The reserves of fire crackers seemed inexhaustible. Perhaps this explains Morris's later firework phobia. 'I always did hate fireworks,' he said, describing the great fire at Tooley Street in London that set the Thames ablaze in 1861.

Dr Wilkinson discovered the names of the boys who had brought in the fireworks. Four more boys were dismissed, among them Augustus Twyford, a popular hero of the school. Sensing trouble, Dr Wilkinson arranged for him to leave the school not via the main entrance but from the Master's lodge. The plan was discovered. Several hundred boys were waiting. 'Tramp, tramp, tramp,' wrote Edward Lockwood, who was one of this contingent, 'eight abreast we doubled along the road leading to the town, and woe to any obnoxious person whom we met, and who found no method of escape.' Back at the College uproar broke out again and authority was defied with a loud chorus of groans, slamming of desks and stamping of feet. In the days which followed, flogging went on continually; at one stage as many as twenty-eight boys were flogged in a batch. But these desperate measures were largely ineffective. Before anything like discipline began to be restored the Headmaster's sacred inner chamber had been ransacked, the stock of birches he kept there had been scattered. Even the manuscript translation of Sophocles on which he had been labouring was burned.

The Rebellion was Morris's first experience of anarchy. It must have affected the way he came to look at the whole question of revolution and mass violence. He was never afraid of physical resistance; he could comprehend that revolution implied bloodshed. What he was opposed to, with a deep repugnance that increased as he knew more of it, was mindless violence. He was repelled by the movement of the mob. At Marlborough, for weeks, he had seen it in the ascendant. He was deeply alarmed at the power of the hooligan; and what more potent proto-Fascist image than the Marlborough boys tramping through the town in military formation eight abreast?

Whose side was Morris on in the Rebellion? He was a natural anti-authoritarian. But he was an observant one. It would not have escaped him that this was not a simple confrontation of boys versus masters, innocence verses brutality. It had its hidden elements of class war. There were the complex sub-plots of boys versus school retainers, boys versus local peasantry. The public-school ethos encouraged social arrogance. This stayed on Morris's conscience and underpinned his thinking. Forty years later he could still describe with fury to his friend Henry Salt (formerly an Eton master) the scene in which a local farmer had been pelted from the Marlborough College windows as he passed below. When the school was assembled to hear him state his grievances there was such a storm of laughter that the inquiry had had to be abandoned. British public schools in the past have often bolstered class disparity and military jingoism with complacent impunity up to the point of a reaction, which, when it comes, can be a hard one. There are numerous small histories of lives of opposition: rejection of class, rejection of conventional public-school loyalties to monarchy and country. Morris himself became a revolutionary Socialist and a passionate anti-imperialist and that was one thing. It is also worth remembering that, in another century, Marlborough educated Anthony Blunt.

The 1851 Rebellion was a personal disaster for Dr Wilkinson. The next term he resigned and became a country clergyman. He was replaced by the Rev. George Cotton, the 'grave young master' who appears in *Tom Brown's Schooldays*. This was to be a much improved regime; but not before the school had been doubly decimated by the removal of almost a hundred boys by parents alarmed by the news of revolution as the lurid tales seeped out. Amongst those withdrawn was William Morris, who left in December from the Fifth Form, having taken his final term's examinations. In these he was placed fifth out of nine entrants, true to form.

Morris returned to Walthamstow and spent most of the next year there, partly at home and partly studying for his Oxford entry with a private tutor, the Rev. Frederick B. Guy, a young master at the nearby Forest School. The Morris family home, Water House, the only one of Morris's childhood homes still standing, is a mid-eighteenth-century buff brick building with a portico flanked by three-bay bow windows. It is a handsome building, mellow, safe, portentous: a watered-down version of Woodford Hall. The tenor of the life there was similarly feudal, though less extravagant. Water House was moated. Behind it was a lawn and beyond the lawn a moat forty feet wide. In the moat arose an island planted with aspens. The water was alive with pike and perch. The boys fished in the moat and skated on it in the winter. The overgrown island made a dank adventure playground. Rendall Morris once marooned himself there, an imitation Robinson Crusoe, creeping back into the house, frightened and cold, at night. The moat for William Morris was a recurring image. It had a double poignancy. First, the antiquarian: the moat is the cliché of the imagined mediaeval scene. For Morris it had a place in his own history, suggestive of so many of the adolescent yearnings of that oddly displaced year:

> Deep green water fill'd the moat,
> Each side had a red-brick lip,
> Green and mossy with the drip
> Of dew and rain; there was a boat
>
> Of carven wood, with hangings green
> About the stern; it was great bliss
> For lovers to sit there and kiss
> In the hot summer noons, not seen.

Descriptions of Morris at this period show his unusual ebbs and flows of mood. For much of the time he was lodging with his tutor in Hoe Lane, Walthamstow, where Frederick Guy coached him between school hours, dividing his time between his official and unofficial pupils. For Morris this was a return to the scene of his earlier schooldays in Walthamstow: a fellow pupil at Guy's, W. H. Bliss, had been surprised to find him lodging so close to his own home. Bliss regarded Morris as convivial, resourceful, hyperenergetic and perhaps a bit alarming. When they played singlestick he insisted on a table between them to ward off the blows when Morris got to fury point. Morris taught him netting and together they made a large net with which they dragged the pond at Water House, fishing out some perch and a great many weeds. He remembered rambles in the forest, on one of which either he or Morris got into trouble by knocking a goose on the head with a large stone.

Morris was already seeming reckless and amusing, with a trace of the self-parody that delighted his later Pre-Raphaelite cronies. But there was something that put people on their guard. 'I don't like the boy William. He seems to see nothing and he observes everything,' noted a female relation meeting him at Water House at this post-Marlborough period. When he arrived at Guy's his tutor had not known what to make of him and indeed had not expected to make any progress with him. In fact they later got on well. F. B. Guy, later a Canon of St Albans, was a High Churchman of some visual sensitivity, with a gentle 'classical, poetic' temperament. Morris enjoyed the six working weeks they spent together in the summer of 1851 in Alphington, a village near Ottery St Mary in Devon. At Ottery he visited 'the queer ante-dated old church,' which he recorded as 'certainly one of the most remarkable and beautiful ones in England'. But in spite of their shared tastes Guy still found vaguely disconcerting the pupil so addicted to winding his legs tightly round the chair legs in the study. He put pressure on them suddenly and then the chair would collapse. This was a life-long problem. Burne-Jones was to look wanly round the chairs in his studio: 'Morris has sat in them all, and he has a muscular movement in his back peculiar to himself, which makes the rungs fly out.'

Morris's jerks and antics were certainly peculiar. His physical oddities bear some resemblance to those of Samuel Johnson whose tics, gesticulations, ejaculations, mimicries were so compulsive. Oliver Sacks, in discussing Tourette's syndrome, has claimed that Dr Johnson's creative spontaneity and lightning-quick wit had 'an organic connection with his

49

accelerated motor impulsive state'. Could the same be true of Morris? Certainly Morris's bouts of playfulness, extravagance, the speed of his inventiveness, the rush of visual images, have many of the elements found in Tourette's syndrome in its innovatory and phantasmagoric form. Morris, like Johnson, could behave well and write soberly; but he too had the compulsion to break out, cavort, career like an out-of-control child and spew forth his inner fantasies. In his old age more than ever: in his last years Morris embarked on writing a new version of the long meandering surreal stories that, ever since his schooldays, had been crowding through his mind.

Water House had (and has) a spectacular entrance, squared in black and white marble, and ascending up a massive chestnut staircase to a second upper hall. Here on the landing, ensconced in a deep window seat, Morris spent whole days reading. His bursts of frenzied energy seem to have alternated with equal extremes of lassitude. There is a self-portrait in the *The Novel on Blue Paper*:

You know, one has fits of not caring for fishing and shooting a bit, and then I get through an enormous lot of reading; and then again one day one goes out, and down to the river, and looks at the eddies, and then suddenly one thinks of all that again. And then another day when one has one's rod in one's hand one looks up and down the field or sees the road winding along, and I can't help thinking of tales going on amongst it all, and long so much for more and more books.

It was a time of limbo, or late teenage angst, when Morris was aware, as he had never been before, of absence. There were the reminders of the absence of his father, a fixed point of authority if not of emulation. William Morris Senior's tomb, with its coat of arms and scrollings, an overloaded sepulchre, still looms over Woodford churchyard.

There was by now another, much more recent, painful change and this was the absence of Morris's sister Emma, who had moved to Downe in Kent following her marriage to Joseph Oldham, the curate who had once tutored her in German. Emma was the sister Morris had adored: 'his favourite sister or chum', May Morris called her. It was Emma he had sat with long ago in the rabbit warren at Woodford Hall, reading the Gothic novel *The Old English Baron* until they were both in such a state of tension they were afraid to cross the park to home. This was the closeness of an easy physicality. Morris recreated it in his Oxford story 'Frank's Sealed Letter': 'I see a little girl sitting on the grass, beneath the limes in the hot summer-tide, with eyes fixed on the far-away blue hills, and seeing who knows what shapes there; for the boy by her side is reading to her wondrous stories of knight and lady, and fairy thing, that lived in the ancient days.'

Later on at Marlborough it was Emma who continued in the role of protector and adviser, filling his tuck box with the Morris home farm products, overseeing his exchanges of rabbits for a fishing rod, replying to his anxious requests for silkworm eggs. This was the fondness he most easily relied on. It was softness that had a kind of bracing quality. He could write to her from Marlborough in a kind of shorthand, such was their rapport.

Edward Burne-Jones was given the impression that Morris felt deserted when his sister married. It seems he went on yearning for such closeness of companionship which, later in his fiction, takes on sexual overtones. Morris's late romantic heroines are sisterly and comradely, hard-running and fast-shooting, sharers of physical as well as intellectual pleasures. The difference is that they are – mostly – to be captured. His desertion by Emma and the breaking of that bonding was the beginning of, for him, a tragic cycle of female intimacy vouchsafed and then withdrawn.

The Duke of Wellington died in 1852. The funeral was on 18 November. His old Marlborough friend Nunns, still in contact with Crab Morris, mentions that the bells that day were ringing muffled. The entry in his diary was given a black border. Morris's fellow-pupils at Guy's set off to London to watch the funeral procession. The entire Morris family travelled to London too. Morris, contrarily and to the great annoyance of his sister Henrietta, stayed at home and took a solitary ride through Epping Forest.

He rode as far as Waltham Abbey, the Norman church for which less than ten years later Burne-Jones designed his most marvellous of windows: 'Christ in Majesty', seated on a rainbow, surrounded by the seven scenes of the Creation. Blood-red sun and yellow moon; five elongated trees; the parting of the waters in clear azures and light greens. He has packed a choir of angels into one of the high roundels. In another, naked, nervous, stand his Adam and his Eve.

CHAPTER THREE

Oxford
1853–55

Morris travelled up to Oxford to take his matriculation examination at Exeter College in June of 1852.

Beside him in the hall, taking the same papers, was Edward Burne-Jones from King Edward's Grammar School in Birmingham. They did not speak, but Burne-Jones remembered him when they met again the next year as undergraduates. His appearance then was striking. 'He was slight in figure in those days; his hair was dark brown and very thick, his nose straight, his eyes hazel-coloured, his mouth exceedingly delicate and beautiful.' Burne-Jones noticed from that first day his peculiar decisiveness, watching how he finished a Horace paper early, folded it and inscribed it 'William Morris'. He seemed very self-contained.

Morris came to regard Oxford with a vehemence unusual even for him. In his classification of the cities it did not rate simply as 'the most important town of England': it had more personal resonances as 'a place, a second home'. When he first arrived in Oxford it was a city in transition. The railway had arrived there, but only very recently, in 1844. Suburban development, which was to make Oxford almost unrecognizable by the 1880s, had only just begun. There was enough of the old city left intact for Morris to adopt it as the paradigm of the perfect mediaeval city: 'A vision of grey-roofed houses and a long winding street and the sound of many bells'. Only Rouen ever matched it in his mind. His memories of that first and almost untouched Oxford fired and fuelled his opposition to what he regarded as its violation: it was his 'jewel' city cast away. Oxford had so fixed a place in his emotional history that 'a kind of terror' always came upon him at returning: 'indignation at wanton or rash changes mingles curiously in me with all that I remember I have lost since I was a lad and dwelling there; not the least of losses the recognition that I didn't know in those days what a gain it was to be there.'

Morris took up his place at Exeter in January 1853. He had expected to enter the previous autumn, but the college was so full that his entry was deferred and he spent a few more months studying with F. B. Guy. When he arrived in Oxford he still found an accommodation crisis in the college; he and Burne-Jones were allocated daytime rooms out in the town, returning at night to sleep in college, billeted in the third room of other students' sets. It was a ramshackle start that may have influenced their gathering despondency. Burne-Jones and Morris made immediate friends and they spent much of their time in that first term in 'gloomy disappointment and disillusion', taking angry walks together in the afternoon, complaining of the sloth and apathy of Oxford. In this they were not especially original. The transition from high hopes to dawning disillusionment with a system so languid as to be almost corrupt was familiar enough to be satirized in that classic Oxford novel of the period, Cuthbert Bede's *Mr. Verdant Green*.

'It was clear we had lighted on a distasteful land in our choice of College.' Burne-Jones's antipathy to Exeter was shared by Morris, who complained of its banality: 'I took very ill to the studies of the place.' Marlborough had a traditional connection with Exeter. Primarily, this was a West Country alliance. Until 1856, when the statutes were revised, Oxford colleges drew their fellows from specific regions of the country. This meant that Exeter was very largely governed by a body of clergymen from Devon and Cornwall. There was also, as at Marlborough, a certain High Church emphasis. Interestingly John Betjeman, who himself proceeded from Marlborough to Exeter in the 1920s, still found it 'the headquarters of Anglo-Catholicism'. College records for 1852 show that eight of the fifty-nine boys who went on to university that year went on to Exeter. One of these was W. Fulford Adams, a distant school friend of Morris's, and later his neighbour in Oxfordshire. Exeter life was all too close to school life. Morris once described Oxford as 'a huge upper public school'. The college divided into two distinct communities: the 'reading men', absorbed in the classics and theology; and the 'fast set', men who rowed, hunted, ate, drank, whored and swore. The fast set at Exeter was then in the ascendant. Burne-Jones found it like 'the Brasenose of old times, very fast indeed'.

53

Now all Oxford undergraduate courses lead to a bachelor's degree with honours. A pass may be awarded to those who do not achieve the honours standard. In the mid-nineteenth century the system was more flexible. Morris had entered specifically to read for a pass degree. His tutor was unimpressed with him, noting in the pupil book 'a rather rough and unpolished youth, who exhibited no special literary tastes or capacity, but had no difficulty in mastering the usual subjects of examination'. The lack of enthusiasm was mutual: Morris's formal studies of the classics were accompanied by groanings all through his Oxford period. 'My life is going to become a burden to me, for I am going, (beginning from Tuesday next) to read for six hours a day at Livy, Ethics, etc. – please pity me.' His hatred of the classics in fact was only nominal. He did not hate the classics, but he loathed how Oxford taught them. Morris's view of the classics was eccentric and possessive. He was always deeply stirred by the thought of epic tale-tellers, seeing himself as a part of that tradition. Later in his life he would set about translating *The Aeneid* and *The Odyssey* with a kind of nonchalance derived from loving them so much and knowing them so well. For Morris, as much as any of the writers and painters of his period, the imaginative worlds of the ancient Greeks and Romans were deeply embedded in his mind. But classics were taught at Oxford with a dryness and pomposity that undermined their wonders. When he came to equate his official Oxford studies with snobbery, aridity and practical uselessness, Morris was attacking a whole style of education and a lack-lustre and self-serving institution. It was anything but an ideal training for the ministry. 'A University education', he wrote caustically, 'fits a man about as much for being a Ship-Captain as a Pastor of Souls'.

The fierceness of his feelings about Oxford education pours out in *News from Nowhere* in the passage about the decline of real learning in the nineteenth century in Oxford 'and its less interesting sister Cambridge'. The commercialization of these cities had corrupted those who taught there:

They (and especially Oxford) were the breeding places of a peculiar class of parasites, who called themselves cultivated people; they were indeed cynical enough, as the so-called educated classes of the day generally were; but they affected an exaggeration of cynicism in order that they might be thought knowing and worldly wise. The rich middle classes (they had no relation with the working classes) treated them with a kind of contemptuous toleration with which a mediaeval baron treated his jester; though it must be said that they were by no means so pleasant as the old jesters were, being, in fact, *the* bores of society. They were laughed at, despised – and paid.

Morris escaped again, as he had escaped at Marlborough, into the study of history. He gives his own account of how, when first at Oxford, he 'fell to very vigorously on history and specially mediaeval history'. There was a tradition of history at Exeter. Amongst its recent fellows was the great historian J. A. Froude, one of the last of the Exeter Devonians; C. W. Boase, elected three years before Morris's arrival as an undergraduate, remained a Fellow for over forty years. It seems possible that Morris was marginally influenced by academic specialism in history at Exeter. But much more important to him was the town that stood around him, the deductions he could draw from the practical history of buildings, the massing and the details of construction, the relation of ornament to form. What had in his childhood been a question of instinct became, in those years at Oxford, a study and a science: he came to look at architecture solemnly as witness to 'the unfolding of medieval thought'. This was a radical and indeed an almost anti-Oxford discipline, a kind of hands-on history. By the middle 1870s, when the Society for the Protection of Ancient Buildings was founded, it was a national movement and Morris was welcoming an enlightened period in which 'the newly invented study of living history is the chief joy of so many of our lives'.

Oxford at Morris's period had an enclosed quality. The city came to an end abruptly, almost as if it had been walled. There was very little brick in it: Oxford was predominantly grey, the grey of stone, with the yellow wash of pebble-dash on the houses in the poorer streets. The castle was dominant, with its 'monster beauty of a keep' and the mill and little network of waterways near by. There was the cathedral so admired by Ruskin for its unaffected Englishness: the true English Norman vaults; the true English Tudor roof; and the west window, with its clumsy painting, 'the best men could do of the day'. University expansion in the seventeenth and eighteenth centuries had brought a scattering of Baroque buildings: one would like to know how Morris had reacted to the early seventeenth-century Exeter College chapel, demolished in the year he came to Oxford to make way for George Gilbert Scott's reworking of the Sainte-Chapelle. But the town was still mainly fifteenth century, small-scale, and possessing the character Morris so much valued: the sense that it had never not been there. Morris looks at

55

Magdalen Buildings and he sees buildings that are 'essentially part of the street, and look almost as if they had grown up out of the roadway'. In this vision of the building as organic William Morris prefigures not just Frank Lloyd Wright and Gaudí but a whole twentieth-century counter-culture movement for 'architecture without architects'.

To Morris and the friends he made there Oxford took on the aspect of the mediaeval citadel, the place beyond the world, a kind of no man's land. It had its Lewis Carroll air of dottiness: could *Alice's Adventures in Wonderland* (1865) have been written anywhere else? Years later Burne-Jones described his Oxford as 'all friends living in the same street, and the street long and narrow and ending in the city wall, and the wall opening with a gate on to cornfields in the south, and the wild wood on the north – and no railways anywhere – all friends and all one's world tied up in the little city – and no news to come – only rumours and gossips at the city gate, telling things a month old, and all wrong'.

At Oxford Burne-Jones and Morris went through a phase of wearing purple trousers. They already spoke a shared language of clothes as social protest, as they later dressed in almost uniform blue working shirts. Burne-Jones came upon the scene as the unconsciously desired male intimate, filling the vacuum left by Morris's own elder brother, Charles Stanley, who was born and died in a week, and by William Morris Senior's early death. He was also in a sense a compensation for the close friend Morris had failed to find at Marlborough. Morris had had his school friends, but none of them were intimate. This new friendship was based on an instant recognition of samenesses of attitude: a restless and prickly perceptiveness, an earnestness. As with forty per cent of Oxford entrants at that period Burne-Jones too was at this stage intended for the Church. The friendship was sharpened by its obvious differences: Burne-Jones from the urban Midlands, Morris from the soft home counties. Their contrast in appearance made them almost cartoon characters, perambulating round the streets of Oxford, one so tall and pale and languid, one so dark and taut.

Edward Burne-Jones was plain Ted Jones in those days. The name Ned came later, apparently invented by Dante Gabriel Rossetti. His upbringing had been the contrary of William Morris's; Burne-Jones had been the solitary child in a terrace house on Bennett's Hill, in the commercial centre of Birmingham. His mother had died the week after he was born and his childhood was punctuated by lugubrious expeditions to her graveside where his father would grasp his arm so tight he almost cried. Edward Richard Jones was a very unsuccessful picture framer and gilder. Part of the house was a showroom, with a workshop in the yard behind it. They were painfully hard up. Burne-Jones had known Morris was comfortably off, since in their first term at Oxford Morris had offered to give him half his money: 'which', said Burne-Jones, 'was nice of him, only I was proud'. But until he was invited to Walthamstow, cocooned in that genteel atmosphere where Mrs Morris dropped her aitches and the butler tried to hide his laughter at the sallies of the two young Oxford gentlemen at table, Burne-Jones had no idea Morris's house would be so grand.

Morris and Burne-Jones arrived in Oxford in the aftermath of the Oxford Movement. For the two previous decades the town had been torn by religious controversy. In so inturned a community the social consequences were intense. In 1845 John Henry Newman, the former Fellow of Oriel and vicar of the university church of St Mary's, had finally embraced Roman Catholicism. Burne-Jones regarded Newman with ferocious admiration. Even as a schoolboy he identified with Newman's radiant austerities, so strikingly prophetic of the Arts and Crafts aesthetic: 'In an age of sofas and cushions he taught me to be indifferent to comfort; and in an age of materialism he taught me to venture all on the unseen.' It was because of Newman that Burne-Jones had been inspired to choose Oxford in the first place. He and Morris had expected to find a town still heady with Tractarian arguments, the religious battleground described so vividly in Newman's Oxford novel. *Loss and Gain: The Story of a Convert* was published in 1848. In the event they were disappointed. It was part of their angry disillusionment with Oxford that the influence of Newman was no longer so alive. But they still endeavoured to recreate that fervour. In their first few terms at Oxford they were solemn, still devout.

In the evenings they read religious works. Morris read and Burne-Jones listened: Morris hated to be read to. They devoured Milman's *Latin Christianity*, Neale's *History of the Eastern Church*, great swaths of the *Acta Sanctorum* and *Tracts for the Times*, the controversial essays written by Newman, Pusey and Keble, insistent upon reclaiming the identity of the Church of England as the 'true Catholic and Apostolic Church'. They both found deeply attractive the Tractarian emphasis on sacraments and ceremonial. Burne-Jones, writing home, adopted the joke persona of Edouard Cardinal de Birmingham. At mealtimes he was reading Archdeacon Wilberforce's latest treatise on the Holy Eucharist. At one point he and Morris confessed to one another they had both been reading Kenelm Digby's *Mores Catholici* in secret. In 1854, when Wilberforce too became a Catholic convert, they very nearly followed him, such was the lure of Rome.

In their first term Morris also read 'The Lady of Shalott' out loud to Burne-Jones in the funny sing-song voice he always used when reading poetry. He laid great stress on the rhymes. Tennyson had written 'The Lady of Shalott' in the early 1830s. In 1842 his 'Sir Launcelot and Queen Guinevere', 'Morte d'Arthur' and 'Sir Galahad' were published. This was part of a whole Arthurian cult, following the rediscovery of Malory's *Morte d'Arthur* in the late eighteenth century by Sir Walter Scott. By the time Morris and Burne-Jones arrived in Oxford Victorian Arthurianism was approaching its grand climax. William Dyce had already started painting his cycle of Arthurian frescoes in the Queen's Robing Room in the Palace of Westminster. Morris and Burne-Jones laid their own claims on the Arthurian myth. Morris's interpretation was primarily a verbal one, although in early days he produced Arthurian paintings; Burne-Jones, all his life, dwelt on themes of the San Graal in his paintings and his tapestries and he was still painting in the irises on his giant canvas 'Avalon' in the weeks before he died. Arthurianism, as Burne-Jones and Morris saw it, was not merely an intellectual exercise. They fell upon it as an extension of religion, adopting the chivalric as a rule of life. Embedded in their visions of the San Graal were the memories of the high emotions of those early weeks at Oxford, and their mutual recognition: 'Nothing', wrote Burne-Jones, 'was ever like Morte d'Arthur – I don't mean any book or any one poem – something that can never be written, I mean, and can never go out of the heart'.

Burne-Jones attributed their closeness to the fact that he and Morris were both Goths, by which he meant they had a shared sense of morality, a shared creative energy. From such different backgrounds they had found, when they converged, they belonged to the same tribe. They encouraged one another to a heightening of vision. This was partly the artist's perception of colour. Morris was a supreme colourist. Burne-Jones saw days in colour. Sunday was gold, Monday yellow, Tuesday red, Wednesday blue, Thursday amethyst, Friday sapphire – and 'Saturday wet', he said, 'ever since I was tiny – but I don't know why'. There was in their relationship a wistfulness, a winsomeness, a consciousness of nonsense not so far from Edward Lear. Morris and

Burne-Jones created a double persona which was not English mainstream but which verged on the surrealist. They liked exaggeration. As
Burne-Jones was to comment after Robert Browning's funeral in Westminster Abbey: 'how flat these English are'.

It was Burne-Jones at Oxford who first saw Morris's quality, saying
he was certain Morris would be a 'star'. At the end of their first year
Burne-Jones described him as 'one of the cleverest fellows I know . . .
He is full of enthusiasm for things holy and beautiful and true, and,
what is rarest, of the most exquisite perception and judgment in them.
For myself he has tinged my whole inner being with the beauty of his
own, and I know not a single gift for which I owe such gratitude to
Heaven as his friendship. If it were not for his boisterous mad outbursts
and freaks, which break the romance he sheds around him – at least to
me – he would be a perfect hero.' But even then Burne-Jones had a sense
of Morris's ferocity: he too noted his eyes, those eyes of such great
inexpressiveness, which took in a whole person, the details of the
clothing, nuances of physiognomy, without being seen to look.

The friendship with Burne-Jones was Morris's first real friendship. It
remained important to him, though it had its ebbs and flows. But to see
this as the legendary and all-excluding friendship, as it has so often been
portrayed, is incorrect. If Morris had a need for the intimate companion
he had an even stronger yearning for the group. He knew a great deal
about chivalric fraternities. *The Broadstone of Honour* by Kenelm
Digby, a rambling and hypnotic overview of the theory and history of
chivalry, first published in 1822, was a book to which Morris was
addicted and, like other books he read and clung to, it idealized the
small band of valiant friends. The search for brotherhood can also be
explained in terms of Morris's own shyness, the enduring and exceptional privateness that coexisted so strangely with his bluffness. As his
daughter May described it: 'No glimpse of the inner life of Morris was
ever vouchsafed even to his closest friends – *secretum meum mihi.*'
Morris felt at his most comfortable in a group, in a setting of male
badinage, of generalized affection. This again he had never properly
achieved at Marlborough. He found it at Oxford in discovering 'the Set'.

The Set, later expanded and referred to as 'the Brotherhood', was
already in place when Morris came to Oxford. It was based at Pembroke, where three undergraduates from Birmingham all had rooms in
the old quadrangle. The Set then consisted of William Fulford and

Richard Watson Dixon, two friends of Burne-Jones from King Edward's, with Charles Faulkner who also came from Birmingham, though from a different school. Fulford and Dixon were meant for holy orders, an immediate link with Morris and Burne-Jones. They were all, in their way, brilliant young men. Faulkner was a highly original mathematician who became a Fellow of University College; he followed Morris into Socialism, leading the Oxford branch of the Socialist League. Fulford was the Set's chief literary figure, small, energetic, dapper, and at the time galvanic; but he seems to have had the precocious sort of talent that quite rapidly burns itself out. Richard Watson Dixon, later Canon Dixon, was perhaps the most interesting of the brethren, himself a considerable poet, correspondent and supporter of Gerard Manley Hopkins, one of the few people who understood the nature of that tormented and complicated talent. (Hopkins, also a musician, set some Dixon poems to music.) The Set was joined later by another friend from Birmingham, Cormell Price. It was Price who founded the United Services College, the colonialist boarding school which educated Rudyard Kipling. Cormell Price is immortalized as the unconventional but respected headmaster in Kipling's *Stalky & Co.*

The Birmingham contingent had been introduced to Morris by Burne-Jones. At first they dismissed him as 'a very pleasant boy' who talked compulsively in his husky shouting voice and liked going down the river with Charles Faulkner, sharing his interest in boats. They saw him as a sportsman, good at singlestick and fencing. It was only gradually they realized he was much more intellectual, and odder, than he seemed. Faulkner commented to Dixon, 'How Morris seems to know things, doesn't he?' and Dixon observed how decisive Morris was, how accurate, without making an issue of his expertise. They saw what a great reservoir of observation lay behind so many of his most casual comments. Morris surprised them with sophisticated knowledge of subjects about which the literary-oriented Set knew nothing. Unlike them, he read *The Builder* magazine; and went to *look* at buildings. Dixon was startled when, the first time he met Morris, he suggested they should go and look at Merton tower.

In the Michaelmas term of 1853 Morris and Burne-Jones moved into rooms in college. Morris's rooms were in the quadrangle called Hell Quad, reached by passing through an archway out of the great quadrangle. This archway was known as Purgatory. The rooms overlooked the Fellows' garden and the chestnut tree, with a sideways vista down

Brasenose Lane to the Bodleian Library where Morris at this period spent many hours examining the mediaeval painted manuscripts. In the 1890s he returned again to study the thirteenth-century Apocalypse which as an undergraduate he specially loved. His rooms at Exeter were gradually filled with rubbings from mediaeval brasses, imprints on paper taken from the brass memorials to knights and their ladies set into the floor of many early churches. A letter he sent to Cormell Price one spring vacation mentions his success in having gone 'a-brassing' near the Thames on the Essex side. Here he acquired two remarkable brasses, one a Flemish brass of a knight, dated 1370; 'another a brass (very small, with the legend gone) of a priest in his shroud; I think there are only two other shrouded brasses in England'. This last brass, about which Morris writes with such authority, came from one of the prettiest small village churches he had ever seen, with the consecration crosses showing red in a red circle. The parson showed them round: 'he was very civil and very, very dirty and snuffy, inexpressibly so, I can't give you an idea of his dirt and snuffiness.'

In those early terms at Oxford a routine had soon evolved. Faulkner's rooms at Pembroke, on the ground floor in the corner of the quadrangle, became the social centre for the Set. They would meet there around nine o'clock most evenings. They talked of Transcendentalism and 'all the host of German systems', continuing the debates of their Birmingham vacations. Burne-Jones had once launched on a defence of the Jesuits; to his great surprise, this met no opposition. They were treading, selfconsciously, on dangerous ground. The little group at Pembroke was old-fashioned Evangelical. Its infiltration by such intense Tractarians as Morris and Burne-Jones set up a *frisson* that was practically sexual. The religious debate had its aspects of flirtation. The Set, so closely intertwined and so high-minded, were intensely conscious of each other's physicality. Dixon, describing Morris as an aristocrat and a High Churchman, emphasized his radiance. 'His countenance was beautiful in features and expression, particularly in the expression of purity ... I have a vivid recollection of the splendid beauty of his presence at this time.'

The Set were Tennysonians. The Oxford intelligentsia of that period was obsessed with poetry in general and Tennyson especially. It was almost a fever, as Dixon recollected it: 'All reading men were Tennysonians; all sets of reading men talked poetry. Poetry was the thing: and it was felt with justice that this was due to Tennyson.

Tennyson had invented a new poetry, a new poetic English: his use of words was new, and every piece that he wrote was a conquest of a new region. This lasted till "Maud", in 1855.' Dixon, with his own poetic sensibility, had watched the effect of Tennyson on Morris. Where the other members of the Set were caught up by the language Morris searched much further, looking for a morality beyond the language: he saw that Tennyson's poems 'represented substantial things that were to be considered out of the poems as well as in them'. It was 'this substantial view of value' that later led Morris to admire ballads so highly. In this context it is certainly ironic that so much well-founded criticism of Morris has been as the writer of the poetry that lulls.

William Fulford was the chief Tennysonian of the group. He loved reading poetry and had a fine deep voice in which he regaled the Set with 'In Memoriam'. Dixon listened entranced, Morris a little less so. He admired Tennyson, but there was defiance in that admiration. He had perceived some limitations. He commented: 'Tennyson's Sir Galahad is rather a mild youth.' In expressing such lukewarmness about Tennyson Morris, whether consciously or not, was challenging the older, more bumptious Fulford, who had installed himself as the leader of the Set. Morris tended to resist overbearing masculinity. He detected a certain male rowdiness in Tennyson. He criticized the hero of 'Locksley Hall': 'My dear fellow, if you are going to make that row, get out of the room, that's all.'

Morris's clique at Oxford was a reading set. In his second year at Oxford the Set began assembling weekly to read Shakespeare in one another's rooms. Morris, Burne-Jones and Fulford were the prize performers, together with Cormell Price, by then at Brasenose. They drew lots for their parts. Morris did a good Macbeth and a good Touchstone, and his *tour de force* was Claudio in *Measure for Measure*. 'He suddenly raised his voice to a loud and horrified cry at the word "Isabel", and declaimed the awful following speech "Aye, but to die, and go we know not where" in the same pitch.' The effect was overpowering. Morris kept his childlike literalness. Reading *Troilus and Cressida* he interrupted the passage where Thersites lists the fools, ending 'And Patroclus is a fool positive'. Morris intervened unselfconsciously, delightedly: 'Patroclus wants to know why he is a fool!'

The horizons of the Set were in some ways wider than those of William Morris. Coming as they did from Birmingham they were closer to industrial realities and social upheavals. Burne-Jones's father had been enrolled as a special constable in the Chartist Riots of 1839, and the maidservant, putting the child to bed, had told him scaring stories of the violence on the streets. Cormell Price had childhood memories of bestial prize fights and remembered one Saturday night walking from Birmingham far into the Black Country and counting, in the last three miles, more than thirty people lying dead drunk on the ground, nearly half of them women. Because most of the pupils at King Edward's Grammar School were day-boys, familiar with the city, taking short cuts through the slums, they were much more aware than Morris, insulated at his boarding school, of Dickensian squalor and industrial reality. Older boys at King Edward's had awakened social consciences and they discussed contemporary social problems. Before they came to Oxford Cormell Price and Charles Faulkner were experts on such topics as sanitation and the Factory acts. Their awareness of poverty and suffering was deepened in 1854 by the terrible cholera epidemic (whose causes were no better understood than the outbreak of the Plague two centuries earlier). The Oxford autumn term was postponed for a week because of it. Morris's story of that period, 'A Dream', has as its background the plague hospital of a disease-ridden city. Morris's memories of Rouen? The sense of perspective in the Set was also altered by the onset of the Crimean War, the closest Europe came to an all-out war between 1815 and 1914.

There was a kind of youth cult in the circles of reformers. The ardour of Morris and his group of friends at Oxford was in some ways very close to that of the Young England movement of the 1840s. The spokesmen for Young England were four Conservative MPs: Benjamin Disraeli, Lord George Manners, Alexander Baillie-Cochrane, George Smythe. They themselves were young. In Disraeli's trilogy of novels, *Coningsby*, *Sybil* and *Tancred*, it is the young men who are reforming activists. Young England sought to emulate ideals of mediaeval England, not in a regressive way but a creative one. They wanted to extract from mediaeval England those elements from which the Victorian age could learn. New societies based on equality of classes; a small-scale quasi-monastic system of community; the return to the country; the revival of physical activity; principles of shared work and work-as-holiday, like the road-building and haymaking in Morris's *News from Nowhere*; architecture as the measure of civilization and the means by which the people reconnected themselves with the past: all these were ideas Morris worked on and developed and in the end, during his Socialist period, elaborated

63

and sharpened almost beyond recognition. It is ironic that Morris's Socialism had roots in the Tory Young England movement. Noteworthy too that such palliative measures as the Whig Reform Act of 1867, which gave the vote to respectable urban working-class men, exacerbated discontent in the voteless lower strata, enabling Tory Young England to make common cause with the labouring classes, in an alliance which in some ways still exists.

Morris said that at Oxford he had been 'a good deal influenced' by the works of Charles Kingsley. Kingsley's books gave him 'some socio-political ideas which would have developed probably but for the attractions of art and poetry'. What exactly were these socio-political ideas? Charles Kingsley at this period was a controversial clergyman, a Christian Socialist and an academic. As Professor of English he had been a colleague of F. D. Maurice's at Queen's College in London. F. D. Maurice had been forced to retire after his denial of the received interpretation of Eternal Punishment: Burne-Jones had heard the news of this with great regret, 'for the Christian Socialists, if Maurice and Kingsley are fair examples, must be glorious fellows'. Both Burne-Jones and William Morris were prone to sympathy for martyrs of the faith. Kingsley too had his history of martyrdom. In 1851, after he had preached a reckless sermon, the Bishop of London banned him from London preaching. What Morris found in him was iconoclasm, courage, an extreme concern with the right use of one's talents and resources. Kingsley spoke to Morris of the conscience of his class.

The books Morris read at Oxford certainly included the first of Kingsley's novels, *Yeast, A Problem*, written in 1848 and originally serialized in *Fraser's Magazine*. Its hero, Lancelot Smith, is a young man with money who has just left Cambridge. Smith makes friends with a Carlyle-reading Cornish gamekeeper. Confronted with real rural poverty he is enlightened and inflamed. It is a powerful study of a young man with a conscience; it is one of the most savage novels ever written about class and the English. It was a book almost made for William Morris. Kingsley then wrote *Alton Locke*, *Hypatia* and *Westward Ho!* All these apparently were 'welcomed gladly by the set', who found in Kingsley's works not only food for thought but the sources of marvellous and almost endless arguments. Kingsley's were books they liked to read together: these took on a special meaning in the context of the group. Kingsley made them conscious of their country as it actually was, and they came to see themselves as young men with a mission, 'as full of enthusiasm as the first crusaders'. This was how Burne-Jones described himself and Morris in their Kingsley days.

In 1855 Morris came of age. Devon Great Consols shares had been prospering and his mother was advised to safeguard the future of her children by putting shares in trust for them. Emma Morris and her brothers-in-law Thomas and Francis were the joint trustees. When he was twenty-one Morris was given thirteen shares. The dividend provided him with income of £741 in 1855, £715 in 1856 and so on. In today's real terms this would be well over £7,000 a year. It was then a lavish income that gave him extra freedom but which was also a cause of some embarrassment, in that his spending power was immeasurably greater than that of the others in the Set. Already here at Oxford one can see the tension in him between his munificence, an extreme generosity that prompted him to buy his friends the books they had been wanting, surprising them, delighting them, and equally strong urges towards anonymity and modesty. There was a sense in which Morris's relative affluence made it even more essential for him to feel accepted by his peers and a part of their activities. This was the beginning of a pattern. All his life he was to see the possibilities in using his wealth in the formation of brotherhoods, keeping them together with financial underpinning. He began to realize that his inheritance of riches made it even more important to find a proper purpose for his life.

In his early phase at Oxford Burne-Jones seriously considered founding a monastery. He was attracted by the brotherhood of chastity. He had been schooled in ideals of endurance. At Oxford one of the favourite novels of the Set had been Charlotte M. Yonge's *The Heir of Redclyffe*. Dixon, in old age, still considered it 'unquestionably one of the finest books in the world'. Like *Yeast* this was a book almost designed for Morris. The hero, Guy Morville, is dark, rich and very wilful. In his tempers he bites his lips and cuts through pencils, as uncouth as William Morris. The theme of this gripping surplice-ripper is, through faith and self-discipline, the schooling of the wild. With *The Heir of Redclyffe* we are in those High Victorian realms of self-sacrifice and sexual abnegation. Guy, after many trials, attains his love and marries her. On honeymoon in Italy he catches fever from the former enemy he nurses forgivingly. Philip recovers. Guy, alas, does not. Idealized, implicit in one of the most full-blown death scenes in any novel of the period, is the Tractarian principle of chastity, the aim of forgoing temporary earthly pleasure in exchange for the spiritual victory and riches in the afterlife. Did Morris read *The Heir of Redclyffe* with an intimation that sexual abnegation was to loom large in his life?

> When death is coming near
> And thy heart shrinks in fear
> And thy limbs fail,
> Then raise thy hands and pray
> To Him who smooths the way
> Through the dark vale.

In his final hours Guy had asked Amy, so soon to be his widow, to repeat their favourite lines from *Sintram and his Companions*. It was *The Heir of Redclyffe* that led Morris on to *Sintram*, the 'winter' story in the collected tales, one for each of the four seasons, by the German Baron Friedrich de la Motte Fouqué. In Oxford Morris and Burne-Jones had come upon a translation of this early nineteenth-century romance. The frontispiece was a woodcut copy of Dürer's engraving of 'The Knight and Death', the knight riding on his horse through a desperation valley of gnarled trees and jagged rock-forms. Though the print was badly made the woodcut fascinated them and they pored over it for hours.

The meanings of *Sintram* fascinated them as well. The solemn mystic story of the hero travelling through the icy landscape, embattled with his own wild and troubled temperament, set up reverberations which would last for life for both of them. They took to it at Oxford not as an escapist narrative but as a blueprint for the living of real lives. *Sintram* too is a chronicle of self-discipline, self-sacrifice. Sintram's mother is a nun, majestic, grey-haired, sexless. She is unable to receive him in her cloister until he is pure in mind and body, as unsullied as the snowy plains around the convent. Sintram, looking at his shield and on that shiny surface coming face to face with his own image, realizes how far he is from that ideal. In a moment of frenzy he reaches for his dagger and cuts off his black hair, 'so that to look upon he was almost like a monk'. The dwarf, his sexual tempter, 'the Little Master', is as horrid as the lubricious yellow midget in Morris's own 1890s' fairytale *The Wood beyond the World*.

One of the Oxford models for William Morris's monastery was in the nearby countryside. Morris and Burne-Jones both knew of the community at Littlemore, where early in the 1840s Newman bought land beside the church with the intention of founding 'a half college, half monastery' developed out of an L-shaped block of six cottages and stable. The stable was converted to make the library. The monastic accommodation at Littlemore was austere enough to have impressed the Italian Passionist priest Father Dominic Barberi: 'nothing to be seen but poverty and simplicity – bare walls, floor composed of a few rough bricks without a carpet, a straw bed, one or two chairs, and a few books; this composed the whole furniture'. Though Morris loved his pleasures there was also in his nature a self-flagellating instinct, and his yearnings for the monastery involved a way of living at the opposite extreme from the home comforts of Walthamstow, with its welcoming window-seat, its apricots ripening in the kitchen garden. He was craving a dramatic volte-face and subduing of the flesh.

Burne-Jones, with his town background, was even more attracted to ideas of a mixed community of monastic and lay members working together in the centre of London, on the pattern suggested in Hurrell Froude's *Project for the Revival of Religion in Great Towns*. Burne-Jones hoped to recruit Cormell Price to this community. He wrote to him in May 1853, 'I have set my heart on our founding a Brotherhood. Learn Sir Galahad by heart; he is to be the patron of our Order.' He described William Morris as being already involved in the project 'heart and soul'. Burne-Jones made it very clear the Brotherhood would be a chaste one. A few months later he was writing to Price still more persuasively: 'We must enlist you in this Crusade and Holy warfare against the age.'

Why this emphasis on chastity? One has to remember that chastity was then in fashion, especially amongst those with advanced aesthetic tastes making their own protest against vast Victorian families. There was the example of the Nazarenes, so called because of their return to the dress and indeed hairstyles of the Bible. This brotherhood of German painters, Lukasbrüder, or the Brotherhood of St Luke, had been founded in 1809. The leaders were Friedrich Overbeck and Franz Pforr. They moved to Rome in 1810, where they took over the disused monastery of S. Isidoro. There they were joined by Peter von Cornelius. In Rome Overbeck became a Roman Catholic. Their work is suffused by a religious solemnity. They believed the moral purpose of art had dissipated since the Middle Ages. They put a renewed emphasis on teaching through the workshops, and living monastically in a community. The Nazarenes were purist but they also had a certain flamboyance. They revived the art of the monumental fresco. They forsook the world to flood it with immense and crowded canvases. Their connection with the English Pre-Raphaelites is patent. There too in the orbit of the Nazarenes is Morris, of the second generation of Pre-Raphaelites, with his combination of reticence and splendours. His mediaevalism edged towards the *outré*: vast chambers hung with tapestries, preposterous stained glass.

Another of the models for William Morris's monastery was the plan put forward by George Edmund Street, one of the leading English Gothic architects and a vigorous Anglo-Catholic. In 1848 he had drawn up his proposals for an English artistic and religious foundation, a society or college in which the students and the masters would be 'under certain religious ordinances and live a life in strict accord with the lofty character of their work'. By the time Morris had arrived at Exeter, Street was diocesan architect of Oxford. There he later built the great North Oxford church of St Philip and St James, known to future generations as Phil-Jim. He and Morris did not at this stage know each other, but in their ideals of artistic celibacy there is an obvious link. The monastic connection ran from William Morris to the later English communities of craftsmen: in its most dramatic form to Eric Gill at Ditchling, putting on the habit of the Third Order of St Dominic, complete with the girdle of chastity. It was not always as convincing as it might have been; but a constant element of Arts and Crafts in England was its purism and separatism, the creation of small rural worlds apart from the distractions of flesh.

For Morris and Burne-Jones the ideal of chastity provided a convenient postponement of decision. They were young for their years, with a hazy sexuality. Georgiana Burne-Jones may have had a vested interest in registering an impression of her husband's early purity, but there is no reason to question her assertion of the sexual *naïveté* prevailing in the Set. She was confident that 'the mystery which shrouds men and women from each other in youth was sacred to each one of them'. She says they had no conquering airs with women: to this extent Burne-Jones and Morris were Mr Verdant Greens. If anything their leanings at this stage were homosexual, but a world away from the knowingness of Oxford homosexuals of the 1890s. They had that particular mid-nineteenth-century romantic openness.

Burne-Jones had been nervous about Morris's reception of his first and best Birmingham friend, Cormell Price. But he need not have worried. Price was stalwart, gentle, handsome, with a face that looked permanently sunburnt, and Morris loved him from the first. It was Crom Price who was the confidant of one of William Morris's rare emotional outbursts, in the earliest surviving letter from his Oxford years. He and Price, at the end of term, had somehow missed each other. Morris wrote from home:

I won't make any excuses: please forgive me. As the train went away from the station, I saw you standing in your scholar's gown and looking for me. If I hadn't been on the other side, I think I should have got out of the window to say goodbye again.

In those few phrases one looks into a small world of male *tendresse*.

A fixed memory of the Oxford of that period is of William Morris reading Ruskin out loud to his friends in the mighty singing voice which was chanting more than reading. He declaimed from *The Seven Lamps of Architecture*, *Modern Painters* and *The Stones of Venice*. He almost hurled these works towards his audience, defying them not to be impressed by Ruskin's descriptions of the slave ship or his eloquent defence of Turner's skies. Morris the omnivorous reader was already familiar with the two published volumes of Ruskin's *Modern Painters* before he came to Oxford. But the second volume of *The Stones of Venice*, published in 1853, was an Oxford book, *the* Oxford book of that whole period when the reading of Ruskin seemed to Morris to have been a 'sort of revelation'. He was particularly dazzled by the chapter in *The Stones of Venice* entitled 'On the Nature of Gothic Architecture: and herein of the true functions of the workman in art'. When this chapter was published in the 1890s in one of the first of the Kelmscott Press editions he explained the great impact it had had on him originally:

in future days it will be considered as one of the very few necessary and inevitable utterances of the century. To some of us when we first read it . . . it seemed to point out a new road on which the world should travel.

Burne-Jones was a natural convert. But to others of the Set Ruskin's verbal torrent, with his passion for the visual, was unfamiliar and at first bewildering. Morris's championing of Ruskin shows how quickly his approval could sway the taste of others. Dixon recollected 'we soon saw the greatness and importance of it'. In *Stalky & Co.* Beetle is reading

Fors Clavigera. Evidently Cormell Price later recommended Ruskin's books to the boys in his charge at Westward Ho.

Morris always insisted that Ruskin came at the right time and that he was the prime mover in the turning of the tide away from a blind faith in materialist progress and towards a perception of the damage to society this implied. Ruskin was in his middle thirties when Morris was at Oxford. His *Seven Lamps of Architecture*, a precise and inspired disquisition on the Gothic, was one of the handbooks of the Gothic revival. In the early 1850s his intervention in defence of the Pre-Raphaelites profoundly influenced public attitudes towards them. Ruskin had by this time acquired the authority of the minor sage. His 'On the Nature of Gothic', part description, part polemic, is a wonderfully lucid essay on morality, eccentric and impassioned, written in a soaring and idiosyncratic Biblical prose. Morris fell upon it, finding in it what he described later as the 'marvellous inspiration of genius' that took Ruskin to 'the centre of mediaeval art'. This insight had to do with art and national culture: it was the perception that the art of any epoch was the expression of its social coherence. Ruskin took his argument to an extreme critique of contemporary morals, appealing to Morris both as mediaevalist and as the conscience-stricken heir of the City finance houses. Ruskin's claim was that the social structures of the Middle Ages allowed the workman freedom of individual expression tragically absent in the Victorian age.

Morris at one stage commented that Ruskin appealed more directly to working-class than middle-class audiences because they could see the prophet in him rather than the fantastic rhetorician. Morris too had the simplicity to cut through the swathes of Ruskinian elaboration to seize his central truths. Ruskin argued against the division of labour in the Victorian factories and the way it inevitably dehumanized the operatives: 'if you will make a man of the working creature, you cannot make a tool'. He attacked the monotony of the Victorian industrial system, with its morally destructive cycles: boredom and monotony at work, sweated or otherwise, followed by pursuit of leisure completely unconnected with the work or work place. In that disconnection social neurosis lies.

Ruskin challenged the traditional view that a designer should not also be a maker: it seemed to him unsatisfactory to the point of immorality for one man's thoughts to be executed by another man's hands. His most startling proposals arose from what he saw as an incorrect distinction between manual labour and intellect:

We are always in these days endeavouring to separate the two; we want one man to be always thinking, and another to be always working, and we call one a gentleman, and the other an operative; whereas the workman ought often to be thinking, and the thinker often to be working, and both should be gentlemen, in the best sense.

Leaving aside the 'gentlemen', this statement is so radical that it still strikes one as relatively modern: Eric Gill preached something like it in the 1930s and so did Raymond Williams in the 1960s. As it has seemed to commentators in the 1990s, no wonder that the National Curriculum is so unsatisfactory – arrived at by Westminster and Whitehall 'gentlemen', more than a century too late.

Morris at Oxford read the works of other English social critics widely. Amongst his belongings still kept at his old college, the jumble of pipes, pens, compasses, spectacles, there is a copy of Carlyle's *Past and Present*. He was affected by Carlyle deeply and lastingly: especially by Carlyle's dour view of the present in relation to the moral vigour of the past. But he was always more attuned to Ruskin's high-flown clarities. He found Carlyle too grotesque: he once said somebody should have been beside Carlyle to punch his head every five minutes. The 'ferocity' of Carlyle's gloom stood as a warning to him. The influence of Ruskin was always to be greater because Ruskin was ecstatic and allowed him chinks of light. Ruskin founded his Guild of St George with the purpose of transplanting on English soil the laws and methods of life already proven in the great cities of Venice and Florence at the high point of their cultural achievements. Ruskin sat down by the roadside, while his Hinksey roadworks were in progress, perching himself on a heap of rubble, learning from a stone-breaker how to break flints. Ruskin's progress was heroic, containing a whole series of such emblematic episodes. Morris's life was also to be a bit like that.

As late as 1850 an Oxford college library refused to purchase any books by John Ruskin. But during the period Morris was at Oxford the town became gradually Ruskinized. Ruskin was himself involved with Dr Henry Acland in the initiative for the University Museum, the building intended to house 'all the materials explanatory of the organic beings placed upon the globe'. Acland was in Scotland with John Ruskin, Ruskin's wife and Millais in that notorious summer of 1853 which led to Effie's nullity suit for non-consummation against her husband. Effie later married Millais. It is strange that in the year in which Morris was absorbing Ruskin's proposals to remedy society Ruskin himself was undergoing such painful and humiliating trials of the heart.

The Museum building was started two years later. The architect was Benjamin Woodward from Dublin, grave, silent, sensitive, and though only middle-aged already terminally ill. That whole Museum project, with its earnest aspirations, its slight touch of melancholy, was true to the spirit of the Oxford of that time. 'The Museum rose before us like an exhalation,' wrote a contemporary don, admiring how every detail of the building, even panelling and skirting boards, gas burners and door handles, was an object lesson in art. He noted the ironwork, 'plastically trained' into flower forms and leaf shapes. In between the shafts of the interior arcades were instructive displays of British rocks, and the columns of the buildings were themselves designed as scientific specimens, showing the character of different materials, stone, granite and marble. They rose like the pillars of a great cathedral in shades of grey and buff and pink and white.

Ruskin saw the Museum as 'the first building raised in England since the close of the fifteenth century, which has fearlessly put to a new trial this old faith in . . . the genius of the unassisted workman who gathered out of nature the materials he needed'. Literally so: the red-bearded O'Shea brothers and their nephew, part of the contingent who had come over from Ireland with Woodward, brought in plants from the Botanic Gardens to use as their sources for the carving of the pillars. When they started to caricature leading Oxford figures they had to be got rid of. Ruskin's theories of creative freedom had been seen to go too far. Ruskin himself, who was frequently on site advising and encouraging, is said to have worked personally on the carving of a column, which one of the workmen later took down. The immense rib-vaulted portal with its lavish marble carving was designed by Hungerford Pollen. Pollen was the artist who had painted the roof of Merton college chapel with a bold cross-hatching of green and black and russet. In their first term at Oxford Morris and Burne-Jones had spent many silent afternoons in the chapel which they rated with the cloisters at New College as their chief local shrine.

It was fortunate for them that they had come to Oxford at a time of such cross-currents. There was the connection between art and the scientists, of which Dr Acland, medical practitioner and Reader in Anatomy and architectural patron, was the supreme example. There was also the connection between art and the Tractarians. Morris and Burne-Jones belonged to the Plain-Song Society which practised regularly in the Music-Room at Holywell. Other members were Woodward and G. E. Street, the architects, and the well-known chivalric painter William Dyce. When they went to the gymnasium in Oriel Lane their instructor was Archibald MacLaren, a sportsman of unusual erudition. He wrote books on physical education and commissioned Burne-Jones to illustrate a collection of fairytales.

MacLaren, about twelve years their senior, was intrigued by Morris and Burne-Jones and would ask them out to his house in Summertown, then in the country. He was partly a father figure, partly older brother. He supported them and teased them. These visits to MacLaren were their first joint contact with the outside world. It was a low white house, with a rose-covered veranda and a little enclosed garden, a model for Morris's many enclosed gardens, real and imagined, boxed in with white walls. There they met MacLaren's young wife, hardly more than a girl. When he saw the studies of landscape and foliage Burne-Jones had been making in the country around Oxford MacLaren was impressed and gave him great encouragement. Morris was at this stage drawing not flowers but buildings: windows, arches and gables. He was arriving at his sense of the centrality of architecture as the basis of all arts.

The Pre-Raphaelite painters had preceded them to Oxford. Here already, in the early 1850s, the Pre-Raphaelites had found their first important patron, Thomas Combe, leading Tractarian and Printer to the University. He purchased Millais's 'Christ in the Carpenter's Shop'; Charles Collins's 'Convent Thoughts', painted partly in Combe's own garden in Oxford; Holman Hunt's 'Converted British Family Sheltering a Christian Missionary from the Persecution of the Druids'. In a way it seems surprising that the first intimation of the Pre-Raphaelites for Morris and Burne-Jones came so indirectly, from the publication of Ruskin's Edinburgh lectures in 1854. 'I was working in my room,' wrote Burne-Jones, 'when Morris ran in one morning bringing the newly published book with him: so everything was put aside until he read it all through to me. And there we first saw about the Pre-Raphaelites, and there I first saw the name of Rossetti. So for many a day after that we talked of little else but paintings which we had never seen.'

Combe had also purchased from Millais 'The Return of the Dove to the Ark', an oil painting exhibited at the Royal Academy in 1851. It shows the homing dove with its sprig of laurel being cradled by two wives of the sons of Noah. They are very young and girlish, one in an emerald green dress, the other in a floating white robe. Very shortly after they first heard of the Pre-Raphaelites, this painting was on show in Oxford, in James Wyatt's picture dealers in the High Street; 'and then', said Burne-Jones, 'we knew'.

In the autumn of 1854 Morris had moved into new rooms at Exeter. These adjoined Burne-Jones's rooms in the Old Buildings of the college, since demolished. They were complicated buildings, gabled, pebble-dashed and rambling. Small dark passages led from the staircase to the sitting-room; steps up to the window seat, steps down to the bedroom. Doors banged in people's faces; there was a certain claustrophobia, a *Charley's Aunt* atmosphere of incipient farce. It was here in the Old Buildings that Morris became a poet. 'Here, one morning,' recorded Burne-Jones, 'just after breakfast, he brought me in the first poem he ever made. After that, no week went by without a poem.'

The news spread around the Set. Crom Price and Richard Dixon went to Exeter, found Morris with Burne-Jones who announced it to them wildly: '"He's a big poet." "Who is?" asked we. "Why Topsy."' Topsy was the name Burne-Jones had given Morris, an in-joke referring to his mop of hair. Topsy was the little slave girl in Harriet Beecher Stowe's recently published *Uncle Tom's Cabin*. It was Topsy who maintained she had no father and no mother and, when questioned on her origin, said 'I 'spect I grow'd'.

Dixon, late in life, remembered the scene vividly:

We sat down and heard Morris read his first poem, the first that he had ever written in his life. It was called 'The Willow and the Red Cliff'. As he read it, I felt that it was something the like of which had never been heard before. It was a thing entirely new; founded on nothing previous: perfectly original, whatever its value, and sounding truly striking and beautiful, extremely decisive and powerful in execution . . . I expressed my admiration in some way, as we all did; and I remember his remark, 'Well, if this is poetry, it is very easy to write'.

Morris himself contributed to the legend of the instant Oxford poet, recording in his long autobiographical letter to Scheu: 'While still an undergraduate, I discovered that I could write poetry, much to my amazement.' In fact it seems unlikely that 'The Willow and the Red Cliff' was the first poem he had written. In the 1920s a small cache of early Morris poems and fragments not published in his first collected volume was retrieved from a drawer of a bureau which had belonged to Morris's sister Emma. Amongst these is a long poem in Tennysonian blank verse about the destruction and rebuilding of the temple. 'The Dedication of the Temple' was the subject for an Oxford prize poem in December 1853. As an undergraduate Morris would not himself have been eligible to enter, but the subject must have struck him as irresistible.

> it is sweet
> To see the many marble pillars stand,
> To see within, the many archèd cross:
> To see the arches other arches make
> In dark and light upon the marble floor.

This is an unmistakably Ruskinian temple. Morris's narrative has a certain vigour although it is obviously immature.

Morris seems to have obliterated from his memory the poems in this collection. Looking at them now, some naïve ballad quatrains seem almost juvenilia, and there are poems that may date back to Marlborough, written out in Emma's careful and affectionate hand. Morris probably considered these false starts. What does seem obvious is that in his second year at Oxford he started writing poetry with sudden new seriousness and much increased facility.

Morris's enthusiasms came in cycles. Each new enthusiasm quickly eclipsed the old one. Morris's own letters show the extent to which the writing of poems had now become obsessive. In his poetic phase the urge to make a poem came nagging at him constantly like one of his compulsive physical activities, a mental equivalent of his netting or his weaving. On Tuesday in Holy Week (3 April 1855) he wrote to Crom Price from Walthamstow enclosing a poem he described as 'exceedingly seedy': the poem begins ''Twas in Church on Palm Sunday'. It is an accumulative poem about kisses, Easter kisses, lovers' kisses, death-bed kisses, unmeant kisses:

> Willow standing 'gainst the blue,
> Where the light clouds come and go,
> Mindeth me of kiss untrue

In another letter he tells Price the idea of 'Kisses' came to him in church: not at sermon-time, but as the second lesson, the history of Judas's betrayal, was being read. One gets the impression that this inner life of poetry, exhausting and compulsive, was making his home life seem more remote and even less congenial. He complains to Price from Walthamstow, 'there are no facts here to write about; I have no one to talk to, except to ask for things to eat and drink and clothe myself withal; I have read no new books since I saw you, in fact no books at all.' His Oxford life had taken over from his old life. When Burne-Jones had come to stay and his mother had embarked on childhood reminiscences, seeing Burne-Jones was fond of him, Morris had been embarrassed and had shut his mother up.

It is curious that Dixon laid so much stress on Morris's originality. 'The Willow and the Red Cliff' is particularly Keatsian, and indeed close to the poetry Dixon himself was writing:

> About the river goes the wind
> And moans through the sad grey willow
> And calls up sadly to my mind
> The heave and swell of the billow.
>
> For the sea heaves up beneath the moon,
> And the river runs down to it.
> It will meet the sea by the red cliff,
> Salt water running through it.
>
> That cliff it rises steep from the sea
> On its top a thorn tree stands,
> With its branches blown away from the sea
> As if praying with outstretched hands
>
> To be saved from the wind, from the merciless wind
> That moaneth through it always,
> And very seldom gives it rest
> When the dark is falling pallwise.
>
> One day when the wind moaned through that tree,
> As it moans now through the willow,
> On the cliff sat a woman clasping her knee
> O'er the rise and fall of the billow

Keats was being read within the Set in those days. Morris always admired Keats with a 'boundless admiration' and liked to refer to him as one of his masters. Wordsworth, he later confessed, was a poet whom at

Oxford he only pretended to have liked. By 1855 he had read a little Shelley and had liked the poems he had read: '"The Skylark" was one: WHAT a gorgeous thing it is!' But a later conclusion was that Shelley had no eyes. What he found and related to so easily in Keats was his supreme visual quality. Morris drew the distinction between poets of rhetoric, in which category he put Milton and Swinburne, and poets who were primarily makers of pictures, visually observant poets such as Chaucer and Keats. Morris too was by instinct a picture-making poet, though he had yet to find his own poetic voice.

Morris had no high opinion of his early Oxford poetry. When it was suggested in the 1890s that some of his unpublished poems should be reclaimed and printed Morris shuddered. He did not want the 'ingenuous callowness' of them revealed to public gaze. In a way what had been more important than the poems themselves had been the context of their writing. Poetry at Oxford had been a group activity. Fulford, booming reader, was himself a poet. Dixon, dark, pale-faced, sad-voiced, shabby, beautiful and dirty, became a poet of small output but strange visionary quality. When Tennyson died not just Morris's name but Dixon's was being bandied around as his possible successor as Poet Laureate. It was an atmosphere of intense creative interplay and Morris, for the first time in his life, was at the hub of it, alert, hectic, exhortatory, beaming, directing operations, giving and receiving. This scenario came to be so necessary to him he would attempt to recreate it in successive bands of brothers grouped around him, most notably in Morris, Marshall, Faulkner & Co.

Morris at Oxford was exuberant and noisy. 'A little more *piano* sir,' Madox, his scout at Exeter, is said to have suggested. There were tales of Morris shouting for his scout out of the window while the man was actually standing in the room. Such tales accumulated. It was while he was at Oxford that Morris's wild temper began to take on the quality of legend. In these rages he was accredited with superhuman strength: driving his head against the wall hard enough to make a deep dent in the plaster; biting practically through the woodwork of a window frame; using his teeth to lift up heavy weights. Dixon described his masochistic habit of beating his own head, 'dealing himself vigorous blows, to take it out of himself'. MacLaren complained that Morris's bills at the gymnasium for broken sticks and foils equalled those of all the rest of his pupils put together. Unimpressed with the quality of the Christmas pudding served at Red Lion Square Morris hurled it down the stairs. These were stories which persisted, in one form or another, until Morris was middle-aged. They were passed round and embroidered, like the tales in Nordic sagas. What was behind them, and indeed how true were they?

It does seem certain that Morris's famous rages at their worst could develop into something more alarming: a kind of seizure in which he partially lost consciousness. The most graphic description comes, again, from Dixon in notes supplied for but played down in Mackail's biography. Morris had gone to stay with him in Birmingham:

When he was to go, we both (I think) misread the railway guide, and drove to the station when there was no train: and there was nothing for it but to wait to next day. I was made aware of this by a fearful cry in my ears, and saw Morris 'translated'. It lasted all the way home. It then vanished in a moment: he was calm as if it had never been, and began painting in watercolours. I wanted to get him some wine: but he said he was all right, and he manifestly was.

There has been such a conspiracy of silence over Morris's true medical condition that it is difficult now to piece the evidence together. But it does seem likely that the incident described by Dixon is a typical example of a relatively minor disappointment and annoyance triggering an involuntary physical response out of all proportion to its cause. It appears that in these states Morris did not actually fall to the ground but remained immobile, unaware of his surroundings for what could be many minutes, in what would now be described as partial seizure. When Bernard Shaw, fascinated as he was by medical phenomena and particularly gleeful at pointing out the weakness in anyone so apparently robust, first broached the subject he used the word 'eclampsia' to describe Morris's condition. This term is now used mainly to refer to quasi-epileptic fits during pregnancy, dangerous if not controlled by drugs. Shaw was using it in a more generalized sense to suggest that Morris's rages in fact were pathological and that Morris's loss of physical control when crossed or irritated was not quite sane. One of the puzzles that remain is whether Morris's 'translation' was followed by amnesia, an involuntary obliteration of the incident from his memory, or whether the almost ingratiating quietness that followed on his outbursts was the result of his dismay and his embarrassment. But Shaw echoes Dixon in his comment that these rages left Morris shaken 'as men are shaken after a fit'.

Inevitably these illnesses engendered a kind of separation from the male friends Morris by now so much depended on. There was his immediate frightening removal into the 'absent' state. Equally, there was the state of anxious tension in the aftermath, the moments of returning to reality. It seems his friends made light of it, sharing his own embarrassments and hoping to contain these incidents by the chaff and horseplay the Set was always prone to. There was a youthful cruelty in their behaviour. After one of his 'storms' in the late 1850s Faulkner stuck a label 'He is mad' on William Morris's hat, before they went out.

What is interesting is the way Morris himself colluded, as if desperate to make himself more socially acceptable. He turned himself almost into a cartoon character for the entertainment of the Set. He was willing to stagger around holding a coal scuttle in his teeth, in imitation of the passengers alighting from a cross-Channel steamer. In London, slightly later, 'He would imitate an eagle with considerable skill and humour, climbing onto a chair.' He went along with the sobriquet of Topsy more than was absolutely necessary, sometimes signing his letters not with his name but with the sign of the small boy's spinning top. Morris's Socialist colleagues were furious at the way the name Topsy was still lingering among his old acquaintances up till the 1890s. They felt that it demeaned him. Bernard Shaw pondered this problem: 'There must have been a moment in which he realised that there was no such person as Topsy.' Indeed there was; but it did not happen yet.

Morris's writings make great use of rages, trances and translations. The Black Knight in *The Water of the Wondrous Isles* casts himself down, rolls about and paws the ground. In the same novel, when Birdalone returns to him, Arthur in thanksgiving sinks his forehead to the earth: he rolls over, his limbs stretch out, blood gushes from his mouth. In 'The Hollow Land', a story of Morris's Oxford period, a dizzying swoon precedes Arnold's benign vision of his love clad in loose white raiment sitting on a great grey stone. He consistently dwells on the prophetic power of swooning. The most vocal of Morris's prophets, the Hall-Sun in *The House of the Wolfings*, is a swooner. It is also significant that she is a woman. Perhaps those who have experienced this sort of other-worldliness have the equipment to get closer to the truth.

*

By the end of William Morris's second year in Oxford hopes for the monastery seem to have been waning. Price wrote: 'Morris has become questionable on doctrinal points, and Ted is too Catholic to be ordained.'

Other things preoccupied them. In the summer vacation of 1855 Morris went to the Royal Academy exhibition in London. It was here he first met Georgiana Macdonald. She was then fifteen, demure, shy, incandescent with intelligence. Burne-Jones already knew her. Her father, the Rev. George Macdonald, a leading Wesleyan Methodist, had been a minister on the Birmingham circuit in the early 1850s. Georgie's brother Harry was at King Edward's Grammar School with Ned. She had once answered the door to him, the small girl in her pinafore. The Macdonald family had now returned to London. Slowly, tentatively, she and Ned had renewed acquaintanceship.

A remarkable female dynasty emerged from that Methodist background of plain living and high thinking. Georgie's elder sister Alice was Rudyard Kipling's mother. Of her three younger sisters Agnes married the artist and later Royal Academician Edward Poynter; Louisa married the Midlands ironmaster Alfred Baldwin, MP for Bewdley, and their son was Stanley Baldwin, Conservative prime minister three times between 1923 and 1937. Even in such a family of formidable women Georgie stood out for her asperity and firmness. Rossetti, who knew these clever daughters as young women, had predicted it was only Louisa who would grow up to be the equal of 'Mrs. Ned'. The oldest daughter, Mary, had died in early childhood, like Morris's elder brother: this was one bond between them. Another was a concentration on essentials so dogged as to constitute a kind of blindness. As a child it had never occurred to Georgie to wonder if her family were rich or poor.

The Academy meeting was an unpropitious start to Morris's friendship with the woman Sydney Cockerell described as his 'spiritual affinity'. Georgie was accompanied there by Wilfred Heeley, a friend of her brother's, another of that close-knit group of Birmingham young men. Heeley said, 'That's Morris,' pointing at the stolid figure standing closely scrutinizing Millais's painting of 'The Rescue'. Heeley introduced them. She thought him very handsome, of an unusual type, reminiscent of the statues of mediaeval kings. He had no moustache in those days so the shaping of his mouth, which she always felt was his most expressive feature, stood out clearly. His hair waved and curled 'triumphantly'.

But his eyes seemed inward-looking: 'he looked as if he scarcely knew me,' she wrote later. At their next meeting the following summer, the impasse had remained. Georgie wondered how this awkward, unresponsive man had ever written the poem of 'Rapunzel and Golden Guendolen'. He did not appear poetic.

Other people at the time observed this same incongruity.

CHAPTER FOUR

Northern France
1855–56

William Morris was not one of the great Victorian travellers. But in the course of his life he made two journeys that had an effect on him out of all proportion to their actual duration. The first of these was the three-week tour he took in the long vacation of his final year at Oxford round the churches and cathedrals of northern France.

It was not his first visit to France. He had already travelled abroad with his sister Henrietta in the summer vacation of 1854. They had been to Belgium, concentrating upon late mediaeval paintings: the van Eycks, Hans Memling, Rogier van der Weyden. They had journeyed on to see the great cathedrals of Amiens, Beauvais, Rouen and Chartres. William Morris had begun to develop his affection for France as the place of good cooking, and also of good drinking. He saw wine as the test of a true civilization: a country that produced such good wine was in his opinion 'a very great country'. That first summer he had smelled the mixed beeswax, wood-smoke and onions that became for him the epitome of Paris; the two of them had looked down from a high building on to the trees in the Tuileries gardens. These were 'so thick they looked as if you could walk on their tops'.

The journey he made in 1855 was different in character. It was emphatically a male holiday and, in theory at least, it was an energetic walking tour, avoiding the railways which Morris soon began defining as ABOMINATIONS. This was also partly an economy measure since Burne-Jones was so poor. Originally Cormell Price was in the party, with Morris, Burne-Jones and Fulford. But at the last minute he was unable to go. Morris tried to make the best of Fulford, saying he would no doubt be a very pleasant travelling companion; 'yet to me', he wrote sadly to Price, 'he is a very poor substitute for you'.

The three of them set off on Thursday 19 July. Fulford had brought a volume of Keats with him and regaled Burne-Jones with readings in the small hotel in London where they slept the night before. Morris met them at the station, and they made the crossing from Folkestone to Boulogne: a wet crossing, not a rough one; none of them felt seasick. They travelled straight on to Abbeville that evening, taking a slow late train and walking a mile to their inn, the Tête de Bœuf, along a mysterious poplar-lined road. On a later visit Morris described, in a passage almost painful with nostalgia, 'the French poplar meadows and the little villages' of 'the waters about the Somme'. He added 'often I longed to be following up the long roads among them more than I can tell you.' Those long straight roads of Northern France remained in Morris's mind as they would remain in the memories of the English veterans of the First World War.

That first night in Abbeville Morris had caught a glimpse of the big church, the church of St Wolfram, looking like 'a very mountain of wrought stone'. This was the first of many glimpses of big churches in a tour that would encompass nine cathedrals, and at least twenty-four non-cathedral churches, as Morris later totalled them up on many fingers: 'all splendid churches; some of them surpassing first-rate English Cathedrals'. The next morning at Abbeville he woke the others early for a wander before breakfast. By midday they had climbed St Wolfram's tower and surveyed the old town with its network of narrow streets and pitch-roofed mediaeval houses. 'We were all three', wrote Morris, 'in exstasies thereat.'

Just before he left for France Morris had been to Ely. What he found there was a familiar cosy English townscape: the 'bit of a hill' on which Ely Cathedral stands struck him as 'very jolly', with its green fields and its gardens and its trees, 'all dotted about with quaint old houses, and bits of the old conventual buildings'. That cathedral in its setting seemed domestic, rather ramshackle, verging on a joke. But Morris's descriptions of French churches are more awe-struck: they have an added gravity, a mystery of foreignness. What Morris perceived as the ultimate in Gothic was the solemn silent Gothic of great northern French cathedrals. They went on from Abbeville in the afternoon to Amiens, where they spent an hour in the cathedral before dinner, returning to it afterwards. Morris 'surveyed it with calm joy'.

Morris used Amiens as the basis for a very autobiographical short story, 'A Night in the Cathedral'. This appeared in the *Oxford and*

Cambridge Magazine the next year. The narrator is a young architectural enthusiast on a walking tour who returns to the cathedral after dinner to investigate it further. He finds to his horror that he has been locked in. This happened in real life in Winchester Cathedral to Morris's mentor G. E. Street, the architect. Like Street, Morris's narrator is overcome by panic, banging on the great doors, shouting to get out. It is partly a rather adolescent Gothick terror tale. There are ghosts in the cathedral: 'stern knights and sad priests rose from their graves, skeletons with armour and robes dangling and folding about them, making the night hideous beyond endurance.' More significantly, in the background of the story, there are strong suggestions of a spiritual crisis. The narrator falls into a trance and he sees visions. Conscious as he is of the beauty of the building he senses that the heart of God has gone from it. He feels he is 'in the presence of awful, cold beauty – inexpressibly lovely, but with no love for me'. He continues:

It was as if some old friend had proved false, or as if I had hitherto mistaken my own nature, and aimed at that which was too high for me. How miserable, how degraded I felt! I could see the beauty, but could not feel it, – at least not as I had felt it of old, when it was almost unmixed delight to me.

There was a kind of agony for Morris in this protracted tour of the shrines of Christianity at the very moment he was thinking of severing his own connection with the Church.

Morris analysed this later as the moment when the influence of John Ruskin overcame his devotion to the High Church and the Puseyites. One can see how he travelled around France that vivid summer with the words of John Ruskin ringing in his ears: 'go forth again to gaze upon the old cathedral front . . . examine once more those ugly goblins, and formless monsters, and stern statues, anatomiless and rigid; but do not mock at them, for they are the signs of the life and liberty of every workman who struck the stone'.

Morris was embarking on a by then conventional Ruskinian Grand Tour, following the tracks of G. E. Street, Gilbert Scott and William Burges, architects steeped in French mediaeval building. In some ways the essay Morris wrote when he returned, 'The Churches of North France: Shadows of Amiens', reads like the work of the Ruskinian disciple: architecturally speaking it is very well observed. But it has another element which shows Morris already breaking free from Ruskin's influence. This difference lies in its narrative expansiveness, its storyteller's concept of the sweep and surge of history, its ebullient delight in the setting and the meaning of the buildings in the landscape, arrived at by looking out as much as concentrating inwards. At Amiens:

We came out from the roof on to the parapet in the blaze of the sun, and then going to the crossing mounted as high as we could into the spire, and stood there awhile looking down on the beautiful country with its water-meadows and feathery trees.

Morris loved the detail in the country. Ruskin, faced with the spread of meadows around Oxford, complained there were too many buttercups and it reminded him of poached eggs.

When Morris first entered Amiens he felt inclined to shout, it seemed so free and vast and noble. But he discovered he liked Beauvais even better. Asked once to say which was his favourite cathedral he replied it was the one he happened to be in. He, Burne-Jones and Fulford, still in their state of ecstasy, travelled on to Beauvais the next day, trekking the last seventeen miles on foot, a problem for Morris who had brought the wrong shoes with him and was suffering from corns. In Amiens, working himself up towards one of his alarming and debilitating rages, 'filling the streets with imprecations on all bootmakers', he had bought himself a pair of 'gay carpet slippers' which he wore *en route* to Beauvais. It was painful progress and he told his mother that the walk had rather knocked him up. But Morris could always be cheered up by a good building and he was especially susceptible to Beauvais's great size, its Gothic grandeur and the fact it was unfinished.

The apse and the choir rise confident, stupendous. What makes Beauvais so disconcerting is that it is a cathedral with no nave, as if some accident had happened or a spell had been cast over it. Morris was strongly moved by its colossal freakishness. On a later visit he described it as one of the wonders of the world: 'seen by twilight its size gives one an impression almost of terror: one can scarcely believe in it.' It hovers as a backdrop to Morris's Oxford story, 'Gertha's Lovers': 'to this day the mighty fragment, still unfinished, towering so high above the city roofs towards the sky, seems like a mountain cliff that went a-wandering once, and by earnest longing of the lowlanders was stayed among the poplar trees for ever'. Cathedrals as cliffs; castles like rocky outcrops: Morris was peculiarly attuned to seeing buildings as geological events.

On the Sunday morning they went to High Mass in Beauvais

Cathedral. It was the full-blown ritual: processions, ancient singing, music from trombones and two organs pealing out so suddenly that the noise made the air tremble. Burne-Jones felt the Day of Judgement had arrived already. 'What a day it was, and how alive I was, and young – and a blue dragon-fly stood still in the air so long that I could have painted him.' Looking back through the whole sequence of experience that shaped him it seemed as if that day at Beauvais represented the first day in his creation, or rather the first day of his later reconstruction. It is fascinating in the accounts of this French journey by both Morris and Burne-Jones to see places where they dovetail. They both looked back on Beauvais with particular nostalgia because it was so central to the evolution process of that summer, part of their self-questioning, a place in their joint history. On the Whit Sunday after William Morris's death Georgiana Burne-Jones sat in the Beauvais cloister reading aloud from Ruskin's 'On the Nature of Gothic' and Morris's own preface to the Kelmscott Press edition.

In the Louvre Morris made Burne-Jones shut his eyes and led him right up to Fra Angelico's 'Coronation of the Virgin' before allowing him to look. Morris was proprietorial in France. In fact he had not wanted at all to visit Paris, knowing how miserable Notre-Dame was looking with half of its sculpture removed and strewn haphazardly underneath the porches. He had suggested skirting round the city, even though this would take longer. But Burne-Jones wanted to look at the pictures in the Louvre, Fulford was also anxious to see Paris, and Morris was bribed with the prospect of a visit to the Hôtel de Cluny, already a museum, hung as it was with mediaeval tapestries. They worked hard at sightseeing for at least twelve hours a day. They saw the Sainte-Chapelle. They were excited to find seven Pre-Raphaelite paintings hanging in the Beaux-Arts section of the Exposition Universelle: one by Collins, three by Millais and three by Hunt, including his 'Light of the World'. Morris said the Beaux-Arts was well worth seeing for the English pictures 'and for nothing else'.

On this Paris visit Morris seems to have been edgy and obnoxious, showing that insularity that sometimes surfaced, unwilling to bend himself to other people's plans. He grumbled and fidgeted. One evening they went to the Opéra to hear Madame Alboni in Meyerbeer's *Le Prophète*. Burne-Jones, who had never seen an opera, was enraptured; 'Morris seemed a good deal bored.' He was still having trouble with his feet. One senses a general relief at their departure, after three nights in Paris. According to Fulford Morris was delighted: 'he has been dying to leave Paris and get to Chartres.'

They had now been in France almost a week, and Chartres was the third of their cathedrals, spectacularly sited, rising like an extraordinary mirage in the fields:

through the boughs and trunks of the poplars, we caught glimpses of the great golden corn sea, waving, waving, waving for leagues and leagues; and among the corn grew burning scarlet poppies, and blue corn-flowers; and the corn-flowers were so blue, that they gleamed, and seemed to burn with a steady light, as they grew beside the poppies among the gold of the wheat. Through the corn sea ran a blue river, and always green meadows and lines of tall poplars followed its windings.

At the end of the corn fields stands the great church, as described in much the most successful of Morris's Oxford stories, 'The Story of the Unknown Church'. The building he depicts is a composite cathedral: some of its features are more obviously Amiens. But in its topography, the cathedral in the corn sea, Morris's Unknown Church is definitely Chartres.

Seen closer Chartres is not in fact a building in the country. The cathedral is the crown of the mediaeval town and Morris spent a day there exploring what he called its 'quaint streets and gorgeous churches', catching glimpses from all angles of those huge and cliff-like buttresses. In Chartres fifty years later, Eric Gill rated his first sight of the North Transept from one of the little alleys on the hillside as one of his most exquisite spiritual and sensual delights. Both to Morris and Gill the townscape had a meaning beyond its aesthetic splendours and surprises. It explained and seemed to justify the social system that had brought it to such a pitch of perfection. Morris has been criticized for misunderstanding mediaeval realities. But he understood them in the way he wanted, as a symbol and a yardstick, and in Chartres he found his prize example of the cathedral built so daringly and quickly, and built by a whole community in consort. The cathedral was rebuilt in the early thirteenth century, after the destruction of the Romanesque cathedral. It was more or less completed in a thirty-year timespan: in the context of history, almost overnight.

In a letter he wrote home to Crom Price, Morris dwells on the 'beautiful statues' of Chartres. The narrator in his 'Story of the

Unknown Church' is the master-mason, working on the carving of the new church rising to replace a burned-down building. The story describes events of 'more than six hundred years ago', and this puts it exactly in the period of the rebuilding of Chartres. The interesting thing about this story of obsession, a highly wrought dream narrative, a dream within a dream, is the way it focuses on the activity of *making*. The mason is carving all the bas-reliefs of the west front of the cathedral with his own hand. And still more interesting is its theme of female creativity: Morris's first depiction of a character he frequently returned to in his novels and his stories, the comrade sister, companion in craftsmanship. In the porch, beneath the mason, his sister Margaret is carving at the flower work, 'and the little quatrefoils that carry the signs of the zodiac and the emblems of the months'. Margaret is about twenty, very beautiful, with dark brown hair and deep calm violet eyes.

The cathedral in his story is the centre of fecundity. Morris's descriptions of the gardens of the abbey – the roses, the convolvulus, great fiery nasturtiums, 'great spires' of hollyhocks – have the pictorial fluency of one of his own chintzes; and as always with Morris his description of the beauties and the fruitfulness of nature is shot through with a sense of the erotic. Wild flowers from outside have crept into the garden: 'lush green briony, with green-white blossoms, that grows so fast, one could almost think that we see it grow, and deadly nightshade, La bella donna, O! so beautiful; red berry and purple, yellow-spiked flower, and deadly, cruel-looking, dark green leaf, all growing together in the glorious days of early autumn'. There is the hint of decadence, the whiff of Baudelaire.

What did Morris make of the glass in Chartres Cathedral? In a letter to Crom Price he mentions it fleetingly. In a later essay he suggests the twelfth century as the beginning of the real history of stained glass as art: 'The windows of that date that are left us are very deep and rich in colour, red and blue being the prevailing tints.'

In the back of his mind one senses the lingering intense reds and blues of Chartres, and the narrative content of those windows: the groupings and the bustlings of knights and priests and peasants, fishmongers and butchers, vintners and cobblers, a community in action. They are like the much later Morris & Co. windows in the way they invite participation: what are they *about*? Together in that summer, in Chartres Cathedral and the smaller churches, Morris and Burne-Jones first discovered the visual formula they would rework so often: the extended single figure, the saint, the king, the prophet, in the tall top section of the window, with a more crowded panel of narrative below.

The carving of the tomb in the nave of the cathedral in the great far-off city: this remained a scene of immense resonance to Morris. He could visualize it stage by stage, from the raising of the marble canopy high above the tomb to the painting and carving of the canopy with flowers and small narrative scenes. On the tomb itself the master mason carves the effigies of his dead sister and her lover, lying with clasped hands like a husband and wife. In Morris's tombscapes in his northern French church stories we stand at the meeting point between Gothick and Gothic: the mid-Victorian Gothic of John Ruskin superimposed on the Technicolor vision of Walter Scott. Light shining through stained glass is a factor in the throbbing other-worldliness, almost the hysteria, of Morris's dream narratives: light flickers on to polished surfaces of marble, heightening intensity, swooping, swooning with emotion – 'till a sound of music rose, deepened, and fainted; then I woke'.

At six in the morning on 27 July they left Chartres in a drizzle which practically hid the spires of the cathedral. Morris, who liked to see a landscape in all weathers, decided this looked splendid; he was over-joyed that they could route themselves to Rouen with very little travel-ling by train. They went across country via Dreux, Evreux and Louviers, partly using 'quaint nondescript' public conveyances, drawn by a single horse, going very slowly, and also travelling by omnibus. From France William Morris wrote home in two directions: to his mother he writes more briefly and more guardedly whilst the long and lyrical accounts of his French journey are sent to his absentee brother, Crom Price. This particular day is parcelled out to both of them; the letter to Price is flowing, garrulous, amusing, giving out a sense of the immediate experience not surpassed even in Morris's vivid *Icelandic Journals*. We probably know more about this July Friday than any day in William Morris's life.

The rain was still falling a little as they left Maintenon and travelled by conveyance to Dreux, a distance of about seventeen miles through countryside that Morris liked better than any of the country he had seen so far in France. It was a matter of the grouping of the trees: all the trees, but especially the poplars and the aspens. He liked the hedgeless fields of grain and the feathery herbs the French farmers grew for forage, whose names he did not know. What he saw was a landscape of foreignness and yet of extreme familiarity, a timeless countryside that launched him into a description of almost biblical rotundity. These French fields were the most beautiful fields he ever saw:

looking as if they belonged to no man, as if they were planted not to be cut down in the end, and to be stored in barns and eaten by the cattle, but that rather they were planted for their beauty only, that they might grow always among the trees, mingled with the flowers, purple thistles, and blue corn-flowers, and red poppies, growing together with the corn round the roots of the fruit trees, in their shadows, and sweeping up to the brows of the long low hills till they reached the sky, changing sometimes into long fields of vines, or delicate, lush green forage; and they all looked as if they would grow there for ever, as if they had always grown there, without change of seasons, knowing no other time than the early August.

Long before they got to Dreux the weather had cleared and it was a bright sunny day.

They were in Dreux in the middle of the morning, exploring the 'very quaint old town' with its waterways and bridges. They discovered the mediaeval belfry, prime example of the sort of foursquare building that enraptured Morris always. It stands in the town centre, stolid, bulky, menacing, like the tower in his poem 'Winter Weather' from which boomed the midnight bell. They admired the church of St Pierre, a good example of French flamboyant Gothic. But Morris, already alert to the depredations of the restorers, complained bitterly about insensitive restorations in the apse. He preferred the shabbier condition of the elaborately carved transept front. This, he wrote, was now looking 'very forlorn and battered but (Deo gratias) not yet restored'.

Morris travelled around France with his prejudices rampant. In this, in his persona of the apoplectic gentleman, he appeared to be older than his age. On the way to Evreux the travellers were forced to undergo half an hour's ride by railway. This too aroused his 'intensive indignation'. At Evreux they had to divide their time between eating their dinner ('alas! for our Lower Nature') and gazing at the gorgeous cathedral, sited so idyllically in a little complex of mediaeval buildings by the Iton river. Morris seems to have loved this cathedral partly because it was a relatively small one. In his letter to Crom Price he analysed the sweep of styles in it: the Norman nave; the early Gothic choir; the 'very rich flamboyant' aisles. He writes with a disarming ebullience and exactness, expecting to be understood even at his most technical. He finds Evreux 'exceeding lovely', adding 'there is a great deal of good stained glass about the Church.'

When they left Evreux, travelling by public wagon, they found that the landscape had altered absolutely. It was getting much more hilly. First they passed through a succession of quite flat and wooded valleys with hills on either side; then they wound up a long hill and on to a large plateau, finally descending into a 'glorious lake-like valley' which led them at last into the little town of Louviers. Morris arrived as the architectural pilgrim:

there is a splendid church there, though it is not a large one; the outside has a kind of mask of the most gorgeous flamboyant (though late) thrown all it, with such parapets and windows, it is so gorgeous and light, that I was utterly unprepared for the inside, and almost startled by it; so solemn it looked and calm after the fierce flamboyant of the outside.

His description of the church of Notre-Dame at Louviers shows his sophisticated comprehension of the Gothic. He alights upon this church as his definition point between the simple grandeur of the thirteenth-century French Gothic and the more ornate, fanciful and feminine French Gothic as it developed over the next two centuries. He knows with immense certainty which Gothic he prefers. For Morris, as it was to be for D. H. Lawrence, the cathedral is repository of awe, strength, male bravura: he sees a great church as the place of the male mystery. In Lawrence's novel *The Rainbow* Will Brangwen's soul shuddered when he opened the door of Lincoln Cathedral: his soul leapt upwards with the pillars; he responded to the 'far-off clinching and mating of the arches, the leap and thrust of the stone, carrying a great roof overhead'. Morris's perception of the Gothic is not so overtly sexual as Lawrence's. But a sense of solemnity and splendour and the glamour of that early technological achievement underlies Morris's own precise, ecstatic understanding of the 'huge free space' of the 'mighty Gothic naves'.

They left Louviers by omnibus. It was a five-mile ride from the town to the station. The sun by then was setting, striking right across a valley which was the most glorious of all the valleys they had travelled through that day. The country was not planted with wheat or corn, but was mainly grassland, set with trees. 'O! the trees!' wrote Morris, with his almost automatic imaginative trick of peopling a landscape: 'it was all like the country in a beautiful poem, in a beautiful Romance such as might make a background to Chaucer's Palamon and Arcite.' They took the train to Rouen, Morris grumbling, cursing the iniquities of 'nasty, brimstone, noisy, shrieking' railway train roaring through the country ignoring the subtleties of cornflowers, convolvulus, white clematis, golden St John's wort. To his extra disapproval the train sneaked into Rouen by a side route, disappointing them of preparatory vistas. They saw nothing of the buildings until they were actually in the town.

With his usual dread of being disappointed by the things he had most prized Morris felt anxious at going back to Rouen after his visit of the previous year. But his fears were apparently dispelled on that first evening. They arrived about eight-thirty, having visited three towns, two good churches, one cathedral. They had travelled for fifteen hours and spent nine shillings each. 'Well here we are in Rouen, glorious Rouen', Morris told his mother. He had seldom enjoyed a day so much.

Why was Morris so possessive about Rouen, going back over and over again to his first sight of it? 'what a wonder of glory that was to me when I first came upon the front of the Cathedral rising above the flower-market': this was what he wrote, in full flood of recollection, in 1878. One of the things that attracted him most was the cathedral's situation in the *mouvementé* centre of the working city. Unlike Chartres, the hushed and isolated place of pilgrimage, raised up above the town, Rouen Cathedral was set within the hubbub of the criss-crossed crowded streets. A contemporary guide describes the town as 'swarming like an ant-hill', a commercial town, a French equivalent of Manchester, the centre of the cotton trade in France.

Morris saw the façade of the cathedral partly in the terms Claude Monet was to see it. In the early 1890s Monet painted that tremendous façade as it was altered by different lights, by switching seasons. He painted it glowing pink and mauve or grey and grizzled. Morris too was highly conscious of effects of light and weather. But he was also conscious of the cathedral in its townscape, as part of the fabric of its local social history, full of community resonance and meaning. In 1895, in a passionate defence of Rouen against a threatened restoration programme, Morris argued for the totality that made it in his view the most beautiful monument of art in 'the two great architectural countries, France and England'. Its artistic value derived from its connections. This cathedral was 'the work of the associated labour and thought of the *people*, the result of a chain of tradition unbroken from the earliest stages of art'.

Morris and his friends spent five nights in Rouen, over the weekend of their second week in France. They stayed at the Hôtel de France. On the first day there they went around the churches; climbed to the top of the view spire which gave them an enormous panorama of the city; clambered around the roof and the lantern of the fourteenth-century church of St Ouen; heard Vespers in the cathedral; finally, after dinner, ascending Mont Ste Catherine and wandering about there until it was quite dark.

Each day they returned to visit the cathedral. Burne-Jones shared Morris's excitement with it, thinking it was the best of all the churches he had seen in France. They had hoped to hear Vespers there each afternoon and were disappointed to find they were sung only on Saturday and Sunday. But Morris was effusive at the quality of singing: 'And weren't they sung, just. O! my word! on the Sunday especially, when a great deal of the psalms were sung to the Peregrine tone, and then, didn't they sing the hymns!'

Morris did not hope for comfort when he looked at ancient buildings. His view of architecture was never a complacent one. He perceived unnerving qualities, the values Ruskin itemized in 'On the Nature of Gothic': primitivism, restlessness, the itch of the grotesque. Like Ruskin he reached out for the savage face of Gothic, its 'wildness of thought, and roughness of work'. Gazing at Rouen Cathedral he was drawing on Ruskin's correlation of the man-made and the natural: 'the look of mountain brotherhood' between the cathedral and the alp. Morris was not Ruskin's uncritical disciple. Here again one can sense twinges of defiance in his attitude. He began to regard Ruskin in the way that he saw Tennyson at Oxford: admirable but not quite watertight. Ruskin's sense of the inherent strangeness in the Gothic was, however, something he agreed with and adhered to all his life.

In one of his late novels, *The Well at the World's End*, Morris describes a church at Goldburg that is partly Rouen, partly Ruskin. This great church formed the whole of the long side of Goldburg market place. These were wayward, savage people. The building was fine, delicate, 'and its steeples and bell-towers were high and well builded, and adorned exceedingly richly'.

The journey now took on a curious momentum. On the Wednesday they left Rouen, hoping to catch the steamer down the Seine to Le Havre. The steamer had been cancelled, so they set off on a twenty-five mile walk to Caudebec. This was 'a glorious walk', but it exhausted them and Morris was again in trouble with his shoes. He had had to go back to wearing the original badly fitting boots he had brought with him. These were patched twice at the sides and by then the heels were loosening. He eventually took them to the cobbler's where he was received by three men and a boy. Morris told his mother what happened next: 'I said when I had taken off my boot (in French of course) "Can you mend my boot if you please" and made a face expecting what the answer would be, well they laid their heads together and presently they (or rather one of them) said, "Monsieur we cannot mend it" – and I went away.'

They travelled by diligence from Caudebec to Yvetot; it cost each of them a penny for the ten-mile journey. They slept at Le Havre and travelled on by steamer to Caen over a very smooth sea. Caen was disappointing. Morris had already heard too much about it: he resisted pre-publicity, preferring a discovery. But the Caen church of St Etienne delighted him, and so did the cathedral at Bayeux and the tapestry. This was described by Morris as 'very quaint and rude' (in the old-fashioned sense, by which he meant unstudied) 'and very interesting'. Part of the cathedral was closed for repairs although they made 'strenuous efforts' to get in.

The last of Morris's great cathedrals was at Coutances. This huge spare thirteenth-century edifice, 'like our Early English, very plain but very beautiful', was more to Morris's taste than it had been to Ruskin's. The town, too, struck him as English in its character, a granite town built up the side of a steep hill overlooking pretty country: 'much like Clay Cross without the Chimnies'. Morris's married sister Emma was now living in Clay Cross.

They went on by diligence to Avranches and Mont St-Michel, finally sailing home from Granville via Jersey. Morris had worked out they would set off in their steamer at the very time on Sunday morning when the Morris family would all be at church. 'I suppose', he told his mother, 'the Monday or Tuesday following will see me at Walthamstow, in a very seedy condition as to my clothes, for my coat is a beautiful russet brown where the sun has caught it, and my beautiful violet ribbon had become so seedy that I was obliged to throw it away at Caudebec, and no words can describe the seediness of my dusty hat.'

In Rouen Morris bought Thackeray's novel *The Newcomes*, in the recently published Tauchnitz edition. Almost uncannily this book mirrors the conflict Morris was undergoing at the time. Clive Newcome horrifies his father, the good Colonel, with news of his decision to become an artist. Morris, in northern France, was on the brink of a similar confession to his mother. He had reached the point of knowing he could not take holy orders. Late one evening towards the end of their French travels, pacing the quayside at Le Havre, he and Burne-Jones made the definite decision to begin together what they called 'a life of art'.

What had brought them to this moment of clarity? Partly it was the national crisis in the background. Burne-Jones, it appears, had been in a state of turmoil over the Crimean War. Earlier that year he had been tempted to take up one of the commissions offered by the government to the university. He felt Oxford had failed him, and he said, 'I wanted to go and get shot in the Crimea very much indeed.' He had been turned down on grounds of health. There was a desperation in their decision. One should not forget the role of the unfamiliar setting in heightening emotion and sharpening the sense of possibilities. For all of them this had been a journey of discoveries and intense extremes. Le Havre itself, the largest port in France, the main port of entry for imported goods for Paris, was a thoroughfare for the *outré* and the exotic. Travellers have left accounts of those quaysides cluttered and resounding with the strange cries and glittering plumage of parrots and macaws. It was an environment conducive to a drama. In France even Fulford, the most level-headed member of the party, was deflected temporarily from taking holy orders, though the Church of England claimed him in the end.

Morris recognized and hated his own vacillating nature, the seesaw of his hyper-energy and his inertia. He returned home from France in a new mood of resolution. He and Burne-Jones had arrived at a new scheme of things in which Burne-Jones would be the artist while Morris embarked upon his training as an architect. He was impatient to leave Exeter College and begin. Shortly after the return he was writing to Crom Price in a high fever of activity. He felt too old already.

I MUST make haste, it would not do for me, dear Crom, even for the sake of being with you, to be a lazy, aimless, useless, dreaming body all my life long. I have wasted enough time already, God knows.

We have no exact record of how Morris told his mother. Later references suggest he made confession in two stages. First he told her he did not intend taking holy orders. She cried and disbelieved him and admonished him, telling him how evil it was to be an idle man without a purpose. There had evidently been an acrimonious conversation; Morris later apologized for speaking 'somewhat roughly'. He excused his clumsiness: he said he had been 'speaking indeed far off from my heart because of my own awkwardness'. His sister Henrietta was severe with him as well. A few weeks later Morris sent his mother a long letter. This letter still exists. It is a careful, anxious letter, intended to repair the damage of that interview but bearing the fresh news that Morris is determined to enter an architect's office as a pupil. He cannot expect his mother's sympathy for this decision. He knows it will bewilder her. But he presents it as *fait accompli*. In this letter he stresses how he himself will pay the premium required to start the pupillage, suggesting that only the extent of his own income allowed him the freedom to make the proposed move.

Morris's decision took him out of the orbit of family influence. It was a break with any world his mother could relate to and a final rejection of any sort of future his father had intended. He knew, with a conviction that strengthened all his arguments, that he was entering a world in which the standards of his Walthamstow childhood no longer applied. He wrote to his mother: 'Stanley and Rendal [*sic*], and Arthur, and Edgar shall keep up the family honour in the World, and perhaps even I myself shall not utterly disgrace it, so may Christ help the family of Morris.' He now stood on the edge of the family, eccentric and self-conscious. It was another step towards the role of social outcast as he embraced it in the 1880s, and a negation of the expected responsibilities of the eldest son.

Morris was in Malvern that September. The Priory bells were ringing for the fall of Sebastopol which after a siege of eleven months had yielded to a final assault by British, French and Turkish troops. Morris warmed to Malvern itself but felt indignant at the way it had been turned into 'a kind of tea gardens for idle people'. He travelled on to Clay Cross to see his sister Emma, noticing flags everywhere, especially on the Burton-on-Trent chimneys. At Chesterfield a flag of victory was flying from the top of their 'particularly ugly twisted tower'.

This was the Malory summer. After France Morris went to Birmingham, staying with Burne-Jones. At Cornish's, the booksellers in New Street, was a copy of Southey's edition of Malory's *Morte d'Arthur*.

Surprisingly these dedicated Arthurians had not discovered Malory before. Burne-Jones found the book first and, unable to afford it, had been reading it *in situ*. Morris bought it straight away.

After Tennyson's versions of the Arthurian legends the toughness of Malory came as a revelation. The ambivalent splendour of Malory's Queen Guinevere, technically guilty but defying judgement, was a picture of womanhood that haunted and dazzled and bewildered William Morris. The Guinevere factor was a strong one in his life. When they began to read Malory he and Ned were overcome with that curious bashfulness attaching to the things they both cared most about. They hoarded the book as if it was a secret until Dante Gabriel Rossetti, older and brasher, pronounced that the *Morte d'Arthur* and the Bible were the greatest books in the world. It entered their mythology. This was one reason why, in the 1890s, Aubrey Beardsley's illustrations for *Morte d'Arthur* so appalled them. Malory was their possession. Beardsley seemed like a marauder. Faced with Beardsley's speedy brilliance they were insular and ponderous. As old men they made their own grand plans for a Kelmscott Press edition with at least a hundred illustrations by Burne-Jones.

Morris spent three weeks in Birmingham. He and Crom discussed the organization of labour. There was a recreation of the atmosphere of Oxford, with reading, talk, chaff, bear fights, hugging one another in these imitation wrestling matches. Morris found a substitute family in the Birmingham network of young men and their sisters that collected round Burne-Jones. Besides Fulford and Price there was their friend from Cambridge, Wilfred Heeley, associated with them in the plans they were then making for the *Oxford and Cambridge Magazine*. Into this cosy, earnest, provincial community Morris seems to have erupted as an oddity and hero. Price's younger sister depicts him in her diary:

Aug. 22 F [Fulford] says Morris is very handsome.

Aug. 22 Fulford, Morris and Jones came over to tea and supper. Morris *is* very handsome.

Sept. 2 Edward and Morris came to tea and supper. We had great fun: Morris got so excited once that he punched his own head and threw his arms about frantically.

The Set reassembled in Oxford in the autumn of 1855. Over the next six months, with the addition of Heeley and Vernon Lushington from

Cambridge, the Set enlarged itself into a Brotherhood of seven, like the seven sons of Jack of the Tofts in Morris's fairytale *Child Christopher*. Morris had not intended to continue with his studies. But his mother had insisted he return to university and Fulford, who had taken his own finals and had been teaching in a school in Wimbledon, returned to coach him for his Final Schools. Morris was anxious about the implications: 'I don't think even if I get through Greats that I shall take my BA., because they won't allow you not to sign the 39 Articles unless you declare that you are "extra Ecclesiam Anglicanam" [outside the Church of England] which I'm not, and don't intend to be, and I won't sign the 39 Articles.' The Oxford rule of compulsory subscription (until 1871) to the articles of faith of the Church of England was a typical example of the hypocrisy Morris was later to castigate so bitterly. But he took his pass degree that autumn, followed by his BA in 1856; and in the end he signed.

Oxford had a history of little magazines. One of the first had been *The Student* or *Oxford Monthly Miscellany* of 1750, a series of literary pamphlets to which Samuel Johnson, formerly of Pembroke College, had contributed. *The Oxford Sausage*, a comic anthology of verses and lampoons, lasted from 1764 to 1776. When the *Oxford Magazine* was launched in 1834 its intentions were high-minded: a leader stated this was 'not intended to be a receptacle for erotic poetry'. But there was no consistent editorial policy. The *Oxford Magazine* had not been a success. The *Oxford and Cambridge Magazine*, the literary vehicle of Morris and the Brotherhood, was announced as a collection of 'mainly Tales, Poetry, friendly critiques and social articles'. There was to be no showing off, no quips, no sneers and no lampoons. Burne-Jones wrote: 'We have such a deal to tell people, such a deal of scolding to administer, so many fights to wage and opposition to encounter that our spirits are quite rising with the emergency.' In its urge to come to grips with contemporary issues the *Oxford and Cambridge Magazine* breathed the spirit of Kingsley and *Yeast*. It was part of the Brotherhood's crusade against the age. But its bias towards the architectural, the painterly, the mystical, the faerie, makes it an oddity amongst the magazines of Oxford. In its serious attention to art its one competitor is the short-lived Pre-Raphaelite magazine *The Germ*.

The original idea of the *Oxford and Cambridge Magazine* was Dixon's. He had hoped to help fund it, but in the end it was Morris who paid for it entirely and, to begin with, edited it too. There is a certain ruthlessness in Burne-Jones's comment that the expenses would fall on Morris heavily, 'for it cannot be published under £500 per annum, exclusive of engravings which we shall sometimes give: he hopes not to lose more than £300, but even that is a great deal.' The publishers of the magazine were Bell & Daldy. Seven hundred and fifty copies of the first number were issued on 1 January 1856. It was successful enough for another 250 copies to be printed. Ruskin was one of its enthusiastic readers, writing to promise to contribute to it later. Tennyson, acknowledging a copy of the January issue which contained the first of a series of articles by Fulford on Tennyson's poetry, praised the 'truthfulness and earnestness' of the undertaking. He liked its intimacy: 'very refreshing likewise is the use of the plain "I" in lieu of the old hackneyed unconscientious editorial "we"'. The *Oxford and Cambridge Magazine* lasted for twelve issues, through various vicissitudes. Morris found his editorial duties tedious and after the first number handed them over to Fulford, paying him a salary of £100 a year. 'Topsy has surrendered active powers as Editor to Fulford,' Ned reported, 'it will be a good thing for all of us, and a great relief to Topsy.' He was now released to concentrate on what he liked much better: the production of his 'grinds'.

The Oxford word 'grind' is so redolent of Morris's final term that it is worth investigating closely. Dixon, once again, was the originator, calling Morris's poems his 'grindy lays'. This delighted Morris and the Set, and from then on poems were known as 'grinds' or 'grindelays'. The word was embroidered upon. Morris proposed calling his book of manuscript poems 'Liber Grindelarum' and his book of prose tales 'Liber Grindelorum'. The 'grind' acquired a more generalized meaning, in the sense of 'the enterprise', 'the work in hand'. The *Oxford and Cambridge Magazine* itself came to be referred to as 'the grind'. It is at this period that Morris's view of work comes into sharper definition: he had come to recognize his work as intense pleasure, the grind not as the burden but as the necessity.

I am to have a grind about Amiens Cathedral this time, it is very poor and inadequate, I cannot help it; it has cost me more trouble than anything I have written yet; I ground at it the other night from nine o'clock till half past four am., when the lamp went out, and I had to creep upstairs to bed through the great dark house like a thief.

This letter, written from the Morris home at Walthamstow that Christmas vacation, shows the force of his compulsion. A few weeks later

Dixon and a friend arrived early in the morning in Morris's rooms in Oxford. Morris was by this time in architectural practice. He had been up all night and had written a whole story. Dixon recollected, 'We were both astonished by the amount he had written. It was a mass of manuscript, sheet on sheet.'

As contributors Morris and Fulford were the mainstay of the *Oxford and Cambridge Magazine*. Mackail, in his 1899 biography, lists Morris's contributions to ten out of the twelve issues: a total of eight prose tales, five poems, the article on Amiens Cathedral, another on Alfred Rethel's engravings and a review of Robert Browning's *Men and Women*. Exact attribution remains difficult since these were all unsigned contributions. But there is later evidence suggesting that Morris was the author of at least three more prose pieces. Morris himself turned against these early writings, resisting later attempts by publishers to bring out new editions. By then perhaps the memories of Oxford were too poignant. At the time he seemed to blossom in the warmth of his friends' appreciation. Fulford, a little jealous, issued a private warning to Crom Price: 'You men at Oxford must not let your love of Morris carry you away to admire such of his writings as don't deserve admiration.' But one of them still noted after issue number seven, in which Morris's Norse tale 'Gertha's Lovers' was completed, 'Topsy has got the real grit in him and no mistake.'

Morris came to have a very poor opinion of literary criticism: 'To think of a beggar making a living by selling his opinion about other people!' It was one of those topics on which his friends could rouse him to a predictable apoplectic response. In moods of anti-intellectuality Morris would claim that poetry itself was 'tommy-rot'. His review of Robert Browning shows how far this was a pose. The article is fascinating, first, on grounds of rarity: it is one of only two extant reviews. It is a very good review, generous and conscientious, and it tells us a great deal about Morris himself and his attitude to poetry. It amounts to a defence of obscurity, suggestiveness:

it does not often help poems much to *solve* them, because there are in poems so many exquisitely small and delicate forms of thought moving through their music, and along with it, that cannot be done in prose, any more than the infinite variety of form, and shadow, and colour in a great picture can be rendered by a coloured woodcut.

Morris, in his final term in Oxford, had in fact embarked on woodcuts. He knew from experience the satisfactions and the limitations of the trade.

His perception of Browning is as supreme love poet. Morris views the non-love poems of the *Men and Women* collection as merely 'a supplement to the love poems, even as it is in all art, in all life'. In putting forward the suggestion that love is the central component of life or art, that life or art in which love is absent can only be considered as 'a wretched mistake', Morris does not sound dispassionate. He writes from his own crossroads of emotional development. This was the stage at which he himself was moving out of the realms of the celibate and into the more problematical dramas of human sexuality. The tone of the review is at times surprisingly personal, even desperate: 'love for love's sake, the only true love, I must say – Pray Christ some of us attain to it before we die!'

In his own poems and stories of this period Morris appears tensely concerned with the erotic. As others have noticed, they are mainly about love, even when ostensibly concerned with other subjects. 'The Chapel in Lyoness' is an Arthurian death scene, a lament by and for Sir Ozana Le Cure Hardy, Knight of the Round Table, lying in the chapel within the gilded screen. The final stanza, in its *Oxford and Cambridge Magazine* version, is a symbolist love song:

> Ozana, shall I pray for thee?
> Her cheek is laid to thine;
> Her hair against the jasper sea
> Wondrously doth shine.

The April number of the magazine included the story by Morris, 'Frank's Sealed Letter', which, apart from his later so-called *Novel on Blue Paper*, is his only prose tale of contemporary life. It is a melodramatic story of physical obsession, chiefly remarkable for Morris's portrait of Mabel, the emasculating woman, cold, proud and heartless with her heavy, sweeping black hair and her 'great dreamily-passionate eyes'. Morris writes almost hysterically of the destruction of the personality of a man who is otherwise purposeful, decisive. Frank is fatally deflected by love's 'wild, restless passions', becoming forlorn, hopeless, fixated on the past.

Morris's 'Lindenborg Pool' story, in the September issue, is based on a macabre tale in Thorpe's *Northern Mythology*. It ends in a nightmare scene of sexual depravity. The narrator is the priest who takes communion to the bedside of a dying man. Small sparkling eyes and nothing else appear above the bedclothes. To thunderous raucous laughter it turns out he is a *swine*. The huge pig heaves out of bed, tearing the holy water from the hand of the priest, scoring him deeply with savage tusk and tooth, so that red blood gushes quickly to the floor. Then pandemonium is unleashed:

right madly skirled the intolerable laughter, rising to shrieks that were fearfuller than any scream of agony I ever heard; the hundreds of people through all those grand rooms danced and wheeled about me, shrieking, hemming me in with interlaced arms, the women loosing their long hair and thrusting forward their horribly-grinning unsexed faces towards me till I felt their hot breath.

The nightmare vision is intensified by the fact that although the women were recognizably female they were dressed like men.

Morris's own fictional representations of sex and sexuality as mystery and terror are especially interesting in the context of more level-headed debate about such subjects elsewhere in the magazine. The August number contains a long essay on 'Woman, Her Duties, Education and Position', reminding its readers these are not esoteric topics but affect directly half the human race. The article makes pleas for a less restricted association between young men and young women, arguing succinctly that girls would choose their loves 'with less haste and more discrimination' were they to have more room for choice. Such arguments Morris accepted intellectually. His later Socialist pronouncements, though guarded, make a case for true equality between the sexes. In *News from Nowhere* he proposes a startlingly radical scenario of easy companionship and non-possessiveness. He went way beyond the confines of his class and culture in his theories of sexual tolerance and freedom. But he was hampered by his chivalric urges. He could not write himself out of the role of bashful hero. In practice Morris was always to be victim of a fatal emotional ambivalence.

Was he unattached at this stage? On the whole it seems most likely. But in a letter sent from Oxford by Crom Price to his father in January 1856 there is a cryptic comment: 'I shall ignore the existence of the female Topsy for the time.'

When Philip Webb first saw Morris he was 'a slim boy like a wonderful bird just out of his shell'. Webb was then senior clerk in George Edmund Street's office in Beaumont Street in Oxford. Morris had signed his articles with Street on 21 January 1856, paying around five pounds to enter on a pupillage expected to take between five and seven years. His lodgings were close to the Martyrs' Memorial, in a house next but one to the site on which, a few years later, the grandiose Randolph Hotel arose. He found himself in an artistic household. Morris's land-lord, Mr Richardson, had been a drawing master. His former wife, a skilled flower painter, had taught Philip Webb to draw. Richardson's maid had the poetic touch, describing the statues of the martyrs as 'Radley, Cumnor, and Littlemore, all out there in the snow'.

Street's architectural office had been Morris's first choice. He had written to his mother, 'I propose asking Mr. Street of Oxford to take me as his pupil: he is a good architect, as things go now, and has a great deal of business, and always goes for an honourable man; I should learn what I want of him if of anybody.' To Crom Price Morris gave additional reasons, showing how much he depended on the ambience of Oxford: if Street would consent to take him on 'it would be glorious, for then I would not leave Oxford at all'.

Street had been in Oxford since 1852. He was at a decisive phase of his career. The churches of St Peter, Bournemouth, and All Saints, Boyne Hill; the theological College at Cuddesdon; the convent build-ings for the East Grinstead Sisterhood, for which Street characteris-tically refused payment: many of Street's buildings of the middle 1850s were original and complex with a brilliance of detail his earlier church buildings had not achieved. He absorbed foreign influences. In 1855, after an intensive tour of Italy, during which he made notes and sketches, his *Brick and Marble Architecture of North Italy* was pub-lished. By the time Morris joined him, Street, ten years Morris's senior, was becoming the star architect of the ecclesiologists.

Morris entered a small office. Street was not a delegator. He believed that architects were born, not made, and he dominated the scene in his own office with his stalwart physique, his serious expression and his curt, decisive way of speaking. An acquaintance once described this as the *opposite* of gush. In Street's office the rattle of the T-square was incessant. His few assistants spoke of his energy with awe and apprehen-sion. He was reluctant to allow them even to design a keyhole. Norman Shaw, who joined him three years after Morris, described the organiza-tional feat by which Street left the office in the morning, took the train to Buckinghamshire to measure an old church, came back in the after-noon and drew the whole church carefully to scale, with his proposed additions, all ready to ink and finish. The whole exercise took him seven hours and a half. It seems strange that this deeply religious, dedicated Gothicist, who was not a born communicator and who in a sense resented his assistants, had such a potent influence upon his pupils and the pupils of his pupils. The family tree of Arts and Crafts architects shows Morris in an unexpected context, in the cohorts of Street descendants who over the next few decades were to dominate the English progressive architectural scene.

ARCHITECTURAL OFFICES:

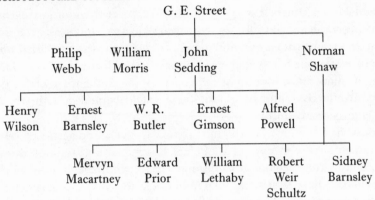

Morris had been handed over to Philip Webb on arrival at Street's office. Webb was to supervise him. He realized immediately how unsuited Morris was to the disciplines and tediums of office life. Much of Morris's time at Street's office was spent in copying a drawing of the doorway of St Augustine's Church, Canterbury. He found this frustrating; there were too many arch mouldings. He pressed so hard his compass points bored holes into the drawing board. Webb's accounts of Morris's behaviour in Street's office, a kind of alternating violence and scattiness, suggest that from the outset he was finding it a strain. Street decided it would be good for him to learn how to compile a professional specification. He was sent to a site at Holywell. The surveyor of the site had discovered a dead goose there. Morris was told this corpse must be allowed for in his document. The recommended phrase was, 'All rubbish, including the goose, to be shot where indicated.' At the time Morris was spending his evenings writing poetry. In the daytime he walked round and round Street's office, thumping his head with resounding blows, reciting nonsense verses:

What is this rattles beneath my old bones,
Not little kids I think but only loose stones.

Webb marvelled at Morris, at his charm and his pugnacity, and his instinct for a building: the way in which he saw and could define the exact difference in feeling between a Chartres and a Reims. But this was much more than an architectural friendship. All Morris's main emotional relationships take triangular form, by design or by invasion. Philip Webb is the necessary completion of the triangle started by the friendship of Morris and Burne-Jones. Webb saw himself as the friend that Morris had selected. He described William Morris as having run him down 'in the chase of his early life'. He later used a startling image of possession: he felt he had been branded with the letter M, like a sheep with its owner's imprint on its back.

Unlike Ned Webb had no female sexual attachments. With very few exceptions his friendships were all male ones. Although not overtly homosexual Webb had links with the gruffly understated homo-erotic factions of the Arts and Crafts. Webb, with his acute shyness and the grizzled, battered features once compared to the bronze head of Michelangelo in Oxford, fell into the role of William Morris's henchman. Theirs was more a mediaeval than Victorian companionship. From their meeting in Street's office they embarked upon a friendship of shared male austerities and a reticent delight in one another's company that lasted forty years and never failed.

Webb was older than Morris, born in 1821; and he had much earlier memories of Oxford. He brought a new perspective which was that of town not gown. His father was a doctor, a 'country saw-bones' with a practice in and around Oxford. Philip Webb was actually born in Beaumont Street, where G. E. Street now had his office. As a child the Oxford he knew was the area around St Giles. He used to watch the old Giles's Fair, with its caravans, its hobby horse and pink flounced lady, from the Webb family house near St Giles's church. Webb's origins were more small-town than William Morris's. In fact few of Morris's friends were his social superiors. What he valued in a friendship was not worldly position but an integrity of outlook he could draw on. In Webb's case he almost envied an upbringing which, though not an intrinsically happy one, had bound him to the place and to the history of Oxford in a way that was entirely personal and irreversible. Webb had almost taken Oxford over in the holidays: 'I explored all the courts and lanes, especially in the vacations, when it was all mine.' Webb showed Morris his Oxford. One morning at six-thirty he woke him up, with difficulty, chaffing him about his night shirt. There was always chaff in his relations with Morris. This was their emotional coding. Morris was defensive about the night shirt: 'That's my style,' he said. They went out, walked past St John's and along the little path that is recorded in Loggan's *Views of Oxford* to Parson's Pleasure, where they bathed naked, as is still the approved mode.

Morris was writing carols. His 'French Noël' is included in the collection *Ancient Christmas Carols* (1860) arranged for four voices and published by Edmund Sedding, brother of John Sedding. Both the Seddings were at one time architects with Street. In his carols Morris's handling of the Christian iconography, Ox and Ass and Babe, shows how close to the religious traditions of his childhood he had in fact remained. Another fragment of a carol from this period was printed in the *Oxford and Cambridge Magazine*:

> Ships sailing through the Heaven
> With red banners dress'd,
> Carrying the planets seven
> To see the white breast
> *Mariae Virginis*.

Morris at this period sometimes had a kind of glow.

What did Morris gain from Street? He acknowledges so little one can only make surmises. But it is impossible to think that he gained nothing from working for a year in close proximity to such a high-minded and virtuoso architect, one of the great Victorian exponents of 'muscular' building: more productive and less fanciful than William Burges; as original and more immediately accessible than his fellow-ecclesiologist William Butterfield. Compared with Butterfield's, Street's buildings are less combative, less clashing. In the buildings he was working on when Morris joined his office he began to show his powers as the supreme structuralist. These are not imitation French-Middle-English Gothic: they are strenuous reworkings, emphatically Street. They are multi-layered buildings: Street works in horizontals, massing up his arcades, clerestories, chancel arches, to arrive at his tremendous spatial rhythms. Street directs his dramas combining colour, ornament, brick and stone, mosaic and tile and sculpture to achieve an effect that is the reverse of fussiness. He is the Victorian counterpart of Vanbrugh or Hawksmoor, lavish, hugely daring, always in control. It is the measure of Street's sophistication that these highly complex buildings seem to look almost organic, rising from their sites as if planted there and growing there. In his *Book of Building*, Sir Edmund Birkett, Street's contemporary, describes the way that buildings of this 'muscular' or 'vigorous' style rise from the ground without plinths or projecting bases, 'as if they were mushrooms'. Red House, the house that Webb designed for Morris on his marriage, is a muscular outcrop, sprung from the orchard, of just this spontaneous kind.

What Morris grasped from Street is surely his technique in creating grand effects from myriad components. A Morris interior is a disciplined amalgam of patterns, colours, textures: wallpapers, friezes, curtain fabrics, wallhangings, painted ceilings, layer upon layer. Morris came to know as Street did, by finding out in practice, that natural materials have their own inherent qualities, dictating the limits of the use designers make of them: he and Street shared the religion of the right use of materials, though Street's first choice was brick whereas Morris preferred stone. Perhaps most of all it was Street's sense of architecture as the centre and the ruling force of all design activity that infiltrated Morris's thinking at this period. He knew about buildings, he was ignorant of architects. Street was the first architect whom Morris saw in action, and Street's purposeful solemnity affected him more than he admitted, perhaps more than he knew. There is something very Street-like, typical of that whole movement of ecclesiological earnestness, in Morris's later pronouncements on the subject. How can architecture not be solemn when it is concerned with 'the moulding and altering to human needs of the very face of the earth itself'?

Street himself believed in handwork. He felt that any architect should himself be able to decorate his buildings with painting and with sculpture; an architect should also be a blacksmith and a textile worker and a designer of stained glass. Street was especially concerned with church embroidery. His views had a galvanic effect upon some pupils. John Sedding, who followed William Morris in Street's office, became one of the most visionary and resourceful of English craftsmen-architects: there is a typical memory of Sedding who, while working on the church of St Clement's at Bournemouth, spent the evenings in his lodgings carving obsessively with mallet and chisel on a block of stone begged from a local stone merchant. In Street's office Morris too had begun his explorations. He started clay modelling, wood carving and stone carving. He was making the first of his illuminated manuscripts, confident with the colouring, more hesitant with lettering. His dexterity surprised those people who had registered the clumsy, rather helpless look of Morris's small hands.

Street appears to have treated him kindly, almost as the favoured son. In 1853, when he went to Lille for the judging of the competition of Lille Cathedral, he took Morris with him. Street had entered a design 'Quam dilecta Tabernacula tua Domine virtutum', with twin spires banded in colours, for which he had high hopes. He and Morris spent three hours looking at the exhibition. Street admired the design entered by Clutton and Burges, but most of the architects' entries struck him as very inferior or worse. He wrote home saying, 'I really think I shall have one of the prizes. Morris says the first.' In the end Street came second. Burges won the competition; but his cathedral, as designed, was never built.

Morris rejected Street as he had disowned his own father. In a way this was inevitable. Street's Gothicism was too set and too conservative. Webb, thinking back, decided William Morris could not have been influenced by Street's work 'except in the negative way of determining to leave the study of what to him was but a change of one kind of Victorian art to another'. Morris detested restoration: Street became a prime restorer. Morris became a Socialist: 'Street, though a very able man, could not perceive that only from the life of the people could come a living art.' Morris later maintained that Street had been a quarreller. This was not wholly fair. It was Morris who had quarrelled and who went on hounding Street in the years to come with a curious, ungenerous compulsiveness.

In August, a year after Morris had returned from his undergraduate tour of the cathedrals, he prepared to move to London. Street's office was being transferred from Oxford to Montagu Place, near Marble Arch. Burne-Jones had already been in London more or less continuously since early in the year and in June had become engaged to Georgiana Macdonald, an event Morris marked by bashfully presenting her with a copy of Turner's *Rivers of France*. Georgie's mother recorded a visit by Morris to her daughter in that summer, a few days after Georgie's sixteenth birthday. He came to tea and sat with Georgie on the balcony till eleven o'clock, talking as it grew dark. It seems that the awkwardness between them was by now gradually dissolving into affection and respect.

Over those months London had been becoming Morris's new emotional centre. His plan was now to find London rooms with Ned, continuing to work with Street but simultaneously spending six hours a day practising his drawing. He realized that this would be a heavy programme. As he put it to Crom Price: 'One won't get much enjoyment out of life at this rate, I know well, but that don't matter: I have no right to ask for it at all events – love and work, these two things only . . .'

What did Morris mean by love? Love for a woman certainly, to worship, serve, be dazzled by. As his letters from France show he was steeped in the Chaucerian ideal of courtly love. But he had a broader concept of love which entailed duty towards oneself and others, to direct one's talents usefully. This letter shows him consciously resisting the temptation of falling into pleasurable, useless dilettantism, 'slipping off into a kind of small (very small) Palace of Art'.

To Morris small was suspect, and it became more suspect. When older, and frustrated, he cried out, 'O how I long to keep the world from narrowing on me, and to look at things bigly and kindly!' His thinking big was a part of Morris's Victorianism. His vast simplicity has puzzled future generations. His solidity could prick the conscience of the aesthetes. The thought of Morris 'has always slightly irritated me. Of course he was a wonderful all-round man, but the act of walking round him has always tired me.' This was Max Beerbohm's fastidious response.

CHAPTER FIVE

Red Lion Square
1856–59

In August 1856 Morris and Burne-Jones moved into rooms in No. 1 Upper Gordon Street in Bloomsbury. Morris's association with this particular area of London continued until he moved his works to Merton Abbey in 1881. The streets and squares of Bloomsbury, fashionable in the early eighteenth century, had deteriorated by the middle of the nineteenth. Their self-righteous air of shabbiness had begun attracting London's intellectual incendiarists and misfits, writers, radicals and artists; sixty years later Gordon Square and its environs were the natural habitat of the Bloomsbury Group. At the time Morris lived there Upper Gordon Street was dingy. One façade could hardly be distinguished from another. Burne-Jones had once got half-way up the stairs and shouted for his dinner before he realized he had entered the wrong house. But Morris and Burne-Jones were by now adept performers at transforming their surroundings: behind a dull façade they could create an inner sanctum of light, shade, texture, colour, memory and history. 'Topsy and I live together', wrote Burne-Jones that August, 'in the quaintest room in all London, hung with brasses of old knights and drawings of Albert Dürer.' To Burne-Jones he and Topsy seemed like babes in the wood.

Since his father died Morris's connections with London had been tenuous. In arriving there to live he drew many threads together: the sense of his own past, his love of history and buildings, his growing perception of the city as the place where good and evil oppose one another fiercely. In his fears for the future of the city Morris was to voice the deep anxieties and ambivalences of his age. Of all cities he was to speak most lucidly and most alarmingly of London, 'the richest city of the richest country of the richest age of the world'.

In the decades before Morris came to live there London had been through a period of unprecedented growth, doubling in size between 1800 and 1840. This expansion continued. Inner London population has been estimated at 1,949,000 in 1841; 2,303,000 in 1851; and it was to rise to 2,808,000 by 1861. So that by the mid-nineteenth century the overflow of people into the London suburbs was accelerating rapidly. In 1851 the population of Outer London stood at 322,000, an increase of eleven per cent over the previous decade; by 1861 it was 419,000, a further thirty per cent increase; ten years later it was 628,000, a fifty per cent increase. With this growth of population came a great influx of energy, commercial and manufacturing activity, created by, feeding upon, this urban concentration. London was the greatest centre of industrial production in Britain and indeed in Europe before, during and after the industrial revolution. London was the largest single market for basic consumer goods as well as the endlessly resourceful centre of luxury trades for the rich. The docks, waterways and railways; the complex construction industries; the large and highly organized distilleries and breweries; the specialist, skilful heavy engineering workshops: the economy of London depended on enormous substrata of activity, intricate patterns of supply and demand which foreigners arrived to marvel at and imitate. Morris, the Dickens addict, was familiar with Count Smorltork, the 'famous foreigner' in *Pickwick Papers*, on his fortnight's visits to London gathering material for his 'great work on England', filling his large notebook with local information on 'music, picture, science, potry, poltic; all tings'.

This was the exuberant and pullulating London that had nurtured Morris's father, allowing him to make his large fortune in the city. Morris too would weigh up London and would seize its opportunities. He too could be fired by activity, excited by a sense of human energy, watching with intense curiosity how people involved themselves in technical and recondite pursuits. Morris shared much of his father's entrepreneurial instinct. His own business success was partly based on London's building boom. The viability of his decorating business, as it was to develop from the 1860s onwards, depended upon the prosperity of London. It was part of the whole pattern of Victorian consumption, the unrelenting cycle of purchase and renewal as a mass of new possessions piled into the edifices of the rich. Morris loved things; but he despised the superfluous. London was, of all cities, the most mindlessly acquisitive. From his early days of living there he started to regard it with a mixture of fascination and dismay.

He came to describe London as 'the spreading sore'. He watched how London swallowed up the countryside around it, polluting the environment: 'mocking our feeble efforts to deal even with its minor evils of smoke-laden sky and befouled river'. Cholera epidemics had been devastating London from the 1830s onwards. Florence Nightingale was nursing at the Middlesex Hospital, not far from Red Lion Square, in the fearful epidemic of 1854, and a few years later the Thames, London's chief sewer and main source of drinking water, began to smell so putrid that people called it 'The Great Stink'. These were the sort of memories that fuelled Morris's long campaigns against pollution. London at its worst he looked on as 'this world-without-end-for-everlasting hole', hardly a place for humans. Sometimes, threading his way through the filthy, squalid city, slithering through streets 'all pasty and slippery', Morris felt he was living in the habitations of the Tockakopoos.

London was a dread, a torment. But for most of his adult life it was the place he lived in. He spoke about it with such force because he knew it in such detail. London was indeed his city, and he never lost his sense of the London that might be. Visions of this other London erupt into his fiction, sometimes edge into his letters: 'London in the older parts like the Inns of Court really looks well in this spring-time with the bright fresh green against the smoky old walls. Spring over, it becomes London again, and no more an enchanted city.' This is a passage from a letter in old age. Morris's imagined London had remained a young man's vision, shot through with nervous tremors, with the terrors and delights of his early months in London, when he and Ned were living within sound of the tin-pot bells of St Pancras: 'well-remembered days when all adventure was ahead!'

At the time he came to London Morris's beauty was still striking. It was the beauty of the innocent. Morris looked as he was, peculiarly naïve. One sister of a friend found him delicate and decorous, his white complexion brightened with dots of pink on the cheeks and his nicely chiselled chin not quite hidden by his beard. Another, seeing him in Birmingham that summer, remarked on the way his hair had grown and blossomed out: 'it is much *greater* than it was before, in fact a mass of curls and waves that will soon sweep his shoulders.' At Oxford he was forced by the college regulations to shave off his moustaches; after he left he never touched a razor. His hair was thick and springy and phenomenally strong. Later in his life he would swing his children from it, like an Edward Lear eccentric. One night in Birmingham the length and wildness of his hair convinced Ned's father's servant that Morris was a burglar arriving at the front door and she would not let him in. There was a sense in which he cultivated wildness, using his faroucheness to bludgeon opposition. That summer he learned the way of silencing the noisy, quizzical, irritating Fulford: 'whenever Topsy wanted to say anything he sprang into the middle of the room and flourished his fists'.

Morris was still the *seigneur*, buying what he wanted. As well as books he was by now acquiring paintings. He wrote to Ned that summer, 'Will you do me a great favour, viz. go and nobble that picture called "April Love", as soon as possible lest anybody else should buy it.' This painting was then hanging in the Royal Academy Exhibition. Burne-Jones nobbled it for Morris. It is now in the Tate Gallery. It is by the Pre-Raphaelite artist Arthur Hughes. The girl in the painting stands in a dark arbour beside a solid tree trunk wound around with ivy. The painting is replete with sexual expectancy. The ribbon of the girl's puffed sleeve presses into her flesh gently. Her skirt is blue, the colour Morris most associated with pleasure and desire.

All through the summer London had been luring him. Morris had been travelling up and down from Oxford almost every weekend, visiting Burne-Jones. Earlier in the year Burne-Jones had met Dante Gabriel Rossetti, the poet and one of the original Pre-Raphaelite painters. He had sought him out at the Working Men's College in Great Ormond Street where Rossetti was then teaching. The next day he had visited Rossetti in his studio in the old house in Chatham Place at the northwest corner of Blackfriars Bridge where he found him working on a water-colour of a monk copying the mouse in an illumination. This was the painting later called 'Fra Pace'. By the summer Burne-Jones had become Rossetti's close disciple. Rossetti had encouraged him, enticed him, helped to make it practical for him to live in London and devote his life to art. Through Ned Morris too now entered Rossetti's orbit. Rossetti had already read a few of Morris's poems: indeed his first conversation with Burne-Jones had been mainly about Morris. On his visits to London they went round as a trio, looking at paintings, going to the theatre, roaming the streets, returning late to Rossetti's studio in Blackfriars, reading and talking until three or four a.m.

Dante Gabriel Rossetti was only six years older than Morris, but his reputation and self-confidence made the age gap appear greater. Like

MacLaren at Oxford he was a combination of the worldly mentor and the much older brother to Morris and Burne-Jones. His background was more exotic and dramatic. His father Gabriele Pasquale Guiseppe Rossetti, born in the Abruzzi and brought up in the part of Italy then ruled by Joseph Bonaparte, had been hounded out for political rebellion once Ferdinand of Sicily recovered power. He had been smuggled out of Italy disguised as an English sailor.

He was a poet, a mystic, an authority on Dante. In 1831 he was appointed Professor of Italian at King's College in London. His house in Bloomsbury became a sanctuary for other exiled patriots. Dante Gabriel's mother, born Frances Polidori, was half Italian, bilingual, a devout High Anglican. Although brought up in England Dante Gabriel Rossetti was southern European in temperament and looks, with his sensual mouth, his oddly bulging forehead, his peculiarly thick nose. His eyes were grave and dark with a smudgy rim around them: Lady Ashburton thought they looked as if they had been put in with dirty fingers. He was almost the same height as William Morris and both of them had a tendency to portliness, Rossetti's accentuated by the plum velvet frock coat he very often wore. Coventry Patmore remarked upon his aura of 'tensity rather than intensity'. He could appear lethargic but people were conscious of his ability to pounce. Rossetti was notoriously, dangerously charming, a sympathetic listener. 'Ah Gabriel was the one to tell things to,' said Ned, 'no, Gabriel, on second thoughts, was not the one to tell things to – and second thoughts are best.'

Morris was swept up in his new friend's affection and charisma. In the world of brotherhoods Rossetti was a veteran. The Pre-Raphaelite Brotherhood had been founded in 1848, the year of European revolutionary ferment. The original members were Holman Hunt, John Millais and Rossetti who had been 'the mind and soul' of that artistic movement, giving it its direction and its impetus.

Rossetti, in his vision of an ideal community of artists, saw this as multi-talented, with one activity spreading out into another. Like the Vorticists, the Omega and other later groupings, the Pre-Raphaelites assumed that art, design and literature have a common creative base. The Pre-Raphaelite magazine *The Germ* was of mixed media, publishing poetry and prose and graphics. Many of Rossetti's poems related to his paintings and from 1848 onwards he was working on the sonnet sequence 'The House of Life', the long meditation on love and religion that drew on his own manifold vicissitudes of living. By the middle

1850s the original Pre-Raphaelite brothers had dispersed, Holman Hunt to the Holy Land, Millais to new worlds of commercial success. Rossetti had been left a little stranded and unconfident. The accolade given to his work in the first issue of the *Oxford and Cambridge Magazine* surprised and delighted him. It was a boost to his morale to meet Burne-Jones, 'one of the nicest fellows in Dreamland, for there most of the writers in that miraculous piece of literature seem to be'. Rossetti was in need of confederates, admirers, and he seems to have envisaged Ned and Morris gathered into a Pre-Raphaelite Brotherhood of the second phase.

Rossetti believed anyone could be a painter. He had faith in the strain of creativity in everyone, lying there latent, ready to be activated: it was only a question of acquiring the technique. Rossetti himself was technically very fluent, working fast and almost carelessly, giving the impression that designing was as easy as drinking wine. He had no doubts about the primacy of painting. He would say that if any man had poetry in him then he should paint it. He argued that poetry in England had got as far as it could get, whereas painting was as yet an unknown art. With such swishes of derision he demolished Sir Joshua Reynolds' *Discourses* and the Royal Academy's whole subsequent tradition of post-Renaissance academic practice. Nor did Rossetti have respect for contemporary architects, considering them tradesmen. He urged and cajoled and finally persuaded. Wrote Morris in July of 1856, 'Rossetti says I ought to paint, he says I shall be able; now as he is a very great man, and speaks with authority and not as the scribes, I *must* try. I don't hope much, I must say, yet will try my best – he gave me practical advice on the subject.' Burne-Jones later suggested that Rossetti had a secret pleasure in setting all his friends to attempt with difficulty what he could so easily achieve himself.

Rossetti was not attuned to politics. As Morris later commented, he was too self-centred, too much the individualist. Besides 'it needs a person of hopeful mind to take a *disinterested* notice of politics and Rossetti was certainly not hopeful'. Under Rossetti's influence Morris swung away from his old Oxford causes: 'I can't enter into politico-social subjects with any interest, for on the whole I see that things are in a muddle, and I have no power or vocation to set them right in ever so little a degree. My work is the embodiment of dreams in one form or another . . .' Rossetti was a lounger. Descriptions of him emphasize his seductiveness of gesture, his deep melodious voice. He drew Morris into scenes of sophisticated languor, the opposite of Oxford with its singlestick and bear fights. In his studio one day Morris was drawing and Burne-Jones was painting when Holman Hunt arrived there: 'a tallish, slim man with a beautiful red beard, somewhat of a turn-up nose, and deep-set dark eyes: a beautiful man'. Rossetti sat down beside Hunt and played with his beard, threading his paint brush through and through the golden hair.

When Morris first arrived in London he continued to work in Street's office in the daytime, going every evening to a life class in Newman Street. Burne-Jones was also a student at the life class. But it became clear that this arduous routine could not continue; soon Morris was setting off again to Walthamstow to announce to his mother he was changing his profession. Again, he seems to have broken the news tactlessly. Again Emma Morris was startled, baffled, grief-stricken. If architecture seemed an unreliable profession painting was even further beyond her comprehension, and she turned and blamed Burne-Jones, who had come to her with Morris, for what she saw as the corruption of her son.

Morris does not seem to have regretted his decision. He was always to have a certain ruthlessness in disowning whatever was no longer any use to him. He came back from the Low Countries in the autumn of 1856 having adopted Jan van Eyck's motto 'Als ich kanne', the motto he was later to incorporate into his first known embroidery in its English version 'If I can'. His own anti-hero in the story 'Frank's Sealed Letter' expresses an almost frightening decisiveness: 'I could soon find out whether a thing were possible or not to me; then if it were not, I threw it away for ever, never thought of it again, no regret, no longing for that, it was past, and over to me.' The only exception to this was sexual love.

In those first few months in London life opened out for Morris. As well as seeing Rossetti almost daily he and Burne-Jones were on friendly terms with Robert Browning, 'the greatest poet alive'. The Brownings were impressed with Morris's dramatic poetry. Rossetti praised 'Rapunzel' as on a par with Tennyson. Morris and Burne-Jones met other brother artists: Arthur Hughes, Thomas Woolner, Ford Madox Brown. They were carelessly abandoning old loyalties. The Oxford and Cambridge Magazine was in a crisis. 'The Mag. is going to smash,' wrote Burne-Jones, 'let it go!' The standard of the contributions seemed to be waning. 'I shall not write again for it, no more will

Topsy – we cannot do more than one thing at a time, and our hours are too valuable to spend so.'

After a few weeks in Upper Gordon Street Morris and Burne-Jones moved on to No. 17 Red Lion Square. This was at Rossetti's suggestion. The rooms here, on the first floor of an early eighteenth-century brick town house, were unfurnished and so cheaper. Rossetti had lived there himself a few years earlier. The place had melancholy associations since Rossetti had shared it with a young, poor, handsome Pre-Raphaelite painter, Walter Deverell, who was terminally ill, probably with Bright's Disease. Whilst Deverell lay dying in the back room Rossetti went on painting in the front room. Once when the doctor came, he had, in a fit of pity, put his hands on Rossetti's head as he sat painting and exclaimed 'Poor boys! Poor boys!' In 1856 Rossetti went to reinspect the premises and found them derelict and dusty. An address either he or Deverell had noted on the walls of a bedroom was still there five years later, 'so pale and watery had been all subsequent inmates, not a trace of whom remained'.

Morris and Burne-Jones were installed in this outpost of itinerant London by the end of November 1856. The move had not been easy because of the great mass of artists' impedimenta: 'books, boxes, boots, bedding, baskets, coats, pictures, armour, hats, easels – tumble and rumble and jumble', as Burne-Jones complained. They occupied three

3 'William Morris in a bath-tub', one of Burne-Jones's long series of Fat Morris cartoons.

rooms. The large front-facing room was their main living-room and studio, as it had been Rossetti's. The central window had been extended high up to meet the ceiling, providing a good painting light. Behind the studio was a medium-sized room. This was Burne-Jones's. Beyond that again was Morris's own room, a small room. The series of cartoons that Burne-Jones drew of Morris often depicted him confined in a small space: laid out on a small bed, squashed into a small armchair. There was a streak of the masochist in Morris that made him almost ask to be diminished. Selfconscious of his riches he accepted the worst room, as if by doing so he could cancel the imbalance. On the ground floor of the house the Fauconniers, a French family of feather-dressers, carried on their trade. Were they responsible for Morris's mania for feathers? In one of his most beautiful drawings of this period, the 'Nympha Florum' design now in the Victoria and Albert Museum, the nymph has an enticing floating couverture of flowers, hair and feathers, like the *pièce de résistance* at the *Folies Bergère*.

Before they moved in Morris had commissioned furniture for the rooms to his design. Rossetti described how Morris was 'rather doing the magnificent there': he was having 'some intensely mediaeval furniture made – tables and chairs like incubi and succubi'. These rough-hewn early pieces were apparently the only furniture that Morris himself was ever to design and they are different in character from the much lighter furniture later produced under his aegis by Morris & Co. The Red Lion Square pieces were made by a local cabinet maker, probably Tommy Baker of Christopher Street, Hatton Garden. The workman designated to take charge of Morris's orders was Henry Price, an Englishman recently returned from cabinet making in America, an enthusiastic if somewhat hamfisted craftsman who later recollected how 'A gentleman who in after years became a noted Socialist, and Poet as is an Art Furnisher called at our shop and got the govner to take some orders for some very old fashioned Furniture in the Mideaval Style.'

The first of the pieces to arrive was, according to Rossetti, a great round table 'as firm, and as heavy, as a rock'. This is the table to be seen in the background of Burne-Jones's cartoon of the furnishing of Red Lion Square and it is now in Cheltenham Museum. It was followed by colossal chairs, the chairs out of a fairytale, 'such as Barbarossa might have sat on'. There was also a large settle, with a long seat beneath it and above it three cupboards with great swing doors. When the settle was delivered it was even bulkier than Morris had intended, creating a

4 *'Nympha Florum'* design for stained glass by William Morris, *c.* 1862.

drama: 'all the passages and the staircase were choked with vast blocks of timber, and there was a scene'. A later large-scale chair was surmounted by a box which Rossetti thought would be ideal for keeping owls in. For a time there was a resident owl at Red Lion Square with which Rossetti quarrelled. Visitors have left descriptions of the chaos of the place: the 'noble confusion' of the room so packed with furniture, metalwork and armour, pieces of tapestry and drapery, half-finished pictures, sketchbooks, oddments of Flemish or Italian earthenware, here and there a hat or coat or pair of boots. Only beside the fireplace was a little open space, like a clearing in a forest or a jungle, where meals were eaten and where there was 'genial converse' when work was done.

Most of Morris's mediaeval furniture was painted. The enormous empty panels demanded decoration; the mediaeval scale of the pieces of furniture inspired mediaeval narratives: 'when we have painted designs of knights and ladies upon them they will be perfect marvels,' wrote Burne-Jones. Morris and Rossetti together painted the back of a chair with figures and inscriptions in 'gules and vert and azure', and then, wrote Rossetti, 'We are all three going to cover a cabinet with pictures'. For the backs of the chairs Rossetti chose two subjects from Morris's early poems: the arming of the knight from the Christmas mystery of 'Sir Galahad' and the magically sensuous scene from 'Rapunzel' with Guendolen leaning from the witch-tower encouraging the Prince to kiss her golden hair.

The Red Lion Square furniture was not the earliest, or best, of Pre-Raphaelite painted furniture. Holman Hunt and Millais had painted a cupboard door 'as a lark' at Worcester Park Farm as early as 1851. In 1855 William Burges was designing the first of his extraordinary decorated cabinets, highly coloured, gilded, gabled, based on two ancient armoires at Bayeux and Noyon, rediscovered by the French mediaevalist Viollet-le-Duc. By 1858, when George Price Boyce attended a meeting of the Hogarth Club in Morris's rooms in Red Lion Square, noting in his diary the 'interesting drawings, tapestry and furniture, the latter gorgeously painted in subjects by Jones and Morris and Gabriel Rossetti', painted furniture had lost the shock of novelty. Through the late 1850s and early 1860s many other artists, including Albert Moore, Simeon Solomon, Henry Holiday and Edward Poynter, were involved in painting furniture at one time or another. Each panel was treated as a miniature canvas, telling a story: Biblical, Classical, Arthurian. These ornate coloured pieces were Pre-Raphaelite cult objects, part of a whole setting of nostalgia and romance. But what was for most of the Pre-Raphaelite artists a passing craze was for Morris a beginning. The Red Lion Square furniture first gave him intimations of what could be possible for him in terms of protest. These crude and naïve pieces were important in the history of Morris's commitment to designing and to making, and the yearning for the real, the substantial, the tangible that underpinned so strongly Morris's interpretation of the holy crusade against the age.

Morris had already long ago rejected prevailing standards of design and manufacture: even as a boy of seventeen he had refused to enter the Crystal Palace to see the Great Exhibition with his family, remaining sulking outside on a seat. At Oxford the depressing state of taste in England had been one of the topics earnestly debated by the Set. In his early protest pieces of the 1850s Morris demonstrated his general dislike of the graceful, curving, and, to him, meaningless furniture fashionable at the time. Their bulky mediaevalism also stood in contrast to the refinements of Morris's own background, the genteel upholstered drawing-rooms of Woodford Hall and Walthamstow. Morris's protest furniture had highly emotional overtones and much of its attractiveness to him lay in the fact that this was a group enterprise, a sociable activity based on a shared language of the visual and verbal. It was furniture as painting and furniture as poem.

Through the spring of 1857 Burne-Jones was painting a wardrobe in

5 Edward Burne-Jones's *Self-portrait* at Red Lion Square, examining Rossetti's painting on the back of a chair Morris had designed.

Red Lion Square with scenes from Geoffrey Chaucer's 'Prioress's Tale'. This was the macabre story of the Christian child who so much enraged the Jews by singing a hymn to the Virgin on his way to and from school that they killed him and cast him in a pit. He went on singing until people heard him and rescued his martyred body. As Burne-Jones worked on this subject he kept up a rhythmic chanting:

> He Alma Redemptoris 'gan to sing
> So loud that all the place 'gan to ring.

Burne-Jones and Philip Webb gave this wardrobe to Morris as a wedding present. It travelled on from Red House to Kelmscott House in Hammersmith. It is now in the Ashmolean Museum in Oxford. Inside the cupboard door are mysterious secret paintings of mediaeval figures, one male, three female. One of the ladies is combing her long tresses. There is a suggestion that Morris, in a hurry, painted the flowers down the side.

Morris's view that there was more to furniture than function was, and still is, extremely influential. It dominated the furniture workshops of the Arts and Crafts movements from the 1880s onwards, forming and sustaining that romantic vision of 'the art that is life'. It resurfaced in the Post-Impressionist painted furniture of Roger Fry's Omega Workshops; the Freudian dream furniture of Piero Fornasetti in the 1950s; the fantastic and nostalgic 1960s painted furniture of Pop. When Burne-Jones's descendants complained of the discomforts of Pre-Raphaelite furniture they were missing the whole point of this storytelling furniture, so redolent with meaning. Comfort did not come into it. As Morris said succinctly, 'If you want to be comfortable go to bed.'

Rossetti was showering praise on his disciples: 'both are men of real genius. Jones's designs are models of finish and imaginative detail, unequalled by anything unless, perhaps, Dürer's finest works; and Morris, though without practice as yet, has no less power, I fancy. He has written some really wonderful poetry too.' Rossetti was correct in his estimate of Morris's potential, though his temperament was more that of designer than fine artist. He was always to be uneasy drawing from the model in spite of his belief that drawing was the necessary basis of any training in design. Through the spring and summer of 1857 he persevered with drawing. The two wistful self-portraits now in the Victoria and Albert Museum date from this period. By June he had embarked on his first painting, a scene from the *Morte d'Arthur*: 'Sir Tristram after his illness in the Garden of King Mark's Palace recognised by the Dog he had given Iseult'. Rossetti was still hopeful: 'It is all being done from nature of course and I believe will come out capitally.'

Painting from nature had been one of the main tenets of the Pre-Raphaelite Brotherhood. In its most extreme form this principle had taken Holman Hunt on his long travels to paint a real scapegoat by the side of the Dead Sea. Here, in the second generation, Burne-Jones went out from Birmingham into the orchards of Warwickshire and Worcestershire to look for the perfect apple blossom for his painting of 'The Blessed Damozel'. It was a windy May and the blossom, once found, blew to the ground before it could be painted. For his land-scape of paradise he travelled out to Walthamstow to paint the cherry tree in Mrs Morris's garden. The lilies were painted from the lilies growing in the garden at Red Lion Square. Morris too worked directly from nature. At Oxford that summer he painted a tree in the Mac-Larens' lovely garden, working with such an excess of concentration he wore bare patches into the grass beneath his chair. He also made a painting of the garden wall at Woodford, carefully delineating all the stones and the red lichens. Webb remembered many other studies at this period which remained 'knocking about'.

'You know', wrote Rossetti to William Allingham, 'he is a millionaire and buys pictures.' The painter was also the purchaser of paintings. After Hughes's 'April Love' Morris had bought 'The Hayfield' at Rossetti's instigation from Ford Madox Brown, paying £40. Rossetti also refers to Morris buying several of his own water-colours: 'indeed it seems as if he would never stop, as I have three or four more commissions from him. To one of my watercolours, called "The Blue Closet", he has written a stunning poem. You would think him one of the finest little fellows alive – with a touch of the incoherent, but a real man.' In fact Morris wrote a poem to two at least of the paintings he purchased from Rossetti: both 'The Blue Closet' and 'The Tune of Seven Towers' appear in his first collected volume, *The Defence of Guenevere*.

'The Blue Closet' is a poem quite close in its detail to Rossetti's painting. This is a narrative of suspended animation, about four desolate ladies stranded in the sea-bound tower room:

Four lone ladies dwelling here
From day to day and year to year;
And there is none to let us go;
To break the locks of the doors below,
Or shovel away the heaped-up snow.

It is a beautiful and odd poem with its vivid sexual imagery, its painterly precision, its Anglo-Catholic symbolism, its Pre-Raphaelite weirdness:

Kneel down, O love Louise, kneel down, he said,
And sprinkled the dusty snow over my head.

He watch'd the snow melting, it ran through my hair,
Ran over my shoulder, white shoulders and bare.

It is almost as though Rossetti has been releasing an erotic charge in Morris. The painter and the poet share the meaning of the code.

In 'The Tune of Seven Towers' the connection is more distant. But again there is the throb of sexual claustrophobia in the morbid scene in the battlemented building with its heavy grey lead roof and the moat in which the white ghosts sit in a row, 'Long hair in the wind afloat'. Both the paintings and the poems reflect the rather juvenile cult of spookiness in Red Lion Square where Burne-Jones had a whole repertoire of Gothick horror stories, pulled together from old French and Gothic sources, tales of white ladies, red knights, black monks and screech owls. There was always the distant promise of the story to end all stories. Burne-Jones warned, 'He who tells that story often goes mad in the telling of it, and he who hears it *always does*.'

At Red Lion Square Morris kept his wood-carving tools in a long, folded white evening tie nailed up in loops against his bedroom wall. Whilst training himself in drawing and painting he was pursuing other crafts as well and immersing himself in mediaeval work, especially illumination. 'In all illumination and work of that kind,' wrote Rossetti, 'he is quite unrivalled by anything modern that I know.' Georgiana Macdonald's younger sister Louisa, then twelve or thirteen, used to spend whole days with Morris and Burne-Jones in their studio, drawing and painting and amusing herself listening. Morris was fond of her, preferring girls to boys, and he gave her a page of an illuminated manuscript, part of a fairytale by Grimm which he had written out in Gothic script with coloured border and a decorated initial letter. He had also given Louisa two volumes of *Froissart's Chronicles* and H. N. Humphrey's *Illuminated Illustrations of Froissart* which he inscribed 'Louisa Macdonald from her friend William Morris' and decorated with his own drawing of a dragon.

Integral to life at Red Lion Square was Mary Nicholson, known as Red Lion Mary. She had been brought in when the original housekeeper, who seemed an exceedingly respectable woman, arrived one day in 'the most unequivocal state of intoxication' and had to be dismissed. Red Lion Mary was a plain woman but relatively cultivated. She could write and spell well and took down the letters Burne-Jones dictated to her. She was competent, resourceful and could carry out all likely and unlikely errands: debt collecting for Rossetti, going round to Little Holland House to borrow draperies as instructed by Burne-Jones. It was because she was so flexible and cheerful that Red Lion Square was endlessly hospitable. She would find space in the crowded rooms to spread out mattresses for visitors and when the mattress supply was exhausted she would construct beds with portmanteaux and boots. She was jealously protective of the young men she worked for, and had aspirations to modelling, suggesting that if her lack of height was the problem perhaps she could stand on a stool. Rossetti, touched by this, included her in his 'Meeting of Dante and Beatrice in Florence'. In Burne-Jones's words 'Red Lion Mary is one of those attendant women, the least prominent, but she is there.'

Red Lion Mary was taught by Morris to embroider his designs for hangings. She was the first of the dozens of women who spent many hours stitching under Morris's direction. She was made to bring her embroidery frame into the studio so that he could supervise her progress closely. She appreciated Morris's dependence and said once, 'I seemed so necessary to him at all times, and felt myself his man Friday.' To that extent Red Lion Mary was the comrade, the genderfree woman who appears in his romances, joining in the battle and serving at the feast.

But Morris irritated Mary. He was querulous, finicky. Once at breakfast he said, 'Mary, this egg was quite rotten. I've eaten it, but don't bring them up so again.' He could be neurotic about imagined noises. One day when she was working in the studio quite silently he shouted at her fiercely, 'Mary, be quiet, don't make that insufferable noise.' It was partly perhaps that having been brought up in strictly stratified households, with servants in their quarters, he felt awkward with a servant in such close proximity, especially a servant so intelligent and confident. Later in his life, when employing his own servants, he kept them at a distance, in contradiction of his democratic views. But the root of Morris's failure with Red Lion Mary was sexual after all. It was a simple matter of feminine favour, of preferential treatment for the men she found attractive. Ned wrote, 'She liked Gabriel and me, and cheated for us always; but Morris she did not care about, and he had always the worst bed, and the coldest water.' He was also allotted less clean sheets and nightgowns, an unkindness compounded with injustice since it was Morris, as usual, who paid.

Red Lion Mary had already summed him up as inexperienced and clumsy. She tackled Burne-Jones on this: 'One day she said to me, "I shouldn't think Mr. Morris knows much about women, sir", and I said, "Why not, Mary? What makes you think Mr. Morris does not know much about women, and when have you seen Mr. Morris with any women?" "I don't know, sir, but I should think he was such a bear with them".' Already at Red Lion Square Morris was paying the penalty of the sexually reticent and was being victimized.

Rossetti, suave, manipulative, lived a life of urban drama, on the edge of poverty, on the fringe of prostitution, aware of and taking advantage of the spread of corruption in the city. He was a compulsive night-wanderer, familiar as Dickens was with low-life London. Already Burne-Jones had been indoctrinated into ways of life more complex, more unnerving, than anything imagined at Oxford by the Set. There was an exotic scene of Rossetti and the moneylender. Burne-Jones arrived at Blackfriars to find him in his studio with a Jew, one of the Ashkenazim. The floor was covered with his clothes: his only dress suit, pairs of trousers, coats and waistcoats. Rossetti swore falsely that all these were new. After long negotiation the Jew rolled up his large parcel, arranging to pay Rossetti three pounds. Rossetti then began on one of the huge breakfasts that made even his admirers shudder. These consisted of tea, jam and 'horrid eggs'.

Rossetti had a certain crudity. But there was also glamour, an aristocratic immunity to squalor of surroundings. He had found a place in Cheapside serving dinners for fourpence: beer, a sausage and a lump of stale bread. Here he used to lean against the counter, pull a copy of *Morte d'Arthur* out of his pocket and read passages aloud while he and his friends ate. When he led Burne-Jones and Morris around London he was charmingly impatient, leaving the theatre in the middle of any play that he found boring, saying, 'This play is a curse.' He went on one evening to the Judge and Jury, a low-level music hall in a vaulted chamber which Burne-Jones compared to the Cave of Harmony in Thackeray's *The Newcomes*. Though Burne-Jones in fact found it duller than the theatre Rossetti insisted that this was 'seeing life'.

Morris and his friends at Oxford had discussed the social problems that urban life created. In their idealistic Gladstonian way they had considered their own responsibility to remedy, to rescue. Now for the first time Morris was confronted with the realities. It appears from a reference in the memoirs of Georgiana Burne-Jones that the rooms at Red Lion Square were an informal rescue centre for the fallen women of the area: Red Lion Mary could be trusted 'like a good woman to shew kindness to another woman whose goodness was in abeyance, and could understand the honest kindness of a young man to such a one, and help him to feed and clothe her and get her back to her own people'.

Ford Madox Brown's diary for 1858 records how he had gone to Red Lion Square with an outfit purchased by his wife at Burne-Jones's request for 'a poor miserable girl of 17 he had met in the street at 2 a.m. The coldest night this winter, scarce any clothes and starving, in *spite of prostitution*, after only 5 weeks of London life.' Burne-Jones gave her money and sent her back home to her parents in the country.

Another, slightly later, account is of a small crowd coming down the street in Bloomsbury with Burne-Jones at the head of it, 'closely followed by a wretched, draggled looking girl whom he had found, not quite sober'. A gang of boys and roughs had been jeering at her, bullying her. Burne-Jones was taking her to look for police protection. But it seems Burne-Jones's role of protector of the prostitute was undermined by that of Rossetti as consumer. Ned once told a story of how Rossetti paid a prostitute five shillings to come after him, having told her Ned was very shy and timid but wanted to speak to her. She was persistent and they marched arm in arm down Regent Street together, to Burne-Jones's great embarrassment.

Did Morris go to prostitutes? It seems unlikely. His later public stance on prostitution was a firm one: his Socialist League statements denounce all views of women as commodity or property. In *News from Nowhere* his Utopia is envisaged as a place of sexual non-possessiveness in which prostitution has no place. All the same there are indications in his novels that he looked on the selling of the female body with a kind of fascinated horror. In *The Well at the World's End* there is a slave market where women are sold like cattle to the highest bidder. These women are bareheaded; they are dressed in uniform yellow embroidered robes, sleeveless and revealing, hardly reaching to the ankles; their naked feet are shod in sandals with white thongs. The description is peculiarly enticing and erotic, with its images of bondage. Each of the slave women 'bore an iron ring about her right arm'.

In the Oxford years Morris had had a young man's taste for the violent and ghoulish. Burne-Jones shared this, with his predilection for 'bogeys', love-horror creatures featured in whole series of Bogey drawings, the repudiation of deep-rooted childhood fears. What Rossetti taught them both was more dangerous, more adult. Rossetti had a sinister obsession with animals, the more grotesque the better. He easily charmed animals: at the Zoo in Paris for example he scratched a wombat, 'who liked it'. Later on, at Cheyne Walk, he filled the house and gardens with improbable menageries. In the 1860s he was seriously thinking of purchasing a lion. Rossetti both indulged and was cruel to his animals. He had a southern European callousness, tying up his dogs and tormenting them; once even chaining a gnu to a tree, from which it escaped and began to chase Rossetti in a scene that could have made a Belloc Cautionary Tale. Working on his painting 'Found' he was increasingly frustrated by the calf that had been loaned him by a farmer, with the cart. The calf kicked and fought all the time he was tied up, for five or six hours daily, then sank into a stupor in the afternoon. 'At these times', wrote Rossetti, 'I have to cut him down and then shake him and kick him like blazes. There is a pleasure in it my dear fellow: the Smithfield drovers are a kind of opium eaters at it, but a moderate practitioner might perhaps sustain an argument.'

Morris learned some of this sadism, and was the victim of it. Rossetti treated him almost as a part of his menagerie. His cruelty to Morris, as recorded by Burne-Jones, began within a year or two of their first meeting. The tauntings alternated with endearments. Morris's unstable temperament reacted to this teasing, making him seem even more rampageous and freakish. Under Rossetti's influence his friends began describing him as 'a domestic Wild Bull'.

They were no longer reading *Yeast*. The book of that period was *Sidonia the Sorceress*, a perversely erotic witch-hunt novel published in Germany by Johannes Meinhold in 1849 and translated into English by Lady Speranza Wilde, Oscar Wilde's mother. It appears that Rossetti introduced Sidonia, the beautiful and sexually insatiable witchwoman, to the Red Lion Square circle with spectacular success. Rossetti himself called Sidonia 'a stunner'. Burne-Jones painted Sidonia twice in 1860; Georgiana Burne-Jones gave the book to John Ruskin, sending a nervous letter, as if doubting its reception; for Morris it was one of his 'sacred books', republished in his Kelmscott Press edition in 1893. This long, trundling, macabre story, with its scenes of titillation verging on the pornographic, centres on the machinations of the vicious Sidonia who is, like the cruel mother in Morris's own fragmentary 'Story of Desiderius', outwardly lovely but in fact 'a painted show'. Morris is revealed in his poetry and fiction as fascinated by such cruel, devious women, from the vengeful Medea in *Jason* to the devilish Queen of Utterbol chastising her waiting-maids in the late novel *The Well at the World's End*. He felt the allure of the lady with the whiplash, a masochistic urge towards abasement and defilement, which counterpoints his image of the woman as the healthy sunkissed sweetheart, the stalwart comrade wife.

Tantalizingly Morris left little record of this period. There are few extant letters. These are also years he skates over in the brief autobiography he wrote for Andreas Scheu. It is difficult to gauge Rossetti's influence exactly. Morris's friends came to depict him as a Svengali figure, dominating the young Morris to sinister effect. Morris's own few words on Rossetti are such mild ones: 'He was very kind to me when I was a youngster,' he wrote in 1882, on Rossetti's death. Yet there are signs that Morris recognized a species of corruption. He saw how Rossetti tempted him towards a moral lassitude. He later became very sceptical of leaders: he would argue that principles mattered more than personalities. He spent much of his life in combating inertia, analysing and decrying its eroding effect upon human capabilities. He set his face firmly against flattery and charm, resisting the ingratiating with a stubbornness that in the end became almost pathological. Morris's hatreds deepened as his relationship with Rossetti became more convoluted. They had their beginnings in Morris's awareness of how far he had succumbed to the glamour of Rossetti when he was young in London in 1856.

In the long vacation of 1857 there was an exodus from Red Lion Square to Oxford. The summer of the Indian Mutiny was also the summer of Rossetti's 'jovial campaign' when he gathered round him a group of brother artists to paint Arthurian murals in the Oxford Union. Morris had been in Oxford with him when the frescoes were first mooted. Rossetti turned down the original suggestion that he should paint a panorama for Benjamin Woodward's new Oxford Museum of 'Newton gathering pebbles on the shores of the Ocean of Truth'. But he and Morris put an alternative proposal to Woodward, whose Oxford Union building was then nearing its completion. This building was a *tour-de-force* of red-brick Oxford Gothic. Scenes from the *Morte d'Arthur* were to be painted in each of the ten large bays above the gallery of the high-roofed, oval-shaped, spectacularly mediaeval hall. Rossetti attempted to enlist established artists, including Ford Madox Brown, William Bell Scott and Holman Hunt, whose initials were inscribed expectantly on the bare panels. But the only artist of experience who finally took part in the scheme was Arthur Hughes. So Rossetti recruited less professional assistants, one of whom, Val Prinsep, could not paint or draw at all, and used the example of Morris to encourage him: 'there's one of my friends going to join us who has never painted anything, but you'll see he'll do a stunning thing'.

Rossetti was enthusiastic about founding a new school of muralists in England. He was impressed by the heroic fresco in tempera, 'Justice: a Hemicycle of Lawgivers', which G. F. Watts was then painting for the new hall at Lincoln's Inn. Watts had given his services free, in return for the cost of his materials. This was by and large the system adopted for the Union, except that Morris paid for at least some of the tempera colours that they used. Morris flung himself into the work. His subject was 'How Sir Palomydes loved La Belle Iseult with exceeding great love out of measure, and how she loved not him again but rather Sir Tristram'. It was Morris's familiar theme of the rejected lover, the tragic triangle. He had apparently made several sketches on the theme of Tristram and Iseult earlier that summer as well as beginning his first oil painting. One of these attempts was given the all-too-jovial title 'Sudden Indisposition of Sir Tristram in the Garden of King Mark's Palace, recognisable as Collywobbles by the pile of gooseberry skins beside him, remains of unripe gooseberries devoured by him while he was waiting for Yseult'.

This was a group endeavour, the secure inbred male ambience in which Morris flourished. Other artists involved in this first phase of the murals were Hungerford Pollen and Spencer Stanhope, Hughes, Prinsep and of course Burne-Jones. The sculptor Alexander Munro was carving a stone shield for the main entrance, to Rossetti's design. Morris was the first to start his panel and the first to finish. He then embarked on painting a design of grotesque creatures on to the huge area of the roof panels and trusses, assisted by a group of enthusiastic amateurs, 'university men' who had stayed in Oxford for the long vacation specially. Charles Faulkner, by this time Fellow and Mathematical Tutor of University College, arrived regularly in the afternoons to help Morris high up on his scaffold. 'Charley', wrote Burne-Jones, 'comes out tremendously strong on the roof with all kinds of birds and beasts.' Crom Price was an assistant: 'Spent afternoon in daubing black lines at the Union roof for Topsy'; 'stippled and blacklined at Union', his diary records. Dixon too had returned to help Morris with his panel, painting in sunflowers by the square yard. The jovial campaign was a reunion for the Set, with all the old knockabout and badinage. Scholars working in the library next door were frequently disturbed by 'their laughter and songs and jokes and the volleys of their soda water corks'. Startling quantities of soda water were brought in, at Union expense, from the nearby Star Hotel. Morris was in a mood of ebullience, pressing his thumb into the wet paintwork with a childlike delight in his own handiwork: 'This is mine and this and this.'

They started work about eight a.m. There was an Oxford ritual of Rossetti and Pollen coming into their rooms to tear the bedclothes off Morris and Burne-Jones. They worked through the day till the early evening, eating sandwiches for lunch. While they worked the hall windows were whitened out so that they could gauge the effects of colour better. Rossetti filled these spaces with wombat cartoons. On the floor of the building was a table stocked with the colours in tempera, with a man whose task it was to supply the artists on the scaffold with the colours that they shouted for. Rossetti said of Morris: 'He had a way of picking up dirt and annexing it.' His smock, his face, his hair were frequently a mass of paint. Burne-Jones caricatured him standing looking upwards at the roof of the Union in his paint-splashed garments. The caption reads, 'O Tempera, O Morris!' Morris's stance is characteristic, with his legs splayed apart and his hands behind his back. A party of visitors from the University cross-examined him about the subject of the paintings. 'Morte d'Arthur,' shouted Morris, disappearing up a ladder into the roof scaffolding. The visitors complained about how rude the workmen were. He had some insuperable problems with his panel. The painting of figures nine foot tall on to a curving wall surface was beyond his skill.

His Tristram scene consists of three figures in a garden. Tristram and Iseult courting, with Palomydes watching in an agony of longing. Rossetti complained Morris's Iseult was unconvincing, Prinsep went further and described her as an ogress. Morris was dispatched to Godstow to ask the eighteen-year-old daughter of the innkeeper to model for Iseult. He was unsuccessful in his suit to 'Stunner Lipscombe'. A 'stunner' was the word used in Rossetti circles for a beautiful and covetable girl, woman or model. Morris got back to Oxford crestfallen to find a jeering placard over his bedroom door:

> Poor Topsy has gone to make a sketch of Miss Lipscombe
> But he can't draw the head, and don't know where the hips come.

Compared with Rossetti's 'Sir Lancelot prevented by his sin from entering the Chapel of the Holy Grail' and Burne-Jones's 'Merlin being imprisoned beneath a Stone by the Damsel of the Lake', Morris's own panel, seen after the 1987 restoration, is certainly ungainly and amateur. He himself later found it embarrassing, calling it 'extremely ludicrous in many ways' and saying he would feel 'much more comfortable' if it disappeared from the wall.

The present decoration of the roof at the Union is not Morris's original but a reworking of the 1870s when Morris provided a 'new and lighter design'. His design of 1857 was dark, complicated, mythical, a mass of vegetation, crowded out with nightmare creatures. He completed the design within a day. Morris became deeply interested in the possibilities, both social and artistic, of the decoration of the surface of a building. It is a subject he considers in great detail in his lectures on pattern design. He understood the function of wall painting in binding a community together through a shared pictorial narrative. He is lyrical about the delights of discovering an unexpected painting in a building, probably remembering such *frissons* in the lonely and eccentric little churches around Essex he had found as a child. The Oxford Union roof was the first of his long series of experiments with pattern: repeats covering the ceilings, covering the walls. This was architectural pattern, related to the building and drawing out its meaning. In the early days of Morris, Marshall, Faulkner & Co. wall-painting commissions were the ones they were most anxious to procure. At Oxford private jokes were infiltrated. On the roof, in the dark angles of the beams, little cartoon portraits of Morris started to appear. These made him look like a miniature version of Henry VIII standing stoutly as he does in Holbein's painting. 'By God, I'm getting a belly!' exclaimed Morris. The 'slim boy' of two years ago was now quite fat.

Morris was carving a block of stone to make the capital of a pillar. Arthur Hughes judged that it was done with 'great spirit and life'. One day, while he was working on this, a splinter flew into his eye and had to be removed by the famous Dr Acland; this accident aroused Morris to a fury which was 'even for him unequalled in its force and copiousness'. At this period, pursuing the experiments with crafts he had embarked on in Street's office, he was drawing and colouring designs for stained glass and life-modelling from clay. Crom Price sat for a portrait in clay, never completed because of the number of times Morris became impatient with it and smashed it up. He was also continuing his research into lost techniques of embroidery, an eccentric enthusiasm at a time when it was seen as essentially a woman's pastime. He had a frame made specially, based on an old pattern. He sought out an old French dyer to dye worsteds for him. Morris was a determined and formidable patron, as Morris & Co. suppliers were later to find out.

From a smith with a forge near the castle in Oxford he ordered a bassinet, a *recherché* kind of helmet. He and Burne-Jones often needed obscure pieces of armour for their drawings. Morris's solution was to have Arthurian armour specially made. Sometimes there were hazards: once, trying on his bassinet, he found that the visor would not lift. Burne-Jones describes Morris, 'embedded in iron, dancing with rage and roaring inside'. The most ambitious of his commissions was a surcoat of ringed mail with a mailed hood and a skirt coming down beneath the knees. The day that this arrived he was so pleased with it he sat down to dinner in it. He looked 'very splendid', Burne-Jones wrote loyally.

Coventry Patmore, visiting the Union late in 1857, described the 'voluptuous radiance' of the murals: their innovation was colouring 'so brilliant as to make the walls look like the margin of a highly-illuminated manuscript'. This was not to last. Within six months the murals had deteriorated badly: the brickwork was uneven and had not been prepared properly. The murals were exposed to damp and dust and to the depredations of the smoke and heat from the gas chandeliers. Nor were they ever finished. Rossetti left Oxford with his panel uncompleted and several of the others still awaited final touches when the project was abandoned in March of 1858. To some of the participants the painting of the Union became a kind of legend of youthful camaraderie: 'What fun we had! What jokes! What roars of laughter!' Georgiana Burne-Jones saw a kind of sacredness in 'those wonderful seething days'. Morris's recollections are not so sentimental, partly perhaps because the episode in retrospect was overlaid by sadder and more complicated memories. In the late 1860s he wrote of it dismissively: 'the whole affair was begun and carried out in too piecemeal and unorganised a manner to be a real success'.

While they worked at the Union the artists at first lodged in the High Street, in a house reached through a courtyard in which grew a fine specimen of vegetable marrow. Rossetti used this marrow as the subject for a drawing. The scene in the lodgings was described by Prinsep:

When the dinner was over and the lodgings' slavey had removed the cloth, Rossetti rose from the table and curled himself up on the horsehair sofa which adorned this 'jolly crib'; Ned Jones got down a pen-and-ink drawing at which he set to work; Morris stamped about the room, emphasising his points by gestures which recalled the quaint illustrations of a mediaeval Missal.

'I say, Top', said Rossetti, who had been humming to himself on the sofa, 'read us one of your Grinds'.

Morris, apparently expecting this request, took out a largish book with a clasp. This he put down on the table. While he read he rested his head on one hand, while with the other he ceaselessly twisted his watch-chain. Prinsep noted his jerky eccentricities of movement. Among the poems he read was the love song 'The Eve of Crecy':

> Gold on her head, and gold on her feet,
> And gold where the hems of her kirtle meet,
> And a golden girdle round my sweet;–
> *Ah! qu'elle est belle La Marguerite*

Such golden female figures recur in Morris's own stained glass and his embroidery, and they are usually girdled. The girdle and the garland had a special meaning in Morris's vocabulary of desire.

Now at Oxford, more than ever, Morris became established as the butt, the comic character, the basis of a legend. The stories multiplied. How Morris was invited to dine at high table at Christ Church and, finding he had left his dress clothes behind, had had to be squeezed painfully into Arthur Hughes's. How Topsy had pleaded illness to avoid going out to dinner with the notoriously boring Dr Acland only to be discovered by the doctor in his lodgings playing cribbage, having already eaten. The Topsy persona developed its own language: 'very, very Topsian' was the way Georgiana Burne-Jones described Morris's unreasonable request in his lodgings in Birmingham for dinner for six people in an hour's time. The stories often focus on greed, physical excess. Morris's increasing girth made him an ever better target. Algernon Charles Swinburne, arriving at Balliol in the autumn of 1857, seems to have picked up what was almost a mania for ridiculing Morris. Swinburne wrote that he 'swears awfully, and walks with a rolling gait, as if partially intoxicated'.

Burne-Jones had embarked on his almost life-long series of Topsy cartoons, dwelling on Morris's contours, his obsessiveness, his foibles and 'the forcible and energetic manner which characterises that unnaturally and unnecessarily curly being'. Rossetti too was drawing caricatures of Morris. These drawings were sometimes sent or taken down to London and passed around by Georgiana and her sisters. In a sense these cartoons are fond but they are also wicked. Morris participated in the joke. Said Prinsep, 'He was the essence of good nature, and stood chaff with extraordinary tolerance.' But it would be difficult for somebody as sensitive as Morris to withstand unscathed such a long barrage of ridicule. It must to some extent have damaged his self-confidence, especially with women, and intensified his feeling that he was the outcast, even in his own close group.

When Rossetti, as a joke, made a Class List for vanity, like the class lists at graduation published by Oxford University, he put himself, Burne-Jones and Swinburne in the first class. He put Morris nowhere, and when Burne-Jones asked why, he said Morris was 'out of the run altogether', and must have a class to himself.

'Topsy raves and swares like or more than any Oxford bargee about a "stunner" that he has seen.' This bulletin was sent by Crom Price to his father in December 1857. The 'stunner' was the eighteen-year-old Jane Burden, whom two years later Morris was to marry. Janey had been brought into Morris's orbit by Rossetti and Burne-Jones who had seen her with her sister at the theatre in October of that year. Rossetti put much time and energy into trawling for 'stunners' whom he could use as models: it was an excitement, almost an addiction, and he had persuaded Janey to pose, asking and receiving permission from her parents. The Oxford Union artists had by this time moved their lodgings from the High Street to George Street. Janey posed in the first-floor sitting-room. At first it appears she posed exclusively for Rossetti who used her as the model for a sequence of studies of Queen Guenevere. When Rossetti left Oxford in the autumn, Janey posed for Morris, modelling for the painting which is now in the Tate Gallery, 'La Belle Iseult'. The relationship between the artist and the model is notoriously delicate, shot through with sexual overtones. Rossetti was used to it, would play upon it, tease it. Morris, less sophisticated, fell immediately in love. Topsy in love was a phenomenon his friends regarded with the usual derision, and they regaled each other with stories of the hours he spent ensconced with Janey in the sitting-room at George Street, reading out loud from *Barnaby Rudge*.

In loving and eventually marrying Janey, Morris made another decisive move away from his own background. Janey came from a poor family, from the ranks of agricultural workers migrating from the villages round Oxford to the town to find employment. Her mother, Ann Maizey, came from Alvescot; her father, Robert Burden, from the neighbouring village of Stanton Harcourt. Janey belonged to the substratum of Oxford society recreated some years later in Thomas Hardy's *Jude the Obscure*. She was born in 1839 in St Helen's Passage off Holywell, in a cramped and insanitary cottage; her mother registered her birth not with a signature but with a cross, indicating illiteracy. Janey's father was a stablehand or ostler at Symonds' Livery Stable in Holywell Street. Her older brother William was working as a college messenger by the age of fourteen. Her older sister Mary Anne died of tuberculosis in 1849. Janey's childhood had been circumscribed. There is a little picture of Janey and her sister Bessie in the Rev. W. Tuckwell's reminiscences of Oxford: a pair of teenage working-class girls around the town. Her view of life was inevitably narrow. She remembered picking violets on the Iffley Road beyond the city. But before her marriage Janey had never been to London or seen the sea. In later life, as I have mentioned, she was evasive on the details of her upbringing. Of Morris's friends it was only Philip Webb, with his own Oxford connections, who understood her background. He knew it was unhappy and he sympathized with Janey's instincts, which others saw as snobbery, to obliterate the past.

Janey's style of beauty too was an attraction of opposites. She did not resemble Morris's mother or his sisters. She did not represent the ideals of female beauty approved of by the people Morris sneered at as 'respectables'. Janey was tall and gaunt, frizzy-haired, exotic, foreign. It used to be suggested that she had gypsy blood in her. Later, travelling in France, her appearance seemed so *outré* that strangers would stare and giggle in the street at her, to Morris's great fury. It is interesting that in their early years at Oxford her younger sister Bessie was generally considered better looking. But her aura of aloofness, the fraught and unearthly quality of beauty that alienated less artistic people, was the element in Janey the Pre-Raphaelites fell upon, making her almost the Pre-Raphaelite icon. In the early days Pre-Raphaelite 'stunners' had been red-haired; after Janey, a 'stunner' was more likely to be black-haired. Morris fell in love with Janey because, to him, she looked right and he was attuned to worship the aesthetically pleasing. Bernard Shaw was malicious but correct when he diagnosed her role later on as 'to be beautiful': she 'knew that to be so was part of her household business'. In acquiring Janey Morris was perfecting an artistic *mise-en-scène*.

Burne-Jones's engagement to Georgiana Macdonald was more or less a relationship of equals. She was the Methodist minister's daughter: in their backgrounds of genteel poverty and intellectual seriousness they were not so far apart. But in their artistic circle this was almost the exception. In the sexual relationships of the Pre-Raphaelites there is a recurring pattern of disparity, a definite male movement *du haut en bas*. This was a chivalric drama of finding and transforming. Lizzie Siddal, unofficially engaged to Rossetti from the middle 1850s, was from a humble, though respectable, background: according to one of the many legends that accumulated round her she was first spotted arranging hats in the window of a milliner's shop in Cranbourne Alley, off Leicester Square. Holman Hunt found Annie Miller working as a barmaid at the Cross Keys in Chelsea and paid for her elocution and deportment lessons, obliterating her past as artists' model, only to lose her to Rossetti in the end. Ford Madox Brown had kept his marriage to Emma, his model, the illiterate daughter of a farmer, a secret from all except his closest friends for two or three years, so that he could educate her. Emma became increasingly neurotic and, early in the marriage, took to drink. A. J. Munby, on the fringe of Pre-Raphaelite circles, a civil servant and barrister and poet who married a scullery maid and wrote poems in praise of the roughest working women, pushed to furthest limits the Victorian correlation of servitude with male 'needs'. As a depiction of sexual electricity arcing across the classes perhaps the prime example is Burne-Jones's tensely erotic painting 'King Cophetua and the Beggar-maid'. He was worried, when he painted it, in case he was making the beggar maid too clean.

One of the poems in Morris's *Earthly Paradise* is 'Pygmalion and the Image'. In Morris's résumé: 'A Man of Cyprus, a sculptor named Pygmalion, made an image of a woman fairer than had yet been seen, and in the end came to love his own handiwork as though it had been alive. Venus made the image alive indeed, and a woman, and he wedded her.' It is a curious and disconcerting poem, raising the moral question of the sculptor's involvement in the making process at the expense of the object of the making. Such obsessiveness is seen to be suspect, an activity 'half loathed, half loved':

> And yet, again, at last there came a day
> When smoother and more shapely grew the stone
> And he, grown eager, put all thought away
> But that which touched his craftsmanship alone,
> And he would gaze at what his hands had done,
> Until his heart with boundless joy would swell
> That all was wrought as wonderfully well.

The Pygmalion factor cannot be discounted in Morris's highly idealized and at times tormented relations with Janey. In the Pre-Raphaelite dream of female transformation there was a certain built-in heartlessness, not lost on Bernard Shaw, so entwined with Morris's household in the 1880s when he was a young man. It was typical of his mischievous intelligence that when he came to write his own version of *Pygmalion* the character he based on Mrs Morris is not in fact Eliza but Professor Higgins's mother, once the Pre-Raphaelite heroine, now the acerbic and elegant recluse.

After meeting Janey, Morris was *énervé*. At a dinner in Oxford, when her name was mentioned in a manner he took to be insulting, Morris bit his four-pronged fork so hard he twisted it and crushed it beyond recognition: this entered the repertoire of amusing Morris tales. In the summer he travelled north to stay with Dixon for the Manchester Art Treasures Exhibition, the first large-scale international show of paintings assembled from the royal and from private collections. Here Morris behaved arrogantly and dogmatically, refusing to look at the Old

Masters, though admitting he was 'absurdly prejudiced'. He enjoyed the fine collection of carved ivories much better, managing to make a 'furtive sketch' of one of them, in defiance of the regulations. When he heard the organ blaring out throughout the exhibition he urged Dixon to leave with him: 'Let us get out of the reach of that squealing thing,' he said.

In Manchester with Dixon, Morris finished a water-colour painting at one sitting. Dixon says he worked on it with 'great enthusiasm'. This now vanished painting he called 'The Soldan's Daughter in the Palace of Glass'. It showed a female figure seated in a heavy wooden armchair, apparently imprisoned in a faery crystal palace constructed of varying shades of bluish glass. Morris himself to some extent seemed to be living in a glasshouse, transfixed by his emotions but unable to express them. 'I cannot paint you but I love you,' he is said to have scribbled on his picture of Janey as Iseult.

Morris was working on that painting through the summer and on into the winter of 1857–8. Although at one time believed to be of Guenevere the portrait is undoubtedly Iseult, whose little hound is depicted lying underneath the distinctly rumpled bed. The bed remained unmade for weeks in the Red Lion Square studio while the work was under way. Morris's painting is by no means amateur, but compared with the paintings Burne-Jones was then producing it has a curiously constipated quality. Morris's tentativeness in relation to Janey is clear from the poem 'In Praise of my Lady' written in the weeks he was in Manchester:

> Her great eyes, standing far apart,
> Draw up some memory from her heart,
> And gaze out very mournfully;
>   – *Beata mea Domina!* –
>
> So beautiful and kind they are,
> But most times looking out afar,
> Waiting for something, not for me.
>   *Beata mea Domina!*

The engagement was announced in the spring of 1858. There is no record that Janey was taken to be presented to Morris's family in Essex. Nor is there any evidence of how or even whether she was groomed to be a lady. But it seems likely that she, like Annie Miller, was put through at least a basic training course. Janey became an avid reader and it must have been at this stage that she learned to play the piano. Morris's present to her on her first birthday after their marriage was Chappell's *Popular Music of the Olden Time*. The response of some of Morris's friends to the engagement was discouraging. Swinburne said that Topsy should be 'content with that perfect stunner of his – to look at or speak to. The idea of marrying her is insane. To kiss her feet is the utmost men should dream of doing.' Rossetti drew a cartoon barbed with malice.

6 '*William Morris presenting a ring to Jane Burden*'. Cartoon by Dante Gabriel Rossetti.

How far Rossetti sabotaged the marriage right from the beginning is uncertain. At this Oxford period he had been in theory committed to Lizzie Siddal for the past five or six years, in a relationship shot through with uncertainties, made more problematic by Lizzie's frequent illnesses, attributed to consumption or 'phthisis' (though in fact she showed no symptoms of pulmonary disease) and Rossetti's permanently impecunious state. He loved Lizzie in his way; but he was always on the look-out. He was overwhelmingly sexually competitive: as Burne-Jones once pointed out, nothing pleased Rossetti more than 'to take his friend's mistress away from him'. He was on terms of particular intimacy with Janey: he had found her, praised her and taught her modelling. He had left her to Morris in the later months of 1857, which he spent in Derbyshire with Lizzie; but there is the mysterious episode of his sudden return to Oxford to draw Janey as Guenevere the following summer, when Morris was in France. That June, when George Price Boyce visited Rossetti in London, he found him agitated: 'He made one or two rough sketches while talking, one of a "Stunner" at Oxford which he tore into fragments, but which I recovered from the fire grate.' Six months later, in December, amongst Rossetti's new work, Boyce noticed 'A most beautiful pen and ink study of Topsy's [Morris's] "Stunner" at Oxford'. In the months before her marriage, Morris's 'Stunner' was apparently much on Rossetti's mind.

Janey later admitted she had never loved her husband. She implied she had really had no choices in the matter, given social circumstances that did not allow the acceptance or refusal of a suitor on purely emotional grounds. Morris's was a good offer, far beyond her expectations; almost forty years later, she said that in that situation she would do the same again.

Janey also maintained that Rossetti had not 'made love' to her before marriage, implying that the amorous advances only started seriously nine or ten years later, when he began to paint her with a new intensity and the passionate sonnets began to rain down. This is probably true; but there are many sorts of lovemaking. Rossetti's looming presence over the liaison of the two sexually inexperienced and socially disparate young people helped to confirm the marriage in its doom.

While Morris was in Manchester Rossetti wrote to tell him 'we have unearthed a new poet who is charming'. The spectacularly red-haired Swinburne was welcomed into the artistic clique at Oxford, Burne-Jones referring to him as 'dear little Carrots' and announcing 'Now we are four and not *three*'. It is unlikely that Morris, when he met him, welcomed Swinburne so effusively into the inner circle. He was always to have reservations about Swinburne. But Swinburne at this stage hero-worshipped Morris, listened admiringly to his sing-song readings and soon began writing a quasi-Morris poem, 'Queen Yseult', which Morris told him was much better than his own.

Morris was preparing his own poems for publication. There was by now a large accumulation. Rossetti, overwhelmed by Morris's productivity, judged he had enough good poems for a volume even at the time he first moved into Red Lion Square. He continued writing fluently all through that Oxford summer, and in October 1857 made a first approach to Alexander Macmillan, head of the publishing firm: 'Having a volume of poems which I intend bringing out, I wish to know if you would undertake to publish them, and on what terms?' In the end the publishers of Morris's *The Defence of Guenevere*, in March 1858, were Bell & Daldy. The poems were published at Morris's expense. There was a certain carelessness about the editing: Morris's nonchalant attitude to proof-reading resulted in a number of misprints and mistakes in punctuation. About two hundred copies of the edition were sold or given away; the remainder lingered. Morris's dedication reads 'To my friend, Dante Gabriel Rossetti, Painter, I dedicate these Poems'.

There are thirty poems in *The Defence of Guenevere*. Compared with Morris's later epic scale of operation – his four-volume *Earthly Paradise*, his translations of *The Odyssey* and *The Aeneid*, his Icelandic sagas – these poems are succinct, almost peremptory. The longest is 'Sir Peter Harpdon's End', a violent mini-drama of the Hundred Years' War, at 748 lines. The pair of Arthurian poems, 'The Defence of Guenevere' and 'King Arthur's Tomb', are nervy, almost jagged, compared with Tennyson's rotund and polished treatment of the same Arthurian themes. Other poems are distilled out of Froissart: these are war poems, small stark incidents of battle and campaigning, violence, imprisonment, betrayal, sudden death. There is also a sequence of short dream poems, lugubrious Pre-Raphaelite scenes in which human figures huddle in unnerving mystic landscapes. There is always gloom in Morris. A dance partner of May Morris's, longing to talk to her about her father's poems, misquoted the title of the one he could remember as 'Sir Guy of the Doleful Damn'.

When Morris was asked in whose style these poems were written he replied: 'More like Browning than anyone else, I suppose.' Browning's fairytale poem *Sordello*, with its spikiness of language and its complex tricks with time scale, was read over and over by Morris and his friends. Morris's early poems are certainly like Browning in the way that they dispense with the preamble: the reader of these poems is shot straight into the action. They are also like Browning in their lack of resolution. These are difficult poems, unsettling and demanding. Not all are successful. Morris's mediaevalism can be a little windy. But at their best they have a brilliance, a freshness and a quirkiness that Morris's poetry did not achieve again.

To W. B. Yeats as a child the supreme expression of happiness was Morris's description of the red brick and grey stone castle in 'Golden Wings':

> Midways of a walled garden,
> In the happy poplar land,
> Did an ancient castle stand,
> With an old knight for a warden.
>
> And many scarlet bricks there were
> In its walls, and old grey stone;
> Over which red apples shone
> At the right time of the year.

In this and many other of the poems in *Guenevere* there is indeed an aura of happiness, infectious delight in landscape and the detail of the buildings in a landscape. Morris writes as a man acutely conscious of the beauty of the earth, both inherent and man-made. But even at this stage he could not be too hopeful. Already in these early poems there are traces of the uneasiness that accumulated later to make Morris so ferocious a protester against the despoliation of the landscape and so passionate a critic of what he came to see as the social iniquities behind that despoliation. In the poems in *Guenevere* there is an enormous tension that derives from the sense of beauty under threat.

In 'Golden Wings' there is a menace in the landscape: the fruitfulness dissolves into barrenness and terror. The apples fall from the trees before they ripen; the 'draggled swans' eat the green weed in the moat; and in a shock image typical of Morris:

> Inside the rotting leaky boat
> You see a slain man's stiffen'd feet.

In his vision of pastoral landscape turned to horror Morris writes as a Victorian, expressing a dread by this time deeply rooted in the

143

contemporary psyche. What is so characteristic and peculiar is the way
in which Morris, in giving precision to this horror, stretches back to his
own version of the mediaeval past. In the poem set in France, 'Concerning Geffray Teste Noire', two skeletons in armour are found among the
primroses in copses of green hazel. One of these is identified as a young
woman. Her small white skull rattles loose inside the helmet. The hair is
still golden, 'not gone to powder', yet.

Morris's great theme is the fragility of happiness. In these poems is
embedded a deep consciousness of the possibilities of happiness in
human relationships: domestic contentment, sexual fulfilment. So many
of these poems reveal Morris's perception of an almost cosily close
eroticism and his sense of how vulnerable, destructible, this is. Sir Peter
Harpdon, the Gascon knight stranded in the derelict castle in Poictou,
thinks compulsively of scenes from domestic life:

> To find her sitting there,
> In the window-seat, not looking well at all,
> Crying perhaps, and I say quietly;
> 'Alice!' she looks up, chokes a sob, looks grave,
> Changes from pale to red.

Alice says she loves him, kisses him. Her little fingers creep through the
tangles of his beard.

The regret for lost possibilities, for wasted intimacies, is even more
explicit in a version of the poem not finally included in *The Defence of
Guenevere*:

> I see her in the dance her gown held up
> To free her feet, going to take my hand,
> I see her in some crowded place bend down,
> She is so tall, lay her hand flat upon
> My breast beneath my chin as who should say,
> Come here and talk apart: I see her pale,
> Her mouth half open, looking on in fear
> As the great tilt-yard fills; I see her, say,
> Beside me on the dais; by my hearth
> And in my bed who should have been my wife.

This was a passage that Swinburne thought so good he tried to persuade
Morris to leave it in.

In the *Guenevere* poems Morris's sexual images are precise, explicit:
lips curl and swell; mouths ache and wander; hands strain; lovers kiss
'like a curved sword', biting with all its edges. The images of peace
become the images of war, and in the most violently erotic poem in the
collection, 'The Haystack in the Floods', there is a harshly described
scene of double threat as Godmar, crying rage, kills Jehane's lover Robert:

> with empty hands
> Held out, she stood and gazed, and saw,
> The long bright blades without a flaw
> Glide out from Godmar's sheath, his hand
> In Robert's hair; she saw him bend
> Back Robert's head; she saw him send
> The thin steel down.

In Morris's strangely symbolic poem 'The Wind' the lovers 'kiss hard'
before Margaret lies down on the grass, marking the moss with the
imprint of her body. Her lover piles her body up high with daffodils, in
one of Morris's more macabre floral arrangements. But Margaret is
doomed, in disarray, the blood starts seeping:

> Alas! alas! there was blood on the very quiet breast,
> Blood lay in the many folds of the loose ungirded vest,
> Blood lay upon her arm where the flower had been prest.

Morris's poem ends, as so many of his stories do, with the awakening from
the dream: the narrator shrieks, leaps from his chair, a heavy carved one,
monumental as the chairs in Red Lion Square, and from underneath the
chair rolls an orange with a gash in it:

> The faint yellow juice oozed out like blood from a wizard's jar;
> And then in march'd the ghosts of those that had gone to the war.

Morris's symbolist poems are sometimes reminiscent of Blake in their
child's language, their apocalyptic visions. They are even closer in their
mood and in the trappings of their period to the poetry of Morris's friend
Richard Watson Dixon: to 'The Wizard's Funeral', with its colossal
black-plumed horses; to the particular Victorian exoticism of Dixon's
desert landscape 'Dream':

> With camel's hair I clothed my skin,
> I fed my mouth with honey wild;
> And set me scarlet wool to spin,
> And all my breast with hyssop filled.

Even the scarlet wool has its connections with Morris. The verbal is the visual; every poem paints a picture. Dixon was at this period taking painting lessons from Rossetti. Both Morris and Dixon were writing wonderfully coloured Pre-Raphaelite poems. They were playing visual tricks of a kind later exploited by the technologies of cinema and video. In Morris's poem 'The Sailing of the Sword', the sword indeed goes out to sea, with a bizarre inner logic. 'The Blue Closet' contains a scene of wonder verbally obscure yet visually credible:

> *Through the floor shot up a lily red,*
> *With a patch of earth from the land of the dead,*
> *For he was strong in the land of the dead.*

'Sir Galahad, a Christmas Mystery' includes a stage direction: 'Enter Two Angels in white, with scarlet wings; also Four Ladies in gowns of red and green; also an Angel, bearing in his hands a surcoat of white, with a red cross.' This reads like the instruction for a Morris & Co. tapestry or one of his more complicated windows in stained glass.

Morris seems to have been nervous about the reception of *The Defence of Guenevere*. Swinburne complained that soon after publication he disappeared from view: 'That party has given us no sign of life as yet; in vain has the *Oxford County Chronicle* been crammed with such notices as the following: "If W. M. will return to his disconsolate friends, all shall be forgiven. One word would relieve them from the most agonizing anxiety – why is it withheld?"'

The few reviews Morris received were mainly unenthusiastic. The most cutting of the critics, in *The Saturday Review*, called Morris's poetry 'all cold, artificial, and angular. It is, in words, just what Sir Isambras on the plum-coloured horse was two years ago.' The reference is to John Everett Millais's brilliant, erratic painting 'Sir Isumbras at the Ford', so widely ridiculed when it was exhibited at the Royal Academy in 1857. The hostility directed at Pre-Raphaelite painting found a new target in Morris's poems. In effect he was the first Pre-Raphaelite poet to be published. Rossetti's collected *Poems* did not appear until 1870; he and his sister Christina had at this stage had only a few poems published in small-circulation magazines. Swinburne was not published until two years later; R. W. Dixon's first collection, *Poems from Christ's Company*, did not come out until 1861. This made Morris particularly vulnerable. Poems that in his circle seemed so normal and acceptable, part of a shared currency, were isolated suddenly and people unprepared for them found them baffling, wayward and uncouth.

They lacked the expected finish. This was a fair comment. Morris was not strict with himself and he had no sense of bathos: some of the poems in *Guenevere* are obvious candidates for that anthology of poetic anti-climax, *The Stuffed Owl*. Another criticism was that Morris lacked the necessary moral grandeur. 'Poetry is concerned with human passions and duties': the consensus of opinion in that supreme decade of the poetry of argument was that, on the basis of this collection, Morris lacked this sense of duty. He was standing aside from the social debate. And certainly *Guenevere* does look a little lightweight in comparison with Tennyson's *In Memoriam* (1850); Matthew Arnold's *Empedocles on Etna* (1852); Robert Browning's *Men and Women* (1855); Elizabeth Barrett Browning's *Aurora Leigh* (1857), her elaborate, impassioned debate on the state of the nation, the position of women, the role of the poet. Morris admired Mrs Browning hugely, considering her greater than her husband, but he was defeated by *Aurora Leigh*, which he described as 'dull'.

As a poet Morris failed to take himself quite seriously. This was partly a result of his great fluency: poetry came too easily. He could not bring himself to view as a profession an activity that really seemed domestic entertainment. Shaw, better than anyone, understood this attitude:

he could sling rhymes without having to think about them, and used to look at me with incredulous disgust when I told him that when I wanted a rhyme I had to try down the alphabet: Stella, bella, sella, della, fellah, hell a, quell a, sell a, tell a, well a, yell a, Campbell, bramble, gamble, ramble etc. etc. He did not consider poetry worth all that trouble; and I agree.

The hostile reviews disconcerted Morris, probably because he saw the truth in them. After *Guenevere* he entered a long silence. He published nothing for the next eight years. He continued fitfully but finally abandoned a cycle of poems on the Trojan War. Nor did he pursue his original intention of using the Arthurian narratives in *Guenevere* as the basis for an epic on King Arthur and the Knights of the Round Table.

No doubt he was discouraged by the publication in 1859 of Tennyson's vastly popular Arthurian cycle *Idylls of the King*. Morris flung himself into other activities: the 1860s saw his emergence as a designer-manufacturer and the beginning of Morris & Co. He was always able to move on from disappointments, with a characteristic 'je m'en fiche'.

Morris's *Guenevere* poems have had their admirers, of an unworldly and discriminating sort. Mrs Gaskell called this a book 'made for quiet places'. R. W. Dixon felt these poems were better, in the sense of being purer and more original, than anything Morris subsequently wrote. There are a few records among Oxford undergraduates of the 1850s and early 1860s of their surprise at the discovery of Morris; his name was included with Southey and Shelley in Gerard Manley Hopkins's little list of Oxford poets in 1865.

When years later William Morris was rediscovered by the Imagists it was these early spare strange poems which excited them. In the tree house in the woods in Philadelphia, Ezra Pound read William Morris out loud to his love Hilda: he literally shouted 'The Gilliflower of Gold' across the orchard and there was 'passionate emotion' in his reading of 'The Haystack in the Floods'.

In 1929 Yeats was in Rapallo, visiting Pound and reading Morris's *Defence of Guenevere* all through 'with great wonder'. He added: 'I have come to fear the world's last great poetic period is over.'

> Though the great song return no more
> There's keen delight in what we have –
> A rattle of pebbles on the shore
> Under the receding wave.

In August 1858 Morris was in France, on the last of his bachelor summer expeditions. His companions were Philip Webb and Charley Faulkner. Webb too had by this time left Street's office and was in private practice in Great Ormond Street. They travelled the familiar route from Abbeville to Amiens where accidentally, on the tower of the cathedral, a small shower of golden sovereigns shot out of Morris's satchel. These would have descended through the mouths of the gargoyles if Webb had not stopped them with his foot. Morris settled down to make a drawing of the choir while the others examined the galleries. 'Looking down', wrote Webb, 'we saw him have a struggle with himself and suddenly go away – he had upset the ink bottle all over his drawing.' Morris on this holiday seems to have been irascible and tense.

They travelled on from Amiens to Beauvais, sketching in the churches and cathedrals as they went, and arriving in Paris on 21 August. They drew some of the capitals in Notre-Dame and the rose and ivy panels in the west porch. They avoided the Sainte-Chapelle, knowing how much the restorations would enrage them. In Paris they lodged at Meurice's in rooms at the top of the building. Webb noticed rats in the gutters of the roofs.

The drama of the expedition was the voyage down the Seine from Paris. A traditional boat had been sent over from the Oxford boatyard Bossom's for the purpose. By the time it got to Paris a hole had been knocked in it. Rage and disappointment at the damage brought on one of Morris's quasi-epileptic fits. He was 'transported' and grazed the skin of his hand against the parapet of the river wall. This 'transport' was succeeded by the usual phase of calm and apparent unawareness of the incident: in a minute or two he turned round and said, 'You fellows seem very quiet; what's the matter?' They arranged for the boat to be mended and set off from the Quai du Louvre. The bridges of the Seine were lined with people watching the three eccentric Englishmen embarked with their three carpet bags and six bottles of wine. They took Morris's copy of Murray's *Guide to France*, marked every five miles with the distances from Paris to the sea.

They stopped at the collegiate church of Notre-Dame in Mantes, the austere and erect church painted by Corot. 'I do love a gaunt church!' exclaimed Webb. Under Webb's influence Morris's own taste in buildings became stricter: in the end his ideal structure was the mediaeval barn. What they liked about the church at Mantes was its aloofness, its size and general amplitude, 'unhelped' by any ornament. Webb was eloquent in the way that only he could be about the particular splendours of that building: the long line of the roof ridges; the areas of tiling; the apse supported so precisely by *arcs buttant*; and the twin towers arising so surprisingly 'with their total change from the horizontal in their lines'.

Where Burne-Jones's imagination was mythical and sensual, Webb's was much more technical: he *understood* a structure, could explain a building lucidly in terms of its materials, its components, arcs and planes. But he too in his way was a romantic and his sense of visual rightness was as fine-tuned as Burne-Jones's. In the education of the senses William Morris depended upon both of these close and life-long friends. The rapport with Webb was also firmly rooted in shared humour, mutual quaintness: they thought of the church at Mantes as a giant Noah's Ark.

The journey downriver was hilarious, eventful. They stopped at towns and made excursions. The boat was light and keelless but Faulkner insisted upon sailing it whenever there was enough wind. In a lock on the upper river, Morris's intemperance angered the lock-keeper who let the water out and left them stranded. Nearing the Pont de l'Arche, Morris said 'I'll show you fellows such a bridge . . .' But the bridge had been destroyed, and this resulted in more rages. At an inn there was another tournament with soda siphons. On 2 September the three of them reached Rouen where they were upset to find the new cast-iron spire of the cathedral under way but not completed: 'The upper part was lying hateful on the ground.' At Duclair they met a tidal wave. Webb was the first to see a wall of water about eight feet high moving towards them. He shouted out 'the Bore! the Bore!' They were rowing for dear life towards the shore when the wave threw them high up on the land. The tide raced on for hours before the boat was launched again. The journey, as recalled by the travellers years later, has an end-of-season quality, a resonance of sadness. There is almost desperation in this jocularity, as of the last sally of the Verdant Greens abroad.

The Red Lion Square regime began breaking up that summer. Burne-Jones had been unwell and was virtually kidnapped by his friend Val Prinsep's mother, the determined Mrs Prinsep, and taken to recuperate in the luxury of Little Holland House in Kensington. Morris disapproved of this, disliking the ambience of fashionable culture in a household where G. F. Watts and Tennyson were habitués, and where 'the very strawberries that stood in little crimson hills upon the tables were larger and riper than others'. Already there were signs of the political divergences which later put a strain on his friendship with Burne-Jones. Morris himself was spending a great deal of time in Oxford. After his return from France, Red Lion Square was given up and the only remaining link was Red Lion Mary who stayed on as housekeeper to Morris's successor, an Oxford acquaintance said to look like Byron. Red Lion Mary continued embroidering for Morris until she eventually married and left service.

Records for this period are sparse, but it seems likely that Morris was busy through the autumn and the winter with the finding of a site for the building that became Red House. He and Philip Webb were certainly discussing plans for a house for Morris while they were in France: scribbled on the back of a map in Murray's *Guide* was Webb's preliminary sketch of a staircase tower. In autumn 1858 Morris had an illness which his friends attributed to unwise eating. Maybe this was an early version of the kidney trouble that affected him so badly three years later. Certainly he ate with gusto and drank recklessly. Rossetti describes a lunch in London in which three of them had finished three bottles of burgundy before three o'clock.

Through the months of his attachment to Janey and engagement, Burne-Jones had been complaining of Morris's intransigence: 'Jones is going to cut Topsy, he says his overbearing temper is becoming quite insuportable as well as his conceite.' By spring 1859 George Price Boyce came upon him in Oxford in a very wild condition. Boyce had rowed to Godstow with Charles Faulkner and Burne-Jones where they saw '"the Stunner" (the future Mrs. William Morris)'. Afterwards they had all, including Swinburne, dined at Topsy's lodgings. He and Swinburne are described as 'mad and deafening with excitement'. They went on to another friend's lodgings for dessert where 'the chaff and row continued with great spirit and cleverness'.

Was Morris growing apprehensive about marriage? There is no direct evidence for this, but an odd small comment from a friend that Morris had lately 'taken a strong fancy for the human' suggests he was appearing more than normally emotional. The wedding was held on 26 April 1859 in St Michael's parish church in Oxford, an appropriately extraordinary building, with its square and ancient late Anglo-Saxon tower. There is a curious irony that five years before Morris's wedding the church had been restored by his old master G. E. Street. No banns were read; the marriage was conducted by licence. Janey was recorded as living at No. 65 Holywell and Morris at his George Street lodgings. She was described as 'spinster' and 'minor'; her husband as 'Bachelor' and 'Gentleman', aged twenty-five. Janey's father and sister signed the register; no member of Morris's family appears to have attended. The event was peculiarly low-key. Charles Faulkner was best man. Edward Burne-Jones was present but not Georgie. Rossetti too was absent. The ceremony was performed by Richard Watson Dixon, now ordained and a curate at St Mary's, Lambeth. He was warned not to refer to the newly married couple as 'William and Mary', but to the joy of Morris's friends this was exactly what he did.

Janey's ring was not a piece of art jewellery but a plain gold band made commercially, bearing the London hallmark for 1858 and the maker's mark JO, probably James Ogden. Her present from her husband was a double-handled antique silver cup. Another gift to Janey clearly dating from this period is the jewel casket painted by Rossetti and Lizzie Siddal. Was this too a wedding present? It is now at Kelmscott Manor. It takes the form of a compartmented coffer, a Pre-Raphaelite doll's house with a steeply gabled roof. It is adorned with mediaeval scenes of courtship, a homely and more secular version of Hans Memling's exquisitely painted Gothic casket containing the relics of St Ursula in the Hospital of St John in Bruges.

Bruges was on the itinerary for a six-week wedding tour that also took in Paris and the Rhine. Morris had been to Bruges before. His first visit had been made in 1854 with his sister Henrietta. He would go again. 'This place was one of the towns which always gave William Morris pleasure,' Webb remembered. He and Janey stayed at the Hôtel du Commerce, the obvious hotel for discriminating tourists. It was in a splendid old mansion of the town, with a strange and charming central staircase. Each upright took the form of a duck with a multicoloured bulrush in its mouth. No doubt Morris and his wife paid one of Morris's ritual visits to the Béguinage, the religious community of lay sisters living in houses grouped around a central courtyard, a small still citadel within the city. One of the things Morris liked about Bruges was its containment: 'You can walk all round the town by the walls.'

How did the honeymoon work out? Morris's later accounts of Bruges are unemotional with no sense of an underlying trauma, in spite of the fact that he and Janey were allotted the same bedroom in the Hôtel du Commerce when they went to Bruges again in 1874. However, Morris's brusqueness and shyness may well have been a problem, combined with his peculiar jerkiness of movement; and Janey must have found it a struggle to respond to his rushes of enthusiasm for esoteric subjects alien to her. Certainly a strong sense of the difficulties men and women have in timing their approaches to each other, and the despair that can be born of such a struggle, lies at the centre of much of what he wrote.

*

In Morris's magic novel, *The Well at the World's End*, Ursula and Ralph, on their quest together, travel through the wilderness and then over grassy mountains until they arrive at a cliff edge by the ocean. A square stone is engraved with an inscription or 'token', the message that can lead them to happiness and truth:

It was now evening, and the sun was setting beyond them, but they could behold a kind of stair cut in the side of the cliff, and on the first step whereof was the token done; wherefore they knew that they were bidden to go down by the said stair; but it seemed to lead no whither, save straight into the sea.

CHAPTER SIX

Red House
1859–65

'The Towers of Topsy must darken the air by this.' Rossetti, writing in summer 1860, referred to Morris's Red House, then nearing its completion. Philip Webb's building was romantic and dogmatic and, at that time, very startling in its colour: a stranger approaching from a distance would be conscious of 'an immense red-tiled, steep, and high roof'. This was Morris's dream dwelling, the house he described as 'very mediaeval in spirit', based on the architectural style of the thirteenth century. Red House was the ultimate Pre-Raphaelite building and Morris was to live there for the next five years.

The site at Bexleyheath in the small hamlet of Upton ten miles from central London had been chosen by Morris and Webb both for its rurality and its convenience. Morris was fond of modest Kent, not unlike his native Essex but much prettier in its variegated country. Below Red House lay the valley of the Cray with the lovely Darenth valley a little further off.

Morris needed the vista of the river or the hill to offset the claustrophobia that easily attacked him. Historic association was another of his cravings and at nearby Abbey Farm were the remains of an Augustinian priory which Wolsey had suppressed. Red House was also close to the ancient Watling Street, the pilgrims' route to Canterbury: Morris, the devoted Chaucerian, referred to the squat and cosy garden porch at Red House as 'the Pilgrims' Rest'. He continued to curse the iniquities of railways, but he was to make good use of Abbey Wood, his local station, only three miles away on the newly opened North Kent line.

One of the great attractions of the site had been its orchard of apple trees and cherry trees. Red House was envisaged as a house within an orchard and Morris and Webb were delighted to discover a site that could be built on with scarcely any destruction of the trees. The apples at Red House became a kind of legend. There were battles of the apples. Charley Faulkner, on a visit to Red House, was besieged in the store of windfall apples in the attic. He defended himself valiantly against all comers and with a well-aimed apple gave Morris a black eye. On hot autumn nights the ripe apples bounced in through open windows from the overloaded branches right into the house.

Webb designed Red House to be an L-shaped building with two storeys, easily extendable around the four sides of the quadrangle. Meanwhile rose trellises filled in the spaces, forming what was in effect an enclosed garden. For the centre of this courtyard Webb designed a typically idiosyncratic feature, a tall, turreted well-house like a giant candle–snuffer. The plan of the house was for its time unusual: the main living-rooms, the studio and drawing-room, were placed on the first floor, with the bedrooms. The large hall, the dining-room, the library and morning-room were placed more conventionally on the ground floor, with the kitchen. But the kitchen itself was unusually generous, a light and friendly room with its window to the garden. Morris and Webb, embryo Socialists, provided exceptional conditions for the servants. The house is plain and functional, beautiful and homely, with the simple solid structure and respect for its materials that recommended it to modern movement architects in the 1930s, whose paradigm building it became. But Red House is also playful, wilful, an amalgam of surprises, gables, arches, little casements of a size to shoot an arrow through. In another sense it is a touching design, childlike, a house in the Dutch toy-town Morris played with as a boy.

This was Philip Webb's first job as an independent architect. The influence of Street, his old master, is apparent in Red House: in its sturdy masculinity, pitched roofs and Gothic arches. Like all Street's domestic buildings it is almost a church building. Red House is also close in style to the small series of rectories designed by William Butterfield, an architect whom Webb admired to the point of filling sketch books with examples of his buildings. Street and Butterfield had used red brick before Webb's Red House. So had Pugin. In some ways Red House is an obvious instalment in the campaign against stucco and pomposity in building, launched by Pugin more than twenty years before. But Webb, perhaps the most obsessive and original of all Victorian architects, poured into this commission the fruits of his own years of quiet observation and his passion for the English mediaeval. In 1857, for example, he had visited Tattershall Castle in Lincolnshire, built in 1440 for Ralph Cromwell, Lord Treasurer of England. This huge square tower, a magnificent example of early brick building, had excited Webb enormously. He noted in his sketch book: 'The keep is of solid and beautifully built brickwork . . . bricks of a beautiful red.'

For Morris too Red House had the thrill of the induction. Morris was such a devotee of buildings, and was so steeped in architectural terminology, it is surprising to remember that this was in fact the only house he ever built. Red House was to him a deeply symbolic building. It has a monastic quality and an apartness emphasized by the quadrangular structure: like Eric Gill's later Roman Catholic communities, with their workshops and houses ranged around a quadrangle, Morris's Red House is symbolic as an act of separation, the retreat from and defiance of the world. But it is also the place the knights ride out from. Red House's inner courtyard has its Arthurian overtones: it is the departure point for the crusade against the age. For Morris the layout and the detail of his building was, and continued to be, personally expressive. The great tiled, barn-like roof with its weather-vane and turret; the fountain splashing up within the courtyard; the inner porch of welcome; the oak staircase rising steeply through the centre of the building: these are visual images, precise, highly emotive, that recur in Morris's poems. Webb understood his feelings with sensitivity rare in the often troubled histories of architects and clients. Red House was a building that arose in all its splendour from an unusual emotional rapport, almost from the intuitive closeness between lovers. Rossetti recognized its sense of extreme harmony, describing Red House when it was completed as 'a most noble work in every way, and more a poem than a house'.

Whilst the Towers of Topsy began to rise in Kent, Morris and Janey lived in furnished rooms in 41 Great Ormond Street. Webb's office, No. 7, was conveniently near. It was here Edward Burne-Jones took his fiancée Georgiana to see Janey, a meeting still vivid in Georgie's mind as an old lady: 'never shall I forget it – literally I dreamed of her again in the night.'

Janey began appearing a little around London. In January 1860 George Price Boyce came upon her at the Hogarth Club. Morris introduced her. Boyce noted in his diary: 'was surprised at the fine and beautiful character of her face.' William Bell Scott's wife Letitia asked her to a party at which she and Morris made a very brief appearance: Janey kept her bonnet on, ready to depart in a rush to catch a train. Letitia was mystified by her appearance: 'I can't think what countrywoman Mrs Morris is like, not an Englishwoman certainly . . . All we little women looked quite diminutive beside Mrs Morris.' At this party Georgie, 'a very little creature', sang the ballad of Greensleeves 'in loud wild tones quite novel and charming'. In the sub-bohemian setting of their London at this period one has the impression that Janey was socially poised, if appearing shy and silent. Mrs Street, wife of the architect, was kind to her: they shared an interest in embroidery. Janey was also 'taken up' by Mrs Prinsep, her dark and foreign beauty being seen as an additional adornment for Little Holland House. Janey seems a statuesque and rather solitary figure, with Morris preoccupied, impatient, ebullient. This was to be largely the pattern of their life.

Red House took a year to build. It was built in the normal way by a contractor. As construction advanced Morris and Janey moved temporarily to Aberley Lodge, a house close to the site, so that he could keep a strict eye on the progress of his building. Supervision by both architect and client must have struck the contractor as peculiarly keen. There were still some workmen in the building in the June of 1860, an unusually wet summer, when Morris and Janey finally moved in.

One of the most potent images of Red House is of Morris coming up from the cellar before dinner, beaming with joy, with his hands full of bottles of wine and more bottles tucked under his arms. At Red House, aged twenty-six, Morris was in his element, the reincarnation of the mediaeval host. The house swarmed with his friends, who were collected from the station in a horse-drawn wagon with curtains made of leather. This coach, designed by Webb, had been specially built. The Burne-Joneses were among the earliest of Morris's visitors. Georgie remembered in detail the arrival at Abbey Wood Station, 'where a thin fresh air full of sweet smells' greeted them as they walked down the platform; the ride in the wagonette sent from the house to meet them; the pull up the hill and the swing along the road for three miles, past the three or four labourers' cottages known locally as Hog's Hole, a name Rossetti seized on with delight. The wagonette stopped at the gates, Webb's stout oak gates with iron hinges. 'I think Morris must have brought us down from town himself,' wrote Georgie, 'for I can see the tall figure of a girl standing alone in the porch to receive us.'

The dynamics of the group of Morris's friends had altered greatly by the time Red House was completed. The young and single people, the fiancées and suitors, were now regrouped as married couples. In June 1860 Ned and Georgie had been married in Manchester. It was four years to the day since their engagement. The long, tense, introspective love of Lizzie and Rossetti had ended in their marriage too, the month before, in Hastings. Lizzie, increasingly addicted to laudanum, had seemed to be dying. Rossetti was stricken with affection and remorse. In the glow of emotion he had written to his mother: 'Like all the important things I ever meant to do – to fulfil duty or secure happiness – this one has been deferred almost beyond possibility.' He had hardly deserved that Lizzie should consent to it. Rossetti, married, with the new zeal of the convert, remained the absent presence in the *ménage* at Red House.

Ned and Georgie were at Red House through the summer and into early autumn. It was a working holiday, the first stage in Morris's plans for making Red House 'the beautifullest place on earth'. Rossetti, left in London, grumbled that not only was Morris out of reach at Upton but that Burne-Jones was with him 'painting the inner walls of the house that Top built'. Burne-Jones had embarked on a mural in tempera for the drawing-room. This was based on the fifteenth-century romance of Sir Degrevaunt, one of four Thornton Romances edited for the Camden Society in 1844 and always a great favourite of Morris's: the Kelmscott Press produced its own edition, with a woodcut by Burne-Jones, in the year after Morris's death. The mural was designed as a sequence of seven paintings; in the event three only were completed. The Red House walls were new and not prepared to take the tempera: the colour soon faded and the pictures became patchy. Technical lessons of the Oxford Union débâcle had not been learned. But enough remains of the paintings to see their spirit. This too was much like Oxford. They emanate from the same close-knit community, conveying secret messages. They are paintings of peculiar intimacy. The scene of the wedding feast includes Burne-Jones's portrait of Morris as the king, in deep blue robe with gold borders. Beside him is Janey in a wimple, crowned as queen.

The Red House drawing-room is large, spectacular and barn-like with its extended height and exposed beams. It is a romantic room and multi-purpose, prefiguring Morris's later theory that, in the best of worlds, life would be lived simply in one huge and lovely room. Its focus is Webb's red-brick fireplace looming vastly and inscribed ARS LONGA

VITA BREVIS. At Red House Burne-Jones and Morris entered a more overtly classical phase. The settle from Red Lion Square was installed in the great drawing-room, and extended ingeniously with a ladder and a parapet to a little door above which led into the roof. This home-made minstrels' galley was meant for Christmas concerts, a throwback to Morris's childhood Christmases at Walthamstow. The three upper doors of the settle had been decorated by Rossetti with his 'Dantis Amor' paintings of the meeting of Dante and Beatrice on earth and then in paradise; the central panel, with its red-haired, red-winged angel, was removed and is now in the Tate Gallery. Burne-Jones sketched in another painting on an inside shutter. This time it was a scene from the *Niebelungenlied*.

Morris painted on the wall below Burne-Jones's mural a tempera imitation of a hanging, a version of those he must have noticed on his continental travels. He painted a design of bushy trees and parrots interspersed with a heraldic pattern of small pennons bearing his motto 'If I can'. Rossetti, on a visit to Red House, found the spaces not yet filled in by Morris irresistible. He added his own version of the motto, 'If I can't'.

Janey and Morris worked together on the painting of the ceiling in the drawing-room. Charley Faulkner arrived to help paint patterns on walls as well as ceilings. Morris began a painting, never completed, on the panels of Webb's canopied cupboard in the hall. The two panels are designed to be read through, as a narrative. The models for the figures, the four men and the six women, are the people of his household: Charley Faulkner, Janey, Ned and Georgie, Lizzie Siddal in their mediaeval poses. The scene is Arthurian, Morris's reworking of a convivial scene from Malory in which Sir Lancelot brings Sir Tristram and La Belle Iseult to the castle of Joyous Gard. The ensemble is charming, though a little stiffly painted. The scene is an open-air one, in the garden of the castle with its fruit trees and its daisies, a Pre-Raphaelite version of *'Déjeuner sur l'herbe'*. This may have been the unfinished cabinet referred to by Dr Furnivall, the founder of the Chaucer Society, who visited Red House and complained about the colours, in particular the yellow and the 'London mud' colour. Morris dismissed this brusquely: 'Don't be a damned fool!'

He and Janey collaborated on the Red House textiles. 'Top has taken to worsted work,' Rossetti jeered. Janey had found by chance in a London shop some indigo-dyed blue serge which had, for Morris, the attraction of the commonplace. It was, as Janey noted, 'material such as can be bought in any shop in any street'. When she brought the blue serge home Morris was delighted with it, setting to work at once designing flowers. The result was an early version of Morris's 'Daisy' pattern, based upon the clump-of-flowers motif he discovered in a British Museum Froissart manuscript. Morris used it in many permutations: as a wallpaper it was lastingly popular, until well into the twentieth century, especially for maids' rooms and the bedrooms of young girls. The pattern appears at its best as an embroidery: the sweet and naïve flowers in white, red and yellow, standing out well against the depth of the blue background. Janey wrote 'The work went quickly and when finished we covered the walls of the bedroom at Red House.'

Morris was a more experienced embroiderer than she was, though evidently Janey had a natural aptitude. 'Morris was a pleased man when he found that his wife could embroider any design that he made, and did not allow her talent to remain idle,' as Georgie rather acidly observed. He taught both women what stitches to use and how to place them. According to Janey, Morris showed her 'the first principle of laying the stitches together closely so as to cover the ground smoothly and radiating them properly afterwards'. Together they built up their knowledge of techniques by unpicking old embroideries. Morris was himself the prime mover in this craft revival. Janey wrote in retrospect of her husband's 'enormous energy and perseverance', in an admiring, perhaps slightly weary tone. There is a skill in the giving of instructions that is itself a kind of creativity. Georgie's experience was that Morris's instructions 'could not be improved upon and that disaster followed their neglect'.

Under Morris's aegis an ambitious scheme developed to decorate the dining-room at Red House with a frieze of figures, each three feet high, embroidered on plain linen, then cut out and stitched on to a background of silk velvet, in the manner of mediaeval embroidered appliqués. Only seven, maybe eight, of these panels were completed. They are all of female heroines, based by Morris rather freely on Chaucer's poem *The Legend of Good Women*. Three are preserved at Castle Howard, assembled as a screen. These are warrior women, bearing swords, spears, flaming torches. They look like fiercer versions of Lizzie Siddal, with their floating manes of auburn hair.

Morris had intended that the embroidered ladies should be linked by symbolic trees. St Catherine, the figure now at Kelmscott Manor, is in fact the only heroine to have her tree beside her. At least she allows us to envisage the effect, and to see how in their period Morris's ideal women looked *outré* and rather awkward. Janey, writing to Rossetti years later, is dismissive about the embroideries of this Red House period on which she had worked with her sister Bessie Burden: 'I had some hand in one of the figures, the other was Bessie's, the two were mounted on a piece of brick-red serge with a comic tree, and tufts of grass at the feet. They were our first rough attemps at the kind of work, I should hate to see the thing about again.' It is interesting that Morris himself uses the same tone in an account written in the 1880s, where he dismissed as 'exceedingly young . . . very medieval' the poems in *The Defence of Guenevere*.

How original was Red House? It was clearly a far cry from the Victorian bourgeois norm described by Morris's friend F. S. Ellis as 'the hideousness of deal doors painted and grained to look like oak or maple, staircases covered with mustard-coloured paper, and squared in blocks to imitate some sort of marble that never existed, hangings usually of a dull heavy rep, and, in the wealthier houses, stuffs equally ugly, if more costly, varied in summer by preposterous sham lace, black horsehair chairs, ponderous yellow mahogany sideboards, and flock wall-papers'. But, seen broadly in the context of architects' interiors of the period, Red House was by no means a revolutionary building. It was not a light and bright house but a complicated dense one, not so different in character from Pugin's elaborately Gothic interiors of the decade before. In terms of a rethinking of volume, form and function, it was less of a departure than E. W. Godwin's Japanese-style furniture of the later 1860s or his minimalist studios in Chelsea. When it comes to artistic aplomb Red House is tentative compared with William Burges's full-blown extravaganzas of the 1870s at Cardiff Castle and Castell Coch. What it has is an extreme visual integrity, a flow of living-spaces, a sense of human scale and human possibilities. It is a building that inspires and enfolds.

We have to wait until well into the twentieth century to find the closest counterpart to Red House. This is Charleston, the farmhouse in Sussex lived in and compulsively decorated by Vanessa Bell and Duncan Grant, their friends and colleagues, from 1916 right up to the 1960s. With its painted walls and furniture, embroideries and textiles, Charleston, similarly, radiates an excitable and a very English artistic amateurism, in which life and art are inextricably merged.

It was this impetuosity, a rawness in technique, that made Red House so startling. The first sight of Red House 'gave me an astonished pleasure', wrote a visitor in 1863, listing out the elements that struck him as 'vividly picturesque and uniquely original': the deep red colour of the brick, the huge tiled roof, the small-paned mediaeval windows, low wide porch and massive door, the sweetbriars in the garden, orchard walks and gnarled old fruit trees. What made it look so different was its *ad hoc* quality, the build-up of elements to form a personal collage. The primitivism of Red House was strangely moving. When William Bell Scott first saw the vast empty hall at Upton, 'painted coarsely in bands of wild foliage over both wall and ceiling', he could scarcely believe his eyes. The execution seemed 'bizarre' to Bell Scott, himself a painter: 'if one had been told it was the South Sea Island style of thing one could have easily believed such to be the case'.

The old Oxford Union badinage was revived at Red House, with bowls along the green alley in the garden and bear fights in the drawing-room. In the middle of one scrimmage Faulkner came flying down from the minstrels' gallery, crashing to the floor with an astounding thud. It was a cheerful time for Morris, always at his safest with too much work to do and a crowd of friends to share it. He allowed himself to drift into his old role of victim: Burne-Jones boiled the thermometer, to trick Morris into thinking the weather even hotter; they sewed up his waistcoat to make him appear fatter, bursting out of his buttons like a greedy Tom Kitten; at whist, Burne-Jones and Faulkner doctored a pack of cards. Morris beamed to see his hand at first; then he lost everything. He bellowed 'You fellows have been at it again!' Janey was drawn into the most cruel of these jokes, which was sending Morris to Coventry at his own table. Faulkner and Burne-Jones would refuse to say a word to him, communicating only through his wife.

A Red House routine evolved. In the morning Janey and Georgiana were busy with their needlework or wood engraving. In the afternoons they went out on drives around the country, taking a map of Kent, and returning with accounts of their adventures to the men left working at home. There were evening amusements: hide-and-seek was played at Red House. Georgie described Janey in her role as seeker, searching out Ned along dark mediaeval corridors: 'I see her tall figure and her beautiful face as she creeps slowly nearer and nearer to the room where she feels sure he must be, and at last I hear her startled cry and her peal of laughter as he bursts from his hiding place.' On sedater evenings they

7 *'Back view of William Morris'*, caricature by Edward Burne-Jones, depicting him as the outcast.

collected round the piano for songs, mostly the old English songs published by Chappell and what Georgie called the 'inexhaustible' *Chants du Temps Passé*.

These early days at Red House surely remain in the 'blindsight' of Morris's proposals in his 1880s' lectures, 'How we Live and How we Might Live'. He envisages as the ideal way of living the 'noble communal hall' where people work together and enjoy each other's company. In that lecture Morris defines true domesticity: 'It is not an original remark, but I make it here, that my home is where I meet people with whom I sympathise, whom I love.' He dwells in vivid detail on ideas of work as pleasure: how in an ideal future 'people would rather be anxious to seek work than avoid it; that our working hours would rather be merry parties of men and maids, young men and old enjoying themselves over their work, than the grumpy weariness it mostly is now'. In this new and smiling world men and women work together. No sexism, no ageism. There are memories of Red House inherent in this too.

Deep in Morris's mediaevalism was his image of woman as co-worker. The idea of the woman at work on the cathedral, as expressed in his 'Story of the Unknown Church', was aesthetically pleasing and sexually compelling, if historically suspect. For the first time at Red House Morris was surrounded by women with artistic aspirations of their own.

163

Georgie, for example, went to wood-engraving classes before she married Ned; she arrived at their first lodgings with a small deal table in the drawer of which she kept her own wood-engraving tools. An obituary described her work as delicate and distinguished, though small in quantity. Rossetti's wife Lizzie was an artist of more formidable powers, a protégée of Ruskin's whose peculiar talents had burgeoned with Rossetti's encouragement. Lizzie Siddal's status was at least semi-professional: she had exhibited with the Pre-Raphaelites publicly. Ford Madox Brown acknowledged her as 'a real artist, a woman without parallel for many a long year'. This is not to say that Red House offered equal opportunities. Georgie's later verdict is probably the true one: 'It is pathetic to think how we women longed to keep pace with the men, and how gladly they kept us with them until their pace quickened and we had to fall behind.' The reasons for their failure to pursue their talents further were the usual ones for women of their period: for Georgie and Janey children intervened, family life, responsibilities of housekeeping. There was also the psychological aspect. Georgie and Janey bowed to the concept of the master talent, as so often in artistic households of that time. But at the very least at Red House there was an unusual empathy between the sexes, the result of shared activities. There was more cosiness, more sense of possibility, more freedom than in the formal households of Morris's family.

At Red House the women dressed in flowing garments. Agnes, Georgie's more conventional sister, teased Janey for the gloom of her Pre-Raphaelite colours, and complained that the doors at Red House were too narrow for her to pass through in her crinolines. The clashes in style between his old world and his new world must have borne in upon Morris in September 1860, only a few weeks after moving into Red House, when he went to give away his sister Isabella. The bridegroom was a naval lieutenant, Arthur Hamilton Gilmore, ten years her senior. The marriage took place in the parish church at Leyton. Isabella wore a wedding dress of Honiton lace with a train twelve yards long.

The garden at Red House had been preplanned and preplanted so that it looked mature before Morris's arrival. Climbing plants, already marked on Webb's elevational drawings, were trained up the red-brick walls: white jasmine, roses, honeysuckle and the passion flower. The jasmine reappears in the earliest of Morris's original designs for textiles, the 'Jasmine Trail' cotton of 1868. The flower beds were bordered with lavender and rosemary. There were midsummer lilies; in the autumn there were sunflowers. Burne-Jones adored the sunflowers: 'Do you know what faces they have – how they peep and peer, and look arch and winning, or bold and a little insolent sometimes? Have you ever noticed their back-hair, how beautifully curled it is?' The poppies too inspired him. He arrived at breakfast one morning with the drawing of a poppy done at dawn.

In one sense the inner garden at Red House was quite formal: a large square subdivided into four smaller square gardens, each with its wattled fence and an opening leading from one garden to another. Roses grew thickly all over the trellis in the summer, forming a succession of floral arbours in a delicate domestic mediaeval style. Red House seems to have had the first Victorian example of 'square-plot and trained-hedge' garden. Morris believed that a garden, one of the necessities for civilized existence, should be both mysterious and familiar, evocative and homely. He set out these principles in 'Making the Best of It', a lecture given in 1879:

large and small, it should look both orderly and rich. It should be well fenced from the outside world. It should by no means imitate either the wilfulness or wildness of nature, but should look like a thing never to be seen except near a house. It should in fact look like part of a house.

In all his latter pronouncements about gardens Morris harks back to his own original garden in north Kent. At Red House the garden literally flows into the building. Morris's insistence on the integration of the garden and the building encouraged a new movement in English garden design. He influenced the theorists: there are many signs of Morris in William Robinson's *The English Flower Garden* (1883); J. D. Sedding's *Garden Craft Old and New* (1891); Reginald Blomfield's *The Formal Garden in England* (1892). The Arts and Crafts garden, in its careful balance of lushness and decorum, owes much to William Morris. Without Morris in fact would there have been a Gertrude Jekyll? One might argue Morris's garden was more influential than his house.

At Red House there were successions of spaces within spaces. From Morris's studio, with its windows facing in three directions, vistas opened out over the garden and the countryside. Through the little horizontal slit over the doorway birds could be observed as they hopped around the red-tiled roof. In one corner of the garden there were stables, with stalls for the horses; the stables, wrote Georgie, had 'a kind of younger-brother look' in relation to the house. At the front and the back of Red House there were deep porches. The porch at the back, almost itself a garden room, contained a solid table, painted red, and a bench along the wall on which people would sit, looking out on to the well-court and the roses on the trellis. These were the perfect places, as in Morris's romances, for conversation, courtship, the intimate exchange. Here one morning, sitting sewing with Janey, Georgie saw in her basket 'a strange garment – fine, small and shapeless – a little shirt for him or her'. It transpired that Janey had been pregnant since the spring. Lizzie too by now was pregnant. Georgie felt a certain tremor as she viewed the little garment: 'looking at my friend's face I knew that she had been happy when she made it; but it was a sign of change'.

In January 1861 in London George Price Boyce, the painter, called in to see Burne-Jones, finding him at work on a pen-and-ink drawing of Childe Roland. Burne-Jones told Boyce that 'he and Morris and Rossetti and Webb were going to set up a sort of shop where they would jointly produce and sell painted furniture'. These were the beginnings of Morris & Co.

As originally constituted the firm was Morris, Marshall, Faulkner & Co., and there were seven partners: Ford Madox Brown, Charles Faulkner and Peter Paul Marshall in addition to the members listed by Burne-Jones. 'The Firm', as it was often colloquially referred to, started business on 11 April 1861. Each of the partners held one twenty-pound share, of which one pound was initially called on, and each member was expected to produce at his own expense at least one or two items for stock. Because of the dwindling success of Devon Great Consols Morris's own finances were now relatively straitened. For the start of trading William Morris's mother provided a hundred-pound loan.

The firm that became the best-known decorating business in Victorian Britain, and a byword for good taste amongst the intellectual classes, began in a small way, though with large views of its potential. It has often been claimed that the Morris firm arose from Morris's own struggles in the furnishing of Red House, and certainly Webb and Morris's experience confirmed their worst fears about the problems of finding furnishings of an acceptable standard ready-made. But this was a subject on which Morris had been fulminating since Oxford; in some ways the idea had predated the house. In April 1861 he wrote to his old tutor F. B. Guy, now the headmaster of Bradfield College, eliciting support for his new enterprise, explaining: 'You will see that I have started as a decorator which I have long meant to do when I could get men of reputation to join me, and to this end mainly I have built my fine house.' Over the relative input of the individual partners there were eventually to be bitter quarrels. Morris showed no sign of doubt that he had always been prime mover in an enterprise he defined less as a modest exercise in artistic shopkeeping, more a full-blown movement of national reform. He later wrote of his perception that all the minor arts were in a state of 'complete degradation', especially in England; 'and accordingly in 1861 with the conceited courage of a young man I set myself to reforming all that.'

Morris could not have been unaware of the official debates on art and manufacture. These had been trundling on since 1835 when Sir Robert Peel's Tory administration, aware of decreasing exports and conscious of the inadequacies of British products in comparison with French ones, formed Mr Ewart's Select Committee 'to enquire into the best means of extending a knowledge of the arts and principles of design among the people (especially the manufacturing population) of the country'. This committee had sat for almost a year, collecting evidence from industrialists, critics and artists themselves. A subsequent 350-page report had stressed as one of the causes of the problem 'the want of instruction in design among our industrious population', and it was in the aftermath of Mr Ewart that the network of national art schools was set up.

Morris must also have known of Henry Cole and Summerly's Art Manufactures of the 1840s. Cole, later Sir Henry, was an indefatigable reformer by committee. The term 'the great and the good' might have been invented for Cole, the instigator of the 1851 Great Exhibition, Director of the Department of Science and Art, and a founder of the South Kensington Museum, precursor of the Victoria and Albert Museum. Under the pseudonym of Felix Summerly, Cole had produced designs in china for Minton's. The success of his Minton's tea set had encouraged him, in 1847, to form a small creative group of painters, sculptors, architects, whose aim was to revive 'the good old practice of connecting the best Art with familiar objects in daily use'. These artists included John Bell, William Dyce, George Wallis, John Callcott Horsley, Richard Redgrave, Owen Jones, Matthew Digby Wyatt. Cole drove them on and almost a hundred items, proposed prototypes for industrial production, were assembled at the third annual Exhibition of British Manufactures at the Society of Arts in 1848.

There are obvious parallels of scope and intention between Summerly and Morris, not least that Cole's group too was a gathering of visually orientated friends. Morris's life-long silence about Cole and his endeavours reflects perhaps three things. First, stylistic difference: the Art Manufactures were ornate in a classical mode Morris always found abhorrent. When Morris chose to be ornate it was in a mediaeval way. Next, the Summerly designers operated merely on the fringes of production, as providers of a service; Morris and his partners saw *themselves* as the makers, or at least as supervisors, immersed in the actual production of what they had designed. Finally, even at this stage, Morris was temperamentally suspicious of the mainstream. Summerly was essentially an establishment enterprise, attempting to reform from inside, working out. Morris's instinct was the opposite: the maverick instinct of reforming by upsetting. With his 'conceited courage' he set out to demonstrate the things that could be done. He felt art, the very life-blood of the nation, too important to be left to institutions and committees. Considering the record of effectiveness of twentieth-century attempts at reformation – the British Institute of Industrial Art of the 1920s; the Council for Art and Industry of the 1930s; the Council of Industrial Design, later transmuted into the Design Council – it could be claimed that history has proved him right.

It was the spirit not of Henry Cole but Ruskin that pervaded Morris's venture. In the Red Lion Square days Morris and Burne-Jones had first met their Oxford hero who befriended them, seized on Burne-Jones's drawings, called them his 'dear boys'. Burne-Jones was ecstatic at the way Ruskin seemed to treat them as his equals: 'Oh! he is so good and kind – better than his books, which are the best books in the world.' In 1860 Ruskin had written *Unto This Last*, his most passionate diatribe against the aridities of Britain, the social divisiveness, the ugliness of cities, the iniquities of luxury. Ruskin was not opposing luxury itself. Like Morris he was a connoisseur of excellence. But he fulminated against élitist luxury, in which the whole population could not share. Ruskin dwelt at some length on conditions of production, insisting that employers should respect their workmen, deal fairly with them and try earnestly to love them. His close and fiercely argued attack on the whole structure of mid-nineteenth-century England, an indictment of the brutalizing cycles of contemporary commerce, was initially serialized in the *Cornhill*, Thackeray's new popular monthly magazine. Here it was considered so potentially inflammatory that, to Ruskin's rage, the fifth instalment was refused.

'How deadly dull the world would have been twenty years ago but for Ruskin.' In Morris's mind Ruskin was indelibly connected with his own early adult decades of activity and hopefulness in which he began to discover his true *métier* and channel his developing sense of social injustices. 'It was through him that I learned to give form to my discontent, which I must say was not by any means vague.' Morris, Marshall, Faulkner & Co. was conceived as an opposition movement: anti-boredom, anti-pomposity, against the inane luxuries that Ruskin had decried. The radical principle of products designed by the people for the people underlay their early plans. They deliberately set themselves up as the alternative to the fashionable firm of J. G. Crace, decorator to the aristocracy, whose High Renaissance suites of rooms at Windsor Castle were the obvious example of the style the Firm deplored. As Rossetti stated clearly right at the beginning, in a letter dated January 1861, 'We are not intending to compete with Crace's costly rubbish or anything of that sort, but to give real good taste at the price if possible of ordinary furniture, we expect to start in some shape about May or June.'

Philip Webb said the early affairs of the Firm were carried out 'like a picnic'. The image reminds one of the scene in *News from Nowhere* in which the gang of road menders look like 'a boating party at Oxford', out for a jaunt with a large basket of cold pie and wine. There was certainly an aura of clubbability in the premises at No. 8 Red Lion Square, so close to Morris's old lodgings, into which the Firm had moved in April 1861. They got back into the swing of victimizing Topsy: once a roll parcel arrived for him made totally of wrapping, the wrapping being gummed through to the core. Faulkner described the meetings held once or twice a fortnight as having more of 'the character of a meeting of the "Jolly Masons" or the jolly something elses' than of a meeting to discuss a business.

Beginning at 8 or 9 p.m. they open with the relation of anecdotes which have been culled by members of the firm since the last meeting – this store being exhausted, Topsy and Brown will perhaps discuss the relative merits of the art of the thirteenth and fifteenth century, and then perhaps after a few more anecdotes business matters will come up about 10 or 11 o'clock and be furiously discussed till 12, 1 or 2.

Work spilled over to the weekends. Red House became an outpost of Red Lion Square. But here too there were temptations and digressions.

Faulkner described a visit there in which 'the day was so beautiful and there was so much to do in the way of playing bowls and smoking pipes that the day passed without leaving time to do anything'.

In its moods of relentless jocularity, its maleness, the Firm had much in common with other second-generation Pre-Raphaelite groupings. Morris had been a member of the Hogarth Club, a social club for artists and architects and writers, their clients and their friends: its inaugural meeting was held in Morris's and Burne-Jones's lodgings in 1858. He had joined the Medieval Society, with Webb, Ford Madox Brown and the leading Gothic-revival architects.

More improbably, in view of his later anti-militarist stance, Morris was a member of the Corps of Artist Volunteers, formed in 1859, a time of real fears of an invasion of England by the French following Napoleon III's annexation of Nice and Savoy. Burne-Jones joined the Corps, as did Ford Madox Brown, Rossetti, Leighton, Millais, Holman Hunt, G. F. Watts: an unlikely line-up, parading through London in their uniforms of grey and silver. Morris was not a malleable soldier, tending to turn right when commanded to turn left, then invariably apologizing to the comrade he found himself facing. This lack of co-ordination was possibly connected with his epileptic tendencies. William Richmond, Hon. Secretary of the Corps, remembered it as being 'supremely comical'. But unlike Rossetti Morris was conscientious in attending drills and camps and was under canvas at Wimbledon on the night of the great Tooley Street fire, near London Bridge. Looking out from his tent Morris could see the sky burning scarlet from the conflagration ten miles away.

To an unusual extent Morris was dependent upon these male networks. He felt lost without his henchmen. He was willing to settle for a role of some indignity, as the group buffoon, if this ensured stability and generated jollity. With his perilously nervous disposition Morris needed a cushioning of noisy bonhomie. All his life, even through his Socialist period, he clung to his familar male groupings. They formed and reformed around him, with some changes in the membership, always keeping a core of Morris's familiar faces. In the Firm, Burne-Jones and Charley Faulkner were still with him, and in touch with Crom Price, who had travelled to St Petersburg to tutor the sons of Count Orloff-Davidoff. The Firm was essentially a recreation of Morris's Oxford Set, with the same male gruffnesses, the emotional reticence, the sense of a shared language, the dependence on tradition. When Morris came to study the Icelandic Sagas, with their extreme male bondings, he was not on such strange ground.

But, although the Firm was formed by and revolved around its friendships, to view it as an amateur concern would be a mistake. It was properly constituted, with a quite professional attentiveness to aims and methods. Though the Jolly Masons' element is obviously present, the minutes of the Firm suggest much close discussion about job allocation and progressing of work. Charley Faulkner had now resigned his mathematics tutorship, together with his Fellowship at Oxford, to come to London to study civil engineering; he spent his mornings in the sewers. The first modern sewage system was then under way in London. Then, to complaints that he reached Red Lion Square stinking, he turned his attention to the business of the Firm. From 1862 Faulkner was one of the two salaried partners, the part-time general manager. One of his responsibilities was the producing of accounts. The other administrative partner in the Firm was Morris, appointed business manager at a salary of £150 per year.

In spite of his Ruskinian misgivings about commerce Morris had a particular stake in the success of the Firm. He had spent about £4,000 on the building of Red House at a time when his income from his shares in Devon Great Consols had reduced itself, from £819 in 1857 and £780 in 1858, to £572 in 1859. He was conscious of his duty in the support of his family: the Victorian consciousness of family responsibility was always strong in Morris, even in his revolutionary Socialist years. More than any other of the partners he regarded the Firm as a full commitment, seeing it as the basis for his future. To raise capital for the Firm he sold off shares in Devon Great Consols, one in 1861 and one in 1862, dismaying his family who thought him 'both wicked and mad' to divest himself of his inheritance. His mother made sure the shares were kept within the family by buying Morris out, transferring the ownership to Morris's brother Stanley. Morris's insistence on providing the Firm with a viable financial basis shows he had already learned a painful lesson: that only a measure of commercial success could allow him to do the work he wanted in the way he chose to do it. This was to prove the great dilemma of his life.

In the early weeks, in April 1861, a prospectus was sent out around all likely clients. Foreseeing how much trade might arise from the new churches being built on the wave of Anglo-Catholic expansion, a Clergy

List was purchased on the Firm's behalf. The circular is headed 'Morris, Marshall, Faulkner & Co., Fine Art Workmen in Painting, Carving, Furniture, and the Metals'. Arthur Hughes, one of the painters of the Oxford Union, is included in the original alphabetical list of partners of the Firm although he had 'rather despaired of its establishment' and had by this time asked to be released. The tone of the prospectus is that uneasy mixture of the unctuous and businesslike found in so many of the manifestos of the later workshops of the Arts and Crafts. It lays out its principles, tactfully asserting that 'The growth of Decorative Art in this country owing to the effort of English Architects has now reached a point at which it seems desirable that Artists of reputation should devote their time to it'. The circular then dwells upon the Firm's great pool of talent, stressing the aesthetic and financial benefits of teamwork in achieving stylistic consistency and minimizing expense.

The prospectus arrives at a grand climax of persuasiveness.

These Artists having been for many years deeply attached to the study of the Decorative Arts of all time and countries, have felt more than most people the want of some one place, where they could either obtain or get produced work of a genuine and beautiful character. They have therefore now established themselves as a firm, for the production, by themselves, and under their supervision, of:

    I Mural Decoration, either in Pictures or in Pattern Work, or merely in the arrangement of Colours as applied to dwelling-houses, churches or public buildings.

   II Carving generally, as applied to Architecture.

  III Stained Glass, especially with reference to its harmony with Mural Decoration.

  IV Metal Work in all its branches, including Jewellery.

   V Furniture, either depending for its beauty on its own design, or on the application of materials hitherto overlooked, or on its conjuncture with Figure and Pattern Painting. Under this head is included Embroidery of all kinds, Stamped Leather, and ornamental work in other such materials, besides every article necessary for domestic use.

In arriving at this list the Firm was drawing on considerable resources of skill and of experience. As painters Madox Brown and Rossetti were already well established. Brown, then forty, was, as indeed he seemed, much the oldest of the partners, the most productive and high powered. His work dominated the exhibitions of the Hogarth Club and he had already designed stained glass for James Powell & Sons. It has been said that the Firm was his original suggestion. Certainly in the early months of operation he assumed the role of its *éminence grise*. Brown had the weight and the artistic authority for whatever mural decoration might be offered. Rossetti, Burne-Jones and William Morris also had between them their extensive, if not wholly successful, experience of the painting of murals at the Oxford Union and more recently Red House.

Philip Webb was an exceptionally knowledgeable architect whose technical skills were rooted, like Morris's, in his fascination with materials. His range extended to furniture, metalwork and glass. For Red House he had designed a collection of table glass with coloured decoration: wavy-edged waterglasses, goblets with trailed decoration and twisted stems. He had also designed brass candlesticks that Rossetti complained were too heavy to pick up. His sketch books for this period are full of details for stained glass, tiles, little objects. Of all the Morris partners his interests were the broadest and his creative powers in many ways the rarest, swerving from the commonsensical to the recondite.

In stained glass Burne-Jones had had the most experience. He had already designed the stained-glass panels for Red House: Fate, with the bandaged eyes, holding aloft the wheel of fortune; Love crowned, whilst tongued flames lick greedily around about him. Burne-Jones had also carried out some large commissions in the years before the Firm was formed and he had evolved a distinctive style. The 'Tower of Babel' window designed for Bradfield College; the 'St Frideswide' window in the Latin Chapel in Christ Church Cathedral, Oxford; the 'Tree of Jesse' window at Waltham Abbey: they show Burne-Jones already in action in the vertical, creating swirls of movement with a precocious skill. These are tall and crowded windows; clear strong scenes of great activity; they pullulate with people, in their scarlets, greens and purples, people gaping at processions, people joining in the feast. It is noticeable that these early Burne-Jones windows, made by James Powell & Sons, are more vibrant in their colour than his Morris windows of later years.

Of the Firm's assembled partners Charley Faulkner and Peter Paul Marshall have the weakest of credentials. But Faulkner, since Oxford, had been proving himself willing to be swept into the action, painting walls and pricking out the decoration for the ceilings. This involved stamping the plaster with small dotted holes while it was still wet. He was to be drawn into firing the glass in the basement at Red Lion Square. The amiable rubicund Scot, Peter Paul Marshall, referred to by

Georgie as 'Big Peter Paul', was a professional surveyor and sanitary engineer, a part-time painter with many Pre-Raphaelite connections. He was married to the daughter of John Miller, an enthusiastic Liverpudlian patron, and was a particular friend of Madox Brown. His artistic talent would never prove a strong one. A small sequence of oil paintings illustrating George Eliot's *Scenes of Clerical Life* were his only known works surviving in 1992. But in the general mood of optimism Marshall was entrusted with a dozen or so minor stained-glass windows in the first churches decorated by the Firm.

The Firm used the first floor of the house at Red Lion Square for its offices and showroom. In the attics on the third floor were the workshops. Rossetti referred to the building as 'the Topsaic laboratory'. The Firm also occupied part of the basement. A furnace was built in what was once the kitchen for firing glass for stained-glass windows and firing the tiles. Plain white tiles were imported from Holland and coloured by hand using enamel paint before being fired again at Red Lion Square. The ground floor of the building had an independent tenant, a jeweller who was sometimes called upon to make the jewellery that Philip Webb designed. Some at least of the furniture was not made at Red Lion Square but farmed out to a local cabinet maker, Mr Curwen. Similarly Webb's table glass was manufactured at Whitefriars Glassworks by James Powell & Sons and ordered as required. Red Lion Square was an assembly point as well as a workshop, a busy, complex centre of ideas and activities.

Families and friends were drawn into it. Charley Faulkner's sisters, Lucy and Kate, helped to paint wistful scenes of fairytale and legend on to tiles designed to decorate fireplaces and entrance porches. Georgiana Burne-Jones painted some of these tiles too. Janey and her sister supervised a group of women embroidering designs on to silk and cloth. A Morris speciality was very mediaeval wallhangings, highly coloured wool embroideries of flowers and figures on a background of coarse and dark-toned serge supplied by a manufacturer in Yorkshire. These were a development of the blue serge hangings invented for Red House. Morris always seized on labour wherever he could find it. He infected his brother-artists with his own enthusiasm. Designs for glass and tiles were made by Albert Moore, Simeon Solomon and by William De Morgan, whose own production of tiles would soon eclipse the Firm's.

The extent to which all this was social experiment is hard to gauge exactly. There were certainly several Pre-Raphaelite precedents. G. E.

Street and his wife worked together on embroideries; Street's sister had founded the Ladies' Ecclesiastical Embroidery Society in 1854. But it seems that the members of the Firm worked alongside wives and sisters to a then unprecedented extent, and in the exhilaration of accounts of Red House and Red Lion Square there is a certain sense of daring. As in Roger Fry's Omega Workshops from 1913 onwards, and even the craft communities of the 1960s, the sense of emancipation was as personal as it was artistic. These were young people conscious of the breaking of new ground.

Morris was also now, with a new blatancy, challenging accepted social patterns by involving himself in the processes of handwork. In the mid-Victorian period this was far from being the usual role of the educated man. Here and there, among the thinking classes, the people who read Ruskin, the subject was raised and would be cogitated over. In *Felix Holt, the Radical* (1866) George Eliot drew a hero who, although educated, deliberately chose the life of an artisan. The division of society into workmen, who used their hands, and gentlemen, who did not, was viewed by the acute as a cause of social evil, perpetrating class antagonisms. This was a debate into which Morris now flung himself with vigour, painting tiles and stitching hangings, demonstrating, remonstrating, combining the craftsman and the impresario. Descriptions of Morris in action at Red Lion Square remind one of his later years of Socialist flurry. In these early days of hope he did not deny the irony. He enjoyed the incongruity of poetry and commerce, saying that the Firm kept a poet just like Moses & Son.

At Morris, Marshall, Faulkner & Co. familiar faces were supplemented by some outside labour. At the end of 1861 five men and boys were in regular employment. A year later there were twelve. The boys were recruited from the Industrial Home for Destitute Boys in Euston Road. This had been set up in 1858, in that era of politico-social concern, to teach trades to youths who otherwise had little future. The connecting link was Colonel W. J. Gillum, a veteran of the Crimean War, who was on the boys' home management committee. It was Browning who originally introduced him to Rossetti. Gillum was one of Philip Webb's earliest clients. His destitute boys made some of Webb's early furniture, including probably the huge, heavy round table now at Kelmscott Manor. In recruiting his craftsmen Morris favoured the untutored. Where successful, such appointments bolstered his conviction that art and skill is latent, ready to be drawn out of the least superficially promising of people. This was to be one of the chief tenets of the Arts and Crafts workshops and it explains their often eclectic mix of members ranging from the ex-Whitechapel cat's-meat barrow boys to the Masters of the Art Workers' Guild.

Sometimes Morris had particular need of a professional. For Red Lion Square George Campfield was recruited. Campfield had worked as a glass painter with the reputable stained-glass manufacturer, Heaton, Butler & Bayne. He had enrolled in the evening classes at the Working Men's College in Great Ormond Street, where Morris first encountered him. Campfield was still employed by the Firm, as foreman of the glass painters, at Merton Abbey at the time of Morris's death. Morris was critical to the point of arrogance about the products of other stained-glass workshops and indeed decorating firms in general. As he wrote to F. B. Guy: 'You see we are, or consider ourselves to be, the only really artistic firm of the kind, the others being only glass painters in point of fact, (like Clayton & Bell) or else that curious nondescript mixture of clerical tailor and decorator that flourishes in Southampton Street, Strand.' All the same he was dependent on Campfield's professional skill and knowledge in establishing the Firm's early reputation in stained glass.

Campfield had the added virtue of resilience. At Red Lion Square he had been the victim of a towering burst of temper, the result of some confusion about the size of a stained-glass window. Morris flung at him the copy of the *Nuremberg Chronicle* Swinburne had once given him. Campfield dodged behind the door. The book dislodged a panel. Faulkner was coming up the stairs and said 'What's this?' In his usual manner, Morris, shamed after the paroxysm, returned to normal rapidly and tried to shrug it off.

The moon shining through the window of the church on to the tomb, 'throwing fair colours on it from the painted glass'. It is a potent image, occurring in Morris's early story 'A Dream'. Even in his Oxford days stained glass had been a part of Morris's imaginative landscape, in the background of his eerie architectural narratives. Stained-glass windows were the first of the successes of the Firm.

The early 1860s saw the surge of Neo-Gothic church building and refurbishment. This was the period of ritualist revival with its new awareness of the role of earthly beauty in lifting the sight of the congregation heavenwards. The Firm was not alone in using the Clergy List to locate likely customers: it was one of a number of small specialist firms burgeoning to supply new orders for church decoration of all kinds. The Firm's earliest large-scale commissions in stained glass came from George Frederick Bodley, then a rising architect. He too was profiting from the swing to ritualism. As the younger architect W. R. Lethaby described him, 'He could do Gothic flavours to a miracle, and his churches are monuments of taste.' Bodley had been George Gilbert Scott's first pupil. He was a member of the Hogarth Club, the Medieval Society, an intimate of Street's. Morris invited him to Red House, never underestimating the importance to his business of the network of geniality.

In the early 1860s the Firm carried out a small series of commissions for Bodley in his own new church buildings: All Saints, Selsley; St Michael's and All Angels, Brighton; St Martin's-on-the-Hill, Scarborough. All these have their glories. The first of them, at Selsley, has a special poignancy since here one can pinpoint a convergence of conditions that in later commissions would never quite recur. Bodley's building itself is a masterpiece of siting, a square-set limestone church with its Tyrolean bell-tower rising steeply on the hillside above Stroud. Morris later insisted that 'The worth of stained glass must mainly depend on the genuineness and spontaneity of the architecture it decorates: if that architecture is less than good, the stained glass windows in it become a mere congeries of designs without unity of purpose.' At Selsley the windows space out down the nave and wind around the apse in a remarkable relationship of architecture with pictorial stained glass. Rossetti's 'Sermon on the Mount' (infiltrated with a portrait of Morris as St Peter); Burne-Jones's delectable 'Adam and Eve' with heads drawn from Ford Madox Brown and his wife; Brown's own graphically forthright 'Crucifixion'; Philip Webb's and Morris's 'Creation', with trees, corn, waters, flying planets. Selsley demonstrates most movingly of what the Firm was capable. These windows have the power of the genuine ensemble.

For Morris the true period for stained glass was the late fourteenth and early fifteenth century, the time when the windows were being installed in the nave aisles of York Minster and at Merton College, Oxford. This glazing he described as 'the highest point reached by the art'. From then on there was a gradual descent in taste and in technique towards the decadence of the seventeenth and eighteenth centuries when a window was treated merely as a kind of painting, given a pictorial opaque enamel mask. Morris poured scorn on the west window of New College Chapel, adapted by Sir Joshua Reynolds from Correggio's painting 'La Notte'. In his pursuit of an alternative method, the 'mosaic enamel method', in which windows were assembled from already coloured pieces, Morris was returning to the techniques of what he saw as a more genuine mediaeval past.

Morris did not himself reinvent these ancient skills. He was dependent, as were his contemporary Gothicist craftsmen in stained glass, on the researches of Charles Winston, a chemist whose study *An Inquiry into the Difference of Style Observable in Ancient Glass Painting* (1847) had stimulated the renaissance of the craft. Nor did Morris ever manufacture his own glass: this he often regretted. He selected his supplies of white and coloured pot metal from Powell & Sons, who had begun to make their glass in the mediaeval manner, overseen by Winston as their technical adviser. Morris soon, however, started to demand a thicker glass: he believed in creative collaboration with his suppliers. The Firm's workshop also added its own silver stain, applying to the glass a silver compound to produce, when it was fired, a yellow staining which could range from lemon yellow to deep amber. When applied to blue pot metal this produced a wonderful green with a metallic sheen.

What distinguishes these early Morris windows from the stained glass being made by other workshops of the period? It is first of all their richness and yet subtlety of colour. In most Neo-Gothic glass the colours are more garish. Morris himself kept a tight control over the colour and, in later years of the Firm, over the leading of each window. The designs were submitted to Morris in cartoon form, 'and the men in the shop have to glassify them under my directions', as he explained. Although they were the work of different artists, Morris windows stand out by their artistic unity, due to their consistency of layout. The figures and the narrative scenes were set in backgrounds designed by Morris and Webb. Their idiosyncratic canopies and heraldry and the use of lettering give them a graphic identity, almost a house style of their time.

Above all they stand out for their quality of storytelling. Morris felt that stained-glass windows should 'tell stories in a simple direct manner', especially important when the congregation could not be relied on to be wholly literate. In many of these early Morris windows the well-known stories from the Bible stand out brightly in the framework of clear glass. They claim the viewer in the way familiar folktales can be transformed in the telling, given a new edge. Their narrative directness makes these windows so effective. They have a vivacity only rivalled in their period only by the brilliant apocalyptic stained glass in William Burges's churches in North Yorkshire.

Burne-Jones emerged immediately as the star performer. But Ford Madox Brown was also prolific at this period: the best of his glass is his vigorously gruesome retelling of the legend of St Oswald for St Oswald's Church in Durham. Morris's own contribution as designer was lower key. Because of his diffidence about his drawing of the figure, in later years he more or less confined himself to angels: the angels with the rebecs and mandolins and cymbals filling every nook and cranny of the topmost traceries. But in the 1860s Morris was producing some large-scale figure windows that, if a little static, have peculiar charm. His 'Three Maries at the Sepulchre' for Brighton has a red-winged Angel sitting rather stolidly on Christ's empty tomb, with its mediaeval heraldry; Morris's three Maries are Pre-Raphaelite heroines, robed and wimpled, bearing gilded caskets. At Selsley his 'Annunciation', based on a van Eyck altarpiece, shows a startled Mary kneeling on a scarlet carpet. The décor is unmistakably aesthetic. The Angel Gabriel is clasping a huge lily which could be a D'Oyly Carte prop for *Patience*. The viewer is projected straight into the story. These windows have the freshness and gaucheness of early Morris poems.

Morris had a further role in the development of the Firm's stained glass. He was its best publicist. The first time William De Morgan went to Red Lion Square Morris dressed himself in vestments and posed as if playing on a regal, a small portable organ, 'to illustrate points in connection with stained glass'. Somehow he stayed dignified. De Morgan noted later, 'As I went home it suddenly crossed my mind as a strange thing that he should, while doing what was so trivial and almost grotesque, continue to leave on my memory so strong an impression of his power.'

In 1862 Morris, Marshall, Faulkner & Co. took space at the International Exhibition at South Kensington. This was the public unveiling of its products. The exhibition was the sequel to the Great Exhibition of 1851 and should have been held in 1861, but the troubled state of politics in Italy had caused its postponement. The 1862 exhibition did not capture the public imagination in the way the Crystal Palace had done, but it was even wider in its coverage, on a large site extending northwards from what is now the Natural History Museum. Its chief innovations were a Japanese stand, which encouraged the growth of *japonaiserie* in Britain, and a Mediaeval Court, devoted to the Gothic. It was here that the Firm, investing twenty-five pounds of its meagre capital, reserved two stands, an area of 900 square feet. They could have managed with one-twentieth of this, said William Rossetti, Dante Gabriel's brother, who considered the Firm's plans foolishly ambitious.

One of the stands was for stained glass. Here Rossetti himself was optimistic on their prospects. 'Our stained glass, at any rate, I will venture to say, may challenge any other firm to approach and must, I think, establish a reputation when seen.' On the other stand was a display of the Firm's decorated furniture. Among the most interesting of exhibits was the cabinet designed by Philip Webb and painted by Morris with scenes from the story of St George and the Dragon. Janey was the model for the distressed princess. This cabinet can now be seen in the Victoria and Albert Museum. With its panorama of grief turned to joy and triumph it is a lovely, youthful, curiously touching piece.

A more ambitious project shown at the exhibition was the so-called 'King René's Honeymoon Cabinet', a hugely complicated piece of office furniture incorporating shelves, drawers and drawing desk. This was designed by the architect John Seddon for his Whitehall chambers and was decorated for him by the Firm with scenes from the marriage celebrations of René of Anjou, the artist-king. The piece of furniture is more grotesque and grandiose than anything the Firm itself would have arrived at; but it gave the artists a good public opportunity to show their combined versatility and talent. Brown, Burne-Jones and Rossetti painted the four panels. Morris and Webb filled in the background of arches and heraldry, criss-crosses and borders, as they were to do in many hundred stained-glass windows. At the top and around the sides of this strange cabinet are six little square panels showing craftwork. The smith in 'Ironwork' is a sturdy William Morris. The scenes are simple, candid, as in mediaeval manuscripts. May Morris put it neatly: 'We are looking through a peep-hole at a medieval town.'

The Firm's stand also contained a somewhat motley collection of furnishing accessories: embroideries, painted tiles, an iron bedstead, a washstand, a sofa, copper candlesticks, examples of Webb's jewellery. There was a last-minute panic to assemble the exhibits. Faulkner wrote to Crom Price *in medias res* in April: 'The getting ready of our things first has cost more tribulation and swearing to Topsy than three exhibitions will be worth.'

In looking back later on these early products Morris wrote, 'we were naturally much ridiculed'. To some extent this may be wishful thinking: he was always embarrassed by the ease of his acceptance by the bourgeoisie. Certainly at the time the Firm received some brickbats. *The Ecclesiologist*, for instance, called its furniture 'preposterous' and its stained glass 'pseudo grotesque'. *London Society* launched into gentle satire:

As we strolled into the court devoted to the exhibition of Messrs. Morris and Co's mediaeval furniture, tapestries, etc. who could have believed that it represented manufactures of the nineteenth century – the age, par excellence, of cog-wheels and steam rams and rifled cannon? Six hundred years have passed since the style of yon cabinet was in vogue. On such a faldstool as this the good St. Louis may have prayed. Can't you imagine Blanche of Castile arranging her tresses at that mirror?

But there was also lavish praise for the Firm's products, even from its professional competitors. Both stands received medals of commendation. The Exhibition Jury singled out the stained glass for 'artistic qualities of colour and design'. At South Kensington £150 worth of goods were sold, and some important new clients were acquired. The English radical conscience is a delicate organism. In Morris, with his edgy personality, it was to reach new heights of sensitivity. The exhibition set the social critic and incipient revolutionary firmly on his path as successful commercial entrepreneur.

The year of the exhibition marked more or less the end of Morris's ambition to become a painter. Red House had been equipped with a well-lit studio and in the 1861 Census Morris had entered his occupation as 'B.A., Artist'. He returned briefly to painting in the 1870s, but amateurishly. His heart was never in it. He later described how he had 'studied the art but in a very desultory way for some time'. Later still, as an old man, he analysed his shortcomings:

I should have painted well so far as the execution is concerned, and I had a good sense of colour; but though I have so to speak the literary artistic memory, I have not the artistic artistic memory: I can only draw what I see before me, and my pictures, some of which still exist, lack movement.

It was a perceptive assessment, largely true. Morris's painting for the St George's cabinet was in effect his swansong. From the early 1860s his artistic energies were channelled into different directions: into the design of repeating patterns, first for wallpapers, then textiles; into a more amorphous but, as it seemed to him, equally creative role as selector and assembler, giving the Firm its general visual identity. He could have described himself as art director if the term had existed then.

The earliest of Morris's wallpapers were designed in 1862. He was not the first of the partners to embark on them: already in January 1861 Rossetti was describing the paper he had made for his and Lizzie's rooms in Blackfriars. This was a fruit design in yellow, black and Venetian red, and Rossetti asked the paper manufacturer to print it 'on common brown packing paper and on blue grocer's-paper', to see which looked the best. Morris's three designs were also based on fruit or flowers. They are gentle flowing patterns which show Morris's belief in the purpose of pattern to impose a rhythm, to soothe and civilize. Morris achieved so easily in these repeating patterns the fluency, the sense of movement, which he found hard to arrive at in drawing or in painting. If they have a fault it is that they are over-sweet. Morris said he 'disliked *flowers* treated geometrically stiffly in patterns'. He set his style against the brightly coloured, heraldic, formal patterns popularized from the 1850s onwards by Pugin and Owen Jones. Morris must have known of Christopher Dresser, whose 1861 lectures to the Society of Arts were published as *The Art of Decorative Design*. Dresser's study of the morphology of plants had led him to the theory that plants could 'furnish the ornamentalist with abstract form'. It is tantalizing that Morris never comments directly on the most important design theorist of his period. But Warington Taylor, Morris's first manager, described with a shudder Dresser's patterns 'in which the leaves and flowers are distorted into the most painful geometrical harsh forms'.

Morris always asked for meaning in a pattern. It acted as a code; it gave a stab of recognition. It was a way of making a connection with the past. These early wallpapers show how he used his patterns as a form of reminiscence. Compared with Morris's later wallpapers they lack sophistication. There is still a certain formality of structure. But compared with the majority of papers produced by his contemporary designers they are full of human interest, tangible with feeling. All three patterns arise from his personal odyssey. The earliest, 'Trellis', is a Red House pattern, based on the rose trellises around the central courtyard: it is a sunny summery pattern; the humming-birds, designed by Philip Webb, are hovering and swooping. But the rose bushes are obviously, ominously thorned. The 'Daisy' is the daisy of the hangings at Red

House, innocent and pretty. The 'Fruit' or 'Pomegranate' is Morris's prize image of temptation. Atalanta's apples. Magic apples of desire in the Garden of the Hesperides. 'Acontius will I wed today,' as the lovelorn hero inscribes the surface of the great, smooth, golden apple with a long sharp thorn in one of the most haunting scenes of Morris's *Earthly Paradise*. Pomegranates are exotic fruits of passion and of loss.

The Firm first attempted to produce Morris's wallpapers at Red Lion Square, using etched zinc plates and transparent oil colours. But this proved too laborious and also unreliable. Morris then had conventional wood blocks cut and transferred production to a commercial wallpaper manufacturer, Jeffrey & Co. in Islington. Jeffrey began to print Morris's wallpapers from 1864 and continued to produce them under his surveillance. Morris never manufactured his own wallpaper designs. He was more fortunate with Jeffrey than with other subcontractors. Metford Warner, acting manager from the beginning, later Managing Director, went along with Morris's ceaseless quest for quality and the meddling in production that this entailed. Warner later maintained that Morris 'allowed nothing to pass until he was quite satisfied it was right both in colour and design'. Because they were not perfect Morris once discarded a whole set of expensive printing blocks. Warner said that people sometimes called Morris a humbug: he always assured them that the term was less applicable to him than to anyone he knew.

However, neither Warner nor Morris himself seems to have confronted the moral problem underlying their commercial success. In any period wallpaper printing by hand would have been a laborious, repetitive, uncreative and demeaning operation. Morris's achievement of excellence depended on a level of activity that, in human terms, he so consistently decried.

The public face of the Firm was always seen to be important. Back in the planning days Rossetti had envisaged 'a shop like Giotto! and a sign on the door!!' The motive was to bridge the gap between the maker and consumer. The sign was to symbolize accessibility.

There is an eye-witness account of Morris, pioneering shopkeeper. Mrs Richmond Ritchie visited Red Lion Square in 1862, guided by Val Prinsep 'one foggy morning to some square, miles away'. Her narrative continues:

we came into an empty ground floor room, and Val Prinsep called 'Topsy' very loud, and some one came from above with hair on end and in a nonchalant way began to show me one or two of his curious, and to my uninitiated soul, bewildering treasures. I think Morris said the glasses would stand firm when he put them on the table. I bought two tumblers of which Val Prinsep praised the shape. He and Val wrapped them up in paper, and I came away very much amused and interested, with a general impression of sympathetic shyness and shadows and dim green glass.

In the history of shopkeeping in London, at a time of the relentless rise of the department store, Red Lion Square evidently had the charm of the erratic. Another later customer, who asked for softer colours, was shown the door by Morris who said, 'There is plenty of mud out there.'

It was this imperious side of Morris as designer that appealed to Max Beerbohm who recreated the Morris of that period calling on a client, Charley Faulkner in attendance, in his 1950s' radio broadcast 'Hethway Speaking', a narrative salvaged from Beerbohm's unpublished manuscript *The Mirror of the Past*. The narrator, a gentleman with a taste for parquet, is bludgeoned with ideas in his own drawing-room in Chelsea. Morris is in quasi-sailor clothes and in nautical mood:

'we'll let you have everything at two per cent above cost of production, by Jiminy, because we're blooming beginners and you're our friend. Hooray! I've got *all* the designs in my head now,' and he struck his forehead a violent blow with his fist. 'I see your whole blessèd room for you, all clear before me. You shall have a great cedar chair – *there*, in the middle – like Odin's throne; and a settle – all along *this* wall – to seat a regiment. And Ned Burne-Jones will do the stained glass for your window – Life of La Belle Iseult; and Ford Madox Brown shall do the panels of the settle – Boyhood of Chaucer; and' – he strode up and down, brandishing his arms – 'there's a young chap named William De Morgan who'll do the tiles for the hearth; and my wife shall embroider the edges of the window-curtains – you know that green serge we've got, Faulkner – glorious. And by Jove we'll' – but here he slipped and sat with a terrific crash on the parquet. 'That's just what I was going to speak about,' he continued, sitting; 'this isn't a floor, it's a sheet of ice: it won't do; we must have good honest rough oaken boards with bulrushes,' he cried, bounding to his feet, ' – strewn bulrushes. And we'll have a – '

'One moment, Morris,' I begged. 'When you say *we*, do you mean simply yourself and Faulkner and the Company, or do you include *me?*'

'But of course I include you,' he said. 'Why, hang it all, the *room's* yours.'

'That's just what I was beginning to doubt,' I said.

Morris's decisiveness in fact attracted custom. Even in the early days visitors to the showroom in Red Lion Square were enthusiastic. A regular customer was the architect George Gilbert Scott, whom Morris was later to turn on in such fury for his want of moral standards. George Campfield's dinner hour was frequently used up in explaining to pros- pective customers the intricacies of the Firm's stained glass. Morris and his partners were both forming and supplying the taste of the discri- minating middle classes for special household products, above the general level of the market. A whole movement in specialist retailing began with what Rossetti had christened 'the Great Shop'. The young Arthur Lasenby Liberty, for instance, began his importation of oriental objects in the aftermath of the International Exhibition; Liberty & Co. opened in Regent Street in 1875. From then on there was a long line of such exploratory shopkeepers: Ambrose Heal in the 1890s; Gordon Russell with his Wigmore Street shop in the 1930s; Terence Conran and the 1960s Habitat; the designer-object shops of the 1980s. The same was true elsewhere in Europe. The first shop inspired by Morris was S. Bing, the famous art nouveau shop/gallery in Brussels. The Sub Rosa shop, which specialized in English textiles, was opened in Stockholm in 1892.

The sunflowers, the herbals, the blue china, the red tiles: Morris and his partners were remarkably successful in alighting upon what became the cult objects of their period. Like the Habitat enamel mugs and chicken bricks, reclaimed into smartness in the London of the 1960s, these were ordinary objects looked at with new eyes. The partners were altering perceptions of shape, texture and colour. The Firm began the fashion for painting woodwork white. Morris was an inspired buyer with a built-in covetousness. In the winter before his wedding he had been in France buying 'old manuscripts and armour and ironwork and enamel'. He had good qualifications as a creative shopkeeper in that he liked buying the things he liked.

'Have nothing in your houses that you do not know to be useful, or believe to be beautiful.' Part of the Firm's success lay in its flair in merging the personal and public. Morris was so convincing because his views arose from his own deeply felt, imaginative concept of home life.

'Kid having appeared, Mrs. Brown kindly says she will stay till Monday . . . Janey and kid (girl) are both very well.'

With those off-hand words Morris announced, to Ford Madox

Brown, the birth of his first daughter, on 17 January 1861. The Browns were at that time in Morris's close domestic circle. Emma had come to be with Janey for the birth. A nurse, Elizabeth Robinson, was taken on, apparently recommended by the elder Mrs Morris. She supplemented the normal Red House staffing: the cook, the housemaid and the coachman-groom. The baby was named Jane Alice Morris: Jane after her mother, Alice after William Morris's youngest sister. She was always known as Jenny. Rossetti wrote jocularly about the 'little accident which has just befallen Topsy and Mrs. T.'

There were grand scenes at her christening, though the weather was tempestuous. One of the guests remembered the wild flapping of the leather cover of Morris's wagonette on the way to Bexley church. After the service a lavish mediaeval banquet was set out at Red House, on a large T-shaped table. The Browns were there, the Marshalls, Georgie and Ned, and Swinburne. Overnight accommodation had the old informal quality of Red Lion Square. Georgie, by now herself pregnant, described how she and Janey 'went together with a candle to look at the beds strewn about the drawing room for the men. Swinburne had a sofa; I think P. P. Marshall's was made on the floor.'

At the christening feast Rossetti sat silent and abstracted, munching raisins from a dish before it was dessert time, and drinking only water. Lizzie's own pregnancy was problematic. She was *énervée*, withdrawn and in poor health. Rossetti's gloom was prophetic. Only a few weeks later, in May 1861, their daughter was stillborn, having been dead already for two or three weeks in Lizzie's womb. Her precarious emotional state tipped over into breakdown. When Georgie and Ned went to see her soon afterwards they found her in a low chair with the empty cradle on the floor beside her, looking like Ophelia as painted by her husband. She had cried, 'Hush, Ned, you'll waken it!' with 'a kind of soft wildness' as they came in.

Over the next three months Lizzie was in a disturbed state. Her dependence on laudanum was now beyond control. She was sent to stay at Red House in that summer and that autumn, while Rossetti was away, as it was clearly dangerous for her to be alone. Her behaviour was erratic. Rossetti wrote desperately to his mother, asking her to find Lizzie and give her a few pounds. It was an anguished time for Rossetti. The tension between him and Lizzie was electric. Peter Paul Marshall, who saw them both at Red House, said that Rossetti appeared 'quite cowed' by Lizzie who snapped at him. It must also have been a trying period for the Morrises, entrusted with her care while Lizzie, increasingly beyond the reach of sympathy, wandered around Red House like a wraith. In February 1862, in Chatham Place, she died from an overdose of drugs. It seems likely her death was self-inflicted. In a paroxysm of despair and guilt Rossetti put his notebook of poems into Lizzie's coffin, to be buried with her in Highgate Cemetery.

What did Morris make of this episode? None of his existing letters mentions Lizzie directly. It is almost as if he obliterated her, as if her tragic history had been in a way too much for him, though one cannot imagine that the pale, red-haired, long-limbed, artistic, neurotic Lizzie did not linger somewhere in his mind. Indeed in his poems there are counterparts of Lizzie, strange, intense, addictive women, suggesting that Morris was able to make use on one level of the experience he rejected on another. Georgiana saw Lizzie as an opposite of Janey, 'Mrs. Morris being the statue and Mrs. Rossetti the picture.' Janey's grave nobility tended to be tempered by the look of human kindness in her eye. Of the two Lizzie seemed more unearthly, with a wistfulness that qualified 'her brilliant loveliness and grace'.

It is also pertinent to wonder how the loss of his child, followed by the death of Lizzie, deepened Rossetti's animosity to Morris. Only four weeks after Lizzie's overdose, on 25 March 1862, Janey gave birth to a second daughter, Mary, so named because she was born on Lady Day, the Feast of the Annunciation, but always known as May. Rossetti's own deprivation seemed the crueller in this household of the daughters. Over the years he appears to have somehow transferred blame for it to Morris. 'I ought to have had a little girl older than she is,' he said eyeing Jenny, then aged seven. Later he made a semi-serious attempt, which the child in fact welcomed, to adopt May.

The Victorian age, in some ways so crude and blatant, had pockets of innocence difficult to comprehend completely from this distance. Georgiana Burne-Jones was on the verge of taking on as nurse to her son Philip 'a very handsome German woman' known as Norma, a model of her husband's; it took years to dawn on her that Norma was a prostitute. There is, still in Morris's circle, the classic scene of horror on Ruskin's wedding night when he discovered that his wife had pubic hair. More than forty years after the marriage of the Morrises, Molly – the granddaughter of one of Morris's northern clients, Sir Isaac Lowthian Bell – discovered with amazement only on her wedding night 'what a man's love was'. After that there are frequent references in her diary to nights of 'wonderful love'. Wonderful for Molly. But how had it been for Janey? It is almost impossible to say.

There is no way of knowing William Morris's sexual history. He was notably, even unnaturally, reticent on sexual questions and the true condition of his marriage was always glossed over by his protective friends. It is obvious his sexual relations with Janey did not mirror Ruskin's failure: after all they had two children in just over two years. All the same, in the light of later history, it seems likely that they were hampered not only by mutual inexperience, but by Janey's innate coolness and by Morris's huge bashfulness. One remembers his paroxysms of embarrassment when talking about serious subjects with his mother, being betrayed by feeling into positive untruthfulness: 'speaking indeed far off from my heart'.

How did he and Janey handle the predictable scenes of nervousness and fumbling? Almost certainly they would not have made use of contraception, given their period and class. Rubber condoms and diaphragms only became available for those able to pay for private medical consultation after 1880. Possibly, after the birth of their two daughters in quick succession, William took to abstention or coitus interruptus as the simplest form of birth control – unless Janey was already pleading the unfitness that made her a semi-invalid within the next few years, so sadly soon after the games of hide and seek at Red House. There is no impression given in the letters of the Morrises, or in contemporary descriptions of the two of them, of physical closeness, still less of mutual passion. They are affectionate and yet they seem apart.

It is dangerous to read too much into a writer's work; writers play tricks with their readers, write themselves into the scenarios they want or even fear. But Morris, one might argue, is a special case. J. W. Mackail, Burne-Jones's son-in-law, who knew much more of the Morrises' secret history than he was able to reveal in his biography, argues that Morris's work was his confessional in a particular, necessary way. 'Shy and reserved in life, as to many matters that lay near his heart, he had all the instinct of the born man of letters for laying himself open in his books, and having no concealment from the widest circle of all.' Certainly in Morris's writing over the next decade he confronts his readers with extraordinary images of fear, pain, impotence and sexual disarray.

The sword in the bed between Sigurd and Brynhild. The bridegroom unmanned in 'The Ring given to Venus', trying night after night to consummate his marriage, grieving and abashed:

For who, indeed, alone could bear
The dreadful shame, the shameful fear,
Of such a bridal?

The most powerful of all these scenes of sexual disaster comes in the poem from *The Earthly Paradise*, 'The Love of Alcestis'. The king of Pherae, Admetus, on his wedding night, comes to claim his bride. The palace is, as usual with Morris, very golden:

> Upon the gilded door
> I laid my hand; I stood upon the floor
> Of the bride-chamber, and I saw the bride,
> Lovelier than any dream, stand by the side
> Of the gold bed, with hands that hid her face:
> One cry of joy I gave, and the place
> Seemed changed to hell as in a hideous dream.

Between the lovers has sprung up, silently, a hideous serpent, the more terrifying because of its mobility:

> A huge dull-gleaming dreadful coil that rolled
> In changing circles on the pavement fair.

Morris gives us some bad monsters: snakes and dragons, apparitions. This is much the worst one because it is so slithery and sexually threatening, the nightmare, even in pre-Freudian days, of any bride. Admetus realizes he has lost the thing he longed for:

> And 'twixt the coils I met her grey eyes, glazed
> With sudden horror most unspeakable.

The serpent lurches over to violate the bride, and she turns upon the bridegroom, blaming and reviling him:

> They coil about me now, my lips to kiss.
> O love, why hast thou brought me unto this?

Even when the serpent slinks away the bridegroom is fatally undermined, cringing in shame outside the chamber: 'Like a scourged hound, until the dawn of day'. Morris tells the story as a dark and complex fairytale, loaded with the symbolism of how passion turns to ashes. There are undertones of female frigidity, the ultimate *vagina dentata* syndrome. The poet explicates the treachery of expectation: even at the point of consummation the hope of happiness is cruelly whisked away.

One of the unfulfilled plans for Red House was a series of tempera paintings by Burne-Jones of scenes from the Trojan War. These would have covered the walls of the staircase whilst below them, in the hall, he intended to paint a great shipload of Greek heroes in the guise of mediaeval warriors, with their shields hanging over the ship sides. One of the things that intrigued Burne-Jones and Morris, then and later, was the mediaeval view of the ancient world. In the 1890s, when Morris came to breakfast, 'we talked hard all morning, mainly of one subject, why the mediaeval world was always on the side of the Trojans, and of Quintus Smyrnaeus, and how Penthesilea came to be tenderly dealt with in ancient tales and tapestries. He was quite happy,' wrote Burne-Jones.

At Red House William Morris took up again the cycle of Troy poems he had begun a few years earlier. It was, like Burne-Jones's murals, an ambitious project destined never to see the light of day. 'Scenes from the Fall of Troy', as originally listed in a manuscript notebook *c*.1857, consisted of twelve episodes, from 'Helen Arming Paris' to 'Aeneas on Shipboard', and including 'The Descent from the Wooden Horse'. In the end only six of the scenes were completed, with two more half-finished. They were not published until May 1915, when May Morris presented them as fragments, in the ultimate volume of the *Collected Works*.

They are strange and intense poems, dealing with events in Troy in the twilight period as the War itself was coming to an end. These are the narratives of the lost epics of the cycle: the Aethiopiad, the Little Iliad, the Taking of Troy. It was the tail end of the Trojan cycle, melancholy in atmosphere and picturesque in detail, that appealed most to the mediaeval mind. Morris superimposes upon the ancient sources the mediaeval versions of the stories: Caxton's *Historyes of Troye*, Chaucer's *Troilus and Criseyde*. The bitterness and bleakness of his narrative of war is also close to Shakespeare's in *Troilus and Cressida*. This of course is the play that the narrator of Morris's Oxford story 'Frank's Sealed Letter' took out with him to Essex to read beside the river. As so often with Morris the source is not straightforward. These are classical stories filtered through the mediaeval. Mackail is correct when he points out that Morris's Troy, spired, gabled, red-roofed and filled with towers, turns out to be a town like Bruges or Chartres.

In Morris's *œuvre* the Troy poems occupy the middle ground between the pared-down, gripping language of the *Defence of Guenevere* and the later narrative rotundities of *The Earthly Paradise*. The empty embittered landscape of Troy, the town of limbo, comes across not unlike a Neo-Romantic painting of the English 1940s; a bomb-shattered scene infused with the sense of melancholy and of passing time. In Morris's handling of the story there are *longueurs*, there is quaintness. There is also from time to time some very forceful poetry. The episode in which Helen of Troy is reclaimed by the Greek Menelaus, her first husband, has Morris writing powerfully on the negation of desire, the paralysis of love, and the weirdness of the moment when sexual denial turns to violence.

There are only a few passages in Morris's poetry in which the violence is so vivid and protracted. Helen, ageing, saddening, is living on in Troy with Deiphobus her new husband, the Trojan prince. They are in their house, at night. Deiphobus lies asleep, with his sword above their bed. Menelaus bursts into the chamber, in his armour. He has arrived in Troy that night concealed within the Trojan horse. In a scene of savage irony he seizes his ex-wife and forces her to fetch Deiphobus' sword and hold him by his feet while Menelaus thrusts him through. The body is pushed out of the bed and Menelaus takes the place of the dead Deiphobus in the blood pool. He speaks to Helen, brutal with reminders:

> I am the Menelaus that you knew
> Come back to fetch a thing I left behind.
> You think me changed: it is ten years ago,
> And many weary things have happened since.
> Behold me lying in my own place now:
> Abed, Helen, before the night goes by!

Morris gauges very well the effect of that black comedy of ravishment. It becomes a fearful and sardonic episode, as Helen is compelled to couple with her first husband on the bed and in the blood of her last husband. Morris reaches out towards Grand Guignol in suggesting that human degradation can get no worse.

Outside there is the mob roar from the city, now taken by the Greeks.

Then the murmur that the Trojans are making a new stand. As in Shakespeare's *Troilus and Cressida* the inner human narrative is framed by the political as the Trojans rally in the dawn, crying chillingly and shrilly: 'Aeneas and Antenor to the ships!' Fresh in Morris's memory would have been those similar scenes of savagery, rape and carnage, perpetrated by the British in north-western India after the siege of Lucknow in the autumn of 1858.

In July 1864 the Irish poet William Allingham set off on a small expedition 'By steamer to London Bridge and rail to Plumstead. After some wandering, find the Red House at last in its rose garden, and William Morris and his queenly wife crowned with her own black hair.'

Morris and Janey still seemed mediaeval, regal. But by now the scene was changing. Allingham, in his diary, recorded the next morning: 'The Red House 7½ a.m. Rose Trellis. Jenny and May bright-eyed, curly pated . . . WM brusque, careless, with big shoon.'

The role of the father was a role that Morris took to. In the early days he spoke of marriage without sentiment but wanted to have children, according to Burne-Jones. It has been suggested Morris was disappointed that his children were both daughters. Georgie, who knew him so well, denied it: writing to Sydney Cockerell, she felt he had a natural affinity for daughters. 'Have you ever tried to imagine a *son* of Morris? I have tried to *try*, and failed!' At the Red House period he petted them, protected them, calling them 'the littles'. A cartoon of that period shows him cutting up their food for them, enfolding the two infants in his ample arms.

Jenny and May grew up with predictably idyllic memories of their Red House upbringing. May, in the 1930s, would still describe her father's appearance as an Icelandic ruler in the great painted chair at the end of the long table. She remembered Swinburne lying in the grass in the orchard, his red hair flying round him, while she and Jenny scattered rose petals on his face. May also made a more cryptic comment about 'certain dream-pictures' of her childhood at Red House which were strangely intense but 'too intimate and tender' to be divulged in public. What did she mean by this? Had the child's antennae, often so over-active, sensed some almost unacknowledged tension in the household? Had there been a 'primal scene' between her parents or her mother and Rossetti which, half-comprehended, had lodged in the child's mind? The Kings and Queens and leather shoon and the mediaeval

8 *William Morris at Red House with Jenny and May.* Caricature by Edward Burne-Jones.

trappings masked emotional impasse, an inner melancholy. Even May seems to have sensed the regime at the Red House, with its perfectionist detail, was based on an ideal too fragile to survive.

By early 1864 the Firm was outgrowing its Red Lion Square premises. Morris himself was tired. Commuting by train from Red House ate up three or four hours every day. The commissions for stained glass had been accumulating healthily: five in 1861, fifteen in 1863. But the lack of working capital was proving problematic, making the firm vulnerable to the booms and busts of the Victorian economy. In the back of Morris's mind would have been the panic year of his father's death and the sudden collapse of Sanderson & Co. A future manager of the firm, George Wardle, called in at Red Lion Square and saw Morris, recollecting, 'He struck me as being a man overworked. Those were early days of the Firm, business was unremunerative, and perhaps a large share of the work had to be done by him.' Business worries also seemed to have affected Charley Faulkner, whom Wardle noticed working at his tile painting. Faulkner had a harassed look 'which spoke hard times'.

In order to concentrate activity and allow for the Firm's future expansion, there was serious discussion about moving the whole firm to Upton and building new production workshops on a site close to Red House. The Burne-Jones family was part of this equation. Their son

193

Philip was now almost three and Georgie once again pregnant. The rooms in Great Russell Street, by the British Museum, were feeling impossibly cramped. On Morris's instructions Philip Webb made new drawings to extend Red House to complete the quadrangle. The Burne-Jones family would also come and live there, partly independently, with their own rooms and entrances, but under one roof and sharing the garden, in a new community of life and art.

That September the Morrises went *en famille* to Littlehampton in Sussex with the Burne-Joneses, Charley Faulkner and his sisters. Kate Faulkner, so talented, strongminded, solitary, was the sister both Morris and Ned especially loved. It was a successful and cheerful seaside holiday and a trial run for the new community. As Georgie put it, 'the evenings were always merry with Red House jokes revived and amplified'. Ned got up and preached spoof sermons. Morris obliged with one of his statutory rages, flinging a pair of broken spectacles out of the window in frustration, imagining he had brought a replacement with him. He had not. Before breakfast the next morning he was seen outside their lodgings, bareheaded, abject, and trying to find his broken glasses in the street.

But the trip to Littlehampton ended disastrously, when a local outbreak of scarlet fever infected the Burne-Joneses' small son Philip. It was a mild case. They took no serious precautions. Then back in London Georgie herself succumbed to it. In her condition the disease was very dangerous and Georgie gave premature birth to a son. The baby lived on for three weeks, while Georgie was delirious, still with a high temperature. Ruskin, a good friend to the family, had the street outside spread with tan-bark, 'deep as a riding school', to keep the clip-clopping of the horses' hooves from reaching her. Just as Georgie appeared to be recovering the child died. Ned called him Christopher because 'he had borne so heavy a weight as he crossed through the troubled waters of his short life'. Morris was out of reach throughout this tragedy, severely ill himself with rheumatic fever, the result of a chill caught on a long wet journey from Upton to Bloomsbury. He was still in bed when Burne-Jones wrote to explain to him that after all these traumas the plan to move to Red House could not proceed.

The sequence of illnesses had unnerved him badly. As George du Maurier summed up the situation: 'Jones poor fellow has given up all idea of building his house; he has had lots of trouble and not done a stroke of work for 4 months – his wife's confinement and scarlet fever, and his own horrible funk about it have quite knocked him up.' Scarlet fever at that period was a disease much feared. It could affect the sufferer's judgement permanently. In most cases recovery was slow. Ned himself was very delicate. Georgie's illness had followed on not so long after his own breakdown of 1861 when a sore throat and a cough had worsened into more dramatic symptoms of collapse and blood-spitting, and Georgie had feared that he was at death's door. 'Who does not know that threading of the streets in a hastily summoned jolting cab, with the one haunting fear for companion?' Compared with Morris, bolstered by his resources, the Burne-Joneses were a more cautious and less competent couple, seeming sometimes like two poor children out in the world alone. Ned's Birmingham background, scraping a living, had left him financially careful. He may have felt the Red House scheme too reckless. Ned, in his heart of hearts, may well have had his doubts about so physically close an involvement with the Firm.

Morris did his best to contain his disappointment, writing to Ned with a shaky hand, still in his bed:

As to our palace of Art, I confess your letter was a blow to me at first, though hardly an unexpected one – in short I cried; but I have got over it now. As to our being a miserable lot, old chap, speaking for myself I don't know, I refuse to make myself really unhappy for anything short of the loss of friends one can't do without. Suppose in all these troubles you had given us the slip what the devil should I have done? I am sure I couldn't have had the heart to have gone on with the firm; all our jolly subjects would have gone to pot – it frightens me to think of, Ned.

Over the next year all plans for expanding the Red House site were abandoned. Morris's own income from the mines showed small improvement. In what amounted almost to a state of crisis he was having to sell off valuable possessions, including the paintings he had bought from Rossetti over the past years. The idea of the working community of artists never materialized in William Morris's lifetime. Later at Kelmscott Manor there were no craftsmen, no workshops, though Morris had occasional wild schemes to move the Press there. Merton Abbey, later still, was essentially a workplace, with very little overlap with Morris's domestic life. The ideal of the integrated life of productivity and family has been a very potent one in twentieth-century Europe and America. It inspired the Arts and Crafts communities in Gloucestershire: Ernest Gimson and the Barnsleys; C. R. Ashbee and the Guild of Handicraft in Chipping Campden; Michael Cardew at Winchcombe. It lived on in Eric Gill's religious communities in a particularly idiosyncratic form: bed, board, small farm and workshop, home and schools and earth and heaven all in the soup together. What is ironic is that, although Morris had conceived it and longed for it, such true integration of working life and family in an idyllic rural setting was something he himself never in fact achieved.

In the summer of 1865 the Firm took a twenty-one-year lease on larger premises at No. 26 Queen Square, just east of Southampton Row, only a minute's walk north from Red Lion Square. Morris made the decision to move back into London with his family, sharing this building with the Firm. He preferred to sell Red House outright rather than rent it because 'he could not bear to play landlord to the house he loved so well'. We have no definite record of Janey's reaction. But the move entailed a definite loss of social status which, sensitive as she was to class, she would have registered. Georgie suggests that the family embarked on the move to Queen Square with some sinking of the heart.

Morris never went back. Apparently he could not face it. But, wrote Georgie, 'some of us saw it in our dreams for years afterwards, as one does a house known in childhood'. Jenny's later description of waiting, as a child of four, in the dining-room at Red House for the conveyance to take them to the station has a Chekhovian ring.

No immediate purchaser for Red House was forthcoming. The estate agents described it as 'A Capital Freehold Residence' the next year when, in spite of Morris's misgivings, it was advertised to let.

CHAPTER SEVEN

Queen Square
1865–69

A manuscript notebook, now in the Fitzwilliam Museum in Cambridge, includes the instruction

> to Cabmen and others
> if you find this book bring it to the owner –
> W. Morris
> 26 Queen Square
> Bloomsbury
> and you will receive one guinea reward –
> NB it is of no use to any one but the owner.

On the reverse are a few verbal doodlings:

> 'Yea by so much –
> Bright with remembered hope –
> Where is thy work?
> Where are thy friends?
> Who were thy friends?'

Morris moved from Red House to the east side of Queen Square in the autumn of 1865. This was a definite return to the great city, and back to the Bloomsbury he knew so well already with its streets of tall houses, interconnected squares and their gardens of straggling shrubs and dusty plane trees. Queen Square, like Red Lion Square, was a place of faded glory, although in the early eighteenth century three bishops and a future Lord Mayor of London had been listed as residing there and in the 1780s Fanny Burney wrote her *Diary* in a small upper room of her father's sociable house. The well-known Queen Square girls' school, known as 'the Ladies' Eton', from which one of the masters, the poet and satirist Charles Churchill, had been ejected for 'irregularities' had finally closed down in the Crimean War. Queen Square was now becoming a place for the placeless. In the 1880s Henry James described it as 'an antiquated ex-fashionable region, smelling strongly of the last century with a hoary effigy of Queen Anne in the middle'. No. 25, the house next door to William Morris, was a Home for Gentlewomen. A census of the period lists fifteen lady residents, unmarried or widowed, mostly in late middle age.

It is perhaps surprising that Morris is said to have kissed the earth of London on returning. But he was resilient, believing in tomorrow, not regretting what was over. Georgie, who observed him carefully, had noted that he said goodbye to Red House 'in his unflinching way'. The large Queen Anne house, for which Morris, Marshall, Faulkner & Co. paid £52 rent per year, gave him scope to develop the Firm's work in new directions and he saved the many hours spent in travelling from Upton by living literally above the shop. The ground floor of the house became the office and showroom. A ballroom erected in palmier days across the courtyard at the back of the house was turned into a big workshop with small workshops around it. Later, a further workshop for cabinet making and upholstery was taken in Great Ormond Yard. Nearby, in Little Ormond Yard, in the 1850s the first lectures had been given to the working men of London. These were the beginnings of F. D. Maurice's Working Men's College. In returning to Bloomsbury Morris had come back to the Christian Socialist country of his youth.

At No. 26 Queen Square a long wide wooden gallery connected the main building to the ballroom. Here the glass painters worked. Jenny and May Morris would peer through the windows watching the craftsmen shifting and bending as they assembled the stained glass. To a child this was entrancing: 'the jewel-like colours of the glass that lay about were so attractive, and the silvery networks of the leading, and above all the shadow and the mystery of the kiln-house.' Sometimes when a trial window was set up for his inspection Morris would lead his little daughters in.

The family occupied the remainder of the house. Now living with the Morrises was Janey's sister, Bessie Burden, who had joined them in the last few months at Red House, after her father died. The 1871 Census shows three servants in the household of William Morris 'Artist and

Painter, Employing 18 men and boys'. The servants were Eliza Searle and Agnes Turner, both aged twenty-two from Cambridge, and Marie Hughes aged thirty. All three were entered as unmarried and Agnes and Marie as illegitimate. The best room in the house was the sitting-room, a 'noble room' according to May, well-proportioned and uncluttered, with its five fine windows overlooking the square gardens. The house had been 'made to shine with whitewash and white paint', the better to show off the Firm's hangings. As Red House had been, Queen Square was intended as a showhouse, to show the Firm in action and to demonstrate to visitors the effect of the ensemble. The child May, in her cot in the nursery high up towards the attics, found the birds in Morris's 'Trellis' wallpaper malevolent-looking and alarmingly alive.

On the first floor Morris had his studio, which May remembered as a place with a big easel and on a chair 'a huge lump of bread with a small hole picked out of the middle'. Morris used bread for erasing. There were bread-crumbs on the floor, and the whole room 'smelt pleasantly of tracing paper'. Far down in the cellar, where Morris kept his barrels, he held arcane discussions with his wine merchant and sometimes the bottler would arrive and transfer the table-wine from the barrels to the bottles. The amber-coloured Rhine wine and the crimson of the claret showed at its best the set of table glasses designed by Philip Webb. Part of this ensemble was Janey, decorative and rather silent, in the soft silk gowns her children loved to stroke.

Before the move to Queen Square Morris had embarked on the vast narrative that was to make him, for a decade, the most popular poet of his period and eventually to put him in the running for Poet Laureate in succession to Tennyson. *The Earthly Paradise* was his homage to Chaucer and that English tradition of ceremonial tale-telling. The structure of the poem, with a Prologue linking the twenty-four stories by different narrators, is clearly derived from *The Canterbury Tales*. In Morris's version a band of Norsemen in the late fourteenth century, fleeing the Black Death, set sail in search of the reputed Earthly Paradise 'where none grow old'. They do not find it, and return disappointed, grey and aged, to the 'nameless city in a distant sea'. Here the ancient Greek gods are still worshipped. The decrepit Wanderers are welcomed. Twice a month there is a feast day in the city at which a tale is told, one of the elders of the city and one of the Wanderers taking it in turns. The elders' repertoire is classical: Perseus, Croesus, Alcestis, the Apples of the Hesperides. The Wanderers' narrative range is more eclectic. They tell tales from the Norse and from mediaeval sources and, increasingly, reflecting Morris's own awakened interests, the Icelandic. He constructed the 40,000-line poem carefully, judiciously, professionally, as he might have constructed a tapestry or building. He wrote it in bursts of concentration, almost frenziedly. It was the grand unloading of the stories which had jostled in his mind since he was a boy.

For five years, from 1865 to 1870, *The Earthly Paradise* loomed over Morris's life and the lives of his close friends. The move to Queen Square had renewed, and cleared the time for, the habit of writing that had been in paralysis since the poor reception of *The Defence of Guenevere*. Georgiana Burne-Jones depicts him in 1865 as 'brooding over the gigantic scheme'. He used the poem, as he employed all his

9 *William Morris reading poetry to Ned.* Caricature by Edward Burne-Jones.

projects, as the means to keep his friends around him, discussing his plans and reading every poem out loud as soon as it was written. 'I remember with shame,' wrote Georgie, 'often falling asleep to the steady rhythm of the reading voice, or biting my fingers and stabbing myself with pins in order to keep awake.' In the early days, dinners to discuss the progress of the poem were held at Queen Square. But Janey, already suffering from the mysterious ailment that turned her into the archetypal Victorian semi-invalid, beautiful and supine on the couch, found these dinners so exhausting that they were put a stop to and *The Earthly Paradise* discussions moved elsewhere.

What exactly was this illness? It is difficult to diagnose. Backache was the symptom most frequently alluded to, plus delicate digestion and a general lack of energy. Was Janey's trouble basically spinal? Or was it gynaecological? Or was it the result of her emotional troubles? Janey's ill health continued intermittently for much of her life, but there is no evidence that she ever suffered from a serious organic disease. Her illness must be seen in the context of its period. A good deal has been written about how Victorian women were 'invalided out' of society; Janey exemplifies the opposite tendency, the illness of convenience, for the women to whom taking to the sofa added a new, exotic dimension, attracting sympathy, cultivating mystery, removing them to realms beyond domestic blame.

In 1866 William Allingham reported a visit to the Burne-Joneses' new house in Kensington: 'Monday July 30, Kensington Square. Studio, Psyche drawings. Book planned. Morris and lots of stories and pictures.' Two days later this zest was undiminished:

Wednesday Aug 1. At dinner William Morris, pleasant, learned about wines and distilling. The Big Story Book, woodcut of Olympus by Ned Jones. Morris and friends intend to engrave the wood-blocks themselves – & M. will publish the book at his own expense. I like Morris much. He is plain-spoken and emphatic, often boisterously, without an atom of irritating matter. He goes about 12.

The Big Story Book was conceived originally as one large folio volume illustrated with 500 woodcuts from drawings by Burne-Jones. Towards this epic project Ned in fact produced over a hundred designs, including seventy illustrations for 'The Story of Cupid and Psyche', fifty-four of which reached the next stage of engraving and printing on wood. Drawings and notes for 'Cupid and Psyche', now at Birmingham City Art Gallery, show the fraternal intimacy of the collaboration: Morris lists the subjects, Burne-Jones provides the sketches with a wonderful fluency, positioning the figures, detailing the furnishings. It is almost an intuitive visual and verbal give-and-take. Burne-Jones and Morris share the thrill of the lugubrious: the black and craggy rocks; the surly, grey ferryman; the swirling Styx. They are attuned so closely that in depicting Psyche they arrive at a shared image of violated innocence. The

10 *'Psyche in Charon's Boat'*. Design by Edward Burne-Jones for the abortive illustrated edition of *The Earthly Paradise*, engraved on wood by William Morris.

dramatic scene of 'Psyche and the Opened Casket' shows the box, like a child's money-box, unclasped and pouring smoke, while Psyche swoons, 'in deadly sleep', upon the barren shore.

Allingham, on a holiday visit to Morris and Burne-Jones at Brocken-hurst in Hampshire, paints a vivid picture of the partnership in action, Morris's impatience, Ned's teasing nonchalance. 'Ned only makes a few pencil sketches. He occupies himself, when in the mood, with designs for the Big Book of Stories in Verse by Morris, and has done several from Cupid and Psyche; also pilgrims going to Rome, and others. He founds his style in these on old Woodcuts, especially those in *Hypnerotomachia*, of which he has a fine copy. His work in general, and that of Morris too, might be called a kind of *New Renaissance*.' Ned plays a trick on Morris by pretending to have been so lazy he had not produced a single drawing for the book. Morris grunts with disappointment. Ned produces his eight or nine designs for woodcuts. Morris laughs and shakes himself.

The cutting of the blocks was meant to be farmed out to Morris's assistants. Janey's sister Bessie cut at least one block. George Wardle, a draughtsman first employed by the Firm to provide copies of the

11 'William Morris making a wood block for "The Earthly Paradise".'
Caricature by Edward Burne-Jones.

patterns on the screens and roofs of Suffolk churches, was asked to make
the wood blocks from Burne-Jones's drawings for 'Cupid and Psyche'.
Morris quickly took these over. 'Mr. Morris', wrote Wardle, 'came
possessed by the idea of cutting all the blocks himself.' He cut with great
ardour but not without frustration because the work of block-cutting
was inevitably slow and Morris was 'constitutionally quick'. But he
persevered and improved and finally his woodcuts passed muster with
professionals as skilled as Charles Fairfax Murray. He cut over fifty of
them. May remembered her father at Queen Square with 'a gloriously,
mysteriously shining object, behind which he would work with bright
cutting tools on a little block of wood, which sat on a plump leather
cushion'. The illustrated *Earthly Paradise* was finally abandoned for
reasons that were largely technical: when two trial sheets of the folio
edition were set up at the Chiswick Press the results were crude. Morris
and Burne-Jones went on hoping they could resurrect the Big Story
Book with pictures at the Kelmscott Press in the 1890s; but the 'Cupid
and Psyche' with its Burne-Jones illustrations did not finally appear for
another eighty years.

At this period Queen Square was a hive of productivity. Rossetti had

paranoid visions of a cupboard piled to overflowing with Morris manu-
scripts. May recalled the house strewn with little rolls of printed paper.
Much later, she realized that they must have been the proofs of *Jason* or
The Earthly Paradise, which tended to put her father into a bad temper.
The first of his poems to be published was in effect a preview of the
main collection: *The Life and Death of Jason*, Morris's Golden Fleece
poem. At 13,000 lines, a length somewhere between *The Aeneid* and *The
Odyssey*, it was too bulky for inclusion in *The Earthly Paradise*. It was
published separately in 1867 by Bell & Daldy, again initially at Morris's
expense. The publishers, however, paid a fee to Morris for the second
edition. For the fourth he transferred to a new publisher, Frederick
Startridge Ellis, to whom Swinburne introduced him. Ellis became a
staunch friend, a fellow-fisherman, a confederate of Morris in pursuit of
fine editions. He remained Morris's publisher until he retired in 1885.
Jason was well received. Even Tennyson, not otherwise a Morris
enthusiast, admired it. The young Octavia Hill judged it as 'true
poetry', whilst regretting the absence of Christianity. (In this she was
naïve. Morris remained the bishop *manqué*.) With the success of *Jason*,
Morris regained the confidence he needed to complete *The Earthly
Paradise*. He wrote to Burne-Jones, beaming: 'Naturally I am in good
spirits after the puffs.'

Why did *Jason* succeed where *Guenevere* failed? It was partly a
matter of the timing. In the eight intervening years the climate had
changed greatly. Tennyson was out of fashion, beginning to sound
empty, and the public had got tired of Tennysonian imitators. Two
years before *Jason*, the publication of Swinburne's impassioned and
exuberant poetic drama, *Atalanta in Calydon*, signalled the tide turning
towards more intellectually contentious forms of poetry. The subsequent furore over Swinburne's *Poems and Ballads*, some of which
were judged obscene, at last brought the methods and ideals of the
Pre-Raphaelite poets and artists into the public domain. George
Saintsbury the critic, looking back thirty years later at his original copy
of *Jason*, with its red buckram binding by then faded to orange on the
spine, explained how at that time, following on Swinburne, William
Morris 'hit the bird on both wings'. Morris took a perfect classical
subject, and gave it a perfect Romantic treatment. It was impossible for
anybody not to recognize that here was 'an entirely new fashion of telling
a story in verse'.

Morris's technique had changed since *Guenevere*. The awkwardness

1 *Emma Shelton*, Morris's mother, probably painted at the time of her engagement to William Morris Senior in 1824. Watercolour miniature.

2 *William Morris Senior*. Watercolour miniature by T. Wheeler, 1824. Both portraits are now in the collection of the William Morris Gallery, Walthamstow.

3 Henrietta, the second of William Morris's sisters, who remained unmarried and converted to the Roman Catholic Church. 4 Isabella Gilmore, his third sister. After the early death of her husband she became a Deaconess and a leading light in the ministry of women in the Church of England. 5 Emma Oldham, Morris's eldest and most loved sister, who married the Rev. Joseph Oldham in 1850. 6 Alice Gill, William Morris's youngest sister, born in 1846.

7 Arthur, the third of William Morris's brothers, a professional soldier who rose to Colonel in the King's Royal Rifle Corps.   8 Edgar, Morris's youngest brother, employed at Queen Square and Merton Abbey.   9 Hugh Stanley, usually known as Stanley, the brother closest in age to Morris, who became a gentleman farmer near Southampton.   10 Thomas Rendall Morris, usually known as Rendall, an unsuccessful soldier who died young.

11 Woodford Hall, Essex, the Morris family home from 1840 to 1848, when the financial crisis following the sudden death of William Morris Senior precipitated their departure.

12 Water House, Walthamstow. Emma Morris lived here with her children from 1848 to 1856, and the house is now the William Morris Gallery.

13 The grandiose tomb of William Morris's parents in Woodford churchyard, showing the family coat of arms granted in 1843.

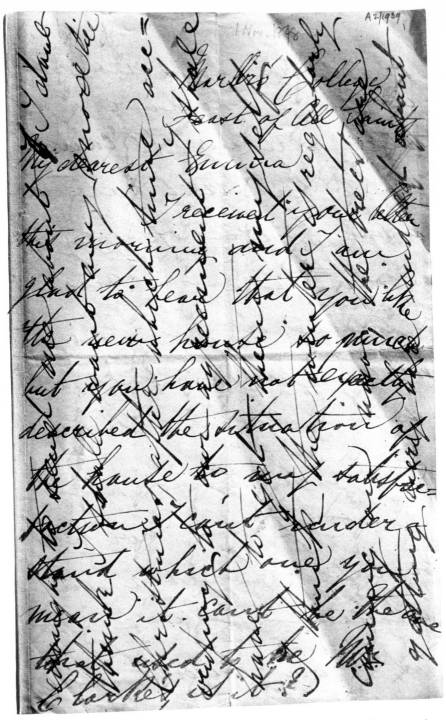

14 William Morris's earliest known letter, sent from Marlborough to his sister Emma when he was about fifteen.

15 William Morris, self-portrait dating from the time he was at Oxford, *c.* 1855.
Pencil drawing.

16 William Morris at twenty-three, a studio portrait taken when he was at Oxford.

17 Exeter College, Oxford, where Morris and Edward Jones (later Burne-Jones) were undergraduates from 1853 to 1855. At the time, major building works were under way. This picture is believed to show rooms they occupied in the Prideaux Building.
18 Oxford High Street in 1860. The historic architecture of Oxford fuelled Morris's passion for the buildings of the past.

19 Charles Faulkner, one of Morris's closest Oxford friends, later a founding partner in Morris, Marshall, Faulkner & Co. Faulkner eventually followed Morris into Socialism.
20 Cormell Price, the life-long friend who became headmaster of the United Services College. 21 Richard Watson Dixon, a fellow poet of Morris's at Oxford who became a Canon of the Church of England and was later 'rediscovered' by Gerard Manley Hopkins.
22 Wilfred Heeley, the oldest member of the Oxford 'set'.

23 St Philip and St James in north Oxford. Work on G. E. Street's famous High Victorian Gothic church began in 1860, soon after Morris joined Street's architectural office. The photograph was taken by John Piper.

24 George Edmund Street, photographed in 1877. Morris absorbed much from Street's architectural practice, but turned against his policy of restoration later, in the campaigns of the Society for the Protection of Ancient Buildings.

25 *Study of William Morris for the head of David.* Pencil drawing by Dante Gabriel Rossetti for the Llandaff Cathedral triptych, 1856.

26 No. 17 Red Lion Square. From November 1856 to spring 1859 Morris and Burne-Jones lived in the first-floor rooms.   27 The Old Debating Chamber (now the library) of the Oxford Union Society, decorated with murals by Morris, Rossetti, Burne-Jones and others in the 'jovial campaign' of 1857.   28 Dante Gabriel Rossetti, *carte de visite*. Morris first met Rossetti through Burne-Jones.

29 *Ford Madox Brown*. Drawing by Dante Gabriel Rossetti, 1852. 30 *Lizzie Siddal* (Mrs Rossetti), pencil drawing by Dante Gabriel Rossetti dated June, 1861, the year after their marriage. 31 *Jane Burden*, drawing by William Morris made in 1858, shortly before their marriage. 32 *Study of Janey as Guenevere for 'Sir Lancelot in the Queen's Chamber'*, by Dante Gabriel Rossetti.

33 Georgiana Macdonald photographed at the time of her engagement to Edward Burne-Jones, when she was sixteen.

34 Edward Burne-Jones, a rare photograph of the aspiring artist at the age of thirty-one.

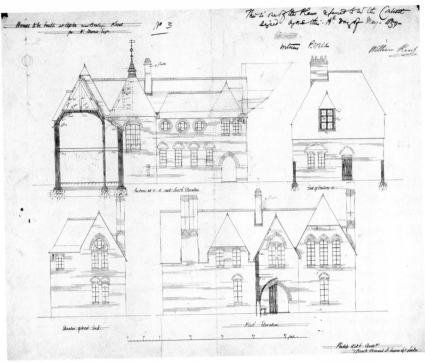

35 Philip Webb's original designs for Red House, Bexleyheath, a building 'in the style of the thirteenth century' that became an inspiration to twentieth-century modernist architects. Pen and ink, 1859.

36 Red House interior. Entrance hall leading to the magnificent oak staircase.

37 Philip Webb portrait, watercolour, by Charles Fairfax Murray, 1873.
In the National Portrait Gallery, London.

38 *Study of Mrs Morris for the head of the Virgin*, for Dante Gabriel Rossetti's Llandaff
Cathedral triptych. Pencil and indian ink, 1861.
39 A less idealized portrait of Janey on a *carte de visite*, early 1860s.

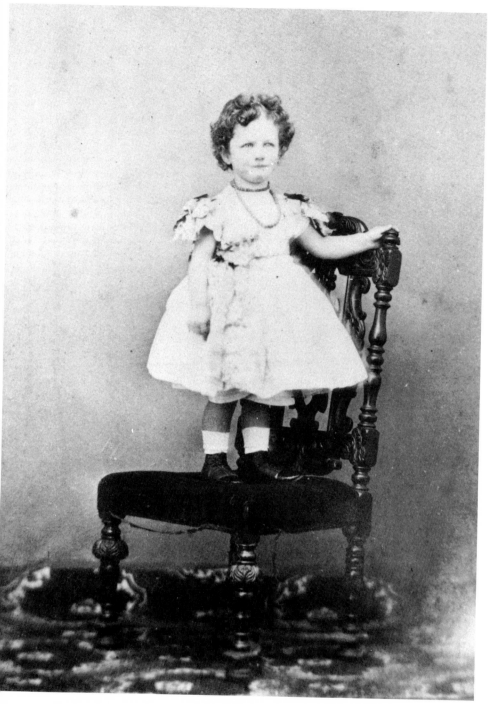

40 The infant May Morris standing on a chair, *c.* 1864. The portrait reminds us that in some respects Morris's daughters had a conventional Victorian bourgeois upbringing.

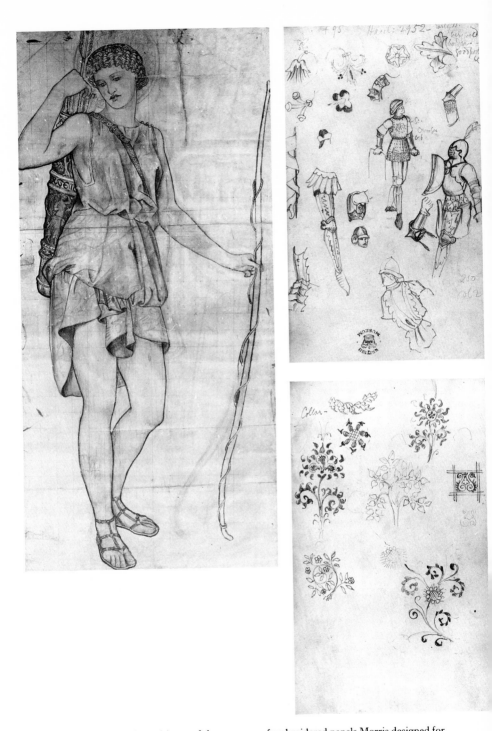

41 Cartoon for 'Artemis', one of the sequence of embroidered panels Morris designed for Red House. The three completed panels are now at Castle Howard, Yorkshire.

42 and 43 *Knights* and *Flowers*, sketches from William Morris's notebooks, probably dating from the Red House period, and now in the British Library.

44 'The Legend of St George', Morris's design for a painted panel for the cabinet designed by Philip Webb, shown at the International Exhibition in London in 1862. The princess is an obvious portrait of Janey. The cabinet is now in the Victoria & Albert Museum.

45 William Morris in his working smock. The smock was adopted by Morris's followers as the uniform of social protest in the Arts and Crafts workshops of the simple life.

46 John Ruskin and Dante Gabriel Rossetti, photographed by W. & D. Downey in 1863.

47 No. 26 Queen Square, where Morris lived and worked from 1865. The site is now occupied by the National Hospital for Nervous Diseases. 48 No. 16 Cheyne Walk on the Thames embankment. Dante Gabriel Rossetti lived here from 1862, after Lizzie Siddal's death, becoming increasingly reclusive. 49 Algernon Charles Swinburne, Dante Gabriel Rossetti, his brother William and Fanny Cornforth at No. 16 Cheyne Walk, *c.* 1863.

50 Jane Morris posed by Dante Gabriel Rossetti, one of a series of portraits taken in the tent in the garden at No. 16 Cheyne Walk in 1865.

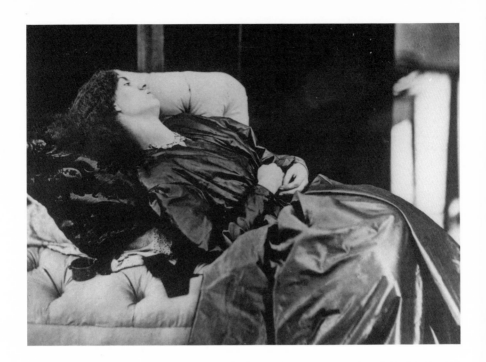

51 Jane Morris in one of Dante Gabriel Rossetti's more voluptuous poses. The photographer
was probably John R. Parsons.

52 *Mrs William Morris reading*, pencil drawing made by Rossetti when he and Janey were at
Scalands, 30 April 1870. The drawing is now in the Ashmolean Museum, Oxford.

53 *Aglaia Coronio*, pastel drawing by Dante Gabriel Rossetti, 1870.   54 Aglaia Coronio, *carte de visite* showing a less glamorous figure.   55 *Marie Spartali*, later Marie Stillman, a model and pupil of Rossetti's and Janey's closest friend. The portrait is by Rossetti, a study for *Dante's Dream at the Time of the Death of Beatrice*, 1870.   56 *Maria Zambaco*, whose liaison with Ned caused a crisis in the Burne-Jones marriage. The portrait is by Edward Burne-Jones.

57 Bad Ems on the river Lahn, the fashionable German spa town where Morris endured six weeks of attendance upon Janey in 1869.

58 The Kesselbrunnen at Bad Ems, the pillared hall in which the spa waters were dispensed.

59 A nineteenth-century photograph of the Icelandic landscape near Reykjavík. The barren
scenery affected Morris deeply and he returned to it repeatedly in his later writing.
60 Eiríkr Magnússon, Morris's co-translator of the Sagas and his companion on his first journey
to Iceland in 1871.

61 Kelmscott Manor. The east front, showing the original sixteenth-century house with the
addition of *c.* 1670 to the right. In Morris's Utopian novel *News from Nowhere* the travellers
finally arrive at a 'many gabled old house built by the simple country folks of the long past times'.

had gone. He had now arrived at his mature way of writing, the style described by Swinburne as 'so broad and sad and simple' in his notice of *Jason* for *The Fortnightly Review*. These days we are so attuned to reading short poems that work as huge as *Jason* seems to have its built-in tediums, like a Bruckner symphony. There are times when Morris seems to be merely pattern-making as the heroic couplets, broken into, overlapping, wend on and on and on. You need to read it slowly, preferably aloud, and to get into the swim of it, to become aware of the strength of Morris's narrative, the glow of visual detail. Morris's Golden Fleece is superlatively golden. Burne-Jones was right about it when he said of Morris's poetry, 'You cannot find short quotations in him, he must be taken in great gulps.'

Morris himself acknowledged his dependence on his *subject* in making his verse flow. In choosing to retell the classic story of Jason's long voyage in the *Argo* to bring back the Golden Fleece from Colchis, Morris found himself a formula, the quest tale, that lasted for the rest of his creative life, through the several volumes of *The Earthly Paradise*, on to the solemn fairytales of Morris's second childhood in the 1890s. From now on, the tales he tells are, in their essence, all the same tale. The child raised in the wild, ignorant of his true origins; the apparition of the maiden with her girt-up gown and sandalled feet (the foot has a curious significance for Morris); the *distrait* and bashful hero; the memory-trick, glimpses of 'something half-remembered in his face'; set-piece scenes of the hero in tremendous confrontation, like the Taming of the Brazen Bulls in *Jason*; and always in the background the ebb and flow of passion, recognition of the lover, love achieved, love lost again. C. S. Lewis, writing in the 1930s, saw this pattern as very odd and as peculiar to Morris. He defines it as 'the endless hithering and thithering of natural desire' joined with 'an irrepressible thirst for immortality'. And indeed in Morris's hands the tale of Jason emerges as an unlikely mid-Victorian hybrid: Keatsian romance and Christian Socialist text.

It is not of course so much the tale of Jason as of Medea. In depicting his most glamorous and devious enchantress Morris was writing from the heart of his obsession for the women of darkness, the shape-changers and spell-binders. His Medea is successor to Sidonia the Sorceress. Burne-Jones at this same period was painting Circe. The exquisite sorceress behind the brazen cauldron was a figment of the Pre-Raphaelite dream. Jason betrays Medea with his new beloved, Glauce:

and once more on that night
She stole abroad about the mirk midnight,
Once more upon a wood's edge from her feet
She stripped her shoes and bared her shoulder sweet.
Once more that night over the lingering fire
She hung with sick heart famished of desire.
Once more she turned back when her work was done;
Once more she fled the coming of the sun;
Once more she reached her dusky, shimmering room;
Once more she lighted up the dying gloom;
Once more she lay adown, and in sad sleep
Her weary body and sick heart did steep.

Morris tells a good story which is also a Victorian version of pornography. Again it was C. S. Lewis who first noticed, or anyway first pointed out, that the eroticism in William Morris's writing is 'patent, ubiquitous and unabashed'.

The fascination about Morris's *Jason* is the distancing. The story as he tells it is almost unbearably familiar although it is based on a remote classical legend. Shaw once claimed that in *Jason* Morris was describing 'a journey by the Thames through the Thames and Severn tunnel to its source' and that was why he liked it. This seems doubtful. But certainly the sense of Morris's deeply felt experience, intellectual, emotional, topographical, permeates the poem. The classical is held in the grip of a well-rounded but in some ways eccentric Victorian sensibility. Morris apologized to his old Exeter colleague, the rector and antiquarian Morgan George Watkins: 'As for my archaeology I'm afraid you will find little of it in Jason, and that my towns belong rather to the Cinque-Cento or Jacobean period than the Homeric or rather pre-Homeric, and that there is more of Lincoln or Rouen than of Athens in them, let alone Tiryns or Mycenae, and that my wine is Bon Bourgogne not Chian, which latter assertion I hope to have the pleasure of proving practically and literally to you.'

Morris, buoyed up by success, threw his weight about a little. Ned complained of haughtiness when *Jason* went into its second edition. Topsy was pleased with the news that his old tutor F. B. Guy was introducing *Jason* into the curriculum at Bradfield. It made him laugh to be 'in the position of nuisance to schoolboys' after his miserable Marlborough years.

If he read it, the review in an obscure American paper must also have delighted him. Under the heading 'Advances of Intellectual Activity among the Working Classes of England' it praised the poem by a rising author 'who earns a precarious living by designing wall-papers for London furnishing firms'.

'M. .rr. .s of Emperor's Square', as William De Morgan called him, was more in public view than he had been in the old premises. A prospective customer arriving at Queen Square in 1865 was attended to by Morris in his dark blue linen blouse. He discussed wallpaper patterns and made out the bill himself. The following year a client interrupted him at work there on a new design, for the 'Pomegranate' paper. As outside commissions multiplied, his staff began referring to him in official correspondence as 'Our Mr. Morris'. Rossetti's famous jibe about the Bard and Petty Tradesman was very near the truth.

12 *'The Bard and Petty Tradesman'*. Caricature by Dante Gabriel Rossetti.

Changes had been made in the Firm's structure. Charley Faulkner had returned to be a mathematics don at Oxford: 'though not much like one I must confess', said Morris. Charley stayed in close contact with the partners through his mother and his sisters, the Firm's neighbours, who lived at No. 35 Queen Square; his duties were passed on to a new business manager, appointed in the last few months before the move. The appointment of a business manager to small idealistic enterprises has its built-in hazards: it was one of the great unresolved problems of the Arts and Crafts workshops. In the history of unlikely recruitments Warington Taylor's must rate as an extreme one. He was a tall, thin man with a large Roman nose and a rapid, excitable manner of speaking. He had been in Swinburne's division at Eton, then was sent to school in Germany where he intrigued the locals by continuing to wear his top hat and Eton jacket. He had become a Catholic, entered and left the army, and as Georgie so delicately phrased it 'had not yet found his place in life'. He was a resolute Wagnerian, unlike Morris who found Wagner ridiculous, resenting what he saw as his belittling of the epics of the north.

When Warington Taylor came to the Firm's notice he was employed in the box office of Her Majesty's Theatre which was then an opera house. He had married beneath him. His daughter died in childhood and his wife took other lovers. Interestingly, when his marriage arrived at a crisis point, it was Janey who was summoned to visit Mrs Taylor and negotiate a peace.

Taylor was surprised and overjoyed by his appointment. He was already attuned to the aesthetics of the Firm. He was eager to immerse himself in its philosophy, the *'intense honest* desire to attain Truth at any risk', seeing the Firm as part of an important artistic movement in the country: 'the same feeling produced Pre-Raphaelitism – it produced Ruskin – it produced Woodward – it has produced Webb the only really great Architect I know'. Always the opportunist, Taylor also saw the Firm supplying conveniently the furniture and fittings, 'the little bits of carpet etc. etc.', he was needing to move into his new home.

Taylor saw immediately that the Firm had lost direction. Since Faulkner left, the partners' meetings were no longer regular. In the middle 1860s the Firm's market in stained glass began a downturn, and the turnover and profits were so low that there was still no possibility of a repayment of the loans made in the early years by Morris and his mother. Morris as businessman was becoming more erratic, more pre-occupied with writing. Taylor acted fast and violently to 'throw regularity and business habits' into the Firm's affairs. Within the first few weeks the rumour spread among the partners 'that he was keeping the accounts of the firm like a dragon, attending to the orders of the customers, and actually getting Morris to work at one thing at a time'.

This was the period at which the black rush-seated chair, the so-called Sussex chair, came into its own as a middle-class cult object and a symbol of Morris himself and of the Firm. Ford Madox Brown had been the original enthusiast for quasi-peasant furniture. From the late 1850s there were rush-seated chairs in all the houses of the partners including Red House, where the Sussex chairs were red. But until the middle 1860s the Firm's simple furniture had been overshadowed by the more ornate, palatial, decorated pieces. It was Taylor's achievement to redress this balance. He encouraged lighter furniture on grounds of practicality: 'What about moveable furniture – light Sir – something you can pull about with one hand?' He supported it too with arguments of ideology, suggesting that 'The old Sussex Black chair, the common chair of Red Lion Square, is essentially gentlemanly with a total absence of ex-tallow chandler vulgarity – it possesses poetry of simplicity.'

Taylor was himself a visionary. He found and admired in the Sussex chair a quality of sweetness and decorum comparable with the delicate rosebuds on early Worcester china or with English willow-pattern plates. His aesthetic, as expressed in his astute and rambling letters, has many echoes in Morris's lectures of the early 1880s. How far was Morris influenced by Taylor's early concept of a style of decoration based on 'nature, serenity and true construction', an English modern style that made a creative connection with the past?

An even more interesting question is the extent to which Taylor affected Morris's political awareness. May Morris went so far as to claim he was responsible for Morris's eventual conversion to full-blown Socialism. Taylor the old Etonian, like Morris the Marlburian, was deeply conscious of the iniquities of the class structure in Britain. He would rant and rail against it. His streak of the outrageous focused on the British middle classes with their phlegmatic minds. He found the women especially despicable. 'I don't understand anyone looking upon the said British mamma as otherwise than a fool.' In the midst of the Firm's commission to redecorate St James's Palace, Taylor was fulminating: 'Just remember we are embezzling the public money now – what business has any palace to be decorated at all?'

Taylor's political unease is mirrored in the outbursts of Morris himself as, over the next decade, he found his own position as rich man's lackey increasingly untenable. There is another echo of Taylor in Morris's famous confrontation with one of his best clients, Sir Isaac Lowthian Bell, who asked him why he was stamping and storming through the rooms at Rounton Grange he had been called in to advise on. Morris turned on him 'like a wild animal', saying, 'It is only that I spend my life ministering to the swinish luxury of the rich.'

Morris enjoyed the good life. Taylor could not allow it. He had too sharp a knowledge of the easy fall from fortune. He was haunted by the spectre of the man as walking sandwich-board. 'Sandwiches', he noted, 'are often decayed gents.' Frustrated by Morris's boisterous self-containment, irritated by his corpulence, he set himself up as Morris's tormentor, attacking his professional fecklessness, his personal extravagances, prophesying the bankruptcy that would result from his lavish expenditure on wine and manuscripts. Taylor left London in 1866. He was dying of consumption and he went to live in Hastings. He was never officially divested of his duties but he remained the business manager in exile, pursuing his vendetta against Morris with increasing vehemence through his declining years.

Were his strictures justified? Was Morris really so inefficient that he would not begin a stained-glass window until forced to, so lax in supervision that a dishonest clerk could easily embezzle a pound or two a week? There is the ring of truth in Taylor's accusations of Morris being 'very nervous' about work, taking men off one job to allot them to another in an *ad hoc* and amateurish way. 'Morris will start half a dozen jobs,' claimed Taylor: 'They are put away, bits get lost, have to be done again: hence great loss of time and money.' Was the time and motion study quite so unknown at the Firm?

There is certainly evidence that Morris was bad at keeping work on schedule. Morris wrote apologetically to the Dean at Jesus College, Cambridge, about the decoration of the nave roof of the chapel, due to be completed by the Christmas of 1866. He asked for an extension till the spring: 'work of this sort cannot be hurried, as the men who are able to do it are very few.' There is also a hint of managerial chaos in his letter to George Campfield, the foreman on the job, enclosing his cartoons and instructions for angels: 'The escapades of our men have enraged the dons and they want to get rid of you.' But just as likely, Taylor's goading may have made Morris the more obstinate. He could easily revert to small child's behaviour. His relations with George Wardle, who took over Taylor's duties in the office, were more equable, and 1866 was the year in which a number of important new commissions for interior decoration, directed by Morris, consolidated the reputation and finances of the Firm.

The redecoration of the Armoury and Tapestry Room at St James's Palace was carried out between September 1866 and January 1867. The Armoury is the first in the sequence of public rooms at the top of the Grand Staircase which lead through to the Throne Room. The Tapestry Room comes next.

Philip Webb designed the detail of the scheme which is almost overpoweringly Gothic and tenebrous, rich, dense and highly patterned. The lower walls are panelled darkly with gilt floral and green foliage decoration. Doors, dado panels, ceilings, windows, cornices are painted. There are touches of fantasy: flowers with sunburst centres. Giant fireplaces are gaudy, like outlandish gypsy stalls. The effect of the exotic was increased by the display of armour installed by the War Office in 1868, including eight full Maltese armour-suits and six helmets, and the royal tapestries themselves in their faded buffs, blues, greens. They are figurative tapestries with huge and lowering figures. These rooms are strange and magical, stagy, a bit preposterous, like the over-ornate palaces in Morris's fairytales. Their originality derives not from their layout, which was in its day conventional, but from their build-up of extravagant detail. The effect of so much pattern is almost psychedelic. The spectator feels dislocated, woozy, trapped in an entirely painted space. The shock of the new, the impact of these rooms on Morris's contemporaries, can be best appreciated by comparing the Firm's work at St James's with the anaemic Banqueting Rooms redesigned two years earlier by the favoured royal decorator John G. Crace.

How had Morris achieved this large commission at the Palace? Indeed how had the Firm succeeded so quickly in its stated aim of ousting Crace? It was the result of Rossetti's well-timed friendship with the First Commissioner of Public Works, William Cowper, later Lord Mount-Temple, a stepson of Lord Palmerston and a man with a burgeoning interest in new developments in art. Lady Mount-Temple gives the background in her memoirs: 'when some rooms in the old Palace of St. James's had to be done up, instead of putting them into the hands of some fashionable upholsterer, as had been done before, he persuaded the great Reformer in Art, William Morris, to undertake the work.' Rossetti had achieved it by charm and audacity.

One day Mr. Rossetti was dining alone with us, and instead of admiring my room and decorations, as I expected, he evidently could hardly sit at ease with them. I began then to ask him if it were *possible* to suggest improvements! 'Well,' he said, frankly, 'I should begin by burning everything you have got!'

Morris's second substantial official commission was for the Green Dining-Room at what was then the South Kensington Museum. Along with Philip Webb he had already been pillaging the collections, studying the stained glass, tiles and painted decoration. Morris once said at a meeting, 'They talk of building museums for the public, but South Kensington Museum was got together for six people, another is a comrade in the room.' He was referring of course to Philip Webb. The initial inquiry came from Henry Cole, Richard Redgrave and Captain Francis Fowke, the architect of the new buildings at South Kensington, who must have seen and been impressed by the Firm's stand at the 1862 exhibition. Stained glass by Morris and Burne-Jones had been purchased for the Museum collection in 1864. One hundred pounds was allotted to the Firm for their preliminary sketches for the 'Western Refreshment Room'.

Fowke's idea was that the buildings of the Museum and their decorative details should be instructive and inspiring, that they should constitute exhibits in themselves, and the Green Dining-Room was the completion of a trio of elaborate refreshment rooms on the ground floor of the Lecture Theatre building. The large central dining-room, now called the Gamble Room, was a Renaissance-style interior, with its columns in majolica, its frieze of *amorini*; the East Refreshment Room or Grill Room, also known as the Dutch Kitchen, was designed by Edward Poynter in a more 'aesthetic' manner, using Dutch blue and white tiling. It was influential as one of the first Victorian decorative schemes to revive the large-scale use of the pictorial tile panel. Ned and Georgie used to dine there together as a treat. But of the three interiors it was the Firm's Green Dining-Room which had the greatest impact. It became the meeting place for the men of taste in London, the equivalent of Gréliches and the Progrès in Paris. Whistler, du Maurier, Poynter, Lamont congregated there, admired it. If you want the first example of the 'greenery-yallery Grosvenor Gallery' interior satirized by Gilbert in *Patience*, this is it.

Webb's design for the room is a complicated interplay of elements, using the technique of layering pattern upon pattern which was to become almost the hallmark of the Firm. The wall surface is divided into four distinct areas: the dado, the panelling, the filling and the frieze. The bottom layer consisted of oak panels, stained deep green. Above it rose a tier of painted panels of the months and the signs of the Zodiac, by Burne-Jones, interspersed with panels of vegetation, like the drawings from a herbal. Higher up again was a layer of moulded plaster panels, each with an olive branch in relief. Above this was the frieze of dogs chasing hares, designed by Webb and based on a font in Newcastle Cathedral. The ceiling was itself divided into panels with sharp-leaved decoration painted in yellow. The pattern was pricked straight into the wet plaster, as it had been at Red House. The Firm's work was now so large-scale that they used a subcontractor. Much of the work of the Green Dining-Room, as at St James's Palace, was carried out by Dunn & Co., a London firm of builders and decorators. But there was still the atmosphere of the jolly working party, with Morris costing, estimating, cross-negotiating, at the hub.

He may have been erratic but Morris kept his clients. The Firm received further commissions for St James's Palace through the 1870s and early 1880s. Morris was discussing details for the curtains for the Throne Room two years before he joined the revolutionary Socialists. His links with the South Kensington Museum continued close, affectionate, interdependent until his death. In a sense his clients clung to him because he was an oddity: there was a certain cachet in employing the author of *The Life and Death of Jason*. Unlike the general run of London decorators, Morris met his customers on their own terms. The Firm's clients were already, or soon became, his friends.

One of the Firm's earliest commissions for domestic interiors was from the water-colourist Birket Foster. For his house, The Hill, at Witley in Surrey, Ford Madox Brown, Rossetti and Burne-Jones provided one stained-glass panel sequence of 'King René's Honeymoon', another based on Chaucer. Morris saw, but never fully exploited, the possibilities in domestic stained glass. He and Philip Webb collaborated on schemes for other friends on the Pre-Raphaelite networks: the studio house Webb designed for Val Prinsep at No. 1 (now 14) Holland Park Road in Kensington; Webb's house for George Howard at No. 1 Palace Green. Between Morris and George Howard, later 9th Earl of Carlisle, the rapport was very close, a subtle intertwining of politics and families and wallpaper and art. They were in touch by 1867 when Morris wrote regretting he had not been able to visit Howard at his home at Naworth Castle: 'I know something of Naworth by Parker's book.' This was John Henry Parker's *Some Account of Domestic Architecture in England*

(1853), a favourite reference book of Morris's. From this he knew that Naworth 'must be a very beautiful and interesting house'.

Since Red House the tenor of Morris's life had been changing. There his friends had come to him. Now there was a movement outwards. Deprived of their large garden with the stables, May and Jenny were reduced to five shillings' worth of donkey rides on Hampstead Heath. Morris spent much of his time with Ned and Georgie in their house in Kensington Square, which he helped to furnish with a large Persian prayer-carpet. They had moved into this house in 1865, after the disbandment of the joint plan for Red House. One evening Morris arrived there with 'a glorious haul of picture-books – black-letter and old engravings – a History of the Cross, a *Biblia Pauperum*, and a Looking Glass of Human Salvation'. He would come to play 'American bowls' in the Burne-Joneses' long garden with Ned, Webb and Faulkner, when he was in town. They would go off and dine together in some 'pot-house' afterwards. Morris liked the male seclusion of London restaurants such as Rouget's in Castle Street, Leicester Square, which provided 'French dinners at moderate rates'. A. J. Munby, an admirer of *Guenevere*, had spotted him there in the early 1860s, noting with surprise his lack of obvious charisma: 'Morris is simple and unpretending in appearance and conversation, and does not express by either the power which his book shows him to have.'

Morris did not enjoy the theatre, finding it too formal. When Allingham took him to see *Black-eyed Susan* at the Royalty in 1867 he was 'bored a good deal'. He preferred his own performances. Allingham was with him at a gathering of friends in Euston Road, in the lodgings the ailing Warington Taylor had returned to for the winter. Philip Webb was there, also Rossetti, lounging. 'I say the rhyme about "There's a louse on my back Twenty years old!" (which I heard Tennyson give). Morris repeats it with furious emphasis and gestures, making us all shout with laughter. Poor Taylor – tall, with eager hatchet face – is ghastly thin but full of mental energy – vociferates, then must stop to cough.'

The Firm was involved in schemes for decorating the chapel in Forest School at Walthamstow. There were other *rapprochements*. It seems Morris's relations with his family in Essex were closer than in the Red House years. The children were the link between the generations, and now their life in Kent was over old Mrs Morris's house in Leyton was used as their usual rural retreat. The family would travel from Queen Square in a cab piled up with luggage to the house May remembered as 'a fine, square, spacious building set in well-bushed grounds, with a wide terrace-lawn and gardens sloping to a wilderness'. With the respectful servants and the amiable throng of his relations Morris was back in the milieu he had earlier chosen to reject. Such hitherings and thitherings of feeling, the basis of his poetry, were always in the background of his life. May describes him taking part in family prayers at Leyton. The tea urn is borne in; the house servants then enter, carrying a long bench on which they sit in a long row; Morris reads family prayers. May reports, with the sharp ears of a child, that her father reads the 'Psalm of the day in the language of King James's Bible, beautifully', but that the prayer by a modern theologian is delivered disapprovingly in short sharp snaps. The urn sizzles. Henrietta's little dog comes in from the garden. Morris's mother stands on tiptoe and fondly strokes the whiskers of her son.

From the relative claustrophobia of Bloomsbury there was more reason to go off on expeditions. In the summer of 1866 Morris, Webb and Warington Taylor went on another working holiday tour of churches in northern France. Janey had recovered enough from her malaise of the previous year to go with them. It was an oddly assorted party. Ned and Georgie had hoped to join the travellers but were prevented by the birth of Margaret, destined to marry William Morris's first biographer, in June. Burne-Jones drew a sketch of himself holding the baby, left stranded on the cliffs, while the rest of them depart. Janey

13 *Edward Burne-Jones (holding the baby Margaret) watches the departure of William and Janey Morris, Philip Webb and Warington Taylor for France.* Caricature by Edward Burne-Jones.

leans over the side of the boat. Morris crouches in the bottom, like a figure in a nonsense rhyme by Edward Lear. Before they took the coach from Sens to Troyes they stopped in Paris briefly. Morris looked for books on the quaysides and went early to his bed.

That same August Morris joined the Burne-Jones family at Lymington. He came down from London to meet them *en route* in Winchester. Georgie described how she and Ned had waited for him at the door of their hotel: 'I remember his swinging towards us along the High Street with a look as if he had easily walked all the way.' They went on together over the water meadows to St Cross church. Webb and Allingham were with them. Back in the city they looked at the cathedral where, according to Allingham, Morris talked 'copiously and interestingly on all things', Webb intervening sometimes on technicalities. They had dinner at the George: 'tough mutton, parsonic waiter, red faced grinning landlady (bill 19s.)'. Afterwards they returned to the cathedral where a verger, 'tall, sallow and melancholy, did not offer his services, but made a remark or two which seemed to imply, in a self-respecting manner, that he was ready to go round with us officially if we cared for him. But, taking slight notice of him, Morris discoursed away and the Verger listened with the rest of us, at one point civilly correcting Morris on a detail.' The next day, back in Lymington, they took Morris and buried him up to his neck in shingle on the beach.

In August 1867 the holidays were spent on familiar ground at Oxford. They saw much of Charley Faulkner whose mother and sisters were also staying there. The Morrises lodged in Beaumont Street, where eleven years earlier Morris had begun his pupillage with Street. The Burne-Jones family took over some undergraduates' rooms in St Giles, empty for the long vacation.

As it turned out this was to be their last joint holiday. Morris still had to travel up to London every day or two to supervise the Firm. The giant edifice of *The Earthly Paradise* was still rising. The words flowed fast, even on a London omnibus. Every evening he would read out to the assembled families in Oxford the day's completed work.

Holiday events lie fossilized in Morris's poetry. One river expedition, through the remote and lovely upper reaches of the Thames via Eynsham and the meadows of the Evenlode, is drawn upon for the introductory verses to the June stories in *The Earthly Paradise*.

What better place than this then could we find
By this sweet stream that knows not of the sea,
That guesses not the city's misery,
This little stream whose hamlets scarce have names,
This far-off, lonely mother of the Thames?

These verses of Morris's are curiously prophetic. Four years later he himself, in leasing Kelmscott Manor, was to set down his roots in the same lost riverland.

Another memorable excursion, on a day of blazing summer, was made down the Thames to Dorchester. Again this river journey is the basis for a passage in *The Earthly Paradise*, the description in the introduction to August of the long-roofed church and the weir by Day's Lock within sight of extensive prehistoric remains on Sinodun Hill. Morris made a double use of the trip for in the course of it he read aloud to his companions his latest version of 'The Story of the Wanderers', the prologue to *The Earthly Paradise*, to the muffled summer sounds made by the barley mowers on the 'trenchéd hill'.

A certain sense of melancholy overlies descriptions of this Oxford holiday. Morris was unwell, probably with a recurrence of his rheumatic troubles. He makes several complaints of lumbago and sciatica in his letters over the next few years. Practical jokes were over, Georgie noticed. There was a new and subdued mood of family responsibility. The prospect of another move, the third in seven years, hung over the Burne-Joneses. The house in Kensington Square had been sold during their tenancy and they had now taken, rather nervously, a larger and potentially much grander house in Fulham. This was The Grange in North End Lane. A few days before they moved, Ned opened his first bank account. 'Naturally', wrote Georgie, 'he chose that of Morris, and was introduced by him to Messrs. Praeds of Fleet Street.' He placed with Praeds the sum of £127 10s. They gave him a cheque book which he did not know how to use.

The final family summer holiday was spent in Southwold, Suffolk, in 1868. Morris was back in the flat lands of East Anglia, great waste spaces of sand dunes and marshy valleys, heather, scrubby bushes, bracken. He described the region later as 'a mournful place, but full of character'. He was moved by its buildings, especially the severe and reed-bound fourteenth-century Blythburgh church. Rossetti, contemplating following the Morrises into this backwater of Englishness, called Southwold a 'deadly-lively (or very quiet) place'. The Morrises travelled with some dubious companions, Charles and Kitty Howell. Howell was born in Portugal. His father was English, his mother Portuguese. He came to England aged sixteen, and was now working as Ruskin's secretary. He also hovered round Rossetti, and was his confidant and right-hand man. Morris too had befriended him, to the extent of signing the register at the Howells' marriage. He became disenchanted, perhaps at the point at which Howell had invoked Morris's authority to trick Warington Taylor into letting him have wallpapers at a special discount price. Morris was scathing about the broad red ribbon Howell wore across his shirtfront and claimed as a decoration of his mother's noble family: knowing Howell, Morris suspected he had stolen it. He may have half-suspected that at Southwold Howell was acting as a go-between, bearing letters to and fro between Rossetti and his wife.

Morris draws upon Southwold, quintessential English seaside, in *The Earthly Paradise*, in the stanzas for October. It is grey, ghostly scenery, a landscape of premonition:

> O love, turn from the unchanging sea, and gaze
> Down these grey slopes upon the year grown old,
> A-dying mid the autumn-scented haze,
> That hangeth o'er the hollow in the wold,
> Where the wind-bitten ancient elms infold
> Grey church, long barn, orchard and red-roofed stead,
> Wrought in dead days for men a long while dead.

Rossetti was now living in dilapidated splendour at No. 16 Cheyne Walk in Chelsea. This was a house he had had his eye on for some time and he was installed there by the end of 1862, eight months after Lizzie's death. 'Tudor House', as it was known, was built on the site of Sir Thomas More's old residence. In the 1860s there was no Embankment and only a narrow road to separate the tall iron gates of the courtyard from the Thames. Tudor House is in fact a spectacular example of the eighteenth-century London town house, with its brick pilasters, arch-headed windows and rhetorical central pediment. Swinburne, George Meredith and Rossetti's brother William all rented rooms there in the early days and Meredith described it as 'a strange, quaint, grand old place, with an immense garden, magnificent panelled staircases and rooms – a palace'. Rossetti, unlike Morris, looked for histrionic qualities in choosing a building. There was nothing of the homely about Tudor House. It seemed a building set apart, a Sleeping Beauty's resting place. Its decorative ironwork formed a carapace. The outsize, metal dragon door-knocker disconcerted visitors. Did one seize the door-knocker by the tail or by the head?

Tudor House was full of mirrors. The sitting-room was lined with mirrors of all shapes, sizes and patterns. Again this was a source of alarm to many visitors, faced in all directions with versions of themselves. It was another point of difference with Morris who thought vanity unmanly and whose own dislike of mirrors was intense. There are dozens of descriptions of the rooms at Tudor House. Rossetti's decorative style was both classic and eclectic, careless and recherché, surely the first example of what in the twentieth century came to be known as 'shabby chic'. The sitting-room with its original fire grate, Chinese black-lacquered panels with gold birds, flowers and animals; the old blue Dutch tiles; the Spode china in the cabinet. Rossetti's stuffy bedroom with thick seventeenth-century crewel-work curtains drawn around the antique four-poster bed. The blue china cases filled with peacock feathers. The props spilling out from the drawers of the studio: the necklaces, feather-work, Japanese crystal. Old stringed instruments lay strewn around; dulcimers, mandolines and lutes. Visitors depict Tudor House as a mixture of junk shop and museum with, as the prize exhibit, Rossetti himself, sturdy, burly, joking, charming, wearing 'a sort of dressing gown' and slippers to usher people into his studio.

He was only just prevented from adding a young elephant to his increasingly exotic collection of animals and birds at Tudor House. Browning asked him what on earth he would do with an elephant. Gabriel replied that he wanted to teach him how to clean the windows: 'Then when someone passes by the house he will see the elephant cleaning the windows, and will say "Who lives in that house?" and people will tell him, "Oh, that's a painter called Rossetti", and he will say, "I should like to buy one of that man's pictures". So he will ring and come in, and I shall sell him a picture.' Where Morris's humour was direct and almost childlike, Rossetti's was more whimsical with underlying menace. This was a sign of the southern melancholy that ebbed and flowed so tragically in his life.

Fanny Cornforth was a part of Rossetti's Chelsea ménage. Fanny was the street girl turned model, the 'cordial stunner' with corn-coloured hair introduced to Pre-Raphaelite circles in the late 1850s, becoming the particular possession of Rossetti. She had been devastated, fretting constantly, at the time of Rossetti's honeymoon in Paris. Now, with Lizzie's death, Fanny was reinstated, coming and going to Cheyne Walk from her own house in Royal Avenue, ruling the roost, cackling, teasing in her raucous Cockney accent. 'F. sometimes says, "Rizetti, I shall leave the room! – I'll put you out in the scullery', Allingham recorded. He found her there at breakfast one morning, dressed in white.

If there seems something incongruous in Fanny's sensual presence in the house that was also a shrine to Lizzie Siddal, hung with her pen-and-ink and water-colour studies, this was nothing new. Rossetti's complex nature encouraged such dualities: he needed a woman both to worship and to make love to, and he did not see these functions as necessarily combined within one woman. Rossetti exemplifies almost at its crudest the Victorian male concept of woman as either Virgin or whore. Mourning Lizzie he was still extremely curious about other people's sexuality, wondering almost obsessively if Byron fucked his half-sister, borrowing from Swinburne *Les Liaisons dangereuses*. In August 1862 Boyce was writing in his diary 'Joined Rossetti at Swinburne's rooms where they were looking over "Justine" by the Marquis de Sade, recent acquisition of the latter. We then went on to the International Exhibition. Had some ices at a stall near the Egyptian things where there was a very lovely girl of whom Gabriel obtained a promise to sit to him.' Masculine effrontery; female capitulation. A lark, a reassurance, and a pattern of his life.

His attitude to loose women was humorous, protective. His Greek friend Luke Ionides recalled a conversation at a dinner party. The high-pitched voice of a well-known artist had proclaimed, 'I had rather any day meet a lioness bereft of her whelps than a woman who has lost her virtue.' To which Rossetti replied softly, 'Nonsense man, nonsense! I've met many and all very nice indeed.' For the other sort of women, the objects of his worship, he had another manner, both more distant and intrusive. In April 1864 Rossetti started painting Marie Spartali, the Greek consul's daughter, the woman once described as 'Mrs. Morris for beginners'. Looking back in her old age she explained to Georgie the particular enchantment of a sitting with Rossetti. He cosseted and flattered with a subtle and disorientating combination of reverence and sexual provocation. It is clear from her description that Rossetti was a master at locating and releasing the unacknowledged urges. Morris worshipped. But he could not communicate. Rossetti could make a woman feel as she had never felt before.

In taking for her lovers first Rossetti and then Wilfrid Scawen Blunt, two of the most famous seducers of the whole Victorian age, Janey Morris can be accused of silliness and shallowness. But she cannot be entirely blamed. She had married out of her milieu. Anyone with Janey's history would be lacking in self-confidence. She had married a man of huge talent and generosity but with his own kind of uncouthness and blindness. Morris admitted his own failures in expressing his emotions: 'I am something of an Englishman and the words won't flow, it's one of the curses entailed on our blood and climate.' These confessions did not make him any easier to be married to. One senses an emotional aridity, with Morris as the classic stumbling English husband. He had wide-ranging interests. He was endlessly preoccupied with writing and designing and with the day-to-day details of the Firm. When, in the 1860s, Janey began again to model for Rossetti one can see in this an almost 1990s' instinct for being her own person, for remaking an identity. This Morris would have found incomprehensible. Nor did he seem to recognize in Janey a craving for danger, for living on the edge.

Janey and Rossetti had never been discreet. As far back as 1860, when he went to see Rossetti in his studio for the first time after his marriage to Lizzie, George Price Boyce had been aware of crosscurrents of intimacy. Gabriel was painting his 'Adoration of the Christ' for Llandaff Cathedral. An Italian from the Parmigiano was sitting. 'Morris and his wife (whom DGR familiarly addresses as Janey) came in.' In 1861 Janey herself was modelling for Llandaff, sitting for the Virgin Mary holding the Christ child. Morris's portrait was used for King David. In 1863 they were all at an evening party held to celebrate Rossetti's move into No. 16 Cheyne Walk and a little later in the year the same group reassembled at Ford Madox Brown's house in Kentish Town. Georgie's memoirs give a detailed description of the scene at this party held in honour of Alphonse Legros and attended by Swinburne, by Christina Rossetti, 'gently caustic of tongue', and by Whistler, with drooping black hair and angry eye-glass looking ten times more like a Frenchman than Legros. With Morris and Janey came Janey's sister Bessie. Georgie depicts a radiant Rossetti passing through the room 'bringing pleasure to great and small by his beautiful urbanity, a prince amongst men'. Whistler, in his diary, provides a more malicious vignette of Rossetti and Mrs Morris at one of the Browns' parties 'sitting side by side in state, being worshipped in an inner room'.

At this stage there was no outright defiance of convention. But Janey and Rossetti gradually edged much nearer. In the manuscript collection of the Victoria and Albert Museum is a small cream-coloured envelope bearing a penny red postage stamp, addressed to Mrs Morris in the final months at Red House. It is postmarked 5 July 1865. Enclosed is a sheet of Rossetti's crested paper, embossed in gold with the initials and the tree. It is headed 'Sunday night' and reads:

My dear Janey
The photographer is coming at 11 on Wednesday. So I'll expect you as early as you can manage. Love to all at the Hole.

The professional photographer was John R. Parsons, a friend of Howell's. The series of portraits, in which Janey was posed as the model by Rossetti, was taken in the garden at Cheyne Walk. The background in some suggests a marquee or a tent. They show Janey standing, sitting, leaning, lying, yearning in an unmistakably erotic sequence, wearing a beautiful and fluent dark silk dress. At this same period Rossetti was drawing Janey's portrait in pencil, chalk and charcoal, looking more demure. Of Rossetti's many portraits of Janey these are the ones she later thought to be his best.

Once the Morrises moved to Queen Square Janey began to pose more often for Rossetti. At first Morris appears to have encouraged this. In March 1868 plans were under way for Rossetti to paint a portrait of Janey, at Morris's expense. For the first of the sittings Bessie as well as Morris was invited to accompany Janey and to stay overnight at Cheyne Walk. This portrait, known as 'Mrs William Morris in a Blue Silk Dress', shows Janey wearing the gold chain necklace and the gold ring set with an emerald listed as jewellery 'used in D. G. Rossetti's paintings' in the inventory made after her death. At the top of the portrait Rossetti painted is the bumptious inscription:

JANE MORRIS AD 1868 D. G. Rossetti pinxit
Conjuge clara poetâ, et praeclarissima vultu,
Denique picturâ clara sit illa meâ

As translated by a poet of the twentieth century:

> Her famous beauty and her poet's fame
> Sufficed, but now she's safe with mine – in paint

Morris, not surprisingly, growled about the portrait when it was eventually delivered and hung over a great Italian chest of cypress wood in the sitting-room at Queen Square. He sent it back to Rossetti to be worked on. When it returned it seemed only slightly better. 'I don't think the frame suits it,' he complained to Janey: 'it wants something more florid, a big dark-toned picture like that.' His inner objections were not confined to the frame.

Through the remainder of 1868 Rossetti was working, increasingly obsessively, on portraits of Janey. Sometimes Morris went with her, even staying a few days there, but it seems by this time a precedent was established for her to go on her own to Cheyne Walk. 'Mariana', 'Reverie' and 'La Pia de Tolomei': all date from this period and all show Janey in the situation of the suffering heroine, isolated, poignant. Pia de Tolomei for example was the daughter of a Sienese nobleman married to a Guelph lord who brought her to live in the Maremma marshes where she was either poisoned or died of exposure to the polluted air. These were the first of Rossetti's long succession of portraits of Janey, the sultry, raven-haired and melancholy figure, semi-enticing, semi-inaccessible. In recent years these portraits have been appropriated as the symbol of Victorian sexual ambivalence. The 'Day-Dream' portrait of Janey appears, for example, on the jacket of Lotte and Joseph Hamburger's *Contemplating Adultery: the Secret Life of a Victorian woman* (1992).

As Rossetti's devotion towards Janey deepened, his ridicule of Morris became wickeder, more daring. Staying in Scotland in 1868 he composed a household drama, set in Queen Square, centred upon Morris as the imbecile and bully. He sent this to Ford Madox Brown:

BROWN How are you Morris? Have you heard how Gabriel is?
MORRIS (dancing) I wish to God Gabriel – no I mean the cook – was in Hell! Don't you Janey dear? Damn blast etc. etc. Oh ah! Don't you know? Gabriel's all right again. Damn blast etc. etc. – of course you'll stay to dinner Old Chap. I don't know though if we have any. Janey dear it's all your fault. Damn blast etc, etc. – (Dinner brought in.)
JANEY (carving) Haven't you heard from Gabriel, Mr. Brown?
MORRIS (nudging her, in a whining tone) Why Janey dear, that's the bit I always have. You know Brown doesn't like it.

JANEY O I'm very sorry dear. Here it is. Will you have the other too? What were
 you saying Mr. Brown?
BROWN I thought Morris might have heard from Gabriel.
MORRIS (who has been helped)
 O ah! Gabri-obble obble Gabri-uuch–uuch–
 Gabri-obble obble obble obble obble –
 (Morris eats. Tableau.)

Through the autumn of that year he kept up a stream of bulletins
lampooning Morris's everyday ineptitudes. On 9 November he recorded
how he called on Topsy 'who was howling and threatening to throw a
new piano of his wife's out of the window'. The reason for his fury was
that it arrived at dinner time. Only a few days later Rossetti was
recounting how he had met Topsy at 'a huge party of Greeks'.

He seemed depressed and complained of deafness, but on a large plug of string
being taken out of his ear, he revived a good deal and even scratched himself in
places apparently inaccessible. When I left, he was being prepared for departure. The whisky cork had already been got out of his hose, and Janey had
neatly succeeded in fishing the paper knife up from the base of his spine. He was
offering to stand on his head that it might drop out.

By this time the gossip was spreading around London. Rossetti,
whose eyesight was mysteriously failing and who was beginning to show
signs of the depression that from then on dogged his life, evidently
confessed his passion for Janey to William Bell Scott, not the discreetest
of his friends. Scott wrote to Alice Boyd, his own mistress, in November, reporting on Rossetti's worrying condition. 'Gabriel had not tried
painting, nor seen any doctor, nor seen the sweet Lucretia Borgia.' This
was his code for Janey. With a sudden flash of insight he connected
Rossetti's problematic eyesight and agitated state to his 'uncontrollable
desire for the possession of the said L. B.' The ladies were chattering.
Bell Scott's wife Letitia, on a mission to Queen Square ostensibly to
discuss an altar cloth, met Janey. Scott comments, 'Even Mrs. Street
had spoken to Letitia about Gabriel being so fond of Mrs. Top.'

Two weeks later Scott himself held a dinner party. He invited Rossetti, the architect William Burges and George Henry Lewes, described
as 'a host of himself in conversation'. (George Eliot apparently was not
there.) Once again Bessie Burden arrived with both the Morrises.
Rossetti's provocative behaviour alarmed even the urbane Scott. 'Gabriel sat by Jeanie [sic], and I must say acts like a perfect fool if he wants

to conceal his attachment, doing nothing but attend to her, sitting side-ways towards her, that sort of thing.' He thought it hardly possible that Bessie, sitting opposite, could have been unaware of what was going on. He commented crisply on Janey's apparent sang-froid: 'Of course a woman under such circumstances, before people, is a sealed book, still I think she is cool.' On the way down to dinner, Rossetti did his best to wrest Janey from Bell Scott, her allotted dinner partner. He put his arm in hers almost automatically, then 'abandoned her as hurriedly for the nearest other lady'. Scott was aware of Morris watching every detail of this scene.

Morris's chagrin and dismay poured out into his verses. Some of these, with conscious irony, form part of the fabric of *The Earthly Paradise*. Other snatches of verses relating to this period are still being discovered, scrawled on to Morris's copious manuscripts and drafts. These are some of the most moving lyrics ever written about love and loss and suffering, paralysis of feeling, damaged confidence. This is the bleakness of 'The Hill of Venus' which Victorian readers would have had no difficulty in relating to the *mons Veneris*:

> . . . time and again did seem
> As though a cold and hopeless tune he heard,
> Sung by grey mouths amidst a dull-eyed dream;
> Time and again across his heart would stream
> The pain of fierce desire whose aim was gone,
> Of baffled yearning loveless and alone.

While Morris was producing such lyrics of despair Rossetti was writing his sonnets of love resurgent. Sixteen of these appeared in March 1869, including the blatantly sensual 'Love-Lily':

> Brows, hands, and lips, heart, mind and voice,
> Kisses and words of Love-Lily, –
> Oh! bid me with your joy rejoice
> Till riotous longing rest in me!

It had become indeed the duel of the words.

Were Janey and Rossetti technically lovers? On the whole this appears likely. It has been claimed that Rossetti was impotent: this claim was first advanced by Hall Caine, Rossetti's factotum in the last months of his life, in a letter to George Bernard Shaw in 1928. There is evidence Rossetti suffered from, and had surgery to remove, a hydrocele, a fluid-containing tumour in the testicle. But there is no proof of Rossetti's impotence. It is also sometimes argued that their correspondence hardly celebrates *grande passion*. This is true of Janey's letters: she was uneducated, her whole manner was understated and subdued. It is less true of Rossetti's letters, and not true at all of the sonnets he transcribed into the black notebook, which Janey kept with her till she died. The main argument against a physical relationship hinges on Janey's later admission to Wilfrid Scawen Blunt that although she had loved Gabriel there had been reservations: 'I never quite gave myself as I do now.' Some modicum of reservation with Rossetti would be likely. He was her husband's friend and Janey at that time would have still had the fear of pregnancy. But people are not always wholly truthful to new lovers, and there are degrees of giving, as any woman knows.

Janey Morris was not a Lucretia Borgia but a Victorian married woman of the middle classes. Her later letters show her as conventional, diffident. She retained a clearly defined, if irritated, affection for her husband and she loved her little girls, by this time six and seven. It is inconceivable that she would have risked the opprobrium incurred at that time by a known liaison between a married woman and another man if physical passion had not been a factor. (The scandal that arose from the liaison between George Eliot and G. H. Lewes was a warning, and in that case Lewes's marriage was already dead.) It is also worth noting that Janey had much more opportunity than other married women. She and Rossetti, the artist and the model, spent long periods alone.

Why was Morris so complaisant? This is the more puzzling and more interesting question. Why did he retreat into a terrible self-pity instead of attempting to retrieve the situation with, if necessary, confrontation and threats? It was partly perhaps the masochistic habit: Morris was long used to playing victim, first for a joke, later for real. It was also the fear of a rupture with Rossetti, destructive to the Firm and the ideal of the male brotherhood. The contortions of chivalry – including the lately rediscovered conventions of 'courtly love' – still hung over Morris and there was a sense in which he could more easily relinquish his wife than disband his group of friends. It was certainly his intense fear of breaching privacies: as Bernard Shaw once pointed out, Morris was unwilling to discuss family affairs even with his own family. Shaw also noted Morris's streak of fatalism that led him to regard coercion as useless: 'He knew that the world is full of precipices; but if people were determined to walk over them it was no use trying to hold them back: over they must go.'

In Morris's attitude to the loss of Janey there are the first signs of his radical view of sexual relations, his belief that human beings are not one another's keepers, and that 'Copulation is worse than beastly unless it takes place as the outcome of natural desires and kindliness on both sides'. Over the next two decades Morris would arrive at a scenario of marriage too open and too generous to be generally acceptable even in the supposedly tolerant Britain of today.

He set out his principles in a letter to Faulkner in 1886:

1 The couple would be *free*.
2 Being free, if unfortunately distaste arose between them they should make no pretence of its not having arisen.
3 But I should hope that in most cases friendship would go along with desire, and would outlive it, and the couple would still remain together, but always as free people. In short artificial bolstering up of natural human relations is what I object to.

Was this a view he had arrived at intellectually? Was it prompted by the stirrings of early Communist ideology? Or was it forced out of his own history of suffering? Would Morris have arrived at this philosophy if Janey had been other than she was?

In May 1868 there had been a festive dinner at Queen Square. Allingham arrived to find 'just alighting, Mrs. Ned in a gorgeous yellow gown.' In spite of Morris's usual objection to 'togs' this was a full-dress party. Allingham wore a velveteen jacket. He listed 'Morris, Ned J (thin), DGR (looking well), Boyce ("has been ill"), F. M. Brown (oldened), Webb, Howell, Mr. Wilfred Heeley, Publisher Ellis and W. A. (ten men).' There were also 'Mrs. Morris, Miss Burden, Mrs. Ned (gay), Mrs. Howell, Mrs. Madox Brown (looks young with back to the window), Lucy Brown, Miss Faulkner (I between these), Mrs. Ellis, Miss Heeley (ten ladies).' It was Allingham's idea to call the banquet 'Earthly Paradise', and Ned wrote this in on the top of the menu. There was a storm of talking, and Allingham left with Rossetti at about one a.m.

Through the rest of the year such gatherings continued, but with a growing undercurrent of hysteria. With that curious parallelism that still dogged them, the troubles of the Topsies were now being overtaken by the Burne-Joneses' marital predicaments, and Morris, the recipient of his friends' sympathy, was also now chief confidant in the high dramas between his friend Ned and the young Greek sculptress, Mary Zambaco, with whom he was appallingly in love. Mary was the daughter of Hadji and Euphrosyne Cassavetti, cousins of the Ionides, leaders of the London circle of Greek merchants and financiers described with amusement by Rossetti as 'the Greeks'. She had married Demetrius Zambaco, doctor to the Greek community in Paris, but she found the marriage humdrum and arrived in London alone with two young children in 1866. Mary radiated accessibility. A young cousin remembered being brought to her dressing-room, having fallen fully dressed into a swimming bath: Mary proceeded to undress in front of him, and 'her glorious red hair and almost phosphorescent white skin' shining out from the gloom of the drawing-room stayed for ever in the mind of the child. Burne-Jones had evidently been equally susceptible. As Georgiana observed tartly, Ned was most affected by two qualities in others: 'beauty and misfortune – and far would he go to serve either'. He had promised to elope with Mary, and then reneged. She had pursued him, proposing a suicide pact in Holland Walk in Kensington, then attempting to drown herself in Paddington Canal.

Rossetti described these dramas with the gusto that often masked deep feeling: 'Poor Ned's affairs have come to smash altogether, and he and Topsy, after the most dreadful to-do, started for Rome suddenly, leaving the Greek damsel beating up the quarters of all his friends for him and howling like Cassandra.' He mentions that Georgie stayed behind. Morris's sympathy in times of crisis was graver and more stalwart. He could not regard his friends' misfortunes as high comedy. Luke Ionides who also later came to ask advice from him vouched for Morris's tonic qualities: 'I would go to him in the depths of misery and after being with him for an hour or two I would leave him feeling absolutely happy. I always compared him with a sea-breeze, which seemed to blow away all one's black vapours.' Though Morris seemed a strong man, Ionides perceived in him the delicate feelings of a tender woman. One day he heard Morris consoling a friend who had been abandoned by the woman he loved. He said, 'Think, old fellow, how much better it is that she should have left you, than that you should have tired of her, and left her.' He responded to such crises with more than robustness: with a discreet and imaginative common sense.

Morris did not in the end go with Burne-Jones to Italy. Burne-Jones was too ill. They got to Dover and returned. Before they departed Morris had taken the precaution of forbidding Janey's sitting to Rossetti in his absence. Even his generosity had its limits. Rossetti noted bitterly, 'Janey has stopped her sittings by order during foreign service – just as I supposed.'

14 *'William Morris attending his wife who lays upon a couch'*. Caricature by Edward Burne-Jones.

The Americans in London were lionizing Morris. In the autumn of 1868 the scholar and art historian Charles Eliot Norton wrote to tell Ruskin he was seeing a good deal of Morris, 'who combines in a wonderful measure the solid earthly qualities of the man of practical affairs, with the fine perceptions and quick fancy of the poet'. He wrote that it was pleasant to see a famous author 'so simple, and so little of a prig'. A few months later Henry James reported to his sister that the 'crowning day' of his London visit had been spent with 'Mr. Wm. Morris, Poet', in Queen Square. He explained that Morris's poetry was only his sub-trade but that his production of 'everything quaint, archaic, pre-Raphaelite' was so small and specialized that it could be carried on within his house. There is a very transatlantic sense of marvel in James's description of the Morrises at home:

Oh, ma chère, such a wife! *Je n'en reviens pas* – she haunts me still. A figure cut out of a missal – out of one of Rossetti's or Hunt's pictures – to say this gives but a faint idea of her, because when such an image puts on flesh and blood, it is an apparition of fearful and wonderful intensity. It's hard to say whether she's a grand synthesis of all the pre-Raphaelite pictures ever made – or they a 'keen analysis' of her – whether she's an original or a copy. In either case she is a wonder. Imagine a tall lean woman in a long dress of some dead purple stuff, guiltless of hoops (or of anything else, I should say,) with a mass of crisp black hair heaped into great wavy projections on each of her temples, a thin pale face, a pair of strange sad, deep, dark Swinburnian eyes, with great thick black oblique brows, joined in the middle and tucking themselves away under her hair, a mouth like the 'Oriana' in our illustrated Tennyson, a long neck, without any collar, and in lieu thereof some dozen strings of outlandish beads – in fine complete. On the wall was a large nearly full-length portrait of her by Rossetti, so strange and unreal that if you hadn't seen her you'd pronounce it a distempered vision, but in fact an extremely good likeness. After dinner (we stayed to dinner, Miss Grace, Miss S. S. and I,) Morris read us one of his unpublished poems, from the second series of his un-'Earthly Paradise,' and his wife, having a bad toothache, lay on the sofa, with her handkerchief to her face. There was something very quaint and remote from our actual life, it seemed to me, in the whole scene: Morris reading in his flowing antique numbers a legend of prodigies and terrors (the story of Bellerophon, it was), around us all the picturesque bric-à-brac of the apartment (every article of furniture literally a 'specimen' of something or other,) and in the corner this dark silent medieval woman with her medieval toothache. Morris himself is extremely pleasant and quite different from his wife. He impressed me most agreeably. He is short, burly, corpulent, very careless and unfinished in his dress, and looks a little like B. G. Hosmer, if you can imagine B. G. infinitely magnified and fortified. He has a very loud voice and a nervous restless manner and a perfectly unaffected and business-like address. His talk indeed is wonderfully to the point and remarkable for clear good sense. He said no one thing that I remember, but I was struck with the very good judgment shown in everything he uttered. He's an extraordinary example, in short, of a delicate sensitive genius and taste, saved by a perfectly healthy body and temper. All his designs are quite as good (or rather nearly so) as his poetry: altogether it was a long rich sort of visit, with a strong peculiar flavour of its own.

The bustling overactive husband; the woman in dead purple: with his novelist's nose for human dissonances Henry James seems to be sensing more than he could have known.

Morris was as patient with Janey's illness as was possible for anyone so naturally restless. But it contributed to his depression at this period. His friends were finding him quarrelsome and awkward. He described himself as 'like a hedgehog with nastiness'. He was only thirty-five, but his mind was much on mortality.

CHAPTER EIGHT

Bad Ems
1869–70

In the late summer of 1869, Morris spent two months marooned in central Germany. 'That is really my address though it looks like chaff', he wrote to Philip Webb from the Fortuna guest house in Bad Ems, a fashionable spa town in the valley of the Lahn a few miles from Koblenz. Janey had been advised to travel there to take the waters. By now her condition was considered very serious. They left Jenny and May at Naworth Castle with the Howards. Morris went to say goodbye to the Burne-Joneses at The Grange where Ned, still showing signs of strain, torn between his wife and his lover, was obviously devastated by Morris's departure. Philip Webb said he felt 'a mutilated body' when Morris and Janey went to Ems. Morris himself was nervous, both about the practical problems of the journey and the risk of unsuccessful treatment: 'it will be bad indeed to have to bring her back no better; I don't know how to face the fear of that.'

They left in late July. Lucy Faulkner and Bessie accompanied them on the outward journey. They travelled via Ghent where Janey was just well enough to drive around the quays and see the van Eyck painting 'The Adoration of the Lamb'. They stopped for a night each at Mechlin, Liège, Aix and then Cologne. Morris was working as they went on 'Acontius and Cydippe', one of the tales for the next volume of *The Earthly Paradise*, hoping to rough it out before they got to Ems. In his agitation Morris had not planned the journey properly, and their arrival at a popular watering-place in mid-season without lodgings entered the family mythology as a prize example of parental ineptitude. As May wrote in her memoirs of her father: 'they were literally stranded at the station, and I scarcely know which to be sorrier for, mother waiting there alone in a state of collapse, or father, frantically seeking for accommodation and coming back to her in a positively desperate state of mind.' But within a few days they were lodged comfortably, though not luxuriously, in their rooms at the Fortuna where, according to the contemporary registers, Herr Morris and his wife were at the time the only guests. The Fortuna overlooked the most architecturally arresting ancient building in Ems, the 'rum old 17th century house' that Morris identified as the old Kurhaus. Town life encroached upon them. The wind-band in the Kurgarten was apt to wake them at seven a.m. 'with Luther's Hymn played in thundering style'.

The mineral springs of Ems (anciently Eimetz) had been famous for centuries. The Romans had known of their curative properties. By the time Morris arrived there a whole industry of medicine and tourism was growing up around them. Dr Edward Gutmann's popular medical guide to *The Watering Places of Europe*, compiled ten years after Morris's

15 *'Resolution; or, the Infant Hercules'*. Dante Gabriel Rossetti's cartoon of William Morris fighting his way out of an invalid shower bath, dated 14 August 1869.

visit, described Ems as 'the *gem* of the German spas' because of its fine buildings and its general air of elegance as well as its standards of medical attentiveness. In its high season 13,000 patients thronged through its streets and promenades. It was especially popular with English visitors. The Hôtel d'Angleterre had been built to greet them, and at a lower level the Englischen Hof guest-house. Bad Ems is the charming spa town in the background of Disraeli's novel *Vivien Gray*. The spa, with its carbonated alkaline waters, specialized in the treatment of chronic catarrh, bronchitis, laryngitis. It also had a special reputation for the condition referred to delicately in the guide books as *les maladies de femme*.

Three of the twenty-one Ems springs were drinking springs. The waters, described by visitors as warm and mawkish with a distinctive taste of weak beef tea, were dispensed at the Kurhaus in a morning ceremony, handed across the counter by the Brünnen-Mädchen in cut-glass Bohemian tumblers. The Kurhaus was very public, an imposing columned hall. The Kesselbrunnen spring rose there in a marble reservoir. The Kraenchen spring issued from a silver tap in a niche of the Kurhaus.

The spring water for bathing was collected into reservoirs for cooling, then distributed by a network of pipes into more than a hundred individual bathing cabinets. In this, much more private, bathing establishment there was a vapour bath, a powerful uterus-douche, applied for disorders of the uterine system, and the pride of Bad Ems, the natural ascending douche, the Bubenquelle, a fountain half an inch in diameter rising from the bottom of a basin, when a stop-cock was turned, to a height of between two and three feet. This fountain, applied strictly under medical supervision, entered the body via the vagina and was claimed to be effective in the treatment of sterility and discharge from the womb. We do not know the details of Janey's medical treatment. But it can be presumed that Bad Ems had been selected because it offered her possible remedies that were not obtainable elsewhere.

As a respite from the treatments Bad Ems offered river walks and pleasure gardens, a regimented landscape of flower beds and terraces planted with horse chestnuts and limes. Indoor entertainment was provided in the Kursaal, a highly ornamental and elaborately finished building consisting of a grand central saloon and upper gallery, hung with cut-glass chandeliers. One of the upper rooms contained a piano for the visitors. Another was taken up with gaming tables where the patients and their companions whiled away the time with *rouge et noir* and roulette.

Of all the places Morris ever stayed in, Bad Ems must rate as one of the least congenial. There was a fearful irony in somebody so active being contained, almost literally held captive, in a spa town with its curious combination of pomp and lassitude. (Resnais's film *Last Year at Marienbad* conveys the atmosphere.) He disliked the town itself which he called 'noisy and uninteresting'; he loathed the other visitors and takers of the waters, who were dismissed as 'a collection of fine feathers and foul birds'. He spoke very little contemporary German, claiming that his knowledge of the language stopped short at Martin Luther's bible. The chambermaids laughed at his attempts to communicate, finding his performances on 'that high dutch instrument as good as a play'. Rossetti's cartoon 'The German Lesson' shows Morris handing a mob-capped maid his breeches, with Janey in the background, looking cynical.

At Bad Ems one can see Morris's English prejudices surfacing. He was frightened of the prices and scared of being cheated: 'As you may imagine,' he told Philip Webb pathetically, 'the folks here are sharks.' They had timed the visit particularly badly. Bad Ems itself sat in a storm-cloud of political upheaval. King William of Prussia was staying in the town, as he did each summer. The French ambassador was rumoured to have visited. Even foreign tourists were aware of local tensions. The next year saw the famous exchange of 'Bad Ems' telegrams with Bismarck, leading up to the declaration of the Franco-Prussian war.

In this uneasy situation Morris did the best he could. Janey's medical routine was intensive. After only a few days Morris was reporting: 'J. has seen the Dr. twice and has had 4 baths and a corresponding amount of lukewarm Spa-water which she drinks in the morning before breakfast.' Her mobility was limited. Carriage rides would leave her shaken. Her backache was so bad that some days she was unable to sit up to write a letter. Diet was difficult: she found the German food too greasy, although both she and Morris took to German beer. In many respects Morris was the perfect husband. He felt for Janey, entered into the details of her treatment, charted her progress in his letters home. He paddled her heroically round the artificially widened stretches of the river Lahn in 'a machine like a butter-boat with a knife and fork for oars'. He found a nice green river bank that could be relied upon to be in cool shadow in the early evening. He would row Janey out and they would rest there and recover: Germany that summer was stiflingly hot. But Morris's many letters to Webb contain an undertone of sheer frustration and the sense of being exiled in a set of circumstances that were altogether alien. The invalid's routine was astonishingly irksome to someone who described himself as being 'in roaring and offensive health'.

One consolation to him was the countryside round Ems. Its hillocky beauty reminded him a little of the Lake District 'without the sour grow-nothing air of that soaking land'. He described the valley of the Lahn as *very* narrow, traversed by its rugged river as wide in some places as the Thames at Clifton Hampden. It was the measure of his homesickness that Morris so frequently related foreign landscapes back to English ones. He admired the roadside terraces, the neat and ship-shape vineyards. The fruit harvest was in progress and Morris drew on that productive German landscape for the introduction to 'The Death of Paris' in *The Earthly Paradise*:

> The level ground along the river-side
> Was merry through the day with sounds of those
> Who gathered apples; o'er the stream arose
> The northward-looking slopes where the swine ranged
> Over the fields that hook and scythe had changed
> Since the last month; but 'twixt the tree-boles grey
> Above them did they see the terraced way,
> And over that the vine-stocks, row on row,
> Whose dusty leaves, well thinned and yellowing now,
> But little hid the bright-bloomed vine-bunches.

But though the valley was so pretty Morris found it claustrophobic. He explained that it was not a place for anyone like him, with his yearning for stretches of chalk down and long vistas, to contemplate settling in and living in. Bad Ems made him slightly frantic: 'one is so boxed in'.

He could not leave Janey alone for long stretches. But one day he managed two hours' stride up a hill road, finding himself in some 'very jolly' country: 'it all runs towards the big gorge in little gorges, the centres of which are all grass and hold the moisture like a cup and are as green as green can be'. He came to a green plateau with alders all around it, with big hills in the distance at one end, and around the other, hills

235

rising steeply with 'great lanky beech woods – as dry as a bone'. Although he did not warm to it exactly, Morris did not underestimate the appeal of German landscape. He saw it as an influence on German character, 'fit for the breeding of German sentiment'. While in Bad Ems, Morris was reading Goethe's *Wilhelm Meister* in Carlyle's translation. He found this long, powerfully philosophic novel heavy going, though acknowledging its genius: 'Goethe must have been asleep when he wrote it: but 'tis a great work somehow.' *Die Wahlverwandtschaften* (*Elective Affinities*), Goethe's novel on the theme of the mutual attraction of the married couple for two other people, would have been appropriate reading for that emotionally fraught summer at Bad Ems.

Morris, the connoisseur of the melancholy forest, crept off into the woods as he used to do at Marlborough. He would take his pocket book and do a little work. The beechwoods around Ems were lonely and dismal except in the brightest weather, and the fine days alternated with the overcast and stormy. 'O Lord,' wrote Morris, 'can't it rain at Ems.' The woods were full of giant ants. Morris drew one to size in a letter: it measures three quarters of an inch. The slugs, four inches long, emerging from the sodden undergrowth, were bigger and more sinister than any Morris had ever seen: most of them were 'a brilliant red-lead colour, but some like bad veal with a shell on their backs'. The warm, wet valley also encouraged adders. One morning out walking, Morris heard a rustle in the leaves behind him: 'out crept one', he wrote to Webb, 'as long as my umbrella of a yellowish olive colour and wriggled across the path as though he were expected; I kept feeling the legs of my trousers all the way home after that.'

The first week or so at Ems was spent on the completion of the first draft of 'Acontius and Cydippe'. Morris then prepared to work it over, to knock it into shape. But he felt hesitant: 'I am not sanguine about it,' he told Webb. Perhaps the tale of the man who came to Delos and saw the noble damsel, 'was smitten with the love of her, and made all things of no account but the winning of her', set up reverberations that proved too much for Morris. In this anguished story the disorientating effects of love are vivid: cries Acontius:

> 'why then like a burnt-out fire,
> Is my life grown?'

236

The meeting of Acontius and Cydippe in the tulip fields is painful with hopefulness:

> There in a silence hard to bear,
> Impossible to break, they stood,
> With faces changed by love, and blood
> So stirred, that many a year of life
> Had been made eager with that strife
> Of minutes; and so nigh she was
> He saw the little blue veins pass
> Over her heaving breast; and she
> The trembling of his lips might see,
> The rising tears within his eyes.

They are parted. Acontius sets out on the quest to find his love again. After many wanderings he finds her in the garden. But now she is a changed person, a wayward cruel woman:

> oftenest the well-beloved
> Shall pay the kiss back with a blow,
> Shall smile to see the hot tears flow,
> Shall answer with scarce-hidden scorn
> The bitter words by anguish torn
> From such a heart.

Morris never approved of 'Acontius and Cydippe'. He told Swinburne later on, 'Acontius I know is a spoony, nothing less, and the worst of it is that if I did him over a dozen times, I know I should make him just the same.' This self-criticism, very true, is the more poignant since Morris knew that in the world's eyes he too was a spoony, a love-sick fool.

In another poem of this period, not published until May Morris's edition of 1915, the personal history is made still more explicit. Here the woman speaks:

> Why dost thou struggle, strive for victory
> Over my heart that loveth thine so well?
> When Death shall one day have its will of thee
> And to deaf ears thy triumph thou must tell.

Unto deaf ears or unto such as know
The hearts of dead and living wilt thou say:
A childish heart there loved me once, and lo
I took his love and cast his love away.

A childish greedy heart! yet still he clung
So close to me that much he pleased my pride
And soothed a sorrow that about me hung
With glimpses of his love unsatisfied –

And soothed my sorrow – but time soothed it too
Though ever did its aching fill my heart
To which the foolish child still closer drew
Thinking in all I was to have a part.

But now my heart grown silent of its grief
Saw more than kindness in his hungry eyes:
But I must wear a mask of false belief
And feign that nought I knew his miseries.

I wore a mask, because though certainly
I loved him not, yet was there something soft
And sweet to have him ever loving me:
Belike it is I well-nigh loved him oft –

Nigh loved him oft, and needs must grant to him
Some kindness out of all he asked of me
And hoped his love would still hang vague and dim
About my life like half-heard melody.

He knew my heart and over-well knew this
And strove, poor soul, to pleasure me herein;
But yet what might he do some doubtful kiss
Some word, some look might give him hope to win.

Poor hope, poor soul, for he again would come
Thinking to gain yet one more golden step
Toward Love's shrine, and lo the kind speech dumb
The kind look gone, no love upon my lip –

Yea gone, yet not my fault, I knew of love
But my love and not his; how could I tell
That such blind passion in him I should move?
Behold I have loved faithfully and well;

Love of my love so deep and measureless
O lords of the new world this too ye know.

Once Morris had done the best he could with 'Acontius' he turned back to another of the tales for the new volume of *The Earthly Paradise*, 'The Land East of the Sun and West of the Moon'. Looking at the poem again critically he decided that it needed rewriting rather than merely tinkering. He needed to finish it before he left Germany to leave himself some time for corrections in London before it went to press. This poem too is a narrative of love found and then lost again, taken from the opening tale of Thorpe's *Yuletide Stories*. It is much more successful than 'Acontius and Cydippe', a Nordic fairy story with a delicate structure of dreams within dreams imposed on it by Morris, and his usual intimations of erotic self-discovery. John the hero, the churl's son, half-dreams of seven white swans, circling round, dropping down on the dewy grass beside him. When he next looks up there are six swan skins on the ground and near by stand seven white-skinned damsels. One stands by herself holding her swan skin. This is Morris's version of the story of *Swan Lake*. The swan-maiden offers bliss undreamed of:

> Like waking from an ecstasy,
> Too sweet for truth it seemed to be,
> Waking to life full satisfied
> When he arose, and side by side,
> Cheek touching cheek, hand laid in hand,
> They stood within a marvellous land,
> Fruitful, and summer-like, and fair.

As in 'Acontius', he loses the beloved. Again the lady changes shape, becomes strange to him: 'Her loveliness grown dangerous'. Again the hero wanders, lost and alienated, landing at Dunwich, travelling towards London, received at St Albans by a little dry old monk who wants to hear the history that he himself feels is hardly worth the recording. Nothing moves him any longer.

> One place was as another place,
> Haunted by memories of one face,
> Vocal with one remembered voice.

Morris turns his fairytale into an agonizing narrative of sexual fixation: at his most despairing the hero casts himself on to the ground, in the snow, writhing and wailing. Then at last the lost love reappears: his weary eyes

beheld indeed,
His heart's desire, his life, his need,
Still on the earth, still there for him.

But almost everything has changed. She is worn, dulled, almost death-like; he is transfixed by his own sense of his guilt in losing her so very long ago.

Is poetry socially useful or superfluous? Morris raises this question in the coda to his poem and it is an interesting one because so often *The Earthly Paradise* has been dismissed as purposeless entertainment, merely bur-ble, a time filler like a television chat show of the 1990s. In 'The Land East of the Sun' Morris shows how John, awaking from his dream, uses art to give creative form to his returning memories by weaving (the image is not accidental) experiences into 'verses smooth'. Morris implies that the writing of a poem is cathartic to the poet while introducing readers to new levels of perception. He was so immersed in 'The Land East of the Sun' that when his publisher, the jovial, tedious and portly F. S. Ellis, called to visit him at Ems he half-resented the intrusion, complaining that Ellis's arrival 'rather put a spoke in the cart wheel' of his muse.

Ellis came for two days. He had been buying books in Hanover. His constant geniality perhaps stemmed from his father, proprietor of the popular Star and Garter Hotel at Richmond. Ellis's own premises in King Street, Covent Garden, where he specialized in manuscripts and rare editions, became a literary Star and Garter, a convivial meeting place for bibliophiles and writers. There Morris had purchased for £26 his first rare book, a fine, clean, crisp copy of Boccaccio's *De Claris Mulieribus* in the 1473 Ulm edition with the famous woodcuts, bound in sixteenth-century vellum stained yellow. It was also at Ellis's bookshop that Morris was reported by the clerks to the proprietor as a suspicious customer, he looked so down-at-heel. Rossetti, contemplating Ellis as his publisher, but worried that he was already publishing the too-productive Morris, wrote a limerick about him:

There's a publishing party named Ellis
Who's addicted to poets with bellies:
He has at least two –
One in fact, one in view –
And God knows what will happen to Ellis.

In the end Rossetti signed up with F. S. Ellis. His sister Christina and Swinburne joined him too.

Morris's own association with Ellis was long-lasting. Morris came to rely on his kindly common sense and his emotional stability: Ellis was in the inner circle of male cronies who surrounded Morris in his later years. He arrived in that sultry late August in Bad Ems, exuding the normality that Morris both depended on and found exasperating. No doubt Ellis reminded him a little of his father. Morris hired two Bad Ems donkeys, rather to Ellis's horror, and they made a mountain journey. They went into the Kursaal, visiting the gaming tables where Ellis staked 'a mild florin' and doubled his money several times. This pleased him. Morris was so bored with these proceedings he vowed not to enter the Kursaal again.

Morris himself was being harassed about money. In the short term, at Bad Ems, he was running out of funds within the first two weeks, writing to Philip Webb to ask him for a loan: 'I want to make myself safe from being kept in pawn, and set to hard labour at Ems (say sweeping up horse-dung, an office religiously observed here), I want £60 somehow.' Webb forwarded the money through his bank. At the same time, through the summer, Morris was pursued by bulletins on the shaky financial position of the Firm. In 1868 a turnover of £2,000 had produced a net profit of only £300: a derisory sum divided between the seven partners. Warington Taylor, by now in a condition of extreme debility, collapsing, swooning, coughing blood, in what was to prove the last year of his life, was still mentally alert enough to fix the blame on Morris in a series of increasingly vituperative memos written through the summer of 1869.

Morris's private income from his shares was not improving. It was static at around £400 in the years 1867 and 1868. He also had his regular £200 salary. But in 1868 he had to boost his income with £200 from the sale of books and £200 withdrawal of capital from the Firm. Warington Taylor calculated that, to sustain his standard of living anywhere near its current level of £1,000 per annum, Morris would soon need to withdraw his remaining £200 of capital. Taylor looked into the future. Writing to Webb, he painted a gloomy picture of how Morris would behave once his capital had gone: 'He will be onto his old game of drawing small cheques from the firm – and at end of quarter express surprise at amount overdrawn – but then he will have nothing to repay it with – and our firm will be gradually ruined.'

In July of 1869 Taylor drew up a household budget for Morris, maintaining that he could not afford more than £6 per week for household expenses and must cut out entertaining: 'what does an extra dinner cost: piece of salmon 5/-, leg of mutton 7/6, vegetable 2/-, pudding – wine – coals? – butter.' He suggested that Morris should be able to manage on a much reduced level of annual expenditure made up of:

Rent	£100
Clothes	£70
Coals	£20
Wine	£80
House	£364
	£634

He must keep only two servants; be careful not to have too many fires burning simultaneously, reduce the quantity and quality of household candles, and cut down on wine consumption to two and a half bottles a day. Otherwise he warned that Morris would soon be bankrupt, reminding him that under the new bankruptcy act his shares in the mines would be seized to pay his creditors. He would have literally nothing left.

Taylor turned to Webb, asking him to impress upon Morris the present realities of the firm's position: 'If you do not act no one else will – everyone treats it as a joke.' When Webb passed on these comments to Morris at Bad Ems he took Taylor's criticisms with extraordinary meekness: 'there is a great deal of reason in what he says, though he is not at present quite master of the details.' Morris sounds defensive. He was certainly aware of his financial precariousness, and of the extra expenditure Janey's long illness had incurred.

Morris received Taylor's diatribes with patience, even gratitude. But how did he respond to the other news from England, the deluge of letters that Rossetti sent to Janey? Ten of these survive and it appears that Morris shared them with Janey as they arrived. Indeed they are full of direct messages of fondness to 'the dear old thing', as Rossetti describes Morris. 'Pray take my love', he writes to Janey, 'and give the same to Top'.

They correspond with all the urgency of lovers. In spite of her illness Janey writes from Calais; Rossetti, as she has instructed him, sends her a letter to the Poste Restante, Cologne. His letters are solicitous. Her health clearly obsesses him. Indeed in their correspondence now and in the years to come they are intertwined in illness, in solicitous inquiry, exchanging news of treatments: theirs was hypochondriac passion, taken to extremes.

Writing to Bad Ems in 1869 Rossetti fills in many details of the progress of her portraits. He is using Marie Spartali as a substitute model, using her hands to finish the Beatrice he painted from Janey: 'I think they will come well enough, though it is provoking to have made a mull of them from you.' These are fascinating letters which show with a great vividness the nature of the love between Janey and Rossetti, the cosiness, the tenderness. If the treatment improves her, he tells her, he will bless the name of Ems. 'It seems quite a shame to call it Bad Ems on the envelope and I should write Good instead if I thought the postman had an intuitive soul.'

These letters from Rossetti also reveal much about the tensions in his relationship with Morris. He lords it over Morris, uses him as errand boy, wondering if Morris has managed to get him the workman's blouses he promised him from Lille. There is severe professional as well as sexual jealousy in the cartoon character he evolves from Morris, imagining him in ecstasies of composition: 'I suppose Topsy is roaring

16 'The M's at Ems', 1869. Rossetti's cartoon of Janey taking the waters while Morris reads on indefatigably from *The Earthly Paradise*.

and screaming through the Parnassian tunnels and junctions in his usual style now, not without an occasional explosion.' One of the savage cartoons he sends to Janey, inviting her complicity, shows Morris reading from his seven volumes of *The Earthly Paradise* while Janey sits in her shower-bath, faced with the simultaneous torture of drinking seven glasses of spa-water. This he calls 'The M's at Ems'.

He pats Morris on the head. He pets him to belittle him. In one of the Ems letters he tells Janey of his purchase of a wombat. The wombats, small Australian marsupials, nocturnal in their habits, were Rossetti's favourite creatures at the London Zoo. The zoo acquired its first wombat in 1830, adding more examples in the early 1860s. Rossetti loved the wombats for their air of vulnerability combined with their solidity and rough and hairy coats. His cult of the wombat as a creature both peculiarly endearing and peculiarly off-putting was part of his general cult of the grotesque, but it gathered particular relevance to Morris as one deduces from the glee with which Rossetti describes his own new wombat purchased from Jamrach, an animal importer with a 'mart for wild animals' in east London, to his confidant Miss Losh: 'He is a round furry ball with a head something between a bear and a guinea pig, no legs, human feet with heels like anybody else, and no tail. Of course I shall call him "Top".'

The wombat became a legend, dozing off one evening in the epergne in the centre of Rossetti's dining-table and awakening to consume a whole box of expensive cigars once the men had left the table. Top, the 'Consummate Wombat', did not last long however. On 21 September he was reported to be galloping round the Chelsea garden, and Rossetti was calling him 'A Joy, A Triumph, a Delight, a Madness' (quoting Shelley's *Prometheus Unbound*). But he died on 6 November. Rossetti had him stuffed.

If most of Rossetti's letters to Janey at Bad Ems are intimate and joky, with a sense of precious secrets, he occasionally writes much more honestly and openly, as if her serious illness has given him permission to throw the marital conventions to the winds:

All that concerns you is the all absorbing question with me, as dear Top will not mind my telling you at this anxious time. The more he loves you, the more he knows that you are too lovely and noble not to be loved: and, dear Janey, there are too few things that seem worth expressing as life goes on, for one friend to deny another the poor expression of what is most at his heart. But he is before me in granting this, and there is no need for me to say it. I can never tell you

17 *Janey and the Wombat*. Caricature by Dante Gabriel Rossetti,
showing Morris as the wombat.

how much I am with you at all times. Absence from your sight is what I have
long been used to; and no absence can ever make me so far from you again as
your presence did for years. For this long inconceivable change, you know now
what my thanks must be.

Morris had never wanted to go to Ems. When he first arrived there he
had started on the schoolboy trick of crossing off the days until the
holidays arrive. By 15 August he was looking at the timetables, checking
on the trains from Bad Ems to Cologne. But Janey's condition was still

245

fluctuating badly. Her lethargy and weakness was attributed by Morris to the daily warm bath insisted on by her physician. It was the end of August before there was a visible improvement. By that time Morris was complaining of 'the fidgetts'. He forced himself out for a long walk in the heat hoping to calm down, walking over the hills and on into the forest, on and on till he imagined he had lost the way. Then the sight of a familiar green-painted seat showed him suddenly how close he was to home. He told Webb 'I drank a small lake of Seltzer water and white wine afterwards and got rid of my thirst, but not my fidgetts.' But he disciplined himself to write 120 lines.

By the beginning of September Janey seemed a great deal better. Plans were made to install a douche at home in London so that she could continue with her treatment. The doctor gave Morris a prescription that closely approximated the Bad Ems waters. The formula consisted mainly of carbonate of soda and common salt. Again this suggests Janey's complaint was gynaecological. Morris told Philip Webb what would be needed: 'a tin box or cistern somewhat conical at its lower end, and flat against the wall, capacity 2 gallons'. The cistern was to be installed up high, but not too high to prevent it from being filled conveniently with jugs. From the cistern a pipe would run, with a tap at the end 'and a flexible tube (common india-rubber)' half an inch in diameter. Morris's directions were precise. He asked Webb to rig this up at once in the dressing-room adjoining his and Janey's bedroom at Queen Square. He added an exotic touch, asking Webb to organize 'a scooped-out wooden stool like those one sits on at the Turkish bath'. Webb entered into the spirit of this enterprise. He returned a diagram, almost a working drawing, showing this Heath Robinson-like contraption with Janey included in the guise of the fat lady. 'If Janey does not understand the fat joke on the other side please explain it,' Webb scribbled on his design.

They finally left Ems in the middle of September. They made the trans-European return journey by themselves, with Morris anxiously negotiating 'two or three troublesome shiftings at custom houses and the like'. Janey survived well until they got to Calais. An unexpectedly stormy Channel crossing undid much of the good the stay at Ems had done her. She arrived back in London feeling very shaken up.

The effects of Ems on Morris were probably profounder than he then admitted. It is tempting to trace back to that summer of the taking of the waters Morris's long preoccupation in his stories with the elixir of life,

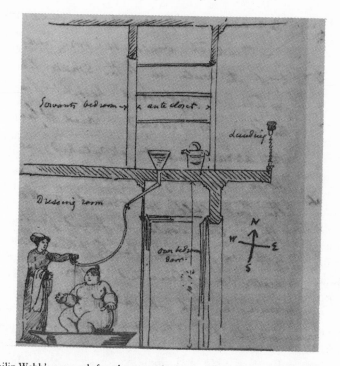

18 Philip Webb's proposals for a home-made shower-bath for Janey, to be installed in the dressing-room at No. 26 Queen Square.

with the healing powers of water, with the symbolism of the well. Magic draughts summed up the unexpected vision, as the hero finds in Morris's last (unfinished) story 'Kilian of the Closes', when he drinks from the gold cup proffered by the fair lady at the Fountain of Thirst.

Morris disliked the idle not just because they bored him but because he questioned their morality. He was soon to enter a new phase in defining the politics of lethargy. He perceived modern society as indecisive, indolent, with no distinct characteristics of its own but floating 'part of it hither, part thither, this set of minds drifting toward the beauty of the past, that toward the logic of the future'. He saw, in a hideous vision of the future, men losing their connections: their creative urges, their critical faculties, their social obligations, the sense of their own histories. This is a passage from his 1880s' lecture 'The Aims of Art':

Art will utterly perish, as in the manual arts so in literature, which will become, as it is indeed speedily becoming, a mere string of orderly and calculated ineptitudes and passionless ingenuities; Science will grow more and more one-sided, more incomplete, more wordy and useless, till at last she will pile herself up into such a mass of superstition, that beside it the theologies of old time will seem mere reason and enlightenment. All will get lower and lower, till the heroic struggles of the past to realise hope from year to year, from century to century, will be utterly forgotten, and man will be an indescribable being – hopeless, desireless, lifeless.

In a terrible way what he prophesied is with us, in the zombie culture of the electronic age.

Morris saw the potential violence in languor. He made the connection between lethargy and fascism. In the 1880s he visited the Tory stronghold of Clouds, the country house in Wiltshire that Philip Webb had built for the Hon. Percy Wyndham. He called this a home for incurables. Its air of listlessness must surely have taken him back to the torpor of Bad Ems, with the invalids assembled in the Kursaal, the orchestra tinkling out the 'Mabel Waltzes' and 'The Last Rose of Summer', and the gathering threat of the Franco-Prussian war.

In Ghent, on his way outwards to Bad Ems, Morris had bought some soup plates and some Delft china oil and vinegar bottles and had sent them back to England. He had made the purchase on the day of Georgie's birthday. The soup plates were for Webb; the cruets were for her. The bottle tops were missing and Morris had asked Webb either to have them replaced or to find suitable silver-mounted corks. Webb was then to present them with Morris's love.

One can tell from the carefulness of Morris's instructions, and his subsequent slightly obsessional fussing about whether the cruets had been broken in transit, that he had come to care deeply about Georgie. This is the solicitude of an exceptional fondness. He had watched with alarm and tenderness as Georgie, much hurt, had kept her dignity through the Zambaco disasters of the year before. There had been histrionic scenes: Howell had brought Mary to The Grange, introducing her to Georgie; Ned had fainted, splitting his head open on the mantelpiece. At the height of the tension Georgie had retreated to Oxford with her children, staying there some weeks, living in lodgings in Museum Terrace like an eternal student, and attempting bravely to recreate her life. Her Methodist upbringing and Christian faith sustained her: she wrote to Rosalind Howard, her great friend, 'sufficient to this time is its evil and also its good, for it is not without that'. She hoped to return home stronger and calmer, holding steadfast to her marriage. She told Rosalind she knew there was enough love between Edward and herself to last out a long life, if they were granted it. It is hardly a coincidence that Morris was soon writing a long narrative poem *Love Is Enough*.

The complex domestic agonizings of this period have been well concealed. Mackail, the Burne-Joneses' son-in-law, in a confidential letter to Aglaia Coronio written after Morris's death, refers to 'those stormy years of *The Earthly Paradise*' and regrets that his account of them in his biography of Morris 'must be excessively flat owing to the amount of tact that had to be exercised right and left'. In 1910, May Morris, working on the introductions to the *Collected Works*, came to Georgie to ask for her father's letters and received a stone-wall answer that may well have been convenient amnesia: 'I turned to my archives, and find that the letters from your father that I have kept only begin in 1876.' But we can retrieve from Morris's unpublished poems of this period some sense of how alienated he and Ned were, and how he turned to Georgie with emotions that, if they were not exactly passion, came very close to love.

There was a painful nostalgia in his feelings. This comes across most strongly in a poem of the *Earthly Paradise* period now in the British Library collection of Morris manuscripts. The verses are written out somewhat frenziedly in pencil:

> We meet, we laugh and talk, but still is set
> A seal o'er things I never can forget
> But must not speak of still. I count the hours
> That bring my friend to me – with hungry eyes
> I watch him as his feet the staircase mount.
> Then face to face we sit, a wall of lies
> Made hard by fear and faint anxieties
> Is drawn between us and he goes away
> And leaves me wishing it were yesterday.

Morris's attitude to cuckoldry was not Rossetti's. These verses show the poet, isolated, lonely, sitting by the fire, tentative, unable to 'bridge the space' between the revelation of his feelings and the 'sad weary face' of the loved woman whom an annotation in the manuscript clearly identifies as Georgie. He jots down words as if to her: '"poets"' unrealities – tears can come with verse we two are in the same box and need conceal nothing – don't cast me away – scold me but pardon me. What is all this to me (say you) Shame in confessing one's real feelings.' These real feelings are bound up in his past. He clings to Georgie, seeing her as his still centre in a time of disorientation and commotion:

> For you alone unchanged now seem to be
> A real thing left of the days sweet to me.

There are poems of hands meeting, lips trembling, cheeks burning, grey eyes 'truer than truth' piercing through his weal and woe. In the verses of these years the gentle grey-eyed girl with her enormous self-containment recurs in a fascinating counterpoint with Morris's other female, the beautiful shape-changer, desirous and wilful. There is the suggestion of a fleeting physicality. We can also surmise that in this sense he was rejected:

> She wavered, stopped and turned, methought her eyes,
> The deep grey windows of her heart, were wet,
> Methought they softened with a near regret
> To note in mine unspoken miseries:
> And as a prayer from out my heart did rise
> And struggle on my lips in shame's strong net,
> She stayed me, and cried 'Brother!' Our lips met.
> Her hands drew me into Paradise.
> Sweet seemed that kiss till thence her feet were gone,
> Sweet seemed the word she spake, while it might be
> As wordless music – But truth fell on me
> And kiss and word I knew, and, left alone,
> Face to face seemed I to a wall of stone
> While at my back there beat a boundless sea.

Perfect self-abnegation and the clarion call of comradeship: they seem to have arrived at a solution from one of the chivalric novels of Charlotte M. Yonge.

Mackail, with his wonderful gift of the hint between the lines, pointed out in his *Times* obituary of Georgiana, who died in 1920 in her eightieth year, that between her and William Morris 'sympathy was as deep and as affectionate, though different in kind, as between Morris and Burne-Jones'.

Morris referred ruefully to these emotional turmoils in a letter to Ned in 1886, at the height of his involvement in Socialist politics: 'If I were but twenty years younger. But then you know there would be the Female complication somewhere. Best as it is after all.'

While the Ms were at Ems, Rossetti was in Scotland, staying at Penkill Castle with Alice Boyd and William Bell Scott, as he had done the previous autumn. He had hoped to find the visit to darkest Ayrshire soothing: Penkill Castle was remote, peaceful, set in its private glen. But in fact the visit was disastrous, with Rossetti brooding about Janey and closer to a breakdown than he had ever been. His sight was still failing, he was sweating excessively, he suffered from insomnia. He was becoming dangerously obsessed with suicide. One day Scott had watched with alarm as he peered grimly into the 'Devil's Punch Bowl', a deep black whirlpool at the base of a waterfall on the Penkill estate. He began to suffer from the delusions that made his later life such an appalling tragi-comedy. When, on a walk, a chaffinch alighted on his hand, he took it for the spirit of Lizzie, returning to prophesy disaster. He and Scott walked back to the castle in silence. He was almost triumphant when he found that in their absence, for no apparent reason, the castle gate-bell had tolled.

He and Howell had entered into a secret conspiracy to recover the manuscript poems Rossetti had placed with Lizzie in her grave. This involved the exhumation of her coffin in Highgate Cemetery. While he was at Penkill he was preoccupied with the arrangements for this delicate affair. Rossetti had decided that his value to posterity lay more with his literary output than his paintings: as a painter he now felt he was being outperformed by Millais and Burne-Jones. In order to advance these claims he urgently needed to publish a substantial new volume. To bulk out what he was planning as a 400-page edition he needed to reclaim his old unpublished poems. There was another reason. The poems he was currently writing were almost all addressed to, or at least inspired by, Janey. The closeness of their relations, known or at least suspected only in their own small circle, could develop into widespread scandal if the object of the poet's adoration were to be publicly identified. Attention could be deflected from the Janey poems if they were published as part of a large collection, with a diplomatic vagueness about dates.

The retrieval of the volume was above board and official. Rossetti had authority from the home secretary, Henry Bruce, who on the strength of old acquaintanceship had waived the necessity for permission from Rossetti's mother, the legal owner of the grave. Rossetti felt the enterprise might well upset his family. The Order for Exhumation was issued on 28 September 1869. Rossetti himself was not present at the graveside, operating the proceedings by remote control, instructing Howell to locate a volume bound in rough grey calf which (he was 'almost certain') had red edges to the leaves. He trusted this would give Howell enough detail to distinguish his poems from a bible, also buried with Lizzie in her coffin. There was the possible extra complication of the body of a Polidori aunt in the same family grave, but this proved to be a false alarm.

Lizzie's body, when the coffin was opened, was reported as being in 'perfect' condition, as Rossetti had been told was probable. He assured himself, and others, that the retrieval of the poems was what she would have wished. At first sight the book of poems appeared to be intact, though 'soaked through and through' with moisture. It had to be doused again in disinfectant. But when Rossetti himself came to examine the volume at the doctor's he found a good deal missing. The poem he had most relied on finding, 'Jenny', an early poem on the theme of prostitution, had a great hole through the centre. He decided, however, that 'with a little rewriting and a good memory', he would be able to resurrect the work. He had offered Howell a drawing in payment for the part he had played in the exhumation. Howell requested a drawing of Janey, which Rossetti agreed to on condition that Howell would let him have it back at any time that he requested it, in exchange for something else.

Rossetti had planned to give away three copies of his completed *Poems*. One of these honoured recipients was to be Janey. He had wanted to dedicate the collection to her too, but realized that this was socially impossible. (Morris had already dedicated *The Earthly Paradise* 'To my wife'.) He told Janey, Scott and Henry Treffry Dunn, his studio assistant, about the opening of the grave. He also confided in his brother William. He did not tell Morris or Burne-Jones, though they found out later via Howell. Rossetti realized that 'the truth must ooze out in time.'

There is one surviving fragment of a letter of this period, a letter dated October 1869, from Morris to Georgiana Burne-Jones. The start of it is missing; the remaining letter opens '. . . about him nearly drives me mad when I am in an irritable humour'. Could Morris have been referring to Rossetti? One can only assume a growing undertow of bitterness in a friendship that continued, on the surface, equably. The next spring he was dining with Rossetti at Rules restaurant in Maiden Lane, off the Strand. They gorged themselves on oysters while discussing the binding of Rossetti's poems. Professionally they depended on each other. Morris agreed to review Rossetti's book. Rossetti asked his brother William to put forward this proposal to the editor of *The Academy* magazine. (Swinburne had already been signed up for *The Fortnightly Review*, the outlet Morris would have preferred.) There was at least the semblance of brotherly back-scratching. Rossetti grandiosely suggested that the enterprise could only be of benefit to Morris's reputation. But Morris confessed to Janey that the prospect of reviewing the poems rather terrified him.

J. W. Mackail, appalled by the ramifications of Morris's review of the poems of his rival, erotically fuelled by the beauty of his wife, shies away from it in his biography of Morris, dismissing the review as 'stiff and laboured', and as 'nearly colourless as anything of his writing well could be'. He is wrong about this. The review in fact resounds with a real admiration of Rossetti's combination of the mystical and lyrical. Morris, with his own rare skills in both the visual and the verbal, had a special understanding of Rossetti's dual talents: 'that a master in the supremely difficult art of painting should have qualities which enable him to deal with the other supremely difficult one of poetry' is, he tells his readers, remarkable indeed. He defended Rossetti's controversial poem 'Jenny' on the grounds that although the subject is a difficult one for a modern poet to deal with it is *necessary* for a modern man to think about: by the 1880s Morris would himself be campaigning on behalf of young girl prostitutes. When it comes to the sonnets at the end of the volume, the sonnets in which Janey is featured so explicitly, Morris calls them 'a magnificent collection', unsurpassed since Shakespeare. (We should bear in mind however that Shakespeare was not Morris's favourite poet.)

Rossetti and Janey were still being seen together around London, the beautiful people of their period. At one party he was watched feeding her with strawberries, divesting each strawberry carefully of cream, which was considered bad for her, before he spooned it in. At another party, at the Browns', the young Edmund Gosse described excitedly how Mrs William Morris, 'in her ripest beauty, and dressed in a long unfashionable gown of ivory velvet, occupied the painting throne, and

Dante Gabriel Rossetti, who, though still almost young, was yet too stout for elegance, squatted – for some part of the evening at least – on a hassock at her feet.'

In the spring of 1870 there was a scheme for Janey to accompany Rossetti to Evans's supper club in a large party that included Ned and Mary Zambaco. Rossetti wrote sympathetically of Mary, telling Janey how exquisite she looked: 'I think she has got more so within the last year with all her love and trouble.' He explains that he liked Mary 'because she said the sweet one was far more beautiful than anyone else in the world'.

The love letters still poured in, some charming, optimistic, as in one beginning 'Funny sweet Janey', dated 4 February 1870:

more than all for me, dear Janey, is the fact that you exist, that I can yet look forward to seeing you and speaking to you again, and know for certain that at that moment I shall forget all my own troubles nor even be able to remember yours.

Other letters from Rossetti were intensely melancholy:

For the last 2 years I have felt distinctly the clearing away of chilling numbness that surrounds me in the utter want of you; but since then other obstacles have kept steadily on the increase, and it comes too late.

Rossetti's swings of mood had always been alarming. He was by no means as ruthless as he seemed. He had an active conscience and lurched uneasily between his Casanova instincts and his family's High Anglicanism. He found some of Swinburne's poetry blasphemous and obscene. After the opening up of Lizzie's grave, which in his blackest moods he construed as desecration, Rossetti became more paranoid than ever, in 'a broken state of health and nerves'. He talked of taking a house in the country as far as possible from human habitation. He favoured Haslemere. But in March 1870 he was installed at Scalands, a house at Robertsbridge in Sussex which belonged to his friend Barbara Bodichon. It was conveniently close to Janey, by now suffering from a throat infection, who had been sent with the children to recuperate at Hastings only twenty miles away.

Rossetti was sharing the cottage with W. J. Stillman, the American journalist. It was Stillman who introduced him to chloral, which he took in the first place as a cure for his insomnia. Chloral had been discovered in 1832 by Liebig, but did not come into general use in medicine until

19 'Rossetti carrying cushions to a startled Janey Morris'.
Caricature by Edward Burne-Jones.

the 1870s. It was then considered harmless in its effects and was used in high bohemian circles much as alcohol was turned to in the London of the 1920s and 1930s, cannabis in the 1960s, as a semi-public secret, the bringer of relaxation and escape. Rossetti was notably careless in his use of medicines: as a young man he should have learned his lesson from the effect of taking three doses of a tonic containing tincture of nux vomica in quick succession. His initial dose of chloral, apparently ten grains washed down with whisky, was increased rapidly and Rossetti became an addict, to the point in 1880 when he was boasting to his friend Hall Caine that he was taking as much as 180 grains a day. This may be an exaggeration: his physician, Dr John Marshall, took the precaution of instructing the chemists to dilute the prescription before dispensing the drug. But Rossetti's wildly fluctuating moods from the 1860s onwards were at least partly caused by the drug habit now begun.

Rossetti and Stillman walked the snowy roads and leafless woods and discussed Stillman's engagement to Marie Spartali, regarded by Rossetti as 'a noble girl in beauty, in sweetness, and in artistic gifts'. Rossetti pursued the gamekeeper's daughter. He grew tearful at finding a 'poor dear little mole' dead by the roadside. He visited Janey at the seaside. On 26 March she and Morris came over for dinner and Rossetti reported to Ellis: 'Top and Janey are here today – the former insolently solid – the latter better than when I saw her at Hastings.' By 14 April Janey was installed at Scalands on what turned into a four-week springtime idyll. Rossetti wrote to his mother to tell her the glories of the weather, the violets, the primroses, the lambs which were growing tails and starting prancing. 'Janey Morris is here, and benefiting greatly. Top comes from time to time.'

The owner of Scalands, Barbara Bodichon, was herself an amateur artist. A woman of very advanced views, she later founded Girton College, Cambridge. Rossetti had described her as 'blessed with large rations of tin, fat, enthusiasm, and golden hair, who thinks nothing of climbing up a mountain in breeches, or wading through a stream in none, in the sacred name of pigment'. He had known her in the years before her marriage when, as Barbara Leigh Smith, she had befriended Lizzie and gone to visit her. Not least of the ironies of the situation was that, years earlier, Lizzie Siddal had been ill in Hastings too. Barbara Bodichon's cottage was a new one, built on her family estate. 'Barbara', wrote Rossetti, 'does not indulge in bell-pulls, hardly in servants to summon thereby – so I have brought my own. What she does affect is any amount of through draught – a library bearing the stern stamp of "Bodichon", and a kettle holder with the uncompromising initials B.B.' Scalands, in its lack of fripperies, was an early model for the English academic female home. But Rossetti reported himself as thriving there. The pains in his head and his eyes had receded, and he was back at systematic work. He had finished his drawing of the gamekeeper's daughter and he started on a portrait of Stillman before he left Sussex. He was also working on a new portrait of Janey, showing her lying on her sofa reading a paper, looking relaxed though pensive, which he considered 'about the best' likeness of her he had done.

Morris sent kindly but rather plaintive letters from Queen Square. On Good Friday he wrote saying he had sent some wine to Scalands. He was bored with being at home alone with Bessie ('at least', he heads his letter, 'Bessy seems to have gone to Church.'). However on Monday he

will go to see his mother. He will be at Scalands on Wednesday afternoon. He writes again to Janey ten days later, and again it is a patient,
calming letter, though he evidently longs for her return: 'I shall certainly come down for a day or two next week and fetch you up when you
are ready to be fetched – do you want any more wine?' Janey meanwhile
had recovered. Rossetti was describing her striding round the Sussex
countryside 'like anybody else'.

A relic of that springtime in Sussex is the sonnet by Rossetti 'Youth's
Spring-tribute':

On this sweet bank your head thrice sweet and dear
I lay, and spread your hair on either side,
And see the newborn woodflowers bashful-eyed
Look through the golden tresses here and there.
On these debatable borders of year
Spring's foot half falters; scarce she yet may know
The leafless blackthorn-blossom from the snow;
And through her bowers the wind's way still is clear.

But April's sun strikes down the glades to-day;
So shut your eyes upturned, and feel my kiss
Creep, as the Spring now thrills through every spray,
Up your warm throat to your warm lips: for this
Is even the hour of Love's sworn suitservice,
With whom cold hearts are counted castaway.

Another of the poems of that period of love in the buttercup fields is
'Silent Noon', later set to music by Vaughan Williams. It bears the
Rossetti hallmarks of lushness, physicality, almost too much emotion.
Rossetti overdoes it. He was still writing fond, dependent letters to
Fanny at this time.

By early May Barbara Bodichon was asking for her cottage back.
Rossetti rented another house not far away, presumably hoping the idyll
with Janey could continue through the summer. But this did not
materialize. Rossetti never occupied the house and in September he
gave the cottage up. Scott made the malicious comment that 'perhaps he
could not manage to get "the hollow chested matron" out to that neighbourhood'. Probably even to Janey the prospect seemed too risky. So
flamboyant a flouting of conventions might have compelled Morris to
sue for a divorce. Since 1857, when divorce became a matter for the

secular courts, the old arcane procedures had been simplified, but the termination of a marriage remained a very cumbersome and solemn business. Janey would have been treated afterwards as socially dubious; and probably Jenny and May would have been removed from her control.

Janey stayed at Queen Square through the summer of 1870 and then, unwell again with lumbago and sciatica, went with her mother-in-law and Henrietta to spend November and December in Torquay. Morris again pursued her with a series of letters which, though uncomplaining, make his sense of loneliness and isolation clear. The children are misbehaving in her absence: 'Such a rumpus this morning. May enjoying a good tease and Jenny expressing herself in boo hoo.' He has gone, accompanied by Ellis, to order 'a suit of Clothes' in the city. The tailor, before measuring Morris, had complimented him on his 'great works'. The next day, he tells Janey, he intends to entrust 'the head which accomplished the E.P. to the scissors and comb of a hairdresser'. These are the minutiae of life, made the more poignant by the knowledge that the structure of his marriage had collapsed.

Was there a confrontation? I do not believe so. Morris was exceptionally reticent in an age not given, as the late twentieth century in Britain and, even more, America, to the practice of analysing feelings, of 'talking the thing through'. But heightened emotion draws out new emotion and there is a passage in a letter to Janey in Torquay in which Morris breaks out of his customary tone of jocularity and carefulness and seems to address her in his real voice:

As for living, dear, people like you speak about don't know either what life or death means, except for one or two supreme moments of their lives, when something pierces through the crust of dullness and ignorance, and they act for the time as if they were sensitive people –
For me I don't think people really want to die because of mental pain, that is if they are imaginative people; they want to live to see the play played out fairly – they have hopes that they are not conscious of.

May Morris identifies this passage as 'a sudden revelation' of her father's 'sacred hidden self, such as he indulged in perhaps even less than most people'. He stops himself instinctively, realizing he is veering out beyond the bounds of his own self-control and his customary truce of *politesse* with Janey: 'Hillao! here's cheerful talk for you – I beg your pardon, dear, with all my heart.'

My interpretation is that by the end of 1870 Morris and Janey had reached a tacit agreement. She would not give up Rossetti. He would allow her freedom, within certain bounds. She would retain her position in the family. Morris ended his letter lovingly, protectively, 'Goodbye dear child'.

In December 1870 the fourth and final part of *The Earthly Paradise* was published. How to view this immense enterprise that had dominated five years of William Morris's life? In a sense it is easier for us to get the feel of it than it was for many of Morris's contemporaries. The sternest of his critics dismissed it as escapism, evasion of the problems of the age, quoting back with derision the lines in his own prologue which introduce the poet as the 'idle singer of an empty day':

> Forget six counties overhung with smoke,
> Forget the snorting steam and piston stroke,
> Forget the spreading of the hideous town;
> Think rather of the pack-horse on the down,
> And dream of London, small, and white, and clean.

A particularly forthright review in *The Spectator* contrasted William Morris's unwillingness to enter the realms of speculation with Tennyson's zest for comment and explanation, which he often provides in the first person, Browning's 'subtle and exhaustive' insights and the toughness of argument always inherent in the work of George Eliot. Her *Spanish Gipsy* is cited as 'the extremest contrast that can be found to Mr. Morris's work in this respect'.

But to a late-twentieth-century reader, with a background of Symbolist writing, surrealist art and cinematic dream sequences, *The Earthly Paradise* seems part of a familiar tradition of non-literal communication, tricks of meaning. Even Morris's creation of his own archaic language, a source of bemusement (or amusement) to his critics, seems less unlikely to anyone brought up on the verbal shock-tactics of an Ezra Pound or a James Joyce. There is a kind of timelessness in Morris's poetry, a sense of being nowhere and yet somewhere drenched with meaning. This is even truer of the strange dream landscapes of Morris's late novels, science fiction scenarios in which we are suddenly brought up against ourselves and an almost forgotten background of experience. It was C. S. Lewis in 1937, of the generation of the First World War, who first argued persuasively for Morris as a poet more demanding than he seems: 'Morris may build a world in some ways happier than the real one; but happiness puts as stern a question as misery. It is this dialectic of desire, presented with no solution, no lies, no panacea, which gives him his peculiar bittersweet quality, and also his solidity. He has faced the fact.'

These are indeed sad stories, as Morris told his daughters, inscribing in the prettily bound copy of *The Earthly Paradise* he gave them to share, some special verses:

> Ah, my dears, indeed
> My wisdom fails me at my need
> To tell why tales that moved the earth
> Are seldom of content and mirth.

The particular structure he gives *The Earthly Paradise* provides it with a double depth of sorrow. There is the outer framework, the prologue and the envoi, and the inner framework of twelve three-stanza poems for each month which relate so painfully to Morris's personal history: 'In the verses that frame the stories of *The Earthly Paradise* there is an autobiography so delicate and so outspoken that it must be left to speak for itself,' as Mackail so very tactfully points out.

The camera zooms in towards more generalized miseries. It is quickly clear that the landscape of the inner sequence of the tales, ostensibly so lush, is just as tragic, just as arid. The tales of *The Earthly Paradise*, read closely, are *all* stories of love's failure. The lover himself fails in steadfastness or trust. They put forward a bleak vision of love as the fatal distraction, the traducer of men's energies.

Why does the narrator of *The Earthly Paradise* tremble? Why indeed? The inert palace of Circe in *Jason*, as luxurious and deadly as a hotel at Bad Ems; the Sirens so seductively recommending languor; the frighteningly Freudian dark cavern's mouth in the sheer rock's side in the poem 'The Hill of Venus' into which a man can vanish and lose all motivation, paralysed by sexual passion:

> All thought in him did fade
> Into the bliss that knoweth not surprise,
> Into the life that hath no memories,
> No hope and fear; the life of all desire,
> Whose fear is death, whose hope consuming fire.

The Earthly Paradise is full of intimations that Morris did indeed perceive, and was beginning to reject with a great passion, the prevailing moral torpor of his age. When he painted these dream pictures of men, normally active, frozen into inactivity he was asking questions about the world he lived in, a society lulled into false complacency by a belief in progress that in effect was spiritual suicide. The blankness at the centre of *The Earthly Paradise* reflects the blanknesses that Morris found around him. This is almost, but not quite, the poetry of sheer despair. What saves it is its constant counterbalancing, most obvious in its last two volumes, published in 1870, of lethargy with action, as if the narrator shakes himself, awakes himself, resolves what can be done.

Those years of *Earthly Paradise* were in a way self-education. They moved Morris onwards steadily towards his years of action in the form of practical political involvement. The genesis of this is explained by Morris in 'How I Became a Socialist', an extraordinary, vivid recreation of his motives and emotions written for the magazine *Justice* in 1894:

Apart from the desire to produce beautiful things, the leading passion of my life has been and is hatred of modern civilization . . . What shall I say concerning its mastery of and its waste of mechanical power, its commonwealth so poor, its enemies of the commonwealth so rich, its stupendous organisation – for the misery of life! Its contempt of simple pleasures which everyone could enjoy but for its folly? Its eyeless vulgarity which has destroyed art, the one certain solace of labour? All this I felt then as now, but I did not know why it was so. The hope of the past times was gone, the struggles of mankind for many ages had produced nothing but this sordid, aimless, ugly confusion; the immediate future seemed to me likely to intensify all the present evils by sweeping away the last survivals of the days before the dull squalor of civilization had settled down on the world. This was a bad look-out indeed, and, if I may mention myself as a personality and not as a mere type, especially so to a man of my disposition, careless of metaphysics and religion, as well as of scientific analysis, but with a deep love of the earth and the life on it, and a passion for the history of the past mankind. Think of it! Was it all to end in a counting-house on the top of a cinder-heap, with Podsnap's drawing room in the offing, and a Whig committee dealing out champagne to the rich and margarine to the poor in such convenient proportions as would make all men contented together, though the pleasure of the eyes was gone from the world, and the place of Homer was to be taken by Huxley? Yet, believe me, in my heart, when I really forced myself to look towards the future, that is what I saw in it, and, as far as I could tell, scarce anyone seemed to think it worth while to struggle against such a consummation of civilization.'

Homer versus Huxley. The lure of Podsnap's drawing-room. The reference is to Charles Dickens's *Our Mutual Friend*. If such subtleties inherent in *The Earthly Paradise* were lost on Morris's contemporaries there are two main reasons. The first was the work's enormous length and its prolixity. This had to do with Morris's way of composition. He wrote verse in great bursts in the midst of a myriad other activities. To George Wardle, who worked alongside him at the Firm, it seemed like magic. As he described Morris in action to Mackail:

His faculty for work was enormous and wonderfully versatile. He could turn his mind at once to the new matter brought before him and leave the poetry or the design without a murmur. How rapidly and accurately he wrote you know, almost without correction, page after page, but I may say that I always admired the easy way in which he turned from this ordinarily engrossing pursuit to attend to any other and resume his favourite work without apparently the loss of a single thread, as calmly as a workman goes to the bench after dinner.

This versatility was a principle to Morris. It was inherent in his bardic view of poetry not as a vocation set apart but a normal everyday useful activity, a form of craftmanship to be pursued ideally in conjunction with other crafts: he once argued that 'if a chap can't compose an epic poem while he's weaving tapestry he had better shut up.' But the lack of regularity told on Morris's poetry, and so did his almost trance-like mode of composition once he had entered his poetic phase. Morris wrote as if spurred on by a speedometer: one day he achieved 750 lines of *Jason*; on another day, a Sunday, 728 lines of 'Gudrun'. 'Topsy goes on writing a furious rate,' said Rossetti, feeling like the mouse beside the mountain. This element of frenzy gave Morris's work its chant-like, almost *Hiawatha* quality. He was his own best critic: 'they are all too long and flabby – damn it!' was his comment on the poems of *The Earthly Paradise*, except for just one, 'The Lovers of Gudrun' in his volume three.

But if he saw his failings, why was he so lax in correcting them? This again is related to his concept of the poet. He believed that the poet, the bard, must be accessible and that blandness was preferable to obscurity. He saw perfectionism as a kind of affectation: a curious position for someone who, as designer and maker, carried perfectionism to extra-ordinary lengths. The second of the reasons for the failure of Morris's contemporary readers to grasp the desperation in *The Earthly Paradise* is the soporific charm of its surface decoration. The Victorian

The Ring given to Venus.

His fingers lovingly enlaced
By other fingers; ~~now and~~ until he
~~illustrated his own ring Certainly~~ Midst darkness his own
~~But two sought that All that he could deem~~ ring did see
~~the esprit but the wildest fevered dreams~~
~~would at last (without a sound)~~
~~Scatches he lay upon the ground.~~

Nought else a while, then back there came
New vision: as amidst white flame
The flower-girt goddess wavered there,
Nor knew he ~~might~~ now where they twain were
~~that let will desire and fathering their it~~
Midst wild desire that nigh did rend
His ~~changed~~ heart: then there came an end
~~of faint flight, and moaning from an~~ And extacy
~~died with a low~~ empty heart

Ah what a night to what a morn!
Ah what a morrow black with scorn,
And hapless end of happy love!
What shame his helpless shame to prove!
For who indeed alone could bear
The dreadful shame the shameful fear
Of such a bridal? Think withal
~~willingly trusted That fairer~~ such a tale would fall
Upon those folks ~~you~~ ears than on most,
Who, as I said erst, saw a host
Of wild things lurking in the night;
To whom was magic much as right
As prayers or holy psalmody.

20 Early manuscript draft of 'The Ring given to Venus', one of the stories in *The Earthly Paradise*. This was the passage chosen by May Morris to illustrate her father's spontaneity of composition in the preliminary stages of a poem.

materfamilias was lulled into believing it ideal public reading for her assembled children, missing its political messages, imagining the sexual element less omnipresent than it is.

It became a cult book, mainstay of mid-Victorian picnics. One reviewer asked why William Morris insisted on bringing out the volumes of *The Earthly Paradise* in winter. It seemed obvious that they ought to be read in summer, and out of doors if possible accompanied by birdsong. Even the intellectuals saw the poem as a respite. George Eliot and G. H. Lewes wrote to John Blackwood from Petershal in the Black Forest, saying, 'We take Morris's poem into the woods with us and read it aloud, greedily, looking to see how much *more* there is in store for us. If *ever* you have an idle afternoon, bestow it on the *Earthly Paradise*.'

The Earthly Paradise was finished and Morris was complaining of feeling slightly lost at his sudden lack of serious occupation. He told Janey with nostalgia, 'I find now I liked working on it better than I thought.' Morris had a peculiar horror of a vacuum, and in fact he always managed to insure himself against one by keeping a new, absorbing interest in reserve. His activities surge onwards in overlapping phases, each of them approximately five years in duration. In the early 1860s his creative concentration was on pattern design and decoration; the later 1860s were the years of *Earthly Paradise*; in 1870 he first went back to painting and then, still dissatisfied with his abilities, returned with a new professionalism and obsessiveness to the art of illuminated manuscripts. Morris's 'painted books' were from then on his chief 'pleasure work' (as opposed to more routine jobs that he called his 'bread and cheese work'). Between 1870 and 1875 he worked on eighteen manuscript books and many trial fragments, a total of over 1,500 pages of laborious handwriting combined with a mass of decorative detail. The first of these books was the exquisite and intimate *A Book of Verse* written out for Georgie's birthday in August 1870.

With his revival of the skills of calligraphy and illumination Morris was, once again, entering new territory. These were techniques that had lain virtually fallow since the invention and development of printing in the fifteenth and sixteenth centuries. Handwriting had degenerated into the copperplate scripts of the professional Victorian law-writers and conveners, no longer employing traditional quills but the pointed metal pens that came into general use from the 1830s onwards. Morris's initiative turned this by then desiccated craft into an art form.

Like his earlier pursuit of old stained-glass techniques and his later retrieval of lost methods of fabric dyeing and hand-weaving, Morris's determined revival of the manuscript was immensely influential on the later practice of the workshops of the Arts and Crafts. It developed from his academic knowledge of the French and English mediaeval painted manuscripts in the Bodleian at Oxford and the British Museum, studied through the years with a hungry concentration. Morris's notebooks of the Red House days are packed with references to these manuscripts and sketches taken from them. May Morris later claimed that nobody in London, except possibly the staff of the department, knew the British Museum Manuscripts collection in as much detail as her father did.

Morris himself owned four sixteenth-century Italian writing books: *La Operina* and *Il Modo de Temperare le Penne* by Ludovico degli Arrighi (Vicentino), *Thesauro de Scrittori* by Ugo da Carpi, and *Lo Presente Libro* by Giovannantonio Tagliente. These were the earliest of printed writing manuals, handbooks for the new breed of trained professional secretaries required to write out documents rapidly and legibly in the new bureaucracies of Renaissance Italy. The four manuals, bound together in a single fat volume in old crimson morocco, contain page upon page of Alphabet examples: fat letters, spindly letters, solemn letters, fantastical letters. They suggest the possibilities of letter-forms as pattern. Some of the pages have a great exuberance, a childlike delight in playing with the alphabet, trying out the variations of weight and speed and density. You sense the same delight in Morris's later typographical experiments at the Kelmscott Press.

Morris painstakingly taught himself both Roman and italic scripts. He produced page after page of trial scripts, experimenting with both round and pointed hands. One of these exercise sheets quotes Vincentino's words 'Modo de temperare le penne'. On the back of a leaf of one of his own manuscripts he wrote himself a note in a crazy personal shorthand: 'let us try some hands now this is not right this is not right good but rather shaky tis somewhat of a puzzle to know how to set to work about it: tis between pointed and round.' On this experimental sheet he tried out first a cursive script and then a slower and more circumspect italic.

When it came to sheer calligraphic technique some of Morris's successors were destined to surpass him. Edward Johnston was much more systematic and original in constructing his alphabets. Morris was too impatient for such conscious analysis of letter-forms and their unified relationships. Graily Hewitt, that perfectionist scribe, detected in his work a certain roughness: the rhythm was disturbed by 'the dash of diagonal strokes he made for his commas and tails to p's and q's'; Hewitt also complained of the unevenness of Morris's pages. As with his poetry he seems to have fixed a limit on the time he would expend on craftsmanship. Morris was constitutionally suspicious of finesse. But in fact his scripts, though not amongst the finest ever written, have a wonderful strength and an ebullience that makes much twentieth-century calligraphy look precious. Johnston, who just missed meeting him but who was shown his manuscripts by Sydney Cockerell two years after Morris's death, understood his quality. He noted: 'Was more impressed than ever by the sweetness and naturalness of his work, the absence of strain and the beauty of it. His writing became *v. beautiful.*'

While he was learning calligraphy Morris was also rediscovering ancient techniques of gilding. The gilding of the letters and the ornament of illuminated manuscripts is a complex, and chancy, craft in itself: a gesso base is laid and the gold-leaf attached and burnished. Traditionally the gesso was prepared from an arcane mixture of slaked plaster of Paris, white lead, bole and such adhesives as sugar, glue and egg. The raised gold was technically very problematic. May remembered sheets of paper strewn about her father's study for years afterwards covered with experimental squares of groundings and gold as Morris tried out recipes given in Theophilus and other ancient books. He compared the methods of contemporary workers in gold and evolved his own solution. One gets the impression that Morris's phases of technical experiment interested him almost more than the arrival. He once showed his young daughters how the gold was laid, amusing them by passing the broad badger gilding brush through 'his forest of thick curls' like a hair brush before laying it gently on the leaf of gold. The brush, slightly pre-greased by Morris's hair, took the gold leaf up evenly and transferred it to a little cushion for him to cut.

Morris liked the solidity of things and he felt a particular security and happiness surrounded by the tools of his successive trades. Now he began to amass the scribes' accoutrements: delicate brushes in all their varied sizes, metal rules and compasses and finely tempered knives and a range of quill pens, from a goose quill to a crow quill. Surprisingly he did not make these quills himself. He threw himself with energy into the hunt for vellum. Some of Morris's manuscripts are paper, but vellum was used for the most splendid: the two versions of *The Rubaiyat of*

Omar Khayyam (now in the British Museum and the Bodleian); *The Odes of Horace*; the enormous and unfinished *Aeneid of Virgil*.

The only skins available in England were prepared with white lead which Morris judged injurious to the colours and the gold. The search for an unsullied source of vellum led to Rome, where the Vatican sustained a still-thriving market in lambskins and calfskins. Morris commissioned his ex-assistant Charles Fairfax Murray, then travelling in Italy, to send him samples and an estimate of the cost of a hundred skins for manuscript pages about nineteen by thirteen inches. He urged Murray to locate a vellum of the hardness and smoothness found in mediaeval books.

It was never Morris's plan simply to reproduce the past. Mediaevalism for its own sake would have bored him. Through his research into old methods and approaches he hoped to salvage something important for the present. This was what, a few years later, he expressed so plainly in his lecture on 'The Lesser Arts': 'Let us study it wisely, be taught by it, kindled by it; all the while determining not to imitate or repeat it; to have either no art at all, or an art which we have made our own.' His illuminated manuscripts give us the best example of Morris acquiring the techniques of past ages and using them creatively to arrive at a new contemporary art form. This series of manuscripts shows Morris at his most mid-Victorian. They have a certain formality, almost a sententiousness. They are also deeply personal, free-flowing and bizarre.

Morris once asked the rhetorical question, the question from a fairytale, of what he considered the most important production of Art 'and the thing most to be longed for'. His immediate reply was 'A beautiful House'. He continued, 'and if I were further asked to name the production next in importance and the thing next to be longed for, I should answer, A beautiful Book.' It is interesting in view of this to notice how very architectural Morris's painted books are. They are complicated structures with their elements of painting and gilding, rising up like little buildings, turreted and towered. Morris is in charge of the deployment of the elements, though he does not himself take part in all the detail. This is book making as teamwork. Even the birthday-present *Book of Verse* for Georgie written out in Morris's cursive hand contains miniatures by Fairfax Murray, ornament by George Wardle, Murray's portrait of Morris and a gouache of two separated lovers by Ned. This highly original sense of a book as a composite of quasi-architectural elements had great influence not just on the productions of Morris's own Kelmscott Press in the 1890s. It motivated the English private presses. It percolated through to influence the avant-garde in Europe in the 1920s and 1930s. Though they imagined they resisted this Victorian and, as they saw it, deeply bourgeois concept, there is certainly something of the Book Beautiful in the Bauhaus-influenced *neue Typographie*.

On many of Morris's illuminated pages the pictorial decoration swims into the lettering. Leaves and grapes and rose hips; honeysuckle trellis; a thousand dotting rosebuds. Some of his pages are like demented wallpaper with flowers spilling out right to the edge. Then there are the inset portraits. Pre-Raphaelite lovers. Red-winged angels. Poignant ladies. A little wild-haired fairy. The general effect is inexpressibly peculiar, at once beautiful and decorous yet fraught and slightly manic. It is easy to relate it to the world of Lewis Carroll in its juxtapositions of the known and disconcerting. It has something of the graphic visionary intensity of Blake. But the way Morris mixes his letters and his images to make a very secret and suggestive visual landscape, a blurring of feeling and a layering of memory, is really much closer to French Surrealism and the haunting picture poems of Karel Teige and the Czech avant-garde.

Morris's calligraphic pages are as they are because of his close emotional identification with the subjects of his manuscripts. In a specific sense he was writing from the heart as, in later days at Kelmscott Press, he chose to publish books reflecting his own interests and tastes. He drew upon the literature of his personal past. The poems to Georgie are – predictably – sad, suffering, full of the strains of disappointment, separation. One of them casts Georgie, all too obviously, as the grey-eyed and unblinking Muse of the North, a composite of womanhood, nurturing, attracting and finally withholding: 'Mother and Love and Sister all in one'. The northernness of the Muse has its significance. *The Story of Halfden the Black*, *The Story of Frithiof the Bold*, *The Story of the Dwellers of Eyr*: of Morris's total eighteen manuscripts of the 1870s twelve are Nordic. They are tales of bleak heroics, fights to the death and tragic feuds in barren landscapes. Morris's choice of subject shows his imagination now veering towards Iceland. But these are Nordic stories in a frame of English flowers. It is typical of Morris that his *Story of the Ynglings*, the Icelandic saga written out in Roman script, includes an illustration of two plump English rabbits drawn by Philip Webb.

Morris worked on his illuminations with those reserves of patience he could always draw upon for any craft activity. May stressed that her father was extraordinarily patient 'with things if not with people always'.

He could school his natural impetuosity if he could see a worthwhile end result. May remembered watching his 'firm broad hand as it covered a gold square half an inch in size with wee flowers of five pin-point dots of white laid with the extreme point of a full brush. The least wavering would have meant a jog or blot, but the blossoms grew with the ease and surety that are associated with a Chinese craftsman who has spent his life with a brush in his hand.' Morris, when illuminating and hand-lettering, entered what was almost an abstracted state, an enclosed serenity of manual activity, like the therapeutic net-making he used to do at school. He saw it himself as a reversion to his childhood, writing to Murray in 1870 to ask him to come and view his 'blooming letters' – 'over which I have been working hard like a baby as I am'.

A side effect of Morris's self-training in calligraphy was a notable improvement in his ordinary handwriting. His friends and employees had formerly found it scrawly and difficult to read. His letter-forms after 1870 are certainly much clearer and the writing flows more easily after so much practice. It is also possible that the change in his writing reflected a new purposefulness in him at this period. The modern graphologist, Elaine Quigley, perceives that in his later writing his 'youthful zest and enthusiasm, with the need to do good for mankind, has matured into a more considered and rational style. Morris is no less committed or involved, but he is more thoughtful about how he handles his thinking and involvement.' She has also pointed out that in some later versions of his signature the 'M' of the Morris has an extended second downstroke 'which shows that by then he knew what he wanted and was prepared to stand his ground in order to get it'. This was certainly true of the two decades to come.

By 1870 the author of *The Earthly Paradise* had become a public figure. The large head with the leonine cluster of dark curls was increasingly familiar from the sequence of photographs and portraits to which Morris was submitting himself, much against his will. He still had his old deep fear of being faced by his own image, a peculiarly virulent dislike of his appearance and a horror of the process itself. Unlike Janey, who blossomed for the camera or portraitist, Morris shied away from such exposure, rationalizing it as time-wasting, unnecessary fuss. The previous year he had been boasting about escaping the clutches of Julia Margaret Cameron: there is no surviving Cameron portrait of Morris. But in 1870, as the press requested portraits, he weakened and agreed to a sitting with John Parsons who photographed him side view in shirt, tie and thick tweed jacket. The picture emphasizes his wiry beard and moustache, and the smallness of his eyes. On Good Friday 1870, Morris received the ultimate accolade of Victorian society and sat for a portrait to George Frederic Watts.

Watts's 'House of Fame' or 'Gallery of Worthies' included, by the end of the century, portraits of almost everyone of importance in English political and artistic life. Watts painted Browning, Swinburne, Carlyle, Matthew Arnold, Leslie Stephen and Tennyson (in two versions). He painted Gladstone, Lord Sherbrooke, Sir Charles Dilke. There are portraits of the eminent churchmen: Dean Stanley, Dr Martineau, the prophet and poet Stopford Brooke. Ned sat to Watts, as did Lord Leighton. Watts was always disappointed that the scientists Charles Darwin and Sir John Herschel escaped his net. Morris grumbled to Janey, then at Scalands, about his sitting, especially unwelcome since he was suffering 'a devil of a cold-in-the-head', which, he told her, 'don't make it very suitable'. The portrait, now in the National Portrait Gallery, is not in fact Watts's most successful. It does not capture Morris's grandeur and mystery. He looks too mild a youth, like Tennyson's Sir Galahad.

In 1870 Morris began on what was his closest approach to a flirtation. The beginnings of his friendship with Aglaia Coronio coincided with the blossoming of Morris's public image. Aglaia's social status had a certain glamour. Her family were well-born Grecian refugees. Aglaia's father, Alexander Ionides, was head of the once-powerful Phanariot merchant dynasty who fled from Constantinople in the 1820s when the family property was seized by the Turks in a wave of savagery and atrocity. Her grandfather was discovered crucified on the door of his own house.

In exile in England, first in Manchester then London, the family had prospered. Aglaia had been born in the same year as William Morris, in Finsbury Circus, then the main religious quarter for the London Greeks. She was brought up in a large, hospitable, cosmopolitan household in south London, at Tulse Hill. By the time of her friendship with Morris she was married to a member of the Greek community, Theodore Coronio, a businessman described as 'handsome in his youth' but a lightweight beside the quick and versatile Aglaia. She had two children, a daughter, Calliope, who was painted by Rossetti, and a son John. In 1869 she had moved to Holland Park, to a house adjacent to the palatial mansion her father had bought with his grandmother's diamonds. This was now in effect the headquarters of the colony. George du Maurier called it 'a stunner' of a house.

The ladies of the colony, from the much intermarried families of the Ionideses, Cavafys, Cassavettis and Spartalis, were exotic and forthcoming to a degree unusual in contemporary London society, free with kisses and caresses, and faintly predatory. Marie Spartali, Aglaia and Mary Zambaco hunted in a trio and were known as The Three Graces. They were sexually competitive, attracted to the famous. Aglaia set out to fascinate Morris. If Burne-Jones was Mary's quarry then Morris could be hers.

Aglaia already had many connections in Pre-Raphaelite circles. Her elder brother Constantine was a patron and collector. Her younger brothers Luke and Alexander ('Aleco') were particular cronies of Rossetti and Burne-Jones. Aglaia's 'poetical appearance', with her shapely figure, pale face and 'dreamful air', drew many admiring comments from contemporaries. She also had a generous and practical streak. There was a busybody quality about her. Georgie's comments on the Greeks in her *Memorials* are, for obvious reasons, muted; but she does pay tribute to Ned's reliance on 'his friend Mrs Coronio, whose perfect taste had helped him a hundred times by finding fabrics and arranging dresses for models.' Aglaia performed similar services for Rossetti. He had borrowed her embroidery frame for his portrait of Janey as 'La Pia', though he does not appear to have actually used it. He had written to Aglaia for advice on locating the right shade of Indian muslin for one of the pictures he was painting of Janey in 1868. Rossetti's drawing of Aglaia herself bears a striking resemblance to his images of Janey. She becomes one of his line of idealized dark women. A photograph on her *carte de visite* shows Aglaia looking dumpier and much more down-to-earth. Rossetti was always to be on good terms with Aglaia. But it is noticeable in his correspondence that he is wary of her Greek effusiveness. He refers to Aglaia with her 'grins and guffaws'. There is a sense of Rossetti fending off.

The first letter we have from Morris to Aglaia is dated April 1870, when Janey and Rossetti were at Scalands. It is likely they had met at least a year or two before. Morris's letter was sent from 26 Queen Square. It reads:

My dear Mrs. Coronio,
If you will be at home I will call on Tuesday, and bring you your worsted.
Ned says you want to know how to read Chaucer; I will bring a vol: in my pocket, and with your leave will induct you into the mystery, which is not very deep after

21 *'William Morris as Paris offering the apple to Aphrodite'*. Caricature by Edward Burne-Jones.

all: many thanks for your kind note – I have done my review, just this moment – ugh!'

This was the review of Rossetti's *Poems*. Morris is already counting on Aglaia's sympathy.

Aglaia had acted as official hostess for her father in his role as Greek Consul-General in London and Director of the Crystal Palace Company, deputizing for her mother whose English was not good. She had great social fluency and a talent, partly used to entertain herself, for bringing people out. Her nephew Alexander described her as 'the conversational star' of the circle: 'In after years I often marvelled at that capacity of hers, which without too much learning, seemed to throw fresh light on any subject she touched.' He remembered a number of sketches Burne-Jones had done to illustrate a conversation with Aglaia about Morris. Disappointingly none of these survive. But Morris's own comments to Janey at this period show Aglaia in pursuit, Morris pleased but half embarrassed: 'I am going to receive Aglaia's bland flatteries on my way to Neds this afternoon. I do rather wish she wouldn't butter me so, if that isn't ingrateful so you needn't chaff me as one who can't see the fun of it.' This letter was sent to Janey at Scalands on 26 April 1870. Later in the year, when Janey was in Torquay, he sent another bulletin: 'I am going this afternoon to get a little sentiment out of Aglaia.' He added: 'she is making quite a fine thing of her bookbinding, by the way.'

Would Morris have been so susceptible if Janey had not virtually deserted him? This is of course doubtful. Would he have taken so much trouble to teach Aglaia to read Chaucer if Georgie had appeared more responsive to his deep-felt attachment? As it was, he reacted to Aglaia's blatant overtures with surprise, even delight, which is not concealed from Janey. Indeed he slightly flaunts it. There is triumph as well as self-deprecation in his tone. When Luke Ionides claimed of Morris that 'women did not count with him' and Wilfrid Scawen Blunt maintained that he knew nothing of the love of women this was the crass philanderer's view. Women counted a great deal with Morris. There were a few women who could persuade him well beyond the point of gruffness. Aglaia Coronio was the chief of these and he opened out to her in a way that could be freer, because less loaded with past history and present complex longings, than his communication with Georgiana Burne-Jones. With Aglaia there developed over the next year or two an immense *tendresse* – not, I think, a sexual relationship. Mackail records in his uniquely deadpan manner, 'the friendship between her and Morris was affectionate and unbroken through life'. This was almost, though not absolutely, true.

Was it Aglaia or was it his own Georgie to whom Ned was referring in his cryptic comments just after Morris's death? Unlike Blunt, unlike Ionides, Ned understood quite well, to the point of jealousy, that Morris had been at the receiving end of love. Morris, he said, had left him 'in low spirits, for he tells me long histories of how much he has been loved of women and what deeds they have done for his sake in Pontus, and Asia, and the furthermost parts of Cyrene, and no man ever likes to hear that; and I believe it all, for why should he tell untruths?'

Morris at this period was casting around for new ways of expression and in 1871 began to write his first and only contemporary novel. In March of that year he read a first instalment out to Georgie, whose response was not encouraging. Morris told Louisa Baldwin he had also sent the manuscript to Georgie: 'to see if she could give me any hope: she gave me none'.

The ramifications of Morris's abandoned novel have much exercised late-twentieth-century biographers and critics, inevitably so since it is the work in which the emotional triangle, the love of two men for the same woman, seems to come most deliberately close to home. Are we to interpret the two brothers as two facets of Morris's own character: the stalwart, decisive, observant, outgoing John set against the nervy, unhealthy, bookish Arthur? Or are they portraits of Morris and Burne-Jones? Or should we, as Sue Mooney has recently suggested, read the story as an implied confession that Morris had loved Georgie from his early days at Oxford but had stood down in favour of Ned, as John in the novel sacrificed his claim to Clara for the sake of his brother? One might say that such a correlation goes too far. But at many points in this lyrical, engaging, if curiously tentative experiment in writing, we are on the edge of an autobiography as delicate and outspoken as anything in *The Earthly Paradise*.

The setting of the novel has its memories of Walthamstow. It is also uncannily prophetic of Kelmscott. The feeling for the earth, the sense of seasons, vegetation, the sweet sounds and smells of summer: this almost transcendental rediscovery of nature was to be a feature of Morris's middle age. In *The Novel on Blue Paper* the almost adult John confronts the onset of experience with the tremulous hope that Morris himself was now affected with again:

the expectant longing for something sweet to come, heightened rather than chastened by the mingled fear of something as vague as the hope, that fills our hearts so full in us as whiles, killing all commonplace there, making us feel as though we were on the threshold of a new world, one step over which (if we could only make it) would put life within our grasp. What is it? Some reflex of love and death going on throughout the world, suddenly touching those who are ignorant as yet of the one, and have not learned to believe in the other?

In this novel Morris is concerned with growth, transition, and for the first time attempts to come to terms in fiction with the thing that so intrigued him in politics and history: the way in which the present can be affected by the experience of the past. But perhaps at this juncture in his life it was too much for him. There is much of Rossetti's character in Parson Risley, the sensualist clergyman, imprisoned in his own past history of weakness. The handsome man, dark and romantic, more like a captain of dragoons than a parson, but 'all spoilt': 'his brow knit into an ugly half-scowl, his eyes with little expression in them but suppressed rage, his nose swelled and reddened', the ever-present threat of 'a reckless cruelty which in rougher times would perhaps have developed and won for him the reputation of an Ezzelin'. Risley is a hate figure. The domestic bitterness that fuelled Morris's novel may have prompted him to abandon it as well.

How far was Georgie's veto disapproval of the subject? Perhaps she found it hard to take. There was so much of all their pasts in it. It may have seemed the unwelcome sign of Morris's continuing, although unspoken, love. But I think her refusal to give Morris hope was mainly a literary verdict given by a friend whose judgement he relied on, the friend and admirer of George Eliot whose *Daniel Deronda* Georgie would soon be judging as 'cleverer than clever and keener than keen'. Morris's novel, though so touching, is uneven and inept with its stagy fallen woman and its jarring anachronistic language. 'Sooth to say'; '"I don't care", quoth John': at moments Morris writes in fancy dress. This was a period of strenuously intellectual fiction. George Eliot's *Middlemarch* was published in the year in which Morris started writing his *Novel on Blue Paper*. *War and Peace* was out, in Russia, a novel he read later in translation, 'with much approbation but little enjoyment'. Tolstoy's *Anna Karenina* was published in 1871. In this context of contemporary fiction *The Novel on Blue Paper* looks jejune.

Morris himself was dismissive of his 'abortive' novel: ''tis nothing but landscape and sentiment,' he told Georgie's sister, Louisa, the next summer when he took the half-forgotten early chapters out of the envelope in which Georgie had returned them. He sent them to Louisa as an example of how not to write fiction. Morris was Louisa's literary adviser, sending her a long critique of the novel – probably *Martyr to Mammon* – she herself was writing at almost this same time. Morris made no attempt to resurrect his story, though he always kept the manuscript. The fragment, amounting to perhaps a third of the planned total, was finally published in 1982 in an edition by Penelope Fitzgerald who named it *The Novel on Blue Paper* 'because it was written on blue lined foolscap, and Morris preferred to call things what they were'.

In the early summer of 1871, Morris began looking for what he called 'a little house out of London'. The reason officially given was that he was anxious about the effect of London on his children's health. Jenny and May still had the residue of their winter coughs. But there were other motives. The house in the country was an attempt to find a civilized *modus vivendi* for Morris, Janey and Rossetti, giving the triangle the stamp of permanence and at least a veneer of respectability. Morris and

Rossetti could be seen as nothing more than brother artists and partners in the Firm.

Morris gave himself the task of searching for this house. He located it in an Oxfordshire estate agent's catalogue. His ideal of the country was the minor English landscape of grey houses in green meadows. His quest inevitably took him to the upper reaches of the Thames. Here he came upon Kelmscott Manor, a beautiful, decorous but by no means little grey stone building in the flat fields south-east of Lechlade. He recognized it with certainty, just as the heroes in his stories recognize the lover. He wrote ecstatically to his old friend Charley Faulkner twenty miles away in Oxford: 'whither do you guess my eye is turned now? Kelmscott, a little village about two miles above Radcott Bridge – a heaven on earth; an old stone Elizabethan house like Water Eaton, and such a garden! close down on the river, a boat house and all things handy.' He told Charley he would be going again the following Saturday to show it to his wife and to Rossetti.

Before he started house hunting, Morris had planned a summer journey without Janey and the children. He wanted to see Iceland, its strangeness and its wildness. Over the past few years Iceland had seeped into his consciousness: he felt the need to see with his own eyes the country in the background of the Nordic stories to which he felt so much attuned. He and Rossetti took Kelmscott Manor in a joint tenancy in June 1871. Early in July Janey, Rossetti and the children were installed. Morris visited briefly before setting off for Iceland, specifying wallpapers and leaving instructions about necessary renovations with Philip Webb. He was torn at departing. He wrote to Janey: 'How beautiful the place looked last Monday: I grudged going away so; but I am very happy to think of you all happy there, and the children and you getting well.' He told her to kiss 'the littles' for him and give them his best love. He ended that letter 'Live well and happy'. It was for its time – and even in ours – a socially unusual solution and Morris's generosity verged on sublime.

Burne-Jones was not so self-controlled. He was sensitive to Rossetti's cruelty to Morris, having already been complaining of Rossetti's propensity for 'girding' at Top. Possibly his own guilts helped to create the confrontation. As Morris sailed away to Iceland in the vessel named *Diana* Ned's pent-up indignation on behalf of Topsy surfaced. He wrote to George Howard, 'With Rossetti I have had the skirmish I planned – first long letters and then a face to face row, but in each case

I spoke my mind to the full – the first time in my life I have experienced that relief with him.'

The skirmish developed into a long and anguished silence between the two friends.

CHAPTER NINE

Iceland
1871

If you look at the map of Europe, you will see in its north-western corner lying just under the Arctic circle a large island considerably bigger than Ireland. If you were to take ship and go there you would find it a country very remarkable in aspect, little more than a desert, yet the most romantic of all deserts even to look at: a huge volcanic mass still liable to eruptions of mud, ashes, and lava, and which in the middle of the 18th century was the scene of the most tremendous outpour of lava that history records. Anyone travelling there I think would be apt to hope, if he knew nothing of its history, that its terrific and melancholy beauty might have once been illumined by a history worthy of its strangeness: nor would he hope in vain: for the island I am speaking of is called Iceland.

William Morris made two Icelandic journeys, the first in the summer of 1871, the second two years later. On each of these expeditions he was away from England for around two months. Although of such short duration these journeys had an extraordinary impact upon Morris, providing much-needed emotional sustenance and suggesting a more positive political direction. It was in Iceland, seeing life lived at the barest limits of survival, that Morris learned the lesson he turned into a tenet of political intransigence over the next decade: 'that the most grinding poverty is a trifling evil compared with the inequality of classes'. The landscape itself, in its barrenness and luridness, so different from England, had the force of revelation. Morris's 'romantic desert' stayed in his mind for ever.

Toothed rocks down the side of the firth on the east guard a weary wide lea,
And black slope the hillsides above, striped adown with their desolate green:
And a peak rises up on the west from the meeting of cloud and of sea.

These lines are from his poem 'Iceland First Seen'.

In leaving his wife at Kelmscott with Rossetti, 'the man of the South', and in setting off to Iceland Morris cut himself off decisively from old allegiances. His new passion for the sagas was itself in effect a discarding of Rossetti and Pre-Raphaelite influence: he regarded the bluntness of the old Norse literature as 'a good corrective to the maundering side of mediaevalism'. In travelling to Iceland with three hearty male companions, only one of whom – Charles Faulkner – was even remotely connected with Rossetti, he was close to recreating the carefree expeditions of his pre-Rossetti period. In its mode of male comradeship the first of his journeys in the 1870s was reminiscent of his undergraduate tour of northern France of sixteen years before.

Besides the faithful Faulkner, Morris's friend since Oxford, his chief companion on his first Icelandic journey was Eiríkr Magnússon, born in East Iceland, the son of a poor parson. Magnússon, a theologian and linguist, had first arrived in London to supervise the printing of the Icelandic New Testament for the British and Foreign Bible Society in 1862. Morris met him seven years later. Warington Taylor introduced them. Magnússon recollected his first meeting in the hallway at No. 26 Queen Square with the 'ruddy-complexioned, sturdily-framed, brawn-necked, shock-headed, plainly dressed gentleman of middle stature, with his somewhat small, but exceedingly keen and sparkling eyes'. He cried immediately 'come upstairs' to Magnússon, bounding up ahead of him to his study on the second floor. From then on they had been meeting three times a week, reading Icelandic and working through the sagas. Morris was already steeped in Icelandic literature, but only in translation. Magnússon had been his link with the original and Morris gradually began to learn the language. Through this shared enthusiasm they had become friends. They were strangely alike. Magnússon was short and stocky with full face and bushy hair. He was noisy and ebullient. In later years in Cambridge, where he became a lecturer in Icelandic and deputy librarian at the University Library, he would nearly lift the roof off his little sitting-room with the volume of his singing of northern folksongs. He shared Morris's restlessness. May Morris described him walking 'up and down the room, Icelandic fashion, as he sang'. In Magnússon Morris met a more pedantic double. Sometimes indeed in Iceland they were taken as brothers. Morris looked a Viking too.

The fourth member of the party was a surprise addition. This was W. H. Evans, an officer and gentleman from Forde Abbey in Dorset whom none of them knew previously. He had had a commission in the Dorset Yeomanry. Evans was planning his own Icelandic journey. Morris had looked him over, decided he was 'a quiet well conducted chap and not stupid', and suggested he should join in with them. As he put it to Faulkner: 'he has the advantage of being used to wild travel, and will go where I choose to carry him'. Evans would also, crucially, share the expense.

Morris made Icelandic plans in great detail, with much gusto. Two months before departure he reminded Charley Faulkner to practise his riding: 'By Gum the great we shall have plenty of it there according to our program.' Morris's own riding practice had already begun. By mid-June he was reporting to Charley that he had bought him a cork bed for camping and arranged to borrow a saddle from his brother and his brother's gun. Morris was the chief organizer of supplies. A provisional equipment list he drew up and cross-annotated in obvious excitement veers from the practical (boots; camp kettle; plates, pewter) to the fantastical (hair-pins for pipe prickers). He gives himself directives: 'have extra pockets made in my coat'. It is *Boys' Own* stuff. He lists camp food greedily: ship's biscuits, soup squares, whisky, sausage, Westphalia ham. Morris was to be the cook of the party. To prepare for this he built himself a barbecue with bricks in the garden of the Burne-Joneses' house in Fulham, over which, like a castaway, he practised making stew.

They set out from King's Cross. Magnússon was very late and quarrelled with his cabman, agitating the already keyed-up Morris who was not an experienced traveller. The journey to Iceland, by train and then by mail boat, was far more pioneering than the journey to Bad Ems. In his overwrought condition Morris stayed awake all night in the third-class carriage, wrapped up in one of the huge blankets that had been brought for bedding in the camp. Day dawned as they left York. The sun rose as they reached Darlington, merging confusedly with the fires of the forges. It was, wrote Morris, 'one of those landscapes in the sky', of which he was to see much more stupendous ones in Iceland. His first sight of the industrial landscape of the north depressed him horribly: the country 'blotched by coal'; the cities 'wretched and dispiriting'. By Newcastle he was longing to return. But Charley went to sleep; Morris woke him; Charley clouted him: they whiled away the journey with the rituals of friendship, the pattern of male foolery that Morris found so necessary. And then they were in Scotland. Morris had never been there. The lush landscape north of the Tweed was unexpected. This was Border ballad country as he had imagined it. The weather was, in contrast, all too true to William Morris's preconceived idea of a grim and austere Scotland: 'a cold grey half-mist half-cloud hanging over the earth'.

Morris's Icelandic travels are chronicled in detail in the journal he kept from the beginning of the journey, intending it for Georgie. Later he kept work diaries and, for a few months in 1887, a narrative account of his political activities. But this is the only part of Morris's life for which we have his own record of day-to-day events, written with a sympathetic female reader in his mind. The journal has a wonderful immediacy, consisting not just in its conventional traveller's descriptions of the passing scene, though these must rate amongst the best prose Morris ever wrote. Its peculiar quality arises from the sub-text, revealing the responses he kept from his fellow travellers, emotions that in a sense subverted the male camaraderie, whole networks of private apprehensions and joys.

Morris, Magnússon and Faulkner had left London on a Thursday. It was Saturday before they had even a sight of the *Diana*, the Danish mail boat that was taking them to Iceland. Morris, 'impatient to an absurd degree to be fairly on the expedition and in the saddle', found the slow journey northwards frustrating beyond belief. Desperation clouds over the descriptions of Edinburgh as they loiter round the station, feeling 'frowsy', and drinking 'ineffably bad coffee' in the refreshment room before taking a train on to Granton Harbour, 'a dull, dull place with the slip-shod do-nothing air that hangs about a small port'. With time on his hands William Morris had a hair-cut, Faulkner egging on the barber to cut it even shorter. Evans arrived at Granton by steamer from the West Country. Magnússon's wife Sigriður, also on her way to Reykjavík to stay with her relations, appeared in the middle of breakfast at the large, dismal hotel on Granton pier. The rainy, blustery days were full of desultory meetings, greetings, partings. Morris started to feel claustrophobic, fatalistic, as if his journey was already ending *there*.

Magnússon's brother-in-law cried out that the *Diana* had been sighted at last approaching Granton harbour. Morris and Faulkner ran out of the hotel like prisoners released, racing down the pierhead to watch the arrival of the long, low, three-masted vessel, formerly a gunboat, flying the Danish flag. Morris, Magnússon and Faulkner took a small boat out to board her. Morris was so excited that he tried to tip the fat, mild-faced steward five shillings; this was a *faux pas*; his largesse was refused. He sat down busily to write a farewell letter to his mother. At the prospect of sailing, his mood had changed completely. He went up on deck at midnight. It was very cold and bright. He watched the moon rising red over the firth. He wrote in the journal: 'I felt happy and adventurous, as if all kinds of things were going to happen and very glad to be going. So to bed.'

Burne-Jones had many doubts about the wisdom of this journey. He was temperamentally suspicious of the Nordic. He saw how ideas of Iceland appealed to Morris's underlying masochism. He seemed to have sensed the impending separation as he became more worldly and Morris the reverse. He wrote to George Howard, 'Morris has gone away sending cheerful bulletins to the last – his ardent temperament is now being chastened on board a vessel that I am glad to hear bears the name of Diana'. It reads as a fraternal epitaph. But as the *Diana* steamed out of Granton harbour and down the Firth of Forth on Sunday 9 July, Morris was ebullient. The decks were being swabbed. It was a sunny morning. He ate a large breakfast of beefsteak and onion, smoked salmon, Norway anchovies, hard-boiled eggs, cold meat, cheese, radishes and butter. They were charged 3s.9d. per day for food: a bargain, explained Morris, made possible by the fact that everybody always had to pay whereas the more queasy couldn't always eat.

'We were soon fairly out and running north along the Scotch coast, a very dull and uninteresting-looking coast too: there is not much sea and the wind is astern, the day very sunny and bright and I enjoyed myself hugely though I was rather squeamish at first.' Faulkner had already succumbed to the sea-sickness that prostrated him for the duration of the sailing. Morris described him lying without moving on the platform by the wheel. Morris was sea-sick too, but intermittently and never so badly as to curtail all activity. At his worst he would go and lie down in the ship's cabin but emerge at intervals to be sick and look about. The ship's activities entranced him with their rituals and rhythms, like the rhythms of a workshop. He watched the sailors 'heave the log', throwing out a line to measure the speed of the ship's progress; this was done every two hours. As they wound the line up they would sing a little shanty which pleased what Morris called his 'unmusical taste'. The coxswain gave the orders. He was 'a queer little man with a red beard, and a red nose like a carrot, and bright yellow hair like spun glass'.

They sailed between the Orkneys and the Shetlands, running into the great swell of the Atlantic. Morris staggered on to the deck to be faced with a high glittering green and white wall rising on either side of the ship. Such extremities of nature made him feel a land-lubber, a cockney: 'it was all very exciting and strange.' Approaching the Faroes, volcanic islands lying to the east of Iceland, he had his first real intimation of the great grey melancholy of the Nordic landscape. It was almost too much for him; 'I confess I shuddered at my first sight of a really northern land in the grey of a coldish morning.' Morris, the professional colourist, was faced with a monotony of greyness: grey water; grey clouds; grey stone ledges, interlayered with grey grass.

It was a relief when they cast anchor in the homely green-roofed harbour town of Tórshavn on the island of Streymoy. The three fishing smacks already in the harbour ran up English colours in answer to the hoisting of *Diana*'s flag. They were from Grimsby, on their way to Iceland too. Boats put off from the shore to greet friends on the *Diana* and there was 'a great deal of kissing on deck'. The most impressive of these boats contained the Governor of Tórshavn. It had eight oars on each side, rowed by men described by Morris as 'the queerest old carles, who by way of salute as the boat touched our side shuffled off their Faroish caps in a very undignified manner'. Besides these caps, they wore stockings or knee-breeches loose at the knee, and a sleeveless surcoat 'like a knight's *just-au-corps*', with buttons down the front. The gnarled old men wore these coats open. 'The boats', Morris wrote,' are built high in stem and stern, with the keel rib running up into an ornament at each end, and cannot have changed in the least since the times of the sagas.' It was just the sort of scene, picturesque, a little sinister, that Morris returned to in his novels of old age.

Tórshavn reeked of fish. Fish in all its permutations, from guts to gutted whole fish, lay in heaps around the town or hung on lines to dry. Morris and his companions, carrying big bundles of sandwiches, set out on a day's excursion in the Faroes. They explored the town, finding nothing to buy there but Danish cherry brandy which was cheap and good. Morris noted Tórshavn women, 'not pretty but not horrible either', and the men in their skin shoes tied round the ankle with neat thongs. He detected in the men's swarthy faces a strange sadness, the expression of the islander, resourceful but cut-off. Tórshavn, homely and haphazard, makes him think again of the Dutch toy-town he played with in his childhood. The long, deep, peaty valley outside the town reminds him of valleys he has walked along in Cumberland. Morris in the Faroes is back at his old trick of relating to strange places in terms of the well known. It had become a hot bright summer day and Morris, on the nature trail through the meadowlands of Streymoy, was picking out the flowers: buttercups, ragged-robin, clover, wild thyme, 'a beautiful blue milk-wort'. He found it strangely moving to discover such familiar plants growing in a place so different from anywhere he had imagined. As so often in Iceland, he searches for the words for these dreamlike recognitions: 'there was real beauty about the place of a kind I can't describe'.

22 Fantastical wood engraving of the Arms of Iceland included in May Morris's edition of the *Collected Works*.

There were no beaches. Part of the oddness to the Englishman familiar with the seaside at Southwold or Hastings was the way that all the islands, whether sloping or sheer rock, went straight into the sea. The buildings almost seemed to be a part of the formation of the islands of the Faroes, emerging from the rockwalls. Morris came upon the ruin of a stone mediaeval church built right into the bowels of a steep cliff of basalt beside the sea. The church looked indescribably remote and melancholy in spite of the flowers and grass and brilliant sun. The 'long-nosed cadaverous' parson who was guiding them over the island dated it as Reformation. Morris argued with him, saying it was clearly not later than 1340. Morris in the Faroes was still the abrasive connoisseur. They then went into the neighbouring farmer's house, a simple-life interior of untreated pine walls, ceiling and floor with 'queer painted old presses and chests' around the living-room. The farmer arrived with his two children and greeted them in the take-it-or-leave-it abstracted Nordic manner Morris became inured to, and indeed began to imitate after his Iceland tour. They drank 'unlimited milk'. They had a picnic on the slopes above the farmhouse. Morris made a sketch of the house and its surroundings. He discarded the sketch later as being 'imbecile'. Feeling the release from the ship-board privations, squashed four in a small cabin, they rolled around like children in the long grass for sheer joy.

But Morris still had Iceland on his mind and was relieved when the signal gun announced they would be sailing after dinner. The evening sea was smooth and, threading through the craggy islands, they had their best views of the Faroes yet. They sailed through the narrows of Westmannafirth, glimpsing the open ocean through breaks in the rocks, and passing the little rocky town of Westmannahavn, where the water was said to be ten fathoms deep right up to the shore.

After that on we went toward the gates that led out into the Atlantic; narrow enough they look even now we are quite near; as the ship's nose was almost in them, I saw close beside us a stead with its homefield sloping down to the sea, the people running out to look at us and the black cattle grazing all about, then I turned to look ahead as the ship met the first of the swell in the open sea, and when I looked astern a very few minutes after, I could see nothing at all of the gates we had come out by, no slopes of grass, or valleys opening out from the shore; nothing but a terrible wall of rent and furrowed rocks, the little clouds still entangled here and there about the tops of them: here the wall would be rent from top to bottom and its two sides would yawn as if they would have fallen asunder, here it was buttressed with great masses of stone that had slipped from its top; there it ran up into all manner of causeless-looking spikes: there was no beach below the wall, no foam breaking at its feet. It was midnight now and everything was grey and colourless and shadowless, yet there was light enough in the clear air to see every cranny and nook of the rocks, and in the north-east now the grey sky began to get a little lighter with dawn. I stood near the stern and looked backward a long time till the coast, which had seemed a great crescent when we came out of the sound, was now a long flat line.

When, a few days later, he gave his account to Janey of the leaving of the Faroes the experience was vivid. It still seemed to him the most impressive sight he had ever seen containing, amongst other things, the element of strangeness that defined, for William Morris, the ultimate experience. He told Janey he had seen 'nothing out of a dream so strange'.

When he wrote to 'the littles' he told them of the porpoises that had assailed the *Diana* the next afternoon, out in the Atlantic. There was a whole school of them, leaping after the ship, jumping out of the water, playful and contorted. They looked like 'oiled pigs'.

At three in the morning on 13 July Morris at last saw Iceland. Magnússon shook him awake. Morris had been dreaming. His dream was of The Grange, the Burne-Joneses' house in Fulham, which in one of those bizarre dreamer's displacements stood in Queen's Gate, South Kensington, instead. When he pulled himself together and heaved himself on deck he found that Papey, the small island at the south-east corner of Iceland and inhabited by Irish monks before the Norse colonization, was coming into view. It was 'a dark brown ragged rocky island' surrounded by small skerries and beyond it was the mainland: 'a terrible shore indeed: a great mass of dark grey mountains worked into pyramids and shelves, looking as if they had been built and half-ruined'. His first response was of awe, alarm, self-questioning. What was he in fact doing there? His internal debate between horror and hopefulness is resurrected in the poem 'Iceland First Seen':

Ah! what came we forth to see that our hearts are so hot with desire?
Is it enough for our rest, the sight of this desolate strand,
And the mountain-waste voiceless as death but for winds that may sleep not nor tire?
Why do we long to wend forth through the length and breadth of a land,
Dreadful with grinding of ice, and record of scarce hidden fire,
But that there 'mid the grey grassy dales sore scarred by the ruining streams
Lives the tale of the Northland of old and the undying glory of dreams?

Weather changes in Iceland with astonishing speed. Grey skies turn into skies of an apocalyptic splendour. Morris, sailing that day along the southern coast of Iceland, felt he was seeing 'the end of the world rising out of the sea'. What began as a wild morning, very black over the water, with bright sun under what seemed like a canopy of blackness, soon began to look more promising. When they left the trading station at

Djúpivogur a streak of blue sky appeared over the land and the dark grey mountains turned indigo in the distance under the half-cloudy sky. By this time the *Diana* had passed the two great glaciers, Vatnajökull ('an ice-tract as big as Yorkshire') and the pyramid mass of black rock and ice which is the Öræfajökull, Iceland's highest mountain. Now for several hours of mist and drift, they lost sight of the land. Then the rain stopped, the cloud lifted and Morris was confronted suddenly with his first Icelandic sunset, 'a wonderful fiery and green sunset, so stormy looking!', apparently erupting from the huge ice-topped mountain Eyjafjallajökull. At about ten o'clock the sun withdrew again behind the mountains, leaving them grey and cold, silhouetted grimly against a long strip of orange sky.

Morris, still transfixed on deck, could now see the Westman islands. As the ship got nearer they looked like 'the broken-down walls of castles in the sea'. At one in the morning the *Diana* arrived at another little trading station, firing a signal gun to summon the people for their mail. Morris felt sorry for the seven men who came out in their 'walnut-shell' to fetch five letters and one passenger, Lilja Magnússon. Morris was tired after another 'dream-like' day. But before he left the bridge he looked north and saw a crimson spot spreading over the orange in the sky – and 'that was the dawn'.

On 14 July the *Diana* got to Reykjavík. It was a fine bright day, though rather cold. There was the ceremonial greeting in the harbour: little boats went out to welcome in the mail boat, flags were run up the flagstaffs of the stores on shore and up the masts of the boats anchored in the harbour. The fleet included not only the schooners and sloops of the occupying Danish navy but also a French war-brig and a gunboat, stationed in Iceland to protect the interests of the 400 French fishing vessels then responsible for most of the deep-sea fishing in those seas. (The British soon took over: Morris's sympathies would certainly have been with the Icelanders in the so-called Cod Wars of the 1950s and 1970s.)

As they sailed into the harbour Morris focused on the townscape. Earlier English travellers had not been complimentary. Lord Dufferin, in 1856, had described Reykjavík as 'a collection of wooden sheds, one story high, rising here and there with a gable end of greater pretensions, built along a lava beach, and flanked at either end by a suburb of turf huts'. Sabine Baring-Gould in 1863 was even ruder: 'There are but two

streets, and these are hardly worthy of the name.' He described Reykjavík as a small town of great squalor built on 'a dirty greenish slope'
between the mountains and the sea, 'patched with houses which, themselves both roof and walls, are of a mouldy green as if some long-since
inhabited country had been fished up out of the sea'.

Morris's own first impressions of Reykjavík were milder. It seemed to
him 'not a very attractive place, yet not very bad, better than a north-
country town in England'. He had his own reasons for bias towards
Reykjavík. He was naturally sympathetic to the campaign to free the
island from Danish control. During his short stay there Morris was
introduced by Magnússon to Reykjavík's leading nationalist, Jón Sigurðsson, president of the Althing, the Icelandic Parliament. They con-
versed deeply and conspiratorially in Icelandic. Morris warmed to
Sigurðsson, the multi-interest Icelander, intellectual, politician, translator of the sagas: 'a shy, kind, scholarlike man'.

Morris's tolerance of Reykjavík, which developed into fondness, was
also a sign of his emotional investment. Reykjavík was the beginning of
the journey Morris hoped would have immense significance for him. He
was patient with its humdrum qualities, describing the small low
wooden houses with black pitch finish and white sash frames; the streets
of black volcanic sand; the little ragged gardens in which the Icelanders
grew their subsistence crops of potatoes, cabbages and huge stems of
angelica. That scene, and that smell, was still with him two years later
when he added the postscript to his journal:

Lord! how that little row of wooden houses, and their gardens with the rank
angelica is wedged in my memory!

Magnússon had arranged for Morris and Faulkner to lodge with his
sister-in-law. She gave them 'a very clean room' in one of the small
standard Reykjavík timber houses standing back from the road in its
garden of potato and angelica, with its hayfield at the back. They slept
comfortably in their blankets on the floor and got up to breakfast on
stock-fish and smoked mutton. They spent four days in Reykjavík,
making their final preparations for the journey, buying cheese and
cherry brandy, gloves and knitted guernseys and arranging about
money. After complicated negotiations they carried away 1,000 dollars
in canvas bags. They made their first purchases of ponies. Reykjavík was
overrun with the small, sturdy, responsive Icelandic ponies: 'such jolly
little fellows the poneys are,' wrote Morris, 'they almost look as if they

would talk.' They bought sixteen to start with, intending to enlarge the complement to thirty as the journey got under way. Morris felt nervous about actually mounting one. But once he did he found it was plain sailing: 'all my fears and doubts vanish as the little beast begins to move under me, down the street at a charming amble.' This was the pony, Mouse, which Morris took home with him to Kelmscott at their journey's end.

There were last-minute hitches. One of the parcels from England, when opened, was found to contain not the bologna sausage ordered from the Co-operative Stores in the Haymarket but instead four boxes of the patent mouthwash FRAGRANT FLORILENE. The Englishmen gaped at each other, wondering if they were drunk or dreaming. Then they rolled around with laughter in the hayfield while the haymakers leaned on their rakes and watched, amazed and almost frightened at the scene.

The weather was uncertain. Morris fidgeted and worried. On Monday before leaving they paid the statutory visit to the governor who addressed Morris politely in French to be answered very haltingly in French mixed with Icelandic. But by mid-afternoon they were ready to be off. The riding horses were brought to the door, the pack horses were standing waiting in the road, Magnússon strapped Morris's mackintosh to his saddle-bow. Morris tied on his tin pannikin and mounted his small beast. They rode out of Reykjavík in a meandering procession accompanied by several of Magnússon's relations and a young lady friend. Morris looked about the street over his pony's 'queer light coloured mane' in great contentment. He gazed down into the harbour and saw that the *Diana* was still there.

Before he set off Morris had written several letters. One was to his mother. Another was to Janey, repeating his injunction to her to be happy. To his daughters he wrote: 'I hope you are very good and are kind to Mama and that you are happy at Kelmscott: it is not much like Iceland I can tell you.' He sent kisses and love, and some wild thyme he had gathered that morning in the fields.

Morris was by no means the first Englishman in Iceland. Eighteenth-century tourists came to marvel at the landscape in a spirit of scientific curiosity combined with the *frisson* of the Gothick picturesque. The museum in Reykjavík has a small collection of water-colours by these English artist-explorers: views of the sulphur mines at Krísuvík erupting mystically, overshadowing the tiny human figures in the foreground; Mount Hekla spurting lava; 'the New Geysir, a hot spring in Iceland thrown up to the height of 130 feet'. In the nineteenth century, Iceland began attracting a different sort of traveller, more muscular and masculine. *Letters from High Latitudes*, Lord Dufferin's breezy account of his forays into the interior, became a best seller of its day and it was followed by other popular travelogues by gentleman explorers who treated Iceland as a grand adventure playground, watching the birds and shooting them, climbing the unclimbed mountains, mapping out the remote areas which were still virgin ground.

This was the spirit in which W. H. Evans travelled around Iceland, an unlikely companion for Morris, whose interests were so much more recherché and intense. He was certainly the first Englishman in Iceland who arrived with such a knowledge of its language and literature and was so instinctively attuned to the sagas. These stories of the heroic figures of Iceland in the tenth and eleventh centuries had been passed down orally from family to family, farmhouse entertainment for the long dark winter nights, and written versions were compiled from the thirteenth century onwards. Morris saw them as the verbal equivalent of folk art: demotic literature on its highest plane.

'From the very first day that I began work with William Morris on Icelandic literature the thing that struck me most was this, that he entered into the spirit of it not with the preoccupied mind of a foreigner, but with the intuition of an uncommonly wide-awake nature.' Morris's saga mentality surprised Eiríkr Magnússon. By the time he went to Iceland he and Magnússon had completed their prose translation of *Gunnlaugs Saga, Grettis Saga, Laxdaela Saga* and some of the poems from the *Poetic Edda*. They had finished *Eyrbyggja Saga* in April, only a few weeks before they left. Their prose version of the *Völsunga Saga*, entitled *The Story of the Volsungs and Niblungs*, had been published by F. S. Ellis in the previous year. Morris regarded this as 'that most glorious of stories', unrivalled in its depth and intensity and passion. When he arrived in Iceland he was already a loquacious propagandist for the epic of the Volsungs: 'This is the Great Story of the North, which should be to all our race what the Tale of Troy was to the Greeks.'

What did Morris like so much about the sagas? He loved them first of all for their story-telling qualities. Morris could so easily get swept up in the action, as people had noticed when he was a small boy. On their first day of translation, tackling 'Gunnlaug the Worm-tongue', Magnússon's suggestion that they should start with some grammar had been swept aside by Morris: 'No, I can't be bothered with grammar; I have no time for it. You be my grammar as we translate. I want the literature, I must have the story. I mean to amuse myself.' He *hungered* for the story. Magnússon describes him as 'the linguistic glutton', reporting that within three months Morris had mastered the language to 'an astonishing degree'. The method they evolved was that they read the story and Morris got the gist of it. Magnússon took it home and wrote a literal translation. Morris used that as the basis for his own version in the Nordic free style which he felt encapsulated the true spirit of the saga. It was risky, inspired but not completely satisfactory. The most purist of its critics have called it 'Wardour Street'.

In a manuscript in the Brotherton Library in Leeds you can still watch Morris and Magnússon in action. Magnússon's literal translation of *The Story of Olaf the Holy*, in his neat librarian's handwriting, has been altered and annotated over in Morris's hastier and bolder script. Morris reaches for the clearer, more dramatic and, quite often, more archaic language, substituting 'bade' for 'ordered', 'befell' or 'betid' for 'happened', 'mickle' for 'great'. ''Tis clear enow that thou art minded to have clean done with orders from me' becomes, in Morris's more concentrated and more poetic version, ''Tis clear enow that thou art minded to wash thine hands of all my bidding'. Often words were invented. As explained by Magnússon: 'The dialect of our translation was not Queen's English, but it was helpful towards penetrating into the thought of the old language.' '*Leiðtogi*', a guide, was translated as load-tugger, taking load = way, as in 'load-star', load-stone', *togi* = tug on. A load-tugger had the accumulated meaning of the person who leads on with a rope. Translating was a word-game, an Anglo-Icelandic Scrabble, which often had the two of them chortling with delight. After many years of practice such coinings of composite words become second nature to Morris. His Icelandic archaising became the magic language of the fairy stories he turned to late in life.

Morris responded to the directness of the sagas. The laconic language mirrored his emotional austerities, as in the *Völsunga Saga*, at the terrible parting of Sigurd and Brynhild: 'there is nothing wanting in it, nothing forgotten, nothing repeated, nothing overstrained; all tenderness is shown without the use of a tender word.' Morris looked on himself as a quasi-saga hero. Magnússon, not normally the most observant of companions, noticed early on how clearly he identified with the defiant spirit and unflinching sense of duty of the warriors he read about. 'In fact', wrote Magnússon, 'he found on every page an echo of his own buoyant, somewhat masterful mind.' Stopford Brooke was less respectful: 'If Iceland was once started in conversation, Morris clung to it like ivy to the oak. Nothing else, for hours together, was allowed in the conversation. It was terrible, and he looked like Snorri Sturluson himself.'

Morris came to Iceland as a place of pilgrimage. His pursuit of the saga sites gave shape to his itinerary. On board the *Diana*, part of his excitement at approaching Iceland had been his first view of such literary landmarks as the grey peak of Svínafell, 'under which dwelt Flosi the Burner', from *Njáls Saga*, and the islands opposite Njál's house at Bergthórshvoll. The first day of their travels took them eastwards to Njál country, the landscape of the most famous of the Icelandic family sagas, the long dramatic story of Gunnar Hámundarson of Hlíðarendi, the brave warrior who marries the morally flawed Hallgerður. Feuds she sets in motion lead first to her husband's heroic last stand and eventual death, and finally bring about the tragedy of Gunnar's friend Njál, the peaceful lawyer, man of wisdom, who is burned to death in his own hall. *Njáls Saga* was the first of the Icelandic sagas to be brought out in an English translation. Morris read George Webb Dasent's version soon after it was published in 1861. Once he knew the original, the translation seemed to him 'too homely': Dasent, he felt, was missing the stark grandeur of Icelandic stoicism inherent in the story. Morris admired especially the saga treatment of male friendship: 'the dealings between the two friends Gunnar and Njál in the noble story of Burnt Njál are matchless for manly and far-sighted friendliness in the midst of the most trying surroundings.' Could the same be said of Morris and Rossetti or Burne-Jones?

He had found the first day's travel gruelling. May Morris reminds us that her father at that period was used to a largely sedentary life and six hours in the saddle were a new experience. He stumbled along nervously following the Icelandic guides Eyvrindr and Gisli. Eyvrindr he described as 'a queer ugly-looking fellow, long, with black eyes and straight black hair, and as swart as a gipsy'; Gisli was, in contrast, short, amiable, forthcoming, very lazy, with light hair and blue eyes. The ferocity of the landscape disconcerted Morris. 'Most strange and awful the country looked to me as we passed through,' he wrote of that first evening: 'a doleful land at first with its great rubbish heaps of sand'. But beyond the lava fields they found a good place for their campsite, a soft grassy meadow bordered by a small clear stream. It was a cold night, but fine and bright, still light enough to read at midnight. Morris noted the odd quality of the Icelandic light which was wonderfully clear but without shadows, unlike daylight. While the tents were being pitched he and Evans went out shooting golden plovers, Evans with enthusiasm, Morris much less willingly. Out on the hillside he kept turning round to look for the campsite and the grey smoke from the fire that was beginning to rise up.

Morris slept badly, hearing the wild song of the plovers, ponies munching grass nearby, the flapping of the tent canvas through the windy night. But Magnússon and Faulkner had already laid the fire and Morris became more cheerful as he cooked his two plovers in the frying pan with bacon. He carried in this breakfast proudly to the others in the tent. Afterwards he wandered over the hills looking at the flowers, noticing how thickly the purple cranesbill grew in the little hollows that had formed in the sweet grass. Later in the day, as they were riding near the sea-shore, he noted with astonishment 'a huge waste of black sand all powdered over with tufts of sea-pink and bladder-campion at regular intervals, like a Persian carpet'. Where W. H. Auden and Louis Mac-Neice, touring Iceland in the 1930s, found 'Stones, More Stones and All Stones', Morris discovered flowers. Or rather, more remarkably, he found flowers persisting in a landscape otherwise barren in its stoniness. In his most romantic moods he would relate this to the instinct for survival of the whole Icelandic race.

He keeps losing things in Iceland. On the second day out he loses the strap that fastened the tin pannikin ('which made such a sweet tinkle') to his saddle-bow. He then loses the pannikin itself, which he had tied on insecurely with a piece of string. A few hours later he loses one of the slippers he has stuffed carelessly into the pocket of his waterproof. There is general hilarity when a kind Icelander returns it the next morning, laying it carefully on the gatepost of his lodging. In Iceland he casts himself in his old role of the incompetent. In his journal and his letters he is consciously buffoonish. He spends his second night at Eyrarbakki, and describes himself in 'a real clean bed, of course of the northern type, ie. a feather bed under you and another over you.' Morris submerged by duvet. It is curious how often Morris thinks of himself in terms of a Burne-Jones cartoon.

They were now travelling east along the south coast of Iceland. From Eyrarbakki they could see Ingólfsfell, the 'great chest-shaped mountain',

ICELAND 1870

23 'William Morris on horseback in Iceland'. Caricature by Edward Burne-Jones.

and along the central ridge the monument to Ingólfur Árnarson, the first settler, who landed in Iceland in 874. Further off but clearly visible was Hekla, the still-active volcano, its cone permanently rimmed around with red from burning. In the eighteenth century Hekla was the hero of James Thomson's poem 'Winter': 'And Hekla flaming through a waste of snows'. East again, and much nearer, was the mountain called Three-corner. To Morris this looked like a huge church with a transept. As he travels, he translates the landscape into Gothic architecture: this is the ex-pupil of G. E. Street. He views the rock formations as ramparts and battlements, deserted streets, ruined cathedrals. One steeply sloping mountain reminds him of a French château roof. Another, when he comes upon it later in the journey, is 'just the shape of the Castle St. Angelo in Rome.'

Morris expects so much from Iceland he risks an anti-climax. At Eyrarbakki in the morning after breakfast he goes into the little yard behind his lodging house and watches the fowls scratching about and feels depressed: 'a queer feeling something akin to disappointment of how like the world was all over after all'. But back on his pony his mood changes completely. They set off in their convoy, sometimes riding over sand and sometimes hard turf-covered ground, and there is a wonderful sense of exhilaration in Morris's description of the ride beside the seaside:

the beach was edged seaward all the way with toothed rocks and skerries on which the long swell broke and ran up into spires of foam, as calm as it looked out to sea: we were in high spirits indeed this morning, which I think was quite the finest we had in Iceland; we raced where the ground was good enough, and talked and laughed enough for twenty.

They stopped at one point and bought milk from a queer little house beside the road. Then they unloaded the horses to cross the Thjórsá river. The luggage was packed into the ferry boat and the ponies driven into the water *en masse*, 'and they swam in a compact body right across to the landing-place, making a most prodigious snorting and splashing'. The river, Morris noted, was at this point no wider than the Thames at London Bridge.

On the fourth day they rode across the deadest of dead flats into the Njál country proper. Morris could make out three grassy mounds, 'something the shape of limpets', humping up from the green meadow. This was Bergthórshvoll. Morris was busily making his connections with the saga. Here was Flosi's Hollow, the place where he and the hundred Burners tethered their horses before firing Njál's house. There was the ditch into which Kári Sölmundarson leapt, to douse himself, after leaping from the building in his blazing clothes. And nearby was the slope where he lay down to recover. They were told by the farmer who guided them around that, only recently, in the excavation of a site for a new parlour, a bed of ashes had been found buried deep in the ground.

One of Morris's favourite passages in *Njáls Saga* was the one in which Gunnar turns over in his tomb and sings a song in the moonlight. It is the typical Icelandic saga combination of the banal and surreal. At Hlíðarendi, Morris investigated Gunnar's Howe, sited so dramatically on the hillside above the traditional site of Gunnar's Hall. They arrived there in the evening. They lay around on the grass beside the howe resting and gazing, then they toiled up the hill to get a better view. It was about eleven at night when they came down and passed the howe again; the moon was up in the west, a little thin crescent, hardly shining at all. There were no clouds in the sky. It is still possible at Hlíðarendi to see how this sombre and other-worldly landscape suited Morris, intrigued him. The poem 'Gunnar's Howe above the House at Lithend' was included in his *Poems by the Way*:

Ye who have come o'er the sea to behold this grey minster of lands,
Whose floor is the tomb of time past, and whose walls by the toil of dead hands
Show pictures amidst of the ruin of deeds that have overpast death,
Stay by this tomb in a tomb to ask of who lieth beneath.

Ah! the world changeth too soon, that ye stand there with unbated breath,
As I name him that Gunnar of old, who erst in the haymaking tide
Felt all the land fragrant and fresh, as amidst of the edges he died.
Too swiftly fame fadeth away, if ye tremble not lest once again
The grey mound should open and show him glad-eyed without grudging or
    pain.
Little labour methinks to behold him but the tale-teller laboured in vain.

Little labour for ears that may hearken to hear his death-conquering song,
Till the heart swells to think of the gladness undying that overcame wrong.
O young is the world yet, meseemeth, and the hope of it flourishing green,
When the words of a man unremembered so bridge all the days that have been.
As we look round about on the land that these nine hundred years he hath seen.

Morris went into his first bonder's house at Bergthórshvoll. He had already noticed as he travelled these traditional turf-walled Icelandic farmers' houses: small, single-storey buildings huddled into the hillside like tiny aircraft hangars, their rounded roofs blanketed in flowery grass. Sometimes several of these houses were built side by side and joined by an interconnecting passageway, with earth piled around the walls as a defence against the winds. Morris loved the approach to these houses, usually down small lanes with smooth turf walls on either side. They gave him a sense of comfort. The pathways, like the houses, were flowery and grassy, enclosing and secure.

He entered, however, with a certain trepidation. Icelandic bonders' houses are dark and extremely cramped. The doors are very low, a hazard even to Morris who, at five foot six, was relatively short. The parlours are small square rooms, often panelled in pine, with the barest of furniture: a table and a chair. There is rarely a bed to be seen, simply a ladder leading up to the *badstofa*, the common sleeping- and living-room. Morris got to like these houses. Indeed he seized upon them as a confirmation that beauty was a matter of the functional and decorous. Following in Morris's footsteps around Iceland, it is fascinating to see the reductionist aesthetic taking a firmer grip upon his mind. Weaving was an essential part of that economy of rural self-sufficiency. In the bonders' houses Morris took note of how the loom was never cast out into an outhouse but regarded as the family furniture. A few years later Morris too would be installing a loom in his own bedroom, rising for a weaving session in the dawn.

In camp at Hlíðarendi Morris was cook for the first time, in the sense of producing a fully fledged dinner for the party. He had always been interested in cookery in theory, regarding it as a branch of craftsmanship and feeling it was too important to be left to women. Morris sometimes claimed that women knew absolutely nothing about clothes or about cooking: 'their twist isn't that way'. Morris set out his stall professionally:

I dealt summarily with all attempts at interference, I was patient, I was bold, and the results were surprising even to me who suspected my own hidden talents in the matter: a stew was this trial piece; a stew, four plovers or curlews, a piece of lean bacon and a tin of carrots: I must say for my companions they were not captious: the pot was scraped, and I tasted the sweets of enthusiastic praise.

The dinner at Hlíðarendi shows Morris testing out his skills not just in cooking as technique but in cooking as performance. He depended on an audience. He could have made a television cook, in another age.

Before heading north towards the Geysirs Morris went out on a wild day trip to Thórsmörk with Magnússon and Evans. Their guide was a distant connection of Magnússon's, Jón Jónsson, a craftsman-farmer and mature student, learning English from *Chambers's Miscellany*. Jón led them too intrepidly. Several times they had to cross the Markarflójt on their ponies; it was turbulent yellowish-white water, running fast and smelling strongly of sulphur. Morris, terrified, held on to the pommel of his saddle with both hands. They rode over the shingle which, he noticed, was covered with bright yellow-green moss, thickly sprinkled with a very beautiful pink and red stonecrop. Then on past overhanging, high cliff-faces with caves in them 'just like the hell-mouths in 13th century illuminations'. Tail-ends of glaciers dribbled over the rocks. To

Morris the cleft mountains looked like a nightmare avenue, 'a horrible winding street with stupendous, straight rocks for houses on either side'. In this desperate landscape even Morris was fainthearted. 'What came I out for to see?': the recurring refrain of Morris's Icelandic journey seemed a mockery to him as he sat by himself on the bare gritty mountain slope with, all around him, 'every kind of distortion and disruption, and the labyrinth of the furious brimstone-laden Markfleet' in the grim valley beneath. He felt cowed. He felt as if he would never get back home again. 'Yet', he wrote, 'with that came a feeling of exaltation too, and I seemed to understand how people under all disadvantages should find their imaginations kindle amid such scenes.'

On the way back to camp Magnússon and Jón and Morris got waylaid by an intellectual local farmer who insisted on discussing minute details of the time scale of *Njáls Saga*, as if it had all happened within living memory. He had been flatteringly anxious to meet Morris, seeing him as an itinerant poet in the Icelandic tradition. When Morris, on departing, overshot the saddle of his pony and landed on the turf, the farmer said respectfully, 'The skald is not quite used to riding then.' Already, to Rossetti's guffaws, an Icelandic newspaper had welcomed William Morris as the English Skald.

Nine days out of Reykjavík they reached the famous Geysir, the site of a series of deep cylindrical holes in the ground which periodically shoot spurts of warm water high into the air. Faulkner did not set out on this expedition with them. He was ill, already showing signs of the nervous debility which worsened in the years before his early death. May Morris maintained that it was only his devotion to her father that had brought Faulkner to Iceland. Morris was seized with an agony of conscience at his illness, torn between sympathy for the friend and brother, and deep irritation at the possible disruption of his plans. Magnússon stayed behind to 'dry nurse' Faulkner. Morris had as sole travelling companion the increasingly moody W. H. Evans whose gung-ho attitude was grating on him badly and whose lack of interest in the sagas seemed 'pathetic'. He reproved Evans for wanting to shoot the swans in Iceland by calling him a British officer. This, as Mackail reminds us, was Morris's most severe term of contempt.

Morris had pretended not to want to see the geysers. As a sight they seemed too clichéd, the first stop for all the tourists who had never heard the names of Sigurd and Brynhild, let alone Njál or Gunnar, Grettir,

Gísli or Gudrun. He grumbled on approaching 'the ugly seared white slope, all dotted across by the hot springs'. He complained that the turf on the edge of the Great Geysir, scored with the trenches cut by previous tourists round their tents, was the only nasty camping ground they had yet found in Iceland. He was incensed to see the place was strewn with feathers and even whole wings of birds, old shiny mutton bones, a lot of bits of paper: Morris was the anti-litter campaigner of his period. But in spite of his bad temper the geysers won him over. They seemed such amiable and unexpected things. He approaches them with caution, sticking a thumb in to test the temperature of the water. On that first evening he peers through the surrounding steam into the 'horrible blue and green depths and the white sulphur sides' of the geyser known as Blesi or 'the Sigher', and he heats a pot of water for their grog in Blesi, 'its own water being extremely foul of taste'.

By the fourth day at the geysers Morris had become proprietorial about them. He knew their idiosyncrasies of behaviour: how Strokkur, 'the Churn', the second biggest geyser, would not gush until he was stuffed with turf. Morris drew a little picture of Strokkur in his journal. Spectators of a later period would have noticed how like a woman's vulva Strokkur looks. Faulkner had reappeared, improved though still a little shaky, and there was 'a joyful meeting'. As an extra celebration at six a.m. next morning the hugest of the geysers, the 'Gusher' or 'Great Kettle', erupted for the second time in the four days, swelling into a great roar in the crater. They were all out in the open air in a moment to watch as the water first spurted six feet above the crater's lip, then fell again, then finally shot up 'as though a spring had been touched' in an eighty-foot column of water and steam, finally subsiding with immense rumblings and thumpings. The spectacular performance had lasted twenty minutes. They stayed in camp that day, hanging out their washing on a line stretched out between their two tents. Faulkner had made some ingenious clothes-pegs out of firewood. They parboiled a quarter of a whole lamb in Blesi and ate it with preserved peas. The moon rose big and red. The three Englishmen and Magnússon sat down beside the Great Geysir for their first Icelandic game of whist.

Now they were heading north again, right up through the interior of Iceland towards the northern coast. This was a three-day ride through country higher, grimmer and more difficult to traverse than they had encountered yet. Morris's journal describes how they have somehow stumbled up to the top of the pass of Hellisskarð:

and there we are in the wilderness: a great plain of black and grey sand, grey rocks sticking up out of it; tufts of sea-pink and bladder campion scattered about here and there, and a strange plant, a dwarf willow, that grows in these wastes only, a few sprays of long green leaves wreathing about as it were a tangle of bare roots, white and blanched like bones.

This Paul Nash landscape soon changed to a steep lava field, a treacherous mass of rocks that varied in shape and size from pieces as big as your fist to two-foot cubes. All these rocks had jagged edges which slowed the party down to walking pace. Every pony was cut and bleeding by the end of the first day.

They forced themselves on through the mist and drifting rain, the wind blowing up 'like knives' from the waters beneath them. Morris glimpsed in the distance the site of the legendary Thorisdale of *Grettis Saga*. Two years earlier he and Magnússon had worked on their translation, *The Story of Grettir the Strong*, and Morris had already identified himself with the brave outlaw hero he referred to familiarly as The Strong Man. At that time his tendency was to humanize the sagas. In 1869, as he had told Charles Eliot Norton, he detected in Grettir a strain he could relate to, 'a sentiment and a moral sense that somehow made the hopeless looking life of our hero endurable'. Now he was not so sure. Seeing Grettir in his context in this wild Icelandic landscape, Morris's view of the saga hero altered. When he got to Grettir's Lair, the Fairwood-fell of *Grettis Saga*, the savage dreadful place made Grettir seem more abstract, god and dragon: 'it gave quite a new turn in my mind to the whole story, and transfigured Grettir into an awful and monstrous being, like one of the early giants of the world.'

They were trekking onwards, upwards, through the country of the ice-flows, taking the pass of Kaldidalur (or Cold-dale) which runs between the two glaciers of Langjökull and Ok. Morris's journal entry reaches new depths of desolation: 'a dismal place enough is Cold-dale, and cold enough even with a warm east wind blowing as to-day; it is a narrow valley choked a good deal with banks of stones and boulders and stripes of unmelted snow lying about even now: the black cliffs of Geitland's Jokul on one side with the glaciers sometimes trickling over the tops of them, and on the other flatter side dismal slopes of stones and sand that quite hide the ice that caps Ok.' At the top of Kaldidalur stood

24 *'William Morris climbing a mountain in Iceland'*. Caricature by Edward Burne-Jones.

(and still stands, with twentieth-century additions) a little heap of stones in the midst of the moon landscape. This is one of those landmarks called a carline: in our terms, a cairn. Traditionally Iceland travellers left a literary offering, a joke or scrap of doggerel, under one of the stones. The author of *The Earthly Paradise* dismounted. We do not know what he wrote. But he did not feel he had acquitted himself well.

On the third morning of the journey through the wilderness, Magnússon awoke him with the news that the ground had been covered by a new fall of snow and that it was sleeting, raining and blowing. Morris felt tempted to stay warm under his blankets. But the horses were hungry, and he groaned and got up and went out into the 'bitterest morning, the wind NW and plenty of it, and of rain'. He and Magnússon tried but failed to make a fire, so they walked up and down eating their breakfast of cold mutton bones and cold water. The horses stood around with their tails turned to the wind and their heads hung down, shaking with the cold. Morris, who had a stomach-ache, felt beaten for once, conscious of being 'a milksop'. He was distraught at having lost his little haversack, containing his journal notes, his pipe, spare spectacles, and drawing materials ('if they were any use'), and turned on the guide Eyvindr, to whom he had entrusted it, in one of his convulsive rages, threatening to kill him. The haversack later reappeared. One senses that this section of the journey pushed Morris to his limits of endurance, both physical and mental. The physiological effects of 'wind-chill' extend to instant demoralization, as is now well understood.

Morris in the Wilderness fears ghosts and sees visions. As he notes: 'The snow-filled crannies of the cliffs took queer shapes sometimes.' One of them was 'just like a medieval crucifix, the body hanging on the arms I mean'.

Such endurance tests are central in the novels of the quest that Morris wrote twenty years later. *The Sundering Flood* is the great river in the wilderness. *The Water of the Wondrous Isles* is full of Icelandic descriptions of 'crow-black' rocks and mountains in the shape of dismal streets. In these curious novels people traverse mountain passes which grow colder and colder and more barren and more fearsome. Morris returns again and again to these dreamlike sequences of little figures in vast landscapes, struggling on towards the heights, tested to the utmost, surprised by their own feats. In *The Well at the World's End*, Ursula speaks to her lover. They have journeyed through a wild land that is definitely Iceland:

Three months ago I lay on my bed at Bourton Abbas, and all the while here was this huge manless waste lying under the bare heavens and threatened by the storehouse of the fires of the earth: and I had not seen it, nor thee either, O friend; and now it hath become a part of me for ever.

This was true of Morris too.

In this first Icelandic journey the traversing of Kaldidalur was a turning point, in the sense of being so daunting that nothing that came later could be unendurable. It would not, I think, be over-imaginative to see it as a turning point in Morris's own history as well. Iceland had an effect that was purgative, cathartic. This was what he had hoped for when he set out on his travels. It was what he acknowledged in the course of the journey through the wilderness, picking his way on his pony through the sharp-edged lumps of lava: 'Certainly this is what I came out for to see.' The starkness of the landscape and his rapport with the people who had managed to make themselves a life in such conditions, a life of much dignity, productiveness and poetry, gave him a new perspective. Iceland seemed to justify the writer's calling: here were people saved by literature. He felt very far removed from his old 'grumbling life' in England. Iceland had hardened him and yet had, strangely, mellowed him. In his final weeks in Iceland he allowed himself to long for the familiar sweetnesses of domesticity.

Magnússon described without irony how Morris was obviously deep in thought one evening as he prepared the dinner in one of the farmhouse kitchens. Magnússon asked the reason. Morris answered 'with that inexpressibly sweet smile that transfigured his face when he was intensely delighted, "I was dreaming of my love-nest at home".'

In Iceland, Morris seems to have abnegated passion in the sense of sexual passion, though not his feeling for humanity. In the British Library, on a little scrap of paper, are these lines, a poem in progress, disjointed, never finished:

Dead and gone is all desire
Gone and left me cold and bare
Gone as the kings that few remember
And their battle cry . . .
Past and gone like last December
Gone as yesterday's winds that were
Gone as the flame of fire
O my heart how mayst thou bear it

From Iceland he gathered strength for a return.

Morris had not been able to write home since they left Reykjavík. On 11 August, three and a half weeks later, the owner of a Danish schooner setting off for Liverpool offered to take a letter. So Morris sat straight down and wrote 'in huge excitement', telling Janey how often he had thought of the sweet fresh garden at Kelmscott with her and the little ones in it and how he had wished her happy. Rossetti is not mentioned, but he asks her to send his mother his best love. It is a letter written in the language that he uses in all communications with Janey from now onwards: uxorious, affectionate, up to a point confiding but without the expectation of a depth of sympathy so obvious in his letters to Georgie and, at this period, Aglaia. He is optimistic, breezy, unintense. 'I am tremendous in health and in very fair good spirits,' 'the poneys are delightful little beasts, and their amble is the pleasantest possible means of travelling'; 'I find sleeping in a tent very comfortable work even when the weather is very cold.' Morris glosses over the privations and neuroses. He jokes about his dirtiness: 'My breeches are a triumph of blackness, but not my boots, by Jove!' Interestingly, he assumes shared political awareness. The siege of Paris and the Commune is on his mind in Iceland: he tells Janey the loose stones on the edges of the lava fields remind him of 'a half-ruined Paris barricade'.

They are now at Stykkishólmur, the seaside trading station on Snæfellsnes, the large promontory half-way up the western coast of Iceland. Morris has arrived in *Laxdæla Saga* country. The previous day, as he tells Janey, he has visited Helgafell, the place where Guðrun, Ósvíf's daughter, died, and found it overlooking 'a great sea of terribly inky mountains tossing about'. This saga of *c*.1245 has as its central episode the love triangle of Guðrun, the beautiful and ruthless woman who is tricked into marrying her lover's best friend and then incites her husband to kill her former lover, an action which leads inevitably to his own death. For many obvious reasons the story of Guðrun held an overwhelming resonance for Morris. He soon abandoned the prose translation he and Magnússon had started, feeling the magnitude and tension of the drama called out for a more poetic treatment. His poem 'The Lovers of Gudrun' appears in the last volume of *The Earthly Paradise* and he returned to Guðrun in his epic of the middle 1870s, *The Story of Sigurd the Volsung*, which rises like a Nordic cathedral, a strong and simple edifice of anapaestic couplets in four colossal books.

Morris had always seen as the key to the enigma of Guðrun the last line of *Laxdæla Saga*. When she is old, her son asks her which of the men she had known she loved the best. She replies, '*þeim var ek verst er ek unni mest*', which Morris translates, 'I did the worst to him I loved the most'. Woman is cryptic indeed, he seems to say. He travels gloomily through the scenery of the *Laxdæla*. His spirits are at their lowest point of the whole journey, roused only by the sight of a huge eagle flying over Helgafell, followed by a raven who kept close behind insolently, buffeting and teasing. Below a little ship was pitching about in what looked like a tremendously rough sea.

As they round the Snæfellsnes peninsula, the furthest point of their itinerary, Morris's spirits rise again. He starts to dream of Philip Webb. He feels on the homeward route. His power of observation if anything increases. What makes him so compelling and believable a travel writer is his delight in the unexpected detail. There are rainbows in Iceland like no other rainbows: flat and segmental instead of arced and soaring. They lie low over the country and they appear to follow you. From the cliff top at Búlandshöfði Morris watches a seal eating a salmon: 'a black head down in the green sea, dubbing away at a big fish'.

As they travel, he keeps noting their mysterious encounters. A clergyman appears from nowhere in the roadway and Magnússon embraces him as a friend long lost. At Ólafsvík they meet 'a funny little white-haired boy with his little breeches buttoned down behind' as in a Richter woodcut; he is holding 'the most ridiculous of cur-puppies' which Magnússon jovially threatens to eat. Lodging with the doctor at Hnausar they are surprised when, after breakfast, the doctor brings in his daughter dressed up in gala clothes, including a spectacular silver belt dated by Morris as not later than 1530. He observes: 'the open-work of the belt was very beautiful, the traditional northern Byzantinesque work all mixed up with the crisp sixteenth century leafage'. Again, the expert eye.

Morris travels with the journalist's and novelist's antennae, responding eagerly to the *outré* and the marvellous. At Skerdingsstadir he stops at a shack to ask the way from a crowd of girls and children mounted three or four per pony; they had been blueberrying and all their teeth were blue. That same evening he cooks in the kitchen of the farmhouse near the campsite: 'a queer little den', just big enough to hold Morris, his pots, the smoke from the stove and a little girl of five whose name was Augustina. The rest of the community stand in the doorway, gaping while Morris, sweating heavily, makes the soup and fries the trout. These are just the sort of scenes that keep occurring in his novels, pinpointing the element of the bizarre in the everyday.

He reports an encounter between Faulkner in their lodgings at Hnausar and a female Icelander intent on pulling off his boots and breeches, according to the ancient rules of hospitality. Faulkner, knowing no Icelandic, does not manage to resist her. As Morris describes it, this is a Chaucerian scene. Rossetti, having the story relayed to him in England, suggested that the reason Morris escaped this treatment was that he was so evidently unreceptive. The female Icelander, said Rossetti, would have foreseen the 'defensive bootjack' being hurled.

305

By 24 August they were in sight of Thingvellir, the plain of the lawgivers, having circled round to meet the road they travelled north by. They stopped on the way at Reykholt where Morris immersed himself in Snorri's Bath, the circular stone-rimmed hot-spring bath beside the house of Snorri Sturluson, the model for all the versatile Icelanders, poet, statesman, scholar, saga writer and author of the chronicles of the northern kings, the *Heimskringla*. On a cold, raw morning, Morris felt grateful for the hot water up to his middle. It would have made a perfect subject for the malice of Rossetti. Snorri's Bath, out in the open, with its green mound in the background, must have struck him as a great improvement on Bad Ems.

Thingvellir was the last set-piece sight of Morris's Iceland journey. It was the place of the first democratic parliament. Here in 930, soon after the colonization of the island by the Norsemen from Scandinavia and Celts from Britain, the Althing or General Assembly had been formed, a gathering of thirty-nine independent chieftaincies. The Althing continued without any central executive authority until Iceland came under Norwegian rule in 1262. This Parliament met at Thingvellir for two weeks every summer. Besides the official procedures of the legislature, there was what amounted to a national festival of sports, verse-readings and trading. Craftsmen set up their stalls and sold from them. A large proportion of that early population made its way to Thingvellir each year.

As Morris approached the great plain, riding his pony through the valley of Ármannsfell, haunt of the land-spirits, and up the narrow mountain pass with scaly sides, he felt the surge of expectation:

My heart beats, so please you, as we near the brow of the pass, and all the infinite wonder, which came upon me when I came up on the deck of the 'Diana' to see Iceland for the first time, comes on me again now, for this is the heart of Iceland that we are going to see: nor was the reality of the sight unworthy; the pass showed long and winding from the brow, with jagged dark hills showing over the nearer banks of it as you went on, and betwixt them was an open space with a great unseen but imagined plain between you and the great lake that you saw glittering far away under huge peaked hills of bright blue with grey-green sky above them, Hengill the highest of them, from the hot-spring on whose flank rose into the air a wavering column of snow-white steam.

It was a sunny afternoon. They rode along the narrow pass, dismounting to lead their ponies down steep slopes. They saw on their left the small peaked hill, known as the Maidens' Seat, from which the women used to watch the games in the Hofmannflöt (the Chieftains' Plain) below. Then suddenly beneath them was the great grey plain itself, stretching out to the west. Morris had hoped for the moment and found it: Thingvellir was 'a beautiful and historical-looking place'. He saw it with his usual *pictorial* sense of history, envisaging the cohorts of the tribesmen, the unfurling of their banners, a crowded, surging, almost operatic scene. The poem that this scene inspired, 'The Folk-mote by the River', blazes with the patterns and colours of the heraldic:

> And first below was the Silver Chief
> Upon the green was the Golden Sheaf.
>
> And on the next that went by it
> The White Hart on the Park did sit.
>
> And then on the red the White Wings flew,
> And on the White was the Cloud-fleck blue.

That night they camped on mossy turf close to the edge of the Öxará river, almost under the shadow of the Great Rift, the cliff rising in the moonlight on the opposite shore. The place was 'all populous with ravens' which kept crying out and croaking up above the tents. Morris used to do his famous imitation of a raven; perhaps he perfected the technique at Thingvellir. That evening for once he was a reluctant cook. Evans had to bully him into lighting the fire and getting the meal ready. He felt easy and lethargic, in too great a haze of happiness. As always in Iceland he slept with pleasant dreams. The next morning they explored the Lögberg (the Hill of the Laws), approaching past the church and through the churchyard to the little mound where the Speaker at Law would stand every year to deliver his judgements. Morris found this mound, raised up on what was almost a small island in the deep rift of the lava, one of the most dramatic places in all Iceland: 'Grim Goatshoe, who picked it out for the seat of the Althing, must have been a man of poetic insight.' He noted how these days the Hill of Laws was covered over 'with sweet deep grass' and that heath berries were growing down the side of its rift.

Morris found much to admire in the primitive democracy of Iceland. So much so that he would explain it in laborious detail to his Socialist audiences of the 1880s, making the implied comparison between

Victorian Britain and this orderly and equitable social system which respected the personal rights of all free men. Morris dwelt especially on the fact that crime in his contemporary sense had no meaning in Iceland, where morality was enforced purely by public opinion. People could be outlawed but they could not be arrested. He returned to these themes of criminality and violence in *News from Nowhere*, the Utopian novel which is infused with Morris's Icelandic ideals.

In early Iceland manual labour was so far from a disgrace that the mythical heroes were famed as much as weapon-makers as they were for fighting. Morris, the handcraftsman, would point out with delight that 'the greatest men lent a hand in ordinary field and house work, pretty much as they do in the Homeric poems'. Great men made hay, mended gates, sowed corn, built houses. Compared with Victorian England these women were relatively liberated, notably so in marriage. Morris referred approvingly to the enlightened Icelandic attitudes towards domestic violence: there were many cases of women who divorced themselves on grounds of cruelty, mental or physical. A blow, he claimed, could be enough.

The difference between this liberal democracy and the zealous cruelty of the later Icelandic regimes was borne in upon Morris as he stood on the cliff at Thingvellir looking down into the dreadful deep pool where they drowned warlocks and witches in mediaeval times. He does not mention that under the Danish occupation, and within living memory, women convicted of adultery were sewn into sacks, weighted down and cast into the Drowning Pool's remarkable clear depths.

It was raining when they left and Morris cleared the remnants of the last breakfast he cooked under a thick drizzle. At Thingvellir they had gathered up two Cambridge men who had made a chaotic journey around Iceland, from Reykjavík to Stykkishólmur by fishing smack, almost without a guide. They all set off together for the final lap to Reykjavík. Morris was already desperate to see what letters awaited him from home. There was a great jump in his heart when they reached the sea and could make out in the distance the familiar beacon on the hill above Reykjavík, the harbour and the ships.

They turned inland again a little: 'thence away', wrote Morris, 'the road was almost like a road in England, and we swung along at a great pace, keeping quite close together, the horses knowing well that they were coming near their journey's end.' He jumped off Mouse, his pony, just six weeks to the minute after he had mounted him beside the railings of the little weedy garden of the small black and white house. This was the house that would recur so often in his dreams by day and night.

None of the expected letters were waiting at the house for him. He remounted Mouse and galloped to the post office. He walked in quite coolly, although trembling inwardly. The postmaster shuffled through the letters and handed him eleven. He checked them quickly through and was reassured to find that at least no one was dead.

Morris read his letters with his usual sense of niggling anti-climax, 'wondering at people's calmness'. The four days they spent at Reykjavík before departure, selling off unwanted horses, distributing the remainder of their stores, drinking toasts with the governor, seemed banal after their weeks of travel. They set sail on the *Diana* on 1 September. Mouse, destined for a life of ease at Kelmscott, travelled with his master. Poor Faulkner collapsed straight away into his berth. Morris was a little sick to start with but recovered. The last he saw of Iceland was the shadows of the rocks looming dimly through the mist. The pilot boat left them and sailed off through the green water. Morris did not expect he would return.

The Faroes appeared less dramatic after Iceland. Morris's sense of proportion had now altered. Approaching Scotland they ran into a fleet of small luggers, the Aberdeen fishing fleet; Morris found the Scottish coast 'wondrous dull' after all the marvels they had seen. Landing at Granton he felt disorientated, suffering a Victorian equivalent of jet-lag. At the railway station he stood bewildered at the ticket office not knowing what to ask for. 'Lord, how strange it seemed at first!' After the tracts of country they had travelled the journey from Edinburgh to London seemed a short one. As he looked out of the window it struck them that the houses and the horses were disproportionately large for the landscape, like the buildings in a stage set.

The last entry in his journal describes Iceland as 'a marvellous, beautiful and solemn place' where he had 'been in fact very happy'. 'Solemn' was the word he used to express the inexpressible. The importance that the journey to Iceland had for him is suggested by the way in which Morris, the atheist, would refer to it afterwards as his 'Holy Land'.

He was reluctant to get going on writing up the promised fair copy of the journal from the account he had scribbled down while travelling.

Two weeks after he got home he was already making excuses to Louisa, Georgie's sister: it would be 'something in its way like looking at a drawerful of old letters'. He evidently felt afraid of doing damage to the spirit of an episode he held so precious by going remorselessly over the detail of the day-to-day events. Morris did not complete the transcription of the journal until June 1873, when he was preparing to set sail to Iceland for the second time.

He was also notably unwilling to have the journal published in his lifetime, though this was several times suggested. His reason was always the same: that it would need a great deal of polishing to make it fit for publication. This is by no means true. Perhaps the real reason was that the resonances were too personal, too painful. The year after his return he had been writing to Aglaia, 'I know clearer now perhaps than then what a blessing and help last year's journey was to me; or what horrors it saved me from.'

Janey, after his death, upheld the publication veto. Probably she had her private reasons too.

CHAPTER TEN

Kelmscott Manor
1871–75

Kelmscott Manor, the 'beautiful and strangely naif house' in Oxfordshire, was from now on the object of Morris's deep affection. Perhaps no other Englishman, apart from the owners of truly ancestral homes, has ever felt such passionate attachment to a building. This is in spite of the fact that Morris never lived there permanently. He was rarely there for more than a few days at a time. The house was too cold to be comfortable in winter, and even through the summer Morris's business commitments kept recalling him to London. But just as he had noticed in Iceland that small farmers felt an almost gravitational pull back to their farmhouses and home-meads, Morris now began to feel that every road led back to Kelmscott. The gabled, grey stone building replaced Red House as his ideal imagined place of domesticity, gregariousness, happiness, fulfilment. He had literally dreamed about this house before he saw it: one of those sharp pre-visions to which Morris was so prone.

The large house is mainly Elizabethan, dating from around 1570. It was built in a shape common at that period, and described by Morris as 'an E with the tongue cut out'. Towards the end of the seventeenth century a second wing was added, projecting out to the north-east. Technically speaking, the house is not a manor: no manorial rights were apparently attached to it. But its scale and its dominant position in the village make Kelmscott an honorary manor. Morris and Rossetti had rented the house and sixty-eight acres of 'closes' or enclosures from the executors of James Turner, whose family had lived at Kelmscott for the past four centuries. The Turner shield of arms, granted in 1665, adorns a garlanded stone fireplace in one of the main rooms. Morris loved the sense of continuity at Kelmscott, seeing it as a house that had 'grown up out of the soil and the lives of them that lived on it'. It seemed doubly organic, deeply rooted in its landscape and connecting with, embracing, a long local human past.

There were no false notes, no jarrings. Architecturally Kelmscott radiated rightness, in the unassuming way that Morris searched for constantly but rarely found. The house was built of the coarse local oolite stone of the Thames Valley; the wall of the north-east wing had been, as he put it, 'buttered over' with thin plaster which, by the 1870s, had weathered to match the original stone exactly. The house seemed uniform in period: in fact practically dateless. It appears in Morris's own novel *News from Nowhere* as an archetypal building, the place which time forgot. He found in it the qualities of carefulness and quirkiness. The roofs had been covered in the simple stone slates of the Cotswolds, 'the most lovely covering which a roof can have'. What gave him great delight was the way in which the slates had been 'sized down' by the roofers, so that they used small ones at the top, graduating to larger ones down towards the eaves. The 'ordered beauty' of the Kelmscott roofs reminded him of birds' feathers, fishes' scales.

The east front is approached through a door in a tall wall, down a flagged path which runs through the front garden to a porch with a gable, like the house in a child's story book. Turning under an arched opening in the yew hedge you are faced with a quite different gabled vista of the north front of the house. The great charm of Kelmscott Manor is its entrances and exits, surprise views, odd heights and depths and jugglings with spaces. Morris thrived on these diversities: the differences in floor levels, the unexpected angles of windows and roofs and the way that the walls 'batter', leaning back a little, in the traditional manner of the ancient Cotswold house. To the south is a small group of farm buildings: a good barn, sheds and a dovecot. Barns were always Morris's passion: the huge tithe barn at Great Coxwell, a few miles away, was one of his most admired buildings in the world. At Kelmscott he liked to see the way these unpretentious buildings clustered in relation to each other, in relation to the manor. As at Red House the outhouses and gardens were regarded with the same affectionate possessiveness as the main building. Morris personalized his yew hedge with a topiary dragon. He named it Fafnir, after Sigurd's dragon. In later years there was a periodic dragon-trimming ceremony when Morris would set about Fafnir with large shears.

The house, as described by Morris, 'lies at the very end of the village on a road which, brought up shortly by a back-water of the Thames, becomes a mere cart track leading into the meadows along the river'. Kelmscott village was then a hamlet of 117 inhabitants, like the similarly close-knit agricultural communities of Janey's own family background, and a near-replica of the remote Oxfordshire village so vividly described, in all its joys and deprivations, in Flora Thompson's *Lark Rise to Candleford*. May Morris, the child at Kelmscott in the 1870s, recollected later how oxen drew the wagons and the harvest was still threshed with flails on the floor of the great barn. In the poem 'The Half of Life Gone', one of the episodes in *The Pilgrims of Hope*, Morris described practices that continued in the countryside around him:

> There is work in the mead as of old; they are eager at winning the hay,
> While every sun sets bright and begets a fairer day.
> The forks shine white in the sun round the yellow red-wheeled wain,
> Where the mountain of hay grows fast; and now from out of the lane
> Comes the ox-team drawing another, comes the bailiff and the beer,
> And thump, thump, goes the father's nag o'er the narrow bridge of the weir.

Of all the many rivers Morris wandered by and fished in from his early childhood onwards, this was much the most domestic, an extension of his garden. As he wrote to Charles Eliot Norton, he was living 'within a stone's throw of the baby Thames'. This small river, in flat meadows and overhung with willows, was Morris's great refuge through the years he was at Kelmscott, and a source of inspiration. The gentle long-leafed 'Willow' is still one of his most popular decorative designs. When he was at Kelmscott his afternoon routine was to go out in his punt with rod and line, in pursuit of local gudgeon. Friends noticed subtle changes in Morris's personality out on the river. His contentment would make him bossy, rather brusque, like the Nordic seafarer he so palpably resembled. As described by his friends, William Morris on the river is a character from Kenneth Grahame's *The Wind in the Willows*, the idyll of Rat, Mole, Badger and Toad; and there is a connection, for Mrs Kenneth Grahame visited May at Kelmscott in 1934, and released a flood of memories of times May and her father used to scull down the Thames and picnic on the banks beyond Radcot Bridge.

Kelmscott had – and has – its church, to the north-west of the village. Morris found it 'small but interesting': early English in style, but with rounded Norman arches which Morris diagnosed as a local architectural idiosyncrasy. He grew to love the little church with its traces of mediaeval wall painting and the elegantly curved inner arches of the windows, a speciality in Oxfordshire churches of the fourteenth century. Kelmscott church, like Kelmscott Manor, appears in *News from Nowhere*, 'gaily dressed up' for the harvest festival with garlands of flowers festooned from arch to arch. They are feasting in the church in Morris's Utopia: 'its best ornament was the crowd of handsome, happy-looking men and women that were set down to table, and who, with their bright faces and rich hair over their gay holiday raiment, looked, as the Persian poet puts it, like a bed of tulips in the sun.' How often Morris uses churches in his fiction, taking over the real buildings as the background to his narratives, confidently, almost arrogantly, as if churches, like museums and libraries, were in his domain.

Westward from Kelmscott runs a string of little villages: Little Faringdon, Broughton Poggs and Filkins. Northwards goes another string: Langford, Broadwell and Kencot. These villages seemed almost replicas of Kelmscott. Each village had its church, often an architectural marvel. Within a radius of five miles from Kelmscott, Morris claimed he could point to 'some half-dozen tiny village churches, every one of which is a beautiful work of art'. There was the lovely thirteenth-century tower and spire at Broadwell; the 'infinitely curious' mouse-size village church at Broughton Poggs. What Morris found most moving in these buildings was their apparent spontaneity, arrived at because of their directness of intention. They were not put up to make money or impress but were built, in effect, by the people for the people: 'These are the works of the Thames-side country bumpkins, as you would call us – nothing grander than that.'

At Kelmscott Morris came to see himself as living at the mystic centre of a country of immense beauty and complex interconnections. He looked beyond the manor to the village. Still within his near vision was the sequence of other small villages around it: Bibury, on the Coln twelve miles to the north-west, which was, to Morris, 'surely the most beautiful village in England'; to the north-east Minster Lovell, in the valley of the Windrush, which according to May Morris 'must have run it very close' in her father's mind. Morris's view of the countryside roamed further outwards from these grey stone villages of Oxfordshire and Gloucestershire to all the variations of land and architecture that made up the texture of England as a whole. It was now that one of his most influential concepts, the ideal of the network of small ruralist communities, began to surface. Here are the origins of garden cities. Morris wrote in those early Kelmscott years: 'but look, suppose people lived in little communities among gardens and green fields, so that you could be in the country in 5 minutes walk, and had few wants; almost no furniture for instance, and no servants, and studied (the difficult) arts of enjoying life, and finding out what they really wanted: then I think one might hope civilisation had really begun.' It is wonderfully ironic that this communistic vision of the future was addressed to Louisa Baldwin, Georgie's sister, who had married an ironmaster and whose young son Stanley, then six, grew up to be prime minister of England three times, trading on the instinctive conservatism of the shires.

William Morris has been depicted as a sentimental moralist. This is to misunderstand him and to underestimate him. From the 1870s he came to define his vision of the country with the sharpness of a man who actually lived there and who knew the intimate detail of the landscape being dangerously threatened by inertia and greed. When he spoke about England, it was Kelmscott he returned to with a passion too accurate to sink into nostalgia. Years later in *The Commonweal*, his Socialist propaganda paper, Morris evoked *exactly* the sights, smells, sounds of Kelmscott in the course of a diatribe against ruthless commercial developers and his other arch-villains, the forerunners of our own Heritage industry, the woolly-minded 'hunters of the picturesque':

Midsummer in the country: here you may walk between the fields and hedges that are as it were one huge nosegay for you, redolent of bean-flowers and clover and sweet hay and elder-blossom. The cottage-gardens are bright with flowers, the cottages themselves mostly models of architecture in their way. Above them towers here and there the architecture proper of days bygone, when every craftsman was an artist and brought definite intelligence to bear upon his work. Man in the past, nature in the present, seem to be bent on pleasing you and making all things delightful to your senses; even the burning dirty road has a look of luxury as you lie on the strip of roadside green, and listen to the blackbirds singing, surely for your benefit, and, I was going to say, as if they were paid to do it, but I was wrong, for as it is they seem to be doing their best.

After Iceland, Morris irrupted back at Kelmscott in the middle of September 1871, 'with the complexion of a trading skipper and much thinner'. May remembered the commotion of his homecoming 'with all that burden of adventure and travel upon him – coming back out of the land of the trolls and awful mountains'. Her mother and Rossetti had by this time been alone at Kelmscott for two months with the children, May then nine and Jenny ten, the children's nurse, two servants imported from London by Rossetti, and the Comelys, the elderly couple who looked after Kelmscott Manor and lived in the adjoining cottage. Philip Comely, gardener-handyman, drove Morris to distraction by touching his hat or pulling his forelock deferentially with every word he spoke.

In Morris's absence, Rossetti had installed himself in the Tapestry Room and its adjoining bedroom, on the first floor of the house. He used the Tapestry Room as his studio. One of the paintings he embarked on there was 'Water Willow', the portrait of Janey surrounded by familiar images of Kelmscott: the house, the church, the boathouse. May's complaint that Rossetti had distorted the perspective might be of interest to a child psychologist. At first Rossetti took to Kelmscott and its surroundings and sent out drowsy bulletins of his contentment at being in this 'loveliest "haunt of ancient peace"'. He described it as if it were a desert or an Eden, a more domestic desert than Morris's fiery wasteland. The garden, wrote Rossetti, was 'full of fat cut hedges'. The squat farm buildings 'look settled down into a purring state of comfort, but seem (as Janey said the other day) as if, were you to stroke them, they would move'. The children were beautiful and gave no trouble, reading a Waverley novel a day from the set of forty-eight that Rossetti had provided for Janey's delectation. It was so hot that summer that Rossetti shed his waistcoats, wearing a blue blouse indoors and only a wrapper out. He and Janey took long walks through the countryside. Rossetti boasted of her 'most triumphant pedestrian faculty; licks you hollow, I can tell you'. Sometimes they could manage six miles in a day. He and Janey had effectively taken Kelmscott over, as Rossetti's summer poem 'Down Stream' suggests with extreme tactlessness.

> Between Holmscote and Hurstcote
> A troth was given and riven,
> From heart's trust grew one life to two,
> Two lost lives cry to Heaven:
> With banks spread calm to meet the sky,
> With meadows newly mowed,
> The harvest-paths of glad July,
> The sweet school-children's road.

But there was an undercurrent of discontent and sadness. Rossetti's reports were soon becoming less euphoric. He began to complain that the countryside round Kelmscott was the flattest and least inspiring he had ever seen. He was haunted by the seventeenth-century hangings which gave the Tapestry Room its name. These showed the Old Testament history of Samson, 'carried through with that uncompromising uncomfortableness peculiar to this class of art manufacture'. (Rossetti did not live to see Morris's own incursions into large-scale pictorial tapestry.) The tapestry at Kelmscott which especially upset him was a 'grisly' composition in which Samson's eyes are being gouged out, while a brass barber's basin lies at his feet containing his shorn locks.

To May, the nine-year-old at Kelmscott, he seemed worrying, a misfit in the house. She was disconcerted by his erratic timetable. He came down to a late breakfast and, forgetting that he ate no lunch, she could hardly believe that a single human being could consume so many eggs. He would then disappear to his studio till evening when he would descend and go out into the dusk, sometimes with her mother and sometimes on his own. The child was aware of Rossetti's depths of loneliness. Whenever she thought of that summer at Kelmscott she

25 ' "Home Again". William Morris sitting bored in an armchair'. Caricature by Edward Burne-Jones after Morris's return from Iceland, 1871.

317

would see in her mind's eye 'the rather broad figure tramping away doggedly over the flat green meadows', or the selfconsciously melancholy artist slumped into his chair in the studio alone. She felt sorry for him and wished she knew how to approach him. She sensed the tensions in the household. She wrote in retrospect, 'Indeed, we youngsters were more conscious of solitariness in our family life than our elders knew.'

Morris arrived into this household bearing treasures for the children: Icelandic girdles and traditional embroidered bodices. As they had travelled around Iceland, he and Faulkner had scoured the steads they stayed in and negotiated prices for desirable objects. Faulkner had acquired some Icelandic silver spoons. Mouse, the pony, was the most popular memento of Morris's travels. He was harnessed to a little basket carriage, a comic creature sandwiched between two wooden shafts. Morris himself used to ride Mouse around the country. He was mounted when Theodore Watts-Dunton first encountered him:

I saw coming towards us on a rough pony so diminutive that he well deserved the name of 'Mouse', the figure of a man in a wideawake – a figure so broad and square that the breeze at his back, soft and balmy as it was, seemed to be using him as a sail, and blowing both him and the pony towards us.

Eventually Mouse got fat and lazy on his diet of lush Kelmscott grass.

Rossetti was conspicuously insistent on being at Kelmscott to greet the returning traveller. He was, however, disappointed in the tales of Iceland Morris endlessly recounted. Rossetti had evidently hoped they would be bawdier. After a few days Morris returned again to London. Before he left, Rossetti made a sketch of him out fishing underneath the willows:

> Enter Skald, moored in a punt,
> And Jacks and Tenches exeunt.

By early October the manor was deserted. Rossetti went back to Cheyne Walk. Janey and the children rejoined Morris at Queen Square. Burne-Jones, who had been ill and depressed all through the summer but now felt much restored after a visit to Italy, kept his distance from Rossetti, put off by his querulousness and his impenetrable gloom. Janey and Rossetti's continuing liaison still scandalized their circle. On 23 October, William Bell Scott sent his wife an account of a dinner party given by Morris at Queen Square: 'I asked Gabriel the evening before if he was to be there, and on his answering no, I said, "Why then?" His

26 *'Enter Morris, moored in a punt'*. Caricature by Dante Gabriel Rossetti of Morris
at Kelmscott in September 1871.

reply was "Oh I have another engagement." This engagement was
actually Janey at his own house for the night. At Top's there were Jones,
Poynter, Brown, Hüffer [*sic*], Ellis and Green. Of course no Janey. Is it
not too daring, and altogether too inexplicable?' Scott, having been
forewarned, did not inquire about Janey. After dinner Morris read to
the party from his new poem *Love Is Enough* during which Scott
dropped off to sleep intermittently, hoping his inattentiveness had not
been observed.

It was a miserable winter. Hard frosts at Kelmscott killed innumerable moorhens on the river. The human problems multiplied. As Georgie has recorded, 'The year 1872 was marked for us and our intimate
circle by illness, trouble and death.' Morris went down to Kelmscott
alone to see the spring in; Janey, Rossetti and the children were to
follow in the summer in what was now envisaged as an established
pattern. But by early June, Rossetti had collapsed with a total mental

breakdown, showing paranoia symptoms. It was a delayed reaction to the savagely hostile review of his poems and his personal standards of morality, by Robert Buchanan. This first appeared under the title 'The Fleshly School of Poetry' in 1871, in *The Contemporary Review*. The article was republished, in a lengthened form, as a pamphlet in the spring of the next year. Rossetti was already hypersensitive to criticism, highly conscious of himself as the reprobate within the hushed High Anglican household of his mother and his sisters. His loves, first for Lizzie, then for Janey, had their inherent frustrations and their overtones of tragedy. The 'Fleshly School' attack was enough to push him to the edge of suicide.

By 7 June, Rossetti's condition was alarming. He was taken in a cab by his friend Dr George Hake from Cheyne Walk to Hake's own house in Roehampton. Rossetti's brother William and Ford Madox Brown travelled with them. It was a problem journey, with Rossetti imagining he heard a loud bell ringing in the cab. The next day he was only with difficulty prevented from provoking a quarrel with a group of gypsies he imagined had insulted him. Later that day he had delusions of voices mocking him in terms of 'unendurable obloquy'. Dr Hake diagnosed a 'serious apoplexy' and a local practitioner confirmed that Rossetti had indeed undergone some form of stroke. His mother and sister Christina were sent for. Dr Hake discovered an empty bottle containing laudanum under Rossetti's bed. He had started on a new and drastic form of treatment by inhalations of ammonia forte when, perhaps fortunately, Dr John Marshall, one of the day's great surgeons, a Pre-Raphaelite aficionado, arrived. Marshall at once started treatment with strong coffee, applied by an unrecorded route. By the time he came round Rossetti had been unconscious for about thirty-six hours. His brother had no doubt that his intention was suicide, but kept this from his mother and Christina. On regaining consciousness Rossetti experienced some loss of power, probably a pressure palsy, in his left leg.

Bell Scott called at Queen Square to break the news to Janey. His emotions were mixed: he and Brown wanted to keep her and Rossetti apart, believing that she had been a main cause of the breakdown; but Rossetti was insistent that a message must be got to her since she had expected him and would by now be mystified. Scott reported to Alice that he found her on the sofa 'and not discomposed' by his intelligence. Janey had great reserves in the concealment of her feelings. She had in fact had 'dreadful dreams' about Rossetti's breakdown and was in an agony to know his real condition. Only Morris would have diagnosed how anxious she was. Gabriel was now back at Cheyne Walk, and Scott recorded that 'on Friday afternoon Jane Morris was taken down to see him by her more than amiable husband'. On one of the cancelled manuscript pages of his *Autobiographical Notes*, Scott also comments: 'Topsy is D.G.'s alias for Morris, on whose magnanimity, as everyone knows, D.G. depends rather more than his friends care to think.'

Anxiety for Gabriel exudes from Morris's letters. He even mentions in a letter to his mother that one of his friends is very ill: 'indeed we thought him dying on Sunday, though there is good hope for him today'. To Brown he wrote: 'Come by all means and talk to Janey: she will be glad to hear anything you have to say about Gabriel.' He went so far as to offer his own services as Rossetti's residential nurse, taking over Brown's own duties in Chelsea or 'in any place Gabriel goes to hereafter'. This was the self-effacement that gained the Holy Graal.

Towards the end of June, Rossetti was well enough for Scotland, though delusions continued. 'All the birds even on the trees are villains making cat-calls,' Scott reported in despair. All this time Janey was anxiously waiting for news of him and hinting she might travel north to see him. But by September he had made up his mind to return to Kelmscott. Dr Hake had reservations, but agreed that it might soothe him. Rossetti wrote to William, 'all, I now find by experience, depends primarily on my not being deprived of the prospect of the society of the one necessary person.' He arrived at Kelmscott on 25 September: 'here all is happiness again, and I feel completely myself'.

The autumn at Kelmscott was difficult for Janey who had to contend with a Rossetti more dependent and even more irregular in his habits of life than he had been the previous summer. After dining at ten he would not be in bed until three or even five a.m., having dosed himself heavily with chloral and alcohol before he could hope for any sleep. She loved Rossetti but the strain of it would tell on her. As she said later: 'That Gabriel was *mad* was but too true, no one knows better than myself.' Interestingly the person who gave her the most support was Philip Webb, Morris's great ally, who had known them all since Oxford. He wrote to her: 'I have always taken a great interest in you and none the less that time has tossed all of us about and made us play other parts than we set out upon. I see that you play yours well and truly under the changes and I feel deeply sympathetic on that account.'

The brunt of it all was borne, of course, by Morris. One of his friends

said that he suffered the natural repugnance felt by the man of rude
health for the unhealthy. But Morris had his own incapacities. There
was more to it than that. He inevitably felt a great dismay and a great
sorrow at the physical debility and the wreckage of talent in an artist and
a poet with whom, in both callings, he had once felt so inextricably
linked. He was deeply irritated by Rossetti's hangers-on, from now on
much more in evidence at Kelmscott. William Rossetti, the literary man
and civil servant, he found pedestrian beyond belief. When Gabriel
objected to Morris's Sigurd story, saying he could not take an interest in
a hero whose brother was a dragon, Morris responded grandly that a
dragon for a brother was preferable to a bloody fool.

By late autumn Rossetti was talking of settling permanently at Kelmscott. This was not a scenario Morris had ever bargained for. In November 1872 his worry and frustration spilled over in a 'rambling and most
egotistical' letter to Aglaia, written from Queen Square.

When I said there was no cause for my feeling low, I meant that my friends had
not changed at all towards me in any way and that there had been no quarrelling: and indeed I am afraid it comes from some cowardice or unmanliness in
me. One thing wanting ought not to go for so much: nor indeed does it spoil my
enjoyment of life always, as I have often told you: to have real friends and some
sort of an aim in life is so much, that I ought still to think myself lucky: and
often in my better moods I wonder what it is in me that throws me into such
rage and despair at other times: I suspect, do you know, that some such moods
would have come upon me at times even without this failure of mine. However
that may be though I must confess that this autumn has been a specially dismal
time with me: I have been a good deal in the house here – not alone, that would
have been pretty well, – but alone with poor Bessy: I must say it is a shame, she
is quite harmless and even good, and one ought not to be irritated with her – but
O my God what I have suffered from finding always there at meals & the like!
poor soul 'tis only because she is an accidental person with whom I have nothing
whatever to do: I am so glad to have Janey back again: her company is always
pleasant and she is very kind and good to me – furthermore my intercourse with
G [Georgie] has been a good deal interrupted not from any coldness of hers, or
violence [?] of mine; but from so many untoward nothings: then you have been
away so that I have had nobody to talk to about things that bothered me: which
I repeat I have felt more than I, in my ingratitude, expected to: another quite
selfish business is that Rossetti has set himself down at Kelmscott as if he never
meant to go away; and not only does that keep me away from that harbour of
refuge, (because it is really a farce our meeting when we can help it) but also he
has all sorts of ways so unsympathetic with the sweet simple old place, that I

feel his presence there as a kind of slur on it: this very unreasonable though when one thinks why one took the place, and how this year it has really answered that purpose: nor do I think I should feel this about it if he had not been so unromantically discontented with it and the whole thing which made me very angry and disappointed. – There, dear Aglaia see how I am showing you my pettinesses! *please* dont encourage me in them; but you have always been so kind to me that they will come out.

Morris in fact would never again be so revealing of his bitter sense of exile from loved places and loved people, or of his feeling that Rossetti, by his presence, had violated his house, and his peace, rather than his wife.

After he returned from Iceland Morris had settled down at once, with a new burst of resolution, to a poem that had no connection with the Nordic. This was *Love Is Enough*, the poem he called later 'a fantastic little book chiefly lyrical'. It is the oddity within his collected works, the one example of a poetic drama based on mediaeval principles. It takes the shape of the formal masque and in it Morris revives the alliterative metres of pre-Elizabethan English drama with the creative curiosity with which he had earlier unpicked his examples of mediaeval stitching and searched back to rediscover past techniques of stained glass.

Seeing *Love Is Enough* in gestation, Rossetti had had high hopes of it, writing from Kelmscott to William Bell Scott: 'The poem is, I think, at a higher point of execution than anything he has done, having a passionate lyric quality such as one found in his earliest work, and of course much more mature balance in carrying it out. It will be a very fine work.' The children were now just old enough to be aware of their father's poetry in progress. May listened with delight and an awakened sensitivity to the 'long swinging lines' of the 'Music' lyrics, the rhymed dactylics Morris uses for the chorus at the deepest emotional centre of the poem.

Morris tells the story of the king who gives up his kingdom for love in the valley. The king is Pharamond, 'whom nothing but love might satisfy, who left all to seek love, and having found it, found this also, that he had enough, though he lacked all else'. In its outline the tale is drawn from *The Mabinogion*, the ancient Welsh cycle composed orally, as the Icelandic sagas were; in atmosphere and detail it is magically Celtic. No poem by Morris is more intensely and elaborately visual, and it had been intended as a picture book with Morris's own borders and woodcuts from Burne-Jones. In some of the editions these little illustrations were to be filled in with colours and gilding, making it a printed illuminated book.

The story of Pharamond and his love Azalais is acted out at the marriage ceremony of an emperor and empress of some distant dreamlike country. Another pair of lovers, Joan and Giles the peasants, stand in the crowd to watch the royal couple. Morris here provides not just a double but a triple vision: the play within the play within the play. The personal echoes are obvious: the interrelated couples and their dances to the music of time. First, Ned and Georgie; Lizzie and Gabriel; William and Janey. Now Gabriel and Janey? William and Georgie? This poem is shot through, more than any other work of Morris's, by an insistent sexual craving in which the sensuality equates with domesticity. When Pharamond is awakened in his bed by Azalais the detail is pure Kelmscott, complete with the embroidery:

> and then, when thou seest
> How the rose-boughs hang o'er the little loft window,
> And the blue bowl with roses is close to thine hand,
> And over thy bed is the quilt sewn with lilies,
> And the loft is hung round with the green southland hangings,
> And all smelleth sweet as the low door is opened.

Already Kelmscott has become the place of consummation in his sensual topography, in the architectural mind's eye.

No wonder this poem caused Morris such agonies of composition. He was writing it at Kelmscott, struggling to bring it 'out of the maze of rewriting and despondency', in that uncertain spring of 1872. The poem was eventually published in November. It was never a popular success. Compared with the generous, addictive *Earthly Paradise* it seemed too intricate, too self-contained. Coventry Patmore, whilst praising its 'lofty and delicate atmosphere', found it obscure. George Meredith was scathing: 'The Songs are of the species of Fitzball's Gossamer Tree; charming in melody, but there is no such thing as a gossamer tree.' Morris's public, once again, missed the undertow of seriousness, the sense of moral effort, the pain of abnegation as King Pharamond rejects his allotted role and struggles down the highway along the misty valley towards an ideal of love that is not simply human but universal, abstract. It is a pretty poem. Also a poem of premonition. This was the high road Morris too was soon to take.

He was not surprised that his public did not want it. Burne-Jones had suggested he might change the ending, shorten it. But Morris had been obstinate, with what Ned viewed as his dangerous inclusiveness, his heroic tendency for wanting all or nothing: 'It was part of that splendid sternness that was in him – was one of his ways – he would do it. If he ever could have felt that the half was greater than the whole, but he never would. I suppose if he'd painted he would never have hidden things with darkness. That was Top, so clear. That was Top, so out in the sunlight. Never wanted to snatch at anything.'

May Morris suggested, rightly, that the poem was too modern for its period. After the First World War the public was more used to the masque and the mystery, after initiation by the purist Elizabethan Stage Society of William Poel. In 1920 *Love Is Enough* received what was apparently its first stage production, by the Hon. Sybil Amherst, at the Ethical Church in Queen's Road, Bayswater, in a double bill with an episode from Shakespeare's *Henry VI, Part III*.

After *Love Is Enough* Morris lost his nerve a little. He felt worried in case his creative powers were flagging and dreaded joining the ranks of the writers who had once seemed promising but whose imagination and enthusiasm dwindled as they aged. But he knew he could not force things. He wrote very little poetry over the next few years. Meanwhile he and Magnússon worked on their translations, planning the *Heimskringla*, the cycle of the Nordic kings, which would occupy them into the 1890s. He explained to Aglaia that, 'though the translating lacks the hope and fear that makes writing original things so absorbing, yet at any rate it is amusing and in places even exciting.' Occupational therapy. Time-consuming but low-risk.

Through the autumn of 1872 Morris had been looking for a new house in London. The decorating side of the Firm had been expanding and more space was needed at Queen Square for offices, additional workshops and an expanded showroom. The conversion of the family's former living quarters seemed to George Wardle 'almost a desecration', and Morris's equanimity surprised him. But Morris had never liked Queen Square. He felt a lodger there. The fact that he was now virtually exiled from the place he cared the most for, with Rossetti in usurpation at Kelmscott, made him almost nonchalant about domestic changes: 'for this long time past', he told Aglaia, 'I have as it were carried my house on my back'. The planned conversion of Queen Square in any case had compensations for Morris who by this time was becoming interested in the technicalities of textile dyeing. He was cheered by the prospect of his own small dyeshop in what had been the scullery and larder in the basement of the house.

The new house he found eventually, after a depressing search around west London, sometimes accompanied by Ned, was Horrington House, 'a *very* little house with a pretty garden', on Turnham Green Road, the main road running between Turnham Green and Hammersmith. Philip Webb called it 'the little shed on the high road'. Janey too was inclined to denigrate it, saying that the house was 'very good for one person, or perhaps two', evidently forgetting that it was larger than her childhood homes at Oxford. Horrington House, now demolished, does not seem to have been environmentally ideal, standing alongside the Roebuck pub where the Hammersmith omnibuses stopped. William De Morgan remembered the ferocity with which Morris complained about 'a beastly tin-kettle of a bell in a chapel close by, which, he said, went *wank, wank, wank*, until he was nearly driven mad'.

But Chiswick at that time was still a roomy, pleasant suburb of fine houses and large orchards; you could smell and feel the river air down Chiswick Lane. Market wagons packed with produce would trundle down the High Road, and Horrington House soon acquired a certain cosiness. Margaret Burne-Jones associated it for ever afterwards with 'quantities of crumpets'. The kitchen was inhabited by a large yawning cat called Jack. The house served its purpose: the family had settled in in January 1873. They later renewed the lease. In all they stayed there for six years.

Morris kept on his study and his bedroom in Queen Square. This gave him a certain freedom of manoeuvre while Janey was at Kelmscott which, over this period, she very often was. He wrote to Aglaia, with a note of innuendo: 'I can always see anyone I want at Queen Sq: quite safe from interruptions: so in all ways it seems an advantage – does it not?' He warned her that his housekeeper was like a troll wife in an Icelandic story, 'big and O *so* ugly!', and with a deep bass voice. But Morris came to like Horrington House much more than expected, finding his workroom there brighter and more relaxing than his dingy study in Queen Square. Indeed a vision of contentment of those years was to be in his 'pretty room at Turnham Green reading some hitherto unprinted Dumas say about as good as the 3 Musketeers'. He was still writing and illuminating manuscripts. This was his chief enjoyment at that period. George Price Boyce, visiting him at his new house, found him at work on the vellum inscription of *The Odes of Horace*, the relatively small-scale and exquisitely detailed, flowing, floreated version that is now the prize of the Morris manuscripts in the Bodleian. Jenny and May were with their father and struck Boyce as 'very interesting little things, very handsome'. In the course of that visit Rossetti too came in.

For the children, and their friends, Morris's workroom in the little house in Chiswick was a place of long-remembered fascination, with the gold leaf and the ox-gall, the 'very little pots of dye stuffs' and the hanks of worsted which hung around the room. The table in the study was a centre of attraction around which the girls would tiptoe in awe and admiration, not daring to touch the tools and the equipment so professionally arrayed. Morris illuminating: 'the bare light room, the plain work-table; the splendid head bending over the gold, and the two young heads laid close, and the curly locks all mingling'. This was one of the images of childhood May dared to keep intact.

Morris, at almost forty, had never been to Italy. Partly this was accidental, but it was also prejudice: 'Do you suppose that I should see anything in Rome that I can't see in Whitechapel?' Here was Morris's streak of insularity; his resistance to Renaissance art which he considered lacking in humanity; and also now, even more so, his resistance to most things connected with Rossetti, whose father had emigrated from Naples not so long before. But, in April 1873, Ned persuaded him to take two weeks' holiday in Italy, travelling to Florence and Siena. They had both of them been ill and very out of sorts that winter. Ned, the Italy enthusiast, believed that Florence had the power to make any sick man well.

Ned remembered, and recorded, the journey as an outright disaster, with Morris still rheumaticky, grumpy and resistant to all possible pleasures Ned proffered: 'He really was Northern not Southern in his nature.' When it came to Italy, his mind was almost closed, and he travelled in a fury of resentment at the widespread restoration of old buildings, with much metaphoric shaking of the fist.

Ned's cartoon account is not entirely fair to Morris, whose own letters convey both curiosity and pleasure. He writes of 'marvels'; stretches of northern Italy 'all full of wonder and delight'. He and Ned had travelled

327

27 'William Morris in bed'. Caricature by Edward Burne-Jones. A barbed comment on Morris's dislike of the classical tradition.

across Europe by train. They left the Alps and journeyed on towards Turin on 'the most beautiful of all evenings'. Morris described 'going (still between snow-capped mountains) through a country like a garden: green grass and feathery poplars, and abundance of pink-blossomed leafless peach and almond trees'. It was a new scene for him, new colours and new contrasts. They emerged from a tunnel in the Apennines and, to Morris's extreme delight, he saw the plain of Florence stretched out below him, with the square-walled old town of Pistoia in the distance. It was like his first sight of the plain at Thingvellir.

He and Ned found rooms in an old inn outside Florence, anxious 'not to form the furniture of a gigantic Yankee-hutch' by staying in the city. By the early 1870s the transatlantic tourist trade in Florence was under way. But Morris and Ned were themselves tourists of a kind, wandering through the market where Morris saw, wide-eyed, lemons and oranges for sale 'with the leaves still on them: miraculous frying going on, and all sorts of queer vegetables and cheeses to be sold'. He found this 'the greatest game'. Morris was, as always, acquisitive in Florence, planning to buy Janey a bottle of the scent made by the monks of Santa Maria Novella and toys for 'the littles' from the jewellers' shop on the Ponte Vecchio. To Ned's disapproval he also set about 'merchandising for the firm', buying a consignment of *scaldini*, the eccentric waisted lead-glazed pots the Florentines used as braziers, and 'a lot of flasks wickered in all sorts of pretty shapes', precursors of the ubiquitous Chianti flasks imported into Britain in the 1950s. These were bought to be resold alongside the Firm's own products from the showroom at Queen Square.

Florence stayed in his mind as an architectural spectacular. When he wrote to the Prefect of Florence in the early 1880s on behalf of the SPAB to protest against the restoration of the thirteenth-century Bargello, he referred to it as 'your most glorious and beautiful city'. On this early visit he had steeped himself in the Florentine Gothic, visiting the many thirteenth-century churches built or rebuilt in what was then the new Gothic style. His favourite of these was Santa Croce, with its frescoes by Giotto. They were chanting the Miserere as he entered. He also saw Santa Maria Novella, the church so highly recommended by John Ruskin in his *Mornings in Florence* (1875). Morris comments particularly on the cloisters: he could never resist the architecture of the enclosed space. He felt an easy rapport with these relatively early and relatively reticent and northern Italian buildings, though he did not ever actually *love* them as he loved Gothic buildings in England or in France. Burne-Jones watched him unravelling the Baptistry in Florence and enjoying how the pillars were made all in one piece, with little metal trees set into them. The detail of the craftsmanship could tell Morris so much. At the time of this first visit the façade of the Duomo was still pristine. The ornate late-nineteenth-century recasting had not begun. Morris stood in the piazza and decided this was 'certainly the most beautiful church in the world outside'.

But once inside the Duomo Morris felt unhappy, threatened. Ruskin too had found the interior 'a horror'. It is huge and bare and classical. Morris liked huge empty spaces. But not Renaissance spaces. His ideal of large-scale building was the Icelandic mead-hall or the mediaeval barn. The reason he felt so inadequate in Florence, happy only 'as a pig is', conscious of his inability to bring his mind 'up to the proper pitch and tune' to appreciate its wonders, was the fact that in essence this is a Renaissance city and Morris could not separate Renaissance buildings from the regimes that commissioned and financed and erected them. These regimes he viewed with an increasing loathing as cruel, bombastic and corrupt.

In a letter to Philip Webb from Florence he expanded upon things he did not dare to divulge to Ned who was, he said, 'so horribly jealous of the least signs of depression'. His objection to Renaissance buildings of north Italy was fundamentally political and induced in him vast sadness: 'change and ruin, and recklessness and folly, and forgetfulness of "great men and our fathers that begat us" – it is only in such places as this that one can see the signs of them to the full'.

It is significant that Morris, in defining the wreckage of civilization as he saw it, reaches back for the language of his Anglican upbringing, quoting from Ecclesiasticus. It is also notable that the person he confides in is the friend who, unlike Ned, became his Socialist colleague. Philip Webb, in Italy, would feel equally oppressed.

We sighted Iceland in the early morning of Tuesday [15 July 1873] about 1 a.m.; a bitter cold morning and the sea rather high, but bright enough: the first sight of land was just a few peaks thrusting up above a bank of cold grey clouds.

Only weeks after Italy, Morris was again on board the *Diana*. All through the troubles of the previous year a craving to return to Iceland had been taking hold. By January he had been writing to Aglaia: 'I fancy the Iceland voyage will be a necessity to me this year: sometimes I like the idea of it, and sometimes it fills me with dismay.' By February the idea had become more of a reality: 'Iceland gapes for me this summer.' He was feeling it would be the making of him, if he could only get away 'in some sort of hope and heart'. At the end of May he was writing again urgently to Faulkner, this time Morris's sole travelling companion, with details of the five pack saddles he had ordered in advance from a saddler who supplied the British army. These seemed better made and stronger than the Icelandic saddles they used in 1871: perhaps the manufacturer had learned something from the Crimea. By 10 July, Morris and Faulkner were again at Granton. Nothing had changed on board, though the captain was a new one and the flag of the mail ship was now black with voyaging. The next day they sailed off, in the same berths they had had the last time. 'Lord how strange I felt to be in the little cabin again!' He told Webb that he felt nervous. The whole journey seemed unimaginably *déjà vu*.

Morris's own position, however, was now different. He was no longer the innocent in Iceland. In London he had come to be regarded as an expert on Nordic literature and culture. This was certainly the way the young Edmund Gosse had viewed him. Gosse, the Norwegian enthusiast and the earliest interpreter of Ibsen to the English, had jumped at the idea of an introduction to Morris: 'Morris, the greatest gun of all!' he told his father. Morris had vouchsafed him a (rare) reading from the journal of his first Icelandic journey which Gosse had found 'very vivid and amusing'. He thought Morris 'one of the most unassuming, homely people' he had ever met. Later Gosse was in the audience at the Society of Arts for a lecture by Magnússon on Iceland when Morris took the chair:

round and burly, with a shock of hair, and encompassed with many rough garments, [he] was with difficulty persuaded to ascend the platform. Once seated in front of the assembly, he was overcome with bashfulness. When he rose to speak, we trembled. He just barely managed to proceed so far as to say that 'Mr. Magnússon is sure to give you, to give us a – a – very interesting – a – lecture' and then he sat down and buried his face in his hands. He was very uncomfortable and restless during the lecture in the middle of which he suddenly rose to interrupt the lecture with a joke inaudible to us, over which he chuckled a great deal. He yawned several times, but towards the end he discovered that, by judicious wriggling, his chair might be made to swing half round and this little exercise entertained him nearly all the rest of the lecture. At one time he disappeared altogether, for having dropped his pocket-handkerchief, he quietly dived off his chair and under the table for it.

Morris was always rather awkward on the platform, but rarely quite so recalcitrant as this.

The crossing on the *Diana* was a rough one. Morris was at one point sitting in his cabin when the bows of the ship went up towards the sky, and a huge lurch sent the passengers 'all in a heap together'. Morris was very sick, though dressed and on the deck, as the ship juddered up the bay to Reykjavík on a wild, bright Friday morning. His spirits were still low. He wrote from Reykjavík to Janey almost in a state of trance: 'It is all like a kind of dream to me, and my real life seems set aside till it is over.' He instructed her to kiss his 'dear little ones' for him, adding, wistfully: 'My dear how I wish I was back, and how wild and strange everything here is. I am so anxious for you too it was a grievous parting for us the other day.'

He and Charley had planned to take a different route this summer: not a trek around the Saga sites but a more adventurous journey north-east across the relatively untravelled tracts of the interior to Dettifoss, the most powerful waterfall in Europe, and to Akureyri, the main port on the northern coast. For two masters and two guides they had allotted eighteen ponies. One of the guides they knew from their last journey: Jón Jónsson,

331

the saddle-smith, Magnússon's family connection. The other was Haldor, from Eyvindarmúli: 'a little fellow with the most good-tempered of faces', evidently a crony of Jón's.

For their first few days of travel they had an unexpected addition: John Henry Middleton, the architect and scholar, whom they had met on shipboard. Faulkner already knew him. He was to become one of Morris's closest and most esoteric friends, an expert on Eastern art, a connoisseur of the occult. He and Morris corresponded about rare books and carpets: a connoisseurs' exchange. He became in succession Slade Professor and Keeper of the Fitzwilliam Museum in Cambridge and director of the South Kensington Museum. As Janey summed him up, people either liked Middleton 'extremely or not at all'. (She liked him.) He was a notoriously enterprising traveller, going to Fez in the same spirit of inquiry that was bringing him to Iceland. But compared with Morris and Faulkner he was hopelessly ill-equipped for the rigours of the journey. Her father told May: 'he had no comforts, positively nothing, as though he had fallen down from the moon'.

Once he was in the saddle Morris's misgivings were over. They took leave of their Icelandic friends 'in a thymy valley', and as he rode away he felt suddenly light-hearted and quite at home as if there had been no break between the journeys. It seemed that the intensity of that first brief visit had made Iceland more familiar than places he saw oftener but cared about much less.

28 *William Morris eating fish in Iceland.* Caricature by Edward Burne-Jones: 'Morris has come back from Iceland more enslaved with passion for ice and snow and raw fish than ever.'

In fact Morris's second journal starts routinely, almost dully, lacking the edge of strangeness, the stimulus of new sights and new events, as he travels the old routes from Thingvellir into *Njál* country. Even Morris has to push himself to sharpen his responses as, for example, when he reaches Gunnar's Howe again: 'all looked somewhat drearier than before, two years ago on a bright evening, and it was not till I got back from the howe and wandered by myself about the said site of Gunnar's hall and looked out thence over the great grey plain that I could answer to the echoes of the beautiful story – but then at all events I did not fail.'

It is only when they venture into totally new territory northwards by the Vatna glacier, and into the black sand desert, that the journal descriptions again get into their stride and Morris conveys his sheer exhilaration at sun shining on the black cones and pyramids of mountains and the long line of the glacier, interrupted so bizarrely with willowy green pastures and occasional small steads. There are ragged sheep on wasteland. 'The raven flies about here making noises like winding up a big clock.'

In terms of drama, loneliness, entering a mythic landscape, Morris's traversing of the black sands at Fljótsdalur on this second Iceland journey is the equivalent of his crossing of the freezing mountain pass of Kaldidalur two years before. It was now early in August. They had left their camp early, passing two little brooks on their way to the dark desert: over one hovered a few terns looking for worms; over the other Morris noticed a solitary stone-bunting. This was the last living thing, except Faulkner, the two guides and their horses, that he was to see for many hours.

As he described the sand: 'It is not a flat but is in great waves.' It was not so much a desert as a sandy sea shuddering, unstable, variable in its texture:

Sometimes it is little pebbles, looking before your horse's feet sink into the sand, as if the whole place were neatly paved, and most strange it is to go over this and see no track till your horse makes one, and most strange when you are travelling in the shadow of a cloud to watch the sunlight brightening some wave of this into such a wan ghastly colour, for the colour else is not very dark grey.

The riders would sometimes be brought up against big stones and rocks strewn across the pebbly sand. Sometimes they met whole barricades of boulders and great mounds of shaly flagstones. It was the country of ultimate testing, a deathscape drawn by Dürer. Jón the saddle-smith said

333

that there were outlaws still hiding in this wilderness. Charley and Haldor laughed at him, but Morris was convinced.

By the end of his travels Morris was exhausted, depressed and very homesick. The going was harder than the previous year's journey. Some days Morris records as much as nine hours' riding. His journal peters out into disjointed notes: 'So to Einarsstaðir – man with coffin lid: up hill thence, very steep, by turf beacons. Think it wrong – a long way across heath (day cold and grey, getting worse and mistier).' This time there is no sense of Georgie waiting to read it: Morris is on the verge of total incoherency. This journey into Iceland had almost been too much for him. Morris was only two years older, but, apart from his poor physical condition, in the intervening period he had suffered enormous emotional strain. So why did he do it? Why does anybody do it, push themselves not once but twice to their limits of endurance? The answer can be found in his entry for the morning of 9 August, 'a most lovely morning', when they left the camp at Haldórsstaðir and Morris experienced a twinge of clarity, almost a vision: 'there was something eminently touching about the valley and its nearness to the waste that gave me that momentary insight into what the whole thing means that blesses us sometimes and is gone again.'

Iceland, once again, gave him what he had hoped for, as he told Aglaia after he returned: 'surely I have gained a great deal and it was no idle whim that drew me there, but a true instinct for what I needed.' He had come back restored. The journey had deepened his initial impression of Iceland and increased his love for it: 'the glorious simplicity of the terrible and tragic, but beautiful land with its well remembered stories of brave men, killed all querulous feeling in me, and have made all the dear faces of wife and children, and love, and friends dearer than ever to me.' He felt almost certain he would not see Iceland again, and this time he was right.

Who – or what – is the 'love' he refers to in his letter? Did he intend Aglaia to construe it as herself? Morris's letters of this period radiate affection for and indeed to some extent dependence on Aglaia. In one letter he imagines her standing in his garden, like one of his desired ladies from *The Earthly Paradise*. But within the next few years some of the lessons learned in Iceland elevated Morris into realms of moral purity in which the pleasures of flirtation and flattering blandishments gradually fell away.

*

Rossetti had stayed on and on at Kelmscott, through the winter of 1872–73 and into the next year, getting gradually fatter, feeling better than in London, importing friends and models and several yapping dogs. Even his mother came to stay at Kelmscott. Rossetti was painting Janey as Proserpine, resentful goddess with the pomegranate, abducted by Pluto to be the Queen of Hades and released to the light for only half the year. This image of Janey became his addiction, and he painted eight versions between 1871 and 1877.

Over the years of Rossetti's occupation, Morris was himself at Kelmscott only rarely, for a few days at a time. Theodore Watts-Dunton, coinciding with him, found him defensive, very edgy. He could not bear the feeling of being the visitor in the house in which he had invested his emotional rights, and in the spring of 1874 he put his foot down with an assertiveness one senses he would not have found possible in his pre-Iceland days. Perhaps an element in this decisiveness was his worry at the effect of life at Kelmscott on his daughters, now no longer 'the littles' in reality but girls verging on their teens. The company was very mixed. Rossetti mentions a housemaid of advanced ideas who was imported from London to pose for a nude siren. May herself gives an account of wild games of hide-and-seek all over the house, 'romping and skirmishing in the garrets', with some visitors including 'a light hearted model who lacked excitement'. Janey at the time was absent. Morris was aware of a lack of parental supervision whilst Janey was at Kelmscott and he was left in London. In one letter he complains he has not seen his daughters for a month.

On 16 April he at last wrote to Rossetti in anger and hurt, enclosing the rent for that quarter but demanding that Rossetti now allow him to cancel the agreement. 'As to the future though I will ask you to look upon me as off my share, and not to look upon me as shabby for that, since you have fairly taken to living at Kelmscott, which I suppose neither of us thought the other would do when we first began the joint possession of the house; for the rest I am both too poor and, by compulsion of poverty, too busy to be able to use it much in any case, and am very glad if you find it useful and pleasant to you.' It was the official end of brotherhood, and there is a certain hysteria in his tone.

Rossetti made a move to take over the lease on his own account but he did not finalize it, and in the end it was Morris who renewed the lease, in joint tenancy with F. S. Ellis, his publisher and fellow fisherman. That spring of 1874 was the last that Rossetti and Janey were together at Kelmscott. Rossetti left finally in July of that year.

In that same month Morris gathered up his family and took them off to Belgium. Not just Janey and his daughters, Jenny now being thirteen and May twelve, but also the two Burne-Jones children: Philip, who was Jenny's age, and Margaret, who was five years younger, then just eight. Janey was, fortunately, in reasonable health. It was Morris who seems to have found the journey arduous, shepherding the party of children on to the cross-Channel steamer and then travelling from Calais to Bruges, first by train and then by omnibus, in heat so blazing it was like being in a Turkish bath. He was glad to be back in Bruges, his honeymoon city. But he complained of lack of time and space for musing, although the children, enchanted by their first taste of foreign travel, were well behaved and apparently attentive to Morris's expert lectures. May commented later: 'It would take a very crabbed grown-up or a particularly lumpish child not to be warmed and stimulated by my father's eager vision of the city of many memories.' She noticed her father look across at her mother, smile at her and say it was worth anything to see the children enjoying themselves so much.

Whenever Morris travels he is eager to communicate. On this short holiday he writes back to his mother and he writes to Aglaia, describing the landscape he has travelled through: the ripening wheat and oats, and the rye that the farm labourers were cutting along the road that leads from Ghent to Bruges. But it is noticeable that, post-Iceland, a new perspective, a new emphasis, is entering his letters. He travels with intensified social awareness, with the eye of a Cobbett or an early E. P. Thompson: 'the country people I thought looked very poor'.

Naworth Castle is a russet-pink crenellated building in wild country in Cumberland, just north of Carlisle. This is a defensive stronghold, built in the reign of Edward III and rising massively from the dark woodland around it, protected by steep falls on three sides. It is a Walter Scott castle in Walter Scott country, a few miles from the ruins of Lanercost Priory. Beyond is the looming bulk of Hadrian's Wall. Naworth has two towers. These are not uniform: one is square; one is more eccentrically turreted. You enter through a gate house. The inner courtyard has the sweetness of containment Morris longed for in a building, redolent of the monastic as well as the military, with a jumble of multi-level steps

336

and doorways set around the marvellous green sward. The Great Hall is the most spectacular in the North. There is a vast segmental fireplace and a retinue of mediaeval oaken beasts with painted banners. When Morris, later on, supplied the long carpet for the Library, he complained he was 'puffing and blowing over it rather'. At thirty feet by fifteen feet, this was then the largest carpet he had ever made.

Morris and Ned were at Naworth in late summer 1873, staying with the Howards. It is easy to see why Morris felt so happy in this intensely mediaeval setting, telling Aglaia that the environment was 'certainly one of the most poetical in England'. He and Ned were lodged in Lord William Howard's Tower, the bulkier of the two towers. Lord William, George's ancestor who converted to Catholicism in 1584, was the original of Walter Scott's 'Belted Will'. Architecturally, this tower is Naworth's real claim to fame. The first floor has timberwork without parallel in England: huge broad ribs, square in section, set across diagonally. On the second floor there is another giant fireplace; and on the third a resplendent fourteenth-century timber ceiling with ornately moulded bosses and beams. Morris wrote euphorically that he and Ned spent their mornings 'in a most delightful room in one of the towers that has never been touched since William Howard of Queen Elizabeth's time lived there'. He was ignoring – or forgiving – the restorations carried out at Naworth by Anthony Salvin after the great fire of 1844.

The Howards were the only people at this period to penetrate what had for years been the closed circle of friendship of the second generation of Pre-Raphaelites and the survivors of Morris's Oxford Set. It was a world in which friendships elided into commerce, and the Howards were also amongst the most financially important, discriminating and at times demanding clients of the Firm. George Howard, who became 9th Earl of Carlisle in 1889, succeeding to Castle Howard, was Liberal MP for East Cumberland twice in the early 1880s. Morris supported his Liberal campaign. George Howard was an amateur painter of some quality, disciple of the Italian landscape painter Giovanni Costa. There is a self-portrait at Castle Howard of Costa *en plein air* at his easel painting the country around Naworth in 1882. Howard spent many months each year, winter after winter, in hotels, pensiones and rented rooms in Italy working very slowly at his careful and romantic views of the Campagna. He was the mainstay, with Frederic Leighton, of the group of English Italianate painters, the so-called Etruscan School which included Matthew Ridley Corbet, George Heming Mason, Henry

337

Holiday, William Blake Richmond and Walter Crane. George Howard was a civilized, charming, enigmatic aristocrat, not unlike his grandson, and namesake, chairman of the BBC in the 1980s. His range of manner varied, as Sidney Colvin noted, from 'the most captivatingly cordial and urbane to the cynically sceptical and ironic'. His passion for all things Italian had modified his hereditary features to such an extent that he himself looked quite Italian. Colvin would say to himself, driving through some market town in Italy, 'My, here is a whole population of George Howards.'

George's wife was even more remarkable. Rosalind came from the intellectual, original, fearsomely quarrelsome Liberal aristocracy, the family that also nurtured Bertrand Russell. Her father, the second Lord Stanley of Alderley, had held appointments in Whig ministries and was known as Sir Benjamin Backbite because of his vicious tongue. Rosalind had inherited purposefulness and vehemence. Her conversation was 'like a flow of lava', which must have made Morris feel nostalgic for Iceland. She was deeply affected by reading J. S. Mill's *The Subjection of Women* (1869) and while still in her middle twenties she confided to her diary her 'desire to be in the place of the great men of all ages who have done much for the world'. She was to become active in women's suffrage and in the temperance movement; the story of how, on moving into Castle Howard when George inherited the earldom, she tipped 1,500 bottles of claret down the drains is almost certainly apocryphal. But it is a measure of her wilfulness that it was widely believed.

The Howards had entered the charmed circle as the friends of Ned and Georgie, in the middle 1860s. They had given help and sympathy to both afflicted partners through the Mary Zambaco affair. Both Ned and Georgie were naturally reticent but each separately found Rosalind easy to confide in. Indeed from both of them she demanded utmost truth, understanding more than anyone the depths of Georgie's fortitude in the face of such great hurt and, at one stage, turning on Ned in anger, reducing him to tears, explanations, repentances and tenderness, in the course of an hour-long scene.

Over the next few years she was also kind to Janey, removing the children to Naworth in her illnesses. She was interested by the Morris children, finding them remarkably clever though shockingly materialist: May, at the age of eight, was apt to assert confidently that the soul was only 'the imaginary part of the body' and that after death there was nothing left but bones. She found it surprising how the girls had been brought up without theology. Janey was touched and grateful at her patronage, but daunted. Rosalind's 'bright presence' and the natural rapport between Rosalind and Georgie, two such strong-minded and articulate young women, tended to make her feel a burden, an outsider, socially and intellectually inadequate.

Rosalind and Morris had approached each other gingerly. He had first arrived at Naworth in summer 1870, at the time of Jenny and May's visit, bearing 'such a diminutive carpet bag'. Rosalind wrote a few hours after his arrival: 'he was rather shy – and so was I – I felt that he was taking an experimental plunge amongst "barbarians", and I was not sure what would be the resulting opinion in his mind.' After a walk in the glen Morris gradually grew more amenable: 'He talks so clearly and seems to think so clearly that what seems paradox in Webb's mouth, in his seems convincing sense. He lacks sympathy and humanity tho' – and this is a fearful lack to me – only his character is so fine and massive that one must admire. He is agreeable also and does not snub me – This I imagine may be attributed to Georgy having said some things in my favour – Not that I think he will like me – but if he puts up with me we shall jog along right.' In fact she was wrong in this. Morris very soon came to like and respect her, joining Ned in a chorus of approval: 'yesterday morning Morris praised her so loudly in my studio that he shook my canvas and made me draw waggly lines.'

This second Naworth visit was planned as a placid one. Ned had been suffering all summer from terrible nervous tensions and sleeplessness: Georgie had sent on her instructions that in Cumberland he was to be treated as a recuperating invalid. No perilous excursions: he was simply to be allowed to wander around and 'breathe in fresh strength from the sweet air'. He and Morris lounged around and took a drive along the border. Morris 'sniffed the smell of the moor and felt in Iceland again'.

The only other visitor was Richard Watson Dixon, now a minor canon of Carlisle Cathedral and shabbier than ever. He was still writing poetry, with little recognition, and was planning his ambitious *History of the Church of England from the Abolition of the Roman Jurisdiction* (1878–1902). He had already asked Morris to intercede for him with George Howard for a vacant living, saying sadly that he had been nearly sixteen years in Holy Orders and had never received more than £150 a year. He was appointed to the curacy of Hayton, near Naworth, the year after his visit to 'the abode of splendour', as he called the castle. He had not seen Morris and Ned for many years and was shocked by Ned's condition, finding him much muted. 'Topsy genial, gentle, delightful', he reported in a letter to their old Oxford friend Crom Price.

The idea of Top as genial, delightful and eternal was the image his friends clung to. But Morris at forty, after coming home from Iceland, chastened by experience, was in fact much changed. It was Rosalind who had seen so quickly, and had been perturbed by, Morris's element of ruthlessness, his ability to overturn expectations, to detach himself if necessary from old patterns of behaviour and even from loved people.

29 *William Morris and Rosalind Howard.* Drawing by George Howard in a sketchbook now at Wightwick Manor.

She recognized it because it was an ability she herself possessed. And it was to Rosalind, soon after he returned to London, that Morris confided, in self-castigation: 'do you know when I see a poor devil drunk and brutal I always feel, quite apart from my aesthetical perceptions, a sort of shame as if I myself had some hand in it.' Previously he had looked at social problems anxiously but with a relative detachment. Now he was moving towards a virtual identification with the poor.

Morris as a designer is so endlessly intriguing because he is not quite the progressive that we once thought him and nor is he the out-and-out historicist, although he feeds on the past for his techniques and in his reworkings of traditional pattern. There is always the interplay of ancient and original, especially obvious in the surge of textile patterns of the later 1870s. The modern critic Peter Fuller correctly defined him as the radical aesthetic conservative at work.

There is the same strange tension in Morris's persona in the middle 1870s, as middle age approaches. There are episodes in which he is still hugging his past to him, confirming its importance. In 1875 we find him taking his MA degree at Oxford, belatedly: this, he tells his mother, is 'perhaps rather a "fad"' of his. He writes back enthusiastically when approached about providing a stained-glass window for the chapel at Marlborough College. He sets off again with Faulkner, on a voyage to Wales, his 'Fatherland', trekking up the Dyfi valley where, in a wistful mood, he thinks he could live simply with a little house and cow 'and a Welsh poney or two'. He behaves in an exemplary manner to his mother, now living at The Lordship at Much Hadham in Hertfordshire. At one of her ceremonial harvest parties May remembered him standing in an orchard piled with mellow, scented apples, his stick in his hand (Morris was already becoming gouty), and his now elderly mother on his other arm.

But while Morris was consolidating he was also shedding. The process which began with the eviction of Rossetti from Kelmscott Manor continued with his determination to reconstitute Morris, Marshall, Faulkner & Co., disposing of the partners and taking the Firm under his own control. The negotiations, which were under way in early 1874, were bitter and protracted. Morris was conscious that right from the beginning of the Firm's operations he had been the driving force. Now more than ever, as the other partners had drifted away into their own main occupations – Rossetti and Brown and Burne-Jones to painting, Webb into architecture, Marshall into sanitary engineering, Faulkner back to academic life – the viability of the Firm depended on Morris. As he told Aglaia: 'I should very much like to make the business quite a success, and it can't be unless I work at it myself.'

He was endlessly short of money. A reply he sent in 1873 to Eiríkr Magnússon, something of a scrounger, explains his situation:

I will do my best to get the money £70 together in about a week's time: if this seems a cold answer, I must ask you to understand that though I seem comfortably off I am always rather lacking of *cash*: my only important resources being what I can get from the Firm here, which has so many irons in the fire that its banker's book often looks very thin.

On top of his £200 per annum Morris was now paid a bonus of ten per cent of net annual profits. But in 1868, for example, the net profit had only been about £300 on a turnover of £2,000. In any case Morris was now feeling that ten per cent of profits did not repay the effort that he put into the company or provide him with the incentive on which the future expansion of the business depended. He could no longer rely on subsidizing his design work with his income from Devon Great Consols, where the decline in profits was accelerating: when, in 1874, Morris began to dispose of his interest in the company, he received only £80 from the sale of eighty shares. The Firm was now virtually his only source of income. He was anxious to move the business on in new directions which, at that time, he saw as producing more designs for wallpapers, chintzes and carpets and finding outside manufacturers to produce them. In his proposals for reorganization he resorts to good capitalist arguments, put forward without irony. In his new mood, Morris felt he had been put upon. He saw it as the time to claim his due.

The counter-argument was advanced by Brown, Rossetti and Marshall who asked Theodore Watts-Dunton, then still Theodore Watts, the solicitor, to act for them. They claimed that since all the partners had invested in the Firm equally, and had since then been paid pro rata for work done at the agreed rate, they now had an equal claim on the Firm's assets. At the start all of them had been the risk-takers and, in the early days especially, the Firm had been dependent on Brown's experience and Rossetti's many contacts. Now, when the Firm at last seemed to be moving into profit, they were to be excluded. It seemed to them unjust.

The arguments dragged on. Brown was especially vitriolic towards Morris. It took years before they reached a semi-reconciliation. In March 1875 Morris finally agreed to pay £1,000 of compensation each to Rossetti, Brown and Marshall. Burne-Jones and Faulkner waived their claim to payment. Webb too disclaimed his payment and went further by forgoing arrears of salary totalling £640. On 31 March, an announcement was made that Morris, Marshall, Faulkner & Co. was formally

30 *'Rupes Topseia'*. Dante Gabriel Rossetti's caricature drawn at the time of the
reconstruction of the Firm. The original partners, *top left*, hold a scroll reading, 'We Are
Starving'. Janey, Karl Marx and Friedrich Engels watch Morris's descent to hell.

dissolved and the business would continue under Morris's sole owner-ship, trading as Morris & Co. One bizarre side issue was that Rossetti requested that his compensation should be settled upon Janey. Morris replied: 'My dear Gabriel, Thanks for letter. I have no objection to make, but we must settle how the thing can be done, as the money must be vested in trustees.' Rossetti later took a macabre revenge, with another of his cruel dramas based on real people. His playlet, *The Death of Topsy*, has Morris finally disposed of at the hand of his manager George Wardle's wife. Mrs Wardle was the former Madeleine Smith, whose trial in Edinburgh for the poisoning of her lover had been the court sensation of 1857, ending in a verdict of 'not proven'. Her sub-sequent married life seemed to be blameless, but for those who knew her history a few small doubts remained. Rossetti's play bore the ominous subtitle, *A Drama of the Future in One Unjustifiable Act*. He posted the manuscript, in an envelope sealed with his monogram, to Janey at Horrington House.

The dramatis personae are: William Topsy Morris (an upholsterer and author of *The Earthly Paradise*), Wardle (his Manager), Mrs Madeline (*sic*) Wardle, First Young Wardle, Second Young Wardle, Third Young Wardle, A Grocer, A Pharmaceutical Chemist, First Cabman, Second Cabman, Edward Burne-Jones (a Man of Genius), Stennett (a carpenter and undertaker), Ford Madox Brown (a Historical Painter), Emma (his wife), Mrs Guppy (a Medium), The Ghost of Warington Taylor, The Ghost of Topsy, The Ghost of Percy Bysshe Shelley.

Scene – London
SCENE I

On one side an Upholsterer's shop, with the name 'Morris and Co.' over the door. On the other side a Grocer's shop. Enter First Young Wardle, carrying a roll of parchment: he goes into the Upholsterer's shop.

1ST Y.W. Papa, I've fetched the deed of partnership which Mr Morris sent to be copied.

WARDLE (*from within*). Give it here, my boy.

Enter Second Young Wardle: he goes into the Grocer's shop.

2ND Y.W. If you please, my Mamma wants a pound of your best coffee.

GROCER (*from within*). Yes, Sir.

Scene closes as Third Young Wardle is seen going towards a Chemist's shop in the distance.

344

SCENE II
(St. James's Hall)

Topsy is discovered lecturing in Architectural Restoration.

TOP (*reads*). 'Our forefathers had thus reared for us, with superhuman labour, temples worthy of Christian worship – nay, almost worthy in themselves of some portion of the homage which the worshippers' – (*Aside through his teeth*, – 'I can't have written rot like this' – *turns the page to skip, but finding he cannot, goes on*) – 'which the worshippers bestowed on that Power which alone could have inspired such mighty achievements.' (*Aside, as before*) 'I know that damned Ned has stuck it in!' – (*goes on*) – 'Little could those great yet humble ones have dreamed that a too puffed-up posterity' – (*Scratches the seat of his trousers, and looks uneasily at the curtain behind him*) – 'would have devoted all their efforts only to the defacement of the noble structures bequeathed to their keeping by godlike minds and hands.' (*Aside through the curtains*) – 'I say, Ned, damn you.'

E. BURNE-JONES (*from behind curtain*). I didn't do it, Top – you wrote it yourself. It's very bad, but go on or the audience will hiss.
(*Topsy goes on, lurching a great deal, and at last concludes amid great applause: he bows and goes behind curtain.*)

TOP. I say, Ned, mustn't they just be fools! I'll pay you out another time, I must get down to the Wardles, as I said I'd take tea there.

E. BURNE-JONES. They always take coffee.

TOP. O do they? will you come?

E. BURNE-JONES. No thank you. I say, Top, one of the workmen has chalked a large T on your back.

TOP. Well, damn you, why don't you rub it out?
(*They have now reached the door, and E. Burne-Jones bolts down the street.*)

SCENE III

A Private Apartment. Wardle and Madeline seated at a table, with cups and saucers etc.

MADELINE. Is the deed signed?

WARDLE. Yes
(*A crash without. Enter* TOPSY.)

TOP. I say, I'm very sorry, but I was laying down my hat on a chair outside, and somehow my hand went through it.

MADELINE. I pray don't mention it, Mr. Morris, it's of no consequence.

TOP (*to Wardle*). I say, old chap, Ned told me just now that someone had chalked a T on my back. (*Tries to see it*) Do you see it?

WARDLE. No, of course.

TOP. Blow that Ned! (*Aside through his teeth*) I should like to tread his guts out.

WARDLE. He hasn't got any.

TOP. O I say, talk about guts – what's become of mine? (*He stands up, and taking a quartern loaf from the table, stuffs it into the waistband of his trousers to show how much room there is, – then pulls it out again and puts it back on the plate.*)

There, now you mind you don't call me fat any more.

WARDLE. I never did, – I always thought you a fine figure.

MADELINE. Mr. Morris, you're letting your coffee get cold. George dear, hand the cup.

TOP (*taking cup from Wardle*). All right old chap (*Drinks*). Hullo! how can I have the gripes now that I've got no belly? Hullo! Blow! (*dies*).

SCENE IV

(*Same as in Scene I*)

Wardle places a ladder against the Upholsterer's shop, and mounting it erases the name of Morris, substitutes Wardle & Co.

FIRST CABMAN (*passing*). Hi! Who's the Co.?

SECOND CABMAN (*passing*). Why, coffee, course.

(*Topsy is carried out on a stretcher, while Stennett is seen passing at the head of a funeral; he stops and gazes intently. Old Brown goes by on the top of an omnibus, and turning round, stares in stupefaction at the altered name over the door.*)

EMMA (*from within the omnibus*). Did you see that, Ford?

OLD B. Yes, Emma (*He raises his eyes and his hands to heaven*)

(*The ghost of Warington Taylor is heard tapping at a Medium's door.*)

SCENE V

(*The Medium's house*)

MRS. GUPPY *seated at a table of Victorian design, with ghosts and others. Enter the Ghost of Warington Taylor.*

GHOST OF TAYLOR. Topsy you fool, come along. Here's a chance for you. Spit on 'em through that table, & let 'em catch it as they deserve.

GHOST OF TOPSY. Get out, it's beastly rot. Do you think I'm going to believe in bogies merely because I'm one myself? And besides, you don't suppose, you idiot, that I'd talk through a blowed table of such a damned shape as that!

(*Indulges in language after his kind*).

MRS. GUPPY. That is the very lowest class of spirit of which I ever had experience. May not the essence of such misused humanity rank even below the soulless beasts that perish? – Who shall say? Well, he is gone my

346

friends, – I dread to think whither. (*She turns to the table*) Shelley, are you there?

GHOST OF PERCY BYSSHE SHELLEY:

> Hi diddle diddle
> The cat & the fiddle –

MRS. GUPPY. Hush – my friends, now indeed we shall hear something.
(*Curtain*)

The scene with Mrs Guppy, famous medium of the period, was an obvious barbed attack on the phlegmatic Morris. The occult was a bond between Janey and Rossetti who used to go to seances together. Janey had a definitely spiritualist tendency, giving vivid accounts of ghost activity at Kelmscott: mysterious carriages being driven to the house. But Morris had a dampening effect on any medium. Burne-Jones recalled: 'Once I went with Mr. Morris to a *séance* at a house where we dined first with the medium, which I always thought was a mistake.'

The disbanding of the Firm affected Morris more profoundly than he wanted to admit. It was another abandonment of brotherhood. His 'recalcitrant partners' had, he felt, behaved so badly that he was at one point tempted to throw the whole affair into the law courts. It was a saddening and disillusioning time. But Morris, though depressed, emerged from it defiant, even a bit triumphant at getting the top side of those who had for ages been teasing and tormenting him and sucking at his brains. The episode shows Morris as the avenger too, ousting Rossetti from his Firm if not his marriage. He wrote in May 1875, 'I have got my partnership business settled at last, and am sole lord and master now.'

In that same year, with a comparable decisiveness, he resigned his directorship of Devon Great Consols, having disposed of most of his shares. Edward Carpenter, the poet and free-thinker, feeling the call to Socialism, discarded his dress clothes. The Victorians were given to these symbolic dramas. On the day he resigned from his Consols directorship Morris deliberately sat down on his top hat.

CHAPTER ELEVEN

Leek

1875–78

Between summer 1875 and spring 1878 William Morris was frequently in Leek, a small industrial town in Staffordshire, a centre of the silk trade. He was there on an intensive course in techniques of textile dyeing, exploring new methods, resuscitating ancient ones, working up to his elbows in the dye vats, 'taking in dyeing at every pore'. Morris had already started his own experiments in vegetable dyeing in the Queen Square basement. He had now persuaded Thomas Wardle, a Leek manufacturer and brother-in-law of the Firm's manager George Wardle, to co-operate with him in large-scale experiments, using the dye vats at Wardle's Hencroft Works. He stayed in Leek at least five times over this period. Two were extended visits lasting two to three weeks. For Morris this was an instructive, even formative experience, for in Leek for the first time he was faced with the realities of things he had previously considered only in the abstract: industrial landscapes, commercial production, the pattern of loyalties within a small community, the man–master tradition, the innate conservatism of the British working class. In Leek he found great joys, his beaming pleasures of activity. But here Morris was also confirmed in his despondency, the sense of waste and sheer disgust that pours out in his later lectures and writings on production and art. The frustrations of Leek are always in the background. He wrote to Rosalind Howard: 'I have been learning several very interesting things here, and love art and manufactures, and hate commerce and moneymaking more than ever.' This was at the end of only his first week.

Leek in fact was a case history of a place transformed by industrial development. Until 1800 it had been a red-brick market town, isolated in the moorlands of Staffordshire. Button making was the main occupation. There were only about 4,000 people in the town. By the time Morris arrived Leek had become, with Macclesfield and Congleton, one of the three richest Midlands silk towns, with more than fifty mills. The population was edging up towards 12,000. Industry was spreading out from the centre of the town towards the River Churnet, running round the west perimeter. The particular purity and softness of the moorland water gave Leek one of the best waters for dyeing in Europe, on a par with St Etienne, Lyons or Basle. Wardle's Hencroft Works was one of several dye-houses established on the banks of the Churnet by the middle 1870s. Wardle set aside one of the two dye-shops at Hencroft for Morris's use. This was not the nightmare landscape of industrial degradation Morris had glimpsed from the train travelling northwards via Newcastle upon Tyne. Leek still had a feel of the domestic and the humdrum that made its creeping ruination more poignant. Morris, arriving with 'a woeful cold', wrote back to Janey, saying that the town itself was not nearly so bad as he expected and the surrounding country very beautiful indeed.

Morris lodged with the Wardles in their substantial house in St Edward's Street, a broad sloping road in the centre of the town, leading to the parish church of St Edward the Confessor, recently and drastically restored by G. E. Street. Thomas Wardle was the second generation of the family in Leek, where his father had moved from Macclesfield to set up his own dye works. The Wardle speciality was tussur, a wild silk imported from India. Thomas had been working obsessively on methods of dyeing tussur successfully and had made a breakthrough in the early 1870s. This made him in effect the tussur king. Thomas Wardle, three years older than Morris, was in many ways his parallel, in other ways his opposite: dedicated to developing his business but still finding time to write papers on local geology, collect carboniferous limestone fossils and pursue his interests in church music, composing chants for canticles and psalms for congregational singing. He was an earnest churchman, a paternalist employer: a pattern of the mid-Victorian manufacturing entrepreneur.

With typical caution he had married a distant cousin, Elizabeth, whose name was also Wardle. Over the years she bore fourteen children, nine of whom survived into adulthood. Morris refers in a letter to Wardle to '"the ruffians", to whom I offer my congratulations on their youth, their holidays and their capacity for noise'. When Elizabeth Wardle met Morris she was already a skilled needlewoman, with

349

energies as formidable as her husband's for local philanthropy and church committee work. Her portraits show a woman who had never been a 'stunner'. Mrs Wardle looks unimaginative, solid, amiable, bossy, with a leaning for frugality. In old age she compiled a booklet, 'Dinners arranged for Young Housekeepers', dedicated to her daughters, her daughters-in-law and her multitude of grandchildren, containing 366 recipes for inexpensive meals.

The ambience of St Edward's Street was new to Morris. The home life of the Wardles was more robust, more outgoing, than he had been used to in the lavish, enervated households of his youth. Compared with the bloom of Red House or the melancholy beauty of Kelmscott, middle-class life in Leek was provincial, predictable, lacking grace. This is Arnold Bennett country, with the small-town claustrophobia that suffuses Bennett's 'Five Towns' stories: Leek lies less than twenty miles from Stoke-on-Trent. In Leek, as in Stoke, the town was the industry. Many employers lived within sight and sound of their works and almost cheek by jowl with their own workers. The mill impinged upon such households as the Wardles', an almost unquestioned part of their everyday life. Morris, the newcomer, was more sharply conscious of the social dynamics of the town and the hierarchies of the workers in the silk trade, from the despised ranks of 'cleaners' (paid seven shillings and sixpence a week) to the progressively more skilled 'doublers' and 'spoolers', 'pickers' and then 'twisters', who could earn twenty-five shillings. Even after the second spate of Factory Acts of the early 1870s the hours of work were long. Morris, who worked frantically, saw no harm in long hours when work itself was pleasure. Nor did he argue that unpleasant tasks could ever be eliminated totally, though in theory he insisted such tasks should be shared out. What he saw as iniquity – and after Leek attacked with a new insight of experience – was a system of production that relied on human beings carrying out tasks that by their nature were repetitive and arduous, often for longer than fifty hours a week.

Morris wrote from Leek to Georgie: 'My days are crowded with work; not only telling unmoveable Lancashire what to do, but even working in sabots and blouse in the dye house myself – you know I like that.' The image of the poet ebullient in the dye vats is so charming that it very soon acquired the muzziness of legend. But it is worth asking what precisely Morris imagined he was doing at Hencroft Works in Leek. His plans for the expansion of the Firm were now involving a number of sub-contractors: Kidderminster carpets were being woven for him; the first silk fabrics and silk and cotton textiles were being produced; and Morris was already trying out potential block-printers of his designs for chintz. On the whole he was satisfied with standards of machine work. In fact, unlike later zealots such as Gandhi, William Morris had no practical objections to the use of machinery *per se* so long as machines produced the quality he needed. What most worried and depressed him was the general low standard of dyeing in the trade. He felt he could surmount this only by getting the techniques of dyeing under his own control.

Morris expected a great deal from his colours. He was learned about colour, as Thomas Wardle recognized: 'I never met a man who understood so much about colours.' Morris's knowledge was acquired from many years of study of colour in painting, in ancient textiles and historic examples of flat decorative pattern, both eastern and western, especially Italian. In his poem *Love Is Enough* the figure of Love appears as 'clad as a Maker of Pictured Cloths'. This is no accident: colour in Morris's writing is the symbol of desire, the root of sensuality, gratification, wholeness. In a sense colour *is* love.

With his deeply emotional feelings about colour he regarded with a bitter rage the relatively recent changes in the industry, as old methods of organic dyeing were abandoned in favour of new chemical dyes. These developments began in 1810 with the introduction of Prussian blue. By the 1870s textile factories in Britain were all using aniline dyes, derived from coal-tar: in Morris's eyes the connection with coal added insult to injury. Aniline dyes were anathema to Morris. He found their colours harsh, and without a sense of history. They looked particularly horrible in candlelight. The colours were precarious, liable to fade. His indignation spews out into his essay 'Of Dyeing as an Art' of 1893:

Of these dyes it must be enough to say that their discovery, while conferring the greatest honour on the abstract science of chemistry, and while doing great service to capitalists in their hunt after profits, has terribly injured the art of dyeing, and for the general public has nearly destroyed it as an art.

Morris, in the vats at Leek, was embarking on a conscious reversal of the tendencies of the last four decades, bringing organic processes back into the dye-house. He aimed to arrive at acceptable versions of the four essential colours for the dyer – red, yellow, blue and brown – by returning to traditional natural dyestuffs, using indigo for blue; walnut roots or shells for brown; weld yellow, the dye from the wild mignonette, for yellow; cochineal and kermes, both insect dyes, and madder, a vegetable dye, for red. Supplies of kermes were to prove a particular problem, eventually solved when Aglaia procured Morris a sample box of kermes from Greece which produced a resplendent deep vermilion, the red of fourteenth- and fifteenth-century tapestries. Morris made use of his connections with Charilaos Tricoupis, the ex-prime minister of Greece, to negotiate for supplies in bigger bulk.

Before leaving for Leek he had had two years of preparation, mastering the theory while he carried out his initial experiments at Queen Square. May wrote: 'The air at home was saturated with dyeing: bits of madder and indigo lay about, papers of the kermes insect brought home and its habits and customs explained; dye-stuffs of the home-country would be inquired.' Pliny's *Historia Naturalis* in Philemon Holland's seventeenth-century translation and Gerard's *Herball* were read out through the evenings to Morris's captive audience at home. The two girls were given their own sets of dyestuffs: broad-stoppered bottles 'filled with queer powders and lumps and grains'. But though Morris's researches were in their way so thorough the full force of the practical problems of dyeing did not strike him until he was faced with the large-scale copper pots full of (aniline) bright colours in the dye-houses at Leek.

In his experiments Thomas Wardle was Morris's confederate. He had his own commercial reasons for wanting a revival of specialist colours, besides having hopes for much new business from the Firm. He and Morris cross-examined old Leek workmen, dyers old enough to remember how they did things in the days before the synthetic dyes were introduced. Morris travelled to Paris with Wardle, in search of yet more ancient dyeing manuals. At the start of the enterprise they were friends together, boyish middle-aged buffers, enjoying the suspense of it. Dyeing like any craft has its element of risk and within the first few days Morris was writing to Aglaia, 'There are more difficulties in getting good colours and fast ones than you can easily imagine; but I hope to come to it soon.'

To Aglaia he sent the most vivid of his accounts of Leek activities. His letter dated March 1876 radiates the contentment of the overstretched:

This morning I assisted at the dyeing of 20 lbs. of silk (for our damask) in the blue vat; it was very exciting, as the thing is quite unused now, and we ran a good chance of spoiling the silk. There were four dyers and Mr. Wardle at work, and myself as dyers' mate: the men were encouraged with beer and to it they went, and pretty it was to see the silk coming green out of the vat and gradually turning blue: we succeeded very well as far as we can tell at present; the oldest of the workmen, an old fellow of seventy, remembers silk being dyed so, long ago. The vat, you must know, is a formidable-looking thing, 9 ft. deep and about 6 ft. square: and is sunk into the earth right up to the top. To-morrow I am going to Nottingham to see wool dyed blue in the woad vat, as it is called; on Friday Mr. Wardle is going to dye 80 lbs. more silk for us, and I am going to dye about 20 lbs. of wool in madder for my deep red.

You can feel Morris becoming obsessive with his dyeing, resenting the excursions that Wardle was arranging. Alton Towers is described as a 'gim-crack palace of Pugin's'. Lichfield is dismissed as 'such a dull town', in an equally dull landscape: Morris always despises what he sees as towns of lassitude. The only building he lights up for is the mediaeval Haddon Hall, the Derbyshire equivalent of Naworth, the austere romantic castle high above the winding river. He tells Jenny that Haddon is 'the most beautiful of the places about there'.

Blue has a special place in Morris's colour spectrum. In his poems and his novels it is the sign of happiness, of holidays. Blue was the colour of his working shirts. One of his ambitions at Leek was the recapture of a reliable indigo. He did not achieve this until he got to Merton Abbey. But all through the years at Leek Morris was a walking Jumbly, his hands dyed an Edward Lear-like blue. His friends in London, who responded to his bulletins from the dye vats with shouts of patronizing laughter, found the idea of his blueness irresistible. 'Mr. Morris is in roaring health,' wrote Georgie, 'and dined here the other day with two dark blue hands bearing witness that he has plunged into work again.' From this period date the many fables of Blue Topsy: Top seated next to Madame Cosima Wagner, on her visit to London, at a formal dinner party; Top turned away by the Faulkners' maid, who thinks he is the butcher when he rings the bell of their house in Queen Square. He was nervous of being forbidden admission to the theatre when he went with the Burne-Joneses to see Gilbert and Sullivan's *The Sorcerer*. Georgie confided in Rosalind her suspicion that Morris's hands were just the start of it: 'I am now prepared to see him blue altogether.' A blue movie Morris? He himself joined in the conspiracy of ridicule by signing his letters to Jenny 'Your old Proosian Blue'.

Textiles had become the latest of his saturation subjects, taking over from illuminated manuscripts as the focus of excitement. His hands were in any case not in a condition to allow him to continue with such fine and detailed work, and the vast *Aeneid* manuscript was not completed, breaking off towards the end of the great Sixth book, the book of the Styx, at the end of the 177th vellum page. Between his visits to Leek he was now occupied with checking the samples Wardle forwarded to London. He wrote to Aglaia from Queen Square: 'We have got a few pieces of printed cloths here, and they are hung up in the big room, where they look so beautiful (really) that I feel inclined to sit and stare at them all day.' Away from Leek he still worked concentratedly on dyeing, searching out supplies of the walnut husks he needed to achieve subtly shaded natural brown dyes. He discovered that the London leather workers were still using them. Even at Kelmscott, out on the river fishing, he was thinking about dyeing. He reported to Wardle: 'I shall make you laugh when I tell you that on Saturday I tried another dyeing material poplar – twigs to wit.' Morris cut himself a handful of poplar twigs and boiled them, and dyed a hank of wool 'a very good yellow'. He told Wardle, who was also a keen fisherman, that on the same day on the river he had hooked a five-pound pike using his *pater noster* line.

Over these three years of intense activity Wardle was his chief correspondent. Morris's letters to Wardle, informing, exulting, cajoling, exhorting, must be amongst the most remarkable business letters ever written. There are sixty of them, wonderfully lucid, very detailed, providing a running commentary on the Leek experiments and revealing Morris's developing awareness of the fundamental problems in reconciling the commercial demands for productive efficiency, delivery and profit with the artist-designer's quite different criteria of creative advances and the dream of technical perfection of the work. The Morris–Wardle correspondence gradually becomes a dialogue, with Wardle taking the father's role, experienced, pragmatic, Morris the wilful, brilliant, exasperating child.

1018 yellow marigold – a bad match, being much too dark: otherwise satisfactory colour not bad and seems well printed.
1019 tolerable match but rather duller and darker than pattern otherwise satisfactory

1112 Indian diaper Deep red and faint purple: I like the colour very much and we are sending a small order for it and would send a bigger, but the price makes it doubtful as a selling matter: it is very important that the red in it should be kept up to its present depth and be no browner.

1106 Flower de luce madder red. The colour is poor and seems to me to be starved; I have dyed it again in madder and soaped it, and I think either pattern would be good for this design.

There is page upon page of such precise demanding comment. Each time a consignment arrived at Queen Square Morris reported back to Wardle, in no uncertain terms. Sometimes Wardle balked at the expense and time involved in an amendment. Morris would then resort to explanations and entreaties. 'I am sure you understand that we want to get something *quite* different from the ordinary goods in the market: this is the very heart of our undertaking . . . don't be discouraged by anything I have said as I think we have done very well so far'. He defended himself for his insistence on high standards because this was in his nature: 'I mean that I can never be content with getting anything short of the best, and that I should always go on trying to improve our goods in all ways, and should consider anything that was only tolerable as a ladder to mount up to the next stage – that is, in fact, my life.' In his faith in human effort as the means to worldly progress, Morris was as much the mainstream middle-class Victorian as Thomas Wardle, or indeed as his own father. You can read his Wardle letters as artist versus industrialist, idealist versus pragmatist. They were also arguments between entrepreneurs.

Nervous agitation surfaced. Morris even lost his temper with Wardle's workmen in the dye-house, writing shamefacedly to Georgie: 'they have been very trying: but I wish I hadn't been such a fool: perhaps they will turn me out tomorrow or put me in the blue-vat.' The worst of his obloquy was directed at Wardle's head dyer, Kay, who high-handedly disregarded Morris's instructions, no doubt resenting the incursions into his own empire of the irascible poet from the south. Morris complained to Wardle: 'I don't suggest sacking him at once in the face of all the present orders, but we can't be forever under his hippopotamus thumb.' Morris's explanation for the problems was that Kay was a printer, experienced in using the natural red dye madder, who knew nothing about fixing dyestuffs with steam, whereas Hayworth, his fellow-worker in the dye-house, was a steam-colour printer who knew nothing about madder. Here at Hencroft Works, Morris first experienced what he came to see as one of the worst evils of contemporary industry, its compulsion to compartmentalize. The lessons learned at Leek were given eloquent expression in one of his earliest lectures, 'Making the Best of It', delivered to the Trades' Guild of Learning at Birmingham in 1879, in which Morris speaks out against 'division of labour': the rigid organization of the factory which keeps the operative virtually chained to a single repetitive task. In terms of human potential, Morris argues, ten hours a day spent turning out crank handles is a crime. The workman must take control of his activities:

He must be allowed to think of what he is doing, and to vary his work as the circumstances of it vary, and his own moods. He must be for ever stirring to make the piece he is at work on better than the last. He must refuse at anybody's bidding to turn out, I won't say a bad, but even an indifferent piece of work, whatever the public want, or think they want. He must have a voice, and a voice worth listening to, in the whole affair.

What did Morris gain from Leek? It was a background of experience that influenced his thinking over the next decade. Leek provided the model for the less than ideal factories that Morris castigates in his lectures and articles of the 1880s and 1890s: 'How we Live and How we Might Live', 'Useful Work *versus* Useless Toil', 'A Factory as It Might Be'. The Leek factories stood for the 'temples of over-crowding and adulteration and overwork, of unrest' to be replaced, in Morris's visionary landscape, by dignified buildings in beautiful gardens with dining-halls and libraries and schools and quiet studios rising around the workshops like the city of Heaven in a Burne-Jones stained-glass window. What he never truly tackles is how to prevent these imagined garden cities becoming, like Lichfield, towns of lassitude.

When Morris argues the need for space and air and a healthy environment for workers in a factory, his mind goes back to the congested, clanging 'weaving sheds of oversized cotton, hothouses for rheumatism'. When he proposes that the workers should involve themselves in landscaping the gardens, he remembers the large reservoirs of water in the textile-printing works and suggests these could be put to more imaginative use. Leek is used as Morris's yardstick. Leek has given his pronouncements their veracity and passion. He knows at first hand the squalor of the housing of the industrial north where the poor huddle beside the factories in houses that strike Morris as the proper size for dog kennels. (If Leek is Morris's yardstick, so is Walthamstow.) He has seen in dreadful detail the damage to landscape caused by uncontrolled

356

factory production: poisoned air, polluted water, squalid industrial waste. These realities disgust him: 'Why', he asks, 'must Yorkshire and Lancashire rivers run mere filth and dye?' Profit and competition. Greed, disdain and cynicism. Morris saw, and was ashamed.

In 1902 J. W. Mackail gave a talk in Leek on Morris. His attitude to Morris's Socialism was equivocal. But even he admitted that Leek had altered Morris. He called his lecture 'The Parting of the Ways'.

In spring 1876 Morris wrote to Aglaia, 'I am drawing patterns so fast that last night I dreamed I had to draw a sausage; somehow I had to eat it first, which made me anxious about my digestion: however I have just done quite a pretty pattern for printed work.' His close involvement with materials and processes had given Morris a new lease of creativity. In the ten years from 1875 to 1885 he produced at least thirty-two designs for printed fabrics, twenty-three for woven fabrics, twenty-one designs for wallpapers as well as patterns for carpets and rugs, embroideries and tapestries. Of these, the sixteen chintzes printed at Leek by Wardle are what most people consider the quintessential Morris. Where his earlier designs for block-printed cotton, printed by Clarkson's of Preston, had been relatively tentative these chintzes of the middle 1870s are wonderfully confident, *mouvementé*. The patterns almost literally flow.

Morris believed that 'rational growth', or at least the hint of it, was the basis of all successful patterns. His lecture 'Some Hints on Pattern Designing' (1881) traces the evolution of repeating patterns from classical times to the Gothic when a change took place in people's perception of pattern. In pattern designing Morris was a Gothicist, adhering to a structure in which every element 'grows visibly and necessarily from another'. His way of constructing patterns resembled his technique in the construction of a poem. He insisted on precision: 'Above all things, avoid vagueness.' In depicting natural growth, the draughtsmanship should not be flabby: the detail of flowers, fruit, foliage should be 'strong and crisp'. At the same time there should be a suggestion of perpetual motion, intimations of eternity: 'Even where a line ends it should look as if it had plenty of capacity for more growth if it so would.' It was this philosophy, the freeing of the pattern, that makes Morris look so different from most of his contemporary fabric designers. There is a relative deadness, formal stiffness, in the patterns of the school of Owen Jones. Morris's fluency had an obvious bearing on the sinuosities

357

of European art nouveau from the 1880s onwards. His influence was even more essential to the British pattern designers of a later generation: C. F. A. Voysey, Charles Rennie Mackintosh, Allan Walton, Edward Bawden, Lucienne Day. Such designers used familiar English plant forms carefully, creatively, working outwards from Morris's tradition, arriving somewhere new.

'Honeysuckle', 'Tulip', 'Marigold', 'Iris', 'Carnation': these William Morris chintzes of the middle 1870s are the patterns of the English spring and summer. They are patterns with an obvious connection to Kelmscott. Morris's surge of activity was as much inspired by his pleasure in his new way of life at Kelmscott as his technical achievements in the dye-houses at Leek. He can hardly write a letter from Kelmscott without filing a report on the condition of the garden, recording the birds and the flowers of the countryside. He writes to Janey to tell her 'the strawberry bed is a mass of blossoms; there are no roses out except the yellow ones on the gable wall of the barn; but a fortnight hence, it will be a wonder for the roses'. Morris's fabrics of this period somehow radiate enjoyment. Her husband had a rare ability to find enjoyment, Janey rather wistfully once said. The fact that he arrived at these exuberant and beautiful fabrics after such a period of despondency says much about the human spirit of recovery. Prodigal Mozart had the same secret. W. R. Lethaby, Morris's disciple, hints at this when he comments that Morris's patterns are not merely delights, 'they are depths'. Over the years they have acquired almost a sanctity. Ernest Gimson used to carry a piece of Morris fabric around with him on his travels, like a talisman. Morris used a tobacco pouch made up of his own chintz. He found in art and nature the sources of resilience. I think his patterns have lasted on right through another century because they still convey to us a little of that hope.

From the 1870s a pervasive vegetation appears in all the products of Morris & Co. In the early stained-glass windows, the floral decoration was confined within small panes; now it spreads into the centre, filling the main areas of glass from top to toe and edge to edge. The magnificent east window at Brampton, close to Naworth, has a jungle in the background: massed blue and bright red flowerheads with emerald green fronds. In Frankby in Cheshire, Adam and Eve are half-hidden by the bushy apple trees that screen their private parts.

In Morris's wallpapers too a new fluency appears in the middle 1870s. Morris drew a distinction between a pattern for a fabric, designed to hang in folds, and the design for a pattern to be used flat on a wall. His chintzes and his wallpapers are not often interchangeable, though later manufacturers have treated them that way. But the wallpapers designed in those Leek years have the same sense of ebullience, the 'natural growth' that curls and curves through Morris's fabrics: they are similarly frondy, both delicate and dense. The 'Larkspur' design and the 'Chrysanthemum' are typical. Blue larkspur, small pink blossoms and buff roses. The dusty pink chrysanthemums of English garden borders. Here again the Kelmscott memories are strong. Within each pattern there are vistas within vistas, a sense of infinite complexity and depth. For both wallpapers and chintzes Morris employs stippling, a technique like the spots in his illuminated manuscripts, which gives an almost three-dimensional effect. Thackeray Turner, the artist, remembered a scene in Morris's workroom when a fashionably dressed young man, finding Morris occupied with painting all the dots in, asked him why this was not a job that he could delegate. Morris answered, 'Do you think I am such a fool as to let another fool have the fun of doing the spotting when I have had the grind of doing the design?'

As Morris acquired technical control over his colours he could be more inventive. His marvellous designs, especially those for embroidery, exploit the potential of the new organic dyes. The 'Honeysuckle' pattern was originally designed as an embroidery for Janey whose own skills had continued to develop. May describes her mother as 'a past-Mistress in her art', which had the practical advantage that Janey could embroider while lying on her sofa. But it was another semi-invalid, Catherine Holiday, wife of Henry Holiday, the artist, who became Morris's favourite embroiderer, in effect his creative partner, from the middle 1870s. She was already technically expert, but Morris's new colours gave her new possibilities, as she explained years later to Mackail:

There was a peculiar beauty in his dyeing that no one else in modern times has ever attained to. He actually did create new colours then in his amethysts and golds and greens, they were different to anything I have ever seen; he used to get a marvellous play of colour into them. The amethyst had flushings of red; and his gold (one special sort), when spread out in the large rich hanks, looked like a sunset sky. When he got an unusually fine piece of colour he would send it off to me or keep it for me; when he ceased to dye with his own hands I soon felt the difference.

359

Morris was evidently anxious, probably with reason, that Janey would feel ousted. Enthusing, in a letter to May, about a new embroidery of Mrs Holiday's, he gives himself a warning: 'but I must take care, or I shall rouse jealousy'. This particular *tour de force* was yellow on light yellow with a border of green-blue.

Morris was by this time at the centre of the burgeoning Art Needlework movement. It is possible to view this as a retrograde movement, a means of keeping women captive with their needles, and indeed some of the larger-scale Morris and Burne-Jones embroideries, for instance the five-panel *'Romaunt of the Rose'* sequence for Sir Isaac Lowthian Bell's Rounton Grange in Yorkshire, kept the ladies of the household occupied for many years. But Morris was concerned with the releasing of creative instincts which would otherwise be dormant. In his determination to break the grip of mechanically worked canvas embroidery, introducing freer designs, more varied colours, he was indeed the prophet of the subversive stitch. He was among the first of the designers when the Royal School of Needlework was founded in 1872 'to restore ornamental needlework for secular places to the high place it once held among the decorative arts'. He and Ned jointly produced three figurative designs for the School: 'Poesia', 'Musica' and 'The Musicians'. Bessie Burden, who remained a spinster, became the Royal School of Needlework's chief technical instructor from 1880. Greatly to Morris's relief she had stayed in Bloomsbury when the Morris family had left Queen Square.

One of the most fascinating legacies of Morris's stay in Leek was the Leek School of Embroidery, which Mrs Wardle founded in 1879 and 1880. Morris had encouraged her interest in stitching, offering to design a rug for her woolwork, sending two exemplary pieces of Cretan embroidery for her textile museum. These, being the borders of women's petticoats, had been 'washed to death', he said. He encouraged Mrs Wardle to analyse the stitches. The colour of the greener of the samples pleased him very much. It is impossible not to see Morris's influence on Mrs Wardle's worthy project which, at its peak, involved thirty or forty local women, some amateur ladies, some paid professionals. The Leek embroideresses used Wardle's tussur silk dyed with his and Morris's organic dyes. The most tangible and moving reminder of this episode is the profusion of Morris-style embroidery in many local churches: altar frontals, vestments, sanctuary mats, banners, alms bags, kneelers, cushions, some superb in quality and still in use.

They opened the Labour Church in Leek in 1896, a few weeks after

Morris's death. It was a former Quaker meeting house, converted for the furtherance of Morris's ideas, providing 'simple feasts' and entertainment for poor children and a Labour Church Camp which took the tired town-workers out on summer holidays under the greenwood trees. The woodwork of the church was painted apple-green, the walls were stencilled with designs by Walter Crane and Larner Sugden, the Leek Socialist architect, on a rich red lacquer ground. This John Betjeman dream edifice was equipped with a blue silk velvet banner bearing the words of Shelley: 'Every Heart Contains Perfection's Germ'. On the speaker's desk rested an embroidered silk book-cover executed by a Leek Embroidery Society member who had carefully stitched in Kelmscott lettering the inscription 'The William Morris Labour Church'.

The move from Queen Square to Turnham Green had brought the Morris and Burne-Jones families closer. Now a routine evolved which continued almost uninterrupted for twenty years, until Morris's death. These were ritual Sunday mornings at The Grange. Morris arrived for breakfast, which he ate with Ned and Georgie. The breakfast was evidently a substantial one. Ned once offered Morris the treat of a fresh ham, saying he wouldn't like to call it pork. Two visiting American girls, in awe of the poet they had heard so much about, were startled to hear him reply, 'When I lust for pig's flesh, I don't care how it is called.' Having eaten, Morris closeted himself for the next few hours in the studio with Ned for work and talk and reading. Ned was never tired of being read to, and in 1875 he and Morris read Mommsen's entire *History of Rome*. Ned left a picture of a visit of this period:

Morris came over this morning according to custom and found me sleeping like many pigs – but we had a nice morning and he is in brilliant spirits and has just finished half the Virgil task. So he was very happy and talked very wisely – and deposed and set up and punished and rewarded and commanded and forbade like the Sultan of Babylon.

After abandoning his manuscript version of Virgil's *Aeneid* Morris had now embarked on a translation. He was working regularly: Sunday, 34 lines, Monday 138, Tuesday 20, Wednesday 34 ('and wrote out 4 pages'), Thursday 92, Friday 58, Saturday 112. According to one entry in his records he translated 488 lines in just one week, a credit to Marlborough classics, after all. Ned was filled with admiration at Morris's 'bright swift writing' and judged the translation 'simply divine'.

What possessed William Morris, in the midst of his myriad activities, to embark upon a task that would have taxed a professional classicist with time to spare? Sometimes even he seems to have diagnosed an overload, describing himself jokingly as being 'in the thick of poetry blue-vats and business', and confessing to Janey, 'I set myself too much work to do, that's a fact.' It was not as if there was a shortage of translations of *The Aeneid* at this period. In the 1860s at least three English verse translations had been published: Miller's, Conington's and Rose's. C. P. Cranch's had appeared in 1872. H. H. Pierce's rhythmic prose translation was published in 1879, four years after Morris's version. Even Mackail produced his own prose version in 1885. Nor was it as if Morris were especially well equipped to take on Virgil. As Mackail, in his biography, stuffily reminds us, he was not, in the proper sense of the word, a trained scholar; the degree he took at Oxford had only been a Pass. But Morris was debonair about the academic purists, claiming he translated Virgil as 'a poet not as a pedant'. His use of the title *The Aeneids of Vergil* rather than *The Aeneid* was a throwback to George Chapman, the sixteenth-century popular translator of Homer under the title of *The Iliads*. Morris hoped to show that Virgil had contemporary relevance, that Aeneas was a hero with whom his Victorian readers could identify. This was part of his newly demotic attitude to poetry. He was less concerned to claim *The Aeneid* as the supreme achievement of classical Latin as to reclaim it for the romantic mediaeval tradition: Dante up-to-date. He wanted to turn *The Aeneid* into a story everyone would read. There was an additional motivation. Morris never quite abandoned an old longing for the reflective life in the hidden depths of England. Translating Virgil was the archetypal occupation of the country parson he might almost have been.

For his translation Morris chose long ballad verse. This, said one of his reviewers, had the effect of setting the whole poem 'to a national and popular music'. Bernard Shaw referred, without enthusiasm, to Morris's 'long lolloping lines'. The poem opens:

> I sing of arms, I sing of him, who from the Trojan land
> Thrust forth by Fate, to Italy and that Lavinian strand
> First came: all tost about was he on earth and on the deep
> By heavenly night for Juno's wrath, that had no mind to sleep.

To a modern reader '*Arma virumque cano . . .*' and the rest seems a little flaccid. Morris has his moments, of which perhaps the best is the

description of Aeneas watching the shades on the shore of the Styx
begging Charon to ferry them across:

> Down thither rushed a mighty crowd, unto the flood-side borne;
> Mothers and men, and bodies there with all the life outworn
> Of great-souled heroes; many a man and never-wedded maid,
> And youths before their father's eyes upon the death-bale laid:
> As many as the leaves fall down in first of autumn cold;
> As many as the gathered fowl press on to field and fold,
> From off the weltering ocean flood, when the late year and chill
> Hath driven them across the sea the sunny lands to fill.
> There stood the first and prayed him hard to waft their bodies o'er,
> With hands stretched out for utter love of that far lying shore.

Morris is quite reliable. But Burne-Jones's drawing of emaciated people
stretching their arms upwards, prefigurements of newsreels of
twentieth-century refugee camps, makes the scene by the Styx much
more alarming and intense. In Morris's translation the sheer music of
that last famous line – 'tendebantque manus ripae ulterioris amore' – is
lost.

Out of this period comes one of those mystery letters Morris has
bequeathed us. It was written in Leek, apparently around March or
April 1876. It shows Morris in the flood of anxiety and sympathy:

Wherein you are spiritless, I wish with all my heart that I could help you or
amend it, for it is most true that it grieves me; but also, I must confess it, most
true that I am living my own life in spite of it, or in spite of anything grievous
that may happen in the world. Sometimes I wonder so much at all this, that I
wish even that I were once more in some trouble of my own, and think of myself
that I am really grown callous; but I am sure that though I have many hopes
and pleasures, or at least strong ones, and that though my life is dear to me, so
much as I seem to have to do, I would give them away, hopes and pleasures, one
by one or all together, and my life at last, for you, for my friendship, for my
honour, for the world. If it seems boasting I do not mean it: but rather that I
claim, so to say it, not to be separated from those that are heavy-hearted only
because I am well in health and full of pleasant work and eager about it, and not
oppressed by desires so as not to be able to take interest in it all. I wish I could
say something that would serve you, beyond what you know very well, that I
love you and long to help you: and indeed I entreat you (however trite the
words may be) to think that life is not empty nor made for nothing, and that the

parts of it fit one into another in some way; and that the world goes on, beautiful and strange and dreadful and worshipful.

It has been suggested the recipient was Georgie, or even Janey. I believe this is Morris in one of his rare moods of fraternal outpouring to the still unsettled Ned.

From mid-October 1875 Rossetti rented Aldwick Lodge, a villa at Bognor in Sussex, and settled himself in to await the arrival of Janey, his model for 'Astarte Syriaca', an important commission for which he had demanded part-payment in advance. The autumn was gloomy and ominous. Wild weather caused the house to shake. Cows wandered through the gardens eating the leaves from fallen boughs. The tide was higher than at any time in the previous eighteen years, and Dizzy, Rossetti's dog, who had never seen the sea, responded with hysteria: first 'violent and indignant' barking, followed by alarming spasms. He staggered on the sea edge, gulping down the water: 'his usual doggy smell has a twang of Tidman's Sea-Salt,' wrote Rossetti, bored with Bognor, and impatient. He forced himself out for walks along the sea-shore and filled several glass bell-jars with sea-anemones and 'wonders gathered from the deep'.

Janey finally arrived in late November. It had been arranged that she should take the train down from Victoria with George Hake, Rossetti's friend and minder, the young son of his doctor. Janey was herself in poor health and the 'Astarte' sittings, wrote Rossetti, proved 'arduous in her delicate state'. Morris had been alone at Kelmscott in November, grumbling poignantly that he was 'rather short of victuals', being left with only one pound of bacon and a tin of kangaroo meat. The gales that had caused havoc in Bognor also afflicted Kelmscott. Morris had enjoyed the battle with the elements out on the flooded river: 'The wind right in one's teeth and the eddies going like a Japanese tea-tray: I must say it was delightful: almost as good as Iceland on a small scale.'

Janey spent only a fortnight at Bognor with Rossetti, returning to London in December. She described the villa as 'dreary', no doubt made the more depressing by the presence of Rossetti's old furniture from Kelmscott. Perhaps she was glad to get away. Rossetti seemed to have given up hope of her reappearance to continue with the sittings and was making his own plans to come to London when, the following March, Janey arrived again, accompanied by May. Rossetti had not

1 Red House at Bexleyheath in Kent, designed by Philip Webb for Morris at the time of his marriage to Jane Burden. The weather vane on the tower bears the message 'WM 1859'. The house then stood in a rural setting of orchards, fields and copses.

11 Red House interior, showing the way the spaces flow from room to room. The tapered
newel-posts of the oak staircase thrust upwards towards the painted ceiling. Red House became
one of the most influential buildings of its period, inspiring both English Arts and Crafts
architects and twentieth-century international modernists. In 1904 the German critic
Hermann Muthesius described it as 'the first to be conceived and built as a unified whole,
inside and out, the very first example in the history of the modern house'.

Left: III The big door with its strap hinges is set in a deep porch, giving a sense of monumental welcome. His architectural surroundings established the young Morris in his persona of the genial host.

Below: IV The first-floor drawing room at Red House, photographed in the 1990s. Morris intended this to be 'the most beautiful room in the world'. The enormous settle was originally designed by Morris for his rooms in Red Lion Square. Philip Webb adapted it for Red House, adding a canopy to make a 'minstrels' gallery' with doors behind to give access to the roof space. The furniture is an integral part of the interior, as it was to be for Voysey, Mackintosh and Baillie Scott.

On the wall behind the settle, Burne-Jones painted a wedding banquet scene based on a romance by Froissart. The massive brick chimney-piece on the west wall is inscribed ARS LONGA VITA BREVIS.

v and vi Contrasting portraits of William Morris, both painted *c.* 1870. *Left:* oil on canvas by Charles Fairfax Murray. *Right:* oil on canvas by G. F. Watts, chief portraitist of the Victorian great and good.

vii The Green Dining Room at the South Kensington Museum (now the Victoria & Albert Museum), 1865–7. This public refreshment room was one of the first important commissions carried out by Morris, Marshall, Faulkner & Co.

VIII *La belle Iseult*, also known as *Queen Guenevere*, Morris's only extant easel painting, now
in the Tate Gallery. This portrait of Janey dates from his period of courtship at Oxford,
1858–9. There is a tradition that while working on the picture Morris scrawled the note 'I
cannot paint you but I love you'. He was always diffident about his abilities in painting or
drawing the human figure.

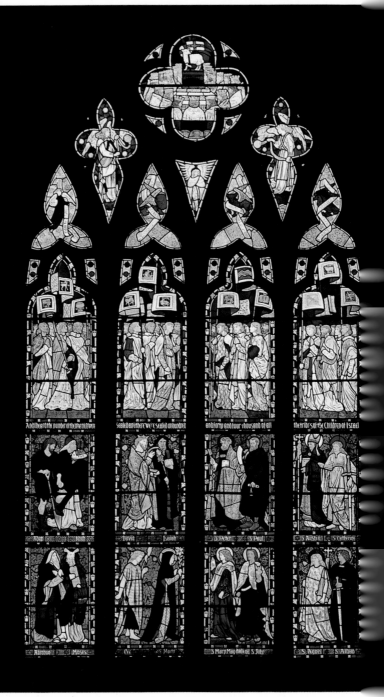

MAGNUS ARTURUS REX   DOMINUS L.UNCELOT DU LAC
POTENTISSIMUS ANGLIAE   EQUES INVICTUS

Left: ix The chancel east window at All Saints, Middleton Cheney, Northamptonshire, 1864–5. The early reputation of the Firm was established largely through its stained glass and church decoration at a time of religious revivalism when many old churches were being renovated and new churches being built.

This spectacular window shows the Firm's policy of artistic teamwork in action. The massed Saints and Martyrs in the topmost tier are probably the work of Simeon Solomon; other designs were provided by Ford Madox Brown and Edward Burne-Jones. *St Peter* (5th on second tier) is by Morris, an obvious self-portrait. He also designed *St Augustine* (7th) and *St Catherine* (8th). On bottom tier, *Eve and Mary Virgin* (3rd and 4th figures), *St Mary Magdalene* (5th), *St Agnes* (7th) and *St Alban* (8th) are all by Morris. The flower and fruit backgrounds, so like his wallpapers, are by Morris too.

Above: x *King Arthur and Sir Lancelot*, the thirteenth and last of the sequence of stained-glass panels made by Morris, Marshall, Faulkner & Co. to illustrate the story of Tristram and Isoud, as told in Malory's *Morte d'Arthur*. Though most of the Firm's stained glass was for churches, they received commissions for domestic stained glass too, and these panels were commissioned in 1862 by Walter Dunlop, a Bradford merchant, for the entrance hall of Harden Grange, near Bingley, Yorkshire. They were sold in 1916 to Bradford City Art Gallery for £100. Morris designed four of the Harden panels, which rework with great narrative clarity and gusto his favourite theme of the triangular love-drama. He here depicts himself as King, resplendent in a sunflower robe.

HAST thou longed through weary days
For the sight of one loved face,
Hast thou cried aloud for rest,
Mid the pain of sundering hours
Cried aloud for sleep and death
Since the sweet unhoped for best
Was a shadow and a breath —
O, long now, for no fear lowers
O'er these faint feet-kissing flowers
O, rest now; and yet in sleep
All thy longing shalt thou keep.

Thou shalt rest, and have no fear
Of a dull awaking near,
Of a life for ever blind,
Uncontent and waste and wide.
Thou shalt wake, and think it sweet
That thy love is near and kind
Sweeter still for lips to meet;
Sweetest, that thine heart doth hide
Longing all unsatisfied
With all longing's answering
Howsoever close ye cling

xi 'Love Fulfilled', a page of the small volume of Morris's own poems written out for
Georgiana Burne-Jones in 1870. Morris was by then immersed in the study of mediaeval
techniques of calligraphy and ornamentation of manuscripts and had evolved his characteristic
script, based on sixteenth-century Italian copy books.
This precious painted book dates from an emotionally problematic period in both their lives
when Morris and Georgie came close in mutual sympathy. J. W. Mackail, Morris's first
biographer, noted his propensity for 'laying himself open' in his writings, and there is plenty in
A Book of Verse for those inclined to read between the lines.

Odd of the Tongue, and others named

THE STORY OF HEN THORIR

Chap I: of men of Burgfirth

HERE was a man hight Odd, the son of Onund Broadbeard, the son of Wolf of Fitia, the son of Thorir Clatter; he dwelt at Broadbolstead in Reekdale of Burgfirth; his wife was Jorun, a wise woman and well skilled; four children had they, two sons of good conditions, and two daughters: one of their sons hight Thorod and the other Thorwald: Thurid was one daughter of Odd, and Jofrid the other. Odd was bynamed Odd of the Tongue; he was not held for a just man.

A man named Torfi the son of Valbrand the son of Valthief the son of Orlyg of Esjuberg had wedded Thurid, daughter of Odd of Tongue, and they dwelt at the other Broadbolstead.

At Northtongue dwelt a man named Arngrim the son of Helgi, the son of Hogni, who came out with Hromund

XII The first page of *The Story of Hen Thorir*, one of the collection of Icelandic stories written out and decorated by Morris, and given to Georgiana Burne-Jones in 1874. The manuscript, now in the Fitzwilliam Museum, Cambridge, shows Morris at a later stage of his progress towards the full-blown 'painted book'. The decoration is more exuberant than in the *Book of Verse*. The initial letter 'T' is enclosed in complex scroll-work, with its reminders of Renaissance illumination, and Morris is paying more attention to the structure and balance of the total page. This architectural approach was to be developed further in the printed books of the Kelmscott Press.

XIII Kelmscott Manor, viewed from the west. This substantial and endearing sixteenth- and seventeenth-century stone building in a remote Oxfordshire village was Morris's ideal of a dwelling. He had seen it in a dream before he discovered it in reality in 1871, entering into what proved to be an uneasy joint tenancy with Dante Gabriel Rossetti.
Morris never lived at Kelmscott permanently but returned there frequently for short visits and for holidays. The landscape around Kelmscott, with its grey stone villages and hidden churches, was a never-failing source of strength.

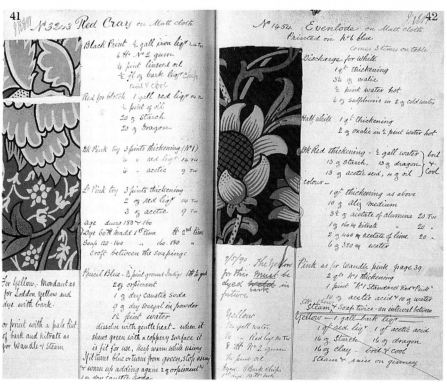

XIV *The Pond at Merton Abbey.* Lexdon Lewis Pocock's watercolour view across the Wandle
to the weaving, tapestry and fabric printing workshops. A less romantic picture is given by
contemporary photographs (see plates 78–84).

XV Pages from the dye book in use at Merton Abbey, 1882–91, giving Morris's precise
instructions for the 'Red Cray' and 'Evenlode' chintzes.

XVI *Prosperine*, the most splendidly sultry of Rossetti's many images of Janey Morris, now in the Tate Gallery. Rossetti identifies Janey with Proserpine, captured by Pluto to be queen of Hades, because of the circumstances of her marriage to Morris. He cast himself as her occasional deliverer into the realms of happiness and light. Between 1871 and 1877 he worked obsessively on eight different paintings of Janey as the goddess. In this, the most voluptuous, the incense-burner evokes her sacredness.

XVII Design for 'African Marigold' chintz, 1876. This design shows Morris's method in sketching out the pattern, then filling in the colour working outwards from the centre. His apparent spontaneity of pattern is arrived at with enormous technical exactitude.

XXIII 'Bird' woven wool double cloth, 1878. The woven fabrics Morris began to manufacture
in the later 1870s are obviously influenced by mediaeval and Renaissance textiles.
XXIV 'Artichoke' carpet, 1875–80. Detail of a design for a machine-produced Kidderminster
carpet, woven to Morris's specifications at Heckmondwike in Yorkshire.

xxv A corner of the Billiard Room at Wightwick Manor, Wolverhampton, showing the 'layered' effect of Morris wallpapers and textiles. The curtains are 'Bird' woven fabric, 1878 (see opposite); the seat is covered in 'Tulip and Rose' woven fabric, 1876; the carpet runner is Morris's 'Tulip and Lily' machine-woven Wilton, *c.* 1875; the wallpaper is 'Pimpernel', 1875.
xxvi 'Flower Garden', woven silk, and woven silk and wool. First produced in 1879.

XXVII 'Cabbage and Vine', or more correctly 'Vine and Acanthus', 1879. This was the first experimental tapestry Morris wove, installing a loom in his bedroom at Hammersmith.
XXVIII Morris began to design hand-knotted carpets and rugs in the later 1870s, hoping to provide a 'modern' English counterpart to the Eastern hand-made carpets he so much admired. This is an unusual almost abstract 'Hammersmith' rug of the late 1880s.

xxix *Woodpecker Tapestry*, *c.* 1885. Morris's most magnificent design for high-warp tapestry was made at the Merton Abbey works at the time of his most intense Socialist activity. The design incorporates familiar motifs: bird forms, honeysuckle, luscious summer fruit, swirling acanthus leaves. The inscription comes from Morris's own poem about Picus, the ancient Italian king who was transformed into a woodpecker. William Morris Gallery.

xxx *The Attainment: the Vision of the Holy Grail to Sir Galahad, Sir Bors and Sir Percival*, the sixth panel of Edward Burne-Jones's *San Graal* series, culmination of the long enthusiasm of the Morris circle for the Arthurian legend. The original version of the Grail tapestry was first woven at Merton Abbey between 1891 and 1894.

xxxi A detail from *The Pilgrim in the Garden*, or *The Heart of the Rose*, 1901. In the middle 1870s Burne-Jones designed a needlework frieze for Rounton Grange, based on Chaucer's *The Romaunt of the Rose*. This symbolist version was produced at Merton Abbey after William Morris's death.

xxxii *The Knights of the Round Table summoned to the Quest by a Strange Damsel*. The first of the *San Graal* panels, now in Birmingham City Art Gallery.

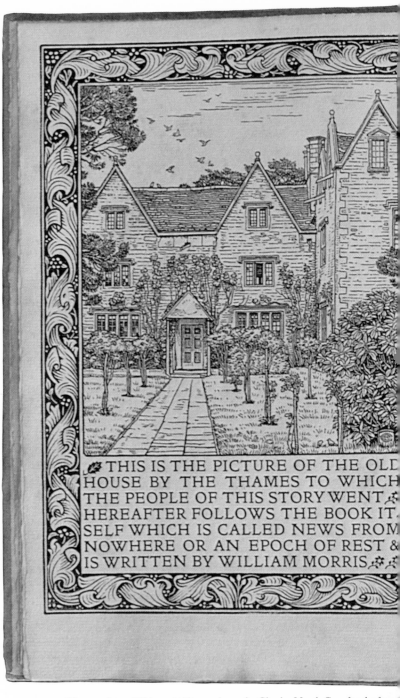

THIS IS THE PICTURE OF THE OLD
HOUSE BY THE THAMES TO WHICH
THE PEOPLE OF THIS STORY WENT.
HEREAFTER FOLLOWS THE BOOK IT-
SELF WHICH IS CALLED NEWS FROM
NOWHERE OR AN EPOCH OF REST &
IS WRITTEN BY WILLIAM MORRIS.

XXXIII *The east front of Kelmscott Manor*, drawn by Charles March Gere for the front
of the Kelmscott Press edition of *News from Nowhere*, 1892. The house becomes the
point in Morris's story, the haven at the end of the long journey, with its stone path le
through the garden where 'the roses were rolling over one another', the blackbirds '

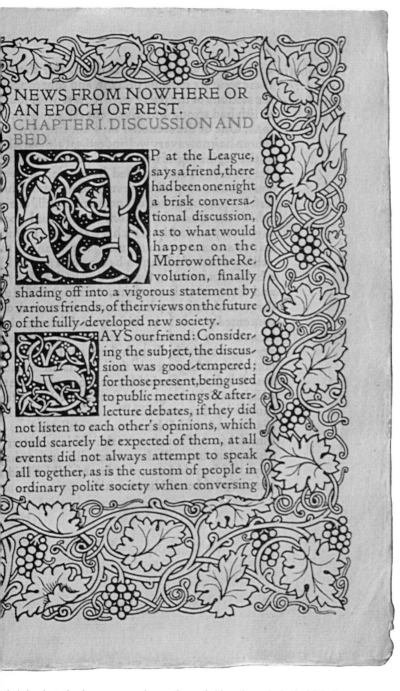

NEWS FROM NOWHERE OR AN EPOCH OF REST.

CHAPTER I. DISCUSSION AND BED.

UP at the League, says a friend, there had been one night a brisk conversational discussion, as to what would happen on the Morrow of the Revolution, finally shading off into a vigorous statement by various friends, of their views on the future of the fully-developed new society.

SAYS our friend: Considering the subject, the discussion was good-tempered; for those present, being used to public meetings & after-lecture debates, if they did not listen to each other's opinions, which could scarcely be expected of them, at all events did not always attempt to speak all together, as is the custom of people in ordinary polite society when conversing

their loudest, the doves were cooing on the roof-ridge, the rooks in the high elm-trees d were garrulous among the young leaves, and the swifts wheeled whining about the gables'. Morris designed the type, borders and ornaments.

xxxiv The white pigskin binding for the forty-eight 'special' copies of the Kelmscott *Chaucer*, designed by Morris in 1895. The pattern is a reworking of the binding by Ulrich Schreier of Salzburg (1478) in his own collection. The binding was done at Cobden-Sanderson's Doves Bindery. The first pigskin copy was delivered to Morris, then ill in Folkestone, by the binder Douglas Cockerell in 1896, a few months before his death.

been satisfied with his first version of the painting. Now, with May as the model for the Attendant Spirit, in the background to her mother posed as the Medici Venus, he began again. On 26 March he wrote to Dr Hake: 'Mrs. M. and her daughter have been staying here, and I have at last started the *Venus Astarte* picture to my satisfaction – the three heads are done and not ill done I hope.'

The 'Astarte Syriaca' is the most voluptuous of all Rossetti's portraits of Janey. It is an enormous picture, six feet high, and shows the goddess as a sexual power-figure, in an alluring and yet disdainful pose. Rossetti had considered a throne, but this was cancelled. He has painted Janey standing, decked in a robe of the shimmering deep green that was Rossetti's favourite colour and the colour of art and aspiration to honour as defined in Cesare Ripa's *Iconologia*, a Victorian artists' source-book Rossetti would have known. The giant goddess is bound around with jewelled girdles, strategically placed under the breast and on the hips. The decorative motif of the girdle is the pomegranate, symbol of passion and regenerated love. Rossetti's sonnet, written to accompany the picture, is unequivocal, verging on the lewd:

> Mystery: lo! betwixt the sun and moon
> Astarte of the Syrians: Venus Queen
> Ere Aphrodite was. In silver sheen
> Her twofold girdle clasps the infinite boon
> Of bliss whereof the heaven and earth commune.

In one of the most tantalizing entries in her memoirs, May refers briefly to that spring in Bognor where she and 'Mother' were 'staying with Mr. Rossetti'. May at this time was very nearly fourteen. She had always been Rossetti's favourite of the children: he found Jenny in comparison too serious and stolid. Rossetti had tended to prefer May as a model: 'not always', his brother William noticed, 'portraying her as being a child'. One would like to know much more precisely how those weeks at Aldwick Lodge affected May and how far they influenced the decision made by Janey, apparently at Bognor and on her own initiative, that the liaison with Rossetti must now end. When she gave her account to Wilfrid Blunt, sixteen years later, she said that she left Rossetti partly for the children's sake.

The other reason she gave was that at Bognor she discovered the extent of his dependence upon chloral. At Kelmscott he had evidently green baize. But Jenny and May thrived there. Up to now they had been rather solitary children, isolated in Turnham Green, regarded as eccentric, but they now formed a little clique of girls of their own age. Of the two Jenny was the more academic. She was the solemn child who kept her study books and dictionaries in what was referred to as her 'book box' under her heavy carved-oak dining-chair at home. A schoolfriend described Jenny as 'tall, stoutish, hefty', with brown hair in a bob, very like her father, with his hasty way of talking, 'as if she wanted to say her say and have done with it'. When asked in the classroom which of her father's poems she preferred, she paused for a moment before answering decisively that it was 'Sir Peter Harpdon's End'. At Notting Hill she soon became one of the prize pupils, commended by the inspectors for her prowess at Latin and English literature at the end of her first year. In the summer of Janey and May's return from Bognor, she passed her Cambridge Local examinations and was obviously destined for one of the early women's colleges at Oxford or Cambridge. She would surely have been taken on at Girton by Rossetti's friend Barbara Bodichon. But in summer 1876 this early promise was suddenly and tragically shattered when Jenny developed epilepsy. Jenny's first fit was apparently triggered off by a boating accident in the River Thames; she had lost her balance suddenly and fallen overboard.

Forty years later Georgie could still describe the drama of the onset: 'there came a note from poor Janey, at Horrington House, asking me to give her the address of a Doctor (they were new to the neighbourhood) because Jenny had fainted suddenly and frightened her very much. How little any of us expected the long drawn out pain and disappointment then begun.' Epilepsy is the condition in which seizures or convulsions are set off by sudden discharges of electrical energy in the brain. At that period it was regarded as an incurable and virtually uncontrollable condition. Even up to the end of the nineteenth century, one in four of those committed to a mental home for life was in fact an epileptic. There was still great social stigma attached to the condition, and widespread fear, arising from the ancient belief that fits were produced by some supernatural force. Here and there, even in the late twentieth century such fears survive. In puberty especially, the illness also had sexual connotations, the 'hysterical epilepsy' dreaded by the parents and guardians of Victorian young girls. The effect on the Morris household was so terrible because Jenny's *grand mal* was so completely unpredictable. Blunt, at Hammersmith, was sitting with Jenny and her mother having

368

tea in the drawing-room when Jenny suddenly fell backwards, 'her head (a tragic circumstance) striking the panel of that well-known and most beautiful cabinet which Morris and Rosetti [sic] had painted together in their youth, the one which represents the miracle of the resurrection of St. Hugh of Lincoln'.

At first Jenny's symptoms were at a relatively low level of severity and frequency. She was treated with the potassium bromides which began to be prescribed for epileptics from the late 1850s. Dr John Hughlings Jackson's investigations into the condition were still at a fairly early stage. At this period surgery was sometimes carried out to remove the superior ganglions of the sympathetic nervous system, involving the excision of neural tissue. There is no evidence that Jenny underwent an operation, but her later photographs show the distinct drooping of the upper eyelids which, in many patients, resulted from this treatment. Jenny's prognosis was in general so gloomy because each epileptic fit is capable of causing further brain damage. These days the condition, now controlled by anti-convulsant drugs, allows a sufferer from epilepsy to lead an ordinary life, apart from the occasional *grand* or *petit mal*. But at that time a steady deterioration was almost inevitable. Jenny's academic career was clearly at an end. She would never be able to marry. As the years went by, her condition fluctuated. Some of her letters written in her thirties are still wonderfully lucid, shot through with the strange candour of the invalid. But from now on Jenny, after all her youthful promise, would be relegated to the margins of society and, even in that enlightened social stratum, treated as a liability, a semi-imbecile.

Her parents' immediate response was to take Jenny out of London, on extended summer holidays. In the middle of July, Janey travelled with her daughters to Deal in Kent, where Georgie and Margaret joined them. Morris wrote from London: 'I am so glad to hear that things go well so far: though of course I cannot help being anxious . . . I think it would be a great pity to hurry them away if the place really seems to suit them, and you can hold out there: I will give you as much of my company as work will let me.' As so often happens, family crisis brought the estranged partners closer.

In September they all went to Broadway Tower, the sixty-five-foot-high folly that Crom Price had rented as a holiday home for himself and friends. The tower, on Broadway Beacon, was built by James Wyatt for the Earl of Coventry in 1800. From the top, on a clear day, you can see across twelve counties and identify four historic battlefields: Evesham,

Tewkesbury, Worcester and Edgehill. Morris, with his tower fixation, found it mad but marvellous: 'I am today at Crom Price's Tower among the winds and the clouds,' he wrote to Aglaia. They all signed the visitors' book, the tribes of Burne-Joneses and Morrises. Jenny's signature is noticeably shaky. Crom Price, by now headmaster of the United Services College at Westward Ho, from that visit onwards took a special interest in her, becoming her adoptive uncle for the remainder of his life.

On the two households Jenny's illness had a muting effect. At New Year Georgie was reporting an unusually uneventful holiday: 'We had no Christmas Eve gathering this year, and indeed have been altogether very quiet – the children are all a little pale and growing and need not to be exerted. We took them to the Circus yesterday but shall not allow them a Pantomime.' At her worst, Jenny would be sent away to be looked after. She was, for a period, a weekly boarder at a nursing home, returning home on Fridays. But the anxiety was ever present and the strain inevitably told on Janey. She confessed to Blunt years later that she had never been able to get used to it. Each fresh fit of Jenny's was a renewal of the agony: 'it is as if a dagger were thrust into me', she said.

Janey claimed it was the worst for her, since she was the person most constantly with Jenny. But it was as bad, or more cruel still, for Morris who felt himself the cause of her condition, the family inheritance descending from his mother to his own symptoms of anger-induced fits. The previous year, strengthened by his Iceland journeys, he had written to Louisa: 'I do verily think I have gone over every possible misfortune that may happen to me in my own mind, and concluded that I can bear it if it should come.' But nothing in Morris's past experience had prepared him for domestic catastrophe of this gravity.

Mackail says very little about Jenny's epilepsy. But the little that he does say shows how grief and anxiety loomed over Morris permanently. 'From this distress his mind was never henceforth free. In all who had the privilege of a close knowledge, his tenderness and unceasing thought and care for her were the most touchingly beautiful element in his nature.' Blunt who, like Rossetti, approached Morris with the superhuman sharpness of the lover of his wife, noticed that he had diverted to Jenny the tenderness once lavished upon Janey, whom he now treated kindly but offhandedly: 'It was touching now at Kelmscott to watch Morris's solicitude for this poor hardly sane girl on whom his chief home love was bestowed.' He poured out his affection. Jenny became Morris's accredited 'deary', his love, almost his double. Janey once described her husband and her daughter rambling on the hills like two happy giant babies. Jenny was always sturdy. A side-effect of the epilepsy treatment was rapidly to make her very fat.

In Iceland Morris had noticed how invalids and the mentally retarded were cared for in their families. This was the resort of poverty. But Morris, particularly after Jenny's epilepsy, pursued it as a principle, maintaining that the ill should not be marginalized and proposing that incapacity itself could cause development of special counter-qualities and skills. As so often, he was a century before his time. It is, ironically, Jenny's illness that provides us with the best documentation of Morris at this period: of the vast quantity of letters he wrote in the next two decades, with their detailed account of his political activity, the best are addressed to Jenny, reclaiming her from social ostracism, fondly, vividly keeping her in touch with momentous events. And in the novels of his final productivity there is also the recurring side-reference to Jenny in the figure of the woman who has fits and sees visions: the epileptic transformed into the goddess or the seer.

The domestic disaster prompted Morris to move outwards. His concern for Jenny gave him new perceptions of wider social distress and injustices and the urge to move society on beyond the reach of them. It was another of the decisive stones in Morris's socialistic cairn. He was breaking out beyond the old cliques of friends and brothers, feeling his way towards quite different ways of living and relating to society. In 'Making the Best of It', a lecture of 1879, Morris expresses clearly his need to be with others who 'meet to forget their own transient personal and family troubles in aspirations for their fellows and the days to come'.

Morris had returned to the epics of courage. His and Eiríkr Magnússon's *Three Northern Love Stories* had been published in the summer of 1875. These were their translations of 'Gunnlaug the Worm-Tongue', 'Frithiof the Bold' and 'Viglund the Fair', a tale Morris referred to as 'another love-saga – very graceful and pretty'. Now he had turned his attention to the last and grandest of his versions of *Völsunga Saga*. He was working on the long poem *The Story of Sigurd the Volsung and the Fall of the Niblungs* through the troubled year of 1876. By March he told Aglaia that he had more or less finished part three. In July, although depressed by Jenny's illness, he screwed himself up to write 250 lines one weekend. It is evident that Morris was forcing himself on with it: the completion of *Sigurd* had become a point of honour. He wrote on when his fingers were so stiff from the dye vats that he could hardly hold his pen.

Wagnerianism then was rife in London. Morris's *Sigurd* was published in November 1876, the year of the first production in Bayreuth of Wagner's complete *Ring*. Morris is of course in some ways England's counterpart to Wagner, with a similarly overpowering eloquence and feeling for the grandiose. The sense of Weird is strong in both. In his notorious belittlings of Wagner, Morris appears at his most pig-headed and parochial. He complained that Wagner's theories on musical matters seemed to him 'as an artist and non-musical man perfectly abhominable [*sic*]'. A letter to Henry Buxton Forman on the subject shows Morris in his mood of facetious insularity, maintaining it is 'nothing short of desecration to bring such a tremendous and world-wide subject under the gaslights of an opera: the most rococo and degraded of all forms of art – the idea of a sandy-haired German tenor tweedledeeing over the unspeakable woes of Sigurd, which even the simplest words are not typical enough to express!'

Wagner was the subject of a flirtatious running battle with Aglaia, who moved in advanced musical circles. Returning from the Wagner cycle in Bayreuth, she had been rash enough to praise the dragon carefully constructed under the Maestro's eye. Morris was enraged that Fafnir, the man-beast of savage legend, should be treated as a species of pantomime dragon, 'puffing steam and showing his red danger-signal like a railway engine'. Morris does not appear ever to have met Wagner, though he was introduced to his wife Cosima in May 1877 when Wagner came to London for his concert series at the Albert Hall. But he went with Ned and Georgie to a morning rehearsal, in seats close beside the Wagners, George Eliot and George Henry Lewes in their box.

Of *Sigurd the Volsung*'s four books the first, 'Sigmund', tells the story of King Volsung's son Sigmund and the fatal marriage of his sister Signy to the King of the Goths. The second and third books, 'Regir' and 'Brynhild' focus on Sigmund's son Sigurd, his betrothal to Brynhild and his marriage to Gudrun, the King of the Niblungs' daughter, under the influence of the magic potion, and the deaths of Sigurd and Brynhild. The last book recounts Gudrun's own death and the fall of the Niblungs. In this poem Morris is in his populist bard element: the narrative swings forward, in its long rhyming couplets, almost too readably, at a tremendous pace. What is very interesting, knowing the way his thoughts were tending by the middle 1870s, is the way in which the Socialist message starts to infiltrate even the Nordic epic. *Sigurd* stands on the borderline between Morris's *Earthly Paradise* and his more overt poems of Socialist polemic, in particular his heroic poem of the Commune, *The Pilgrims of Hope*. In *Sigurd the Volsung* Morris is already the poetic rabble-rouser, using the emotive words and rhythms to play upon the heart-strings, as in the account of the naming of the purple-swaddled baby, son to the dead King Sigmund, by the old wise man:

. . . there rose up a man most ancient, and he cried: 'Hail Dawn of the Day!
How many things shalt thou quicken, how many shalt thou slay!
How many things shalt thou waken, how many lull to sleep!
How many things shalt thou scatter, how many gather and keep!
O me, how thy love shall cherish, how thine hate shall wither and burn!
How the hope shall be sped from thy right hand, nor the fear to thy left
    return!
O thy deeds that men shall sing of! O thy deeds that the Gods shall see!
O SIGURD, Son of the Volsungs, O Victory yet to be!'

Men heard the name and they knew it, and they caught it up in the air,
And it went abroad by the windows and the doors of the feast-hall fair,
It went through street and market; o'er meadow and acre it went,
And over the wind-stirred forest and the dearth of the sea-beat bent,
And over the sea-flood's welter, till the folk of the fishers heard,
And the hearts of the isle-abiders on the sun-scorched rocks were stirred.

But the Queen in her golden chamber, the name she hearkened and knew;
And she heard the flock of the women, as back to the chamber they drew,
And the name of Sigurd entered, and the body of Sigurd was come,
And it was as if Sigmund were living and she still in her lovely home;
Of all folk of the world was she well, and a soul fulfilled of rest
As alone in the chamber she wakened and Sigurd cherished her breast.

In 1933 W. B. Yeats read this passage out loud to his daughter Anne at Riversdale near Dublin. He read it twice in fact, but he could hardly read for tears.

Morris was disappointed at the time by the lukewarm reception the public gave to *Sigurd*. It is easy to see why. He threw so much of himself into it, so many of the loves and the obsessions of those years. And technically surely *Sigurd* is his masterpiece, best viewed perhaps in terms of the stupendous Victorian Gothic building: Street's Law Courts? George Gilbert Scott's St Pancras? Not that this is a comparison Morris would have approved.

In 1877 Morris was approached as the possible successor to F. H. C. Doyle as Professor of Poetry at Oxford. The Chair of Poetry was one of the oldest chairs in Oxford, established in 1708 by Sir Henry Birkenhead in protest at the laziness of dons reluctant to lecture. It was a largely honorary appointment, which then lasted for ten years. The Professor was expected to deliver three annual lectures besides the Creweian Oration given in Latin in alternate years. He also judged the Newdigate and the Sacred Poem Prize which had inspired a very early Morris work. The election to the Professorship of Poetry was not in the gift of the academic hierarchy but was arrived at democratically by the body of the University. The appointment then, as now, aroused wide speculation because it was, uniquely, made by Convocation, the whole panoply of Masters of Arts of Oxford University who cared to turn up and cast their votes. It was hoped that the post could be filled by an Oxford man well known as both a poet and a critic. Matthew Arnold had been the incumbent before Doyle. The two obvious candidates were now Swinburne and Morris. Swinburne had to be discarded on moral grounds. James Thursfield, on behalf of Convocation, wrote to Morris to ask if he would stand.

All Morris's ambivalent feelings about Oxford, his loved but suspect city, are contained in the reply he sent to Convocation. He apologized for his delay in answering: 'I found it hard to make up my mind what was right to do.' He explained that hardly anything would please him more than such recognition from his own university. Nor would laziness or business preoccupations prevent him from standing, if he thought he could be 'of any real use'. Even the prospect of a contested election, much as he disliked such things, did not really frighten him. But he simply felt unqualified to fill a post which demanded either deep and wide scholarship or else 'pieces of beautiful and ingenious rhetoric' which could disguise the lack of it. Morris's letter is wonderfully double-edged. He continues:

It seems to me that the *practice* of any art rather narrows the artist in regard to the *theory* of it; and I think I come more than most men under this condemnation, so that though I have read a good deal and have a good memory my

nowledge is so limited and so ill-arranged that I can scarce call myself a man of
tters: and moreover I have a peculiar inaptitude for expressing myself except
1 the one way that my gift lies.

Ie could not resist adding that he doubted whether the Chair of Poetry
vas more than an ornamental one, and whether 'the Professor of a
vholly incommunicable art is not rather in a false position'. John
Campbell Shairp, the Scottish literary critic, formerly a Rugby master,
vas finally elected. Mackail, who must have known him, describes him
drily as a man 'of unimpeachable orthodoxy, of a most kindly and
ourteous nature, and of some merit both as a critic and a poet'.

Iow far did Morris see himself as a public figure? May gives us the
impression that public work caused him agonies of boredom and frustra-
ion. It was work 'for which no one knew better than himself he was
insuited'. Early in 1876 he wrote to Magnússon: 'I was born *not* to be a
hairman of anything.' Yet at this very period Morris was embarking on
iis long succession of chairmanships, secretaryships, treasurerships,
nduring and even inviting the repetitive detail of committee work that
vent on until the last weeks before his death. He was certainly not
ineffective on committees. His administrative energy impressed the
painter W. B. Richmond, a fellow public worker in the 1870s: 'We are
in two Committees together', Richmond noted, 'and his power of grasp
ind quick facility for seeing a loose screw are sometimes wonderful.'
The truth seems to be that Morris was prepared to school himself for
asks he instinctively found dislikeable, the long-drawn-out discussions,
he grind of personalities, the aridities of minutes, the tedious scroung-
ng for subscriptions, if the end was likely to justify the effort. It was a
means of channelling his new idealistic energies. It was also a facet of
Morris's masochism. So much of his work had always come so easily. In
middle age he started to seek out, as if compelled to, forms of work he
ound much harder, even self-sacrificial. His immersion in the onerous
ommittee work of the late 1870s leads logically onwards to his 1880s
abours for the Cause.

Morris became honorary secretary of the Society for the Protection of
Ancient Buildings when it was founded in March 1877. 'Anti-Scrape',
he name by which the society is still familiarly known, was Morris's
invention, first appearing in a begging letter written to a friend soon
fter its formation: 'By the way you have not yet joined our anti-Scrape

375

Society: I will send you the papers of it: the subscription is only 10/6.'
The idea of a watchdog body to preserve the fabric of the nation's
ancient buildings had been in Morris's mind for some months previously, as it had been in Ruskin's from the middle 1850s. Indeed the
germ of it comes straight from Ruskin's *The Seven Lamps of Architecture* (1849), one of the books that Morris had idolized at Oxford. The
SPAB adapted Ruskin for its public circular:

Take proper care of your monuments, and you will not need to restore them.
Watch an old building with an anxious care; count its stones as you would
jewels of a crown; bind it together with iron where it loosens, stay it with timber
where it declines. Do not care about the unsightliness of the aid; better a crutch
than a lost limb; and do this tenderly, reverently, continually, and many a
generation will still be born to pass away beneath its shadow.

The immediate spur to the foundation of the SPAB was Morris's visit
to Burford Church, *en route* with his family to Crom Price's tower in the
summer of 1876. This mainly Norman and fifteenth-century church,
perfectly sited by the river in what must then have been an idyllic
Cotswold village, was being restored by Street in a way that infuriated
Morris. When he reached Broadway Tower he made notes for a letter of
protest and appeal which, though never sent, was the basis for the start
of the society next year. Morris's responses were impetuous and personal. Compared with Ruskin's, his diatribes on inept restorations have
an extra edge of vehemence because he decried them not just as the
theoretician but the craftsman. On being shown some nineteenth-
century pseudo-Gothic carvings in a cathedral, he burst out: 'Why, I
could carve them better with my teeth!'

What strikes one about all Morris's movements for reform is how
traditional they were in operation and structure. The first SPAB meeting was held at Queen Square on 22 March. Those present included
Spencer Stanhope, George Price Boyce, Henry Wallis, Alfred
Stephens: the Pre-Raphaelite cronies. Apologies for absence were sent
by Ned, Edward Poynter, George Howard, Lawrence Alma-Tadema
William De Morgan and Thomas Wardle. Again, the names are from
Morris's close circle. As well as hon. secretary, Morris was *pro-tem*
treasurer. He, Philip Webb and George Wardle were appointed as the
committee to draw up the aims of the society. In those early years, the
SPAB was operated almost as a military campaign, with Webb as chief
of staff and Morris as the general. Reluctant general maybe? Page two of

376

the first set of minutes is adorned with the familiar William Morris doodles, a cascade of leaves and berries, intimations of outdoors.

But in those first few weeks many decisions were taken. It was agreed to approach bishops and clergy and all other 'custodians of ancient buildings' to seek their co-operation. Connections were set up with art and antiquarian societies. The society made it its business to locate *all* the ancient buildings still left unrestored in order to attempt to forestall their alteration. Morris's friends were all made use of in recruiting other members. Morris wrote to Rossetti to enlist his support, perhaps remembering the ancient building they had shared.

As he draws up the manifesto you can see Morris's own architectural history come surging through it. The queer half-hidden Essex churches of his childhood; Canterbury Cathedral; Ely, Peterborough, Lichfield; the simple little grey stone village churches around Kelmscott. Morris's best-loved churches were the buildings which, for the past two decades, had been increasingly at risk from the drastic restoration programmes unleashed by the ecclesiologist reformers. Churches not conforming to their architectural principles were in danger of alteration or even demolition. Morris was all too aware of how the east end of Christ Church Cathedral had been demolished and rebuilt by George Gilbert Scott in the Norman style. It was such emanations of architectural high-handedness that the SPAB set itself to combat. Morris argued that, in the past, church buildings had been added to in the styles prevailing at the time of the additions: the effect, even if sometimes ramshackle, was genuine. Now, as ignorant architects attempted to bring a church back 'to the best time of its history', without being equipped to distinguish between what was admirable and what contemptible within each period, elements of sheer fakery impinged disastrously. Morris wrote, 'it seems to me not so much a question of whether we are to have old buildings or not, as whether they are to be old or sham old.' This was in a message to Thomas Carlyle, who was moved by it to join the SPAB.

Morris was quick to evolve effective propaganda tactics. His methods were by and large those still in force in the twentieth-century architectural pressure groups formed on the model of the SPAB. The intensive study of case histories of buildings followed by the blast off to the press. The first of these was sent to the editor of *The Athenaeum* on 4 April 1877 protesting about the proposed restoration to Tewkesbury Abbey. This last-minute intervention was unsuccessful and the abbey was thoroughly overhauled by Scott. Two months later Morris wrote to *The*

Times on the subject of the restoration of the choir of Canterbury Cathedral. It is a sharper letter. Morris has already taught himself the language of political invective in defending the stone screen installed originally under Prior Eastry's thirteenth-century regime:

I suppose that the proposed imitation, restoration, or forgery of Prior Eastry's rather commonplace tracery is only the beginning of the evil day at Canterbury, and that before long we shall see the noble building of the two Williams confused and falsified by the usual mass of ecclesiastical trumpery and coarse daubing that all true lovers of art and history dread so sorely; that, in short, the choir of Canterbury will go the way of Ely, St. Cross, and Salisbury.

In pursuing his campaigns Morris shows perhaps surprising purist narrowness, attacking individual work and naming names, castigating the restoring architects with a zealousness that verges on the cruel. Many he knew well. In the campaign for Southwell Minster he embarked on a ferocious public confrontation with his old master, the Gothicist G. E. Street, whom Morris believed 'would restore every building in England if he could, and to our minds with the necessary result of ruining them'. Their exchange of correspondence about Southwell shows how hurt Street was. Morris's *bête noire*, George Gilbert Scott, received the worst of his invective. Morris accused him of the most commercial cynicism: 'convicted out of his own mouth of having made an enormous fortune by doing what he well knows to be wrong'. Scott's final years of illness were made the more despondent by SPAB hostility. When he died Morris described him as 'the (happily) dead dog'.

Not that Morris spared himself. In line with SPAB policy his firm sent out a circular in April 1877 announcing it would no longer be able to supply stained-glass windows for mediaeval buildings which were subject to restoration or improvement. The only exceptions were churches which already had examples of Morris & Co. work or buildings not considered 'monuments of ancient art'. This may well have been the reason for the decline in commissions from twenty-one in 1877 and 1878 to fourteen in 1879 and only eleven the next year.

At the time Morris was so involved with the foundation of the SPAB he was also committed to a more overtly political body, the Eastern Question Association, a liberal pressure group formed to promote resistance to Disraeli's alliance with the Turks. The 'Eastern Question' was a

378

blanket term which covered a long-running international issue: the rivalry between Russia and the other Great Powers for control of the Ottoman Empire, now in its decline. Great Britain, an ally of Turkey, feared the growth of Russian influence and its effect on the European balance of power. The EQA was founded at a time of panic when it appeared that Disraeli and the Tories were heading for war with Russia, taking the Turkish side. George Howard was one of the moving spirits. Morris and Charley Faulkner offered to help fund it. Morris became treasurer of the EQA in November 1876.

Dismay at the reported atrocities which followed the Turkish suppression of rebellion in Bulgaria had been building up in Britain, and indeed in Europe, through the summer. In all about 15,000 people were massacred, eighty towns and villages completely destroyed and ten monasteries sacked. The scale and ferocity of Turkish action caused an outburst of enlightened opinion against Turkey. The Bulgarians were defended by Garibaldi in Italy; Dostoevsky, Turgenev and other liberals in Russia; Victor Hugo in France; and in England Trollope and the young Oscar Wilde, then up at Oxford, who sent Gladstone a copy of his sonnet, 'On the recent massacre of the Christians in Bulgaria'. Gladstone, the former Liberal prime minister, came out of his retirement at Hawarden, north Wales, to explore alternative solutions to the problem. His pamphlet *The Bulgarian Horrors and the Question of the East* was a devastating critique of Disraeli's Turkish policy. In a month almost a quarter of a million copies had been sold. The effect of the crisis can be gauged by Georgie's comment in a letter to Rosalind: 'We take the Times and Daily News now, instead of no paper, and keep an eye on the war by that means, it is dreadful in its interest and has wakened up that piece of Europe as it never was before.' Georgie could have added that Ned and Morris had an extra bias against Turkey because of their connections of amity and commerce with the London colony of Greeks.

As a cause, the EQA just then was ready-made for Morris, providing the outlet for the views that were almost bursting from him: views on commerce, profit-mongering, the likely end of art. Looking back seven years later he analysed the part his EQA involvement had played in his education as a Socialist:

About the time when I was beginning to think so strongly on these points that I felt I must express myself publicly, came the crisis of the Eastern Question and the agitation which ended in the overthrow of the Disraeli government. I joined heartily in that agitation on the Liberal side, because it seemed to me that England risked drifting into a war which would have committed her to the party of reaction: I also thoroughly dreaded the outburst of Chauvinism which swept over the country, and feared that once we were amusing ourselves with European war no one in this country would listen to anything of social questions; nor could I see in England at that time any party more advanced than the radicals who were also it must be remembered hallowed as it were by being in opposition to the party which openly proclaimed themselves reactionists.

On 9 September 1876, a few days after the publication of his pamphlet, Gladstone addressed a rally in his Greenwich constituency at Blackheath. In spite of dreadful weather 10,000 people attended and the crowd was visibly swayed and moved. Six weeks later Morris wrote a strong letter of protest to the editor of the *Daily News*: 'Sir, I cannot help noting that a rumour is about in the air that England is going to war; and from the depths of my astonishment I ask, On behalf of whom? Against whom? And for what end?' He employs all the tricks of politician's rhetoric in pouring scorn on Disraeli's 'shameful and unjust war – how shameful and unjust no words can say'. He swipes out at the absentee members of Parliament, 'too busy shooting in the country', and the apathy of England, the exception being the 2,000 working men who rallied in Clerkenwell the Sunday before. He pulls out the stops of the personal and private:

I who am writing this am one of a large class of men – quiet men, who usually go about their own business, heeding public matters less than they ought, and afraid to speak in such a huge concourse as the English nation, however much they may feel, but who are now stung into bitterness by thinking how helpless they are in a public matter that touches them so closely.

Morris writes emotively of murdered babies in Bulgaria. This is not the idly dreaming poet. Nor does it read like the letter of the political *ingénu*.

The EQA had been brought into being by the clever and manipulative Liberal MP for Sheffield, A. J. Mundella. Morris, the well-known author of *The Earthly Paradise*, was an excellent recruit for a campaign that Mundella had hoped would be distinctive in its character: not just the old gathering of tried and trusted Liberals but supported by 'the Bishops, the Parsons, the Peers, the Literati'. He intended that the EQA should be a movement of radical chic. Morris was on display at the

EQA's first National Conference, held in St James's Hall in London on
8 December. Georgie was in the audience: 'The hall was crammed
everywhere: the women sat apart in the end galleries, so that we could
see all the body of the building filled with a black mass of men, and it
looked very impressive. The Conveners of the Conference were in the
orchestra, Morris in the front row.' Ned kept away in case fatigue should
prove too much for him. The meeting lasted for *nine hours*, and
Gladstone spoke at length. Among the conveners were Charles Darwin,
Robert Browning, J. A. Froude, C. E. Maurice, G. O. Trevelyan, John
Ruskin, Anthony Trollope, W. T. Stead, Auberon Herbert; about 700
people came in all. Morris sent the news to Thomas Wardle in Leek that
the meeting had been 'a very solemn and impressive affair' and regaled
his daughters with his imitations of Gladstone in full flood of oratory,
holding his audience with his piercing gaze. This gaze Morris compared
to the eye of a great falcon, which mesmerized its victim or the listener;
'and he turned his own head slowly round from side to side, with his old
mimetic gift, to show how it was done'.

On 24 April 1877 Russia declared war on Turkey. The EQA held a
series of meetings to protest against any action by the government that
might implicate England in the conflict. On 2 May Morris wrote apologetically to Janey to say he was delayed by the 'great stew in political
matters' from joining her at Kelmscott. That night there was a meeting
of the Workmen's Political Associations and Trade Societies of the
Metropolis at Cannon Street Hotel in support of five anti-Turkish
resolutions which Gladstone had tabled in the House of Commons.
Morris was 'going there to swell the crowd'. He commented afterwards
that some of the working men spoke well: 'They seem to have advanced
since last Autumn.' He was especially impressed by Thomas Burt, trade
unionist and Liberal MP for Morpeth, who addressed the meeting
eloquently 'with a strong Northumbrian tongue'.

Five days later Morris was present at the massive EQA conference in
St James's Hall held to demand parliamentary action on Gladstone's
anti-Turkish resolutions. Ned intended to be there: 'Tonight', he wrote,
I am going to help to kick up a row at a public meeting.' But, perhaps to
his relief, the hall was so crowded that he was turned away. On 11 May
1877 Morris issued a manifesto 'To the working-men of England' which
he signed 'A LOVER OF JUSTICE' and in which he spoke out against
Disraeli's 'unjust war', drawing on his hidden reserves of bitterness:

Who are they that are leading us into war? Let us look at these saviours of England's honour, these champions of Poland, these scourges of Russia's iniquities! Do you know them? – Greedy gamblers on the Stock Exchange, idle officers of the army and navy (poor fellows!) worn-out mockers of the Clubs, desperate purveyors of exciting war-news for the comfortable breakfast tables of those who have nothing to lose by war, and lastly, in the place of honour, the Tory Rump, that we fools, weary of peace, reason and justice, chose at the last election to 'represent' us: and over all their captain, the ancient place-hunter, who, having at last climbed into an Earl's chair, grins down thence into the anxious face of England [Benjamin Disraeli, Earl of Beaconsfield], while his empty heart and shifty head is compassing the stroke that will bring on our destruction perhaps, our confusion certainly: – O shame and double shame, if we march under such a leadership as this in an unjust war against a people who are *not* our enemies, against Europe, against freedom, against nature, against the hope of the world.

Working-men of England, one word of warning yet: I doubt if you know the bitterness of hatred against freedom and progress that lies at the hearts of a certain part of the richer classes in this country: their newspapers veil it in a kind of decent language; but do but hear them talking among themselves, as I have often, and I know not whether scorn or anger would prevail in you at their folly and insolence: – these men cannot speak of your order, of its aims, of its leaders without a sneer or an insult: these men, if they had the power (may England perish rather) would thwart your just aspirations, would silence you, would deliver you bound hand and foot for ever to irresponsible capital – and these men, I say it deliberately, are the heart and soul of the party that is driving us to an unjust war: – can the Russian people be your enemies or mine like these men are, who are the enemies of all justice? They can harm us but little now, but if war comes, *unjust war*, with all its confusion and anger, who shall say what their power may be, what step backward we may make? Fellow-citizens, look to it, and if you have any wrongs to be redressed, if you cherish your most worthy hope of raising your whole order peacefully and solidly, if you thirst for leisure and knowledge, if you long to lessen those inequalities which have been our stumbling-block since the beginning of the world, then cast aside sloth and cry out against an UNJUST WAR, and urge us of the Middle Classes to do no less . . .

It seems as if Morris, through the late 1870s, was shedding one persona and making himself a new one, deliberately preparing for a new role in the world. Public speaking, unlike letters to the press and pamphleteering, was still an ordeal to him. But, as he did with each new craft, he now set himself determinedly to acquire and practise the technique. In the midwinter of 1877 he was anxiously preparing and

ehearsing the first of the hundred or so full-scale lectures he delivered
between 1877 and 1896. This lecture, on 'The Decorative Arts', was to
be given to the Trades Guild of Learning at the Co-operative Hall in
Castle Street, off Oxford Street. Morris, writing the lecture at Turnham
Green, had contemplated calling Sarah, the cook, up from the basement
to read her extracts 'after the example of Molière', but he thought better
of it, afraid that he might 'kill her with surprise'. He did however test
out his voice production on George Wardle, taking him to Castle Street
and reading *Robinson Crusoe* out loud to him in the empty hall. Ned
gave Morris good advice on what he called the 'penny lecture', advising
him on gestures and adjustment of his spectacles and offering to draw
diagrams to illustrate the lectures, an offer which apparently was scorn-
ully refused. Ned did not go to hear him, feeling much too appre-
ensive on Morris's behalf. But Webb sent a good account of his
performance to Janey and the children, saying that the lecture had been
full of truths and knock-me-down blows'. It had been 'tender and
beautiful and withal hopeful to poor folk if not to Kings and Lords'. In
Webb's view the working men in Morris's audience had seemed pleased
at being addressed as adult men and not as children. This lecture, which
moved Webb to tears and which still strikes me as one of the most
orceful and direct of Morris's lectures, was later published as 'The
Lesser Arts'.

In the early months of 1878 it still seemed that war was likely. Morris
felt that Queen Victoria was 'crazy for war in spite of all denials': he
disliked the Queen, referring to her either as the Empress Brown or
Widow Guelph. Protest meetings continued. In early January the EQA
had had 'a glorious victory' in Trafalgar Square: 'though', wrote Morris,
I believe some blood was shed (from noses)'. On 16 January the most
dramatic of the meetings, the Workmen's Neutrality Demonstration,
was held at Exeter Hall. The aim of the meeting was to protest publicly
against England being dragged into war. Morris described the evening
gathering to Janey as 'magnificent: orderly and enthusiastic; though
mind you, it took some very heavy work to keep the enemy roughs out;
and the noise of them outside was like the sea roaring against a light-
house.' There was also opposition to the overflow meeting held in
Trafalgar Square. The demonstration had been organized by Henry
Broadhurst, one of the new breed of trade union leaders, a former
stonemason who was secretary both of the Parliamentary Committee of
the Trades Union Congress and the Workmen's Committee of the

383

EQA. Broadhurst had asked Morris to provide 'an inspiriting song' to open the proceedings. At home two evenings before, Morris had obligingly composed 'Wake, London Lads!', to be sung to the tune of 'The hardy Norseman's home of yore'. It is almost a northman's hymn. There are five verses, culminating in the lines:

> Wake, London Lads! the hour draws nigh,
> The bright sun brings the day;
> Cast off the shame, cast off the lie,
> And cast the Turk away!

As they entered the hall a song sheet awaited every member of the audience. Georgie arrived with Ned, Crom Price and the Faulkners. She wrote: 'When we took our places in the orchestra the whole hall before us was spotted with the white leaflets of the new poem.' The Rev. G. M. Murphy, 'a Nonconformist minister of much note in South London', took the audience through it, reading it out verse by verse in the old Methodist fashion. After this the choir of working men and women sang the song through twice, to familiarize the audience with the words and tune. According to Broadhurst, 'the effect when the burning words were thundered forth by the vast assembly was electrifying', and 'Wake, London Lads!' started a new fashion for political meetings to open with a similarly stirring song. In Exeter Hall the crowd stopped at the end of each verse and 'cheered lustily'. They were about half-way through when Morris and the platform party came in.

Morris was on his feet at this meeting. His performance at an earlier meeting at Lambeth in December had been hesitant, but by now he had apparently gained confidence. 'Mr. W. Morris spoke in strong terms against the "war-at-any-price" party', *The Times* reported the next day. He praised Gladstone ('Cheers') and ridiculed the Court and Disraeli ('Cries of "No, no", and "Three cheers for the Queen"'). When Morris was reminded by the chairman that 'it was undesirable in a Constitutional country in which Ministers were responsible to the people to introduce the name of the Sovereign into political discussions, he concluded by expressing his regret that fortune had placed at the head of affairs in England a man without genius (cries of "Oh! Oh!"), but only a galvanic imitation of it'. The nation must present 'a steady resistance' to Disraeli's shiftiness. As Morris sat down again the air was still ringing satisfactorily with renewed cries of 'Oh! Oh!'

After 'Wake, London Lads!' there were weeks of anti-climax. In the war fever that followed the Russian occupation of Constantinople and the sending of the English fleet to the Dardanelles, the Liberal opposition lost its nerve. Morris described it as taking 'a bad beating' in Sheffield, at a meeting called to object to the government's call for a £6 million appropriation for the war fund. He was present at the scenes of turbulence in Stepney where a public meeting of 1,000 people turned into 'a bear garden': after some rather poor 'fistcuff work', the EQA adherents were obliged to leave the hall. The opposition was up to tricks, as he told Janey: 'they had 400 roughs down in waggons from Woolwich Dockyard, and generally played the gooseberry: people on our side had to hide away in cellars and places and get out anyhow.'

Morris felt let down by the shilly-shallying of Liberals in Parliament: 'I am full of shame and anger', he told Charley on 5 February, 'at the cowardice of the so-called Liberal party.' He went to the House himself, confronting members in the lobby, and arrived on another day as part of the deputation of the Workmen's Neutrality Committee expressing solidarity with the Liberals still remaining firm against the war. He described this scene to Jenny: 'We were received in a room called the Conference-room, which has a sort of screen across it; and the scene (apart from the seriousness of the situation) was as good as one of your plays, my dear.'

The worst of his frustrations concerned plans for a last-ditch meeting at the Agricultural Hall in Islington. By this time the English fleet had left Constantinople. It seemed urgent to refocus attention on England's still unresolved problems vis-à-vis the Turks. Morris and some members of the workmen's committee had gone to see Gladstone to ask him to attend the meeting. Gladstone had agreed 'and', as Morris wrote to Janey, 'was quite hot about it, and as brisk as a bee'. Morris went straight off to the hall and booked it. The details of the programme were well under way when nervous Liberal MPs had harried Gladstone, persuading him the meeting was unwise. Morris saw the EQA as being 'foremost in the flight', and felt personally humiliated when the meeting was cancelled. He told Janey: 'I am that ashamed that I can scarcely look people in the face though I did my best to keep the thing up: the working-men are in a great rage about it, as they may well be: for I do verily believe we should have made it a success'. From now on Morris was disillusioned with the Liberals. The EQA seemed 'full of wretched little personalities'. George Howard might as well come back from Italy to England 'for the boat race as the general election', Morris told him bitterly. By early April 1878 war panic had finally died down. Morris said: 'I should not wonder if the Jingoes were dissapointed [*sic*] after all. EQA as good as dead.'

Morris felt his political career had ended for the present. In the strict sense this was true. But his EQA experiences built up to prepare him for the much more concentrated period of political activism ahead. He had been caught up in the euphoria of fellowship and developed a certain zest for confrontation. 'There will certainly be a fight, so you will come up if you can,' he wrote to Charley, in Oxford, when the EQA had planned a big Hyde Park demonstration. Politically speaking he had tasted blood.

Through that winter Janey and the girls had been in Italy. Rosalind had suggested they should join the Howards at Oneglia, between Alassio and San Remo, on the Italian Riviera. Rosalind had found a house for them, the Villa del Cavo, near the Howards' own villa, and had undertaken to lend Janey one of her own servants to help them settle in. Janey, pleased but rather overawed by this munificence, had written to assure Rosalind that she could manage the long railway journey quite easily. She would travel lying down, 'which I fancy is always possible'. She had added, 'Jenny and May are famous sailors, and can do anything for me on board the steamboat, they are always helpful, not tiresome in any way.'

They had left in November, and Morris had dreaded it. 'It will be a curious time', he told his mother, 'when Janey and the children are gone.' He had taken the train to the coast with them and lingered unwisely on the ferry. 'Wouldn't it have been funny if I had got taken to Calais?' he said in his first letter to Oneglia: 'in that case I would certainly have made the best of it, and gone on to Paris too.' Left at home he worries constantly about his family's welfare, admonishing Janey not to let her 'celebrated thrift' lead her to poison herself with bad wine, and posting the two pounds of tea that she has asked for ('which is expensive but it don't matter'). In one letter Morris wishes he could enclose a pike. He finds Jenny and May news that he is certain will interest them: not just bulletins on his political excitements but detailed domestic agenda. 'Mouse', at Kelmscott, 'looks shaggy and well in his winter costume, and the 2 pussies are as clean as ever.' Margaret Burne-Jones's green parakeet, given her by her adoring father as 'a tooth-taking-out reward' has died, he tells his daughters, 'after a short illness: I am glad my dears that you have not yet taken to pets: for they are a *nuisance*'. He talks to the littles as if they were still at home with him. He has begun house-hunting in west London, having now decided to move out of Turnham Green. At Christmas Morris goes on a visit to his mother's where the family is assembled. Lacking Janey, the intrepid hair-cutter of the family, Morris's sister Isabella cut his hair for him. On his next visit, his mother's maid, Rogers, provided the same service in the presence of his 'kinswomen' and a noisy parrot, 'which last was delighted, and mewed and barked and swore and sang at the top of his vulgar voice'.

Out in Oneglia Jenny celebrated her seventeenth birthday. Morris sent her his 'very best love' and wished that she would 'always be as happy as a bird'. In fact all was not well at the Villa del Cavo. Rosalind reported to her mother Lady Stanley: 'The Ms are not quite so happy as I hoped they might be. Garden a perfect paradise but somehow the girls do not take so kindly to Italy as I hoped.' May, evidently going through an awkward phase, announced one day that she would rather be in Iceland. Janey looked strained and very tired, an impression confirmed by Lady Cavendish, a visitor of Rosalind's taken to call on Janey, whom she described as 'haggard and wistful-eyed, with a heavy bush of black hair penthouse-style over the forehead'. Rossetti was haunted by her handwriting from Italy, which reminded him of 'poor Lizzie's', in the worst of her illness. Not that he was providing much consolation, feeding Janey with news of Top's political activities and comparing him with George Odger, the shoemaker and London trade unionist who attempted repeatedly to enter Parliament: 'He is the Odger of the Future, my dear Janey, depend on it, and will be in parliament next change.'

Jenny's condition, which had seemed so much improved in the previous summer, had worsened dramatically since she got to Italy. To Rosalind her health seemed 'dreadful', and she was always conscious of Jenny's strange disorientated look: 'She sleeps alone and has fits in the nights sometimes, but they say she never gets out of bed with them and so there is no risk. It is frightful to see her whole life so shattered – for she was *very* clever and now she seems so dazed as if there was always a mist over her brain. I think Jenny was partly over-worked at school – but I think it was not only that.'

In March Jenny had a fit while sitting in the garden in Oneglia. Rosalind had never seen an epileptic fit before and was aghast. Morris, terribly alarmed to hear the news, attempted to contact the London specialist in charge of Jenny, John Russell Reynolds, the expert in nervous diseases who from 1893 was president of the Royal College of Physicians. Reynolds was away. All Morris could do was write a letter to be forwarded. In desperation he requested new supplies of Radcliffe's nostrum of bromides to Jenny's old prescription to be sent out to Oneglia. Morris's own analysis of the prescription told him it was 'hashish or bhang like Monte-Christo and the Arabian Nights'. His own plans to get to Italy firmed up under this crisis. He told Janey he would definitely be coming out in April, selling books to finance the journey if he had to. He set out towards the end of the month, leaving London on the night-mail train, travelling via Paris. Morris's trials and his loneliness all through the winter had given him a new appreciation, almost a sense of the sacredness, of family. The reunion was almost unbearably moving, as he wrote to Georgie: 'Can't you imagine what a time it was for me when I looked out of the window at Oneglia and saw those three all standing together?' The scene of the three figures on the platform was recorded like a sepia photograph or magic-lantern slide.

Morris was himself by no means well on his arrival. For the past few years he had been suffering increasingly from gout, a constitutional disorder connected with an excess of uric acid in the blood and bringing on a painful inflammation of the joints. Those most susceptible have always been male, middle-aged or older. Gout has especially afflicted bon vivants. Morris's near-contemporary Charles Darwin suffered from it: gout was the Victorian Grand Old Man's disease. That past December, staying with his mother, Morris's reckless consumption of two glasses of port on Christmas Day had brought on 'signs of the toe-devil' next morning. Georgie blamed the exertions of political activity for Morris's condition of exhaustion that winter and the attacks of gout that continued to assail him. During March he was imprisoned at the house at Turnham Green 'being lame with gouty rheumatism, or rheumatic gout: I can't get down stairs, but I find the long room very comfortable'.

The journey to Italy had tired him. He would have preferred to stay on in Oneglia, wandering in the olive groves above the sea. But arrangements had been made to take the party on to Genoa. By then his gout was definitely under way again. He collapsed on arrival at Genoa station. A porter had to carry Morris on his back. Then, as Morris told Georgie: 'things began to dance before my eyes, my knees went limp, and down I went, thank you, and enjoyed a dream of some minute and a quarter I suppose, which seemed an afternoon of public meetings.' As Morris faints, like one of the heroes of his poems, a strange panorama of his past activities comes flooding through his mind. An inquisitive crowd collected, and he had to wave away the helpful Italian who clamped a brandy bottle to his lips. Finally: 'I had to be Guy Fawkesed upstairs at the Hotel, chuckling with laughter, till they landed me in this present palatial suite of rooms.'

They were not in a condition to appreciate Italy, though Morris courageously dragged himself round Venice, which he called 'the hobbler's Paradise', in beautiful, bright, clear and quite hot weather. It was now the beginning of May. On the first day in Venice he had travelled in a gondola past and then up to the ducal palace, though unable to 'crawl across the Piazetta [sic]'. But by the sixth day he had 'managed to hobble into St. Mark's'. They visited Torcello, the small island just off Venice with its many dusty relics, its green bushes and its 'small cots of fisherfolk'. Morris, a few months before, had made his first visit to Ireland. Torcello was similarly green and unassuming, another of those William Morris wondrous isles.

When they got to Padua they hit storms which left the garden of trellised vines in the Arena Chapel looking wonderfully fresh. Morris appreciated Padua which had a kind of homeliness compared with Venice: 'What a beautiful and *pleasant* place it is with the huge hall dividing the market place, and the endless arcades everywhere.' He and his daughters were caught in a shower and sheltered in a convenient arcade: 'as the pavement was clean and dry', Morris told Georgie, 'I sat down with great content with my back to the wall'. A dyer's hand-cart loaded with blue cotton, which Morris's expert eye could see had just been finished, took refuge beside them. Morris was sorry that his lack of Italian prevented him from conversing with one of the men, 'who looked both good-tempered and intelligent'. In the evening they went to a queer old botanic garden and heard the birds sing. The rain had cleared now. A great storm cloud still hid the Alps, but the small mountains to the west of Padua were clear and blue. Morris began to long to be back in hilly country. He breathed in the sweet damp smell of the hay.

Verona was their last Italian city. Milan had originally been on the itinerary, but Janey had by this time picked up a slight fever, so they decided to cut their travels short. Morris was still not feeling quite himself, but almost managed to rise to the occasion in Verona, finding its general beauty and interest 'beyond all praise'. On a lovely cloudless evening, the view from the Arena struck him as superlative: 'I don't know', he told George Howard, 'when I have been so moved by any place.' In his later unfinished Roman tale, 'The Story of Desiderius', Morris rebuilds Verona as the huge and glorious city, a network of fine buildings and generous public squares, built on the two sides of the white water, with vistas across the sand dunes to the domes and towers of Ravenna in the distance. In this fiction, however, the beautiful city is also a place of cruelty and tyranny, and oppression of the poor.

It was now five years since Morris's previous visit to Italy. The reservations he felt then in the appreciation of Renaissance architecture had deepened in the intervening period, the years of his visits to Leek, his indoctrination into real politics, the devastating grief of Jenny's illness. There no longer seems much point in concealing his deep prejudices, which are as much political as aesthetic. 'Let me confess and be hanged,' he writes to Georgie from Verona:

with the later work of Southern Europe I am completely out of sympathy. In spite of its magnificent power and energy I feel it as an enemy; and this much more in Italy, where there is such a mass of it, than elsewhere. Yes, and even in these magnificent and wonderful towns I long rather for the heap of grey stone with a grey roof that we call a house north-away.

Gout has the effect of bringing emotions to the surface. Morris, creeping painfully around Italy in the early summer of 1878, is a heroic and prematurely ageing figure, the 'gouty old fogy' of his letter to Aglaia. He writes as if frequently on the edge of tears. When he first saw Lake Garda in the sunset he was so transfixed that for a minute he had wondered whether he had actually fallen asleep 'and was dreaming of some strange sea where everything had grown together in perfect accord with wild stories'. May and Jenny were with him at Lake Garda, and their impressions were filtered through their father's. May wrote later that these scenes remained so bright because they saw them 'through the emotion he felt and took no trouble to conceal'.

Out of the heat of Italy, Morris's gout improved: 'I am still plaguy lame,' he wrote, 'a very limpet, but am not so devil-ridden as I was.' Maybe the improvement was also psychological as the train took them through the Alps and into France. Travelling home through the Burgundy country on a windy sunny day Morris himself felt almost merry. Only Janey felt nostalgia for Venice and the gondola, the most perfect form of locomotion she had ever found.

CHAPTER TWELVE

Kelmscott House
1879–81

In April 1879, after weeks of agitated correspondence with Janey in Oneglia, Morris took the house that was to be his London home from then on until his death. This was the late eighteenth-century brick mansion, a handsome but conventional Georgian town house, on the Upper Mall in Hammersmith. Like all Morris's London houses it was a compromise building: 'a convenient and seemly shelter from the weather, a place to keep books and pretty things in', not a house in which he had a great emotional investment. May claimed he never felt it was his real home. When he took the house it was known as The Retreat. This name Morris objected to on grounds that it made the building sound like an asylum: 'people would think something was amiss with me and that your poor Mama was trying to reclaim me'. He renamed it Kelmscott House, in deference to his other Kelmscott, the grey stone country manor of infinitely preferable architectural provenance. It pleased him to think of the two Kelmscotts being linked by 120 miles of the same river: the Thames flowed under this window at Hammersmith, conveying his loved landscape of grey gables, meadows, willows, and bringing these mystic memories right into the Great Wen.

The Hammersmith house had excellent credentials. In its days as The Retreat, George MacDonald, the radical preacher, poet and novelist, had lived there. MacDonald's forte as a writer was the creation of dreamworlds: *Phantastes*, the first of his fantasy novels for adults, was published in 1858. In his Hammersmith years he wrote the most famous of his children's books, *The Princess and the Goblin* (1872), a luminescent tale of good and evil, gender difference, death and transformation which, as reviewers were quick to recognize, had 'charms for others besides children'. MacDonald's books, like Morris's 1890s' novels,

391

influenced the whole genre of twentieth-century fantasy novels. It is strange to think of these suggestive magic stories being composed over three decades by two such solid adult writers in that straight up and down London house.

In the MacDonalds' days there was an energetic social life. They were a family of eleven children, and relations and radical literary friends thronged into the house to watch the Oxford and Cambridge Boat Race passing. The four-mile race, from Putney to Mortlake, had become an annual fixture in 1856. One MacDonald child remembered being sent to fetch a cab for Tennyson from the high road, half a mile away. Each winter at The Retreat there was an open day for the tenants of Octavia Hill's model dwellings for the poor at which the MacDonald children acted plays, almost always fairytales written by their mother, and the long day ended with games and country dancing. These were gatherings not just of the poor but of intellectual and artistic do-gooders: the radical historian C. Edmund Maurice; the Rev. Samuel Barnett, who founded Toynbee Hall; Arthur Hughes and his wife; also Georgie and Ned. In 1868, Ruskin had attended the first of these receptions, confessing himself shocked by the poverty-stricken appearance of the guests, in particular the men arriving without collars. He had led off the final Sir Roger de Coverley with Octavia Hill.

When Morris saw the house it had been empty for some months. The MacDonalds had made a hurried exodus to Italy, for the sake of an invalid daughter, and the house was showing signs of neglect and disarray. William De Morgan, taken by Morris to view it, was distinctly unimpressed by the decoration of the principal rooms with their blood red flock paper and long book cases, painted black, and 'a ceiling of azure blue, dotted with gilt stars, considerably tarnished'. An even gloomier report of it was written by Rossetti who, faced with the prospect of a move from Chelsea on the expiry of his lease, had been to view the MacDonalds' house himself. He sent subversive letters to Janey in Oneglia, pointing out the disadvantages of a house which, although basically 'a nice one', was badly overlooked by the new road from the Hammersmith High Road and where dead, saturated leaves formed 'a complete swamp' in the garden. The house was obviously dangerously damp. The worst thing about it, according to Rossetti, was 'a frightful kitchen floor, perfectly dark and very incommodious – the kitchen stairs being a sort of ladder with no light at all, in which smashes would I think assail the ear whenever a meal was going on'. The Hammersmith house became the new bone of contention, as both wrote impassioned letters to Janey in Oneglia: Rossetti vitriolic against it, Morris more and more in favour. He reassured Janey that 'the house could easily be done up at a cost of money and might be made very beautiful with a touch of my art'.

Morris's house-hunting letters are wonderfully revealing of the current state of play between himself and Janey. They are affectionate and careful. Morris takes great trouble to involve her in the detail of decisions, to spell out the pros and cons. He does not gloss over the problems about Hammersmith. It is far from the centre of London, but what are the alternatives? 'I don't think either you or I could stand a quite modern house in a street, say at Notting Hill: I don't fancy going back among the bugs of Bloomsbury: though 'tis a healthy part and we might do worse: we might as well live at York as at Hampstead for all we should ever see of our friends.' He asks her opinion on a possible house in Earls Terrace in Kensington: 'delightfully accessible', but the rent, at £140 per annum, strikes him as ridiculous for a meagre building with so few amenities; it is 'after all a *lodging*, not a house'. In the age-old balancing act between what is desirable in property and what is affordable, Morris's attentiveness to Janey's views is interesting, first of all because he is the professional, the architectural expert and the well-known decorator. His own London houses were inevitably showplaces, permanent exhibitions of Morris & Co. style. His respect for Janey's views is also very striking after the past years' history of marital waverings that has tested him so much. In these letters, remarkably, he dwells upon her comfort and her needs and their contentedness together. He puts it over to her as a joint decision: 'it would not do for either of us to agree to go into a house, in which one or other would pray for an earthquake to knock it down.'

Morris's letters are ebullient, encouraging, enclosing maps and measurements, infecting Janey with his own sense of the possibilities of Kelmscott House. He promises her 'a very nice room' looking out into the garden, 'and sufficiently to yourself to be comfortable'. There are also two good rooms for the 'maidens'. No doubt the urgent need of space and privacy for Jenny was one of the reasons for the move from Turnham Green. Morris describes the position of the house, 'certainly the prettiest in London', with its views south down the river through the elm trees, planted in the seventeenth century when Catherine of Braganza spent several summers on the Upper Mall in a house known as the

Dowager Queen's House. He is even optimistic about the 'dreary room' at the back of the building, the MacDonalds' rough and ready dining-room: 'we should only want it as a subsidiary "larking room", so needn't mind much when it is duly whitewashed: besides we might keep hens in it; or a pig, or a cow; or let it for a ranter's chapel'. There is a coach-house and stabling: he envisages a pony and trap, and cheerfully agrees to Janey's well-timed request for a third maid. People will come to see them there more than they used to, 'if only for the sake of the garden and the river: we will lay ourselves more for company than heretofore'. They could make a bed for Crom, when on his holidays in London; Kate Faulkner has already agreed to come and stay with them. They are now only half an hour's walk from The Grange. As with most of his moves Morris has faith in the new building ushering in a new and better era. He writes to Janey, having come to an agreement with MacDonald: 'So let us hope we shall all grow younger there, my dear.'

In May 1878, when they returned to London, he was only forty-four and Janey thirty-seven. But both were looking aged. Morris portly, going grey, and Janey more than ever angular and anxious. From nervous strain and fever in Oneglia she suffered hair-loss, and she was 'several inches smaller in the waist', signing herself 'Scarecrow' in the first letter she wrote to Rossetti after her return. She tried to delay seeing him, telling him, 'I care nothing at all about my altered looks for my own sake, only I hate to appear before you as a Guy after this long absence.' Rossetti gallantly said he did not care. As soon as she saw Kelmscott House, Janey had warmed to it. 'I thought it a very pleasant place,' she wrote to Rosalind, 'and the garden much bigger than I expected with many paintable bits in it.' She suggested to George Howard that he should set up his easel and make an Etruscan landscape out of Hammersmith. Possibly Janey was misplaced with the Pre-Raphaelites: George's sunlit *campagna* paintings were greatly to her taste.

Morris had proposed to MacDonald an initial rent of £85 a year, well below the going rate of £120 to £140 for a good house with a garden slightly out of central London. He had argued that the necessary refurbishment would involve a great deal of expense. Morris had first called in the Firm's own estimator, Vinall, and then Dunn & Co., the Firm's usual contractor. By this time the reorganization and diversification of the Firm was paying off, and Morris's annual income was increasing. He was calculating on a basis of £1,200 of disposable income the next year.

It was to rise to about £1,800 in the early 1880s. He spent almost £1,000 on the redecoration of Kelmscott House excluding furnishings and fabrics. The work continued through the summer and the early autumn. In early November 1878 the family finally moved in. Philip Webb heard the news at an SPAB gathering, 'between the yells and mingled gabble of a full antiscrape meeting'. He felt a little worried in case, when asked to dinner, he might absentmindedly catch the train from Paddington towards the other Kelmscott. He was glad that he could now return to its real owners the magnificent French cabinet he had had in his safe-keeping because it was too tall for Turnham Green.

The best space in the house is the forty-foot-long drawing-room with five windows facing south across the river. MacDonald had used it as his study, with the notorious red wallpaper and shabby blue ceiling. Morris, who had seen it as potentially 'one of the prettiest rooms in London', transformed it by covering the walls with the heraldic blue 'Bird' woollen double cloth, one of his new fabrics being woven at Queen Square. On the blue carpet were strewn floral Eastern rugs, strategically placed to avoid the heavy traffic: Morris ruled that 'Eastern carpets were not made to be trodden on with hob-nailed boots'. The Red House painted cabinet stood beside the fireplace. May described this as 'a splendid note and gathering in of all the colour in the room'. Philip Webb's big-pillared grate was installed in the open fireplace. This had originally been designed for Queen Square. At right angles to the fire was the hooded settle first used at Red Lion Square. The room was a composite of objects from these remembered places. They gave it an emotional harmony, almost a melancholy born of such deep connection with the past. There was the 'discreet glimmer of old glass' in display cabinets sunk into the walls and, on a long narrow table, a few Far-Eastern pots and plates. As in all Morris's interiors from Red House onwards there was a sense of reduction to essentials: 'No pictures of course – the simple scheme of the room did not allow of such broken wall-surface – no occasional tables, no chairs like feather-beds, no litter of any sort'. Unlike the interiors of, say, the Greek colony in London it did not exude luxury or encourage intimacy. This was a hospitable but not flirtatious room. For the teenage May it held the promise of an entrée to a hitherto closed world of intellectual male vigour: 'Plenty of "quarter deck" in which to march up and down when discussions got animated and ideas needed exercise.'

The second large room at Kelmscott House is the dining-room, sixteen feet tall with its huge curved window facing north over the garden on the ground floor. At first sight this had seemed the least promising of rooms there. Morris had reported: 'The Macs have done their best to make it look dismal.' It had the dourness of so many Scots interiors. Rossetti had expanded in a letter to Janey: 'The dining room (a fine room) was I understand in constant use by fits and starts, a perpetual table being laid for everyone to cut and come again.' Morris continued to find this room oppressive, disliking its classical proportions and its Adam mouldings, but he repented of his original threats to keep a pig in it or rent it to a Primitive Methodist and put his mind to imposing his own style on it, just as he had done in every room he occupied, back to his rooms at Exeter twenty-five years before.

He papered the walls with 'Pimpernel', a looping, scrolling pattern in soft deep greens with small piercingly blue flower-heads. Morris had designed the pattern two years before in his new mode, formal yet free-flowing, giving a sense of maximum enclosure without being claustrophobic. It created in the room a dream quality: a sense of pleasant dislocation. This was the 'enchanted interior' that Sydney Cockerell saw on first arriving at Kelmscott House. In the dining-room, at least, some pictures were permitted, and Rossetti's portrait of Janey hung above the fireplace. One wall was taken up by a white dresser lined with pewter plates and fine blue china. Opposite was Morris's great Italian cypress-wood chest decked with precious pieces of oriental met-alwork and guarded by a pair of ornate brass peacocks with long jewelled necks. May described the exoticism of the scene: 'Above this table of Eastern riches rose up a carpet spread like a canopy across the ceiling'. This is the rare Southern Persian carpet now in the Victoria and Albert Museum. Earlier in 1878 Morris had been impressed with an exhibition of Eastern art at the showroom of the carpet merchant Vincent Joseph Robinson, who had shipped over a complete room from Damascus and recreated it in London: 'it is all vermillion and gold and ultramarine very beautiful and is just like going into the Arabian Nights.' The dining-room at Hammersmith was Morris's own Damascus room.

The decorations of Kelmscott House can be regarded as the ultimate example of Morris's style in its maturity. It is interesting how far his ideas have by this time been assimilated into the general vocabulary: visitors to Hammersmith would confess themselves surprised by the vibrancy of colour or the detail of arrangement. But there is none of the outrage expressed by earlier critics of Red House. No one now accused

Morris of savagery or rawness: partly because by now they are so skilful, Morris's interiors no longer have the power to shock. Bernard Shaw, who first visited the house as a young man in the middle 1880s, left a credible, if self-congratulatory, account of its combination of the wayward with the decorous:

Some people, going into Morris' house, and finding it remarkably unlike their own house, would say 'What a queer place!' Others with a more cultivated sense of beauty, would say 'How very nice!' But neither of them would necessarily have seen what I saw at once, that there was an extraordinary discrimination at work in this magical house. Nothing in it was there because it was interesting or quaint or rare or hereditary, like grandmother's or uncle's portrait. Everything that was necessary was clean and handsome: everything else was beautiful and beautifully presented. There was an oriental carpet so lovely that it would have been a sin to walk on it; consequently it was not on the floor but on the wall and half way across the ceiling. There was no grand piano: such a horror would have been impossible. On the supper table there was no table cloth: a thing common enough now among people who see that a table should be itself an ornament and not a clothes horse, but then an innovation so staggering that it cost years of domestic conflict to introduce it.

Shaw saw the house in Hammersmith as the expression of Morris's 'artistic taste of extraordinary integrity', and understood how far this was a facet of his ruthlessness. Morris was undistracted, not seduced.

Morris's own rooms, his bedroom and his study, were on the ground floor, facing the river. Later photographs confirm May's description of her father's quarters as 'almost frugally bare', with no carpets or curtains in the study and a plain deal board on trestles as a writing table. No wallpaper: the walls were almost entirely lined with books. The only indulgence was his multitude of boxes. He had what was almost a passion for containers. In the corner of the study was a fine inlaid Italian cabinet. Smaller decorative boxes – snuff-boxes and coffers – would appear from time to time among the piled-up papers and books on his desk. His childhood love of certain perfumes had stayed with him, and May kept poignant memories of her father dabbing a flask of Sainsbury's lavender water on a big bandanna handkerchief and 'inhaling the sweet smell with an absent kind of relish' as he wandered around Janey's room upstairs.

The garden had been one of the attractions of Hammersmith. Morris, writing to Janey, had listed out the trees: '1st a walnut by the stable; 2nd a very fine tulip-tree halfway down the lawn. 3rd 2 horse chestnuts at the end of the lawn'. Beyond that was a small orchard with good fruit trees, a greenhouse and a kitchen garden with more fruit trees round the walls. It was a long garden, and Morris had attempted to divide it out into separate small spaces, in a way that reminded Georgie of Red House. Morris did his best with it, ordering new gravel for the walk that wound right round the garden and planning new oak planking for the borders, hoping the effect would not be too like Chatsworth. He urged on the gardener, 'poor old Matthews', an aged retainer he shared with his neighbours the Richmonds. Matthews was hopelessly slow, but Morris, who was tender-hearted with employees, could not bring himself to sack him: 'even on selfish grounds', he wrote to Janey, 'a new system of horticulture will be more than the garden or I can stand'. But although the town garden gave him intermittent pleasure Morris had been spoilt with gardens, real gardens in the country. He complained about the London cats which used it 'as a pleasure ground' and said that the soil was chiefly composed of 'old shoes and soot'.

Materially speaking the Morrises had entered a new period of comfort. There are three household servants entered in the Census a year and a half after they moved to Hammersmith: Annie (38), cook; Elsa (25) housemaid; Elizabeth (29) parlour maid. Their standard of living was on a par with that of other neighbouring families of the artistic middle classes: the Richmonds at Beavor Lodge, the Holman Hunts at Draycott House in Putney, the Burne-Joneses at The Grange. This was the network of studio society in which 'Jennyanmay', as they had been known in their old days at the High School, still had their closest friends.

These friends were invited to Kelmscott House. Large parties would arrive to watch the Boat Race, as in the MacDonalds' days. It was not Janey's favourite event: 'there is a dreadful thing called a "Boat Race" in our part of London, which I am only too glad to avoid,' she wrote to Wilfrid Blunt. But Morris made efforts to entertain the visitors. At one of the parties, once the race was finished, Morris joined in the most delirious game of Prisoner's Base that Helena Swanwick had ever played. Helena, one of the 'Jennyanmay' circle, spent many Sunday afternoons at Hammersmith, marvelling at 'Mrs. Morris reclining on a couch in all her strange beauty, her long, pale hands moving deftly over some rich embroidery'. Janey got on well with young girls; there was always something girlish, almost unformed in her nature. Other friends would sometimes point out her basic simplicity of nature, suggesting that in fact her beauty was a burden and that within that enigmatic gaunt exterior 'a bright chatty little woman' was struggling to get out. Certainly on these undemanding afternoons she flourished. Helena would wait for her 'delicious chuckling laugh', as they talked and Janey stitched on, so expertly 'voiding' the lines of the leaves and petals on her frame. Then later, 'There would come exciting moments when she would rise and fling the great *portière* down and spread it out,' to judge the overall impact of the piece.

May was beginning to go out to little dances in the studio houses of Hammersmith and Kensington. Helena also remembered the evening the Morris parents went out deliberately, leaving their daughters to have a dinner party for their friends. Such scenes of life at Hammersmith show how intent they were on providing a context in which May's life could continue as near as possible to normal, and Jenny's illness be most plausibly contained.

One typical enterprise of this period was *The Scribbler*, the home-made literary magazine that occupied Jenny, as editor and chief con-tributor, for eighteen months from the winter of 1878. She elicited pieces from May and from other friends and relations, including Rudyard Kipling, the young cousin of the Burne-Jones children, who was then about fourteen. Kipling, as a child, was impressed by 'Uncle Topsy', and especially taken with his story-telling faculty, giving an account in his memoirs of a surprise visit by Morris to the nursery when Kipling was staying with the Burne-Joneses. 'We settled ourselves under the table which we used for a toboggan slide and he, gravely as ever, climbed on to our big rocking horse. There, slowly surging back and forth while the poor beast creaked, he told us a tale full of fascinating horrors, about a man who was condemned to bad dreams. One of them took the shape of a cow's tail waving from a heap of dried fish.' Morris's Icelandic sagas are packed with such strange detail. We may ask how Uncle Topsy, swaying on his rocking horse, awakened Rudyard Kip-ling's own love of the macabre.

Though life at Kelmscott House was equable and cosy, to some extent consciously so, the outside urban world impinged more obviously than at Turnham Green or even at Queen Square. This was partly because of the house's position on the river. When she first arrived there, Janey had been unable to sleep because of the noise of the river steamers passing in the night. Down the Thames to the east they were all conscious of the flare of London industry and the vague throbbing of traffic and

399

machines. Morris himself, in his ground-floor study, was particularly vulnerable. Upper Mall itself appeared so quiet and respectable but it was on the edge of disreputable London. As Rossetti had warned Janey, the area between the high road and the river held 'a labyrinth of slums'. May described how 'ragged mites from the neighbouring riverside slum would tumble around, turning our garden steps too into their play-ground', squealing and screaming until Morris, 'enduring until the exact moment came when he could endure no longer', would go out and implore them to go away and play elsewhere. Once, as he walked down Rivercourt Road, a small chubby urchin swinging on one of the iron gates jeered: 'Have a ride – Morris!' In Hammersmith he was confronted by the socially inadequate, and by the suicidal for whom the Thames had a terrible allure. In the diary he kept in 1881, he noted that a man pulled out of the water by the iron railings died in spite of attempted resuscitation. A few days later he was summoned to the coroner's, as a witness of the scene.

If Morris had not been alive already to the iniquitous divisions in society, his Hammersmith house would have had all the ingredients to bring about conversion. The view from his Georgian study window came to haunt him. He imagined a long line of hungry desperate poor people, etiolated figures of a Gustave Doré engraving, pressing close to his window, almost in the house. The nerve-racked despair that was now taking hold of Morris erupts into the lecture he gave first in Burslem Town Hall in 1881, on 'Art and the Beauty of the Earth':

Look you, as I sit at work at home, which is at Hammersmith, close to the river, I often hear go past the window some of that ruffianism of which a good deal has been said in the papers of late . . . As I hear the yells and shrieks and all the degradation cast on the glorious tongue of Shakespeare and Milton, as I see the brutal reckless faces and figures go past me, it rouses recklessness and brutality in me also, and fierce wrath takes possession of me, till I remember, as I hope I mostly do, that it was my good luck only of being born respectable and rich, that has put me on this side of the window among delightful books and lovely works of art, and not on the other side, in the empty street, the drink-steeped liquor shops, the foul and degraded lodgings. What words can say what all that means?

The middle 1870s were Morris's dyeing years, the late 1870s his weaving years. He set himself to acquiring a deep knowledge of the processes of weaving silk and woollen fabrics, hand-knotting rugs and carpets and making the high-warp tapestry that, from early in 1877, was becoming his 'bright dream'. His intention was not necessarily to divest himself of sub-contractors. Even when he had set up his own weaving-looms, he continued using the Macclesfield company Brough, Nicholson & Co. for large orders for silk fabrics. Alongside their own hand-knotted carpets the Firm also supplied machine-made Brussels, Wilton and Axminster carpets produced by the Wilton Royal Carpet Factory Co. His greatly increased technical knowledge allowed Morris to lay down standards for outside manufacturers convincingly as well as to develop many more of his own products. As with dyeing, his mastery of weaving was to give him a new measure of control, and again he found enormous satisfaction in the physicality and the built-in rhythms. 'I am writing in a whirlwind of dyeing and weaving, and even as to the latter rather excited by a new piece just out of the loom, which looks beautiful, like a flower garden.' Work could be a form of ecstasy.

Silk weaving had begun in 1877 at Queen Square. 'I very much want to set up a loom for *brocade* weaving,' Morris had written in the spring of that year, enlisting Thomas Wardle's help in the recruitment of a weaver from Lyons skilled in the figured silks that were a speciality of the region. In June Louis Bazin, referred to as 'Our Froggy weaver', had arrived. Morris rented workshop space in Great Ormond Yard for weaving, enlarging the windows in an upper storey to provide good lighting. Bazin arrived with his own loom, not a hand-loom but a Jacquard, the mechanical loom invented in France at the beginning of the nineteenth century, involving the punching of the pattern on a series of cards which were then fed into the loom in the correct order. It was not a way of working which encouraged the creative input of the workman but it allowed more freedom to the designer and produced fabrics more consistent in quality than the traditional draw looms could have done. Here we see Morris less concerned in practice with the ideal conditions of production as with optimum quality of product. When it came to a battle of fanaticisms excellence of product usually won.

Bazin made a slow start. Morris was shy with him, as he was with most employees. F. G. Guy, the young son of Morris's ex-tutor, worked at Queen Square that summer before going up to Oxford. His naïve but watchful diary reveals how William Morris 'did not feel as if he wanted to face Froggy at first', delegating the job to George Wardle and retreating to his room. The language was a further barrier to progress.

Morris would not grapple with it, complaining to George Howard, 'many a time in the day have I cause to curse that basest of jargon so grossly misnamed the Frankish or French tongue'. The imperious demands of the new master evidently upset Bazin: he succumbed to what seems to have been a nervous illness and, to Morris's further irritation, spent some time in hospital. Guy's diary reported Morris in near despair as Bazin attempted to produce a figured silk adapted from the 'Willow' wallpaper design. On 21 September, although Bazin was improving at operating the machine, 'the [willow] pattern did not seem to be coming right, and it seemed as if the cards had got misplaced somehow or other. The cards were making an absurd pattern and WM did not know what to make of it. WM returned to Kelmscott by the 6.30 train.' But at last by late autumn the weaving was progressing. An assistant to Bazin was employed, and more weavers gradually taken on, mostly decrepit old men from Spitalfields made redundant from the declining London silk trade. May found them pathetic to watch at work. They were later to find working conditions in Morris's factory at Merton Abbey more congenial, liking its 'queer old sheds by the willow-shaded stream'.

In Morris's woven textiles of this period his designs became noticeably more formal, more heraldic. The reason for this is partly technical: symmetrical patterns with repeats turning over around a series of central vertical axes come naturally to the loom. Morris at the time was also examining historic textiles at the South Kensington Museum, especially the Italian late-mediaeval patterns. He was building up his own collection of samples: he lists at this period four pieces of brocatelle, c.1520; a collection of cut velvets, 'various dates from about 1560, very curious and valuable'; a lady's jacket 'knitted of green silk and gold, pretty'; scraps of a fine piece of gold cloth. He was also looking hard at natural forms, not just plants but local wild life, telling Thomas Wardle, 'I am studying birds now to see if I can't get some of them into my next design'. 'Bird'; 'Bird and Vine'; 'Dove and Rose'; 'Peacock and Dragon': for Morris's succession of bird fabrics of the later 1870s he draws on both his scholarly research and his natural observation in a way that is typically Victorian and also, in its beauty and good humour, peculiar to Morris. These birds are recognizable domestic birds but also highly allusive mythical creatures, like the omniscient bird in the strange poem, 'The Watching of the Falcon', in *The Earthly Paradise*:

And while he thought of this and that,
Upon his perch the falcon sat
Unfed, unhooded, his bright eyes
Beholders of the hard-earned prize.

Morris's new involvement in the technical processes of weaving released new creative energies, as dyeing had done earlier. His weaves are in a way more interesting than his chintzes because of the permutations of the textures: silk and cotton, wool and silk. Perhaps the most splendid is 'St James's', Morris's design for the palace, in woven silk damask combined with figured silk. Morris designed some special *broché* silks for dresses but these met with resistance from the London dressmakers who had their own favourite sources of supply. However May's and Janey's best gowns were of 'Anemone', a rich black silk brocade designed by Morris. Janey also had two dresses made from the fabrics for St James's Palace: the golden silk damask, described by May as 'fit only for her stately figure', and the green 'Oak' silk with its 'moonbeam lights'.

Morris had been designing floor coverings since the middle 1870s. The first of his designs to be registered in June 1875 was in fact for a printed linoleum called 'Corticine floor cloth' in an African marigold design. His first designs for the machine-made carpets produced for him by outside manufacturers were registered in that same year, and he was gradually able to arrive at better colours by stipulating that the carpets should be woven in the yarns he and Wardle were developing at Leek. But when it came to making his own carpets these were not loom-woven but hand-knotted carpets, made on the Eastern model. Such carpets had not been made before in Britain on anything like the scale Morris envisaged. Again he was entering new creative territory. He explained that his aim was 'to make England independent of the East for the supply of hand-made Carpets which may claim to be considered works of art'.

Like his love of illuminated manuscripts Morris's ardour for the carpets of the East had begun when he was young. Carpets answered to his craving for the rare and the exotic: the carpet, magic artefact of Eastern narrative, became part of Morris's personal reverie. He had been collecting fine examples of old carpets since his days at Red House, and had built up such reserves of expert knowledge that by the 1870s the South Kensington Museum keepers were coming to Morris for advice on their own purchases. As his plans for carpet making were advancing, his enthusiasm for prize examples of old Eastern art intensified. In 1877 he wrote to Wardle: 'I saw yesterday a piece of *ancient* Persian time of Shah Abbas (our Elizabeth's time) that fairly threw me on my back: I had no idea that such wonders could be done in carpets.' In Venice in the following spring he got so heated bargaining with a dealer over two fine Persian carpets that George Howard had to intervene and the gondolier, watching idly from the doorway, was surprised to see the '*grande poeta*' so beside himself. One of these two purchases was destined for the Tapestry Room at Kelmscott House. On the way back home through Paris Morris was still pursuing carpets, as Janey told Rosalind, showing her irritation: 'we had but a dreary day there going in a cab to different curiosity shops, finding many fine carpets full of holes, but fortunately buying none.'

Before Morris started on the making of his carpets there was the usual inquisitive, investigative phase in which he analysed an ancient Persian carpet in great detail, teaching himself from it the processes involved. Next he had a frame set up in the attic in Queen Square, anxiously supervising the first trial squares. In 1879 production was moved to Hammersmith, where several carpet frames were installed in the coach-house and stables. A professional carpet weaver from Glasgow came down for a few weeks to give technical assistance, and Morris's first carpet makers were recruited. There were usually to be about six of them, all female. They were expected to hand-knot two inches of carpet a day. The carpets were marketed as 'Hammersmith' carpets. A hammer and a zig-zag, to represent the river, were woven into the border: a primitive logo, curiously close to the hammer-and-the-sickle adopted by the USSR in 1923.

When a large carpet came off the loom at Hammersmith, the family would be called across the garden to view it before it was sent to the showroom. For the first few years in Hammersmith, as at Queen Square, family life went on close to work. Kelmscott House, and the stables, were vulnerable to flooding and one Sunday afternoon a rescue operation was mounted by the Morris family and several Sunday guests to save the Naworth carpet, still in progress on the loom, from an abnormally high tide. There was no attempt to integrate the workers with the family, as there would be later with May and her embroideresses or as would be attempted in more socially radical Arts and Crafts communities of c.1900. But the impression visitors were given was of a peculiarly domestic industry. When Octavia Hill went to Kelmscott House to visit Morris she wrote excitedly: 'He took us all over the garden and into his study, and such an interesting carpet factory . . . It was just in his own garden. The tapestry he had been making himself in his own study was beautiful!!'

In the early design stages Morris delegated little. He drew out the design on a piece of scaled-up paper, filling in one section only if it was a repeat design, and colouring the drawing very prettily in gouache. The Victoria and Albert Museum has dozens of these delicate part-finished designs, showing Morris's work in progress: they give one a remarkable impression of his technical assurance and visualizing skill. May commented perceptively how these 'designs in little were beautiful for their mosaic-like filling of rich colour – a strange contrast to the lovely tangle of flowers in the illuminations of earlier days'. She remembered clearly 'with what relish he added the firmly drawn outlines of white or pale orange'. Working out new ways of colouring for the special technical demands of carpet making seemed to them both a hugely enjoyable new game. For his pattern designing Morris kept an all-purpose set of ordinary water-colours in tubes: Prussian blue, yellow ochre, gamboge, raw umber, Venetian red, crimson lake, Chinese white, lamp black and Chinese ink. 'What a lot of raw umber and Chinese white we used sometimes!' wrote May in a glow of sentimental recollection of a time when she herself was discovering her *métier*. Her role was as her father's technical assistant, helping in the tracing and enlargement of the designs to full size on to point paper under his instructions. These were the kind of tasks allotted to the fifteen-year-old Frank Brangwyn, who started his career as an apprentice at Queen Square in 1882.

How successful was the episode? How Eastern were these carpets? It has to be admitted that Hammersmith rugs and carpets have little of the finesse of the Persian examples that Morris had in theory set out to emulate. This was partly their technique: Morris, being realistic about his makers' capabilities, and also aware of the limits of his market, did not attempt to use the ancient Persian knotting method. His carpets are made using the coarser Turkish, or Ghiordes, type of knot. Morris's smaller-scale rugs, which were often duplicated and which soon became a decorator's cliché, are amongst the most disappointing of his products: they often seem uncomfortably cramped and almost crude, like a poor man's miniature carpets. Unlike, say, the abstract rugs made later in the Omega Workshops, they lack their own creative life. It is in the later large-scale and unique handmade carpets, centrepieces of the firm's ambitious country-house interiors, that Morris's designs and techniques merge triumphantly. Even these are not, in any real sense, Eastern-style carpets. The idiom is different, the iconography is English, with its oak leaves and fritillaries, its river birds, its reminiscences of English woods and meadows. The colouring is particular to Morris. The enormous 'Clouds' carpet, now at Regent House in Cambridge, is a marvellous example: a bright peacock-blue background, Morris's celebration colour, with a flowing, tangling pattern of deep greens and fawns.

A letter to Janey, sent from Hammersmith in summer 1880, shows Morris at his happiest. 'Breakfast is over and I have been carpeteering: the Orchard, spread out on the drawing room floor, though not perfect as a piece of manufacture is not amiss; as a work of art I am a *little* disappointed with it: if I do it again it shall have a wider border I think ... The 3 yellow bordered pots are not so flat as they should be: I fear the worsted warp is to blame for this: I shall use cotton in future, and perhaps dye it blue roughly.' Morris had a broad vision, broader than most of his Victorian contemporaries. Unlike anyone else he had this concurrent capacity for practical experiment. It is in his combination of the thinking and the doing that Morris's true originality is found.

Morris regarded tapestry as the summit of what could be achieved in textiles. He saw it as essentially wall decoration, 'a mosaic of pieces of colour made up of dyed thread'. Morris liked its exactness: in a tapestry, he argued, 'nothing vague or indeterminate is possible'. He admired the depth of tone, the richness of colour and the subtle variations of tone feasible in tapestry; and especially he warmed to 'that crispness and abundance of beautiful detail' characteristic of mediaeval embroidery and weaving. It was this vividness of detail he had noticed when he first saw the Bayeux Tapestry. To Morris the mediaeval tapestry was the equivalent of a Chaucer poem, precise in its narrative, human in its range of reference, eloquent, alive. Tapestry, like stained glass, was a story-telling medium. It was public art, immediately accessible. Morris loved woven pictures, even as a child.

He had kept these ambitions in abeyance until the Firm's carpet making was progressing satisfactorily. To his annoyance Queen Victoria had preempted him. In 1875 The Windsor Tapestry Works had been established, under the Queen's patronage, on royal land at Old Windsor.

Morris complained to Wardle: 'The *Widow Guelph* has been enticing customers from us and has got an order for tapestry that ought to have been ours.' However, by the end of 1877 he and Wardle had entered into practical discussions about plans for making tapestry. It appears that Wardle's aims were more commercial than artistic. Perhaps he saw a Leek equivalent of the royal works at Windsor. Morris felt this would be pointless: 'Let's clear off what you say about the possibility of establishing a non-artistic manufactory: you could do it of course; 'tis only a matter of money and trouble: but, cui bono?'

Morris's own plans were artistically purist and once again he had no obvious points of reference. As he told Aymer Vallance in an interview on 'The Revival of Tapestry Weaving' in *The Studio*, the looms in use at Windsor, which Morris had investigated, were horizontal looms operated by a weaver working opposite the picture he was making. Morris considered this method mechanical and artistically limiting. He intended to pursue the high-warp or *haute-lisse* method, as used to make the mediaeval Flemish tapestries, in which the weaver works from *behind* the tapestry, watching the progress of the picture through a mirror. This method gave the weaver more creative freedom. Morris also liked to think that Penelope and other ancient tale-tellers had created picture stories on just such an antique loom. Though the high-warp loom was still in use in Paris, at the Gobelins works where Morris much despised its products, there was no more local source of information and Morris, once again, fell back on ancient technical manuals, in this case a book from the *Arts et métiers* series published in eighteenth-century France.

Morris knew in theory the qualities he looked for in a maker of tapestries. He had listed them out in a letter he sent Wardle:

1. General feeling for art, especially for its decorative side.
2. He must be a good colourist.
3. He must be able to draw well; i.e. he must be able to draw the human figure, especially hands and feet.
4. Of course he must know how to use the stitch of the work.

He continued, 'I have no idea where to lay my hands on such a man, and therefore I feel that whatever I do I must do chiefly with my own hands.' Morris had an experimental loom erected in his bedroom at Kelmscott House. He got up very early and worked at his loom almost every morning through the summer of 1879.

Morris left a small black diary of the progress of the tapestry that started as 'Acanthus and Vine' and was later to be renamed 'Cabbage and Vine' as the acanthus leaves became wilder, like a wondrous vegetable quite beyond control. 'Cabbage and Vine' is a 'verdure' pattern, swirling: based on pairs of leaves and pairs of birds. Morris began it on 10 May. Some mornings he worked for one hour or for two hours; some days he records as much as six or seven hours; occasionally he spent a day of nine or ten hours at the loom. In June there is a note in the margin: 'a month: weather very bad all this time, often dark'. May would sit at the end of his long bench and watch him working as the great curling leaves grew on the warp threads 'under the nervous swift-moving fingers'. Morris bent his head from time to time to peer between the warp threads and check on the design reflected in the mirror on the right side of the web.

The record breaks off on 17 September. The 'Cabbage and Vine' was by no means completed. But Morris had acquired the basic technique he needed. 'I have taught myself the art of tapestry-weaving, the signs of which might amuse you,' he wrote in October to William Bell Scott. He set up another loom at Queen Square and transferred a young craftsman, J. H. Dearle, from the stained-glass painting workshop to the tapestry department. Dearle was still with Morris & Co. in 1930, at which point his retirement began to be discussed. Two unskilled young boys were taken on as tapestry apprentices. The foundations were laid for the development of high-warp tapestry at Merton Abbey in the 1880s on a grander scale.

Morris had discovered a new kind of therapy. Tapestry weaving became almost a drug to him. He was back at the loom in his bedroom in the morning brightness of the summer months of 1881. The manual activity would soothe him. Where his loom was there his home was. The well-known Burne-Jones cartoon of Morris weaving, the back view exuding great waves of concentration, shows him almost literally grafted to the loom. In moments of stress he would be seized with a great longing for the life of the small-timer, the artist-artisan, with its limited horizons and its occupational certainties: 'Lord bless us how nice it will be when I can get back to my little patterns and dyeing, and the dear warp and weft at Hammersmith!'

The Empress Brown is hard at work at her rival establishment: I am sure she expects to get the whole of the ornamental upholstery of the Kingdom into her hands: let her tremble! I will under-sell her in all branches.

Morris's personal dislike of Queen Victoria, amounting almost to a physical revulsion from a queen so unaesthetic, was for its period unusually strong.

In the spring of 1877 his position as a general household furnisher was strengthened when the Firm leased a shop at No. 264 (later 449) Oxford Street, on the corner of North Audley Street. The not especially distinguished red-brick block was new. It gave the Firm a reasonable frontage with two windows, though references to clerks working in back passages suggest that, as in most shops, the staff areas were relatively cramped. Morris claimed to be lukewarm about his company's incursions into the commercial heart of London, saying that 'a shed with a half dozen looms in it' would have pleased him more. But there is no doubt that a shop so close to Morris's most fashionable competitors – Liberty's in Regent Street, Morant's in Bond Street – contributed enormously to the future expansion of the Firm.

At Queen Square the atmosphere had been relatively casual. One day Georgie arrived there just after the Princess of Wales had paid a visit: both Mr. Morris and Mr. Wardle were out and she had been received by underlings'. The regime was given a new professionalism by the appointment of two brothers, Robert and Frank Smith. To start with, one brother was employed to manage the new shop whilst the other Mr Smith remained at the old showroom. Morris wrote from Queen Square to Charley Faulkner's sister Lucy: 'You are very welcome to any information our Misters Smith can give you either he of Oxford St. or he of here.' But when Queen Square was closed down, as the Firm moved out to Merton, both Smiths seem to have gravitated towards Oxford Street. The smooth service disconcerted some of Morris's old clients. De Morgan complained about the airs and condescension of the 'shopmen' at Morris's: 'I wish to goodness', he remarked as he left, 'they would not treat us as if they were all Ptolemies.'

As Morris became involved in new forms of manufacturing the shop's range of its own exclusive merchandise increased. By the early 1880s Morris & Co. could offer: 'Painted Glass; Embroidery, and material for same; Arras tapestry; Hammersmith carpets; Axminster, Wilton and Kidderminster carpets; Damasks for wall-hangings, curtains and furniture in wool, wool and silk, cotton and silk, and all silk; Stamped velvets; Printed cloths for wall-hanging, curtains etc; Wallpapers'. No other London decorating firm could compete with such a range of products either made in its own workshops or produced to its strict specifications by outside suppliers. At Morris & Co., as at Heal & Son later, the great selling point was the sense of a personal artistic control. A review in *Building News* in 1880 emphasized 'the spirit of individuality and unity' pervading the shop in Oxford Street: 'we do not see a variety of conceptions in different styles, nor a number of patterns by various artists; all the work is exceptionally good, and is due to Mr. Morris himself we believe.'

Morris's 'merchandising for the firm' had been continuing. The regular, repeatable furniture and furnishings were supplemented by Morris's own choice of special objects, which gave the shop its feeling of serendipity. The *Building News* reviewer, on his visit, noticed 'two fine Vases of Oriental design and glazing, and a Spanish lustre': all these 'of bold design'. On his visit to Venice Morris had attempted to commission some glass from one of the small workshops at Murano. He, Janey and the girls stood in the little shed, with its sudden fiery glow as the furnace door was opened. May remembered how her father drew the outline of a tumbler on the dusty floor. The glass blower then produced a sample: 'a simple little glass of slightly coloured, bubbly metal'. But at this point the negotiations stopped because the craftsman was not convinced that Morris was in earnest. On another day they met a barrow piled with glasses in the street and Morris indicated that he was prepared to buy some. The man asked him how many. 'Oh, a thousand or two,' Morris had replied.

He had kept many of his original clients, the friends and fellow-artists from Pre-Raphaelite circles for whom patronizing Morris had become a habit. He and Ned were occupied with the decorations of the Howards' London house, No. 1 Palace Green, into the early 1880s, and the account books at Castle Howard reveal that house's huge consumption of Morris & Co. wallpapers through the 1880s and 1890s. Sixteen rolls of 'Sunflower' for the Yellow Schoolroom; 9 rolls of 'Daisy' for the Boys' Schoolroom; 24 rolls of 'Bird and Anemone' for the High Saloon, covering over the eighteenth-century frescoes by Pellegrini. Morris's 'Venetian' pattern was chosen for the Gatehouse. Morris and Rosalind, the supplier and the client, opened up new realms of possibility in that relationship:

Item, I can do the most ravishing yellows, rather what people call amber: what would you say to dullish pink shot with amber; like some of those chrysanthemums we see just now?

The poet as salesman. Morris's persuasive use of language gives an almost flirtatious quality to their exchange. When he sends Rosalind samples from Oxford Street he marks them 'recommended' and 'specially recommended'. He conveys the feeling that choice is as important to him as it can be to her.

Morris's aristocratic clientele had been developing. In January 1877 he had visited the Duke of Westminster to discuss the decoration of Alfred Waterhouse's new chapel at Eaton Hall. Perhaps this was the encounter described by Luke Ionides between Morris and an unnamed duke: 'Everything', said Morris, 'was so frightfully ugly I didn't know where to begin.' Later that year, Morris had been summoned to the Countess of Charleville at Tullamore, near Kildare in southern Ireland. He set off on the mail train to Holyhead from Euston carrying his patterns of carpets, silks and chintzes. On the road south of Dublin he noticed the extreme poverty of the villages he passed through: 'the cotters' houses in outside appearance the very poorest habitations of man I have yet seen, Iceland by no means excepted'. In 1880 the radical spokesman and vilifier of the Widow Guelph was recalled to St James's Palace first to decorate the entrance and staircases, then to work through the main sequence of great State Rooms culminating in the Throne Room. In 1881 Morris wrote to Janey, 'Work at St. James all finished and happily, with good profit: so don't spare to ask for cash if you want it when shall I send you some?'

By the early 1880s Morris had also acquired more customers from the ranks of rich industrialists and provincial entrepreneurs, the traditional clientele of the Pre-Raphaelite painters. These are the patrons whose collections, undervalued for a century in the galleries of Birmingham, Manchester, Newcastle, Bradford and other provincial cities, have now come into their own. The purchasers were solid successful men of business with a yearning for the culture of faërie and mediaevalist romance. This was a particular form of rich man's snobbery, the wistfulness of practical people for the world of the imagination. When the lawyer Walter Bagehot commissioned Morris & Co. to decorate his house in Queen's Gate, London, he boasted 'the great man himself, William Morris, is composing the drawing room as he would an ode'. In these close-knit families one commission could generate commissions spreading outwards to sons and daughters as they married. William Morris designed for the whole dynasty of the northern ironmaster Sir Isaac Lowthian Bell, as we have seen. Towards these faithful clients

Morris evinced mixed feelings. He was becoming more conscious of his falseness of position in 'ministering to the swinish luxury of the rich'. As his sympathies with the poor and disadvantaged deepen, his outbursts against his clients show the edginess he felt, to the point of neurotic shrillness. He complains about the 'sadly stupid', 'monstrously rich' Catherine Lorillard Wolfe, the American philanthropist: 'hurrah therefore for the social revolution!' He rejects the demands for after-sale service from Mrs Clark at Brentford, who had purchased Morris's curtains: 'really,' he tells Jenny, 'when one sells a body porridge one should not be expected to put it in their mouth with a spoon'.

Perhaps it was as well for the fortunes of the Firm that by the 1880s customers extended far beyond those with whom Morris had personal dealings. Morris & Co. had become a household word: supplier of furnishings to the new artistic middle class. When the Bedford Park estate was laid out in west London, mainly in the Queen Anne style, the majority of residents selected Morris wallpapers and chintzes: so much so, wrote Moncure Conway in his *Travels in South Kensington*, 'that a branch of the Bloomsbury establishment will probably become necessary in the vicinity of Bedford Park'. Morris products contributed to a style, a 'look', an alternative aesthetic. They combined to create the fantasy land that had delighted W. B. Yeats as a child when he moved to a house in Bedford Park.

We were to see De Morgan tiles, peacock-blue doors and the pomegranate pattern and the tulip pattern of Morris, and to discover that we had always hated doors painted with imitation grain, the roses of mid-Victoria, and tiles covered with geometrical patterns that seemed to have been shaken out of a muddy kaleidoscope. We went to live in a house like those we had seen in pictures and even meet people dressed like people in the story-books.

It is ironic that Norman Shaw, chief architect of Bedford Park, was one of the few people who knew Morris and disliked him. He thought Morris was a humbug, overcharging for his wallpapers, 'full of cranks and general stubbornness . . . Being an advanced Socialist he cannot do with much less than from 100% to 250% clear profit in his work, and so his work is dear!!!' Reginald Blomfield, fellow architect and admirer of both men, pointed out their basic incompatibility of temperament: 'Morris was impetuous and fanciful, he was not called "Topsy" by his friends without reason; Shaw was a cool-headed Scot, of first-rate ability, with immense power of concentration, with no strong instincts for poetry.'

A whole cultural history could be written in terms of Morris furnishings. They have always been the safe choice of the intellectual classes, an exercise in political correctitude. North Oxford of the 1880s was all Morris. Morris's *Daily Telegraph* obituary recorded: 'when married tutors dawned upon the academic world, all their wives religiously clothed their walls in Norham-gardens and Bradmore road with Morrisian designs of clustering pomegranates.' Those were days of 'green serge gowns and Morris papers. Every lady of culture had an amber necklace,' wrote Elizabeth Wordsworth, the first principal of Lady Margaret Hall.

Edward Johnston the calligrapher used Morris's 'Willow Boughs' in all his houses. Oscar Wilde had an embossed Morris wallpaper in the smoking-room of his house in Tite Street: 'when you poked it with your finger, it popped and split'. There were Morris furnishings in the house of Stewart Headlam, where Wilde was taken on his return from Reading Gaol. Hubert Bland was puzzled by the 'strangely designed wallpapers' and 'sad coloured velveteens' of the Fabian aesthetic. Beatrice Webb chose Morris wallpaper and furniture, hoping to make her home in Grosvenor Road as beautiful as possible considering her 'limited cash and still more limited taste'. Bernard Shaw commented, astutely, that Morris's sense of rightness, so obvious in his own interiors at Hammersmith and Kelmscott, could easily go wrong in other people's hands. The Pankhursts were brought up with Morris in the background: when a penniless Italian refugee arrived on Sylvia Pankhurst's doorstep in the 1930s she called him 'William Morris' because he was an artist. Frances Partridge remembered 'dark and jungly' Morris patterns in her parents' fine old creaking house in Bedford Square: birds eating strawberries on her mother's curtains, parrots on the wall of her father's drawing-room where she would find him in bed in frogged pyjamas. Aldous Huxley was a child in 'chintzy rooms, modern with William Morris'. In the Keynes family house in Harvey Road in Cambridge the walls of 'the rather dark dining room were clad in deep blue and crimson William Morris paper of such quality that, except for occasional patching, it never needed renewal'. In another house in Cambridge, Sydney Cockerell's study was heavily curtained in Morris fabrics, a suffocating shrine. T. E. Lawrence, a fan of Morris, was in ecstasies on visiting 'the perfect Morris house' at Broad Campden in the Cotswolds. This was the ancient Norman Chapel converted by Ananda Coomaraswamy and hung with Morris tapestries. The low galleries were screened with

Morris chintz, the long refectory tables and shelves were 'full of the Kelmscott printings'; the purpose-made oak lectern displayed the Kelmscott *Chaucer*. Coomaraswamy's act of homage was completed by the purchase of the 'very hand press Morris himself had used'.

In the late 1920s, Kenneth Clark chose Morris paper for the bedroom of the house he moved into with his wife in Tufton Street in Westminster: the house, he wrote, was otherwise 'irredeemable'. To his colleagues' disapproval at the ultra-modernist *Architectural Review* in the 1930s, John Betjeman had his top-floor office papered in a Morris wallpaper, 'ingeniously enlivened by the addition of coloured transfers of butterflies and insects'. G. D. H. Cole, the twentieth-century Socialist theorist, was devoted not just to Morris's writings but to his wallpapers and his fabrics, which he sensibly praised for their qualities of wearing. Howard Coster photographed the Coles at home in 1938. Cole stands in a booklined study, his elbow on the table. Mrs Cole, later Dame Margaret, the Labour party activist, sits reading ensconced in an armchair covered in Morris's 'Corncockle' chintz. Her brother, Raymond Postgate, had a whole shelf of Morris's Kelmscott Press books.

What has been the reason for such longevity that even the well-educated middle classes of late-twentieth-century Britain and America can measure out their generations in William Morris rooms? It is partly that no one has approached Morris's sheer mastery of pattern. When Lethaby says that Morris was 'the greatest pattern-designer we ever had or ever can have', it is difficult to disagree. But there is more to it. The thing that has made Morris's patterns so enduring is their extra quality of reminiscence, the secret inner messages that May herself, more susceptible than anybody to her father's nuances, understood so well. May wrote: 'to some people a "Morris paper" is one definite thing they themselves have chosen perhaps long ago, pieces of pattern so full of life that, as part of the background of childhood or of young married days, they keep a remembrance of it with gratitude and pleasure, feeling the *nearness*, the human-ness of Morris's work.'

In a way that has enormous relevance to Morris, Freud was to disinter the meaning of the object, the significance of pattern recollected through our histories. His consulting room in twentieth-century Vienna was crowded with ancient artefacts and textiles, books and objects, photographs and plaques, many given by friends, all holding many memories of people, of places and the mesh of past events.

Freud's patients were conscious of an almost sacred hush in the apartment. The famous couch was piled high with pillows and covered with a precious Shiraz rug.

In 1878, when Morris was in Venice, St Mark's was one of the few buildings that gave him real pleasure. Once he had managed to limp into the interior he had found 'deep satisfaction, and rest for the eyes'. But he had been incensed at the restorations already under way in the building he considered 'a marvel of art and treasure of history'. Mediaeval mosaics were being stripped out of the baptistry. In his fury Morris smashed up George Howard's hat, imagining it was his own.

The restoration of the west front of St Mark's was the subject of the SPAB's first convincing venture into foreign propaganda. St Mark's was the great issue of the autumn of 1879. Morris was the strategist and chief spokesman for this campaign, which brought the society out of the shadows of vaguely well-meaning liberal activity and into the forefront of public consciousness. The society had been aware of dangers threatening innumerable important foreign buildings. Right from the beginning the manifesto was translated into French, German and Dutch, as well as Italian. Foreign honorary secretaries had been appointed, where they could be found, to alert the SPAB to obvious atrocities, and British committee members and their friends brought back their own reports when travelling abroad. But now for the first time these uncoordinated international activities found a proper focus. As Morris would soon become so painfully aware in the context of Socialist politics it was difficult to galvanize public activity without a well-defined and emotionally charged cause.

Morris's initial moves display more energy than tact. In his first public letter on behalf of the society, to *The Daily News*, he criticized the Italians for their 'headlong rashness' and accused them of cultural vandalism in preferring 'gilding, glitter, and blankness, to the solemnity of tone, and the incident that hundreds of years of wind and weather have given to the marble, always beautiful, but from the first meant to grow more beautiful by the lapse of time'. The Italian response was indignant, and Morris soon learned to soft-pedal, in this and in subsequent SPAB campaigns. St Mark's gave him an education in diplomacy, so far as that was possible. Two thousand signatures were collected for the petition. Protest meetings were held in Oxford, Birmingham and Manchester. The society strengthened its base as Morris gathered in support from the most influential people of the day.

He wrote ingratiatingly to Ruskin, imploring him to write a letter to *The Times* expressing his indignation: Ruskin sent a personal message to the Oxford meeting, held at the Sheldonian, and provided notes for an exhibition of photographs of the threatened building to publicize the SPAB campaign. Morris also wrote to Browning, asking him to speak against the proposals and stressing the strength of his personal involvement: 'to me such a thing happening would mean never going to Venice again'. Browning refused to speak: 'I never speak,' he informed Morris. But he offered a good deal of moral support. Crom Price was contacted to provide the names of his colleagues in the public schools. Even Ned was prevailed upon to speak in public at Oxford, for the only time in his life. Through Morris's zeal the issue was seen as rising to a level above mere party politics. Gladstone signed the petition. So did Disraeli, by now Lord Beaconsfield. In this context there is a fascinating reference in a letter from the artist Charles Keene to Joseph Crawhall to the flurry of activity within the 'Anti-Restoration Society' over the proposals for St Mark's: 'Have you had a circular? I see that eminent Conservative (for the nonce), Burne-Jones, has been haranguing about it at a meeting – and W. Morris too, – pestilent Reds, at the same time.'

Morris put enormous time in on the SPAB, especially in these formative years. He was the dominating figure at the annual general meetings, both reporting in detail on the progress of case histories and rousing the troops in a series of long speeches that show Morris at his most powerful and lucid, putting forward the case for ancient buildings as 'real and living history', which must be guarded 'both from thoughtlessness and sordid destruction, and from rash falsification'. Without such food as genuinely old buildings can give it the consciousness of history will starve and fade. In the intervals between these formalized orations Morris was writing constantly on SPAB business: official letters to the press and the SPAB file reports on individual buildings blister with his purposeful and vitriolic prose. In the background were long hours of discussion and drudgery. The minutes show how conscientiously Morris attended the evening SPAB committee meetings, held weekly, in the early period, at Morris's own premises in Oxford Street. In eight months, between April and November 1878, Morris was at twenty-eight meetings, missing only nine. In 1879 he is registered as present at twelve out of the total nineteen committee meetings. He was also involved in SPAB sub-committees, in particular the Restoration

26, Queen Square,

Bloomsbury, London,

Nov 8th 1879

My dear Browning

I dont know if
you have heard of the proposed
rebuilding of the front of St
Marks at Venice, which terrified
us suddenly & not a little, since
though we knew it would one
day come, we thought would
be put off year after year —
it is now only a matter of

Morris's letter to Robert Browning, asking him to join the public protest against the restoration of St Mark's in Venice.

Committee, and the separate St Mark's Committee, formed partly as a sop to the Italians, to monitor developments in Venice independently of the SPAB. All this was at a time when Morris was immersed in much of the administrative detail of his recently reconstituted firm. It is not perhaps surprising that Morris's poetic output in these years of such flurry of activity was meagre. In October 1879 he wrote to Georgie:

As to poetry, I don't know, and I don't know. The verse would come easy enough if I had only a subject which would fill my heart and mind: but to write verse for the sake of writing is a crime in a man of my years and experience.

Morris's main literary outlet now lay in his public speeches and the lectures: at least eight in 1879, including two in Birmingham and the protest meeting over St Mark's in Oxford; six in 1880, one of which was a speech at the Annual Meeting of the Women's Protective and Provident League at the Society of Arts in London in which Morris seconded a resolution on women's rights. These may appear small totals in comparison with the workload of Morris's Socialist period, with 91 recorded public engagements in 1886, 105 in 1887, 94 in 1888. But at this point Morris was not confident enough for extended extempore speaking. At the time of the Eastern Question Association protests he told Janey: 'I even tried to flit a few words at a small meeting we had at Lambeth yesterday: I can't say I got on very well, but I did manage to get a few words out and get to the end.' His public lectures were all written out carefully in lined exercise books, often corrected over. Many of these scripts are in existence. They are strangely moving documents, showing the time and energy that Morris would expend on them. 'I have been working my head off,' he told Janey, in the middle of composing 'The Beauty of Life' lecture he was due to give in Birmingham. A tremendous anti-jingoist diatribe '"Our country right or wrong?". The tribal banner!' was completed late at night at Kelmscott House in Hammersmith. Morris signed it in triumph at two-thirty a.m.

These early lectures show his thought processes in progress. They convey a strong sense of Morris's growing desperation. The lectures have innocuous titles: 'The History of Pattern Designing'; 'Some Hints on House Decoration'; 'Some of the Minor Arts of Life'. But as some of his audiences – the provincial art societies, professional institutes – were startled to discover, these lectures were only partially on these subjects. When he spoke to the Nottingham Kyrle Society his audience was 'polite and attentive': 'but', he told Janey, 'I fear they were sorely puzzled at what I said; as they might well be, since if they acted on it Nottingham trade would come to an end'. Morris starts his lectures quietly, almost technically, giving his views on, say, surface decoration, tracing the history of Byzantine textiles, giving his audience an expert guided tour of the palaces of the Assyrian kings. From here he would launch onwards, outwards, into a passionate analysis of the relevance of art to society and his hopes and fears for civilization itself. Morris on the platform is in a sense unstoppable: like the child who writes down his house number, street, town, country, continent, the World, the Universe.

He often complained of performance nerves. He was never to be an easy speaker from the platform and these early lectures, as he grappled with the techniques of delivery and struggled to establish a rapport with his audience, were an evident ordeal. Those who loved him watched anxiously as he fiddled with his watch chain, shifting nervously from one foot to another, 'feeling the ground', as a cat does to establish its terrain. He spoke with heavy concentration, seeming almost literally to be digging out his words. Georgie found it strange how Morris, who called himself the 'word-spinner', could be so verbally inhibited in public: 'in his early addresses the difficulty was painful, but sheer weight and volume of meaning burst the barriers at last'. Here there is an interesting parallel with Morris's twentieth-century political champion, E. P. Thompson, who found his own public voice relatively late in life, in the early 1980s, becoming a thrillingly eloquent supporter of the new East–West anti-nuclear initiatives in the revival of CND.

Morris attributed some of his problems to the fact that his lectures were all repeat performances: 'after all I have only one thing to say and have to find divers ways of saying it'. It is largely true that Morris only ever gave one lecture; what is remarkable is that within that format so much light and shade and human vulnerability comes over. In many respects the content echoes Ruskin; but Morris in performance is more original and volatile, not so much the sage. Morris's range of reference is less predictable than Ruskin's. His lectures have a ruggedness, a close-to-home approachability that is not bonhomie but something deeper felt. Already Morris is showing what he means, or thinks he means, by human fellowship. He lectures doggedly, feeling it his duty to speak on the most serious of subjects that a man can think of: 'for 'tis no less than the chances of a calm, dignified, and therefore happy life for the mass of mankind'.

In 'The Art of the People', a lecture Morris gave in 1879 in Birmingham Town Hall at the annual prize-giving of the Birmingham School of Design, the familiar structure is already in place. The innocent start, with its scorpion tail of warning: 'I am among friends, who may forgive me if I speak rashly'. The detailed exposition of the specialist subject, in this case derivations of art and the distortions of history: 'History (so called) has remembered the kings and warriors, because they destroyed; Art has remembered the people, because they created.' So far so formal. Morris is ascending gently, playing with aphorisms, not yet on the attack. He then arrives at a level central plateau, asking questions, stirring memories, citing his own experience: 'the little grey church that still so often makes the common-place English landscape beautiful, and the little grey house that still, in some parts of the country at least, makes an English village a thing apart'. How were these things arrived at? What gives them such significance? What can they still tell us about human happiness? Human happiness: 'that last word brings me to the very kernel and heart of what I have come here to say to you, and I pray you to think of it most seriously – not as to my words, but as to a thought which is stirring in the world, and will some day grow into something.' Just over half-way through his lecture Morris is launched into his great theme tune, which recurs with variations in all the lectures he ever gave:

That thing which I understand by real art is the expression by man of his pleasure in labour. I do not believe he can be happy in his labour without expressing that happiness; and especially this is so when he is at work at anything in which he specially excels.

Dogs hunting, horses running, birds flying: Morris arrives at a transcendental vision of frenetic activity, in which human labour takes its place in the natural cosmic order. He stands in Birmingham Town Hall not as the failed parson but as the visionary prophet, offering vistas 'of the spring meadows smiling, of the exultation of the fire, of the countless laughter of the sea'.

By the end of his speech Morris is established as grandiloquently tactless, like the Old Testament Amos. He has condemned fiercely the environmental despoliation of 'your Black Country yonder'. He has accused the British manufacturers, who included a good proportion of his audience, of cynical exploitation of the countries of the Empire, supplying them with goods which were sub-standard and in any case unneeded: giving 'to the people whom we have made helpless scorpions for fish and stones for bread'. In this speech above all a modern reader feels the need for a video-recorder to capture the expression on the faces of Morris's quasi-artistic middle-class provincial audience when he states: 'I have never been in any rich men's houses which would not have looked the better for having a bonfire made outside of it of nine-tenths of all that it held.'

His peroration is a furious indictment both of the social classes Morris himself came from and could be seen in some sense to belong to still. His lectures have an added force because they are self-scourging. In his examination of the slavery of consumption Morris does not exonerate himself:

For those of us that are employers of labour, how can we bear to give any man less money than he can decently live on, less leisure than his education and self-respect demand? or those of us who are workmen, how can we bear to fail in the contract we have undertaken, or to make it necessary for a foreman to go up and down spying out our mean tricks and evasions? or we the shopkeepers – can we endure to lie about our wares, that we may shuffle off our losses on to some one else's shoulders? or we the public – how can we bear to pay a price for a piece of goods which will help to trouble one man, to ruin another, and starve a third? Or, still more, I think, how can we bear to use, how can we enjoy something which has been a pain and a grief for the maker to make?

Employer; craftsman; shopkeeper (with an establishment in, of all places, Oxford Street); compulsive purchaser: Morris was all these things.

In the autumn of 1879 Morris, at Kelmscott Manor, wrote Georgie what amounted to a farewell letter:

I am sitting now, 10 p.m., in the tapestry-room, the moon rising red through the east-wind haze, and a cow lowing over the fields. I have been feeling chastened by many thoughts, and the beauty and quietness of the surroundings, which latter, as I hinted, I am, as it were beginning to take leave of. That leave-taking will, I confess, though you may think it fantastic, seem a long step towards saying good-night to the world.

At the time of his disillusionment with the Eastern Question Association he had forsworn active politics. Now, only eighteen months later, he was once more in the thick of it, as treasurer of the National Liberal League, founded in the late summer of 1879. This was a largely working-class association, a regrouping of the EQA protesters. George

Howell was the chairman and Henry Broadhurst the secretary. On 17 October Morris was writing to the editor of the *Daily News* to inform his readers of the organization which, 'though but in its infancy', had already begun its 'missionary labour'. The league's aims, Morris wrote, 'are based on Liberal principles at once decided and broad'.

The National Liberal League was a disappointing episode. In the election of 1880 it played a crucial role in organizing the London workers in support of Gladstone; Morris, Ned and William De Morgan campaigned for Sir Charles Dilke, before his fall from grace in the divorce courts. Morris was to make a carpet for Charles Dilke. But with the decisive Liberal victory Morris suffered characteristic depression and a dwindling of the old confrontational vigour, beginning to look back with nostalgia to the activism of the EQA and its glow of camaraderie. He wrote to Anthony Mundella, re-elected as Radical MP for Sheffield and Morris's old ally in the EQA: 'I wonder sometimes as I walk through the streets and look at the people if they are the same flesh and blood as made things so pleasant for us in the spring of '78; and I feel inclined to say, what the deuce then *was* it all about?'

One of the new Liberal MPs was Henry Broadhurst who had led the singing of 'Wake, London Lads!' back in what now seemed the heroic days of ferment. Morris wrote to congratulate him on his election, wishing him all health and happiness in his 'new sphere of usefulness'. But Broadhurst was in fact a prize example of the type of man that Morris meant when he spoke about the possible dangers of social corruption that awaited politically successful members of the working class: 'When a man has gifts for that kind of thing he finds himself tending to rise out of his class before he has begun to think of class politics as a matter of principle, and too often he is just simply "got at" by the governing classes, not formally but by circumstances, I mean.' Broadhurst, the ex-stone-mason, was too easily manipulated by Mundella and lulled into forgetfulness of the old class loyalties. A preposterous, pathetic passage in his memoirs gives an account of his friendly reception by the royal family: 'I left Sandringham with the feeling of one who had spent a weekend with an old chum of his own rank in society rather than one who had been entertained by the Heir-Apparent and his Princess.'

Looking back on the NLL, Morris explained that he once thought 'one might further real Socialistic progress by doing what one could on the lines of ordinary middle-class Radicalism'. He had come to realize this was a fallacy: 'that Radicalism is on the wrong line, so to say, and will never develope [sic] into anything more than Radicalism: in fact that it is made for and by the middle classes and will always be under the control of rich capitalists'. These rich capitalists, whilst not opposing *political* development, will not allow social ones 'if they can help it'. Morris became disillusioned with a parliamentary system in which those with vested interests would always keep control.

He also finally rejected Gladstone, his old hero. Formerly he used to claim that Gladstone was a genuine progressive, only encumbered by reactionary colleagues. Now he started to view him as a shifter of his ground: refusing to reverse Disraeli's policy, which he had once attacked as morally outrageous, in the annexation of the Transvaal. 'I am in hopes', wrote Morris, 'the matter will be taken up somewhat by people outside parliament for inside it all or nearly all people seem to be behaving ill.' He was also apprehensive of the government's policy in Ireland after the notorious Coercion Bill was passed in 1881. This and the 'Stockjobbers' Egyptian War', in which Alexandria was shelled by British warships, destroyed completely any hopes for the Liberals Morris had ever had. By this time he had resigned as treasurer of the NLL with a disgusted flourish, saying how much he hated 'everything vague in politics as well as in art'.

In that same year Morris, still casting around for a political agenda to which he could commit himself, helped in the foundation of the Radical Union, an amalgam of London radical working-class groups. 'Set agoing the Radical Union', he noted in his diary on 15 January 1881. At this point, according to George Wardle, he was hoping to organize 'a strong political party out of the radical elements or out of the trades unions'. The intention was to set up a convincing alternative to the Liberals. Morris was a member of the executive committee and some of the evening meetings were held at Queen Square where the leaders of the working-class Radical clubs repaid his hospitality by confronting him with their current theories on profit-sharing. Why could Morris & Co. not be run more like the Maison Leclaire in Paris, a contracting and decorating firm whose proprietor, Edmé Jean Leclaire, had introduced full profit-sharing in 1840? Morris took such criticism seriously enough to discuss past profit-sharing experiments in detail with Wardle who pointed out that any full-blown system of profit-sharing in the Morris workshops would involve a huge increase in book-keeping, a thing that Morris loathed. However, over the next year or two, a bonus was evolved which benefited half a dozen of the key employees.

Morris's Radical Union initiative was not successful. The working-men Radicals themselves were unresponsive, being too preoccupied with local and trades union politics to be interested in Morris's wide-ranging views. Wardle, who attended many of the meetings, remembered them as uniformly lacklustre: especially dispiriting was a meeting held at Lambeth Baths. But what is interesting about the episode is that it shows Morris at the beginning of his serious attempts to exert political influence over individual members of the working class.

Morris was entranced with the idea of the journey up the Thames by boat from one Kelmscott to the other. The first river expedition was in August 1880, and the journey up river was repeated the next year. On the morning of departure he had got up very early. As he wrote to Georgie: 'Little things please little minds; therefore my mind must be little, so pleased am I this morning . . . item, it is scarcely a little thing that the sky is one sheet of pale warm blue, and that the earth is sucking up the sun rejoicing.'

Before breakfast he and Jenny had gone out to see the houseboat, called *The Ark*, hired from an Oxford boat firm. A rowing boat, the *Alfred*, had been hired as well. Morris described *The Ark* as 'odd but delightful', like a largish steamer with a small omnibus on board. To May it appeared 'a sort of insane gondola'. There was room for two rowers in the front. Morris liked the new view of the country *The Ark* gave him and the feeling of such close proximity to his surroundings: 'what a joy (to a little mind) to see the landscape out of a square pane of glass, and to sleep a-nights with the stream rushing two inches past one's ear.'

Three boisterous bachelors were in the party: Crom Price, William De Morgan (alias 'Meorgan'), and the Hon. Richard Grosvenor, a friend of De Morgan's and a member of the SPAB. Since Oneglia, Janey had been in a precarious condition with fainting fits and back pains. Not long before, she had consulted Rossetti about the efficacy of seaweed baths at Ramsgate in which, as she explained, 'One is made into a kind of pie with the sea-weed'. But she had gathered enough strength to join the river trip. Morris watched her on board fondly, busy with her embroidery, 'lying down and working quite at home'. May and a young friend, Elizabeth Macleod, completed the party. The housemaid, Eliza, from Kelmscott House, went with them for the first part of the journey, returning home by train from Hampton Court.

On their first night they got as far as Sunbury, arriving in the dark. They went to the Magpie Inn for a late supper of pickled salmon, poached eggs and ham. On arrival at the inn, Morris exclaimed, 'What a stink.' The waiter had answered: 'It is nothing sir I assure you.' Richard Grosvenor intervened: 'Is it a sewer?' The waiter replied, 'Yes sir quite sure.' The exchange, and many similar, were noted in the journal to which almost all the travellers contributed accounts of jokes and quips and Morris's expletives. This log book is almost frenetically cheerful, with the particular Victorian male humour Morris always found consoling: on *The Ark* he is with the 'jovial crew' again. 'Note by our Communist,' runs one entry in the journal: 'A mountain before a plain: a plain before a suburb; a suburb before a dust-heap; a dust-heap before a sewer; but a sewer before a gentleman's house.'

Crom and Morris spent the first night in *The Ark* whilst the rest of the party braved the inn. The next day Morris, relieved to be leaving 'Cockney waters', gazed around with unexpected pleasure at unfamiliar stretches of river between Chertsey and Staines, 'full of strange character in many places'. They lunched luxuriously on the bank a little beyond Laleham 'with its enormous willows and queer suggestions (at any rate) of old houses on the banks'. They had a picnic tea on the grass at Runnymede 'on such an afternoon as one can scarcely hope to see again for brightness and clearness'. Morris, in his contentment, reaches out for the superlatives, as he did in Iceland and in northern France. They reached Windsor and he described it as a wonderful place, in spite of 'all drawbacks'; he distanced himself from Queen Victoria and her tapestries. Dick Grosvenor took all of them except Janey on a tour of Eton, to the buildings and playing fields. Here again Morris overcame political objections: 'in spite of drawbacks it is yet a glorious place'. Jobs were handed out. Crom Price was appointed 'boteler by acclamation (his own)' and provided liquor for the party. The log book reports how when they stopped at Surly Hall to take in water and soda water, Crom was inspired to give 'an entertainment gratis with an umbrella and shawl and a champagne bottle'. Nine years later this atmosphere was recaptured uncannily in the famous comic novel of a river expedition: *Three Men in a Boat* by Jerome K. Jerome.

Morris was cook on board *The Ark*, secreting himself in the cabin, then emerging 'like the high priest at the critical moment pot in hand'.

When they arrived at Maidenhead the Regatta was in progress. Both banks of the river were crowded with spectators. They had to drop the tow rope earlier than planned and the crowds jeered to see *The Ark* advancing slowly with Morris sitting on the roof steering while De Morgan laboured at the sculls. They travelled on in the shadow of Cliveden Woods. Here Morris's social conscience was alerted: he found the woods 'rather artificial' and remembered Mr Twemlow, the poor relation of Lord Snigsworthy in *Our Mutual Friend*. But when he got to Cookham he felt that he was back in 'the real country, with cows and sheep and farm-houses, the work-a-day world again and not a lacquey's [*sic*] paradise'. His feeling for the rural reality of Cookham was a satisfaction Stanley Spencer was to share. Late that night, in the streets of Marlow, where they had delivered the ladies to their lodging house, Crom and Morris saw 'the streamers of the Northern Lights flickering all across that part of the sky'. It was 'very mysterious and almost frightening' to see them shining down upon the English summer greenery. The last time Morris saw the northern lights they had been shining on the harbour of Tórshavn, in 1871.

They travelled through what was still fresh countryside for Morris, a new England of the riverbank. He thought it 'very beautiful'. At Hurley Lock, after they had waited to be passed by the big passenger-steamer that travelled regularly down the Thames between Kingston and Oxford, he stood up in the lock and saw to his delight 'a long barn-like building two Gothic arches and then a Norman church fitting on to it and joined into a quadrangle by other long roofs'. It was Lady Place, originally a monastery, then a Jacobean mansion, by this time reduced to a farmhouse, 'somewhat gammoned'. They went ashore and spent an hour 'in great enjoyment' examining the buildings. They found 'a huge dovecot', one of Morris's loved structures, with carefully moulded fifteenth-century buttresses. The church was still recognizable in outline but had been 'miserably gammoned' too.

They left London on a Tuesday. By Friday they reached Henley, stopping by a bank to eat the dinner Morris had prepared for them. Here they were invaded by swans 'who retired without breaking any man's arm', says the journal. 'Miss Macleod took a baby on board the Ark; Price offered to adopt it and was feeding it on the spot with honey out of a spoon.' *The Ark* then ran aground on a mud bank at Wargrave where 'all the males of the party gave conflicting orders in loud tones', De Morgan finally taking off his boots and socks to push her off. At seven-thirty *The Ark* arrived at Sonning, where they ate an excellent supper at the White Hart: 'lady howling song overheard; great hilarity.'

Mrs. M. and Miss Jenny slept at the Inn, Miss Macleod and Miss May at the clergy house, RCG and DM at Mrs. Brown's (note by R.C.G. domestic insects), WM and Price in the Ark.'

It was at Sonning, on their second expedition the next summer, that the young Violet Hunt, who had been at school with Jenny and May, spotted them in midstream. She stood on the parapet of the old bridge watching the progress of the oddly assorted pair of craft. Her account imbues the scene with a mythic quality, part comic, part grotesque:

I recognised the occupants of the first boat that waited a little as the other negotiated the archway. In a flash I realised that they were the right people to be rowing in this bit of purely medieval England. Standing up and shouting indecorously worded advice to the other boat was the man who loved a battle shout better than a symphony, the Defender of Guinevere [sic] and of Gudrun, straddling, legs apart in the boat as erstwhile waggishly depicted by his pals on the ceiling of the Oxford Union, the Viking in the blue byrnie, the maker of my mother's dining-room table; now, in the afternoon of his life, self-styled, 'the idle singer of any empty day', the Hector of Hammersmith and Varangian Guard of his own Metropolitan District – William Morris. . . .

Behind him, sitting up very stiffly, as a weary queen on her dais of Turkey-red cushions, was the historic Janey – 'Pandora' – 'Proserpina' – 'Aurea Catena' – 'Astarte Syriaca', and 'La Pia' of the *Purgatorio* – gaunt, pale, ashen-coloured hair and all. 'Scarecrow', as she called herself but still a 'Stunner', to use the Pre-Raphaelite term of praise, she looked just then, in the morning glare, very like the forlorn wife of Nello Di Pietro, the lady undone by the miasma of the marshes:

Siena mi fe, Maremma mi disfecemi.

By now they were approaching more familiar territory, travelling via Wallingford where Morris drank five lemon squashes at a sitting, and pulling in at Dorchester. Here the whole party, 'except Mrs. M.', alighted and walked up to Dorchester Dykes, with its view of Dorchester Abbey in one direction, and in the other Sinodun Hill. Morris recognized the exact spot where they had stopped for refreshments on the Oxford summer holiday with Charley and his family thirteen years before.

Nearing Oxford he noticed with dismay how the banks of the river had been spoiled since he last saw them. The party stayed overnight in Oxford where, as De Morgan comments, 'in spite of Mr. Morris's dreadful revolutionary sentiments we slept in the King's Arms'. In Oxford, Janey left them and went on by train to Kelmscott to prepare the house for the arrival of the voyagers. As *The Ark* proceeded up the river towards Kelmscott Manor, Morris saw the sight that always roused emotion in him: 'they were haymaking on the flat flood-washed spits of ground and islets all about Tadpole; and the hay was gathered on punts and the like.'

It was Monday. *The Ark* had taken six days to reach Kelmscott, trundling through the English countryside. Morris wrote to Georgie:

Night fell on us long before we got to Radcot, and we fastened a lantern to the prow of our boat, after we had with much difficulty got our boats through Radcot Bridge. Charles was waiting for us with a lantern at our bridge by the corner at 10 p.m., and presently the ancient house had me in its arms again: J. had lighted up all brilliantly, and sweet it all looked you may be sure.

The journey up the river, and especially that homecoming, was drawn upon by Morris for the novel *News from Nowhere*. When his fictional travellers reach their destination a little crowd is waiting to greet them on the bank. Out of this crowd steps forward a tall handsome stately lady: 'for stately is the word that must be used for her'. She is waving her hand gracefully in welcome. Inevitably her hair is black and wavy and the lady has deep-set grey eyes.

CHAPTER THIRTEEN

Merton Abbey
1881–83

'The fictionary sounds likely to become a factory.' In the middle of the summer of 1881, William Morris signed the lease for the seven-acre site at Merton Abbey that enabled him at last to move his workshops from Queen Square into more spacious and much airier surroundings in suburban South London, and to bring most of the Morris & Co. products under his own control. It was a decision that tied Morris more firmly to London as a centre of activity, in a way that sometimes felt like the signing of a death warrant. The Firm was now a sizeable and very complex enterprise: three years after the move to Merton over a hundred workers were employed. The factory at Merton was destined to outlast Morris by almost half a century. Morris & Co. finally went into liquidation, a pale shadow of its earlier creative vigour, in May 1940, a few months after the outbreak of the Second World War.

When he arrived at Merton Abbey, Morris had been searching for a site for many months. Morris's partner in his quest was the dome-headed, whimsical and brilliant art potter William De Morgan, voyager on *The Ark*, an acquaintance since Red Lion Square days and now a Morris crony through their mutual involvement with the SPAB. De Morgan had begun his researches into lustreware in much the same spirit that Morris had begun on his stained glass and his textiles, studying the chemical manuals of his schooldays and building a kiln attached to an old chimney, which caused a disastrous fire in the roof of his original premises in Fitzroy Square. He had since moved to work-shops in Chelsea, but these were not only ill-organized 'but very ill-demorganized', unable to accommodate De Morgan's prolific produc-tion of grotesque and marvellous Persian-style lustre animals, birds and plants. He and Morris set out to locate the FICTIONARY, as they called the imaginary factory they planned to occupy jointly, in a mood that was half serious, half spoof. They travelled around like a pair of eccentric millionaires, raising the hopes of many owners of clearly unsuitable properties by going over the premises minutely, allocating the rooms and even bringing away bottles of water for analysis to make certain it was suitable to dye with. Morris was delighted when an eminent analyst reported that a sample taken from pipes supplying all Lambeth was unfit for human consumption and could only result in zymotic disease.

They had looked in the country and lingered longingly at Blockley, a deserted silk village in Gloucestershire, where Morris found a mill with the last notice of wage reductions still posted to the door. This was the silk mill on which C. R. Ashbee cast covetous glances when he was moving his Guild of Handicraft out of London to the Cotswolds in a Morris-inspired exodus in 1903. Morris, like Ashbee, dismissed Blockley as not practical, but sometimes he regretted it: 'I know I was right,' he wrote later, 'but cowardice prevailed.' Morris and De Morgan also considered premises at Hemel Hempstead and an old print works at Crayford south of the Thames, not far from his lamented Red House at Bexleyheath. These were 'big and solid' buildings, going very cheap, but Morris discarded them as being inaccessible, with signs of increasing rural despoliation all around. A few days later Morris and De Morgan went over Merton Abbey. Here too the surroundings were depressing. Indeed Merton itself seemed to Morris 'Drury Lane transplanted to the country'. But Morris had a quick instinct for a building. 'This will fit us like an old shoe,' he said.

Merton Abbey was a former silk-weaving factory on the site of Merton Priory, destroyed at the time of the dissolution of the monasteries. A fragment of the ancient masonry still stood at one corner of the large and untidy garden: the site had 'a sort of melancholy charm'. There were many historic associations. Nelson had lived at Merton Place with Emma Hamilton, his mistress, and their daughter Horatia. 'Paradise Merton' Emma had described it in the last letter she sent Nelson before his death in the Battle of Trafalgar in 1805. Merton had been a centre of the textiles industry throughout the seventeenth and eighteenth centuries when large quantities of cloth were processed in the River Wandle, a tributary of the Thames. Before the invention of chemical bleaching, cloth was lightened by soaking and exposure to sunlight. The meadows were scored over by drainage ditches and the lengths of cloth stretched over the ridges in between. On a neighbouring site Littler & Co. were

already printing silks for Liberty's of Regent Street. The previous
occupant of Morris's site was Thomas Welch, a manufacturer of printed
table-cloths, winner of a medal in the 1851 Great Exhibition that Morris
had refused to enter. After viewing the site he wrote excitedly to Janey:

first, it would scarcely take one longer to get there from Hammersmith than it
does now to Queen Sq: next it is already a print-works (for those hideous red
and green table cloths and so forth) so that the plant would be really useful to
us: 3rd the buildings are not bad: 4th the rent (£200) can be managed, if we can
settle all that, as at present what is offered for sale is the tail-end of a lease and
the plant. 5th the water is abundant and good. 6th though the suburb as such is
woeful beyond conception, yet the place itself is even very pretty: summa, I
think it will come to taking it, if we can get it on fair terms.

De Morgan found a separate site at Merton Abbey, where he put up his
buildings and kilns, remaining until 1884 when his health, always
precarious, showed serious signs of breaking down.

Merton Abbey had something of the resonance that Morris always
looked for in a place. As May comments, 'one can scarcely imagine him
settled in a neat brick factory with all the latest fittings – among
utilitarian buildings of unengaging aspect'. The factory at Merton was
rambling, almost ramshackle: to a visitor from France it looked like a
large farmhouse. The long, tarred weatherboarded sheds conglomerated
round the water. There were ducks on the river and the streams were
thick with trout.

As one came through the yard from Merton High Street on the right
was a two-storey building which already housed a dye-house on the
ground floor. This Morris reorganized with eight new sunken vats, six
feet in depth, for dyeing his own fabrics, and a succession of smaller vats
for dyeing yarns. 'The dyeshop with its bright copper becks, gay wool
and silks, the men in aprons and clogs, the white steam curling about the
roof, the sunlight outside and the willow boughs close pressed against
the windows': this was the detail of the scene May recollected, the
shining skeins of silk drying outside the dyeing sheds, under the shadow
of the willows. The upper floor of this building, reached by an outside
wooden staircase, was allotted to stained glass, still one of the staples of
the Morris & Co. business, with a darkened display area for viewing
finished windows and a stack of Burne-Jones's and Morris's cartoons.

Further to the right, nearer the river, was the weaving shed where
Morris's hand-operated Jacquard looms for woven fabrics were

installed. A reporter for *The Spectator* was aware of great activity: 'the hand-looms are working busily, the shuttles flying to and fro between the webs with a speed like lightning . . . There are many looms, and beautiful-coloured threads are being woven into beautiful materials on every side.' The weaving shed was also a place of immense clangour as Morris himself was anxiously to recognize. When Emma Lazarus, American essayist and poet, author of the sonnet on the Statue of Liberty, visited England in 1883, Morris took her around Merton. Coming out of the weaving shed 'into the peaceful stillness of the July landscape, Mr. Morris reverted with a sigh to the great problem, and asked why man should be imprisoned thus for a lifetime in the midst of such deafening clatter in order to earn a bare subsistence, which the average professional man pockets in comfortable ease.'

33 *The Stained-glass Workshops at Merton Abbey*, viewed from the dye-house across the River Wandle. Drawing by E. H. New, late 1890s.

Across a timber bridge, on the south side of the river, was the third and largest of the worksheds. Here the tapestry looms and carpet looms were sited. Morris's 'bright dream' of tapestry became reality at Merton and three high-warp looms were ranged along the run of ground-floor windows, with the weavers looking outwards, to give them the best light. This was the only Merton workshop in which women were noticeable. The *Spectator* reporter described it as 'a large, low room' which did not appear crowded.

In the middle sits a woman finishing off some completed rugs; in a corner is a large pile of worsted of a magnificent red, heaped becomingly into a deep-coloured straw basket. The room is full of sunlight and colour. The upright frames face you at right angles, with a long row of windows looking close upon the bright shining river ... The strong, level afternoon light shines round the figures of the young girls seated in rows on low benches along the frames, and brightens to gold some of the fair heads. Above and behind them rows of bobbins of many coloured worsteds, stuck on pegs, shower down threads of beautiful colours, which are caught by the deft fingers, passed through strong threads (fixed uprightly in the frames, to serve as a foundation), tied in a knot, slipped down in their place, snipped even with the rest of the carpet, all in a second of time, by the little maidens.

It was a romantic scene but it was sustained by a firm grasp of economics. In May 1881 Morris noted in his diary that he had had a talk with George Wardle about carpets: 'each full waged girl must do 9 ft of 4 × 4 per week to pay'.

The entire upper floor of this third workshop was for fabric printing. Morris's relations with Thomas Wardle had by this time deteriorated badly. Through the early months of 1881 their correspondence became openly acrimonious as Morris rejected batch after batch of the printed textiles supplied by Wardle on grounds of their poor quality. The colours did not match the samples that he had approved. When 'African Marigold' and 'Red Marigold' arrived, they were such a travesty he said they were unsaleable. He turned upon Wardle: 'I laboured hard on making good designs for these and on getting the colour good: they are now so printed and coloured that they are no better than caricatures of my careful work.' In his private diary his comments about Wardle are even more unguarded: 'Tom Wardle called: foolish palaver'; 'Tom Wardle there; he unreasonable bullying and boastful.' Wardle had become a new hate figure to Morris. One of his main motives in the

move to Merton Abbey was to extricate himself from a business relationship far beyond repair. Morris now stretched his own printing-tables
down the length of the long workshop. The printers pressed their blocks
into the dye pads on the trolleys set on tracks right down the workshop,
like a tramline in the sky. The rhythmic clunk of the blocks as they
descended on the outstretched length of fabric was another of the
characteristic Merton sounds. The cloths were washed in the soft waters
of the Wandle both before and after dyeing, and in fine weather the
prints were left outside for the ground of the fabric to clear after dyeing,
a process known as 'crofting'. May described 'the bleaching ground, a
meadow Father had set with poplars, how charming it looked when
yards and yards of coloured chintz lay stretched on the grass!'

Edging on to Merton High Street were two domestic buildings. One,
a porched red-brick building, was used as offices and storeroom and
a dormitory for the young weaving-apprentices. The other, a small
eighteenth-century house, painted white, had two rooms, including a
bedroom, which were Morris's own: his Dickensian 'Quilp residence',
the family had named it, the equivalent of the bachelor quarters he had
used intermittently in the old days at Queen Square. The garden was
neglected but promising and Morris set to work on it, planting new trees
and having the lawn rolled to make a carpet of green from the house
down to the river. There were flowering shrubs and a broad border
which included tall blue larkspur and orange lilies. Morris planted a
multitude of 'daffies' amongst the willows by the river. He described in a
letter from Merton: 'a beautiful almond tree in blossom relieved against
our black sheds looking lovely'. The site burgeoned with primroses and
violets in the spring. The kitchen garden was divided into plots and let
out to 'certain of the workmen'. Such idyllic combinations of craftsmanship with tillage were pursued, though never with entire success, in
future more advanced communities of the Arts and Crafts.

The semi-domesticity of Merton was emphasized by the presence of
Morris's youngest brother Edgar, born ten years later, in 1844. In so far
as the Morrises had black sheep in the family, it was Edgar, who had
'no vice but never could keep money'. In 1877 he was married and
apparently near-destitute. Morris noted that 'Edgar and his missis and
baby' were amongst the Morris clan assembled at Much Hadham for the
snowy Christmas when Janey was in Oneglia. Morris had been kind to
Edgar and taken him to Kelmscott on a fishing trip with F. S. Ellis, his
publisher and Kelmscott co-tenant, the next spring. He had tried to find

employment – a 'port in a storm' – for Edgar at St Andrew's Home for Working Boys in Soho, a charitable institution for orphans founded by Maude Stanley, Rosalind Howard's unmarried elder sister. When negotiations failed, he himself took Edgar on in a relatively menial capacity at Queen Square. In 1881 he recorded in the work diary: 'Edgar taking stock of wools: 1100 and more'. Edgar had been involved in the search for the new factory and at Merton was the nominal head of the dye vat. In practice he worked as a general factotum, dealing for example with Eiríkr Magnússon's relations when they visited, and locating a large willow to fill the gap left in the row of trees along the river after a gale at Merton. Edgar was consulted by Morris about a mysterious new tree with white blossoms resembling a Portuguese laurel: 'Edgar says it is Dog-wood, but I can't find it in Gerard.' Edgar too apparently had an affinity with plants.

He stayed on and on at Merton. In the early 1890s Wilfrid Blunt noticed him, 'a dreamy man in workman's clothes, with his shirt sleeves turned up, and his arms blue with indigo to the elbows'. Morris's indigent brother was a slight, shambling and pathetic mirror-image, an ambivalent link back to the lost past.

While Morris was embarking on his search for his new premises, Janey had been wintering in Bordighera on the Italian–French riviera, a balmier resort than Oneglia, with palm trees and exotic vegetation. She had left with the Howards in early January. At first they had stayed in a hotel rudimentary enough to make her think seriously of returning home, but they then moved into the Villa Margherita from which Janey sent Rossetti much more optimistic accounts of sunny, perfect weather and the nearby sea-shore 'where there are most accommodating rocks forming splendid places for rest with wraps and cushions'. Morris appears to have approved the expedition, though reminding Janey to make sure she paid her way on it: 'I can't go owing money to Earl-Kin'. Henry James visited the villa and met Janey, finding her even more *outré* now, in her early forties, than she had seemed when he first saw her at Queen Square. He wrote to Fanny Kemble: 'I didn't fall in love with Mrs William Morris, the strange, pale, livid, gaunt, silent, and yet in a manner graceful and picturesque, wife of the poet and paper-maker, who is spending the winter with the Howards, though doubtless she too has her merits. She has, for instance, wonderful aesthetic hair.'

This time Jenny and May were not invited. Rosalind had an instinct for self-preservation. They were left at home in Hammersmith to keep house for their father. 'I think it does them good to be made responsible beings sometimes,' wrote Janey hopefully. Morris reported countless games of dummy and an evening when they planned to entertain 'the Grange' to dinner, with Jenny as hostess. He told Janey that the girls were both being very good, 'though May is whiles a little pale'. May, now eighteen, had in fact been looking pallid ever since the onset of Jenny's epilepsy. She seemed taller than she was because of her thinness; Janey at one stage was alarmed enough to prophesy that May would not 'drag through a long life'. ('So much the better for her!' she added dourly.) Perhaps provoked by his flood of attentiveness to Jenny, May was now intense in her devotion to her father. His study in Hammersmith had already become a hushed and sacred place for her. May, consciously or not, was educating herself to become her father's helpmate in enrolling at the National Art Training School at South Kensington, which offered professional courses to people intending to earn their living as designers or teachers of art. This school was the precursor of the Royal College of Art. May chose embroidery as her special subject. Her first recorded project was an embroidered cover for Ellis's printed vellum edition of *Love Is Enough*.

Morris as single parent is endearingly protective. He enjoyed his daughters' company. He escorted them round London. Philip Webb sent a report to Bordighera of a hearty evening at the Faulkners' with Morris and the girls 'when we cracked all the jokes in the parlour door that we could'. It was typical of Webb's cranky humour to describe the cracking of jokes in terms of cracking walnuts. On other nights Morris dined out with friends, reverting to his bachelorly habits. He dined palatially with Constantine Ionides, eating connoisseur's food in art-lover's surroundings. He revived his old friendship with William Bell Scott who, as Morris wrote to Janey, 'looked very old: *is* near 70 he told me: he was very quiet – as indeed we all were, save Letitia, who gabbled – but not unkindly'. Morris was conscious these days of his circle of friends dwindling, losing energy. At the Richmonds', he met Oscar Wilde and found him much less black than he was painted: 'Not but what he is an ass'.

Janey's relations with Morris's mother and his sister Henrietta seem to have been affectionate, if a little guarded. But there are signs that her husband's self-confidently middle-class family daunted her *en masse*. She seems to have stayed at Much Hadham very little. Morris now, as in previous years, took advantage of her absence to fulfil his family duties on his own. He travelled down to Hadham 'to see the last of Arthur before he goes to India'. Arthur, the successful and conventional brother, unlike the feckless Edgar and the also somewhat problematic Rendall, was now a Captain in the 60th Foot, the King's Royal Rifle Corps. He had recently returned from South Africa, where his regiment had fought in the Zulu War, and was now on his way to join his new battalion in Ferozepore, Peshawar and Chakrata. Morris wrote to Janey: 'Isy is to be there and Alice, and the whole clamjamfry of them.' Theoretically Morris might abhor the middle classes. But he was still attached to the clamjamfry of the Morrises with a despairing tangle of emotional ties.

The uniformed bemedalled figure of his brother Arthur posed, at this period, the most awkward of his private challenges. Arthur typified the spirit of imperialist expansionism that Morris, who regarded the British army as the partner in corruption to capitalist interests, now so violently and so publicly decried. Arthur was, in conventional Victorian eyes, the epitome of manliness. Morris believed in manliness, but in another version. Where Arthur's manliness was concerned with the defence of the *status quo*, Morris saw manliness in more imaginative terms as a force for human progress, an ideal of democracy. He believed it was no use for people to aspire to political freedom unless they used it as an instrument for leading reasonable and 'manlike' lives. There was no showiness in Morris's concept of the manly. It was an austere, almost unworldly virtue. Morris tolerated Arthur, his bluff, scarlet-coated brother. He continued to regard him with a certain caustic fondness. But when it came to views of life Morris was more attuned to his silently enduring Nordic heroes. Say Ogier the Dane.

In the first week in May 1881, Janey started on the journey home from Bordighera. Morris travelled to Paris to meet her, through the glittering and shining Kentish meadows, then across the very flat, 'grey and hazy' sea. The following spring Morris, with Tennyson and Browning, T. H. Huxley and Herbert Spencer, was to sign a petition of protest against the Submarine Railway Company's plan to build a Channel Tunnel, on grounds that this would involve England 'in military dangers and liabilities, from which, as an island, it has hitherto been happily free'.

In Paris, Morris installed himself at the Hôtel Windsor and Janey 'turned up in early morning' the next day. They spent five days in Paris, where the weather was appalling. But the dress of the women in Paris impressed Morris. One day they took the boat to St Germain for Morris to cast a newly knowledgeable eye over the techniques of high-warp tapestry still in use at the Gobelins works.

Later in the year Morris led a more domestic expedition around Gloucestershire. He and his party set out from Kelmscott in a little cavalcade, travelling by water to Lechlade, then transferring to a trap and driving to Cirencester, which turned out unexpectedly pleasant: 'to us country folk a rather splendid place and full of shops'.

He gave Georgie a glowing account of that energetic day trip, which started with an inspection of the large, mainly late Gothic parish church, 'romantic to the last extent, with its many aisles and chapels: wall-painting there and stained glass and brasses also'. Morris liked the fact that it was a hybrid building, with 'tacked on to it an elaborate house, now the town hall'. He told Georgie:

I could have spent a long day there; however, after mooning about the town a bit, we drove off again along the long stretches of the Foss-way (Roman) over a regular down country, the foot-hills of the Cotswolds, pleasant enough, till we came to the valley which the tiny Coln cuts through, where we set ourselves to seeking the Roman villa: said valley very beautiful, the meadows so sweet and wholesome. Two fields were grown all over with the autumn crocus, which I have not seen wild elsewhere in England, though there was plenty of it near Ems. The Roman villa was very interesting, for a show place with a gimcrack cottage ornée [sic] in front of it, and the place was lovely: we spent our time with the utmost recklessness, so that by then we had had tea at a nice little public by the bridge, and were ready to start down the Coln towards Fairford, it was 6.30, and getting towards twilight. However we saw the first two villages well enough and had some inkling of the others: the scale of everything of the smallest, but so sweet, and unusual even; it was like the background of an innocent fairy story. We didn't know our way till we had reached the last of the Coln villages, and kept asking and knocking at cottage doors and the like, and it was all very delightful and queer.

Morris, on his travels, is the tale-teller, still as alert as he had been in Iceland for switches of scale and mysteries of landscape, turning the gentle, familiar Coln valley into a gnarled Hobbit land.

One senses that Morris was now losing his appetite for travel far afield, obsessed both by his work and his anxiety for Jenny. As her state of health fluctuated so alarmingly, Morris, like a second mother, cosseted and watched her. Except for his journey round the fjords during his last illness, Morris never again travelled very far from home. In January 1882 he took Jenny to stay in Ned and Georgie's absence at Rottingdean in Sussex in the Burne-Joneses' house on the bracing Sussex coast. This new acquisition had already been the subject of sarcastic correspondence between Janey and Rossetti who referred to North End House as the 'mansion' near Brighton that Ned had bought in a fit of grandeur: 'He appears to be culminating.' Ned's style in conversation was 'getting beyond the pussy-cat and attaining the dicky-bird'. Janey was clearly envious of the house's situation: 'the sea-air is the only thing that braces up the nerves.' Kelmscott, low-lying and enervating, did not suit her. She went so far as confessing to Rossetti: 'I wish I had such a place, and that Kelmscott was off my hands.'

In Sussex in that winter, Morris and Jenny kept close and quiet. They went shopping in Brighton. They took a long drive across the Downs, seeing from the brow of the hill above Falmer (now transformed into the University of Sussex) the distant town of Lewes 'lying like a box of toys under a great amphitheatre of chalk hills'. Eric Gill, who came to live in Sussex in 1907, admired this same view. Morris found the Burne-Jones house 'very pleasant and agreeable': it suited him 'to a T,' he said, telling his absent hostess he felt very well and happy, in spite of constant nagging anxiety for Jenny. He had brought a large task with him: his next Birmingham lecture, 'Some of the Minor Arts of Life'.

Through these years Janey was being constantly reminded of Rossetti's dependence. He still showered her with letters, desperate for evidence of her continuing affection. Sometimes he wrote pathetically: 'If you read this letter, do not answer hardly, for I cannot bear it.' When she replied kindly, he wrote again: 'Your letter is a great comfort to me, as the removal of your long interest in me would be the one thing I could not bear at all.' Searching through an old cabinet he found forgotten photographs, group pictures of the Morris and Burne-Jones families taken in the garden. 'There are only 3 containing yourself,' he informed Janey. 'Two are not quite satisfactory, but one is divine.'

He now lived enclosed by the memories of Janey, as he had once surrounded himself with memorabilia of Lizzie. In 1881 he delivered the large portrait now known as 'The Day Dream', based on a sketch made nine years earlier at Kelmscott and showing Janey sitting a little precariously in the fork of a tree. The portrait was painted partly from a model, and Rossetti was sad that he had had to draw the feet, in Grecian sandals, from someone else. But she holds a honeysuckle, as from Kelmscott garden, and wears Janey's wonderfully shimmering green dress. The portrait was commissioned by Constantine Ionides. Aglaia had busied herself in a sisterly way with its progression, visiting Rossetti's studio and offering advice. She suggested that the shadow of the face against the sky was rather heavy, and Rossetti obligingly altered it. This was a new version of the Arthurian triangle: one man and two women; Rossetti placating both his goddess and his client.

In 1881 Rossetti had been going through his poems for a new collection, *Ballads and Sonnets*, which Ellis & White published in October. Again this was a reconnection with the past. He consulted Janey on the question of diplomacy: 'A dozen copies of my new book have been sent to me. Do you like me to send one, and to what address? Or two, for yourself and Top?' It was almost a replay of the scenes that followed the traumatic opening of Lizzie's grave. Rossetti evidently sent his book to Morris who wrote him a letter of bluff congratulation: 'I don't think I need say more than that those pieces of this vol. which I have not seen before (you remember you read me the first at Kelmscott) seem to me well up to your mark and full of beauty and interest.' Perhaps it was no accident that Morris singled out not one of the love poems but 'The King's Tragedy', a ballad based on the assassination of King James I of Scotland, as the poem he had most admired.

Occasionally, Janey still visited Rossetti. After Bordighera she sat to him for 'Desdemona's Death Song', a wistful composition of a squatting Desdemona-Janey being prepared for her funereal bedchamber, wrongly suspected of adultery. She holds a hand mirror. In the background immense Venetian hangings swirl. Hall Caine, by now installed as Rossetti's resident factotum, remembered the mystery surrounding Janey's rare appearances at Cheyne Walk. Rossetti would send a little warning note: 'The lady I spoke about has arrived and will stay with me to dinner. In these circumstances I will ask you to be good enough to dine in your own room tonight.' Janey was the only intimate friend of Rossetti's whom he never met. Later, pressed by Bernard Shaw, Caine remembered the breakfast-time gossip he heard from Fanny Cornforth, reinstated as Rossetti's housekeeper in his final years in Chelsea. 'She was especially hard on Mrs. Morris and made charges which I knew must have been lies. One morning Rossetti entered the breakfast room unexpectedly and heard something of all this. He laughed at it and denied it all, and then with a look at me, said, "But who believes anything said by the 'Helephant'".'

Janey had her last meeting with Rossetti in 1881. He was now in a state of extreme paranoia. She went to spend the afternoon with him at Cheyne Walk and dined with him. After dinner he took her back to Hammersmith in a cab. She wanted him to come inside to see the girls; he almost agreed, but turned back at the last minute, when he was half-way across the little courtyard, suddenly overcome with nervousness. 'He was in high spirits that day,' Janey had remembered, 'but I never saw him again.'

In September 1881, for a change of scene, Rossetti took a trip to the Lake District with Hall Caine. Fanny was there too and there was much cavorting. They all three ascended the Great Hough, a fell 1,200 feet high, and added a stone to the cairn, as Morris had done in the Icelandic wasteland. Rossetti descended on his posterior, while Fanny above him 'lay down and roared in paroxysms of mirth'. Depression returned suddenly and he went back to London. On 17 December he suffered a paralysis of the left arm and leg. Dr Marshall blamed the chloral, which he instructed must be 'decisively, instantly and entirely cut off'.

The young doctor called in was Henry Carr (later Sir Henry) Maudsley, the recently qualified nephew of Henry Maudsley, founder of the hospital which now bears his name. Maudsley accompanied Rossetti to apartments in Birchington-on-Sea in Kent where he gradually substituted for the chloral a combination of laudanum, morphia by injection and whisky in unlimited doses. By the end of January the chloral was dropped altogether, never to be resumed. Maudsley left on 27 January. The paralysis of the left arm continued and another doctor, Dr Harris, diagnosed 'some degree of softening of the brain'. On 8 April, Dr Marshall and Dr Harris agreed that the symptoms clearly indicated uræmia, blood-poisoning from uric acid, and treatment was begun by sweating and applying hot poultices to the loins, treatment Rossetti loathed but endured with patience. On 9 April, he 'threw his arms out; screamed out loud two or three times and died'. In 1882 there was no apparatus for the clinical measurement of blood pressure. But the manner of his death suggests that he was suffering from arterial degeneration and that this, not the withdrawal of chloral, was the cause of Rossetti's death.

The day before he died, he had talked of Janey and asked Hall Caine to make sure she had 'anything of his she cared for'. She had first choice

of pictures and various mementoes, in particular the costume jeweller
he had used in her portraits. This collection is now in the Victoria an
Albert Museum, an extraordinarily evocative cache. Rossetti of cours
also left Janey with his letters: 'love letters', she told Blunt, 'and ver
beautiful ones'. She was proud of these, but worried about leaving ther
where Morris or the girls might find and read them. She sometime
contemplated building them into a wall at Kelmscott Manor to kee
them to herself.

We cannot tell how Janey's patent grief affected Morris. He himse
wrote generously and regretfully, mourning Rossetti deeply in a letter t
Bell Scott:

What can I say about Gabriel's death, but what all his friends or almost al
must feel? . . . He had some of the very greatest qualities of genius, most (
them indeed; what a great man he would have been but for the arrogar
misanthropy that marred his work, and killed him before his time: the grain (
humility which makes a great man one of the people, and no lord over them, h
lacked, and with it lost the enjoyment of life which would have kept him aliv
and sweetened all his work for him and us. But I say he has left a hole in th
world which will not be filled up in a hurry.

Morris fighting valiantly for the broad, unbiased view. Shaw, man
years later, diagnosed that Morris, once he 'found D.G.R. out', in th
end came to dislike him. But Shaw was too impatient to tease out tru
situations. In this, as in so many of his comments about Morris, h
misses the nuance.

In January 1882 Jenny was twenty-one. Through that summer an
autumn her condition worsened, with severe and repeated epileptic fit:
Morris was beside himself with worry. Mackail, who knew much mor
of the detail than he stated, wrote: 'This household anxiety coloured a
the world to him.' The fits preyed on his mind: 'It is not putting the cas
too strongly to say that for the time they thoroughly shattered his nerve
There was the added grief of news from Iceland, where the threat (
famine followed a bad year in 1881, an 'extraordinarily late and incle
ment spring' in 1882, with much loss of crops and livestock, and
measles epidemic, a final trick of fortune, which had laid the populatio
low. Morris took what action he could, galvanizing the Iceland Relie
Fund and writing a lucid and emotional letter on behalf of the Ice
landers, a public relations exercise at which he was well practised, to th

editor of the *The Daily News*. 'I suppose', he said, 'that few, if any, of your readers who have not been to Iceland can imagine what a very poor country it is. The best of it is what we should call mere waste.'

The devastation of his adopted country; the affliction of Morris's loved daughter, and her transformation from solemn, glowing promise into a relative grotesque, mental and physical. All this, in the same summer of Rossetti's death, created in Morris a terror and an anguish that deluged out to Georgie. He has not been well, he tells her. He feels he is almost at a point of collapse:

indeed I am older, and the year is evil; the summerless season, and famine and war, and the folly of peoples come back again, as it were, and the more and more obvious death of art before it rises again, are heavy matters to a small creature like me, who cannot choose but think about them, and can mend them scarce a whit.

There was much to be done at Merton Abbey to prepare it for operation. When Morris took the site the buildings were dilapidated and neglected. Foundations needed strengthening and waterproofing; the roofs needed retiling and the floors re-laying. Webb was called in to raise the ceiling level of the weaving shed to accommodate the looms. It was late in 1881 before the buildings were ready to receive the workers and equipment from Queen Square. Morris's diary shows his impatience over that first Christmas:

[22 December] To Merton Abbey; looking about; place still very untidy; weavers getting on badly; but dye house all right.
[27 December] To Merton Abbey. Neither weavers nor John there. I muddled about: trees being planted – our weavers are bad belike – the 13 foot carpet loom being got up.
[30 December] To Merton Abbey: dyed patterns of madder – the Dutch seems best: men getting to work again; Goodacre the new dyer there.

In the following March there was alarm as the London and South Western Water Company brought a private bill before Parliament to sink wells and tap the springs of the Wandle at its source at Carshalton. The effect, as Morris expostulated, would have been to 'reduce it to a muddy ditch', a disaster not only in terms of his own business, which relied to such an extent on Wandle water, but an act of environmental outrage. 'I think you will believe me when I say that such a loss of a beautiful stream would grieve me more on public than on private grounds,' Morris wrote to James Bryce, the Liberal MP for Tower Hamlets, seeking his support. In the event the bill was rejected when it came before the House of Commons Select Committee. But not without causing fresh commotion at Merton where the preparations and amendments in some of the workshops continued through the whole of 1882.

The fabric-printing departments were the most problematic since for Morris & Co. this was a new process. On 19 December the printing shed was still disorganized, though a start had been made on 'Brother Rabbit' and Morris was only finally able to report that the wheels were going round at Merton and 'the printing seems likely to go on swimmingly' in the first week of January 1883.

At Merton Morris managed finally to master the indigo discharge process that had evaded him at Leek and exacerbated his relations with Thomas Wardle. This technique was the reverse of the conventional printing on to the plain surface of the cloth. Instead, the bolts of cloth themselves were dyed a uniform dark blue and the pattern was created by the application of bleaching reagents, which either removed or reduced the blue colour as required. More colours would be introduced by further dyeings, mainly of red and yellow. These were superimposed on the half-indigo to produce delicate shades of green, purple and orange. It was a skilled and risky business. To start with, it demanded Morris's intensive supervision, as he explained to Jenny: 'the colour mixer Kenyon is a good fellow, but rather a muddler, and often to be sure that a thing is properly done either [George] Wardle or I have to stand over him all the time.' The printing of 'Strawberry Thief' gave him sleepless nights in his Quilp-like Merton lodgings. This design, derived from his observation of the thrushes creeping under the nets in the garden at Kelmscott, stretched the indigo discharge process to its limits with a criss-cross of extremely subtle colours: blue flowers, luscious red strawberries, the thrushes' flecked brown breasts.

Of the nineteen patterns registered by Morris & Co. between May 1882 and September 1885 seventeen were designed for indigo printing. Once again the acquisition of a new technology, or rather a revival of an ancient technique, stimulated Morris artistically. 'Rose and Thistle', 'Bird and Anemone', 'Brother Rabbit': these are complex, finely detailed, confident designs, very English in their range of reference, their observation of the life of the hedgerows, their fondness for the sleek, evasive creatures of the woodlands, but also clearly influenced by

Morris's study of historical textiles. His own collection contained many similar small-scale repeat patterns, of the kind used for fifteenth-century Italian silks. By 1883 Morris had begun upon a project that was surely to be the high point of his achievement in textile design, the series of gently flowing patterns based on the tributaries of the Thames. These are 'Windrush', 'Evenlode', 'Kennet', 'Wey', 'Wandle', and 'Medway'. They show Morris at his most thoroughly Victorian: the brother of Darwin in his botanical precision, the scientific exactness of his vision; the cousin of Browning in his build-up of complexities of meaning. These are not merely patterns but something more demanding: they are packed, poetic commentaries, edgy intimations of the stretches of the river that had meant so much to Morris since he was a child.

Morris planned at Merton to enlarge his range of influence, reach out to the less affluent. He was sometimes shocked by the amount his products cost, especially Morris & Co. furniture. As he wrote later to James Mavor, his Socialist colleague, 'the cheapest chair we can sell costs about 7⁸/0 (and *they* are made 4 or 5 dozen at a time too) a workman can get a chair for 1⁸/6, and as you very well know he *must* buy them as cheap as he can.' He realized how far his so-called simplified interiors were beyond the reach of even the lower middle classes, the suburban sub-strata of clerks, shop and office workers, let alone manual workers. He put his hopes on an extended range of cheaper fabrics. A prospectus of 1882 emphasizes how 'a great number of furniture prints of our own design' are now available, and that these, combined with Morris & Co. wallpapers, 'now form a great mass of uncostly surface decoration'. He also now introduced cottons for women's clothing, writing to May: 'there is a new block come in for the printed dresses, and we can dye piece cotton goods for such like things famously so, give your orders ladies, as even the humble can indulge in simple articles'. But Morris's romantic egalitarian vision of classless women wearing inexpensive floral cotton dresses was always out of reach. The nearest realization was in the Britain of the 1960s when Laura Ashley built up a quasi-Morris business, designing, mass-producing and finally retailing its products with great commercial acumen.

It was Morris & Co. tapestry that most impressed the visitors who made the pilgrimage to Merton singly or in parties. Morris understood the value of the factory visit and was evidently willing to set time aside for prospective customers and serious inquiries, showing the work in progress and explaining his ideas. The tapestry aroused such curiosity because of the unique process and because of its sheer scale. Now for the first time Morris was set up to make gargantuan panels in tapestry: 'The Attainment' from the *Holy Grail* series woven in the 1890s is eight feet high and almost twenty-three feet long. Now, too, the Firm's own dye-house gave him total control over the colour. This was the link missing in the stained-glass operation, where Morris was still buying in his raw materials. With the Merton tapestry, as George Wardle explained it, 'he was at once the colour maker and colourist'.

The first Merton Abbey tapestry was an aberration. Morris had paid £150 to Walter Crane for a cartoon originally drawn to illustrate 'The Goose Girl' in a new edition of *Grimm's Fairy Tales*. The illustration, Crane at his most fantastical, shows a farmyard maiden sitting with a flow of silken tresses in a flurry of white birds. The tapestry version is six feet wide, seven feet high. Crane's nursery scene, charming in a picture-book, looks absurdly whimsical on so large a scale. Morris admitted disappointment, telling Jenny: 'I thought the Goose Girl was not bad, my dear, on the whole: but when all is said it was not a design quite fit for tapestry.' But why had he commissioned it, at a fee much higher than the £25 paid to Burne-Jones in those days? And why was it not obvious to Morris that the tapestry was less than successful at an early stage? Was his judgement affected by emotional factors? Walter Crane had been in sympathy with Morris's Liberal causes in the 1870s as well as with his anti-imperialist stance. Crane, like Morris, was despairing of a social system that forced such a high proportion of the population to endure lives of poverty and squalor. Should we see 'The Goose Girl' as an exercise in Socialist solidarity?

Morris returned to Ned for the next Merton Abbey tapestries, a pair of goddess figure panels, 'Flora' and 'Pomona'. These were successful tapestries, often repeated. At least eleven versions of 'Flora' were woven and six of 'Pomona' over the years. Some of these were relatively cut-price versions, small in scale. But the originals, now in the Whitworth Art Gallery in Manchester, are almost ten feet high, seven feet wide, lavish compositions with flower and fruit borders and inscriptions at the top and bottom of the panels set in mediaeval scrolls. They are clearly derived from the large-scale verdure tapestries of sixteenth-century France and Flanders. Morris supplied the backgrounds to Burne-Jones's goddess figures: dense vegetation, a jungle effect similar to his Hammersmith tapestry 'Cabbage and Vine'. These are goddesses encased, caged in, by foliage: *Earthly Paradise* visions, beckoning yet inaccessible objects of desire. Morris wrote the verses that were woven into the tapestries. This is Pomona, as evasive as his Gudrun:

> I am the ancient Apple-Queen,
> As once I was so am I now.
> For evermore a hope unseen,
> Betwixt the blossom and the bough.

In August 1883, sixteen months after Rossetti's death, Janey met the man who would soon become her second lover. They met at Naworth Castle, the building Morris had described as the most romantic in all England. Rosalind Howard had asked her there on purpose to introduce her to Wilfrid Scawen Blunt. Morris had been at Kelmscott and had now returned to London. Blunt mentioned the meeting in his official, published diary: he had spent a week at Naworth in Mrs Morris's company 'and we had made friends'. In his more lubricious Secret Memoirs, left to the Fitzwilliam Museum in Cambridge and annotated helpfully by Blunt 'for reference of anyone preparing a new edition of My Diaries', he gives a fuller version of the start of the affair with Mrs Morris, which he typically puts over in terms of doing her a service: 'She must have been 42 when we first became intimate, and though still a beautiful woman was already on the decline and sad. Rossetti had just died and I was able to console her and give her an opportunity of pleasure she was grievously in want of, for I doubt if she had ever quite indulged it with him.'

Blunt was Janey's exact contemporary but he was far beyond her, and indeed far beyond Morris, in worldly experience. He was one of the most glamorous figures of his period, a poet and explorer, a political adventurer, a wealthy radical with highly idiosyncratic anti-imperialist views. Blunt had started life as a diplomat but left the Foreign service when he married. He and his wife set off on a succession of intrepid and exotic journeys through Arabia and Mesopotamia. The most remarkable of these expeditions was their crossing of the Nefud desert to the small feudal town of Hail where they were welcomed by the emir, who presented them with some of his brood mares and gave their caravan a safe conduct to Baghdad. Blunt's wife, Lady Anne, was Byron's grand-daughter. Her mother was Ada, Byron's only daughter, who died young. Blunt's diaries reveal clearly his histrionic tendencies: he

447

modelled his own career on that of Byron as poet and as profligate. It has even been suggested that he married Lady Anne primarily for the Byron connections. This would have been in character. As a hero-worshipper Blunt had his ruthlessness.

Wilfrid Blunt was an obsessive philanderer. His daughter Judith, later Lady Wentworth, wrote bitterly of his intrigues with women, 'cynically regarded by him as so many pawns and pieces to be exchanged, thrown away or manoeuvred at will in a skilful game of chess'. She was exaggerating slightly, but not much. The first of his *amours* had been 'Skittles', alias Catherine Walters, the ambitious daughter of a Liverpool sea-captain who became the most famous courtesan of the late Victorian age, mistress to several dukes and, inevitably, the Prince of Wales. Skittles was *en route* from Paris to Biarritz to join the imperial circle of Napoleon III and the Empress Eugénie when Blunt first met her. She was his indoctrination into the world of the dangerous liaison. He was then twenty-three.

His subsequent amorous history is detailed in the secret account which still, after all these years, seems shocking in its coolness. In the range of love affairs that extended so improbably from Skittles to Mrs William Morris, Blunt is the narcissistic voyeur of himself. He enjoyed the danger of the doubly forbidden, and many of the women he pursued with such great skilfulness belonged to his own close circle. They were the aristocratic married women of the inbred social circles of the Wyndhams, the Pollens, the Noels. He liked the excitement of the clandestine affair progressing within the formal public setting of the country-house weekend: smouldering glances across the dinner table, snatched kisses in the rose garden. Blunt was one of the role models for Hector Hushabye in Shaw's play *Heartbreak House*. His affairs were often simultaneous and long-lasting, ebbing, flowing, intertwining over several decades. He always disliked a final termination. Blunt was the classic stockpiler, careful to keep a reserve of old liaisons in condition to be rekindled if a new liaison failed. Sometimes he would turn on himself in self-disgust, promising repentance. His mother had been a Catholic convert. She had sent her son to be educated by the Jesuits at Stonyhurst. The sense of sin was strong in Blunt, as it had been in Rossetti. Sometimes his guilt led him to consider suicide. But each time he made vows to abandon what he called 'his old ways of pleasure', Blunt would lapse again, making suitably Byronic entries in his diary: 'Love is to me what a dram is to the drinker. I cannot live without it though I know it is destroying me.'

448

Rosalind Howard had been one of Blunt's few failures. This makes her role as procuress for Janey a curiously interesting one. Their history went back to 1871 when Blunt had re-met her, after many years, on a cross-channel steamer and had felt aware of the quickening of interest, to which he was always hypersensitive, somewhere between Folkestone and Boulogne. It was part of Blunt's technique to act fast in such conditions: to create sexual tension in the very process of identifying it. But for once it seems that Blunt had misinterpreted the signals. Back in London, in April 1872, he had gone to see her at 1 Palace Green, the Howards' town house, designed, as I have mentioned, by Philip Webb and newly decorated by Morris and Burne-Jones. Rosalind was dressed to match the décor. Blunt recorded the meeting in his diary. One of his more likeable traits is his ability to see how close he is to the absurd:

I found her prepared for my visit as for a special occasion, dressed in what was then an unusual and fantastic garb like that worn on the stage by Marguerite in Faust, – mediaeval and designed as I thought and it doubtless was to attract attention but not to my eye becoming. It was therefore without real excuse that after luncheon when we were alone and our conversation had turned for a little while on sentiment I made bold to kiss her. A man who ventures this and finds it unexpected is always in the wrong and deserves what ever reproof he may encounter in return. I had been abrupt and I deserved she should be angry. She should not have been thus treated and she said so in crude words, a torrent of reproaches. If I had then loved her and could have told her so in penitent excuse all might have yet been well, for, the wild words spoken, she offered me her hand and with it her lifelong friendship. But the facility of my recent loves (and there had been two others in Madeira which I have not told of) had turned my head and I in my turn grew angry and refusing the alms she offered rushed out of the house slamming the street door behind me. It was an inexcusable rudeness which ended what might easily have been a connection full of pleasure, for Rosalind was no ordinary woman, and might even perhaps have given me more than her regard, if I had had but patience. It was not till ten years had passed that we met again and I made my peace with her, writing her that penitential sonnet which begins:

> 'If I were angry once that you refused
> The bread I asked and offered me a stone . . .'

This torrid sonnet was included in Blunt's collection of *Love Sonnets of Proteus*.

In the end maybe Rosalind regretted her dismissal of Blunt. By the 1880s she and Blunt were back on terms of emotional, if not physical, intimacy. She seems to have offered him Janey as an act of friendship, a version of largesse, perhaps even an apology. Five years later she was also to offer him Blanche Hozier as a comfort and delight to him on his release from prison, writing invitingly from Castle Howard, 'Blanche Hozier comes about the 15th [July], and when you want frivolity, you will find abundance of it in its most pleasant form with her.' This too was a suggestion Blunt could not resist. But in seeing Rosalind as pandering to Blunt's insatiably erotic appetites one should consider how far she was also hoping to help Janey by providing a new emotional focus for her life. She had seen much of Janey, first at Oneglia, then at Bordighera. She understood the strains that Jenny's illness had imposed on her and, not having Georgie's automatic loyalty to Morris, she may have had a clearer grasp of the long history of incompatibilities between Morris and his wife. Now Rossetti was dead and Morris immersed in politics. Janey was faced with long vistas of emotional aridity that might well have driven her to breaking point. Rosalind was a busybody and a suffragist. Her introduction was made as much to give hope to Janey as to amuse Wilfrid Scawen Blunt.

From his own account of the affair Blunt's chief interest in Janey, apart from the dilapidated remnants of her beauty and a certain melancholy charm, was her long and complicated connection with Rossetti. Blunt was a Rossetti-worshipper as well as Byronist. In his opinion Rossetti was the greatest Victorian poet, Tennyson excepted. With his strong streak of vulgarity he liked the thought of holding the addressee of Rossetti's 'House of Life' in his own arms. It was a macabre triangular relationship. Blunt fantasized that Rossetti returned to be voyeur. 'He always seemed to move there a ghost in her home watching us. It was for me a love with the "what had been" rather than the "what was", and, though essentially physical and real and indulged as often as we met, it never got possession of my whole thoughts or had the power of making me unhappy, the true test of the *grande passion*. I do not remember ever having called her by her Christian name and ever having told her that I loved her. In her first letters to me she began them "Caro mio", a reminiscence of those she must have written to Rossetti.' When not indulging their love Blunt was encouraging Janey to discuss her ancient love affair: 'We talked about Rossetti, and I asked her whether she had been very much in love with him. She said, "Yes, at first, but it did not last long."' Blunt added in pencil: 'It was very warm while it lasted.' He goes over such details with a prurient zeal.

Blunt was not in love with Janey. Nor did he ever claim to be. He once wrote: 'ours is a very curious friendship, for we have little really in common on the outside of things, and she is so silent a woman that except through the physical senses we never could have become intimate'. So how was it that this compulsive philanderer, who was often abroad and only saw her rarely, apparently made Janey happier than she had ever been? Soon after they met she went to visit him at Crabbet Park, his family estate near Horsham in Sussex, and wrote afterwards to thank him with the reawakened delight of a young girl: 'Please believe that I enjoyed myself only too much. I am often amazed at the capacity for enjoyment still left me, and I have never felt it more strongly than in your house.'

To judge from Blunt's own diaries he had a real interest in women, the interest one often finds in men who are pursuers: a fascination with women's histories, psychology, the details of their lives. He was inquisitive where Morris was so diffident. He understood precisely how a woman's body works. Blunt, assuming Morris's sexual disengagement, commented in his diary that Morris talked to women in exactly the same manner as he addressed a journeyman carpenter: the description rings true. Women released in Blunt a fluency and daring. Morris resisted exactly what Blunt revelled in, that moment when a conversation turns to 'sentiment'. Janey, starved of sentiment, responded to him gratefully. Blunt had, in abundance, what Morris lacked, not in his poetry but in his everyday behaviour: the imaginative quality in love.

Was Morris aware of Janey's new liaison? He did not meet Blunt until the summer after Naworth, in late July of 1884. After that they were fairly frequently together. In a way Blunt began to hero-worship Morris too. It is difficult to think that Morris had no suspicions. He was ultra-sensitive to Janey's emotional state. Blunt himself, in his well-practised way, assessed the situation:

She was a loveable and noble woman, but he knew he had never touched her heart. Yet he was observant. What had taken place between her and Rosetti [sic] he knew and had forgiven. But he had not forgotten it. I used to think too that he suspected me at times (for her intimacy with me was not very explicable) even to the extent of jealousy. More than once, after having left us alone together, I noted that he had returned suddenly on some pretence to the room where we were, blundering with loud footsteps and as if ashamed of a suspicion which he had not been able to control. Finding nothing, he was far too generous not to put the thought aside either with her or me – And yet there was reason.

451

May, who had suffered from her mother's lovers, wrote later, 'I'm afraid I always thought Mr. Blunt, with all his qualities, an Egotist and vain.'

In the early 1880s the Firm was still expanding. The Oxford Street showrooms were extended to the first floor, to provide much more display space. In 1883 Morris & Co. moved into Manchester, hoping to find new customers in the Liberal-artistic circles of the north, renting shops first in John Dalton Street and then in Albert Square, and setting up workshops for cabinet making and upholstery. The Firm already had its agents in America, but now made a more definite effort to expand its sales abroad, taking a large stand at the 1883 Foreign Fair at Boston. George Wardle was in attendance. The 'Goose Girl' tapestry and the cartoons for 'Flora' and 'Pomona' were on view. Morris realized the Merton Abbey move had been a gamble and that in effect this was a make-or-break time. He told Georgie confidentially:

I am much encouraged by your interest in our Merton Crafts, and shall do my best to make it pay so that we may keep it going, though, as I have told you, I can't hide from myself that there is a chance of failure (commercial I mean) in the matter: in which case I must draw in my horns, and try to shuffle out of the whole affair decently, and live thereafter small and certain if possible: little would be my grief at the same. This is looking at the worst side, which I think one ought to do; but I *think* we shall on the whole succeed: though a rich man (so-called) I never either can or will become.

The publicity material of the period puts much emphasis on the special ethos of the company. The Boston brochure was less of a commercial catalogue, more of a Morris lecture about history and nature. The links with the ancient were emphasized, the probity of technique and the purity of dyestuffs. It certainly contributed to the success of the whole enterprise that Morris & Co. products were presented in a quasi-religious hush. But how idealistic *was* the Firm now in reality? Were its working conditions so different from those prevailing in the rest of British industry? Or had its ideals been stymied by a move that had seemed in itself so idealistic and the need to secure new customers and markets at a time when business in general was slack? Morris himself would maintain that his purism had prevented the company fulfilling its commercial potential: he told Scheu, 'I believe that if I had yielded on a few points of principle I might have come a positively rich man'. But why was Merton Abbey so far from the scenarios proposed in his own lectures? At a time when William Morris was on the verge of becoming a committed Socialist, these are particularly interesting points.

As the visitors to Merton immediately noticed, the general environment was far and away more pleasant than the norm, with the Wandle winding in and out 'with happy joyous murmur' and the amiable ducks with their bright-orange webbed feet. There was an obvious geniality about the enterprise, a sense of the skills of the workmen being valued and an overflow of Morris's philosophy of working. It was surely not mere sycophancy that prompted one of the block printers to confide in Isabella, when she visited her brother, 'Mr. Morris believes in us men using our brains as well as our hands and does not want to turn us into machines.' Nevertheless many of the processes at Merton – fabric dyeing, the Jacquard loomweaving, the block printing itself – gave little or no scope for creative innovation. The workers worked obediently to Morris's instructions, performing laborious and largely repetitive tasks.

There was no serious attempt to bring out the latent creative talent of each workman, no equivalent of the tailor-made tuition of some later workshops of the Arts and Crafts. Although Morris had originally put so great a stress, in his early correspondence with Thomas Wardle, on the need for an artistic input from the weaver, most of the tapestry weavers at Merton were occupied solely with filling in large areas of the backgrounds, drapes and robes. Where artistic decision was needed as, for instance, in the figure portraiture, this was left to J. H. Dearle and one or two trusted assistants. The weaving shed, although orderly, was noisy, claustrophobic; the Morris & Co. madder sometimes even polluted the waters of the Wandle. Industrially speaking, Merton Abbey was still not so many miles away from Leek.

Young boys were recruited for tapestry making. Morris had perceived, 'The work of weaving is a kind which experience proves to be best done by boys. It involves little muscular effort and is best carried on by small flexible fingers.' Some of the apprentices in the photographs at Merton, dressed in their regulation starched collars, dark striped trousers and black coats, seem not to be older than twelve or thirteen. Much was made by Wardle of the fact that these boys were recruited randomly. One was found wandering in the London streets by Richard Grosvenor; another was the nephew of the housekeeper at Merton where the boys were lodged and fed and given what Wardle described as 'a certain weekly stipend'. Morris wrote so imaginatively on education. He was soon to propose so lucidly in lectures and in papers that factories themselves could be places of learning: factories could provide 'work light in duration, and not oppressive in kind, education in childhood and youth'. But there is no evidence of any further education or even improving recreation for these Merton boys. They were certainly not taken into the bosom of the Morris family as the boys of the Guild of Handicraft were later loved and nurtured by the Ashbees – though one has to remember Ashbee's Uranian inclinations. Morris was less emotional on youth and comradeship. The mediaevalized conditions in the tapestry shed, so romantic to a visitor, were constricting to the workers. The action was in itself monotonous. The weavers sat unhealthily cramped on a low bench. Some of the weavers developed stomach complaints. A Morris & Co. weaver died of a gastric ulcer whilst working on a tapestry in 1929.

One of the tenets of Morris's lectures was that workers should be given a voice in their own factories and control over their products. In practice there was little sign of this at Merton, only the limited system of profit-sharing among the 'upper clerks', already in place before Morris left Queen Square. The majority of Morris & Co. workers, although apparently paid more than the ordinary market wage, had no financial stake in the company, and were subject to the fluctuations of the market; the level of their wages was maintained at 'the highest which each particular product could afford'. Many were paid on piecework, the very system Morris had perceived as so socially destructive at Leek. Wardle's argument for piecework at Merton was that it allowed the workmen control over their own time: they could 'occasionally knock off for an hour's work in the garden'. But presumably each hour of horticulture cancelled out an hour of potential earning time. The Merton piecework system was a just one, according to Wardle: 'Any objections or claims made by a workman was listened to as if it came from an equal and decided according to the equity of the case, as fairly as it might be.' But a fair hearing for claims over piecework was a far cry from the full participation of the workers that Morris had been arguing for as the ideal. Merton was a humane factory for the time, affected for the good by its proprietor's charisma. It is surely true that, as Wardle claimed so loyally, 'No one having worked for Mr. Morris would willingly have joined any other workshop or, having passed through any other, would have given up Mr. Morris for that.' Then, as now, people will put up with much if the proprietor is visible – and visibly better at the job. But this was benign patriarchy, not social experiment. Merton Abbey contained the traditional confrontation between employer and employed.

Why was this? Morris was certainly not blind to the gulf between his theory and his practice at Merton Abbey. But he shilly-shallied. The official reason, and the one accepted by his friends and his supporters, was that a more experimental structure could only be a partial solution, a mere drop in the ocean of capitalist evil. George Wardle later maintained that Morris's true ideal had indeed been a communistic Merton involving 'one purse and one table and one workshop, one interest only for workman and foreman, and this as part of a universal system of communistic life'. When people asked him why this was not in fact attempted by Morris, George Wardle would reply: 'The answer to this, though very simple, needs apparently to be given. It is that *you cannot have socialism in a corner.*' It is certainly true that Morris distrusted the partial solution, seeing it as self-indulgent. The basis of the story told against him by Rossetti, that Top was too mean to give a penny to a beggar, shows the force of Morris's logic: pennies were of no real benefit to beggars. Here again we see Morris well ahead of his time.

There is an important parallel drawn between Merton and the productive Puritan communities established in seventeenth-century America. They had soon discovered, as the Cistercian monasteries had done before them, that their viability ceased at the point at which they were indistinguishable from other merchants or producers. The argument is Wardle's, but clearly drawn from Morris is its reliance on historic precedent:

They could not exist according to their ideal except by complete isolation and independence of the outside world, a condition rarely, if ever possible, and obviously quite impossible in such a business as Morris's which existed only to supply the demands of an unsocialistic society, and was also compelled to draw all its material from the same. Since the buying and selling were both controlled by external conditions, production also was bound to follow them. Mr. Morris would gladly have had it otherwise but the problem for him was not how to defeat the invincible but how to make the best of adverse conditions.

Morris had the commercial acumen to realize that, trading conditions being as they were in Britain in the early 1880s, a communistic Merton would soon run into the ground.

Morris was also wary of improving the conditions of his workers to such an extent that he made them social misfits. Pressed by Emma

Lazarus on the question of the lack of joy in labour in evidence at Merton, Morris told her he would be doing no service to his work-people in the current climate by raising their expectations unrealistically: 'except with a small part of the more artistic side of the work I could not do anything or at least but little to give this pleasure to the workmen; because I should have had to change their method of working so utterly, that it should have disqualified them from earning their living elsewhere.' Tackled by his fellow art worker and Socialist Thomas Cobden-Sanderson about the rate he paid his workmen, he replied that if he were to pay them higher 'they would all at once become capitalists'.

Cobden-Sanderson detected cowardice in Morris. This was certainly a factor in his reluctance to dismantle, or even much amend, a way of working which had evolved carefully over the past two decades, since the days of Red Lion Square. He knew how much he himself depended on known personnel, known skills and rhythms: part of his own joy in labour was the sense of his proximity to techniques he had mastered and completely understood. Mackail observed so truly that Morris was less interested in making money than in making the things he chose to make. He could have gone further and said that William Morris was obsessed with making the things he wanted, as *slowly* as he wanted, by the methods he preferred.

There were other reasons, buried more deeply in the psyche. His personality had areas of reticence and awkwardness, even when with his peers and protected by the panoply of old and trusted friendships and male jokes. Like so many British middle-class converts to the left, he found fellowship much easier in the abstract than the imminent. He was still conscious of his childhood hierarchies, the passages between the servants' quarters and the gentlefolk. There was also the cash nexus, the emotionally complex relationship between the employee and the person on whom he depended for his livelihood, often felt the more acutely by the one who did the paying. Morris tended to be gruff and self-conscious with his employees. He had very little flair for social experiment, none of the devilry of an Edward Carpenter in over-throwing the inhibitions of his class. When he came to know Carpenter, Morris felt almost envious of the little village house in Derbyshire with seven acres where Carpenter lived in close community, social and sexual, with labourers from Sheffield. As Carpenter wrote ecstatically in *Towards Democracy*:

I am the poet of hitherto unuttered joy,
Children go with me, and rude people are my companions.
I trust them and they me.
Day and night we are together and are content.

Morris knew himself well enough to realize that such egalitarian trans-
ports were far beyond his reach.

There was surely a further very fundamental reason, strangely disregarded in many accounts of Morris, for his fear of embarking on any
course of action that would jeopardize his own income. Morris was
intensely conscious of having a family to support, a family including an
invalid daughter and an ailing wife. This was an argument he had
advanced to Cobden-Sanderson: 'that there was his wife and the girls;
and how could he put upon them.' In 1879, on a spare sheet of his
'Cabbage and Vine' notebook, he had made some conscientious little
lists of his projected household expenditure:

Household expenses including Kelmscott	364
Rent	100
Wine acc.	50
Dress for 4 persons	100
	615
add more HE [Household expenses] £3 week	156
	770
T R M & E [servants]	80
Societies	50
	900
Books	100
Travelling	100
Rates and taxes and insurance	100
	1200

Janey's medical treatments, from as far back as Bad Ems, had been
expensive, and Jenny's became more onerous as her condition worsened
and she needed a permanent companion/nurse. By 1884, at a time when
Morris & Co. profits were rising, and Morris was involved in the
Socialist fray, he made the situation more explicit in a long letter of
self-defence to Georgie. For the past year or two his Morris & Co.
earnings had amounted to about £1,800 per annum (as against Wardle's

457

£1,200 and the Smith brothers' £600 each). In addition his annual
literary income was about £120. He felt more than ever buffeted
between the political and personal, tempted to sacrifice his income for
his comrades in the cause. But he tells Georgie categorically that what
prevents him is his responsibility to 'those other partners called my
family: now you know we ought to be able to live upon £4 a week, and
give the literary income to the revolutionary agitation: but here comes
the rub, and I feel the pinch of society for which society I am only
responsible in a very limited degree. And yet if Janey and Jenny were
quite well and capable I think they ought not to grumble at living on the
said £4, nor do I think they would.'

There was a bitter sweetness about Merton. Morris loved it, spent
much time there. In the early 1880s he was at Merton two or three times
a week. He travelled by Underground from Hammersmith to Farringdon, then took the London, Brighton, and South Coast Railway from
Ludgate Hill to Merton Abbey, where the station had opened in 1868.
This journey took around two hours. Sometimes, when unassailed by
gout, he preferred to walk to Merton through Roehampton, a slightly
longer journey but 'not all pure waste like the sweltering train-business'.
There were diverting vistas in Roehampton: once when passing by the
Convent of the Sacred Heart, he spotted a whole bevy of 'holy dames'
emerging and getting into rowing boats on the lake there, an unexpected
harmony in black and white.

Wardle noted that, however troublesome the journey, Morris was
always in a good mood when he arrived at Merton: 'The latter part of
the journey perhaps, through the fields, was soothing and then there was
the short passage from the Station through the garden of the Abbey and
the prospect of being soon at work, which together may have restored
the equilibrium.' However there remained 'a certain *impetus*' in Morris's
manner, 'as if he would still go at 20 miles an hour and rather expected
everything to keep pace to him'. This was his usual nervous delayed
response to railway journeys. Wardle had noticed the same symptoms at
Queen Square. When Morris arrived at Merton he would first discuss
the new developments. Then he toured the workshops, checking on
progress. After this he settled down to his own drawing-board. Wardle
described how there was always at least one design under way, and often
more. If Morris was working on a repeating pattern, the design was
interrupted for the technical assistant to produce the repeats from it,
and he liked to have a pattern in reserve. Wardle was always impressed

Sunday June 1st. 1884

Dearest Georgie don't be alarmed: certain things occurred to me which being written you may pitch into the fire if you please.

The question of sharing of profits in order to shake off the responsibility of exploitation is complicated by this fact, that the workman is exploited by others besides his own employer: for as things now go every thing is made for a profit, & every thing has to pay toll to people who do not work, and whose idleness enforces overwork on those who are compelled to work: everyone of us therefore, workman or non-workman, is forced to support the present competitive system by merely living in the present society, and buying his ordinary daily necessaries: So that an employer by giving up his individual profit on the goods he gets made would not be able to put his workmen in their proper position: they would be exploited by others though not by him: this to explain partly why I said that cooperation to be real & must be the rule and not the exception.

How to be done with it I will put my own position, which I would not do to the public because it is by no means typical, and would therefore be useless as a matter of principle. Some of those who work for me share in the profits formally: I suppose I make the last year or two about £1800, Wardle about £1200, the Smiths about £600 each; Debney & West £400 all these share directly in the profits: Kenyon the Colour-mixer, & Goodacre the foreman dyer have also a kind of bonus on the amount of goods

34 Letter written by William Morris to Georgiana Burne-Jones, 1 June 1884. The free flow of the handwriting suggests the ease and openness of his communication with her.

by his great fluency: 'He drew as quickly and accurately as he wrote.'

Technically speaking, he had organized Merton in the way he wanted it. In a sense he had created it in his own image. It was full of his own tangibilities and beauties: the yarns in the dye-house; the partly printed chintzes stretched out on the long trestles; the improbable tapestries growing on the high-warp loom. Yet Morris came to see it almost as a liability. In 1882 his collected lectures *Hopes and Fears for Art* were published, the sum of his pronouncements to date on art seen from the Socialist point of view. No doubt this helped to concentrate his mind on the conundrum:

it sometimes seems to me as if my lot was a strange one: you see, I work pretty hard, and on the whole very cheerfully, not altogether I hope for mere pudding, still less for praise; and while I work I have the cause always in mind, and yet I know that the cause for which I specially work is doomed to fail, at least in seeming; I mean that art must go under, where or how ever it may come up again. I don't know if I explain what I'm driving at, but it does sometimes seem to me a strange thing indeed that a man should be driven to work with energy and even with pleasure and enthusiasm at work which he knows will serve no end but amusing himself; am I doing nothing but make-believe then, something like Louis XVI's lock-making?

He admitted to Georgie that the dilemma was only theoretical since 'I shall without doubt go on with my work, useful or useless, till I demit.'

Up to and through 1880 William Morris had been aware of, and had felt frustrated by, the almost total impasse in English politics. He saw how the Labour movement had been paralysed by the severe trade depression of the 1870s. He had watched how the working-class leaders had been virtually swallowed up into the Liberal opposition between 1874 and 1880, while the Liberals were out of power. But he gradually sensed the situation to be changing. In January 1881 he had written an optimistic New Year letter: 'my mind is very full of the great change which I hope is slowly coming over the world'. That change, as he saw it, was an altered class perspective: he trusted the new year would 'do a good turn of work towards the abasement of the rich and the raising up of the poor which is of all things most to be longed for, till people can at last rub out from their dictionaries altogether these dreadful words rich and poor'.

In June of that year a new organization, the Democratic Federation was founded in London, inviting delegates from 'advanced political organizations, trade societies and clubs' throughout the country. It protested against the fact that the vast number of members returned to the House of Commons in the 1881 elections represented 'any interest in the country but that of the working class'. The Federation proposed a social and political programme aiming to 'unite the great body of the people, quite irrespective of party'. Morris, too, was then envisaging some new social scenario, 'some kind of culture of which we know nothing at present'. His letters to Georgie, his main confidante that summer, burn with anger and also a not yet fully focused visionary hope.

In July 1881 Morris was much dismayed by the sentence of sixteen months' hard labour, given at the end of his trial at the Old Bailey, to a Viennese dissident in exile, Johann Most, the editor of the anti-Bismarck news-sheet *Freiheit* which circulated illegally in Germany. After the assassination of Tsar Alexander II, Most had published an article which Morris described as 'a song of triumph'. Morris did not associate himself with what Most said, but he saw the hounding and harsh sentencing of Most as a terrible example of British tyranny, hypocrisy and class injustice: 'These are the sort of things that make thinking people so sick at heart that they are driven from all interest in politics save revolutionary politics.' During Most's trial, outside the Old Bailey, the Democratic Federation member Jack Williams had been selling English-language editions of *Freiheit*. By the autumn Morris was writing, 'it is good to feel the air laden with the coming storm.'

In a blazing passage in his lecture 'The Prospects of Architecture', Morris had already identified the testing time and sacrifice demanded to bring about the birth of the new art:

for between us and that which is to be, if art is not to perish utterly, there is something alive and devouring; something as it were a river of fire that will put all that tries to swim across to a hard proof indeed, and scare from the plunge every soul that is not made fearless by desire of truth and insight of the happy days to come beyond.

This was the river Morris was now to cross.

CHAPTER FOURTEEN

Westminster Palace Chambers
1883–84

At the beginning of 1883 Morris underwent what he was always to refer to as 'conversion'. This was not, as has been often claimed, a blinding revelation. Morris himself understood, and explained very straightforwardly, the nature of a change of attitude which had been gradual and inevitable. The sequence of events of his whole life had led on logically to his espousal of the Socialist cause. His pampered but solitary childhood; his edgy years at Marlborough; his rejection of religion during Oxford; the emotional breakdown of his marriage; the severe epilepsy of the daughter he loved and had such hopes for; his accumulating doubts of the value of the work he had embarked on with such success and with such great enjoyment: Morris's 'conversion' was a drama that had a built-in momentum and a quality of splendour. The New Testament word in Greek – *metanoia*, 'mental reorientation' – is more appropriate. May, who was close to her father at this period, observed it as 'some disturbance of the earth'. It affected fundamentally the tenor of his thinking and it removed him, in his forty-ninth year, to a very different milieu. On 17 January 1883 Morris joined the Democratic Federation. By a strange irony only four days earlier he and Edward Burne-Jones had been appointed Honorary Fellows of their old Oxford college, Exeter. On 14 March that same year in Maitland Park Road, north London, Karl Marx was to die at the age of sixty-five.

There is an eye-witness account of Morris almost at the moment of the crossing of his 'river of fire'. Andreas Scheu, the Viennese refugee anarchist and furniture designer, saw him at a Socialist gathering in London:

In the early winter months of 1883 the Democratic Federation had arranged some meetings at the Westminster Palace Chambers. I attended the first of those meetings (I forget the exact date), Mr. Hyndman in the chair. The order of the day was the passing of some resolutions on the question of education, normal working-day, and the housing of the working classes. The business had scarcely been started when Banner, who sat behind me, passed me a slip of paper, 'The third man to your right is William Morris'. I had read of but never seen Morris before, and I looked at once in the direction given. I was struck by Morris's fine face, his earnestness, the half searching, half dreamy look of his eyes, and his plain and comely dress.

No. 9 Palace Chambers was itself the sign and symbol of Morris's conversion. The Democratic Federation then met in the gloomy, stuffy basement of a ponderous building opposite the Houses of Parliament in Westminster Bridge Road. The meeting room was sparse and badly furnished, lit by a couple of sputtering candles stuck into tin candle-sticks. This was the décor of protest, first of many similar Socialist committee rooms with which Morris came to be familiar from then on.

For several years, since his disenchantment with the Liberals and Radicals, Morris had been, as he put it, 'on the look out for joining any body which seemed likely to push forward matters'. His friend and publisher F. S. Ellis, calling at the shop in Oxford Street in 1881 or 1882, found Morris writing furiously. He had told him, 'I'm going in for socialism: I have given up these Radicals.' Morris later said that at this period he had always intended to join any organization that distinctly called itself Socialist. The difficulty in the London of the early 1880s lay in actually locating any declared Socialist group. Socialism at this period was still really an abstraction. There *was* no Socialism as political reality. The politics of protest were a confused amalgam of the London working-men's and Radical clubs, the remnants of the Chartists and the more recent influx of foreign refugees from Austria and France after the Commune, from Bismarck's Germany and from the repressive Russian regime. These refugees formed little groups of insurrectionists *manqués* collecting unhappily in Soho pubs. Even the Democratic Federation was at that time tentative. It had not declared totally for Socialism. Morris joined it in the expectation that it would.

What is remarkable about him at this period is the leap of the imagination still possible for a man of his standing in apparently settled middle age. He took the future on trust. He had few Socialist contacts. At this stage he knew no Socialist theory. He was in at the beginning, in the formative years of English Socialism, working on his instinct, truly the pioneer. Looking back a decade later he explained that he had joined the Democratic Federation because it was the one body that could offer, even hazily, the hope of a society of real equality, without masters and men, without rich and poor:

> If you ask me how much of a hope, or what I thought we Socialists then living and working would accomplish towards it, or when there would be effected any change in the face of society, I must say, I do not know. I can only say that I did not measure my hope, nor the joy that it brought me at the time.

The Democratic Federation had been founded by Henry Mayers Hyndman, a maverick politician from a wealthy family, of the kind that still erupt into socialist politics. He was educated at Trinity College, Cambridge; he had read for the bar and then become a journalist. He was eloquent, quick-witted, cultivated, musical. A craftsman who went to call on him was ushered into his drawing-room and startled to be given a professional rendering of 'O! for the Wings of a Dove' by Hyndman on his flute. Shaw defined him, brilliantly, as 'an *assuming* man', allying him with a long line of free-thinking English gentlemen-republicans during the last half of the nineteenth century: Dilke, Burton, Auberon Herbert, Wilfrid Scawen Blunt, Laurence Oliphant, 'great globe-trotters, writers, *frondeurs*'. H. M. Hyndman is another of the William Morris doubles. He and Morris had many similarities of background. They came from the same generation: Hyndman was eight years younger. Both appear as bearded patriarchs, older than their years. Both were emotional, industrious and solemn in their commitment to the cause. But there were immense differences, summed up by the fact that Hyndman, aristocrat and actor, continued to wear his gentleman's top hat, whereas a decade earlier Morris had sat on his.

In the 1870s Hyndman had met Marx. At that time he was a Liberal, and on the staff of the *Pall Mall Gazette*. Hyndman first read Marx's *Das Kapital* in the French edition on a business trip to Utah in 1880. He returned from Mormon country a convinced Marxian Socialist, and published an optimistic article, 'The Dawn of a Revolutionary Epoch', in the monthly magazine *The Nineteenth Century* in January 1881. At the inaugural conference of the Democratic Federation in June of that year all the delegates were given a booklet by Hyndman called *England for All*. This was Hyndman's exposition of the Marxist viewpoint, based on *Das Kapital* but not mentioning Marx's name, an omission that infuriated Marx himself and earned Hyndman the lasting enmity of Friedrich Engels, Marx's Manchester collaborator and the keeper of his flame. Engels dismissed Hyndman as 'an arch-Conservative and an extremely chauvinistic but not stupid careerist, who behaved pretty shabbily to Marx, and for that reason was dropped by us personally'. Marx called him a 'weak vessel' and accused him of having only a superficial understanding of his views.

Hyndman's *England for All* was, nevertheless, the key text in forming English Socialism at that period, when its principles were so relatively undeveloped, and in introducing Morris's contemporaries to the surplus-value theories of Karl Marx. Edward Carpenter, for instance, explained how it had filled a need in providing 'a definite text for the social argument. The instant I read that chapter in *England for All* – the mass of floating impressions, sentiments, ideals, etc., in my mind fell into shape – and I had a clear line of social reconstruction before me.' Morris himself recommended Hyndman's sequel *The Historical Basis of Socialism in England* to a possible recruit for the Federation, telling him that Hyndman's book was 'well worth reading and very easy to read'.

At the start of the Democratic Federation, Hyndman had soft-pedalled on his Socialist policies. The main thrust had been towards land nationalization and especially the problem of coercion in Ireland. With his journalistic sensitivity to timing Hyndman had been making the most of current interest in the ideas of the American economist Henry George and his book *Progress and Poverty*, putting the case for Single Tax reform. Henry George's impassioned lectures, when he came to England, roused his working-class audiences to wild applause. But by 1883, when Morris joined the Federation, its political stance had been gradually changing. Its original Radical club membership dwindled and now more committed Socialists came in. Hyndman managed to transform the Federation into a more overtly Socialist body. Its membership was strengthened with new working-class recruits who were later key figures in the movement: Harry Quelch, for instance, a journeyman packer then employed in Cannon Street; John Burns, a working engineer who joined a few months after Morris. Burns became the first person of working-class origin to reach Cabinet rank in a British Parliament.

Already, in its first two years, the Democratic Federation was arriving at that mix of class and culture that has given British socialism such a bizarre character. Hyndman had also been recruiting a number of disaffected young men from the English public schools. James Leigh Joynes was an assistant master at Eton, forced to resign after he had accompanied Henry George himself on a campaign in Ireland and both had been arrested. Joynes's *Adventures of a Tourist in Ireland* (1882) tells the controversial tale. Morris's Democratic Federation membership card, made out to 'William Morris designer', was signed by H. H. Champion, the son of General Champion, who had recently resigned his commission in the Royal Artillery. Champion, now installed as Hyndman's right-hand man, had been at Marlborough like William Morris. On the intellectual wing of the Federation was a powerful polemicist who joined the party almost simultaneously with Morris, the 'hard-shell' Marxist economist, Ernest Belfort Bax.

Socialism at this time was far from being a mass movement. The Socialists were still a small and almost unknown body. May Morris quotes the contemporary jibe that the entire movement would fit into a four-wheel cab. The late E. P. Thompson has suggested that William Morris was one of only about 200 people making that particular journey into English Socialism in 1883. The Democratic Federation had the sense of apartness, the motleyness of membership, the zeal and the self-righteousness of the primitive sect. When Edward Pease, then a young stockbroker, made his exploratory tour of the London political meeting-halls he found at Palace Chambers what he described as 'the oddest little gathering'. It consisted of 'twenty characteristically democratic men with dirty hands and small heads, some of them obviously with very limited wits, and mostly with some sort of foreign accent'. Nevertheless he joined the Federation. He said he had been carried away by 'the spirit of the affair'.

This spirit, such as it was, must be attributed to the confident and charismatic leader of the Federation. It was Hyndman who paid the rent of its office and the salary of its secretary. He held it together and he called the tune, seeing the necessity for keeping its members in suspense, at a high pitch of drama and intrigue. Hyndman in fact was a brilliant catastrophist. When the Democratic Federation started, he convinced himself and his followers that they would see the Revolution in 1889.

Morris joined what he referred to as 'the only active Socialist organisation in England' with the deep and pervading contentment of the man who has at last found his proper *métier*. He writes of it in terms of the rebirth, the homecoming, the recognition that the thing so much desired has in a sense been always there. In his *Commonweal* poem, *The Pilgrims of Hope*, written two years later, he returns to the experience, describing the enrolment of the hero as a Communist in glowing, mystic terms. Once again we are in a world of doubles. The message of welcome is delivered by a thickset, short man dressed in shabby blue:

> He spoke like a friend long known; and lo! I was one of the band.
> And now the streets seem gay and the high stars glittering bright;
> And for me, I sing amongst them, for my heart is full and light.
> I see the deeds to be done and the day to come on the earth,
> And riches vanished away and sorrow turned to mirth;
> I see the city squalor and the country stupor gone.
> And we a part of it all – we twain no longer alone
> In the days to come of the pleasure, in the days that are of the fight –
> I was born once long ago: I am born again tonight.

'I see the deeds to be done': these words of course have a particular significance for Morris, the hater of imprecision and vagueness. Part of his joy at his own enrolment in the cause of Socialism was the knowledge that now he was faced with a definite task, indeed a whole series of clearly defined labours, some of them inevitably taxing. The prospect was not unlike the discovery of some arcane and challenging new craft, and indeed Morris applied similar methods, the same close analysis, the driving concentration, to his new discipline, 'the joy of strife'.

He set himself doggedly to acquiring the Socialist theory he badly felt the lack of. When he joined the Democratic Federation he had read a little of John Stuart Mill, in particular Mill's essay 'Chapters on Socialism', published posthumously in *The Fortnightly Review*. This had convinced him, contrary to Mill's own arguments, that Socialism was a *bona fide* movement and that it was indeed possible to bring about a Socialist society in his own time. In retelling the story of his conversion, Morris claimed that Mill's writings 'put the finishing touch'. But Morris explains how he was at this same period 'blankly ignorant' of Socialist economics. He had 'never so much as opened Adam Smith, or heard of Ricardo, or of Karl Marx'. He began to remedy this by reading *Das Kapital*, in the French version, in the early months of 1882. On 22 April, Crom Price's diary records: 'Top to breakfast at Ned's – extra brilliant after overcoming some drooping spirits on account of Jenny . . . was full of Karl Marx which he had begun to read in French – praised Robert Owen greatly.'

He did not find Karl Marx easy. He later confessed that though he thoroughly enjoyed the historical sections, the chapters on pure economics caused him 'agonies of confusion of the brain'. May, who watched his struggles, commented perceptively that it was difficult for someone with her father's deeply emotional attitude to the people and the land 'to delve with sustained enthusiasm' into the intricacies of the 'scientific socialism' of Marx with its hard technical arguments and economic formulas. But he persevered, and the following year was still carving out time from his onerous lecture tours and Socialist committees to study Marx's theories of work and wages. As he wrote self-deprecatingly to Andreas Scheu:

I feel myself very weak as to the science of Socialism on many points; I wish I knew German, as I see I must certainly learn it; confound you chaps! What do you mean by being foreigners? Why did you allow our (no *their* for I am not a Saxon) forefathers to corrupt their low German tongue with that blooming French-Latin? Item, I want statistics terribly: you see I am but a poet and an artist, good for nothing but sentiment.

While he was reading Marx, Morris was also steeping himself in Cobbett's writings. He wrote to Ellis & White, in the summer of 1883, 'Could you lay hands for me on the works of William Cobbett – any or all of them.' Something which distinguished him from many of his intellectually narrower new Socialist colleagues was this greed for new experience, Morris's enormous catholicity. Cobbett, the early nineteenth-century roving radical, self-educated son of a southern English farmer, was a man after Morris's own heart in his view of the countryside, irascible but genial, and in the vigour, almost the innocence, of his response. Presumably Cobbett's *Rural Rides* (1821 onwards) and his *Advice to Young Men* (1829) were among the acquisitions Morris described to Jenny: 'such queer things they are, but with plenty of stuff in them, somehow they rather remind me of old Borrow'. He was certainly amusing himself with *Cottage Economy* (1822), a practical manual in which Cobbett gives instructions on bread making and beer making, keeping bees and rearing poultry and other activities of the simple life. Morris loved the little details, telling Jenny of the chapter on straw-plait making. 'The article on the pig is touching,' he added wistfully. Cobbett's prose style, which Hazlitt called his 'plain, broad, downright English', was the kind of romantic functionalist writing that Morris was to emulate in his Socialist journalism of the next decade.

We see Morris at this period as omnivorous, receptive. Sir Thomas More's *Utopia*, which he had been re-reading; the Owenite and Co-operative experiments; the English rural radical tradition of the eighteenth and nineteenth centuries; the writings of his mentors Ruskin and Carlyle; Marxism as interpreted by Hyndman, argued out in the Democratic Federation meetings: in Morris's Socialism of the early 1880s a broad range of influence converged. In 1883 he was reading Sergius Stepniak's *Underground Russia*, with a heady mixture of terror and excitement. He recommended it to F. S. Ellis: 'Read Underground Russia if you want your blood to boil.' The book was important to Morris in making him aware of a vast new territory of repression and outrage. Stepniak was a Russian aristocrat, born Sergey Mikhailovich Kravchinsky. He renamed himself, for reasons of convenience and political correctness, 'Stepniak', literally 'a man of the steppes', an intellectual Cossack, a free roamer. Despairing of the revolution, Step-niak left Russia in 1874 and travelled around Europe, but returned to St Petersburg four years later, living through 'the Terror' that had cul-minated in the assassination of the Tsar. The translation of his highly emotional account of repression in Russia, unflinching to the point of being lurid, had only just been published in England. Morris com-mented: 'it sounds perfectly genuine: I should think such a book ought to open people's eyes a bit here and do good'. He identified Stepniak as 'one of the Nihilists'. Morris's enthusiasm for a foreign publication about which, had it been English, he would surely have been more cautious, shows his mood of the moment. Ned later maintained that *Underground Russia* had been one of the 'inciting causes' of Morris's Socialism.

Morris certainly allied himself in his imagination with the contem-porary Russian struggle. In the long, inspired and confidential letter he wrote to C. E. Maurice in the summer of 1883 he explained his view that the whole basis of society, with its contrasts of rich and poor, was so 'incurably vicious' that it should no longer be endured by either rich or poor. 'Now it seems to me', he continued, 'that feeling this, I am bound to act for the destruction of the system which seems to me mere oppression and obstruction; such a system can only be destroyed, it

469

seems to me, by the united discontent of numbers.' In taking upon himself the task of 'spreading discontent among all classes', he was acting in the spirit of the *narodniki* – the populists. In 'Art and Socialism', a lecture he first gave in early 1884, Morris speaks the international language of the heroic resistance, with a fervour Stepniak would have approved:

will you say that here in this quiet, constitutionally governed country of England there is no opportunity for action offered to us? If we were in gagged Germany, in gagged Austria, in Russia where a word or two might land us in Siberia or the prison of the fortress of Peter and Paul; why then, indeed – Ah! my friends, it is but a poor tribute to offer on the tombs of the martyrs of liberty, this refusal to take the torch from their dying hands! Is it not of Goethe it is told, that on hearing one say he was going to America to begin life again, he replied: 'Here is America, or nowhere!' So for my part I say: 'Here is Russia, or nowhere.'

To say the governing classes in England are not afraid of freedom of speech, *therefore* let us abstain from speaking freely, is a strange paradox to me. Let us on the contrary press in through the breach which valiant men have made for us: if we hang back we make their labours, their sufferings, their deaths, of no account. Believe me, we shall be shown that it is all or nothing: or will any one here tell me that a Russian moujik is in a worse case than a sweating tailor's wage slave? Do not let us deceive ourselves, the class of victims exists here as in Russia. There are fewer of them? Maybe; then are they of themselves more helpless, and so have more need of our help.

Stepniak the Nihilist was a natural revolutionary. He had been distributing pamphlets, organizing discussion groups and holding secret meetings since he was a very young man. As he boasted, he could always be found where there was talk of an insurrection and habitually travelled with a knapsack bulging with revolutionary leaflets. In *Underground Russia* he paints a vivid picture of conspiratorial St Petersburg where those wanted by the police met secretly in crowded upstairs rooms. Encouraged by the sympathetic reception of *Underground Russia* Stepniak was soon to come to England, settling first in north London and then in Woodstock Road in Bedford Park, among the Morris & Co. patrons. He makes an appearance in the London revolutionist novel, *A Girl among the Anarchists*, written by Isabel Meredith, the pseudonym of Helen and Olivia Rossetti, the daughters of William Rossetti, in 1903. Stepniak is their Nekrovitch, 'a man of strong intellect, and of the strong personal magnetism which is so frequently an adjunct of genius. Physically he was a huge powerful man, so massive and striking in appearance that he

470

suggested comparison rather with some fact of nature – a rock, a vigorous forest tree – than with another man.'

It would be an exaggeration to suggest that Socialist activities in London in 1883 had the built-in melodrama of the Terror in St Petersburg. Nor would it be correct to depict Morris at this period as a would-be Stepniak: he could never be so out-and-out. There was a part of him that remained the child of Walthamstow, now suffering from gout. But as he came to know Stepniak he loved him and respected him. They shared a quality of insurrectionist innocence and a poetic sense of great events arising from small clandestine meetings in insalubrious corners.

When Edward Carpenter first went to Palace Chambers he found what he described as 'a group of conspirators'. There in that dismal basement was Hyndman, occupying the chair, 'and with him round the table, William Morris, John Burns, H. H. Champion, J. L. Joynes, Herbert Burrows (I think) and others'. The Democratic Federation in conference. There is more than a touch of *Underground Russia* here.

The usefulness of William Morris as a recruit to a new and already definitely suspect body was as obvious to Hyndman as it had been to Mundella in the days of the Eastern Question Association. To Bernard Shaw, who first met him at a social gathering of the Democratic Federation, he was 'our acknowledged Great Man'. There were those who were mystified by Morris's activities. Not all early Socialists had read *The Earthly Paradise*. Shaw, and others, were puzzled by the fact that Morris kept 'a highly select shop in Oxford Street where he sold furniture of a rum aesthetic sort, and decorated houses with extraordinary wallpapers'. There was always to be a rift between the political progressives and the aesthetic avant-garde. But anyone could recognize Morris as a man of stature. 'Here, obviously', wrote Hyndman, 'was no needy and greedy proletarian, no embittered revolutionist, no disappointed politician or cynical publicist.' Morris was 'a University man who had achieved for himself a European fame'. Moreover Morris's integrity shone out of him. Once he began to talk on any subject which interested him, he was caught up in it completely in a way that was inspiring and totally convincing. 'His imposing forehead and clear grey eyes, with a powerful nose and slightly florid cheeks, impressed upon you the truth and importance of what he was saying, every hair of his head and in his rough shaggy beard appearing to enter into the subject as a living part of himself.'

Whether Hyndman had expected Morris to involve himself in such detail in Democratic Federation affairs seems doubtful. He would probably have been happier with Morris merely as a respected figurehead. But this was not Morris's way, and with the zeal of the convert he insisted on taking his full share in what Hyndman termed 'the unpleasant part of our public work', proving quickly that he meant to labour 'in grim earnest' on the same level as the party rank and file. Hyndman commented, with some exasperation, that Morris was never satisfied unless he was doing things which he was actually very little fitted for, tasks less sensitive people could have performed better. Shaw watched from the sidelines sardonically as Morris told Hyndman he had no capacity for leadership, and was ready to do anything that he was told: 'I smiled grimly to myself at this modest offer of allegiance, measuring at sight how much heavier Morris's armament was; but Hyndman accepted it at once as his due. Had Morris been accompanied by Plato, Aristotle, Gregory the Great, Dante, Thomas Aquinas, Milton and Newton, Hyndman would have taken the chair as their natural leader without the slightest misgiving, and before the end of the month have quarrelled with them all and left himself with no followers but the devoted handful who could not compete with him, and to whom he was a sort of god.'

In May 1883 Morris was already on the Democratic Federation executive. He had demurred, but Bax had talked him into it: 'so I am in for more work,' he told Jenny happily. He added with a sigh of long experience, 'money is chiefly lacking as usual'. The Democratic Federation elected Morris its treasurer, as the EQA had done before. The early summer was spent in hammering out the detail of the declaration of principles adopted at the second annual conference in June and published as a manifesto, *Socialism Made Plain*. This statement of intent proposed immediate adoption of what Hyndman had called 'stepping stones to a happier period': improved housing for urban and agricultural workers, free compulsory education for all classes, including free school meals; an eight-hour day; state ownership of banks and railways; abolition of the national debt; nationalization of the land; organization of agricultural and industrial armies under state control on co-operative principles. The nationalization of the means of production and distribution was demanded in a manifesto that was in effect the first thoroughgoing exposition of Marxism by an English political group. As a member of the new executive Morris signed the statement. The result of his insistence that no task was too lowly was that Morris was in charge of its distribution too.

Hyndman signed the manifesto as chairman and H. H. Champion as ion. secretary. The other signatories give an accurate reflection of the ocially and temperamentally erratic composition of the Federation in hese early years. There was Scheu, the artistic anarchist from Vienna, oon to be become a salesman for Jaeger. May described him as 'a fiery nd eloquent speaker of striking aspect in his brown close-fitting Jaeger lothing, his fine head like nothing less than one of Dürer's careful tudies of a curly-bearded German warrior'. There was the old Chartist, ames Murray; a West End tailor, James Macdonald; Herbert Burrows, London Radical club activist, editor of a collection of Mazzini's vritings; Jack Williams, a working man who 'knew the stress of poverty', remembered by May as 'an untiring orator in the Parks and lsewhere, full of energy, with a big voice delivering simple phrases that le knew how to direct to his fellow-workers with telling effect'.

James Joynes, the gaunt ex-Eton master and proselytizing vegetarian, vas also on the new executive. The Federation at that time had a strong quota of New Lifers and professional cranks. Joynes's sister, Kate oynes, married another absconding Eton master, Henry Salt, who gave up his post to devote himself to humanitarian causes. 'Socialism! Then blow us up! There's nothing left for it but that,' cried the Eton headmaster, Dr Warne, when Salt declared himself. Salt broadened the base of the Federation meetings with his esoteric range of intellectual interests: naturism; classicism; the reassessment of Shelley's libertarian iews. Salt attempted, but failed, to make a vegetarian of Morris who argued predictably (and accurately, viewed from a future century), 'If our whole system were to become vegetarian altogether the poor would be forced to live on vegetarian cag-mag, while the rich lived on egetarian dainties.' Henry Salt's teetotalism impressed him even less.

The Democratic Federation executive brought Morris his first experience of the female political co-worker. Helen Taylor was John Stuart Mill's step-daughter, an early supporter of the Women's Suffrage movement. She had lived with Mill at Avignon, assisting him with writing *The Subjection of Women* (1869) and later editing his *Autobiography*. Helen Taylor had been in at the beginning of the Democratic Federation, and since 1880 she had also been a member of he SPAB. Now in her early fifties she was the leading lady of the protest movement: Morris reported with amusement that when Helen Taylor entered the room at Council meetings the Socialists rose to their eet, as if she were the Queen. May, who disliked her, found 'her lofty air' a little old-fashioned, like a Tennysonian heroine, and 'in ou higgledy-piggledy gatherings a little out of place'. Morris seems to hav admired her energy and competence. In one of his letters he calls her ' big gun'. But it seems he never warmed to her. Morris had a mor imaginative view of women's role than most of his contemporaries. Th ideal of the woman as co-worker appears in his writing from the ver early days. But the feminist reality appears to have unnerved him, a successive Labour politicians and even editors of the *Guardian* new paper have found. The political female, working in the hurly-burly, wa clearly disconcerting to a Victorian conditioned to view women in term of Pre-Raphaelite enchantment. It was to be the same with two oth powerful women Morris encountered in the Socialist circles of the earl 1880s, Annie Besant and Eleanor Marx.

Soon after Morris joined, the Democratic Federation began on i programme of 'street-preaching', holding regular open-air progagand meetings, following the lead of the Labour Emancipation League Hyndman had at first not been in favour; but the proposals were carrie through by Scheu, Joynes, and others, including Morris who liked th directness of practical preaching wherever and whenever there might b the hope of converts. He told Jenny how salvationist forays were esser tial, 'since those who suffer (more than we, or they, can tell) fro society as it is, are so many, and those who have conceived any hope tha it may be changed are so few'. Even the language in which he writ about it is a link back to Morris's biblical past. Morris spoke regularly a these Sunday morning meetings, forcing himself out, even with gou and in all weathers. Some were far afield, at one of the Federation established pitches: a favourite site was by the Reformers' Tree in Hyd Park where Socialist literature would be sold. Morris was more ofte preaching close to home in Hammersmith, once a Hammersmith branc of the Federation started. Shaw would often appear with him on h neighbourhood street corners, 'conducting what most of the passers-b took to be prayer meetings'. At this date it was only the Free-thinke who held regular outdoor Sunday meetings. Gathering an audienc could be problematic. May writes poignantly of her agonies in accom panying 'the dear father', as she called him, on his Sunday forays, tryin to swell the crowd.

A child's view of Morris out street-preaching appears in the memoi of Georgina Sime, who came across him on a snowy day in Hamme smith, on her way out to a tea party:

474

came across a group of men, one of whom was talking while the others, who had evidently been engaged in shovelling away the snow, stood leaning on their spades and listened attentively to what he was saying to them. He too was leaning on his spade but both in dress and appearance he was different from the rest of the group, men of the unskilled labouring class who were in those days always thankful to earn a shilling or two by clearing away snow or doing odd jobs. They were all shabby but their shabbiness ranged from that of decent indigence to that of absolute poverty. The man who was talking, not with but to them, was William Morris, and he was dressed, as I remember him, in dark trousers, with a moujik blouse of his own famous blue linen, buttoned at the neck and belted at the waist, with loose sleeves down to the wrists. From the bloused body rose the dark head with its thick, strong, black hair. His hands, as he leant on the handle of his spade, were those of an artist, speaking hands; even then, child as I was, I noticed them. And from his strong throat a round, rough, sonorous voice was borne to my ears . . .

Sometimes the snow would fall on him or on one or another of his audience, but he continued speaking as if no interruption had occurred or possibly could occur, and the men round about him, leaning motionlessly on their spades, listened with an absorbed interest, as if the sound of that voice were the one thing in the world worth listening to. No one paid the least attention to me as I stopped short at the edge of the 'square' and looked in, and the scene, without any kind of persuasion on my part, engraved itself upon something inside me for life. I can see it now – the dark sky above, flecked with murky clouds, the tall trees, the snowy ground, the silent houses from which no face was visible at any window, the speaker immersed in what he was saying and the little group round him immersed in what they were listening to, drinking it in and making it their own.

Morris's more formal speaking was also on the increase. This was the beginning of his heavy programme of propaganda visits up and down the country. In 1883 he was in Manchester, Birmingham, Oxford and Cambridge; in 1884 he spoke in Manchester, Leicester, Oxford, Cambridge, Bradford, Birmingham, Leeds, Sheffield, Preston, Newcastle, Edinburgh and Glasgow. This in addition to several dozen London lectures. On some of his provincial visits Morris would be speaking several times to different audiences. All his energies were focused now on spreading Socialism. He told C. E. Maurice he was pledged not to deliver any lecture in London *except* for the Democratic Federation, in the autumn of 1883. The content of his lectures had now changed. In his own mind he divided off the lectures of his pre-Socialist period, the lectures collected in *Hopes and Fears for Art*, from those he delivered from 1883 onwards, after he had 'studied socialism from the scientific point of view'.

The first of these overtly Socialist lectures was 'Art, Wealth and Riches', composed for Manchester. Morris took great trouble over it ''tis to be a short one,' he told Jenny, 'but will give me a fortnight's work I know.' Wearing evening dress, Morris gave this inflammatory lecture before a joint *conversazione* of the Manchester societies at the Manchester Royal Institution in Morley Street on 6 March 1883, and was pleased with the hostility of its reception: 'a letter from one of my friends there says the philistines are much moved by it, that there have been two leading articles about it in the papers already, and a correspondence beginning: so you see one may yet arrive at the dignity of being hissed for a Socialist down there: all this is encouraging.' The rising opposition gave him the satisfying opportunity to clarify his case in *The Manchester Examiner*. He wrote to the editor:

It was the purpose of my lecture to raise another question than one of mere art I specially wanted to point out that the question of popular art was a social question, involving the happiness or misery of the greater part of the community ... What business have we with art at all unless all can share it? I am not afraid but that art will rise from the dead, whatever else lies there.

Morris cannot resist the Stepniak-style threat. He was on an ascending spiral of controversy. Working on his next lecture he told Jenny it would be to some extent a repeat of Manchester: 'only I intend making this one more plainspoken; I am tired of being mealy-mouthed'.

On 2 July Morris and Ned went to Oxford to be received as Fellows of Exeter. They dined ceremonially in hall. Four months later Morris returned to give the lecture 'Art and Democracy' (later published as 'Art and Plutocracy') that finally branded him a Socialist. He had been invited to address the Russell Club, a society of Liberal-to-Radical Oxford undergraduates, in the hall of University College. The original proposal had been that both Hyndman and Morris should make speeches as representatives of the Democratic Federation. But Hyndman, the known revolutionary, had been vetoed by the Master of the college, James Franck Bright, and his cautious colleagues, anxious about the possible effect on the Oxford undergraduates. Morris sent his comments via Charley Faulkner, still a University College Fellow:

As to Hyndman lecturing in your hall I would ask you to lay before the Master the fact that I am quite as much a Socialist as he is; that I am an officer of the same association, and am distinctly going to lecture as a delegate from it: also that if the subject is to be stirred at all, it is surely worth while to listen to a man who is capable of giving a definite exposition of the whole doctrine, which as you know I am not capable of doing in a scientific and detailed way. I am rather anxious about this matter, as if Hyndman is shut up I shall feel rather like a fool and as if I were there on false pretences. For the rest Hyndman is an educated man if Trin: Coll: Camb: is capable of educating (which is doubtful), and though he is perhaps not as polite as the Devil is usually said to be, is at least politer than I am: neither has he horns and hoofs, as I am prepared to swear: neither (as a Sec. of the SPAB) will I allow him to blow up any *old* building in Oxford.

It was a warning. The declared revolutionist still couches it in Oxford-versus-Cambridge jokes.

The meeting took place on 14 November 1883. The college hall was crowded. The lecture was attended by the Master of University College, the Warden of Keble, and the Warden of Merton. Ruskin, by now aged sixty-three and looking more than ever like an ancient prophet, was in his second term of office as Slade Professor of Art and was in the chair. He had already refused Morris's suggestion that he should join the Democratic Federation. His timbers, he said, were enough shivered already: 'It is better that you should be in a cleft stick, than make one out of me.' Morris began his lecture relatively quietly, with a disquisition on the state of art and architecture, a question which, he says, may well seem a solemn one when asked 'here in Oxford, amidst sights and memories which we older men at least regard with nothing short of love'. He progresses to an impassioned attack on the ruination of his beloved cities and beloved country landscapes. This is one of his great lectures. Morris launches into a prophetic passage on the themes of great concern to modern environmentalists:

To keep the air pure and the rivers clean, to take some pains to keep the meadows and tillage as pleasant as reasonable use will allow them to be; to allow peaceable citizens freedom to wander where they will, so they do no hurt to garden or cornfield; nay, even to leave here and there some piece of waste or mountain sacredly free from fence or tillage as a memory of man's ruder struggles with nature in his earlier days: is it too much to ask civilization to be so far thoughtful of man's pleasure and rest, and to help so far as this her children to whom she has most often set such heavy tasks of grinding labour? Surely not an unreasonable asking. But not a whit of it shall we get under the present system of society. That loss of the instinct for beauty which has involved us in the loss of popular art is also busy in depriving us of the only compensation possible for that loss, by surely and not slowly destroying the beauty of the very face of the earth.

By now he is at the mid-point in his lecture and one can sense the shudder going through the hall when Morris, analysing competitive production, announces: 'I am "one of the people called Socialists".'

From then on Morris's anger is increasingly unguarded, his attacks on the middle-class liberals more pointed. The speech culminates in a violent, long passage, the blackness of his vision of commerce in England as a regimented chaos:

I tell you the very essence of competitive commerce is waste; the waste that comes of the anarchy of war. Do not be deceived by the outside appearance of order in our plutocratic society. It fares with it as it does with the older forms of war, that there is an outside look of quiet wonderful order about it; how neat and comforting the steady march of the regiment; how quiet and respectable the sergeants look; how clean the polished cannon; neat as a new pin are the storehouses of murder; the books of adjutant and sergeant as innocent-looking as may be; nay, the very orders for destruction and plunder are given with a quiet precision which seems the very token of a good conscience; this is the mask that lies before the ruined cornfield and the burning cottage, the mangled bodies, the untimely death of worthy men, the desolated home.

It is a fearful image, cruel in its detail, and it shows how desperate Morris had become.

At the end of the lecture Morris turned towards his audience asking for support, demanding mass conversion, in the manner of the popular religious revivalist. Those who were there remembered for years afterwards how the platform sat aghast as he pleaded for an 'organised brotherhood' in Oxford:

One man with an idea in his head is in danger of being considered a madman; two men with the same idea in common may be foolish, but can hardly be mad; ten men sharing an idea begin to act, a hundred draw attention as fanatics, a thousand and society begins to tremble, a hundred thousand and there is war abroad, and the cause has victories tangible and real; and why only a hundred thousand? Why not a hundred million and peace upon the earth? You and I who agree together, it is we who have to answer that question.

As Morris ended speaking there was a deathly hush. The Master, Dr Bright, rose in an anguish of embarrassment to say that the college had no idea that Mr Morris was the agent of any Socialist propaganda. What they had intended was simply to give an eminent man the opportunity of expressing his opinions on art under democracy, a subject with which Mr Morris was 'unusually well acquainted, and a knowledge of which, in the existing condition of social questions in England, was a most desirable part of the education of every young man'.

Ruskin got to his feet and smoothed the situation over. But, as Morris had intended, the damage was irreparable. Mackail, the Oxford man himself, understood the complicated psychology. The college authorities had never been convinced that Morris, as a man of means and a man of letters, could be a Socialist in the same sense as his Democratic Federation colleagues. They had persisted, 'with a sort of obstinate innocence', in believing his address would be general and harmless. 'When they found that he had really meant what he said, their feeling was one which approached consternation.' The establishment in England still responds from time to time with a similar amazement to the solemn onslaught by the man of its own kind.

These dramas at Oxford were reported widely. Not all the press comment on Morris's speech was hostile. He wrote to thank W. T. Stead, for instance, for his 'sympathetic report' of the meeting in *The Pall Mall Gazette*. But there were the inevitable snide attacks on Morris for his inconsistency in living as a capitalist and at the same time speaking in support of the Socialist cause. A fortnight later he wrote to Georgie, 'I have been living in a sort of storm of newspaper brickbats, to some of which I had to reply: of course I don't mind a bit, nor even think the attack unfair.' Indeed in his reply to the editor of *The Standard* he freely admitted his position was a false one:

Your Correspondent implies that to be consistent we should at once cast aside our position of capitalists, and take rank with the proletariat; but he must excuse my saying that he knows very well we are not able to do so; that the most we can do is to palliate as far as we can the evils of the unjust system which we are forced to sustain; that we are but minute links in the immense chain of the terrible organisation of competitive commerce, and that only the complete unrivetting of that chain will really free us.

A side-effect of Morris's Oxford declaration was the support of his workmen at Merton. Their sympathy, he told Georgie, pleased him 'hugely', especially the fact that seven of his men insisted on joining the Democratic Federation. But was this conversion spontaneous, or was it affected by the wish to please their master, from whom they drew their livelihood? This was a question neither Morris nor the later Arts and Crafts workshop proprietors were inclined to pursue.

In these years of his conversion Morris changed his personality, withdrawing from his old haunts and his old friendships. It is to some extent a hidden period. When Mackail asked Morris's friends for their accounts of it he discovered that no two people could agree. They evidently found Morris's transformation baffling. The loved friend, whom they had teased and even patronized a little, now seemed removed into new realms of moral earnestness and obduracy. He had become a threatening and even fearsome figure, with the other-worldliness of the Old Testament ascetic. Walter Crane recollected Morris's art worker colleagues being 'startled and flustered' by the unexpected vehemence of one of Morris's lectures, given near Tottenham Court Road. As they left the lecture hall an old friend said apprehensively, 'He bears the fiery cross!'

Morris's tendency to be completely taken over by the interest of the moment was now apparent more than ever. Socialism was the question that swallowed up all other questions, as Morris admitted: 'like Aaron's rod'. George Wardle found the subject all-pervasive when he returned from a trip to America on the Firm's business, following up the Boston Exhibition of 1883. Politics dominated all Morris's conversation, to some of his old friends' enormous irritation. 'Chat with Top on Socialism as usual,' Crom Price recorded, groaning, in his diary. Top was also reported to have 'argued with Mrs Howard until the room rang' one evening at dinner at The Grange.

Morris evidently hoped his friends would follow him. Charley Faulkner and Philip Webb were soon to do so. But he underestimated the gulf that existed in many people's minds between support for a respectable Liberal cause and a declaration as a full-blown Socialist. William De Morgan, Morris's supporter in the EQA campaigns, complained: 'I was rather disconcerted when I found that an honest objection to Bulgarian atrocities had been held to be one and the same thing as sympathy with Karl Marx, and that Morris took it for granted that I should be ready for enrolment.' Morris was also rebuffed by Swinburne when he asked him, first, to join the Democratic Federation and, next, to write a song for them, to be set to music, 'for singing at meetings of the faithful'. Swinburne, though an equally committed libertarian, felt he could be more effective acting independently, 'as a single and private workman'. He wrote back to Morris tactfully but firmly: 'I do trust you will not – and if you ever do me the honour to read my "Christian Antiphones" in "Songs before Sunrise" I must say I don't think you will - regard me as a dilettante democrat, if I say I would rather not join any federation.'

The relationship affected at the deepest level was Morris's first friendship, made long before their Pre-Raphaelite period, with Edward Burne-Jones. Crom, devoted to all of them, watched anxiously as Morris's arguments with Ned and Georgie became more polarized: 'the little rift of opinions will I trust get no wider'. He could not bear to contemplate a serious quarrel between Morris and 'The Grange'. But Crom would have realized that as Morris was moving leftwards now, fashionable and famous, had been progressing inexorably rightwards: in another ten years Ned, who once called himself Republican, would be reincarnated as Sir Edward Burne-Jones.

Ned had two official reasons for opposing Morris's Socialism. The first was that it was out of character, an aberration in someone who was before all things a poet and an artist': this was Swinburne's argument, that public protest was a dissipation of energy that an artist as individualist could not afford. Ned's other fury was that the Socialists exploited Morris:

When he went into it I thought he would have subdued the ignorant, conceited, mistaken rancour of it all – that he would teach them some humility and give them some sense of obedience, with his splendid bird's eye-view of all that has happened in the world and his genius for History in the abstract. I had hopes he would affect them. But never a bit – he did them absolutely no good – they got complete possession of him. All the nice men that went into it were never listened to, only noisy, rancorous ones got the ear of the movement.

In this Ned was at least partly right.

In some more private comments, Ned admitted his own selfishness. He could see that Morris, believing what he did, had really no alternative: 'How can some men help having an ideal of the world they want, and feeling for it as for a religion, and sometimes being fanatical for it and unwise – as men are for the religion that they love?' Part of Ned's dismay was the sense he had of Morris entering unfamiliar and, to him, much threatening territory: 'It must be, and Morris is quite right, only for my sake I wish he could be out of it all and busy only for the things he used to be busy about.' Ned's response betrays his guilts,

accumulated consciousness of the betrayal of his old ideals and also o
his marriage. Years afterwards Ned spoke of this episode as 'the only
time when I failed Morris'.

The established routine of Morris's visits to The Grange buckle
under the weight of his Socialist commitments. As well as evening
lecturing and Federation meetings he was expected weekly at wha
Hyndman described as their 'little Supper-Clubs' where Marxis
theories were explored, expounded, and where Morris once regaled the
gathered Socialists with a vivid account of the Battle of Agincourt. The
Socialists would meet their fellow dissidents in London at Wedde's
Hotel in Greek Street, Soho, the 'favourite rendezvous for men an
women of advanced political and social opinions of all schools at tha
time'. From now on the Wednesday evenings at The Grange wer
cancelled, and although the Sunday working mornings still continued
there were subtle alterations. The breakfast now was altered from
eight-thirty to nine to give Morris more time for his Federation work
and even then he often had to leave in the middle of the morning to star
on his street-preaching. 'Consider', wrote Georgie, 'what it must hav
meant for him to leave the Grange unsped by sympathy'. The dignity
with which he made his exit was, she said, 'fine to see'.

Georgie did not fail him, though her feelings were divided. The long
explanatory letters, expansive and confiding, that Morris addressed to
her all through the 1880s show how greatly he felt he could rely on her
clear judgement and her staunchness of support. His letters to Aglaia
become notably more cursory, even rather rude. Only Georgie wa
allowed to cross-examine and upbraid him for his all too obvious lapse i
literary work. Early in 1883 he had been at work on a new version i
English of the epic *Shah Nameh*, the Persian equivalent of the Icelandi
Heimskringla, an oriental narrative of heroes and high deeds. But thi
enterprise had been soon abandoned in the onrush of Socialist activit
and Morris had written nothing since. He was reaching a point at whicl
he regarded both his poetry and his design work as irrelevant: 'Poetr
goes with the hand-arts I think, and like them has now become unreal.
he told Georgie in August 1883. He would not abandon his writing an
his 'pattern-work': he still took pleasure in them. But he could no longe
see them as his 'sacred duty'. He explained how he committed himself t
myriad apparently less significant tasks because he saw these as con
tributing to a much greater whole.

Morris shows how far he understood his own compulsions and hi psychological need for some continuing and concerted course of action. A few weeks later he was telling Georgie: 'The one thing I want you to be clear about is that I *cannot help* acting in the matter, and associating myself with any body which has the root of the matter; and you know, and it may ease your kind heart respecting me, that those who are in the thick of it, and trying to do something, are not likely to feel so much of the hope deferred which hangs about the cause as onlookers do.'

Before Christmas Morris paid the statutory visit to his mother at Much Hadham. He was delivering Jenny and her nurse-companion Miss Bailey who were staying there over Christmas and New Year. How far was Mrs Morris conscious of her son's activities? On that duty visit to The Lordship, his family's conventional and comfortable house, was Morris recollecting his denunciation a few weeks earlier when writing to the Manchester philanthropist Thomas Coglan Horsfall: 'I have never under-rated the power of the middle classes, whom, in spite of their individual good nature and banality, I look upon as a most terrible and implacable force.' Whatever his visions of the inevitable demise of the banal middle classes, Morris hid them from his family. His letters to his mother remain dutiful and indeed they strike one as genuinely fond. Morris had a particular ability to sustain on one level what he so bitterly rejected on another. Should we see this as the flaw in him? Or was it, rather, a facet of his greatness that he settled for, and stuck to, the only *modus operandi* possible for him?

It was probably this Christmas when Morris, left in Hammersmith, was faced with a problem more essentially Victorian, a question that only Mrs Beeton could have solved. A complimentary festive package had arrived from Morris's wine supplier, presumably containing one of the enormous three-layered Christmas pies the Victorians were so fond of: pigeon inside chicken inside turkey. Morris turned in despair to his Hammersmith neighbour Clara Richmond, wife of the painter W. B. Richmond:

At the last moment we have received a present from Mr. Diosy, a square box, which I know from experience contains a *pie* which none of *us* can eat: I wonder if in your house which contains young people & to which rash people may come, there might be found a resting place for its contents? in any case don't be offended with me for making the venture, but if you fear it; be so kind as to ask Lowe to bury it in *my* garden. So treated the *Pie* will at least have given a momentary pleasure to one human being, for it will have given

Mr. Lowe the pure joy of digging another hole, which occupation I know from experience is his chief delight in life.

Morris laid his many talents on the Socialist altar. He wrote to Jenny in the autumn of 1883, 'Item I have designed a membership card for the Dem: Fed: people. Item I have made a little poem for them, a copy of which I would have sent you, my dear, but that it has gone to the printer straight.' The membership card is a curious amalgam of the Gothic and nineteenth-century demotic, with its Socialist imperatives, 'Educate', 'Organise', 'Agitate', written out on swirling pennants on an oak-leaf verdure ground. Morris has misjudged the scale of it: it should have

35 Membership card for the Democratic Federation designed by William Morris.

been a tapestry. It set a kind of house style for late-nineteenth-century Socialist graphics: a similar quasi-mediaeval wistfulness would permeate the publications of the Fabian Society and Socialist League. Morris's 'little poem' for the 'simple people' was 'The Day is Coming', a rousing call to action which again set a style of revolutionary bonhomie:

Come hither lads, and hearken, for a tale there is to tell,
Of the wonderful days a'coming when all shall be better than well.

And the tale shall be told of a country, a land in the midst of the sea,
And folk shall call it England in the days that are going to be.

The poem made such an immediate impact that, according to *The Christian Socialist*, it was read from the pulpits of several London churches, and it was later published as the first of Morris's collected *Chants for Socialists*.

In January 1884 the Democratic Federation launched a weekly propagandist paper, *Justice*. It was financed initially by Edward Carpenter who provided £300, described by May Morris as 'a large sum of money'. This finance was not to last for long. Her father undertook to make good the paper's recurring losses which turned out to be substantial. His publisher and dealer, F. S. Ellis, recollected: 'He was not overburdened with ready money at the time, and even sold his cherished books to provide funds.' The first editor of *Justice* was an Irishman, Charles Fitzgerald, a retired army officer who had been a war correspondent on *The Daily News* at the time of the Russian-Turkish campaign and who later disappeared in suspicious circumstances, presumed to have been murdered by the Turks. Fitzgerald soon proving an erratic editor, Hyndman took over the editorship himself.

Justice was to set a tradition of Socialist journalism in this country. It was an embryo *New Statesman* in the range and idiosyncrasy of talent Hyndman managed to attract. One of its leading contributors was Bernard Shaw, already writing his bohemian novels and training himself to produce a regular five hundred words a day. May Morris, soon to succumb to Shaw, described him at this period as 'a certain gaunt pale-faced auburn-bearded young Irishman who had original ideas on music, Shelley and everything under the sun and expressed them with a relentless wit'. Another Hyndman protégé, James Joynes, the ex-Eton master, was already a productive freelance journalist and specialized in satiric political verses. A few months after *Justice* started publication Joynes and E. Belfort Bax co-founded the monthly Socialist review *To-Day*. Shaw's novel *The Unsocial Socialist* first appeared as a serial in *To-Day* where Morris read it and admired it. This was the beginning of Morris's close and complex relationship with Shaw. The imperious Helen Taylor contributed to *Justice*: her specialist interest was in land reform.

Hubert Bland, later a mainstay of Fabian polemics, was a frequent contributor. He had already become a jobbing journalist at the instigation of Bernard Shaw. Like Shaw he had embarked on a career as a philanderer. Sexual adventuring of a crude and callous pattern was curiously common amongst the young men of the Democratic Federation. It was part of the bravado of early Socialism and the crusade for the free, untrammelled life. Bland's unfortunate wife Edith, who also wrote for *Justice*, was the main source of income for the household. As Edith

Nesbit she was the author of the famous children's books *The Railway Children* and *The Wouldbegoods*. There is a portrait of Morris as Socialist leader in the Blands' collaborative novel, *Something Wrong* (1886).

Morris himself contributed to almost every issue of Hyndman's *Justice*. For him it was the start of what amounted to a whole new career in Socialist journalism. Over the next six years he produced almost 500 editorials and signed articles, first for *Justice* and then for *Commonweal*. These total around 500,000 words which, as Nicholas Salmon has pointed out, would fill an additional six or seven volumes of Morris's present twenty-four-volume *Collected Works*.

The first of Morris's contributions to *Justice* was a satiric fantasy on modern society in which the poultry of an unnamed country hire a conference hall to discuss 'the all-important question, *with what sauce shall we be eaten?*' Morris called this 'An Old Fable retold'. With many ruffled feathers the assembled cocks and hens formulate a resolution that sidesteps the question: 'A rumour has reached us that while there were doubts as to the sauce to be used in the serving up, slow stewing was settled on as the least revolutionary form of cookery.' But why should the poultry be eaten at all? The tale, ostensibly so amiable, so bleak in its conclusions, stands midway between an Aesop's Fable and George Orwell's *Animal Farm*.

As well as writing for the paper Morris undertook its selling. Distribution then, as always, was the great unresolved problem of the Socialist press. The wholesale newsagents would not take on the paper, so the Federation members began to sell it in the streets, marching through Ludgate Circus, Fleet Street and the Strand shouting out '*Justice*, the organ of Social Democracy, one penny!' Jack Williams remembered the peculiar social mix of the Federation's sales force:

There was Hyndman, in his immaculate frock coat and high hat; there was Morris, dressed in his usual blue serge suit and soft hat: Joynes in his aesthetic dress; Champion looking every inch the military man; Frost looking every inch the aristocrat; Quelch and myself in our everyday working clothes. I am sure we made an impression on that day.

The first issue of *Justice* declared the Democratic Federation's independence from all existing parties, expressing a particular personal defiance of Gladstone, Joseph Chamberlain and Lord Randolph Churchill. It explained the two main aims of its domestic propaganda: to preach discontent among the workers and to show the educated classes that

Socialism had a 'scientific' basis and was striving to put an end to anarchy. The force of Morris's views, expressed in print and in so challenging a context, could no longer be evaded. His association with *Justice* set up new reverberations of alarm and disapproval through the circles of his acquaintances and friends. Tennyson, at Haslemere, was shocked to hear of William Morris's Democratic Socialism and asked William Allingham to procure him a copy of *Justice* so he could see the worst. Allingham made his own comment: 'Morris's *Justice*, I partly agree with and partly detest. It is incendiary and atheistic, and could upset everything . . . I want reforms and thorough-going ones, but not by the hands of atheists and anarchists.'

Morris apologized to Jenny, at Much Hadham with his mother, for not sending her the first issue of *Justice*: 'I fear the element in which you are is altogether too respectable for me to send you a copy down there; so that must keep.'

In February 1884, in the weeks of the great cotton strike in Lancashire, Morris travelled up to Blackburn for what was his, and the Federation's, first involvement with the broad mass of the working classes. As Morris admitted in a lecture of this period he had still not even been inside a worker's house, let alone seen a large-scale master-worker confrontation, and the opportunities this offered for the spread of the Socialist agitation. Jack Williams and James Macdonald arrived by train from London as an advance propaganda party, taking the largest hall in Blackburn and assembling 1,500 strikers to hear the leading Democratic Federation speakers. Macdonald described how 'They waited patiently while Morris and Joynes and Hyndman spoke, to hear the message the delegates had brought them about their own particular business. Their interest was aroused in the message of Socialism.' Morris too had felt exhilarated by the meeting. A branch was formed at Blackburn, establishing what was to be a long-lasting Democratic Federation presence in Lancashire.

A month after addressing the Blackburn cotton-strikers Morris was beginning 'velvet-weaving' at Merton. A special loom was built for this woven silk velvet, Morris's most expensive fabric: he told Janey 'it will be very grand'. 'Granada' is a splendidly exotic design on a burnt-orange ground, brocaded with gilt thread. Only twenty yards were ever woven, and it cost £10 a yard.

*

On 18 March 1884 Morris was again in the forefront of a Socialist demonstration:

On Sunday I performed a religious function: I was loth to go, but did not dislike it when I did go: brief, I trudged all the way from Tottenham Court Road up to Highgate Cemetery (with a red-ribbon in my button-hole) at the tail of various banners and a very bad band to do honour to the memory of Karl Marx and the Commune.

It was now a year, almost to the day, since Karl Marx died. It was the exact anniversary of the Paris Commune which began its short existence on 18 March 1871. Morris's great emotional rapport with the Commune was partly a natural feeling of affinity with the first attempt at proletarian revolution, also perhaps a slight overcompensation for his relative lack of interest at the time. The procession to Highgate had begun with about a thousand marchers from combined London Socialist and radical groups, accumulating more supporters as they marched so that by the time they arrived at the cemetery, where they found 'a heavy guard' of policemen, they were a crowd of 3,000 or 4,000. Unable to enter, they adjourned to 'an uncomfortable piece of waste ground' near by where they sang the 'Internationale' and speeches were made. Morris told Janey there had been 'a rather feeble attempt by the hobbledehoys to interrupt the proceedings which our people checked with the loss of one hat (Mr Williams')'. After that they marched off their patch of ground triumphant, 'like a royal procession', with policemen on each side.

Through that summer of 1884 William Morris was playing a key part in the London Democratic Federation agitations. Hyndman was determined to take advantage of the growing pressure for franchise reform, involving the extension of household franchise to the counties. The Democratic Federation did not organize its own demonstration but Morris was part of the contingent that attached itself to the big franchise rally of Radical and Liberal working men held in Hyde Park on 21 July, timed to take place as the bill reached the House of Lords. Here too Morris saw scenes that were to haunt him, as the crowds of working people thronged through the London streets on their way to demonstrate. There is still a sense of shock, almost a physical repugnance, in the way he describes these ragged, pallid crowds. He views them with great horror but also with a certain detachment. They are not in reality 'his' people yet.

In Hyde Park the Democratic Federation was staging a meeting-within-a-meeting. The 5,000 working people had assembled to hear the

Liberal trade union leaders, Joseph Arch and Henry Broadhurst, Morris's old ally. The Democratic Federation set up a rival pitch where Hyndman, H. H. Champion, Jack Williams and John Burns addressed the crowd. John Burns, with his genuine working-class background, his dark good looks and his powerful physique, was already proving a great asset to the Democratic Federation. He was a charismatic speaker, although Morris would complain about his 'claptrap style'. At the meeting in Hyde Park the Democratic Federation speakers launched into an attack on the Liberal leaders for their pusillanimity. They denounced working-class Liberalism as ineffective. Inevitably a fracas ensued. Some of the crowd, infuriated, turned upon the speakers, hooting and screaming, destroying the Socialist banners, forcing them off the little hillock they were speaking from and threatening to throw John Burns and others into the Serpentine. Morris, though not a speaker, was vulnerably placed. An account of the battle in Hyde Park was later given by Sam Mainwaring, the engineering worker who founded the Labour Emancipation League:

Morris fought like a man with the rest of us, and before they had taken us half way to the water we had succeeded in making a stand, and I remember Morris calling on Burns to finish his speech. Being on ground level, and our opponents still fighting, Burns said he wanted something to stand on. That day we had only our first pamphlet, 'Socialism Made Plain', of which Morris had a large bag-full at his side. These we placed on the ground in a heap, and Burns mounted and continued his speech, while Morris, and a dozen more of us, were fighting to keep back the more infuriated of the people. Some of our friends found fault with Burns for using language to irritate the crowd, but Morris's opinion was that they would have to be told the truth, and that it was as well to tell them first as last.

Morris's own account bears out Mainwaring's, adding the detail that a Democratic Federation member, a German, had done his best to lug him away to safety, to Morris's indignation, telling him that he was '*an old man*'.

Morris had learned a practical lesson from the Hyde Park attack: that speakers should have an organized bodyguard around them when they met in potentially dangerous locations. But had he learned some broader lessons? At this point what was Morris actually expecting? After eighteen months in the Socialist movement was he becoming more convinced that in the looming struggle between the classes 'rose-water' solutions would not be enough? Temperamentally Morris was not for violence. Many times he spoke out decisively against it. But over these months one detects in him a certain hardening of attitude, almost a resignation to armed conflict as a necessary phase.

He saw a surging international movement towards freedom, a triumphant reversal of the straggling lines of working men and women that he had been aware of on the day of the demonstration in Hyde Park. In a letter to William Allingham a few months later he predicted that the change would be brought about as workers were educated to be conscious that they were the 'organic' section of society whereas other classes were merely parasites:

When they have learned this they will abolish all other classes and become themselves the *State*, that is for all and each. This movement must of necessity be international (a Socialist does not recognise a possible enemy in a foreigner as such), but in all probability England will go first will give the signal, though she is at present so backward: Germany with her 700,000 Socialists is pretty nearly ready: France sick of her republic of stockjobbers and pirates is nearly as far on though on different lines: Austria is ready any moment to shake off her government of Jew bankers and police spies; America is as you say truly finding out that mere radicalism is bringing her into a cul de sac. Everywhere the tale is the same: the profit mongers are finding the game too vast and intricate to keep up.

In his writings of this period the words that Morris reaches for are 'seizing' and 'possessing', 'claiming' and 'destroying'. He could even face the prospect that possessing and controlling the means of production, which he saw as the key to the freedom of the workers, could entail 'ruin and war'. This possibility, he argued, had to be accepted 'coolly and as a necessary incident'. Morris was quite explicit on the question of violence in a letter written in July 1884 to Robert Thompson, an American Christian Socialist in London: 'we must not say "We must drop our purpose rather than carry it across the river of violence".' The river was the image still burning in his mind.

The Democratic Federation Merton Abbey Branch was flourishing. The meetings were held in an upper room in the little office building, where there was already a circulating library for the benefit of employees. Emma Lazarus, who had donated a volume, wrote effusively of the library in which 'the books were as richly bound as though intended for the poet's private shelves in consonance with (Morris's) theory that the working man must be helped and uplifted . . . by developing and feeding his sense of beauty'. Early in 1884 Morris addressed his men, telling Jenny that his lecture 'came off successfully'. Joynes also spoke at Merton Abbey, and a few weeks later Hyndman. Morris was proud of the reception they gave Hyndman: 'the men are getting on very well and I hope we shall spread the light from there. There was a funny old ex-chartist present: an old man of 70: he said it made him feel 20 years younger.' At outside meetings Morris watched out for 'our Merton folk' with a Socialist-paternalist anxiety.

On 14 June 1884 the Socialist message came closer to home when the Hammersmith Branch of the Democratic Federation was formed at Kelmscott House. Besides Morris there were ten founder members, the most heavyweight of whom, Andreas Scheu, delivered the inaugural address on the objects of Socialism. Morris followed this up two weeks later with a short address on 'the condition of workers as slaves, serfs and wage slaves, and showed that Socialism was the only possible remedy to the evils arising from competition and the private use of capital'. As with the main body of the Federation the membership was socially a very broad cross-section, with collective memories that stretched back to the European uprisings and the Chartist movement of 1848. Besides Scheu with his experience of anarchist Vienna, another early Hammersmith recruit, George Lockner, could remember Socialism in Berlin when the party there consisted of only nine members. E. T. Craig was an old Chartist and survivor of a co-operative commune established on an absentee landlord's estate at Rulahine in Ireland. 'Craig', wrote May, 'had been a sturdy and valiant fighter; he watched the young movement with a keen interest.' He would make speeches at the Hammersmith Branch meetings 'in a pipe-like voice which sometimes recovered its old chest register in a sort of bellow that beat upon one's ear drums'. He would come into the garden at Kelmscott House and talk about the old Co-operative days and about phrenology, analysing the characters of the Socialists according to the bumps on their heads. The Hammersmith Branch minutes were kept meticulously by Emery Walker, the process-engraver and expert on typography, who was soon to become one of Morris's inner circle. They had first met in the train coming back from a Socialist meeting at the Monarch Coffee House in Bethnal Green Road. Morris discovered he lived in Hammersmith and had invited him to call. The Hammersmith

Branch already leaned towards the literary and bibliophilic. Morris was appointed treasurer again.

The first membership list includes 'Miss Morris' and 'Miss J. Morris'. In his account 'How I Became a Socialist' Morris had written proudly of his daughters' sympathy with his aims in life. Too much should not be made of Mrs Morris's absence. Janey, by temperament, was not a political person, in the Rosalind Howard or Helen Taylor sense. She was bound to respond with a mild exasperation to her husband's intense preoccupation with the class she herself had risen up from: this may partly explain her susceptibility to the aristocratic milieu of Wilfrid Scawen Blunt. To so private and fastidious a woman, the Socialist incursions into her own household must sometimes have been taxing, and there are occasional signs of resentment as the relatively tentative Socialist activities at Hammersmith become a tidal wave. But there is no evidence in Morris's letters that Socialism is an issue of friction between them. He assumes her interest and to some extent he depends on her support. The picture of Janey cringing and disdainful at Morris's 'rag-tag-and-bobtail' Socialist followers was a legend maliciously put about by Bernard Shaw, whom Janey had her own reasons to dislike as May came increasingly under the spell of his Irish charm and blatancy in 1885. At dinner after a Socialist meeting Janey had pressed a second helping of pudding upon Shaw who, hard up, was obviously hungry. When he had consumed it, she said: 'That will do you good: there is suet in it.' Janey knew that Shaw was vegetarian. In the subtle war between G. B. S. and Mrs Morris, perhaps this was his revenge.

The Hammersmith Branch was very different in character from other Democratic Federation branches. It was more domestic. Here Morris was still the seigneur. The beauty of both the interior and its occupants gave it a certain strangeness, often commented upon by the Socialist comrades: 'like going to Persia after living in Canada'. To those unused to it, Morris's way of living had the sophisticated bloom of the exotic fruit. The young Dollie Radford went through the wind and rain to hear Morris's lecture 'How we Live, and How we Might Live', which she described in her diary as 'a beautiful address'. She was asked to supper afterwards. 'His house is beautiful; and his daughter May is *most* beautiful: no wonder that Rossetti painted her so often'. Morris talked excitedly 'of many things and people. Verse forms – Browning – Swinburne – plays – and Gladstone. Was rather surprised indeed at the way in which he did speak of Gladstone'. She got home very late and very wet, more than ever convinced of the 'seriousness and beauty of the Socialistic movement', singing the praises of Morris above Aveling and Hyndman. She responded to him romantically, as the poet, and conceived an ambition to act in the entertainments of this most highly cultured Federation branch.

Politically the branch asserted its autonomy, discussing and sometimes rejecting Federation policy. For instance, Hammersmith came out against the Federation statement of intent, 'All State churches to be disestablished and disendowed'. On 18 August 1884 a motion was carried that the branch 'should be self-supporting in the matter of the general conduct of meetings, as soon as possible'. In the building up of what were virtually his own branches, first at Merton, then at Hammersmith, Morris was beginning to assert a new authority. He was writing his own sub-text to the Socialist movement. It is difficult not to see this as his moral insurance against the growing crisis within the Federation as a whole.

In the Federation office at Westminster Palace Chambers, the tensions were now surfacing. Hubert Bland had been aware of the undertow of drama: 'There was always a good deal more friction than fraternity at Palace Chambers.' He attributed this to the innovative temperament: 'The type of man who has the intellectual and moral courage to join a new and unpopular movement has also fully developed the faults of the qualities – obstinacy, vanity, a sort of prickly originality, and a quick impatience of contradiction.' By the summer of 1884, bitter dissensions were coming to a head.

The fundamental argument was over the means of achieving Socialism. It was between the members who believed in some sort of parliamentary action, the view of the impatient, opportunistic Hyndman, and the more purist Socialists who supported a longer-term programme of social agitation and education, leading to a more informed and therefore more genuine consensus in the end. The division was not so much of class as of temperament. The working men John Burns, Jack Williams and Harry Quelch and the ex-gentleman H. H. Champion all supported Hyndman's parliamentarianism. The less flexible, unpragmatic Morris was in the latter group. He was now, and he remained, vehemently anti-Parliament, seeing no prospect of reforming from within an institution he knew from his own experience to be thoroughly corrupt. Ranged with Morris against Hyndman were

493

Andreas Scheu, Joseph Lane of the Labour Emancipation League and E. Belfort Bax. In August 1884 Morris was one of the committee of four who had the task of drafting out a new party programme. This was in effect a challenge to Hyndman's leadership. As Morris told Scheu in some triumph, the new programme, though not perfect, 'was better than the old one, and is not parliamentary'.

Another cause of rupture was Hyndman's foreign policy. Morris had noted from early days how Hyndman was a dangerous mixture of the Socialist and jingoist. Earlier the Federation had been at one in its condemnation of the British occupation of Egypt, and Morris and Hyndman were joint authors of an article in which they reviled the military action as 'the Bondholders' Battle'. But in 1884 they parted company on General Gordon, besieged in Khartoum. Hyndman's submerged patriotism surfaced. His 'old Adam of Jingoism' revealed itself as he argued that beleaguered General Gordon must be rescued, not ruling out resumed military action. Morris proposed a motion, which was unanimously adopted at a weekly meeting of the Federation, that any new expedition 'under the pretence of rescuing General Gordon' must be opposed. In the months to come, Hyndman's 'tendency towards National assertion' became even more extreme.

There was the additional complexity of the Marxist succession as the Democratic Federation moved inexorably towards internal crisis. Engels, solemnly protective of the family of Marx, watched with some anxiety as Marx's youngest daughter Eleanor, his beloved 'Tussy', now on the verge of thirty, joined the Democratic Federation. In the summer of 1884 she announced her 'free marriage' to Edward Aveling, a scientist and freethinker who had been a leading light in the Secularist movement and who was already gathering a reputation for sexual and financial shiftiness. Aveling too had now become a Democratic Federation member. Engels saw Hyndman as a megalomaniac adventurer intent on taking over the whole of British Socialism, including what remained of Marx's dynasty. In June 1884 he wrote to Karl Kautsky in anger and depression:

Hyndman is thinking to *buy up* all the little movement here . . . Himself a rich man, and in addition having at his disposal resources supplied by the very rich artist-enthusiast but untalented politician Morris . . . he wants to be sole master . . . Hyndman is a skilful and good business man, but a petty and hard-faced John Bull, possessing a vanity considerably in excess of his talent and natural gifts. Bax and Aveling have most excellent intentions, but everything has gone to pieces, and those literateurs alone cannot do anything. The masses still will not follow them.

If Engels was vitriolic about Hyndman, Morris was by this time, if possible, still more so. They had once worked together closely. They were, after all, joint authors of *A Summary of the Principles of Socialism*, the Democratic Federation handbook, its cover designed like a North Oxford wallpaper of willow leaf and vine. But, as with Thomas Wardle, the more intimate the working relationship the more violently Morris could repudiate that closeness, with an almost obsessive physical dislike. His disenchantment with Hyndman had first shown itself in the summer of 1883, when he had written to Georgie about Hyndman's opportunism: 'As you know, I am not sanguine, and think the aims of Socialists should be the founding of a religion, towards which end compromise is no use, and we only want to have those with us who will be with us to the end.' By the following March Morris's suspicions about Hyndman had developed into hatred of his sanctimoniousness. On the day of the procession to Karl Marx's graveside, Morris saw him as 'all hollow to the last degree'. It was not only Morris who showed signs of disenchantment. To Morris's supporters within the Federation Hyndman was beginning to appear a liability.

For the sake of the cause Morris tried to contain his rising indignation. In June he had told Georgie that 'to desert the regiment because the sergeants are sometimes drunk, or the Captain often swears, would not commend itself to my reason'. He took the situation seriously: 'I cannot deny that if ever the DF were to break down, it would be a heavy thing to me, petty skirmish though it would be in the great war.' In July he had summoned Ernest Belfort Bax to Hammersmith and entreated him 'to be more "politic"', in case stories of its internal dissensions damaged what public credibility the Federation had. Morris wrote to Scheu, 'I cannot yet forego the hope of our forming a Socialist *party* which shall begin to act in our own time, instead of a merely theoretical association in a private room with no hope but that of gradually permeating cultivated people with our aspirations.' Morris did not want a parliamentary party, but he nevertheless hoped for a 'party' in the sense of a gathering of people with real public power of influence. It is a hope that has surfaced and resurfaced on the outer fringes of British left-wing politics.

One of Morris's main anxieties about a split, if a split should come, was that he himself would be turned to as a leader in preference to Hyndman: 'if I have any influence amongst our party (if party it be) it is because I am supposed to be straight, and not to be ambitious, both of which suppositions are, I hope, true.' History is riddled with politicians who disclaim interest in power only to seize it as soon as it is offered. This was not true of Morris. His letters of this period show him moving towards leadership with a deep reluctance, based on his conviction that he is neither ready for nor suited to the task. He wrote to Scheu: 'I know enough of myself to be sure that I am not fit for the rudder: at least not yet . . . I have not got hold yet of the strings that tie us to the working class members: nor have I read as I should have.' Morris saw how the day-to-day political commotion was damaging his intellectual concentration: 'my habits', he explained, 'are quiet and studious and if I am too much worried with "politics" ie intrigue, I shall be no use to the Cause as a writer'. He saw his real value as his capacity to stand back and take the broader view.

In early August, after the Hyde Park demonstration, there was the dramatic conference of the Democratic Federation in which the party changed its name to the Social-Democratic Federation (SDF). Hyndman was displaced as president as a result of Lane and Scheu's argument that a truly democratic party demanded a succession of chairmen, not one personally powerful president. Hyndman nominated Morris to succeed him. Morris, not surprisingly, declined. The anti-Hyndman faction on the Executive Committee was now strengthened by the election of Joseph Lane, Edward Aveling and Eleanor Marx Aveling (as she now styled herself). The tenor of the Palace Chambers meetings altered, becoming more high-powered and even veering to the feminist, a change which Morris viewed with curiosity. He asked Scheu, 'What do you think of Mrs. Aveling in the chair?' He was now even less hopeful of a peaceful resolution. Two weeks into August he was writing, 'I am afraid we are but at the beginning of our troubles.' He was planning two days of recovery at Kelmscott. He had slipped on the grass and sprained his ankle. The injury was followed by a recurrence of his gout. He had hobbled downstairs to the Palace Chambers basement at the rate of 'a mile in two hours'.

Shaw, the outside observer, now a member of the newly formed Fabian Society, made an acid reconstruction of the internal struggles between the Hyndman party and the Marx-Aveling faction in October of 1884:

What we have got at Palace Chambers now is a great deal of agitating, very little organizing (if any), no education, and vague speculations as to the world turning upside down in the course of a fortnight or so. Aveling . . . is on for education, but he is hard up, heavily handicapped by his old associations and his defiance of Mrs Grundy in the matter of Eleanor Marx, personally not a favourite with the world at large, and quite excluded from all influence in the management of *Justice*.

He depicted Morris still pacifying, wandering along between Hyndman and Aveling 'rather uncertainly'. A benign bewilderment was his public stance. But his private letters show he knew the situation was irreparable. The crisis was developing into a clear-cut contest between Hyndman and himself. In October he was asked to join Aveling in redrafting the Federation Manifesto. He shuddered at the prospect: 'my flesh creeps at the difficulties'. Early in December he was aghast at Hyndman's ambitious manoeuvrings: 'I really begin to think he *will* be prime minister before he dies.'

Looking back at the episode from the 1930s, May emphasized the distress it caused to Morris. 'Some people', she wrote, 'find a state of warfare in the family exhilarating, but my Father was the last man to enjoy living in such an atmosphere.' It is certainly true that Morris suffered great depression. It is more than likely that we can attribute to this period of Socialist dissension the fragment of a letter in which Morris quotes Falstaff's sad opinion that sighing and grief blows men up like a bladder: he remained conscious of being far too fat. But neither May nor later commentators with a vested interest in promulgating the 'dear old Morris' legend make proper allowance for his streak of ruthlessness. He did not seek the quarrel. But once quarrels were upon him Morris could pursue them with a strength of purpose and a weight of anger, as he had shown at the time of the dismantling of Morris, Marshall, Faulkner & Co. If he had started earlier in politics, what a resolute leader he might have become.

In the middle of December Morris was in Scotland for four days on a Socialist lecture tour. His sharp eye for a landscape and delight in surprise local encounters had survived the turmoil of the past two years. The omnibus in which he travelled from Newhaven to Edinburgh was half full of Scottish fishwives with their babies. The fishwives 'were not beautiful ones like Christie Johnson [*sic*]', the fisherman's daughter in Charles Reade's novel *Christie Johnstone* (1853) who rescues and then

497

marries a drowning artist, a heroine after Morris's heart. But the women were 'clean and neat, and were dressed in the proper style with jackets of bright chintz'. The passing urban scene was not, however, so uplifting. The standards of house building struck Morris as 'terrible' in Edinburgh and Glasgow, 'and in short almost wherever one comes across a house in Scotland'. He found an architectural crudeness in Scotland, describing the buildings as 'so coarse and *raw*'.

Morris was lecturing in Edinburgh and Glasgow. Andreas Scheu was now living in Edinburgh, trying to find work as a furniture designer as well as furthering the interests of Jaeger. The theories of Dr Gustave Jaeger, who insisted that woollen clothes and bedclothes were healthier than cotton or linen, were finding favour with the intellectual avant-garde in Britain. Morris had written to Scheu a few weeks earlier to say, 'I don't know whether you will be pleased shocked or amused to hear that Oscar Wilde has gone in for Jägar [*sic*] with enthusiasm'. Shaw was to take up life-long Jaegerism too. Scheu, in Edinburgh, was still pursuing Socialist politics. He and a young Scottish engineer, John Lincoln Mahon, had founded the Scottish Land and Labour League. This was affiliated to the SDF, which had no branch in Edinburgh. But its apparently independent status had aroused the wrath of Hyndman, who viewed it as a schismatic, as Morris had foreseen and indeed had forewarned Scheu. Then and subsequently English Socialism had no feeling for Scottish types of radicalism – at least, until Keir Hardie, the Ayrshire miner-journalist, found the Westminster route to power in 1892 when he took his seat in Parliament, still wearing his cloth cap.

Morris addressed the Scottish Land and Labour League, then still in its infancy, on 13 December 1884. He gave the lecture 'Misery and the Way Out' in the SLLL clubroom in Picardy Place. A first-floor dwelling had been converted by Scheu to make the meeting-hall. A sympathetic Edinburgh merchant had contributed. Morris would have appreciated that this clubroom 'was decorated with fine taste and furnished with specially designed cane-bottom chairs'. Bruce Glasier, an architectural draughtsman, son of a Scottish crofter, came across from Glasgow to hear Morris. Glasier, who became Morris's most devoted Socialist disciple, was a founder of the Glasgow branch of the SDF. It is surprising to realize the youth of so many of these Socialist activists: Mahon, the co-founder of the SLLL, was only eighteen. Glasier, when he met Morris, was twenty-five, eager, naïve. He left the most observant of all the recollections of Morris at this period: 'A kind of glow seemed to be about him, such as we see lighting up the faces in a room when a beautiful child comes in.'

Glasier watched Morris seated on the platform:

He seemed in a remarkable way to open wide his whole being to the audience. This impression of his expanding or opening out when facing his hearers often struck me afterwards as very characteristic of him. He always sat with his broad shoulders held well back, his knees spread well apart, and his arms when not employed spread wide upon his knees or upon the table: his loose, unscarfed shirt front, his tousy head, and his ever restless movements from side to side adding to the impression of his spaciousness. He was then fifty-one years of age, and just beginning to look elderly. His splendid crest of dark curly hair and his finely textured beard were brindling into grey. His head was lion-like, not only because of his shaggy mane, but because of the impress of strength of his whole front. There was in his eyes, especially when in repose, that penetrating, far-away, impenetrable gaze that seems to be fixed on something beyond that at which it is directly looking, so characteristic of the King of the Forest. This leonine aspect, physiognomists would doubtless say, betokened in Morris the same consciousness of strength, absence of fear, and capacity for great instinctive action which gives to the lion that extraordinary dignity of mien which fascinates observers. I noted, also – but not until afterwards was I aware of the inveteracy of habit – the constant restlessness of his hands, and indeed of his whole body, as if overcharged with energy.

Morris was pleased with his reception. The little meeting-hall had been 'cram full', he told Jenny, and they had 'fished two additional members, not much you will say, but things go slowly in Edinburgh'. The next day he travelled on to Glasgow, to deliver his lecture 'Art and Labour' before the Glasgow Sunday Society at St Andrew's Hall. It was atrocious weather, but Morris had an audience of about 3,000 in the largest hall in Glasgow. According to Glasier, Morris remarked on the high proportion of 'eager, intelligent faces' near the platform, some of them university and art-school students, artists and literary people, but the vast majority Glasgow artisans. Here, in this great hall, he had more room to spread himself. He read his lecture, 'or rather recited it', keeping his eye upon the written text but every now and then walking to and fro carrying his manuscript, 'schoolboy-like', in his hand. Sometimes he paused, left his text, and talked to the audience in a more intimate way, 'man to man'.

After the lecture Morris had adjourned with members of the Glasgow SDF, including Glasier, to their meeting-room in a low-ceilinged warehouse flat in Watson Street off the Gallowgate. It had been Morris's intention on this visit to counteract the influence of Hyndman who, on his own recent visit to Glasgow, had been vilifying the SLLL and Andreas Scheu. However, Morris's hopes of action as a peacemaker between Edinburgh and Glasgow receded when W. J. Nairne, the Glasgow SDF secretary, read out to the dozen or so assembled members a letter from Hyndman in London, reiterating his attacks on Scheu. Morris himself spoke, at first diplomatically. But Nairne then swung into the attack, needling Morris: 'Does Comrade Morris accept Marx's theory of value?' Morris's reply was politically tactless: 'I am asked if I believe in Marx's theory of value. To speak quite frankly, I do not know what Marx's theory of value is, and I'm damned if I want to know.' This comment has been quoted, or misquoted, to prove Morris's ignorance of Marxist economics and his general political lack of grasp. It is obvious from Morris's lectures and his letters that he understood precisely Marx's theory of value, even if he did not regard it as the be-all and end-all of Socialist thought. To construe his remark as a considered statement would be silly; it was surely the reflex reaction, to a solemn committee man, of a tired and temperamentally irascible middle-aged man goaded beyond control.

However, battle was now joined. Returning from Glasgow Morris sent Janey, who was out of London, a furious account of the affair: 'when I got up north there I found Hyndman had been behaving so atrociously, that I was determined to stand it no longer . . . the fact is he is a precious rascal . . . The question only is now whether we shall go out of the SDF or Hyndman: we are only fighting for possession of the name and the adherence of the honest people who don't know the ins and outs of the quarrel . . . All this is foul work: yet it is a pleasure to be able to say what one thinks at last.'

The first day of confrontation took place on 16 December. Before the SDF executive meeting Morris had assembled what he referred to as 'the cabal'. This consisted of Joseph Lane, the Avelings, Bax, Sam Mainwaring, Robert Banner, W. J. Clarke and the firebrand John Mahon from Edinburgh who had travelled down to testify, if necessary, against Hyndman. Morris told Scheu, 'I found Aveling and all quite ready for battle: they all promised to stick together, and we arranged our part as well as we could.' Hyndman's main supporters, H. H. Champion, Harry Quelch, Jack Williams, James Murray, Herbert Burrows and John Burns, had already taken their places in the Palace Chambers basement. Morris wrote, 'Everybody felt when we came in that something was going to happen. H. was very much the boss from the first.' As so often in politics the meeting was ostensibly concerned with a side issue. Hyndman had demanded the expulsion of W. J. Clarke, a member of the executive council whom he accused of being an anarchist.

It was a typical Palace Chambers commotion, ending in a vote of seven for Clarke's expulsion, nine against. 'The cabal's defiance of Hyndman was expressed obliquely, but "H" knew well enough what we meant.' Morris counted this meeting their first victory, writing with relief to Andreas Scheu: 'what a pleasure not to have to shake hands with Hyndman again'.

The next scene in the drama was on 23 December. Morris's 'cabal' had secretly summoned Scheu from Edinburgh to attend this meeting, which lasted through the evening until midnight. Motions of no confidence in Scheu and of no confidence in Hyndman were discussed heatedly without any definite conclusion being reached. Morris responded to these events with resounding gloom. He wrote to Georgie: 'Last night came off to the full as damned as I expected, which seldom happens . . . It was a piece of degradation, only illumined by Scheu's really noble and skilful defence of his character against Hyndman: all the rest was a mere exposition of backbiting, mixed with some melancholy and to me touching examples of faith.' Morris now, on the verge of a definite withdrawal, faced with the inevitability of taking on a leadership he felt himself unfitted for, moved back into a familiar mood of yearning for the simple rural life. In those tense days before Christmas he travelled north to Chesterfield to talk to Edward Carpenter about the implications of the split. Carpenter's version of the simple life at Millthorpe in Derbyshire seemed to him at that moment the embodiment of dreams:

I listened with longing heart to his account of his patch of ground, seven acres: he says that he and his fellow can almost live on it: they grow their own wheat and send flowers and fruit to Chesterfield and Sheffield markets: all that sounds very agreeable to me. It seems to me that the real way to enjoy life is to accept all its necessary ordinary details and turn them into pleasures by taking interest in them: whereas modern civilization huddles them out of the way, has them done in a venal and slovenly manner till they become real drudgery which people can't help trying to avoid. Whiles I think, as in a vision, of a decent community as a refuge from our mean squabbles and corrupt society; but I am too old now, even if it were not dastardly to desert.

On Christmas Day Morris was quoting Blake, in self-justification and a glimmering of hopefulness:

> I was angry with my friend
> I told my wrath my wrath did end:
> I was angry with my foe;
> I told it not: my wrath did grow

On Boxing Day he wrote to his mother to apologize for lateness in sending Christmas messages. He told her, without details, that the past week had been crowded: 'I have had a very unusual amount of work of a very tiresome kind.'

The end came on 27 December 1884. Hyndman had packed Palace Chambers for the meeting, which started at six and finished at ten-thirty. Members of the Labour Emancipation League, affiliated to the SDF but regarded by Hyndman as probable opponents, were kept outside the main committee room. According to Morris, 'There was a good deal of speaking, mostly on their side, for Hyndman had brought up supporters, who spouted away without the least understanding what the quarrel was about. It finished by H. making a long and clever lawyer-like speech; all of which, as in the House of Commons, might just as well have been left out, as either side had made up their minds how to vote from the first.' At the end the vote was taken. The result was ten to eight, with a majority of two for Morris's 'cabal'.

Morris then made a surprise move. After a few words in his personal defence, he read out a statement of resignation and he and his supporters solemnly walked out of Palace Chambers. There was a shocked reaction. Many Hyndman supporters followed Morris out, assuring him that this was never their intention. The volatile Jack Williams, the labourer raised in a succession of workhouses, was in tears.

Being in the majority Morris could of course have stood his ground. By patient opposition he could perhaps have purged the SDF of what he saw as its Hyndmanite excesses. Morris has been criticized for lack of any long-term strategy in causing this fissure in British Socialism in such very early days. He himself estimated SDF membership as only 400 in London, 100 in the provinces at the end of 1884. The SDF membership could only suffer damage when Morris formed a rival body, the Socialist League. Morris acted as he did because he felt an urgent need to redefine Socialist policy: Hyndman was pursuing policies of notoriety and intrigue that were giving Socialism, already, a bad name. Morris was reluctant to embark on a long programme of obstruction, tabling motion after motion, amendment after amendment. Shaw understood the streak of the dictatorial in him, writing with the hindsight of the 1930s: 'It was as clear to Morris as it has been later to Mussolini and Hitler that no business can be done in this way.' He was nevertheless in an agony of worry. Crom Price saw him at Hammersmith a few days after Christmas: 'WM uncomfortable about the split among Socialists: "feels like a dog with a tin kettle tied to his tail"'.

He had been neglecting Merton. Although, in the turmoil of these two Socialist years, he had continued to supply designs whenever needed, he had delegated the day-to-day running of the works at Merton Abbey to George Wardle, as he had virtually handed over the London end of the firm's business to the brothers Smith. Now Philip Webb, writing from Italy to commiserate with Morris in his troubles, pressed the claims of Morris's art work as a necessary outlet: 'work for Merton Abbey, when you can turn to it, would I think be your safety.' There are signs of Morris tending to agree. On 28 December, the day before the Socialist League was inaugurated, Morris was at Merton, gathering strength from the view out of his window over 'the winter garden'. The workmen were spreading some pieces of chintz on the bleaching ground. The psychological strength of Morris lay in these alternative delights in so close-packed a life.

CHAPTER FIFTEEN

Farringdon Road,
One: 1884–87

It was Saturday evening when Morris led his little group of Socialists 'out into the wilderness'. The phrase is Edward Carpenter's. On the following Monday, 29 December 1884, he took temporary premises for the new body at 37 Farringdon Street, returning to a familiarly shabby part of London, the hinterland of small workshops and offices between Clerkenwell and Holborn. 'This morning', he told Georgie, 'I hired very humble quarters for the Socialist League, and authorized the purchase of the due amount of Windsor chairs and a kitchen table.' He felt like 'a young bear' with all his troubles before him, relieved and released but at the same time apprehensive. He foresaw that the new body would be 'but a small one for some time to come'.

The Socialist League was formally inaugurated on 30 December. Morris pushed onwards with his usual speed and energy once a new creative challenge appeared on the horizon. He and E. Belfort Bax were hard at work composing the Manifesto at Kelmscott House in Hammersmith on New Year's Day. Crom Price arrived for dinner to hear loud voices 'in hot discussion' reverberating through the house from Morris's study while Janey and the girls were upstairs in the sitting-room 'looking rather dismal'. There were new anxieties about Jenny's state of health. Price recorded in his diary: 'Finally Top ascended with Bax – one of his co-conspirators, a man of interesting studious face of extreme pallor. He made some amazing sweeping assertions and then departed, and I then had a long chat with WM on the prospects of the new Socialism.' Morris struck him as still hopeful, full of plans for the journal which was to supplant *Justice*. This was the Socialist League's *Commonweal*. But he admitted to Crom that the total of committed Socialists in Britain was still very small. Crom returned to The Grange, where he and Ned had an anxious conversation about Morris's new departure, both feeling certain that it would lead to 'worry and perhaps broken health, and certainly neglect of art'.

In fact the Manifesto itself shows William Morris at the height of his artistic expressiveness, passionately lucid for the cause into which he now channelled his main creative energies:

Fellow Citizens, We come before you as a body advocating the principles of Revolutionary International Socialism; that is, we seek a change in the basis of Society – a change which would destroy the distinctions of classes and nationalities.

The Manifesto maintains that civilization as it stands is fatally divided into two classes: those who own the nation's wealth and its means of production, and the producing class, the workers. The conflict between the two is ceaseless and *both* classes of society lead degraded lives. The League rejects all previous forms of government: Absolutism, Constitutionalism, Republicanism, all of which have been tried and all of which have 'failed in dealing with the real evils of life'. State Socialism, 'by whatever name it might be called', is also dismissed as ineffective because it is a half-hearted system, merely making concessions to the working class while leaving the current system of capital and wages still in operation. The Manifesto argues carefully and powerfully for a total overthrow of the *status quo*:

The Socialist League therefore aims at the realization of complete Revolutionary Socialism, and well knows that this can never happen in any one country without the help of the workers of all civilization ... We are working *for* equality and brotherhood for all the world, and it is only *through* equality and brotherhood that we can make our work effective.

It is striking how early on Morris perceived that 'Socialism in one country' contained a fatal flaw.

The Manifesto was published in the first issue of *The Commonweal* in February 1885 and was signed by the twenty-two members of the League's Provisional Council, listed alphabetically: W. B. Adams, Edward Aveling, Eleanor Marx Aveling, Robert Banner, E. Belfort Bax, Thomas Binning, H. Charles, William J. Clarke, J. Cooper, E. T. Craig, Charles J. Faulkner, W. Hudson, Frank Kitz, Joseph Lane, Frederic Lessner, Thomas Maguire, J. L. Mahon, S. Mainwaring, James Mavor, William Morris, Andreas Scheu and Edward Watson.

SECOND EDITION.

THE

COMMONWEAL.

REGISTERED FOR] THE OFFICIAL JOURNAL OF THE SOCIALIST LEAGUE. [TRANSMISSION ABROAD.

VOL. I.—NO. I.   FEBRUARY, 1885.   ONE PENNY.

INTRODUCTORY.

WE beg our readers' leave for a few words in which to introduce to them this Socialist journal, THE COMMONWEAL. In the first place we ask them to understand that the Editor and Sub-Editor of THE COMMONWEAL are acting as delegates of the Socialist League, and under its direct control: any slip in principles, therefore, any mis-statement of the aims or tactics of the League, are liable to correction from the representatives of that body.

As to the conduct of THE COMMONWEAL, it must be remembered that it has one aim—the propagation of Socialism. We shall not, therefore, make any excuses for what may be thought journalistic short-comings, if we can but manage to attract attention to the study of our principles from those who have not yet thought of Socialism, or who are, as often happens, bitterly hostile to them through ignorance; or if we can help those whose feelings are drawing them towards the cause of the workers, but who need definite instruction as to its aims and ... awaken the sluggish to strengthen the waverers, to

THE MANIFESTO OF THE SOCIALIST LEAGUE.

FELLOW CITIZENS,

We come before you as a body advocating the principles of Revolutionary International Socialism; that is, we seek a change in the basis of Society—a change which would destroy the distinctions of classes and nationalities.

As the civilised world is at present constituted, there are two classes of Society—the one possessing wealth and the instruments of its production, the other producing wealth by means of those instruments but only by the leave and for the use of the possessing classes.

These two classes are necessarily in antagonism to one another. The possessing class, or non-producers, can only live as a class on the unpaid labour of the producers—the more unpaid labour they can wring out of them, the richer they will be; therefore the producing class—the workers—are driven to strive to better themselves at the expense of the possessing class, and the conflict between the two is ceaseless. Sometimes it takes the form of open rebellion, sometimes ... mendicancy and crime; but

36 Detail from the front page of the first issue of *The Commonweal.*

There was an implied critique of Hyndman in the statement that there should be 'no distinctions of rank or dignity amongst us to give opportunities for the selfish ambition of leadership'.

Bernard Shaw made the comment that the Socialist League was 'entirely dependent on one of the most famous men of the nineteenth century who was not only a successful employer and manufacturer in the business of furnishing and decorating palaces and churches, but a eminent artistic designer, a rediscoverer of lost arts, and one of the greatest of English poets and writers'. As so often, Shaw's remark depended for its effect on suppressed detail. Morris's public reputation gave the League its credibility, as the weight of his authority and obvious integrity had helped the public image of the Democratic Federation in previous years. His financial support of the League was also crucial. Without Morris there could have been no *Commonweal*. He was the League's treasurer in much more than name. But to suggest that the League apart from Morris was a gathering of nonentities is untrue. Indeed on leaving the SDF Morris had taken with him its two most formidable intellects, E. Belfort Bax and Edward Aveling.

Bax, 'the learned and distinguished philosopher' as May Morris described him, was twenty years younger than Morris but like many of his colleagues seemed prematurely aged, a Herr Professor figure who was steeped in German philosophy and culture. He had studied music in Stuttgart and had been a journalist in Berlin. Bax's German was excellent, as Morris's was not: he had written a commentary on *Das Kapital* that Marx himself had praised. He was interested in the wider moral implications of Socialism and was working on a book, *Religion of Socialism*, published in 1885. Bax was Morris's chief collaborator at this period, co-editor of *The Commonweal*. Together they wrote a series of articles, 'Socialism from the Root Up', later published as *Socialism: Its Growth and Outcome* (1893). May left a vivid picture of the oddly assorted pair at work at Hammersmith on the make-up of *The Commonweal*:

Bax, with his fine regular features and bushy moustache – as a young man he must have been handsome as a schoolgirl's dream of a German minnesinger – tall and thin, in his black velveteen coat, sitting in a comfortable armchair by the fire, smoking, with perhaps a glass at his elbow; my Father, as you know his picture, short and square and blue-clad, sitting at the writing-table, his splendid head bent over the paper, with perhaps a dry grin on his face at a vagary of Bax's.

Morris looked forward to these sessions which he referred to as 'compulsory Baxination'. He forgave – May noted disapprovingly – the 'cold blooded and egoist strain' in the fiercely anti-feminist Bax. Through these early years of the Socialist League, Morris was still painstakingly learning his Marxism from Bax. In 1887 he recorded in his short-lived Socialist diary a visit to Bax in Croydon where they wrote their first article on Marx – 'or rather he did it: I don't think I should ever make an economist even of the most elementary kind: but I am glad of the opportunity this gives me of hammering some Marx into myself.'

Bax was one of the few Englishmen accepted in the circle of Friedrich Engels, 'the Grand Lama of Regent's Park Road'. Unlike Morris he was a regular attender at Engels' famous Sunday evenings where the Marxists in exile congregated. Even closer to Engels was Edward Aveling, the Socialist League's other intellectual heavyweight. Through his relationship with Eleanor Marx, he was an adopted member of the 'Marx-Engels family' and, at this time in his early thirties, a brilliantly precocious scientist with a fellowship at University College, London. He had written numerous books and pamphlets on Darwinism and secularism.

507

He was an agile polemicist and a resourceful orator: his voice was 'like a euphonium', wrote May. He had great range and confidence, and was one of the few people who could find, and explain convincingly, an intellectual connection between Charles Darwin and Karl Marx. Aveling was, however, anything but trustworthy. Morris seems to have turned a blind eye to this shiftiness, defending Aveling against Hyndman's accusations of financial irregularities at the time of the split within the SDF. Morris was no doubt swayed by Aveling's obvious usefulness: within the first few weeks of the League's foundation Aveling was delivering a strong series of lectures on Marxism at the South Place Institute. May was outspoken in her dislike of 'this strange little lizard of a man' who was 'spewed out of every Socialist and Secularist Society because in money matters and sexual relations he was almost incredibly shameless, conscienceless and heartless'. It was a view that Morris was forced to accept finally, though he died two years before Eleanor's suicide.

There are no harsh words for Eleanor, described by May Morris, who admired and was in awe of her, as 'that gifted and brilliant woman, who worked long and valiantly for Socialism'. The dark and dark-eyed Eleanor, with her eloquent intensity and serious application to detail, was of real value to the Socialist League too, not just as her father's daughter though that heritage was potent, but as an active worker, writing, speaking and researching. Morris, although never really at his ease with her, supported her courage in living with Aveling openly, renouncing false bourgeois conventions that she claimed were in themselves a form of immorality. Surely one can see the influence of Eleanor in the proposal in the Socialist League Manifesto:

'Our modern bourgeois property-marriage, maintained as it is by its necessary complement, universal venal prostitution, would give place to kindly and human relations between the sexes. Marriage would become a matter of simple inclination. Women would share in the certainty of livelihood which would be the lot of all; and children would be treated from their birth as members of the community entitled to share in all its advantages. Nor would a truly enlightened public opinion, freed from mere theological views as to chastity, insist on its permanently binding nature in the face of any discomfort or suffering that might come of it.'

Morris's own experience has been written in as well. Early in 1885, on a visit to the Marx-Aveling household in Great Russell Street, Havelock

Ellis found Morris there already, sitting by the fire 'in a friendly fashion'. Ellis felt certain that Morris was giving the Avelings financial support.

In the early years of the Socialist League, Morris was much involved with the 'Marx-Engels' family. It is pertinent to wonder what influence Engels himself, the *éminence grise* of Marxism in England, had had on the foundation of the League. During the weeks before the SDF split, Morris certainly visited Engels for discussions; on one of those visits he had seized with delight upon a copy of the Old Norse *Edda* on the table in the room. This inspired him to read Engels some passages from Sigurd. Engels' house in Primrose Hill became a base for the opposition to Hyndman. On the morning of the crucial meeting Morris had been summoned by Aveling to meet Engels to discuss plans for *The Commonweal*. Morris's attitude to Engels is difficult to gauge exactly. He is mentioned very little in Morris's correspondence, although in reporting this interview to Scheu Morris shows signs of resentment at his autocratic manner. Engels had advised him not to attempt to bring out a weekly paper since he and his confederates were 'weak in *political* knowledge and journalistic skill'. One senses an impasse. Engels settled for Morris as a compromise leader: at least he was not Hyndman. But he could not relate to the imaginative force of Morris, his characteristic and erratic combination of Marxism with visionary libertarianism. Engels was prepared to make the best of the new Socialist League triumvirate. But he was not optimistic. Writing to Edouard Bernstein two days after Morris's visit, he called Morris, Bax and Aveling 'the only honest men among the intellectuals – but men as unpractical (two poets and one philosopher) as you could possibly find'.

The Socialist League founders were a curious amalgam. As well as its literary-intellectual faction there were the displaced foreigners, Frederic Lessner and Andreas Scheu, and the element that Shaw described so neatly as 'Chaucerian'. The Chaucerians in the League were the self-taught workmen: Joseph Lane, by trade a carter, with a wide knowledge of political theory, a leader of the London Land Tenure agitation movement; Frank Kitz, a dyer who eventually worked for Morris at Merton, a bluff, jolly, beer-drinking veteran activist, a fine burly figure with fresh face and curly hair; Sam Mainwaring, the engineer with his big full beard like Morris's. Tom Mann remembered how 'After attending propagandist meetings William Morris frequently walked back with Mainwaring, and it was said of them that they looked like the skipper

509

and first mate of a ship.' Here Morris felt at last he was surmounting the class barriers and learning from his Socialist League colleagues about the way they actually lived and how their minds worked. He wrote of Kitz, for instance:

like most of our East-enders he is certainly somewhat tinged with anarchism or perhaps one might say destructivism: but I like him very much: I called on the poor chap at the place where he lived, and it fairly gave me the horrors to see how wretchedly off he was; so it isn't much to wonder at that he takes the line he does.

The Fabian Society had just been formed in London. Morris had steered clear of it, instinctively disliking its uniformly middle-class membership and cultural correctness. He allied himself with Comrade Kitz and Lane and Mainwaring more easily because of their aura of 'primitive simplicity'. Compared with the Fabians they seemed the real thing.

At the end of January the League was well established enough to hold a 'Socialist entertainment' in Ladbroke Hall in London, the first of many fund-raising events that drew upon its multifarious talents. According to Georgie, who attended, the evening was in aid of one of the comrades who was 'out of work and poor'. Besides various readings and musical selections, a three-act comedy by Palgrave Simpson and Herman Merivale was performed. Morris read two poems and made an extempore speech about Socialism as well as giving himself the task of selling the first issue of *The Commonweal* around the hall. At the end of the evening the whole assembled company sang Morris's song of the uprising, 'The March of the Workers', to the tune of 'John Brown'.

The strongest of Morris's objections to Hyndman had been his scare tactics, his way of drumming up panic. With wild talk of the imminence of the revolution, Hyndman had tried to frighten the powers-that-be with 'a turnip bogie which perhaps he almost believes in himself'. The reference is to the hollowed-out turnip lit up to frighten children at Hallowe'en. Morris too at this stage saw revolution coming, but more gradually. The Socialist League Manifesto shows him as determined that, 'when the crisis comes, which the march of events is preparing, there may be a body of men ready to step into their due places and deal with and direct the irresistible movement'. His stress on education was with the intention that the new and just society would already be in place, once revolution happened. Forster's Education Act of 1870 meant that even working-class children were now being educated to a certain level, and by 1880 schooling in Britain was generally compulsory. But there was a yawning gap in political perceptions. Morris saw how fundamentally he needed to change attitudes. He realized the urgency of spreading information amongst the middle classes as well as to the workers. This was one of the functions of *The Commonweal* which first appeared in February 1885 as a monthly, becoming a weekly the following year, financed by Morris, and finally outlasting him as the official organ of the Socialist League.

Morris had had his qualms about becoming editor but could see no alternative. Over the next six years the work on *Commonweal*, recurring so relentlessly and with such drudgery of detail, would take its toll. But it is of course the breadth of mind and quirkiness of Morris, both editing and writing, that gives *Commonweal* its particular flavour, producing one of the best-written, least predictable political broadsheets of this or indeed of any other period. It is more moving and much more entertaining than *Justice* in those first few years. Morris was not exaggerating when he wrote, at one of *Commonweal*'s all too frequent crisis points, 'it does seem a pity to drop the only satisfactory English-written Socialist print'. *Commonweal*'s appearance too was unusually purist. It was printed on high-quality paper, with good functional typography to further Morris's purpose, as laid down in his opening editorial, 'To awaken the sluggish, to strengthen the waverers, to instruct the seekers after truth'. Morris provided a pattern for the masthead, a ruralist motif of intertwining willow leaves. In later issues appears the design based on the angel wings of Freedom, a classic of revolutionary art nouveau by the Socialist League member Walter Crane.

The first issue of *The Commonweal* had been impressive, containing, besides the Manifesto, Morris's own 'Chant of the Workers', an article by Bax on Imperialism versus Socialism, Eleanor Marx Aveling's survey of the International Movement, and reminiscences of Peterloo by the old Chartist E. T. Craig. But, as with so many ventures in publishing, it is in the second issue that the paper gets into its stride. *Commonweal* for March 1885 has an extraordinary line-up of contributors, reflecting Morris's own energy in seeking out support from amongst the European Socialists. Engels' important article 'England in 1845 and in 1885', later included in his preface to the English edition of *The Condition of the Working Class in England in 1844*, made its first appearance in this issue of *Commonweal* together with articles by Bax and Stepniak, Bernard Shaw, Paul Lafargue, Marx's son-in-law and leader of the Collectivists in France. There were messages of greeting to the Socialist League from Wilhelm Liebknecht, August Bebel, Pierre Lavroff, Leo Frankel, Karl Kautsky, Tichomikoff, F. Domela Nieuwenhuis. Morris himself contributed the poem 'The Message of the March Wind', the first instalment of his love poem of the Commune, continued and expanded in future issues under the title *The Pilgrims of Hope*.

He had written to Janey after the first instalment: 'not bad I think' was his verdict on the poem. Twelve further episodes were to follow, the last appearing in July 1886. *The Pilgrims of Hope* is certainly not bad. It has an endearing confidence, a robust narrative flow. But nor is it by any means Morris's best poem. It is very loosely written, verging on the sentimental. It is difficult to relate it to the poetry of macabre intensity that Morris achieved in *The Defence of Guenevere*. The peculiar interest of *The Pilgrims of Hope* lies in its openly autobiographical character and its astonishingly vivid picture of Morris's Socialist milieu of those days. The poem is ostensibly set in the early 1870s, the period of the Paris Commune. The love story is, as usual, triangular: the anguished relationship of a husband and wife and the husband's comrade and best friend. But the background of Socialist committee rooms, street preachings, arrests and court-hearings, the shabbiness of scene and the exhilarating atmosphere, swift changes of mood from tedium to passion: all this is rooted in Morris's experiences in the London of the middle 1880s, first in the Democratic Federation, now in the Socialist League:

> Dull and dirty the room. Just over the chairman's chair
> Was a bust, a Quaker's face with nose cocked up in the air;
> There were common prints on the wall of the heads of the party fray,
> And Mazzini dark and lean amidst them gone astray.
> Some thirty men we were of the kind that I knew full well,
> Listless, rubbed down to the type of our easy-going hell.
> My heart sank down as I entered, and wearily there I sat
> While the chairman strove to end his maunder of this and of that.

The lassitude of atmosphere, the dank depressing décor: the absolute antithesis of Morris & Co. The poem stresses, in a powerful way, what Morris was rejecting. It spells out his spirit of abnegation. May could never read it without surges of emotion, knowing how accurately it reflected his own hopes and disappointments in the Socialist movement, voicing the inexpressible, revealing 'the deeper matters working in him to which he never gave definite utterance'.

The Pilgrims of Hope marks a definite stage in Morris's evolution as a writer, which partially explains the poem's carelessness, its evident roughness of composition. Now he saw himself more than ever as the people's poet, the prolific and anti-perfectionist bard. He explained to a young Norwich Socialist and aspiring poet, James Frederick Henderson, how ideas of romantic individualism had been almost unavoidable when he was young: 'we were born into a dull time oppressed with bourgeoisdom and philistinism so sorely that we were forced to turn back on ourselves, and only in ourselves and the world of art and literature was there any hope.' This now seemed to him selfishness, and a creative cul-de-sac. He envied the ease with which Henderson, at the age of eighteen, had been able to acquire a true sense of perspective: 'You on the contrary have found yourself confronted by the rising hope of the people, and have been able to declare yourself a soldier of the Cause.' Working for the cause must matter more than '*mere* poetry-writing': this was the way Morris had come to view it. The work he spoke of with respect was now campaigning poetry, writing given 'backbone' by political activity. The genre looks forward, so much so that its 'badness' evokes the work of committed poets fifty years later, an obvious example being W. H. Auden's 'Spain'.

Morris's own role on *Commonweal* was wider and more demanding than it had been on *Justice*. He was not just the paper's poet and chief editorial writer but was also the composer of the 'fillers', odds and ends of notes and comment which he described as 'twaddle', put in at the last minute to balance up the page. It was his task as editor to co-ordinate contributors, largely inexperienced, many of them unusually volatile in temperament, and to assess the many unsolicited and sometimes semi-literate contributions that came in.

> Too long from factory, mill and field
> Has come your patient cry –
> 'Tis time that they should see you wield
> A force 'gainst which they have no shield.

Morris printed Herbert Burrows's poem 'To the People' and many others showing a clear influence of his own Socialist chants and marches. A whole long tradition of Socialist folk poetry, stirring and sentimental, can be traced back to Morris and *The Commonweal*. The distribution of the newspaper was nominally in the hands of J. L. Mahon, the young engineer from Edinburgh, now installed as London Secretary of the Socialist League. But Morris was involved in the complex logistics by which packages of *Commonweal* were sent away by train to Manchester, Sheffield, Birmingham, Preston, wherever its potential readers lay. There is something very poignant in the painstaking paperwork – cash account forms, receipts, sales records – often in Morris's own writing, in the Socialist League archives. The sums are very tiny. Over the first six issues the average number sold of any issue was 3,500. The average publication cost per issue was fifteen pounds, the average takings were seven pounds. It was up to Morris to keep the publication in the black.

37 Advertising sticker for
The Commonweal.

There was a certain wildness about *Commonweal*. Its promotional leaflet made no bones about its aims: 'It speaks out plainly without fear or favour *on behalf of the Suffering*. It shows you plainly your *actual position*. It tells you what you are, that is *down-trodden Slaves*, and what you *ought* to be – the *Rulers of Yourselves* – that is the Working Nation!' The tone of it made many of Morris's old friends blench. Some of those who had managed to accept his Socialism as a mild eccentricity were shocked into resistance when *Commonweal* arrived on their own doorsteps, bearing Morris's revolutionary message in irrefutable cold print. Catherine Holiday, Morris's much admired embroideress, wrote from Hampstead to the Socialist League cancelling her subscription: 'We do not wish to continue "The Commonweal".' There is a still more painful letter in the Socialist League papers: 'please address the Commonweal to *Mrs*. Burne-Jones, not to "Mr".' Morris realized how far he had now become the outlaw: 'as a Socialist', he wrote, 'I stink in people's nostrils'. Though Georgie still protected him, Morris was deeply conscious of stinking in the nostrils of The Grange.

Janey and May had spent the early spring of 1885 in Bordighera with the Howards. They returned at the end of April to find Morris 'up to his eyes in Socialist propaganda'. He had seen his most urgent task as the establishment of a network of Socialist League branches. He had only been certain of his home branches of Hammersmith and Merton at the time he left the SDF. Since then he had been writing a mass of explanatory, conciliatory letters and travelling the country, drumming up support. In the early weeks there were affiliations from several London branches. The Labour Emancipation League and the controversial Scottish Land and Labour League joined the Socialist League. Morris also won over the Leeds Branch from the SDF. In February he had visited Oxford where his old friend Charley Faulkner had formed a Socialist League branch from the remnants of an old Radical club. Faulkner, who had shared so much of Morris's history, shows the same signs of joy at his own middle-aged conversion: 'It makes me feel fresh again to be aiming at something in which I can feel an interest, after the miserable dreary twaddle of university life.'

It was now thirty years since they had been undergraduates together and indeed thirteen months since Morris's Socialist affidavit shocked the assembled Oxford hierarchy in University College hall. He arrived back in Oxford on a bright morning, this time with the Avelings, and they walked around the town. The beauty of the city, and the persistent ruination of that beauty, struck him with the usual pang. Charley had invited 'a great many very young persons' to dinner before the Socialist League meeting and their 'ingenuous visages' made Morris feel quite old. The meeting took place in the Music-Room in Holywell, a place redolent of memories for Morris since this was not only the room in which the Architectural Society met when Morris was himself a student, it was directly opposite the workmen's cottages in which Janey used to live. It was a riotous meeting at which Morris delivered his first long unscripted speech to a hundred declared friends, some 250 'indifferents' and twenty or thirty obvious enemies, who howled and stamped at Morris's catchwords and, during question time, let off 'a bottle of chemical which made a horrible stink'. There was scuffling. Charley, nervous in the chair, broke off the meeting. The disrupters were so angry with their ringleader for being ineffective, they went round and smashed the glass in the windows of his college rooms. Morris meanwhile continued the discussion with the more sympathetic of the undergraduates, some of whom took him into the moonlit New College Cloisters. Did they know that this was the corner of old Oxford Morris loved the most?

Two political issues dominated Socialist League propaganda at this period. One was the Sudan War, a focus of public attention since the fall of Khartoum and the death of General Gordon in January 1885. Morris called it 'a wretched Commercial-piratical war', a shameful consequence of the capitalist system. The second issue was the threat of conflict between Britain and Russia in April, after the Russian forces' defeat of the Afghans. The Socialist League line was that *all* sides were 'great rascals'. Morris had his own commercial reasons for fearing wars and rumours of wars: they had a bad effect on business. But as a Socialist he welcomed them. He held to the hope that some good must accrue to the cause of Socialism from 'any row on a big scale'.

Both these issues were on the League agenda in April when Morris set out on the longest of his journeys of 1885 to Glasgow and Edinburgh. His links with the Socialists in Scotland were always to be particularly close. He gave readings for Socialist charity in Glasgow; he spoke to the branch in Edinburgh, reporting 'some very good and thoughtful men' among the members; then the next morning he was back in Glasgow for a conference with the members there, 'who seemed a good lot, but wanting instruction badly'. He spoke again in the evening, sold a good deal of League literature and signed up some new recruits.

He took the train back south, still alert enough to notice the marvellous scenery between Carlisle and Settle. He wrote to Jenny: 'I was really quite surprised at the beauty of the country; I think it is the loveliest part of all England: I will tell you about it when I see you. If ever we "retire from active service", I must sit down somewhere near Kirkby Stephen.' The railway took him right up in the mountains, through the sheepwalks. He could see snow still lying in the pockets of the upper crags. But Morris's euphoria vanished beyond Skipton, with the sight of smoke cloud hanging over the hideous manufacturing cities of the north. He stopped at Chesterfield to stay the night with Edward Carpenter in his Derbyshire landscape of hills and dales and woodland. 'Carpenter seems to live in great amity with the workmen and the women; they all live together in the kitchen, and 'tis all very pleasant.' The kitchen had always been his favourite of rooms.

On the journey Morris was reading 'a queer book called "After London"'. He told Georgie, 'I rather like it: absurd hopes curled round my heart as I read it.' The book, by Richard Jefferies – *After London: or Wild England* – had only just been published and it became a cult book of its time. It describes a devastated England, in which the land has been laid waste by catastrophe and people have returned to a barbaric cruelty. Jefferies' book is deeply pessimistic. Morris did not associate himself with that black vision. When he wrote his own futuristic novel, *News from Nowhere*, civilization has emerged from its dark tunnel on to an optimistic, shining fertile plain. But Jefferies' book spelled out what Morris had known instinctively, that political equilibrium must be preceded by upheaval, silence, a kind of blankness as though of a 'nuclear winter'. Barbarism was in fact a necessary stage towards the future that he longed for. Reading Jefferies he was plunged into impatience: 'I rather wish I were thirty years younger: I want to see the game played out.'

By far the most remarkable of Socialist League branches was at Hammersmith. This, formerly a branch of the SDF, was reincarnated on 7 January 1885, with Emery Walker continuing as secretary. Its premises were part of Morris's Kelmscott House in Hammersmith. The branch was virtually a continuation of the house. The meetings were held in the long narrow room, approached through the yard with the sycamore tree. This room, originally the stables, had first contained the looms for Morris's 'Hammersmith' carpets and had then been used by Morris and by May as a studio workroom where they could set up their large designs and working drawings. Photographs show that the Coach House, in the days of the Hammersmith Socialists, was indeed the 'frugal meeting place' described by May with its bare floor, basic matting and whitewashed walls. It was furnished with benches and stick-back chairs with a plain kitchen table on the platform. There were no curtains, but the view through the large window behind the lecturer's head gave glimpses of the Morrises' town garden. The scene has been

517

38 Walter Crane's design for the membership card of the Hammersmith Branch of the Socialist League, showing a Morris-like smith hammering at the anvil.

much described. It is in fact one of the most described scenes in late Victorian London, appearing in the memoirs of the period, often reverentially, sometimes a little caustically.

There was a certain atmosphere of fiefdom. Elizabeth Pennell wrote: 'At Hammersmith we began to suspect that socialists could boast an aristocracy when through the door communicating with the house Morris and his daughter, Miss May Morris, would appear with something of state, accompanied by favoured "comrades".' George Gissing spent an evening at the Coach House while gathering material for his novel *Isabel Clarendon and Demos* (1886). He found a ready-made extravaganza: 'Positively I felt *en plein roman*.' He too took particular note of May, talking 'familiarly' with the working men:

She is astonishingly handsome, pure Greek profile, with hair short on her neck; wore a long dark fur-trimmed cloak, and Tam O'Shanter cap of velvet. Unmistakeably like her mother, – the origin of Rossetti's best type.

May, now twenty-three, had grown into the role of her father's chief assistant. She had already proved herself invaluable to him in his design work, and was soon to take over the artistic direction of the embroidery department at Morris & Co. Now he came to depend on her support for him in politics. In the months she had been away in Bordighera he had sent her very detailed, combative and amusing accounts of his Socialist activities, telling her, 'I shall be so glad to see you, and we will have *such* talks, and you shall study the gospel properly.' He was obviously longing for her to return. The relationship between Morris and May has something in common with the closeness between Freud and his daughter Anna. It was partly suffocating, in the intensity of its demands, but in another sense a kind of freedom. It released her latent talents and brought her into contact with ideas and activities far beyond the reach of most young women of her period and class. When she looked back a few years later she felt grateful for those 'early days of independence' after living 'dutifully' under her mother's wing. From now on, May is a part of Morris's Socialist history, working for the Cause and almost always at his side.

Sunday was the main day of activity at Hammersmith. In the middle of the morning the small group would set out from Kelmscott House carrying the red embroidered banner (designed by Walter Crane and worked by May) and install itself at one of the recognized positions where the speakers were likely to attract listeners without being in danger of being 'moved on'. The Hammersmith Branch's main sites were at Turnham Green, at Walham Green and at Beadon Road near Hammersmith Broadway. Their favourite pitch was beside Hammersmith Bridge, where the bridge itself provided some protection and where they could hope to attract the passing trade. This meeting ground was shared with the Salvation Army. Morris would work himself up into an agitated fury when the Salvationist service overran.

May paints romantic pictures of Socialist street-preaching by the river on a fine May morning: 'the little group of the "faithful" clustered round the banner, the women strolling round, giving out leaflets and offering *Commonweal* for sale; my father in his loose blue serge suit and soft felt hat speaking, a little nervously at first, but warming to his work as the crowd drew closer'. In fact the street-preaching was not always so idyllic. There are records in the Hammersmith Branch minutes of disappointing meetings such as the one attended by only nine people, eight of whom were Socialists already and at which not a single *Commonweal* was sold. There are also reports of the Sunday morning meetings being interrupted by the police. It was a very chancy business. At his age Morris must have found it wearing. He was sometimes reluctant, confessing once to Georgie, 'It is a beautiful bright autumn morning here, as fresh as daisies: and I am not over-inclined for my morning preachment at Walham Green, but go I must also to Victoria Park in the afternoon. I had a sort of dastardly hope that it might rain.'

May was put in charge of the reading room and newsroom, provided at Kelmscott House at E. T. Craig's suggestion. This was open on Sundays from ten-thirty to one. Walter Crane had suggested a reading list for young Socialists and Morris presented a number of volumes, including a copy of Shelley's *Poems*. May's responsibilities included the training of the Socialist Choir which rehearsed on Friday evenings and was often in attendance at the Sunday morning meetings. The choir had the services of an old army bandmaster. It was he who composed the rousing chorus to Morris's 'March of the Workers'. At a later stage, the Hammersmith Choir was conducted by the young Gustav Holst, an admirer of Morris's writing who attended the lectures in the Coach House. Holst was sometimes to be seen around the streets of Hammersmith, perched on the official Socialist cart playing a harmonium. In 1930, his Prelude and Scherzo, *Hammersmith*, was written in memory of those old Socialist days.

The highlight of the week was the Sunday evening lecture in the

The Socialist League.

HAMMERSMITH BRANCH.

KELMSCOTT HOUSE, UPPER MALL, HAMMERSMITH.

LECTURES

On Sunday Evenings, at 8. Admission Free.

JANUARY 1st.

C. J. FAULKNER.

"Property, or the New Bigotry."

JANUARY 8th.

SIDNEY WEBB,
(FABIAN SOCIETY).

"The Irish National Movement, and its bearing on Socialism."

JANUARY 15th.

WILLIAM MORRIS,

"The Revolt of Ghent."

On SATURDAY, JANUARY 21st,

Will be performed by the

COMMONWEAL COMPANY,

"The Tables Turned, or Nupkins Awakened;"

A Dramatic Interlude by WILLIAM MORRIS.

Tickets 6d. each, to be obtained from any Member of the Branch.

At 8 o'clock on WEDNESDAY, JANUARY 18th, MRS. ANNIE BESANT will deliver a lecture on

"The Evolutionary aspect of Socialism."

This Lecture will be the first of a course to be given on Wednesday Evenings, by representative Socialists of various Schools.

Further particulars will be announced shortly.

Churchman, Printer, 18 King Street, Hammersmith.

(side text:) AND AT OPPOSITE WALHAM GREEN STATION AT 11.30.

Poster advertising the lectures and entertainments programme of the Hammersmith Branch of the Socialist League.

Coach House. This took place at eight p.m. The Hammersmith Sunday evening lectures were, as May points out, 'an institution as fixed and reliable as the Bank of England', under the secretaryship of Walker, and the speakers represented all possible shades of Socialist thought, from Anarchist to Scientific Socialist to Fabian to Progressive. Almost every important Socialist thinker of the period spoke in the Coach House, most of them many times. Stepniak, Kropotkin, Lawrence Gronlund, Graham Wallas, Annie Besant, Sidney and Beatrice Webb, Sydney Olivier, later Ramsay MacDonald and Keir Hardie. Walter Crane gave memorable illustrated lectures, using a blackboard and chalk. The most regular performers were Bernard Shaw and Morris himself. In Morris's absence May would stand in for him. Sydney Cockerell was impressed to hear Morris's beautiful daughter giving a paper on 'Socialism' on his first visit to the Coach House in November of 1885.

The subjects of these lectures were much more heterogeneous than in any other Socialist meeting-room in London. Stepniak might be speaking on the Russian working classes, Shaw might be addressing 'The Seven Deadly Virtues'. On one Sunday, Morris would be providing an erudite analysis of 'Industry in the Fourteenth Century'; on another, John Burns might be giving an account of 'Six Weeks in Pentonville', based on his own experience. The audience was as variable as the speakers, ranging from the wizened E. T. Craig, who sat in the front row brandishing his ear trumpet, to Oscar Wilde, seen attending a Hammersmith lecture looking like 'a basket of fruit, ripe and enticing' and wearing a large dahlia. Young London intellectuals were attracted there by Morris's own writing and peculiar charisma. In later years, the Coach House evenings retained a magic of memory, a buzzing in the conscience, for two writers as dissimilar as H. G. Wells and W. B. Yeats.

Wells, who came in a red tie, caught the mood of those meetings. Morris almost mesmerized him:

He used to stand up with his back to the wall, with his hands behind him when he spoke, leaning forward as he unfolded each sentence and punctuating with a bump back to position. Graham Wallas, a very good looking young man then with an academic humour, was much in evidence, and Shaw, a raw, aggressive Dubliner, was a frequent speaker. There was a sprinkling of foreigners, who discoursed with passion, and a tendency to length, in what they evidently considered was the English tongue.

After the lecture, chosen members of the audience would be invited to stay behind for dinner. They were ushered into the family dining-room, with its 'Pomegranate' wallpaper and its Rossetti portrait. They sat in two long rows down the scrubbed wood table with Morris, looking more than ever like a Viking, at the head. Morris's art worker cronies in the Socialist movement, Walter Crane and Emery Walker, were almost always there, with the guest speaker of the evening. There would also be an intermingling of the people Yeats described as 'more or less educated workmen, rough of speech and manner, with a conviction to meet every turn'. Earnest young men from the universities, curious to learn more about Socialism, gravitated to Hammersmith, and Morris, perhaps seeing in them a reminder of his younger self, would include them in these suppers. C. R. Ashbee and his friend from Cambridge, Goldsworthy Lowes Dickinson, went to hear Edward Carpenter talk on 'Private Property' and listened enthralled as the debate continued backwards and forwards across the table in Morris's dining-room. Lowes Dickinson was brave enough to question Morris about basic principles of Socialism. Ashbee wrote in his journal excitedly:

Old Morris was delightful, firing up with the warmth of his subject, all the enthusiasm of youth thrilling through veins and muscles; not a moment was he still, but ever sought to vent some of his immense energy. At length banging his hand upon the table: 'No' said he, 'the thing is this, if we had our Revolution tomorrow, what should we Socialists do the day after?' 'Yes, what?' we all cried. And that the old man could not answer: 'We should all be hanged because we are promising the people more than we can give them'.

These suppers could easily go on beyond midnight. Morris drank his own claret and became a little garrulous. 'Why do people say it is prosaic to be inspired by wine?' he asked his guests one evening. 'Has it not been made by the sunlight and the sap?'

There is a postscript to the Socialist suppers. It was at the end of one of these long evenings that Shaw and May Morris embarked on what Shaw insisted on describing as a Mystic Betrothal for decades to come. According to his own later all too debonair account of it he was on the threshold of Kelmscott House when May came out from the dining-room into the hall: 'I looked at her, rejoicing in her lovely dress and lovely self; and she looked at me very carefully and quite deliberately made a gesture of assent with her eyes.'

There is no doubt that May fell in love with Shaw. It is also clear that

Shaw had no intention of marrying May or indeed any of the other women with whom he was involved simultaneously. Shaw was an accomplished and compulsive flirt.

To engage her in any way – to go to Morris and announce that I was taking advantage of the access granted to me as comrade-Communist to commit his beautiful daughter to a desperately insolvent marriage, did not occur to me as a socially possible proceeding. It did not occur to me even that fidelity to the Mystic Betrothal need interfere with the ordinary course of my relations with other women.

It was only weeks later that Shaw, at the age of twenty-nine, was indoctrinated into the delights of sexual intercourse by Jenny Patterson, an intelligent and fascinating widow ten years his senior. May noticed Mrs Patterson's advent with disapproval, accusing Shaw of being 'rather a disloyal friend'.

But in their early days the relations between May and Bernard Shaw had been electric. If this was a flirtation it had been a prize one, made headier by its context of the dramas and ironies of the Socialist scene. May's letters to 'Comrade Shaw', as she addressed him teasingly, knowing how he hated it, fizz with an awakened self-confidence, almost a sense of triumph. Shaw evidently had the knack of making women feel intelligent, desirable, generating sexual interest and excitement in a way that Morris so patently did not. What is so interesting about the episode, coming as it did at the time of William Morris's complete preoccupation with the Socialism movement, is the way it mirrors Janey's reawakened passion for another glib politician philanderer, Wilfrid Scawen Blunt.

By July 1885, the time of the first Socialist League conference, membership had climbed gradually to a total of about 230. Not all these were paid-up Leaguers: keeping track of members and eliciting subscriptions were insoluble problems for the League. But eight branches in England were now established, at Hammersmith, Merton Abbey, Stratford, Bloomsbury, North London, Oxford, Leeds and Bradford, with the affiliated Labour Emancipation League and a central branch for floating members. The branches of the Scottish Land and Labour League were also still attached. Over the next twelve months new branches were opened at Mile End, South London, Marylebone, Croydon, Hackney, Clerkenwell, Manchester, Oldham, Leicester, Birmingham, Norwich and Dublin. The Socialist League had been looking for new and more permanent London headquarters with a lecture room capable of seating 300 people, a reading-room and work space for League printing and publishing. In the summer of 1885 they moved north from Farringdon Street to No. 113 Farringdon Road.

The hot-headed young John Mahon had been removed from his post as secretary. Morris had written him a firm but anxiously paternal letter saying, 'the truth is the position has been a difficult one, requiring a great deal of arrangement to fill successfully, it is no wonder if you didn't quite succeed'. In July 1885 he was replaced by Henry Halliday Sparling, a young Socialist struggling on the fringes of literary London. When not employed in the Farringdon Road offices, much of his time was spent in the British Museum Reading Room, on unspecified research. Sparling's mixture of literary pretensions and class bitterness reminds one of Leonard Bast, the clerk in E. M. Forster's *Howard's End* (1910). Elizabeth Pennell heard him lecturing at Hammersmith 'like a romantic schoolgirl'. All accounts of him make him sound a little helpless. He attempted to conceal his obvious social disadvantages behind a façade of cocksureness and knowingness. Harry Sparling, referred to endearingly as 'Spätzle', starts appearing in May Morris's correspondence in the late autumn of 1885.

The League was seizing all opportunities to raise what would now be called its public profile. The records of Morris's engagements through the summer show that he was lecturing every few days. He was still deeply conscious of his own inadequacies and especially anxious about his difficulty in communicating directly with the workers. He forced himself onwards, using all his willpower, into situations that dismayed and disconcerted him. Shaw the Fabian watched with a mixture of admiration and derision Morris's self-inflicted programme: his 'very rough jostles with real life'. In Farringdon Road the Socialist League was on the edge of the East End and the acre upon acre of poverty and squalor soon to be combed over by Charles Booth for his seventeen-volume *Life and Labour of the People of London* (1891–1903). In summer 1885 Morris had given his lecture 'Work as It Is and as It Might Be' to the Socialist League Mile End Branch in Stepney. He wrote to Georgie:

On Sunday I went a-preaching Stepney way. My visit intensely depressed me, as these Eastward visits always do: the mere stretch of houses, the vast mass of utter shabbiness and uneventfulness, sits upon one like a nightmare: of course what slums there are one doesn't see. You would perhaps have smiled at my congregation: some twenty people in a little room, as dirty as convenient and stinking a good deal. It took the fire out of my fine periods, I can tell you: it is a great drawback that I can't *talk* to them roughly and unaffectedly. Also I would like to know what amount of real feeling underlies their bombastic revolutionary talk when they get to that. I don't seem to have got at them yet – you see this great class gulf lies between us.

Morris had based his life on sensuous appreciation. These surroundings provided the antithesis. And to him, as later to George Orwell, the *smell* of the poor was a humiliating shock.

That was also the summer of the 'Pall Mall Scandals' when W. T. Stead had exposed the selling of children into prostitution in a series of articles in *The Pall Mall Gazette*. His suggestion that the London police were implicated in the trafficking exacerbated an already tense situation between the police and the Socialist groups. The Socialist League Manifesto had spoken out against 'universal venal prostitution'. Amongst many meetings of protest at disclosures that caused shockwaves through the country, at all levels of society, was a Socialist League gathering, addressed by Morris on 5 August at the new Farringdon Hall. Here he argued that the recent exposures showed 'one side of the rottenness of well-to-do Society'. How much did he remember of the undercurrent of prostitution in the old days with Rossetti at Red Lion Square? On 22 August the Hammersmith Branch sent a contingent to the mass Demonstration for the Protection of Girls in Hyde Park. The Cobden-Sandersons found Janey there as well as Morris. This is our only record of Janey demonstrating. She was marching in the procession of the Ladies' National Society. Morris was meanwhile sitting in the brake of the Socialist League.

The police had been become very heavy-handed in their attacks on Socialist meetings. The first serious incident had been in May 1885 at the International Socialist Working Men's Club in Stephen's Mews, Tottenham Court Road. The police had broken in, wrecked the furniture, confiscated books, and arrested fifty or sixty members. The focus of attention then moved to Dod Street in Limehouse, an old Radical meeting ground, where several cases of obstruction were brought against speakers for the SDF. In spite of past dissensions the London Socialist groups gave mutual support in times of crisis. A Defence Club was set up, with Morris as the treasurer. The Socialist League offered its help to the harassed SDF. On 20 September a crowd of 10,000 assembled at Dod Street to uphold the right of free speech. The meeting was addressed by Hyndman and a Radical, John Mathias, at one end of Dod Street and, at the other, by the Socialist League speakers, John Mahon and Frank Kitz. The meeting had ended, and the crowd was dispersing, when the police had swooped, arresting two banner-bearers and marching them off with some brutality. There were eight arrests, including Kitz, Mahon and Charles Mowbray the ex-tailor, one of the most vehement of the leaders of the campaign for the rights of open-air free speech.

The next day Morris anxiously attended the Thames Police Court, prepared to stand bail. The presiding magistrate, Thomas William Saunders, gave a vicious sentence of two months' hard labour to Lewis Lyons, a poor East-end Jewish tailor convicted for supposedly kicking a policeman. There was an immediate outcry in the court of 'Shame!' followed by a mêlée in which, according to Aveling's account in *Commonweal*, the police 'commenced an assault upon all and sundry' and especially Eleanor. At this point 'William Morris, remonstrating at the hustling and the thumping, became at once the chief thumpee. There has rarely been seen anything more brutal than the way in which two or three able-bodied young men fell upon the author of what one of the newspapers called the "Paradise League".' In court Morris turned furiously on a policeman, who maintained he had hit him and broken his helmet. Morris was then arrested for disturbance. He was kept waiting for two hours before he was himself brought up before Saunders. *The Daily News* reported the dialogue that took place between Morris and the magistrate when Morris denied that he had ever hit the policeman:

MR. SAUNDERS: Have you any witnesses? . . .

MR. MORRIS: I do not know whether there is any one here who saw it . . . I quite confess that when I heard the sentences passed on the prisoners my feelings got the better of me, and I did call out 'Shame' . . . Then this policeman came and distinctly hustled me. When you are pushed you naturally push again, but that is not resisting the police, I turned round and remonstrated with the policeman, but I distinctly assert that I never raised my hands. He was very rough, and I am quite prepared to bring a charge of assault against him.

MR. SAUNDERS: What are you?

PRISONER: I am an artist, and a literary man, pretty well known, I think, throughout Europe.

MR. SAUNDERS: I suppose you did not intend to do this?

PRISONER: I never struck him at all.

MR. SAUNDERS: Well, I will let you go.

PRISONER: But I have not done anything.

MR. SAUNDERS: Well, you can stay if you like.

PRISONER: I don't want to stay.

He was then liberated, and on getting into the street was loudly cheered by the crowd who had gathered there.

Morris himself reported the incident to Janey good-humouredly, playing down the danger: 'The behaviour of the police, their bullying and hectoring, was quite beyond belief, and I have no doubt they mostly swore through a kitchen table. Kiss my dear Jenny and give her the news.'

George Gissing, the fellow writer, was appalled to read about the incident. He wrote to his brother:

Do you see the report of the row the Socialists have had with the police in the East End? Think of William Morris being hauled into the box for assaulting a policeman! And the magistrate said to him: 'What are you?' Great Heavens! . . . Alas, what the devil is such a man doing in that galley? It is painful to me beyond expression. Why cannot he write poetry in the shade? He will inevitably coarsen himself in the company of ruffians.

Funny Folks printed a cartoon of a policeman blacking Morris's boots in Dod Street, the implication being that the famous poet had received preferential treatment. The cartoon is entitled 'The Earthly Paradox'. *The Pall Mall Gazette* ran an interview with Morris on 23 September in which he said, 'I shall probably go to prison yet . . . if the authorities maintain their present attitude. But I honestly confess that I do not take kindly to the idea of going to gaol. For I do not like to have a door locked upon me, nor do I like to be stopped from going where I want to go.' At the end of the interview the reporter asked him, 'Have you an important literary work in hand at present, Mr Morris?' 'I cannot say that I have – I cannot find time.' 'Then it may be public gain if you are cast into prison?' 'Ah, but there is the oakum to pick.' Oakum picking was the useless toil prescribed for convicts and the residents of workhouses. Oakum was the loose fibre arrived at by laborious untwisting of old rope.

The Dod Street arrests and the publicity surrounding them undoubtedly helped the Socialist cause. The next Sunday a huge crowd,

40 *'The Attitude of the Police'*, a cartoon circulated in 1886, after the Dod Street arrests, satirizing the authorities' lenient treatment of Morris in the courtroom.

estimated at between 30,000 and 50,000 people, demonstrated first of all at Dod Street and then overflowed into the open space in front of West India Docks. This too was territory forbidden by the police. But the ban was defied as Hyndman and John Burns spoke for the SDF, Shaw for the Fabians and the Rev. Stewart Headlam for the Christian Socialists. Aveling's voice rang out for the Socialist League. The police stayed on the sidelines. Their change of stance was partly the result of the government's realization that banning street-corner and open-air meetings would alienate the Free Churches, losing hundreds and thousands of potential Nonconformist votes in the forthcoming elections. In the Dod Street affair, the Free Churches, the Salvation Army, the Church Army formed an uneasy (mostly Liberal) alliance with the atheistic Socialists. It was a notable, and in some ways ironic, victory for free speech.

But for Morris himself the strain of those weeks had frustrating repercussions. Earlier in the year his gout appeared to have receded: he had had no *time* for gout, he was writing in April. But by October it had returned, in both his feet, and he reported himself 'leg-tied completely' and 'reading trashy novels', though even with gout he had had to draw the line at Ouida's *Strathmore*.

He spent the next weeks more or less flat on his back, not suffering bad pain but so lame he had to be wheeled through from his bedroom to the dining-room at Kelmscott House. One wooden leg, he maintained, would be better than two gouty ones. He remembered he had been 'much like this in Venice, only not so lame'. He was enormously frustrated, having to cancel or rearrange his lecture tours and conscious of his failure to provide the Socialist League with the leadership it desperately needed through that autumn with a general election looming and with growing dissensions within the League itself. He was, as always, an uncooperative patient. May complained to Shaw that she was having to accompany her father to Oxford for a lecture: 'I go to "take care of him". Taking care of him is a real farce: I give him wonderfully sage advice as to his health which I need not say he does not follow.' In late November he and Janey were in Rottingdean, staying with Ned and Georgie in discouraging weather. He had managed to stumble out on to the sea front for ten minutes but spent most of his time incarcerated, playing backgammon and cribbage and draughts and yet more backgammon with Janey, who was enervated with a cold.

At first he had tried to persuade himself the problem was purely technical and that a better-controlled diet would solve his goutiness. But he was forced to see that he was suffering from more general exhaustion: 'I have had such a busy and anxious summer and autumn that I am a little overdone which must be expected with a middle-aged man verging towards the elderly.' Morris's younger brother Rendall had died the year before, at the age of forty-five, having sold up his commission and involved himself in dubious plans to set up a poultry farm in Acton. Morris had commented earlier on Rendall's obesity. There is some evidence he had become an alcoholic. Rendall died even younger than their father had, leaving eight children who were almost immediately deserted by their mother. They were brought up by Morris's sister Isabella. He had every reason to feel conscious of passage of time and fickleness of health.

Christmas 1885 was especially despondent. Jenny, now in a nursing home, came back to join her parents and May at Hammersmith. They had hardly any visitors. The weather was dark and foggy. There was desultory music, May playing in duet with her mother on the mandolin, described by Morris as 'a funny twangling sort of thing'. May worked herself up into a *crise de conscience*, contemplating the lives of the haves and have-nots. 'When some people are merrymaking there are always such violent contrasts: to see the crowds of starvelings in the streets watching with interest the shopping of people with money,' she wrote gloomily to Andreas Scheu. Even her father was in a sudden state of disillusionment: 'As to the British working man, to say the truth – he could hardly be faster asleep than he is now . . . I sometimes fear he will die asleep, however hard the times grow, like people caught frozen.' This was Morris's Boxing Day message to F. S. Ellis, his most austere and hopeless of pronouncements of that time.

But Morris's resilience never ceases to astonish. Tiring of backgammon he had now begun what for many people would have been another life's work: a verse translation of Homer's *Odyssey*.

Eighteen eighty-six and 1887 were years of political turmoil in Britain. The long-lasting trade depression and resulting unemployment exacerbated social discontent. At this period Morris was right at the centre of the revolutionary ferment, a shining if, to the comrades, puzzling figure of integrity and boundless hopefulness. He was still very obviously the 'benevolent gentleman' he once described himself but, speaking at large meetings, marching in demonstrations, providing a channel for the swirling mass-emotions of the protesting working classes in his rhythmic chants and revolutionary hymns, Morris was beginning to be a necessary public figure in the movement. He was acquiring a mystique. In an unusually self-analytic letter he recognized his own deep-rooted need for such extremism:

I do not love contention; I even shrink from it with indifferent persons. Indeed I know that all my faults lie on the other side: love of ease, dreaminess, sloth, sloppy good-nature, are what I chiefly accuse myself of. All these would not have been hurt by my being a 'moderate Socialist'; nor need I have forgone a good share of the satisfaction of vainglory: for in such a party I could easily have been a leader, nay, perhaps *the* leader, whereas amidst our rough work I can scarcely be a leader at all and certainly do not care to be. I say this because I feel that a very little self-deception would have landed me among the moderates. But self-deception it would have been.

Those who, over the years, had their own reasons for playing down Morris's Socialism have argued that it was a passing phase, an aberration, as we have seen. It has been claimed that Morris the revolutionary Socialist was a case of mistaken identity. There is no evidence for this. Morris's private correspondence for this period can now be read in sequence. His personal letters, as much as his public pronouncements, show the strength of his commitment. It was as if his Socialism searched out the hidden reserves in Morris's nature:

And I cling to the love of the past and the love of the day to be,
And the present, it is but the building of the man to be strong in me,

as he wrote so movingly in *The Pilgrims of Hope*. In these years of drama, as he struggled to hold the already disintegrating Socialist League together, Morris had never been so much himself.

Morris was still committed to the idea of 'making Socialists'. The Socialist League was keeping to its programme of educating, organizing, agitating, planning for the new society to succeed the revolution. The League's participation in the November 1885 election, which resulted in another victory for the aged Gladstone, consisted simply of a leaflet *For Whom Shall We Vote?* This leaflet was brought out for all future elections and it blazoned out the message, 'DO NOT VOTE AT ALL!' It promised the non-voters their reward at some unspecified future date: 'the time will come when you will step in and claim your place, and become the new-born Society of the world'. This need for faith, without an easily assimilated programme, was one of the built-in communication problems for the Socialist League, identified by Engels in one of his despairing comments on the Socialists in England: 'You will not bring the numerous working class as a whole into the movement by sermons.'

Morris's disgust with the parliamentary system increased further after the episode of the 'Tory Gold'. It was revealed that two SDF candidates, Jack Williams in Hampstead and John Fielding in Kennington, had been funded by the Tories to 'make running' (as Morris put it) for the Tories by spoiling the Liberal vote. At the same time Hyndman, in a drunken orgy of manipulative schemes, had gone to the Radical Liberal candidate, Joseph Chamberlain, and threatened him with further Socialist opposition to Liberal candidates if he did not undertake to support the Eight Hour Bill in the next parliamentary session. Chamberlain refused. This sequence of events underlines the difference in outlook between Morris and Hyndman. He had none of Hyndman's stage-villain quality of daring. The episode inflamed him against Hyndman's methods once again: 'The Hyndman muck-heap is going on seething . . . humbugs are as hard to kill as cholera-germs.' The 'Tory Gold' issue undermined the uneasy truce between the Socialist League and the SDF.

This was one reason why Morris was not present at the meeting at which serious violence first broke out in London. The day of mass riot is now known as 'Black Monday': 8 February 1886. A meeting of the unemployed was held in Trafalgar Square by an organization calling itself the Fair Trade Association, subsidized by the Tories. The SDF arrived intent on taking the meeting over. Morris was determined that the Socialist League should stand apart from what seemed likely to be 'a mere faction fight', though as he reported to John Carruthers many Socialist League members in fact attended. Amongst them was May, who watched from the sidelines, after she had had to promise her family to keep away from scenes of likely trouble. The meeting was called for three o'clock, but hours before that Trafalgar Square was filled. At two o'clock the Socialists took over the square and the crowds from the East End, blocked together to form 'an immense mass of poverty stricken humanity', were addressed from the balustrade of the National Gallery by the leaders of the SDF.

Then Hyndman, Champion, John Burns and Jack Williams headed off with a great crowd of 8,000 or 10,000 people down Pall Mall towards Hyde Park. As they marched past the grandiose buildings of London

533

clubland, the 'power architecture' Morris often denigrated, the real tensions started. When they passed the Liberal Reform Club some of the servants pelted them with shoes and nail brushes. They returned the fire with a barrage of stones. The unemployed were jeered at from the windows of the Tory Carlton, and hooted in reply. As they went up St James's Street they discovered metal bars and loose paving stones and many of the Club windows were shattered, including those of the New University Club from which Hyndman had only recently been expelled. In Piccadilly people began looting shops. Hyndman noticed some East Enders, who had helped themselves to new garments, changing into them in Green Park. Another more inflammatory meeting was then held in Hyde Park, after which all the groups of rioters turned eastwards up North Audley Street and into Oxford Street, breaking plate-glass windows and looting as they went. Morris estimated that they missed by half a minute the Morris & Co. shop at No. 449 Oxford Street.

The effect of the riot was a public panic not unlike the widespread fears that followed the race riots in provincial cities in the 1980s. Over the next few days, in dark smoggy winter weather, London behaved as if in a state of siege. Morris noticed, with amusement, the police advising shopkeepers in Hammersmith to put their shutters up. Some shopkeepers in Kilburn were even closing down. There were rumours that an East End army was marching, under cover of a London pea-souper, towards the west.

Morris's considered view appears in a letter to the Rev. John Glasse in Edinburgh:

As to Monday's riot, of course I look at it as a mistake to go in for a policy of riot, all the more as I feel pretty certain that the Socialists will one day have to fight seriously. Because though it is quite true, that if labour could organize itself properly the enemy could not even dream of resisting, yet that organization could not possibly keep pace with the spread of discontent which will accompany the break-up of the old system, so that we shall be forced to fight . . . Yet I do not agree with you that Monday's affair will hurt the movement. I think it will be of service: any opposition to law and order in the streets is of use to us, *if the price of it is not too high* . . . For the rest an English mob is always brutal at any rate until it rises to heroism. Altogether taken I think we must look upon this affair as an incident of the Revolution, and so far encouraging: the shop wrecking was partly a grotesque practical joke (quite in the English manner) at the expense of the upper classes.

His conclusion was that 'contemptible as the riot was, as a riot, it no doubt has had a great effect, both here and on the continent: in fact the surprise of people in finding that the British workman will not stand everything is extreme'. Perhaps he had been wrong about the working classes being frozen into lethargy? His immediate response was to forgive Hyndman and express solidarity with the SDF in times he was expecting would prove 'both helpful and rough'. The Council of the Socialist League made official overtures of 'heartiest sympathy' for Hyndman, Champion, Williams and Burns, the SDF members who had now been served with summonses. Morris personally stood bail for Jack Williams and John Burns.

After the riot, police surveillance of the Socialists became more systematic. Home Office files released in 1987 show how warily police officials were viewing the infiltration of British politics by the dangerous species of foreign anarchists, 'a violent set and utterly unscrupulous'. Arrangements for policing the SDF meeting in Hyde Park on 21 February were thorough: 200 police constables at Triumphal Arch, fifty at Marble Arch, fifty at Grosvenor Square, fifty at St James's Palace, with a double patrol of 150 in the park and forty-six mounted police in reserve. The officers were adjured to keep the situation calm, restraining their constables from an undue show of vigour with their truncheons 'as a set off against the window breaking' of the week before. However, at the actual demonstration, police were 'compelled to draw their batons and use them without mercy on all who encountered them', according to *The Times*.

Ned had written in alarm after the reports of violence and Morris wrote to reassure him: 'Many thanks, my dear Ned, for your anxiety but lay it aside for the present. I shall not shove myself into assemblies that are likely to turn into riots.' A few months later he was sending soothing messages to Janey via Jenny: 'I had a brisk day yesterday, though tell your mother, no policeman's hand touched my sacred collar.' It was obvious to everyone that Morris was laying himself open to physical dangers as the confrontations between the police and the Socialists intensified in the aftermath of the riots.

Morris showed great courage. In the wave of arrests of Socialists he did what he felt he had to do, without drama and without fuss. Sam Mainwaring gave an account of his response to the news that Frank Kitz had been arrested:

I went to the office of the S.L. in Farringdon Road, and informed the members – who were having a social evening at the hall – of the arrest, and that he wanted bail. Carruthers and Morris left at once with me, and when we arrived at West Ham Police Station I introduced them to the inspector on duty as the sureties for Kitz's appearance on the following Monday.

The officer put the question: 'What is your name?' Our comrade answered, 'William Morris'.

'What are you?' queried the officer. But before Morris could reply to this question, Carruthers stepped up to the desk, and in a vehement manner said: 'Don't you know? Why, this is the author of *The Earthly Paradise*.'

Morris turned to his friend with an astonished look and said: 'Good heavens, Carruthers! You don't expect a *policeman* to know anything about *The Earthly Paradise*, do you?' And, turning to the inspector, said: 'I am a shopkeeper, carrying on business in Oxford Street.'

Morris found the combination of inefficiency and sanctimoniousness of the police courts unbearable. It is often the object of his squibs of satire in *Commonweal*, and he paints a bitter portrait of a self-important magistrate, the 'white-haired fool on the bench', in *The Pilgrims of Hope*. The longueurs of the courtroom tried his patience almost beyond endurance. Shaw came upon him once looking 'desperately uncomfortable at a police court, going to bail for some of the comrades. I found him rubbing it all off by reading *The Three Musketeers* for the hundredth time or so.' But he saw his attendance as his duty, the simple logical consequence of his commitment to the cause.

On 11 July 1886, Sam Mainwaring of the Socialist League and Jack Williams of the SDF were summoned for obstruction at Bell Street, Edgware Road, one of the pitches of the Marylebone Branch of the Socialist League. They were committed for trial the following month at the Middlesex Sessions, having had a previous warning. On 18 July it was Morris who was summoned for the same offence. The summons maintained that William Morris of Kelmscott House, 26 Upper Mall, Hammersmith, 'did wilfully obstruct the free passage of the public footway and Highway at Bell Street, Marylebone' by placing himself upon a stand 'for the purpose of delivering an address thereby encouraging a crowd of persons to remain upon and obstruct the said Highway and footway at 12 noon'.

The arrest of Morris was the culmination of the third successive Sunday police raid on Bell Street, and the police were evidently intent on treating this as a test case. Morris knew he was making himself conspicuous. To the police the author of *The Earthly Paradise* was an embarrassment factor. By appearing in Bell Street he challenged them to act. Before he began speaking, he had told the crowd to keep quiet and orderly in the event of police interference, explaining that he had come to Marylebone to maintain the right of the Socialists to speak in the streets in the same way that people holding other opinions were allowed to do. Morris got into the stride of his speech on monopoly and corruption. The scene was reported in sympathetic detail in *The Commonweal*:

He was impelled to talk to them that morning because the present condition of things was a bad one. He had been asked by a lady the other day why he did not talk to the middle-class. Well, the middle-class had their books with plenty of leisure to read them; the working classes had no leisure, no books. (At this point Chief-Inspector Shepherd appeared outside the crowd, and said that he could not get in. This was false, however, and the inspector was immediately made way for by the people, who groaned him heartily as he approached the speaker. Having come to Morris he told him to desist, which Morris refused to do, on which the inspector took his name and address and left the crowd, when the speaker proceeded without further interruption.) The middle and upper classes were enabled to live in luxury and idleness on the poverty and degradation of the workers. There was only one way in which this state of things could be altered – society must be turned downside up. A true society meant to every one the right to live, the right to labour, and the right to enjoy the fruits of his labour. The useless class must disappear, and the two classes now forming society must dissolve into one whole useful class, and the labour class become society. In conclusion, he appealed to them to do all they could for the Cause; to educate themselves, to discuss the social question with their fellows, and prepare themselves for the great social revolution.

Morris's speech lasted thirty minutes, and his remarks were frequently cheered. The people then passed quietly away, after having subscribed to the Defence Fund. During the time this meeting was going on, a meeting was being held by the religious people a little way down the street.

Morris's case came up before Mr Cooke, the magistrate at Marylebone Police Court, on Saturday 24 July at two p.m. Giving evidence against him was Chief Inspector Charles Shepherd, who described a crowd of about 300 men assembled around Morris, including Jack Williams and many other known Socialists' walking about round the meeting distributing bills and selling their papers *Justice* and *Commonweal*, obstructing the footways and leaving no free passage for foot or horse traffic. The second witness, Inspector William Gillies, gave evidence somewhat unconvincingly, maintaining that a cart was stopped for three or four minutes by the crowd. The judge turned to Morris and said that 'as a gentleman' he would at once see 'when it was pointed out to him, that such meetings were a nuisance' and in future would surely desist from taking part in them. Morris was fined one shilling plus costs.

Morris attended the subsequent trial of Mainwaring and Williams at the Middlesex Sessions, from 11 to 13 August 1886. They appeared before Assistant-Judge Peter H. Edlin. Morris described the proceedings dejectedly to Jenny:

May and I were in the court all day yesterday, and a sorry exhibition it was, except for our comrade Mainwarings' speech which was very good: in fact I was proud of his bearing altogether. The Judge was abhominable [sic], really a kind of Judge Jeffries the Younger. You would have thought that our friends had at least committed a murder under aggravated circumstances so bitter an advocate he was against them. They were sentenced to pay £20 each or else two months and besides that to be bound over (with one surety each) to keep the peace for 12 months: that means that if they can't find a surety or if they get hauled up for obstruction again, they will have an extra 12 months prison – and all this for what no reasonable man can call even the smallest crime. It is too disgraceful: being working-men they cannot themselves pay so heavy a fine, and though we could find the money I don't think either of them would agree to that. It is a pity that Dickens wasn't alive & there to touch up the little blackguard of a judge, for that is what he is. However, as I told some of our lads yesterday, they musnt [sic] grumble, as all this is the why and wherefore of their being Socialists.

Charley Faulkner was called as a defence witness. He had been at Bell Street at the Socialist meeting. He denied there had been any obstruction whatsoever. May wrote the long, indignant and acerbic report, 'Vindictive Sentence', in *The Commonweal*.

Morris's fury was fuelled by embarrassment at seeing the English class system in blatant operation even in the law courts. The working-class Socialists in London complained bitterly of the preferential treatment given to those regarded by the police and magistrates as their social superiors. On 12 June, for example, as *Commonweal* reported, Charles Mowbray and Joseph Lane had gone to speak at Stratford but because they were 'not middle-class men or Radicals, the police immediately interfered'. There is evidence of the security forces' circumspect attitude to Morris in the Public Record Office. It appears in Home Office file only recently released under the 100-year rule. A note in red ink instructs the filing clerk, 'Keep 1/11 to 13 re. William Morris.' The files are stamped: 'Home Office, 28 August 1886'. The subsequent files, 14–18, were destroyed.

All through 1886 Morris was travelling, journeying compulsively like one of his own *Earthly Paradise* wanderers or Odysseus himself, displaced from his own country. Part of the task of making Socialists was seeking them out in distant parts. During that year Morris made ten separate expeditions out of London. In February he was in Sheffield, Bradford and Liverpool, where he spoke on 'Socialism in relation to the London riots', bringing the eye-witness report out to the provinces. In March he spoke in Norwich which he felt 'as likely a place as any in England for the spread of Socialism', in the grip of unemployment as its old weaving industries dwindled and its new shoe-making factories faced increasing competition from abroad. In April Morris was addressing the Socialist League in Dublin. He had hardly returned before he set off again to Shipley, Bradford and Leeds. In May he was in Birmingham, lecturing on 'The Political Outlook' on a wretched wet night when he held his own against a counter-attraction in the Exchange Buildings 'in the form of the Performing Fleas'. In June Morris went north to Arbroath, Edinburgh, Glasgow, Bridgeton and Dundee, delivering six lectures in six days. In September he was in Manchester, fulfilling his annual lecturing engagement at Ancoats for his Socialist-philanthropist friend Charles Rowley, founder of the Ancoats Brotherhood. From there he travelled on to Sheffield where he was still hopeful of building up a Socialist League branch. In October he was back in Norwich, consolidating the progress he had made seven months earlier. The making of Socialists demanded not only great persistence but also a degree of social mobility since sometimes he was staying with Liberal industrialists, local academics, old Pre-Raphaelite contacts, at other times with working-class comrades in their homes.

A few days after Norwich he went to speak in Reading at the British Workman club. In November he lectured in Lancaster and Preston, addressing the Preston Eclectic Society on 'The Dawn of a New Epoch' in the schoolroom of the Unitarian chapel. The venues for his lectures were the ramshackle collection of Socialist meeting-rooms, often hired rooms in coffee houses and temperance halls. Morris grumbled very little. It is almost as if he took a perverse pleasure in surroundings so different from those he was accustomed to. This is a facet of his martyrdom for the

Cause. As he travels around England there are poignant descriptions of food seized in transit: one evening he was dining off two Abernethy biscuits on top of a tram. On a journey in September between Edinburgh and Manchester he missed his connection. He was too late and harassed to stop anywhere for food: 'all I could do', he wrote to Jenny, 'was to rush to the buffet and catch up whatever came first to hand 2 mutton pies as it happened but I was very hungry and they were very good.'

Morris's visit to Dublin is particularly interesting, coming as it did at a crucial time in the controversy over Home Rule for Ireland. Gladstone had put forward his Home Rule Bill, in a three-and-a-half-hour speech to the House, only the day before. The Bill, alas eventually defeated, provided for an Irish Parliament and executive in Dublin with its own powers of legislation, except over certain reserved areas such as foreign policy and defence. Morris, and the Socialist League, had supported the policy of decentralization, seeing 'a gross form of exploitation in progress in Ireland'. Now, and in the future, the League would routinely take part in all demonstrations organized by Irish nationalist supporters. May was on her way to an Irish nationalist protest meeting when Wilfrid Blunt spotted her 'looking like a French revolutionist going to execution' on the Socialist League cart. However, Morris had strong reservations about the Gladstonian policy for Ireland as well as doubts about the calibre of the Irish leaders themselves. He viewed Ireland always as an apology for Iceland, a place that retained an integrity based on simplicity and indeed on poverty, a country all too easy to exploit. He analysed the situation anxiously:

On the whole, I fear it seems likely that they will have to go through the dismal road of peasant-proprietorship before they get to anything like Socialism; and that road, in a country so isolated and so peculiar as Ireland, may be a long one. On the other hand, it will lead them straight to ruin unless they can keep out of the world-market – which they can scarcely do. Undoubtedly the Irish are bent on doing all they can to further Irish manufactures, however artificially, and to that end are sure to drive new railways through the country, and so to stimulate that profit which throws the peasant into the hands of the usurer, and makes peasant-proprietorship a miserable make-shift – a piece of reaction leading nowhere, save *down* the hill. So that after all things in Ireland may go quicker than we now think.

Morris took the boat overnight to Ireland, rousing himself at five-thirty to watch the clouds rising over the Wicklow mountains. The sea was 'deep green with plenty of white horses'. The wind was so strong that it blew his spectacles off. When he arrived in Dublin he found the city already buzzing with discussion of the contents of Gladstone's bill which Morris had viewed cynically: 'It was as I supposed it would be a piece of constition [sic] making of the most ingenious kind.' In Dublin he had his usual heavy programme of speech-making under the auspices of the Dublin Branch of the Socialist League: 'The Aims of Art' one evening, 'The Political Outlook' the next afternoon, and in the evening the opening speech in the debate 'Socialism: What Is It?' The Art lecture was a shock to several Irish 'respectables' who walked out early in the proceedings. The Socialist debate, in terms of propaganda, was even more successful. A mischief-maker turned the gas lights out, plunging the Dublin Saturday Club into darkness, as was reported in the local press. Morris liked the 'sort of cosy shabbiness of Dublin', combined with its wonderful clear air. He was surprised by the political good sense he found in Ireland: 'On whatever point the Irishry are wild, they are quite cool, sensible, and determined on the Home Rule question.' He had a comfortable passage back to England, eating his dinner on the boat and completing fifty lines of his *Odyssey* translation. That whole summer he travelled with his Homer in his knapsack, pulling it out like an enormous piece of knitting to occupy himself *en route*.

Even in London he was still in a strange land. Morris would be seen wandering the streets of Shoreditch and Whitechapel, his eyes kindled, exploring and observing. An *habitué* of the International Club, a meeting place of the European revolutionary exiles in an old dilapidated Georgian house near Shoreditch church, was surprised one day to find 'a peculiar calm pervading the usually hectic atmosphere of tobacco smoke and revolution'. A stranger was sitting on a bench with a crowd of Jews, Frenchmen, Russians, Spaniards, Germans as well as English anarchists grouped round about him. This man was introduced as 'Comrade Morris – another comrade'. He was wearing his usual suit of rough country-farmer's tweed. Sometimes Morris would be sighted, still in the East End, perched on a stool at a street corner expostulating on the ruin of the landscape: 'God made the country, men made the town and the devil made the suburbs.' In his travels we see Morris as urban investigator, social researcher and also romantic traveller on a voyage of discovery through the almost unknown regions of the city, alert to the curious, conscious of the *flavour*. Sixty or seventy years later he would have carried a copy of Pevsner in his pocket too.

As a speaker in the East End, Morris was reckoned unpredictable. 'A jeer from a sceptic would upset him, and then he would pour out a torrent of fiery invective, which was at once beautiful and heroic, and utterly lost on the majority of the audience.' The same commentator, Owen Carroll, was in the crowd at Somers Town one Sunday morning when Morris, in full flood, his head thrown back, his eyes shining, his beard dancing, was interrupted by a man in the crowd shouting: 'If you believe so much in what you say, why don't you give your money to the poor?' This was not a new question. It was of course the question that had dogged Morris, in public and in private, ever since he became a Socialist. Carroll's account, based on hasty notes he made at the time, shows how deeply it still shook him:

Morris's face instantly grew dark. I had never seen him in a rage before . . . For a moment he stood speechless, glaring down at the interrupter like an angry lion. Then the resentment died in his eyes, giving way to pity and he made his defence:

'I started in business for myself over thirty years ago. I am as rich now as when I began, despite my ability and industry. I have paid my men good wages – better, indeed than they could get anywhere else; I have taught them to make beautiful things, and some of the work which has passed through our hands will last even after our bones have mingled with the dust. I have treated my workmen not as an employer, but as a comrade.

'I am not a rich man, but even if I were to give all my money away, what good would that do? The poor would be just as poor, the rich, perhaps, a little more rich, for my wealth would finally get into their hands. The world would be pleased to talk about me for three days until something new caught its fancy. Even if Rothschild gave away his millions tomorrow, the same problems would confront us the day after.'

The crowd applauded him, won over by his earnestness. Morris knew the arguments so well because he lived them. Relative wealth and poverty; art and commerce; creative solitude and the mass movement: these were all dualities Morris recognized and knew he must endure.

There is an open-mindedness in Morris at this period. He travels as a writer, wide-eyed, impressionable. He watches his responses, with the writer's double vision. Morris dreams and tells his dreams. He writes to Jenny of the dream he had that all of them were out together in the high street near the end of Rivercourt Road watching 'shooting stars which were red and green and yellow like the lights on the new Hammersmith Bridge, when all at once one fell to earth in the middle of the road'. The questions he asks are not the tight close questions of the politicians. They are much less guarded, wilder, looser, more unnerving, questioning the basic patterns of behaviour between people, challenging accepted views of man's relation to nature, damning the highhandedness with which human beings appropriate the earth. It is this imaginative, creative content in Morris's thinking and writing that removes him so decisively from the Fabians and parliamentarians in late Victorian Socialist politics and allies him with the intellectual Anarchists.

The Anarchist element in Morris has been consistently, and deliberately, written off in accounts of Morris's politics from the 1950s onwards, most of which have emphasized his Marxism to the exclusion of all else. Even E. P. Thompson's *William Morris: Romantic to Revolutionary*, the book that so magnificently rescued Morris as a serious political figure when it was first published in 1955, misses his qualities of waywardness and danger. Thompson was later to stress that William Morris was an 'original Socialist thinker whose work was complementary to Marxism'. But he underestimates the extent to which Morris, from the middle 1880s, was not just in sympathy with but was on terms of warm personal friendship with the leading London Anarchists.

Sergius Stepniak, living in exile in Bedford Park, was a neighbour of the Morrises. He was highly visible at London Socialist gatherings: Bernard Shaw had met him at a meeting in Hyde Park very soon after he arrived in London, in the early summer of 1884. His lectures for the Hammersmith Socialist meetings were compelling, if not entirely comprehensible: Sydney Cockerell found his accent impenetrable even after Stepniak had been in England six or seven years. May remembers him as being much talked of in the family. All of them were fascinated by his remote and tragic history. Stepniak had 'an air of impenetrability'. Holbein should have drawn him, with his characteristically Tartar physiognomy: the 'strange dignified head with the strong angles of its racial characteristics and the finely set mass of dark hair'. Stepniak had a childlike simplicity of vision that was also present to some extent in Morris. He would remove the books he wanted from the British Museum, but the books would always be returned. The idea of goods in common always haunted William Morris. He agreed with it in theory but in practice was fiercely possessive, especially of the objects and manuscripts he loved. He once accused Sir John Maple, of Maple's store in Tottenham Court Road, of selling a carpet from another manufacturer blatantly imitating one of Morris's designs. Maple blandly admitted it, but said he thought it was fair that 'the sun should shine a little on him too'. Morris said nothing except 'good morning'. George Wardle, who witnessed the scene, thought he was shocked into agreement with the argument that all the world's design was owned in common. An early example of the Stepniakian view.

Morris was also on affectionate terms with Prince Peter Alexeivich Kropotkin, most important of the Anarchist theorists of the period. Kropotkin arrived in London in 1886, after four years of imprisonment in France. His *Memoirs of a Revolutionist* gives a detailed and evocative account of his upbringing in a rich aristocratic family in Russia. As a boy he was picked out to be one of the personal pages to the Tsar. He had served in the Russian army and, during military campaigns in Siberia, had trained himself as a geographer: he shared Morris's interest in the surface of the earth. They shared other things as well: revolutionary seriousness combined with an obsessive love of family and the small change of domesticity. Morris first met Kropotkin, then in his middle forties, in his first few weeks in London, at the Socialist League commemoration meeting for the Commune at South Place, and they established an immediate rapport. There was rivalry between the Socialist League and the SDF to enlist him. Morris wrote to John Mahon, 'I am almost afraid that the Fed: have got hold of Kropotkin . . . But of course he is an old bird and not caught by chaff.'

Kropotkin did not join either party. He kept his independence. But, even more than Stepniak, he became an intimate of the Morrises at Hammersmith. Janey was very fond of him: 'You would like him as much as we all do,' she told Wilfrid Scawen Blunt. Morris was surprised and delighted by Kropotkin's obvious devotion to his new baby, whose progress was endlessly recorded in his letters: 'the good man adores *baby*'. Kropotkin was invited many times to lecture at the Coach House. It was the intellectual tenor of his Anarchism that attracted Morris. Kropotkin was an anarchist and Prince, unlike the cruder English working-class anarchists beginning to infiltrate the Socialist League. Morris and Kropotkin told each other stories. Morris retold for Jenny the fable with which Kropotkin had kept spellbound the guests around the table at a Sunday lecture supper:

There was a little colony of Russians in the Far West of America right among the Redskins: one day the Redskins fell on them and burnt their fields and lifted their cattle. Now if they had been Yankees they would have shouldered their rifles and gone after the Indians and shot as many of them as they could, and so have established a regular deadly feud between them. But the Russians bided their time and watching an opportunity, got hold of all the women of the tribe and brought them home to their own block houses where they kept them fast but treated them well. Then the Indians came to them and said: 'Have you got our women?' 'Yes.' 'How are they?' 'O pretty well thank you.' 'Well, give them back to us!' 'Wait a bit.' 'If you don't we will fall on you and kill you.' 'No you won't because then we will kill *them* first.' 'Well, give them back to us.' 'Presently, but you must do something first.' 'What?' 'Why you must till our land again that you burned.' 'We don't know how.' 'Never mind, we will teach you.' So the Indians turned to, and as they worked between the plough-stilts and otherwise the Russians stood by and encouraged them; crying out: 'There! Good fellow, how well he works! How clever he is!' and so on. Then, the work done, they got their women again and they had a feast together, and were very good friends ever after. Isn't that a pretty little story?

Kropotkin for Morris represented the acceptable face of London Anarchy. Indiscriminate anarchic violence always repelled Morris. It was Socialism distorted: 'I cannot for the life of me see how such principles, which propose the abolition of compulsion, can admit of promiscuous slaughter as a means of converting people,' he would write in 1893. But his friendship and his conversations with the intellectual Anarchist *émigrés* in London in the 1880s reinforced Morris's libertarian views, expressed with a new fluidity and passion in his lecture 'The Society of the Future', first given as one of the Hammersmith Branch lectures in the Coach House on 13 November 1887, the very evening of 'Bloody Sunday' in Trafalgar Square. Now Morris defined his ideal of the society of the future as the freedom and cultivation of the individual will, which civilization at best ignores and at worst denies:

I demand a free and unfettered animal life for man first of all: I demand the utter extinction of all asceticism. If we feel the least degradation in being amorous, or merry, or hungry, or sleepy, we are so far bad animals, and therefore miserable men.

Towards the end of his lecture he endeavoured to give his audience a more concise and complete' idea of the society into which he would like to be reborn:

545

It is a society which does not know the meaning of the words rich and poor, or the rights of property, or law of legality, or nationality: a society which has no consciousness of being governed; in which equality of condition is a matter of course, and in which no man is rewarded for having served the community by having the power given him to injure it. It is a society conscious of a wish to keep life simple, to forgo some of the power over nature won by past ages in order to be more human and less mechanical, and willing to sacrifice something to this end.

Morris's concept of the ideal life in small communities, hazy when he first explained it in the early 1870s, has clarified itself, becoming simul-taneously more generous and perilous. It is now much more far-reaching in its social implications. Each community would keep its individual character, 'within the limits allowed by due social ethics, but without rivalry between each other, looking with abhorrence at the idea of a holy race'. In these communities the family of blood relationship would 'melt' into the wider family of the community and of humanity. The pleasures of this new open society would arise from 'the free exercise of the senses and passions of a healthy human animal, so far as this did not injure the other individuals of the community'. Such pleasurable vistas of permissiveness must have caused some consterna tion even in the virtually shock-proof audience in the Coach House Janey was interested in the theory of Utopian communities. Her response to her husband's views on the free exercise of healthy human animal passions can only be conjectured. Morris's vision of the decentralized society, drawing moral sustenance from primitive simpli cities, has its obvious Icelandic echoes. It may have been sharpened by his envious visit to Carpenter at Millthorpe, when Carpenter lent him Thoreau's *Walden*. But the obvious connection is with Kropotkin's genially anarchic blueprints for the future as expressed in *The Conquest of Bread* (1892) and *Fields, Factories and Workshops* (1899).

By the end of October 1886 Morris had completed the tenth book of *The Odyssey* and felt confident of finishing twelve books by the year end. He wrote to Jenny, 'It really would be rather convenient to me to have a little gout in order to do some literary work.' Simultaneously with the translation he was working on a new story, the finest of his short prose narratives, *A Dream of John Ball*.

John Ball, the work *The Times* so carelessly referred to in Morris's obituary as 'A Dream of John Bull', was written as workaday Socialist polemic, appearing as a serial in *The Commonweal* from November 1886 to January 1887. It is the mature and confident reworking of a form of story that had fascinated Morris from his Oxford period onwards: the first-person narrative in which the narrator dreams himself back into the past. The dreamer finds himself in a countryside he almost recognizes, but which seems strangely altered. It gradually dawns on him that he is in the Kent of the Peasants' Revolt of 1381.

Morris's story operates on several different levels. In this it is like one of his designs for textiles or for wallpapers, superficially easy to read but revealing hidden depths and complexities the more closely you examine it. There is plenty to arrest the cursory reader of *Commonweal*: richly detailed descriptions of landscape and of buildings; a masterly account of a mediaeval battle of the long bows and the crossbows, violence erupting in the quiet of the country; a wonderful example of that William Morris speciality, the atmospheric scene in the great church. But what repays many readings is the density of texture, the planes of activity, the shifting levels of communication as the narrator penetrates further into his invented, and idyllic, fourteenth-century past:

So we turned away together into the little street. But while John Ball had been speaking to me I felt strangely, as though I had more things to say than the words I knew could make clear: as if I wanted to get from other people a new set of words. Moreover, as we passed up the street again I was once again smitten with the great beauty of the scene; the houses, the church with its new chancel and tower, snow-white in the moonbeams now; the dresses and arms of the people, men and women (for the latter were now mixed up with the men); their grave sonorous language, and the quaint and measured forms of speech, were again become a wonder to me and affected me almost to tears.

But strong men do not weep, or they did not weep, in any case, in the Britain of the 1880s, the decade in which Morris's brother Arthur was well on his way to attaining the rank of Colonel in the King's Royal Rifle Corps. What makes *John Ball* so subversive is its element of role change, upsetting expectations of male and female behaviour. This is why the story seems in some ways curiously modern, a fable for our time. In *John Ball* Morris questions the accepted interpretation of 'manhood', while challenging his own deep-rooted reticence. The rebels weep into their beards to hear John Ball's great call to fellowship. Manliness is a matter of being *moved*. The women in Morris's story do not flirt and do not flutter: they answer the men with 'clear straight' looks. The rebels advance with a banner on a cross-pole, Morris's most marvellous banner, like the Adam and Eve in an early stained-glass window, showing 'a man and woman half-clad in skins of beasts seen against a background of green trees, the man holding a spade and the woman a distaff and spindle rudely done enough, but yet with a certain spirit and much meaning'. Beneath the linked figures, 'symbol of the early world and man's first contest with nature', runs the message on the banner:

> When Adam delved and Eve span
> Who was then the gentleman.

John Ball himself, the rebel priest, refers respectfully to his 'unwedded wife', with whom he dwelt in love after he joined the priesthood. The narrative shimmers with half-hints and provocations, a startling early exercise in sexual politics.

Readers tended to read into it the things they wanted. Morris commented early on how it was 'much admired by people of various opinions', and decided to have it reprinted as a book. The 1888 Reeves & Turner edition was reprinted many times, and *A Dream of John Ball*, set in Morris's Golden type, with Burne-Jones's frontispiece, is one of the most poignant of all the books produced in the 1890s by the Kelmscott Press. Morris liked to read, or rather chant, the story to an audience. He read it to his family, preceded by *Brer Rabbit*. He read it to the Socialist meetings: 'we all felt as though it were John Ball himself who was speaking to us and we were the yeomen assembled around him,' wrote an impressionable member of the audience at the Glasgow Branch of the Socialist League.

The story quickly entered Socialist history. Beatrice Webb, in her diary, describes Sidney's courting of her on the late express train from Sheffield by telling her the story of his examination triumphs and reading her to sleep with 'John Ball's Dream'. John Ball stayed in the minds, and was very often quoted, by the architects of the Labour party in the twentieth century, R. H. Tawney and G. D. H. Cole. Harold Laski, visiting Northumberland miners in the Great Slump of the 1930s, found copies of *A Dream of John Ball* and *News from Nowhere* 'in house after house', even when most of the furniture had been sold.

Why has *John Ball* had such a lasting impact, even through periods when much of Morris's writing was forgotten or ignored? And why can it still prick the conscience of a Labour party in Britain, in the 1990s and

548

in a very different mood? The reason is surely the sheer strength of Morris's argument for fellowship, a term modern politicians are aware of losing sight of in an age of opportunism and individualism. With his childlike lucidity, Morris arrives at a statement of the unanswerably obvious: 'fellowship is life and lack of fellowship is death'.

Fellowship was always easier in theory than practice. In the early summer of 1886 May had announced her engagement to her fellow-comrade Henry Halliday Sparling. From May's point of view the Mystic Betrothal to Shaw had been seriously waning. The break seems to have come a few months earlier, at the point at which Shaw's mistress, Jenny Patterson, with sublime lack of diplomacy, had joined the Hammer-smith Branch of the Socialist League. May and Sparling had been thrown together as colleagues at the Farringdon Road offices. They had, for instance, gone together as delegates to 'a merrymaking and speechifying' at the International Working Men's Educational Club in Commercial Road in November of 1885. May told Scheu how at this Club the Socialists 'spoke in various languages and sang "Rose Freiheit" and played a one-act revolutionary play very earnestly and simply, though ending in the funniest Liberty Fraternity and Equality Tableau I ever saw'. In such surroundings love had blossomed, and by April May was reporting, 'We are among the brightest and most unsubstantial of clouds.' The announcement to her parents had, however, not been easy. She wrote to Scheu of the 'extreme terror' with which she had informed 'first the father and then the mother of our "folly"! Such a chicken hearted creature I found myself to be.'

May's fears had been well founded. Morris tried hard with Sparling, already his comrade in the office and his brother in the Cause. By Christmas he was managing to refer to him as 'my future son-in-law Sparling'. He wrote around his friends to solicit work for him in library research and jobbing journalism. But his comments on 'Master Harry' tend to be a little slighting. Morris evidently felt the tall, thin, immature Sparling, with his unattractive mixture of the pretentious and the ingratiating, was no substitute for Bernard Shaw whom he accepted as on his intellectual level: the sparring partner, almost the adoptive son.

Janey's woe at the engagement was patent. Sparling was the son of an Essex farmer, socially not so far above Janey's own relations. As well as Sparling's inexperience and charmlessness Janey's objection was a basic one of class. In August 1887 she wrote to Rosalind, 'May is away at

Kelmscott Manor alone learning cooking and how to live on a few shillings a week. She is bent on marrying without waiting till her future husband gets employment. I have said and done all I can to dissuade her, but she is a fool and persists.' A few weeks later, staying at Naworth, she poured out her indignation to Rosalind and Blunt.

With a callous enjoyment of everyone's discomfiture Blunt weighed up the situation as he saw it:

Mrs. Morris's daughter May wants to marry a socialist with whom she has fallen in love. She [Janey] describes him as stupid and helpless, but I do not see how she is to prevent it. The girl has been brought up in the mill of Socialism. She is 25 and has a will of her own. I am in favour of the marriage – Mrs. Howard opposes it. This led to a grand discussion. Morris himself it seems says he has no authority to interfere but at the same time will not give any money or let the young man live in his house.

May's fiancé was, however, taken to be presented to Mrs Morris senior who made the best of it, commenting to Jenny: 'I thought the young gentleman very young, I should have said he was no more than twenty, he seems good tempered and gentle.' May would be the ruling spirit, she assumed.

CHAPTER SIXTEEN

Farringdon Road, Two: 1887–90

By the New Year of 1887, as the last episode of *John Ball* was published, the concept of fraternity was noticeably waning at the Socialist League. Even from the beginning Morris had been aware of the 'positive genius' for misunderstanding within the highly strung and drama-seeking membership. In its first year of existence there had been a whole succession of resignations, often for the most trivial of causes. The explosive Joseph Lane had resigned (temporarily) because of the rejection of the offer of a friend of his to put up a brass name-plate outside the League's building in Farringdon Road. In autumn 1885 John Mahon had resigned in protest at the waste of time at meetings of the Council and its 'unwarranted and extravagant expenditure of money'. By the following summer Thomas Binning, the compositor, sent another ferocious resignation letter, complaining of 'loose and disorderly' conduct of Council meetings dominated by an esoteric clique of London members: 'If the League means business let it not waste time on metaphysical subtleties such as the precise shade of difference between "Rules" and "Arrangements". Let us first catch our hare before we begin to discuss how it could be cooked.' There was a general air of inefficiency and lassitude. Will Binning wrote in despair to head office: 'I should like to remind you, for about the fifteenth time, that the contribution I handed to you on June 9th has not yet been acknowledged.' The Socialist League records, now in Amsterdam at the International Institute of Socialist History, bulge with similar complaints. Hubert Bland, a visiting member of the Fabian Society, found the scene depressing in the 'large barn-like loft' in Farringdon Road: 'When we called there we generally found it occupied by a touzle-haired young man in shirt-sleeves and slippers smoking a pipe over the fire. The very look of the place gave an impression of feebleness and want of method. Nobody seemed to have anything to do there.'

How far should we blame Morris for the indolence and growing element of anarchy within the Socialist League? William Morris was in all but title the League's leader. But used as he was to giving the instructions in his own workplaces in Oxford Street or Merton, he was all the warier of seeming to assert himself in Farringdon Road where he was the good Socialist and so nobody's master. He was further inhibited by being conscious of how far the League leaned on his financial support for *Commonweal* and his generosity to individual League members. He could see how easily a Socialist party could be polarized into gentlemen and others: those who got arrested and those who stood them bail. Morris was determined not to act the gentleman. Accounts of his relations with working-class members of the Socialist parties and the workers who rose to question him at lectures show Morris terrified of being overbearing, replying much more patiently than he was used to with his social and intellectual equals. His careful and tactful letters to the less well educated of his correspondents bear this out. But this very carefulness made Morris the more vulnerable to anyone who sought to bully or exploit him. It is a theme that has fascinated many British writers, serious and comic: the point at which the master, abnegating his authority, puts himself at the mercy of the erstwhile servant class. Morris, with his convictions, could do nothing else. The reasons for his failure to give the Socialist League the lead it so transparently needed at this juncture lay way back within his upbringing, and his complex, often agonized attitudes towards authority and class.

Morris's own fluidity of outlook had the effect of encouraging into the haven of the Socialist League those whose views were more extreme than his own. This could be seen as lack of foresight, and in the end it did the League much damage. But again it was the hopeful suspension of judgement that was, for Morris, a part of 'fellowship'. Henry Charles, Joseph Lane, Frank Kitz, Sam Mainwaring and Charles Mowbray, leading Anarchists among the founder members of the Socialist League, were still prominent members. In 1887 all but Kitz were on the Council. In the general atmosphere of permissiveness their talk was getting wilder:

It will be a cold day for those who prey upon our vitals if we ever serve them as they serve us ... we can assure the humbugs and parasites of this neighbourhood that their dominion of cant will be strenuously attacked, and will be in danger of being destroyed.

This was Frank Kitz, reporting on repression of a riot in Norwich in *Commonweal*. Kitz, who had acquired a basic knowledge of chemistry, had already been involved in 'a small circle for the making of explosives'; he had retained some of the desperado attitudes of the Anarchist Communist Group he once belonged to, led by Johann Most.

His colleague Joseph Lane wrote *An Anti-Statist Communist Manifesto* which called for complete abolition of the state and revolutionary violence, couched in blood-and-thunder language: 'The study of history has taught us that the noblest conquests of man are written on a blood-stained book.' This manifesto was finally rejected by the Council, but Lane was confident enough to publish it himself. The mood of accusation and counter-accusation was intensified by evidence that a member of the executive committee, Karl Theodore Reuss, was a police spy. Reuss had been expelled from the League in May 1886.

Some sort of a line would have been easier to hold if Morris could have counted on the Avelings and Bax. But the middle-class intellectuals in the League were already showing signs of going their own way. Frustrated at the lack of contact with the masses, and attributing the SDF's greater success in the attraction of recruits to the fact that it held out a more positive programme, they were veering once again towards parliamentarianism: the very issue that had caused the breakaway. One of the key defectors to the parliamentarians was Alexander Donald, the barrister and literary scholar from Edinburgh, considered by Morris to be a good speaker but 'a regular intriguer'. Morris was already showing a new anger, caught as he was in the cross-fire of parliamentarians and Anarchists. His guarded affection for Aveling was turning to dislike and he wanted to be rid of him. 'I wish he would join Hyndman and let them have a hell of their own like the Texas Ranger.' He would soon be describing him as 'that disreputable dog'.

Morris's reflex when in danger was to return to the familiar old activities, known faces. This was happening already at the Socialist League. In May 1886 *Commonweal* became a weekly. Aveling relinquished the deputy editorship, to be replaced by Sparling, the son-in-law-to-be. Morris had an almost mystic belief in the extended family: in his stories his sons-in-law are always promising. But Aveling, whatever his personal faults, was a professional polemicist, a skilled and confident

553

performer of powerful intellect. Sparling was not of the same calibre. 'Harry and I are at the present moment engaged in spinning out notes for the 'Weal – making bricks without straw, I call it!' May wrote coyly in November 1886. *Commonweal* was now too much of a family affair.

The same instinct to play safe surfaced disastrously in Morris's choice of his successor for the thankless post of Socialist League treasurer in the early spring of 1886. Philip Webb was one of the period's great architects. He had already proved himself Morris's loyal lieutenant at the Society for the Protection of Ancient Buildings. He had been for many years a stern and committed Socialist. That he loved Morris must of course be borne in mind. But Webb, a man turned-in, neurotic and so shy as to be almost *incommunicado*, was an inept choice for a post in which communication skills were of the essence, in a Socialist League already riven by rumour and dissent.

Within two years Morris had virtually lost hope of his own party. He would struggle along with it from a sense of duty. But his optimism lay with the broader Socialist movement in the country. He wrote to John Carruthers, a Hammersmith Branch colleague, now one of his main allies: 'As for Socialism I must say that in spite of all faults and follies of the *party* I am encouraged by the *movement*: the dry bones are certainly stirring.' He added ruefully: 'I wish only I were more able in dealing with men.'

By the beginning of 1887 there was certainly more national awareness of the Socialists. The depressed state of trade, leading to widespread unemployment, had left the workers with more time and inclination to listen to the Socialist view. Gladstone's defeat over Irish Home Rule and the advent of Lord Salisbury's Tory administration, with what Morris described as its 'extra reactionary measures of coercion for Ireland', made the Radicals reconsider their position and, according to Morris's possibly over-euphoric account of it, 'many of them turned Socialist'. It was certainly true that police opposition to the Socialists, much of it heavy-handed if not blatantly vindictive, had aroused some public sympathy and had the effect, in the atmosphere of heightened drama, of increasing the Socialist efforts for the Cause. In January Morris began writing a Socialist Diary. This account, which he told Jenny might in the end be published, was intended 'as a kind of view of the Socialist movement seen from the inside, Jonah's view of the Whale, you know, my dear'.

The diary is the detailed day-to-day account of Morris's activities from the end of January to the end of April 1887. It is now in the British Library, written out in a schoolboy exercise-book in William Morris's flowing script. Apart from the Icelandic diary of the early 1870s, which it resembles in its candour, its flashes of indignation and its cushioning of humour, this is the best evidence we have of the real tenor of his life. The diary covers the period at which he was at the height of his Socialist activity. In 1887 he attended at least 105 meetings of the Socialists and the architectural and artistic pressure groups, speaking or lecturing at almost all of them, otherwise taking the chair. The diary opens with his account of one of these engagements at the working-men's club at 11 Merton Terrace, off the High Street, almost adjoining Morris's Merton Abbey works:

I went down to lecture at Merton Abbey last Sunday: the little room was pretty full of men mostly of the labourer class: anything attacking the upper classes directly moved their enthusiasm; of their discontent there could be no doubt or the sincerity of their class hatred: they have been very badly off there this winter, and there is little to wonder at in their discontent; but with a few exceptions they have not yet learned what Socialism means; they and Frank Kitz were much excited about the Norwich affair, and he made a very hot speech: he was much exercised about the police being all about the place, detectives inside and so on: I fancy their game is to try to catch the club serving non-members with beer or in some way breaking the law. But there is no doubt that there is a good deal of stir amongst the labourers about there; the place is wretchedly poor.

What shines out from this diary is how conditions in England still have power to shock Morris. Even after four intensive years of Socialist activity he is by no means hardened. He still blenches as he travels. The obvious comparison would be, again, with Orwell. The 'good luck only' of being born prosperous still rankles as he travels around England with such great reserves of stamina, watchful and concerned but never sentimental, recording the depressing details of the scene.

On 25 January he was at Hammersmith, at the Radical Men's Club very close to Kelmscott House, faced by an audience that 'had clearly no ideas beyond the ordinary party shibboleths, and were quite untouched by Socialism . . . The frightful ignorance and want of impressibility of the average English workman floors me at times.'

On 4 February he stood in for a missing speaker at the debate on the class-war at the Chiswick Radical Club: 'the room was not large; about twenty people there at first, swelling to forty perhaps before the end'. Morris described this gathering as supine: 'my Socialism was gravely listened to by the audience but taken with no enthusiasm.'

The following Sunday Morris was addressing the Hammersmith Branch open-air meeting at the Beadon Road site:

I spoke alone for about an hour, and a very fair audience (for the place which is out of the way) gathered curiously quickly; a comrade counted a hundred at most. This audience characteristic of small open air meetings also quite mixed, from the labourers on their Sunday lounge to 'respectable' people coming from church: the latter inclined to grin: the working men listening attentively trying to understand, but mostly failing to do so: a fair cheer when I ended, of course led by the three or four branch members present. The meeting in the evening poor.

On 12 February he reported in the diary he had been on League business for five nights in the row, a programme that included taking the chair at a meeting at Cleveland Hall, near Great Portland Street, headquarters of the 'orthodox' in London, 'a wretched place once flash and now sordid in a miserable street'. Morris had the arduous task of keeping peace between representatives of the orthodox Anarchists, the Collectivists, the anarcho-Communist *Gruppe Autonomie*, the SDF and its new rival, the Socialist Union, as well as 'our people', the Socialist League. He wrote caustically, 'It was rather hard work getting through all the speeches in the unknown tongues of French and German, and the natives showed their almost superstitious reverence for internationalism by sitting through it all patiently.'

On 20 February Morris visited the Mitcham Branch. He spoke to them extempore in the Socialist League club-room, 'a tumble down shed opposite the grand new workhouse built by the Holborn Union: among the woful hovels that make up the worse (and newer part) of Mitcham, which was once a pretty place with its old street and greens and lavender fields. Except a German from Wimbledon (who was in the chair) and two or three others who looked like artisans of the painter or small builder-type, the audience was all made up of labourers and their wives: they were very quiet and attentive except one man who was courageous from liquor, and interrupted sympathetically: but I doubt if most of them understood anything I said.' Morris admitted he felt downcast 'amongst these poor people in their poor hutch', the ceremonial opening of which he had attended a few months before.

62 *Jenny Morris* and 63 *May Morris*, drawn by Dante Gabriel Rossetti in 1871.
64 The attics at Kelmscott Manor photographed by Frederick Evans in 1896. These attics
appear in *News from Nowhere* as 'quaint garrets amongst the great timbers of the roof, where of
old time the tillers and herdsmen of the manor slept, but which a-nights seemed now to be
inhabited for the time by children.'

65 *Mrs William Morris sewing.* Pencil drawing by Dante Gabriel Rossetti.

66 William Morris photographed by Elliott and Fry on 21 March 1877. This was the year after he entered active politics as Treasurer of the Eastern Question Association.

67 Morris & Co. showroom at No. 449 Oxford Street, opened in 1877.   68 Thomas Wardle, proprietor of the dye works in Leek where Morris carried out his experiments with vegetable dyes in the mid 1870s.   69 Elizabeth Wardle, Thomas Wardle's wife, with some of her pupils. Encouraged by Morris, she founded the Leek School of Embroidery c. 1880.

70 Family group photographed in the garden of The Grange, summer 1874. *Back row, right to left*: Philip Burne-Jones, Edward Richard Jones (Ned's father), Edward Burne-Jones, William Morris. *Front row*: Georgiana Burne-Jones, Jenny Morris, Margaret Burne-Jones, Jane Morris, May Morris.   71 The Morris and Burne-Jones children in a tree in the summer of 1874, a few weeks before Jenny and May Morris entered Notting Hill High School.

72 William Morris's mother, photographed in 1879 when she was in her mid-seventies.

73 Kelmscott House on the Upper Mall, overlooking the River Thames at Hammersmith. The Morris family lived here from 1878 until after William Morris's death.

74 The Oxford and Cambridge Boat Race passing Kelmscott House in 1892.

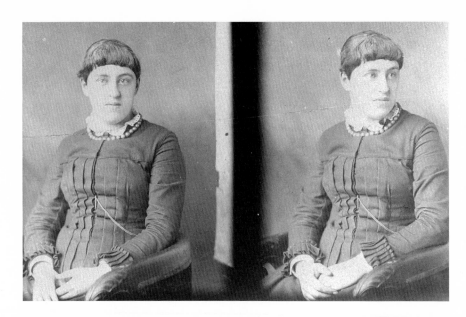

75 Jenny Morris in October 1879. She was then eighteen and had been under treatment for epilepsy for the past three years. Her weight gain is obvious and she appears a little glazed, presumably as a result of sedation.

76 Jane Morris photographed on a visit to Siena in 1881 with Thomas James Sanderson (later Cobden-Sanderson), Jane Cobden and her sister Annie, Sanderson's future wife.

77 William De Morgan, who accompanied Morris on his search for the site for a factory.
He built his own pottery at Merton in 1882.

78 The stained-glass studio at Merton Abbey where detailed working drawings were prepared from the artist's cartoons. At this period almost all the Morris & Co. glass was designed by Edward Burne-Jones.

79 The weaving workshops at Merton Abbey, where Morris & Co. woven furnishing fabrics were produced. Three Jacquard-type hand looms can be seen in use.

80 High-warp tapestry weaving in progress at Merton Abbey, a technique which had lapsed in England and which Morris reintroduced with notable success in the 1880s.

81 Workers hand-blocking chintzes in the Printing Shop at Merton.
82 Lengths of cotton being washed in the Wandle. This took place before and after dyeing.

83 Young women hand-knotting the Morris & Co. 'Hammersmith' carpets, originally made in the coach house at Kelmscott House in Hammersmith, and then at Merton Abbey.

84 Boy apprentices in the high-warp tapestry workshops at Merton Abbey, working from the back of the weft. The looms are positioned to take advantage of the natural light.

85 William Morris photographed by Eliott and Fry in the late 1880s, in the most arduous period of his Socialist involvement.

86 Wilfrid Scawen Blunt in the clothes he wore in prison in Kilmainham gaol, Dublin, in 1888.

87 May Morris photographed by Frederick Hollyer.
88 May on an outing with Henry Halliday Sparling, whom she married in 1890 after a long engagement. Also in the party are Gustaf Steffen, the Swedish sociologist and economist, then London correspondent of the Gothenburg paper *Handelf och Sgösartstidng*, and his wife Anna, regular attenders of the Socialist lectures at Kelmscott House.

<u>Marylebone</u> *Police Court* 113

COPY

Metropolitan Police District, to wit.

To *William Morris*

of *Helmscott House 26 Upper Mall, Hammersmith*

WHEREAS *information* this Day hath been *laid* before the undersigned, one of the Magistrates of the Police Courts of the Metropolis, sitting at the Police Court, *Marylebone*, within the Metropolitan Police District, by *George Draper, Superintendent of Police* for that you, on the *18th inst* Day of *July* in the Year of our Lord One Thousand Eight Hundred and Eighty- *six*

within the said District, did *Wilfully Obstruct the free passage of the public footway and Highway at Bell Street, Marylebone by placing yourself upon a Stand for the purpose of delivering an address thereby encouraging a crowd of persons to remain upon and obstruct the said Highway and footway at 12 noon.*

THESE ARE THEREFORE TO COMMAND YOU in Her Majesty's name to be and appear on *Saturday* next, at *2* o'clock in the *After* noon, at the Police Court, aforesaid, before Me or such other Magistrate of the said Police Courts as may then be there, to answer to the said *information*, and to be further dealt with according to Law.

GIVEN under my Hand, and Seal, this *20* *L* Day of *July* in the Year of our Lord One Thousand Eight Hundred and Eighty- *Six* at the Police Court, aforesaid.

6 Summons. GENERAL FORM.

X M. 10,000 7 | 84 5887

Signed Mr. M. Cooke

89   Police summons issued to Morris on 20 July 1886 for wilful obstruction at Bell Street, Marylebone.

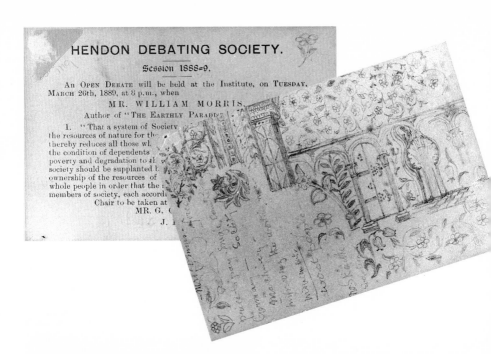

90 William Morris's own card for a political debate in Hendon on 26 March 1889. The reverse is
used for speech notes and Morris's characteristic floral and architectural doodles.
91 Andreas Scheu, the Viennese anarchist emigré and furniture designer, *c.* 1885. Scheu was a
close associate of Morris in the Democratic Federation and then the Socialist League.
92 Edward Carpenter, free-thinker, sandalmaker and poet, author of *Towards Democracy.*

93 Prince Peter Kropotkin, the Russian anarchist and early ecologist, who settled in north London in 1886. 94 Sergius Stepniak, the Russian nihilist who was a friend of Morris's.
95 Eleanor Marx photographed in about 1880, shortly before she and Edward Aveling announced their 'free marriage'. Both were to follow Morris into the Socialist League in 1885.
96 Henry Mayers Hyndman, founder of the Democratic Federation (later the SDF).

97 John Burns in his workshop with an apprentice *c*. 1888. Burns and Morris were colleagues in the early days of the Democratic Federation.   98 *Walter Crane*, portrait by G. F. Watts, 1891. His watered-down *art nouveau* set the style for the graphics of the Cause. 99 John Bruce Glasier, the young Glasgow Socialist who became Morris's most ardent disciple.   100 W. B. Yeats who, as a young man, attended Socialist lectures at Kelmscott House.

107 The first-floor drawing room at Kelmscott House, with *Prioresses' Tale* wardrobe painted by Edward Burne-Jones for Morris's marriage, and settle designed by Philip Webb, originally in use at Red Lion Square. Also visible are two 'Morris' armchairs.

108 The Coach House, adjacent to Kelmscott House and first used as a carpet workshop before being converted to the lecture room of the Hammersmith Socialists.

109 A Kelmscott Press group photograph of the early 1890s. Morris and May in front row, centre. Walker behind Morris; Sparling behind May.

110 Two of Morris's pressmen, William H. Bowden and W. Collins, at work on the folio edition of *The Works of Geoffrey Chaucer*, which occupied the Press from 1892 to 1896.

111 Sydney Cockerell, appointed Secretary to the Kelmscott Press in 1894.

112 Edward Burne-Jones, now Sir Edward, photographed by Barbara Leighton *c.* 1890.
113 Georgiana Burne-Jones reading. Photograph by Frederick Hollyer.   114 Emery Walker,
the process engraver and typographer. A long-standing Socialist ally of Morris's and his chief
adviser on the development of the Kelmscott Press.   115 Frederick Startridge Ellis, Morris's
publisher since the 1860s, one of the staunchest of the friends of his old age.

116 John Carruthers, engineer and maverick economist, author of *Economic Studies*, and a devoted associate of Morris's in the Hammersmith Socialist Society. Carruthers was his companion on his final journey through the Norwegian fjords.

117 May Morris at work. She became, in her own right, the leading embroiderer of her period
and founded the Women's Guild of Arts.
118 William Morris in his study in the early 1890s. Photograph by his son-in-law
Henry Halliday Sparling.

119 Morris in the years of his ill-health, photographed in the study at Kelmscott House in Hammersmith. The chair is covered in the 'Violet and Columbine' woven wool and mohair fabric he designed in 1883.
120 Funeral cart in which Morris's coffin was transported from Lechlade to Kelmscott Church, 10 October 1896.

121 Family group at Kelmscott in the years after Morris's death: May, her mother, Jenny and
Jenny's nurse-companion.
122 May and Miss Lobb on holiday in the mountains in the 1930s.

123 Philip Webb's design for William Morris's tombstone in St George's Churchyard at Kelmscott. He emphasized the grass as a tribute to Morris, lover of the rural landscape. Pencil drawing, 1896.

A few weeks later he was disappointed further by the reception of his lecture on 'Monopoly' at the Chiswick Hall Club, where he had 'a scanty audience *and* a dull. It was a new lecture, and good, though I say it, and I really did my best; but they hung on my hands as heavy as lead.'

On 22 March he gave his 'Feudal England' to an audience of nine people at Hammersmith Radical Club. With that unselfconscious mixture of the public and the private that makes this diary such compelling reading Morris notes his fifty-third birthday two days later: 'no use grumbling at that'.

On Sunday 27 March Morris tried again with his lecture on 'Monopoly' at the Borough of Hackney Club in Haggerston Road, one of the earliest of workmen's clubs in London. This was 'a big club numbering 1,600 members; a dirty wretched place enough giving a sad idea of the artisans' standard of comfort: the meeting was a full one, and I suppose I must say attentive; but the coming and going all the time, the pie-boy and the pot-boy was rather trying to my nerves: the audience was civil and inclined to agree, but I couldn't flatter myself that they mostly understood me, simple as the lecture was.' In the afternoon he was booked again to speak at a free-speech demonstration in Victoria Park. On his way he bought three pennyworth of shrimps. He ate these with ginger beer and bread and butter in a coffee shop which turned out to be 'not as dirty as it looked from the outside'.

What are we to make of Morris driving himself onwards from one nerve-racking meeting to another through the icy winter months of 1887? It was the worst weather he could remember since the 'Great Frost' of 1855. Winds were bitter and the recurring hard frosts made the open-air sites 'underfoot misery'. The unheated meeting-halls, 'tumble down sheds' and 'little dens' around the London suburbs, made the spreading of Socialism an endurance test: this may partly explain the paucity of the attendance at so many of the lectures. Even the Coach House was uncomfortably cold. The physical discomforts would have been made much more bearable if Morris's campaigning had been visibly successful. But it is clear from the diary that Morris was often in an agony of discontent, disappointed by the calibre and potential of his audiences whom he always expects to have a greater grasp of principles of Socialism, and frustrated by his own inability to communicate his message at the necessary basic level. After the Socialist Commune celebration he was covered in shame by his performance: 'I spoke last and, to my great vexation and shame, *very* badly; fortunately I was

557

hoarse, and so I hope they took that for an excuse; though it wasn't the reason; which was that I tried to be literary and original, and so paid for my egotism.' As he repeatedly told Georgie, Morris acted as he did because he felt he had to. The question that arises from the Socialist Diary is whether Morris's considerable energies for the Socialist cause could have been put to a more constructive use.

It is interesting that at this very period Morris's remarkable sister Isabella, now a widow, was making her independent contacts with the people living at poverty level in the London slums. In 1887 she became a deaconess in the Anglican church and founded the Rochester Diocesan Deaconess Institution which trained young women deaconesses and sent them out to do practical work among the London poor. Morris had supported Izzy in the face of considerable opposition from the family and she asked his advice on the decoration of the Deaconess Institution chapel in Park Hill, Clapham. She remembered: 'I got my brother William Morris to come and tell how I might make the chapel beautiful; he was in one of his happy tempers . . . he took the order off with him, and said his people would come and do it all and give me no trouble.' The sanctuary, when finished, was 'hung around with beautiful red velvet and high up with yellow Turkish muslin'. Morris's 'Windrush' chintz, in madder, was provided for the chapel walls and the floors were covered with a Japanese rush matting which unfortunately proved all too hospitable to the fleas brought in by the deaconesses from their poor parishes in Battersea.

Isabella Gilmore was a radical in seeking an active role for women within the government of the Church of England. Her vision and tenacity was very like her brother's. But she was no believer in class equality. Indeed she deliberately recruited well-bred girls as deaconesses, believing only 'ladies' had the discipline she needed for what was almost a female military operation going out into the 'wilderness of South London', caring for the sick, comforting the grieving, organizing holidays for the convalescent, establishing Ragged Schools, setting up Industrial Charities and Provident Clubs. Isabella's deaconesses were a curiously effective combination of nurse, social worker and amateur policewoman. They wore blue or grey merino dresses under large black cloaks; their lawn caps were surmounted by plain cottage bonnets tied with bows under the chin. Out in the streets they always wore a long gauze veil. This uniform made them immediately recognizable in the community, and gave them an instant authority: the deaconesses became adept at intervening in a drunken brawl. They were permanent fixtures, involved in the day-to-day life of the poor parishes, with a definite, indeed an endless, task to do. This made it relatively easy to establish a relationship. Isabella had no difficulties in communication: 'Tongues go fast enough,' she wrote, 'and sometimes merrily enough in cottage and Mission rooms, and often in a tram. I once passed a very merry hour between two fat costermonger women friends coming home from the Borough Market to Battersea, much to the amusement of the inmates.'

Morris once said to Isabella, 'I preach Socialism, you practise it.' He recognized that she achieved the thing he found so difficult, establishing a genuine rapport with the working class as individuals.

It was as a Socialist spokesman at mass protests that Morris, from now on, began to flourish. He could communicate most forcefully, and most emotionally, at a little distance from the crowd. The last, longest and most vivid of the entries in the Socialist Diary is his account of the series of mass meetings in Northumberland on behalf of striking miners in spring 1887. The strikers were protesting against a twelve and a half per cent reduction in wages. In its purism the Socialist League had tended to steer clear of strikes, which it regarded as short-term sensationalism, tending to deflect attention from the real issues. But when John Mahon wrote to Morris, then lecturing in Glasgow, asking him to travel south via Newcastle to attend the Easter Monday miners' meeting, Morris had reluctantly agreed. He was swayed by the fact that the SDF was involved in the agitation already: he was damned if he would 'let the SDF reap' where the Socialist League had sowed.

Morris arrived in Newcastle on Easter Sunday evening. He met Mahon and Alexander Donald, and he stumbled upon Hyndman who had been lecturing that evening. The strike was already in its eleventh week. Next morning the three of them set off for the collieries early, travelling by train through the 'wretched looking country'. There was no smoke, since the collieries were idle, but they noticed that all the roads were black with soot. The hideous Northumberland wasteland struck Morris as 'a "backyard" on a giant scale'.

At Sedghill, seven miles north-east of Newcastle, they stopped at a miner's cottage while Mahon went ahead to finalize the plans for the meeting at Horton the next day. Morris described the scene in the cottage: 'The goodman was a tall strong man his face wrecked by an accident which had blown out one eye and damaged the other: he seemed a kindly intelligent man, and gave us all information carefully, speaking without any bitterness against the masters . . . The man's wife and daughter were about, tidy and good-tempered women, his house was very clean as a cottage in the country, and so apparently were most of the others inside.' As in Iceland the people had surmounted their surroundings. In a letter to Jenny he adds the extra detail that in most of the cottages you could see through the open door 'a swell but ugly bedstead in the place of honour' in the centre of the room.

Morris and Mahon then travelled on to Blyth, on the coast, where they were to collect a detachment of the strikers. Morris could see the masts of the ships from the train as they arrived. A considerable crowd was waiting in the market place. Morris addressed them from a trolley for almost forty minutes. They set off in a rather 'draggle-tailed' procession because they could not afford a band. About half-way to Horton they picked up a band and banner and a lot more marchers. The excitement transfers itself to Morris's prose style as they 'soon swelled into a respectable company: the others had got there before us and lots more were streaming up into the field: the day was bright and sunny, the bright blue sea forming a strange border to the misery of the land'.

They marched six miles, accumulating followers at the villages they passed through. They were 2,000 strong when they arrived at Horton, converging with two other large detachments from other collieries. Groups of men and women were still streaming up the field from all directions. The crowd was estimated at 6,000 or 7,000 in all. The miners objected when they noticed some reporters and yelled to 'pit them out' unless they undertook to report every word of the proceedings. John Fielding of the SDF spoke first as chairman, then Mahon, then Morris, then Hyndman and then Donald. Morris was doubtful at first about mounting the 'rather perilous plank' above the rail of the wagon and suggested addressing the crowd from the wagon itself but the crowd would not have it: 'If yon man does na stand on the top we canna hear him.' So he climbed up on the plank. Someone in the crowd stuck an upturned noticeboard on a pole to provide a makeshift amateur lectern and passed it up to Morris who leaned on it as he spoke, and was 'pretty comfortable'. The men in the crowd near the wagon had sat down to give the crowd at the back a better view. Morris also noticed many women at the meeting, 'some of them much excited'. The mood of the assembly buoyed him up and gave him confidence. He told Jenny: 'It was very inspiriting to speak to such a crowd of eager and serious persons, and I did pretty well and didn't stumble at all.'

Morris's speech, as reported in *The Newcastle Chronicle*, was robust and to the point, expressing solidarity, inflammatory without being irresponsible. He urged the miners to rebel. But he warned against rebelling in 'a blind, unguided, unorganized manner' which would destroy the whole of our present society. Their rebellion should be conducted 'in such a way that it would be a kind of insurance against the violent deaths of the members of the upper classes'. At least his Hammersmith neighbours would survive.

Morris's résumé to 6,000 striking miners of the possible shape of the coming revolution is particularly fascinating at this juncture, thirty years before the Russian Revolution, forty years before the British General Strike, and indeed a century before the confrontation between Mrs Thatcher and Arthur Scargill at Orgreave in 1988:

If there was such a thing as a general strike he thought it was possible that the masters of society would attack them violently – he meant with hot shot, cold steel, and the rest of it. But let them remember that they [the men] were many and the masters were few. Masters could only attack with a certain instrument and what was that instrument? A part of the working classes themselves.

Morris at this point turned towards the policemen at the meeting:

Even those men that were dressed in blue with bright buttons upon them and white gloves – (voices: 'Out with them') – and those other men dressed in red, and also sometimes with gloves on their fingers, what were they? Simply working men, very hard up, driven into a corner and compelled to put on the livery of a set of masters ('Hear, hear' and prolonged hooting.) What would happen when they saw the workers were in earnest? The cannon would be turned round, the butts of muskets would go up, and the swords and bayonets be sheathed, and these men would say, 'give us work; let us all be honest men like yourselves'.

There were resounding cheers at the end of Morris's speech, after which there was a rush to catch the train for Newcastle. Morris set off with Donald and with Hyndman. Next day, back in London, he reached the Council meeting 'in time to come in for one of the usual silly squabbles about nothing'. In its flatness this reads like the ending to one of his dream narratives, the awakening to find oneself at home in one's own bed.

Morris wrote of himself in his Socialist Diary as a person who loathed 'all Classical art and literature'. It seems a perverse statement from a man then just completing his translation of *The Odyssey*. But Morris rated Homer as a supra-classicist. When *The Pall Mall Gazette*, in a Victorian equivalent of *Desert Island Discs*, asked Morris to provide a list of his 100 essential works of literature he included Homer in the uppermost category: 'the kind of book which Mazzini called "Bibles"; they cannot always be measured by a literary standard, but to me are far more important than any literature'. These were books that were in no sense the work of individuals but had 'grown up from the very hearts of the *people*'. With Homer, Morris listed the English Bible; Hesiod; the *Edda*; *Beowulf*; the *Kalevala*, *Shah-nameh* and *Mahabharata*; collections of folktales, headed by Grimm and the Norse legends; and Irish and Welsh traditional poems.

Morris had toyed with translating Homer's *Iliad*. But on balance he had decided to begin with *The Odyssey*, imagining he might yet return to do *The Iliad* in future. In fact he never did. In settling for *The Odyssey*, Morris had decided to translate it into the long, loose, rhyming couplets he had used for *Sigurd*. He claimed that he found it harder work than his *Aeneid* because of the 'great simplicity' of the original, which had no redundant words in it, no word without a precise meaning. In attempting, as he was, a close and literal translation he felt hemmed in by Homer's austerity.

However, he wrote 110 lines on the journey north to Edinburgh in September of 1886. He snatched two hours to work at it in Glasgow, between lectures. He was also working on *The Odyssey* in February 1887 on a so-called holiday with Ned and Georgie at Rottingdean. Sparling watched with fascination Morris's continuing capacity for working on so many projects simultaneously. While he was translating *The Odyssey*, he was writing his substantial lecture 'The Aims of Art' and the narrative fiction *A Dream of John Ball* as well as innumerable articles for *Commonweal*. He was also still producing some designs for Merton Abbey. 'He would be standing at an easel or sitting with a sketchbook in front of him, charcoal, brush or pencil in hand, and all the while would be grumbling Homer's Greek under his breath, "bumble-beeing" as his family called it – the design coming through in clear unhesitating strokes.' In April 1887 the first volume was published by Reeves & Turner. By August, Morris was complaining, 'I have now committed the irremediable error of finishing the Odyssey, all but a little bit of fair-copying. I am rather sad thereat.' The second, and final, volume was published in November. He admitted that he hoped to make 'a few pounds' from it, to recoup some of the money he had paid out to the Socialist cause.

The Odyssey, as much as The Aeneid, was a growth industry in mid-nineteenth-century Britain. In the 1860s there had been five major published versions, from Worsley's Spenserian stanzas of 1861 to Lovelace Bigge-Wither's accentuated blank verse. In the following decade there were the verse translations of Bryant, Mordaunt Barnard, Cordery and Schomberg, besides a prose version by Theodore Alois Buckley. In the 1880s Morris had been preceded by A. S. Way and C. H. Palmer. How does Morris's Odyssey appear in such a context? This is Morris's opening:

> Tell me, O Muse, of the Shifty, the man who wandered afar,
> After the Holy Burg, Troy-town, he had wasted with war.

Here is his account of the reunion of Odysseus and Penelope:

> So he spake, and her knees were loosened, and molten the heart in her breast,
> When she knew the soothfast tokens that her lord made manifest.
> And weeping she ran straight to him, and cast her arms about
> Odysseus' neck, and kissed him on his head and thus spake out . . .

It is respectable, even affecting. But compared with the better contemporary versions, G. A. Schomberg for instance, it sounds a little muzzy. It lacks the resonances of some later poetic-prose translations: Samuel Butler's (1900), for example; T. E. Lawrence's of 1932. Besides, as Oscar Wilde so rightly commented, Morris's Odyssey is 'far more Norse than Greek'.

It is foolish to be too critical of Morris. He was not, after all, in the academic rat-race. Maybe Mackail's lukewarm comments on the project arise from the fact that he was a professional scholar whose own verse translation of Homer appeared in 1905. Morris translated The Odyssey because he wanted to translate The Odyssey: it amused him and it gave him a respite from his political work.

The most interesting thing about it is the evidence it gives us of Morris's continuing fascination with the idea of the quest, the journey through outlandish territory, impelled onwards by some supernatural force. He perceives right at the heart of Homer's narrative the tale of Odysseus's early wanderings: 'a sort of fairy story with cannibals and giants and sorceresses and clashing rocks'.

A month after the completion of *The Odyssey*, Morris had started on a very different enterprise: a Socialist 'interlude', *The Tables Turned*; *or Nupkins Awakened*. This political mini-farce was first performed in the Socialist League hall in Farringdon Road on 15 November 1887 to raise funds for *Commonweal*, and it marked William Morris's début not only as a playwright but as an actor. He stepped into the role of the Archbishop of Canterbury offered to, but refused by, Walter Crane. This was the closest Morris ever came to the real-life role of bishop his mother had envisaged for him, though some members of the audience complained he looked more like an archimandrite of the Greek Orthodox Church. Shaw, who watched his performance with a critical eye, noted that he had not troubled with stage make-up, insisting that all that was required for stage illusion was a distinctive symbol for the character: the twentieth-century modernist view. 'A pair of clerical bands and black stockings proclaimed the archbishop: the rest he did by obliterating his humour and intelligence, and presenting his own person to the audience like a lantern with the light blown out, with a dull absorption in his own dignity which several minutes of the wildest screaming laughter at him when he entered could not disturb.'

The Tables Turned is a topical extravaganza with resemblances both to the mediaeval morality play and the zany political satire that flourished in Britain in the 1960s. It is almost a Victorian *Beyond the Fringe* or *That Was the Week That Was*. The plot is based on a Socialist trial for sedition and incitement to riot and murder, before Mr Justice Nupkins, a prejudiced and sycophantic judge. The day is saved by the outbreak of the revolution and the judge is himself sentenced to a life of rustic exile: he must learn to use a spade and dig potatoes and renounce the pompous jargon of London legal life. In the final scene the Socialists dance around him singing the freedom song 'Carmagnole'. Some of the characters are real people. The judge is a cartoon version of Sir Peter Edlin, before whom Sam Mainwaring and Jack Williams had stood trial at the Middlesex Sessions the year before. Tennyson is brought in as a defence witness. He is asked:

'My lord, have you been present, in disguise, at a meeting of the Socialist League in 13 Farringdon Road?'

'What's that to you? What do you want to know for? Yes, I have, if it comes to that.'

When asked for a description he says:

They sat and smoked; and one fool was in the chair and another fool read letters ... and now and then an old bald-headed fool and a stumpy little fool in blue made jokes, at which they laughed a great deal.

As Tennyson Morris had cast a Socialist League member, A. Brookes, who 'happened to combine the right sort of beard with a melancholy temperament, and drilled him in a certain portentous incivility of speech'.

He involved himself in all the details of production, instructing H. A. Barker, the Leaguer who was playing the Socialist ensign, at what exact angle he should carry the Red Flag. Another Socialist actor remembered the strong language the producer used at his rehearsals and how fiercely Morris stamped and shouted when anything went wrong. Harry Sparling took the leading role of Jack Freeman, the fiery Socialist, and May was Mary Pinch, the labourer's wife accused of stealing three loaves of bread. The scene of rural idyll gave her the opportunity to sing 'Come, lasses and lads' to her own guitar accompaniment. The play was an uproarious success. Shaw recollected he had never attended a first night so ecstatic:

I can still see quite clearly the long top floor of that warehouse in the Farringdon Road as I saw it in glimpses between my paroxysms, with Morris gravely on the stage in his bands at one end; Mrs Stillman, a tall and beautiful figure, rising like a delicate spire above a skyline of city chimney-pots at the other; and a motley sea of rolling, wallowing, guffawing Socialists between.

At the end of the performance Morris could be seen 'capering forward with a joy lit face' as he joined with the cast in the singing of the final hymn of thankfulness for Socialist victory.

The play received one professional review, from Shaw's dramatic critic colleague William Archer in *The Pall Mall Gazette*. He headed his notice ARISTOPHANES IN FARRINGDON ROAD, and he applauded the play's subversive form. After the accolades, evidently unexpected, it was decided to give repeat performances and *The Tables Turned* was seen at least ten times in London through the winter of 1887–88. There was even an idea of performing a version in translation to the Socialists in France. His success with comic dialogue encouraged Morris to continue with the genre. A whole series of topical moral confrontations was by now beginning to appear in *Commonweal*: 'The Rewards of Labour', 'The Boy Farms at Fault', 'Honesty is the Best Policy', all published in 1887, and 'Whigs Astray' (1889). As usual he could not resist including a self-portrait. In one he appears as Mr Olaf Evans, 'a kind of artist and literary man' given to reading aloud from his epic poem 'The Birth of the Bruce'; in another he is 'Owen Marx Boukounine Jones, an architect (unsuccessful)'. The dialogues are political extravaganza pieces curiously expressive of the character of Morris: intellectual and knockabout, genial and black.

Why did Morris not write more for the theatre? Shaw suggests it was because the English theatre was not ready for him. If only he had started a Kelmscott Theatre instead of a Kelmscott Press . . . It is pertinent to ask what effect *The Tables Turned* had in the end on the work of Shaw himself whose first play, *Widowers' Houses*, was produced in 1892. Conventional views of literary values, and the tendency to play down Morris's Socialist writings, belittled *The Tables Turned* and indeed ignored much of Morris's more wayward and original work. In 1912 May wrote to John Drinkwater who was then assembling the material for his critical biography: 'It is written in lighter mood for a Socialist entertainment. You will scarcely want to include it in your appreciation of my Father's experiments in poetic drama.' How wrong she was.

Eighteen eighty-seven was a winter of particular unrest in London. There was still great unemployment and new agitation surrounding the Irish nationalism question. From October the British Socialist and Anarchist groups had been united in their protests against the sentences of execution given, after a year's imprisonment, to the seven so-called 'Chicago Anarchists'. Morris saw this in terms of the battle between capitalists and the body of the workers: 'You probably know how much more violent and brutal such contests are in America than England, and of how little account human life is held there if it happens to thwart the progress of the dollar,' he wrote to Robert Browning, attempting to enlist his support for the campaign. The chief of the Metropolitan Police, Sir Edmund Henderson, had resigned after the 1886 London riots to be replaced by Sir Charles Warren, a hardliner. In the mood of mounting dissidence Warren had determined to ban public meetings in the most popular venue, Trafalgar Square. When *The Daily News* had printed a leader in support of his decision, Morris had protested in a letter to the editor, speaking with the authority of a specialist knowledge of positioning of buildings and the public use of space:

Sir – Apropos of the fitness of Trafalgar Square for public meetings, allow me to describe it briefly for the benefit of such of your readers as have not been in London. It is a large sunken area, capable of holding several thousand persons, of extremely easy access, and with wide streets leading from it in every direction, so that a meeting can easily disperse from it without choking the streets. It is dominated by the raised footway and balustrades on three sides, and the Nelson Column rises from the midst of the fourth side, affording good speaking platforms for the orators, while at the same time a crowd once in it is helpless for any harm if there is a good force of police in attendance. It is a place that nobody wants to walk through or loiter in except poor houseless persons driven to use it as a dormitory. In short, it is the most convenient place in all London for a large open air meeting, and to speak plainly, that is the reason why Sir C. Warren, acting, as you have practically told us, under instructions from the Tory Government, has closed it to the public.

Three days later, on 13 November, the day to be known as 'Bloody Sunday', Trafalgar Square was the scene of the most ruthless display of establishment power that London has ever seen.

The run-up to Bloody Sunday had the inexorability of the sequence of events that preceded the Tiananmen Square massacre in Beijing in 1989: Morris was correct in his diagnosis of the vulnerability of the crowd within the square. For some weeks before the unemployed had been straggling into the West End, down St Martin's Lane and into Trafalgar Square under a black flag. These became known as black flag processions. Once they reached Trafalgar Square the police would break them up. Through October the Socialists joined these demonstrations and the red flag replaced the black. The police repeatedly cleared the square of demonstrators, making arrests, taking away the flag. The Radical Federation's defiant announcement of a meeting against coercion in Ireland at three p.m. on Sunday 13 November had the predictable response: a proclamation by Sir Charles Warren definitely forbidding organized processions to Trafalgar Square.

On that Sunday about 10,000 unemployed workers, Radicals, Anarchists and Socialists assembled in different areas of London to begin their march towards the square. Morris marched with his Socialist League comrades, assembling at Clerkenwell Green with various other Socialist groups, including a branch of the SDF. Before they set off Morris and Annie Besant addressed the workers, about 5,000 in total; they were told to press forward to the square in an orderly manner and like good citizens. They did not realize when they set off, behind their band and banners, that the police had been stationed in force at strategic points around a radius of about a quarter of a mile from the square. As Morris explained bitterly in the next issue of *Commonweal*, Warren's strategy was carried through with such precision and efficiency that not one of those processions could escape falling into the meshes of this net: 'Into the net we marched.'

The attack on the Socialist League contingent came when the columns of marchers had crossed Shaftesbury Avenue and were just about to enter the crossroads at Seven Dials, on its way through to St Martin's Lane. The police attacked first from the front and the flank, completing the demolition of the column with a charge at the rear. 'It was all over in a few minutes,' wrote Morris: 'our comrades fought valiantly, but they had not learned how to stand and turn their column into a line, or to march on to the front. Those in front turned and faced their rear, not to run away, but join in the fray if opportunity served. The police struck right and left like what they were, soldiers attacking an enemy.' There were wild screams of indignation from the women living in the slums to the left. The band instruments were captured and the banners and flags destroyed, leaving no rallying point. The procession of protest disintegrated. All the marchers could now do was to straggle on into the square in little groups or on their own.

These scenes were repeated as other columns of protesters approached Trafalgar Square from different directions. Warren had deployed 2,000 police, reinforced by four squadrons of cavalry and 400 foot soldiers, each carrying twenty rounds of live ammunition. The column from west London, attacked as it came opposite the Haymarket Theatre, was demolished in two minutes by police rushing out from the side streets and immediately batoning everyone in reach, whether they resisted or not. Many reports confirm an unfocused brutality. According to a *Times* reporter, 'the police, mounted and on foot, charged in among the people, striking indiscriminately in all directions and causing complete disorder in the ranks of the processionists. I witnessed several cases of injury to men who had been struck on the head or the face by

:he police. The blood, in most instances, was flowing freely from the wound and the spectacle was indeed a sickening one.' Over 200 marchers were treated in hospital, only a fraction of the many people injured. Among those arrested were the Radical MP, R. B. Cunninghame Graham, and John Burns who only weeks earlier had been delighting the Socialist League audience, after *The Tables Turned*, with his song from *The Mikado* performed in Japanese costume with a Japanese umbrella. Both Cunninghame Graham and Burns were clubbed badly by the police in the course of their arrest.

Morris finally reached Trafalgar Square to find the police, horse and foot, completely in control. He wearily watched the ceremony of the Life Guards forming at the bottom of the square and marching up towards St Martin's where the magistrate, 'a sort of country-gentleman-looking imbecile', stood and read the Riot Act to the already docile crowd. The soldiers were cheered as well as hooted by people who seemed to imagine they would not be so brutal as the police. In his speech to the miners at Horton Morris had held out hopes that when the crisis came both the soldiers and the police would lay down their arms and come over to the workers. Now, in his bitterness, such visions of class solidarity waned and he said of the Life Guards: 'these gorgeous gentry are just the helmetted flunkies of the rich and would act on their orders just as their butlers or footmen would.'

The terrible scene stayed in his mind to haunt and taunt him. It appears, a grim image of deadening brutality, in *News from Nowhere* in which the events of 'Bloody Sunday' have been brought forward to 1952:

A strange sensation came over me; I shut my eyes to keep out the sight of the sun glittering on this fair abode of gardens, and for a moment there passed before them a phantasmagoria of another day. A great space surrounded by tall ugly houses, with an ugly church at the corner and a nondescript ugly cupolaed building at my back; the roadway thronged with a sweltering and excited crowd, dominated by omnibuses crowded with spectators. In the midst a paved be-fountained square, populated only by a few men dressed in blue, and a good many singularly ugly bronze images (one on top of a tall column). The said square guarded up to the edge of the roadway by a fourfold line of big men clad in blue, and across the southern roadway the helmets of a band of horse-soldiers, dead-white in the greyness of the chilly November afternoon.

The immediate effect of 'Bloody Sunday' upon Morris was to make him both more hopeful and more deeply pessimistic. He saw it as the first stage in inevitable uprising: 'As to the Trafalgar Square business I think it was a serious one; distinctly a sign of the recrudescence of the reaction which in its turn is a sign of the advance of the revolution,' he told William Bell Scott. But the ease with which the columns of the workers had been demolished by co-ordinated army and police action had shocked him and forced him to realize how uneducated the Socialist forces were in practical terms, how untrained and unprepared. It is notable that Morris, with his literary imaginings of the clashes of the swordsmen, the armed conflicts of the sagas, had no concept of the power of non-violent resistance, later to be used so effectively by Gandhi in India and by the anti-nuclear Committee of 100 in Britain in the 1960s, perfectly passive demonstration in the same Trafalgar Square.

May, who was so much beside her father at this period, points out that his protests both about the police brutality and the lack of solidarity between the Radical and Socialist parties were written 'from an angry heart, with no sense of exhilaration, no anticipation of the nearing of that greater freedom of life that he dreamed about and worked for'. Morris still believed in a revolution, but the promised days of happiness seemed ever further off.

The following Sunday there was a sequel. A relatively low-key demonstration was held in Hyde Park to protest against the Trafalgar Square outrages. Meanwhile mounted police were stationed in the square, dispersing and pursuing those who struck them as suspicious. In Northumberland Avenue, just south of the square, they knocked down a young Radical law-writer, Alfred Linnell, who subsequently died. The injustice of this random death inflamed the Socialists. For Linnell's funeral, finally held on Sunday 18 December after weeks of legal altercation about whether or not a horse had actually kicked him, a procession of protest and mourning was arranged. Morris composed a 'Death Song' which was sold for one penny for the benefit of Linnell's orphans with an effectively emotional Walter Crane woodcut, showing a mounted policeman with a truncheon and bearing the swirling banner 'Remember Trafalgar Square'.

The procession started in Soho, where Linnell's body had been lying at an undertaker's. In the early afternoon the coffin was loaded on to an open hearse with four horses by the six pall-bearers, William Morris, Cunninghame Graham, W. T. Stead, Herbert Burrows, Frank Smith

for H Buxton Forman   William Morris

SOLD FOR THE BENEFIT OF LINNELL'S ORPHANS.

ALFRED LINNELL

Killed in Trafalgar Square,

NOVEMBER 20, 1887.

A DEATH SONG,

BY MR. W. MORRIS.

Memorial Design by Mr. Walter Crane.

PRICE ONE PENNY.

41 Song sheet designed by Walter Crane for 'A Death Song', written by William Morris for Alfred Linnell's funeral, November 1887.

and Annie Besant. On top of the coffin was a black shield inscribed 'Killed in Trafalgar Square' and behind the shield were three flags, green, yellow and red, for the Irish, the Radicals and the Socialists. The band led the way, playing the 'Dead March' from *Saul*: a 'poor attempt', *The Times* sarcastically reported. Two mourning coaches and a wagon-ette containing the choir followed behind. The procession purposely avoided the square and took a route along the Strand, past St Paul's, Cheapside and Cornhill towards the cemetery ground near Linnell's home at Bow. As it wended its way east, more people joined the huge procession. It extended almost a mile by the time the hearse arrived at Mile End Road, with a mass of banners, mostly red, and several bands competing in slow marches. Great masses of people lined the wayside. A connoisseur of funerals marching behind Morris said he had not seen such a crowd of mourners since the Duke of Wellington's in 1852. 'There was to me', Morris wrote, 'something aweful (I can use no other word) in such a tremendous mass of people, unorganised, unhelped, and so harmless and good tempered.'

Progress was slow. They reached the cemetery at four-thirty. By then it was already a dark winter's afternoon and rain was beginning to fall. The coffin, covered with its black cloth, was set down within a few yards of the grave which had been decorated with evergreens and holly. On the coffin was a mound of wreaths from the Socialist and Radical supporters, including one from 'The Women of the Bloomsbury Branch of the SL'. The Rev. Stewart Headlam, leader of the Christian Socialists, read the Church of England burial service by the light of a lantern in the by now steadily pouring rain.

When the coffin had been lowered into the grave, several speeches were made, the majority of which were overtly political. It was Morris who gave much the most dignified and human of laments:

There lay a man of no particular party – a man who until a week or two ago was perfectly obscure, and probably was only known to a few . . . Their brother lay there – let them remember for all time this man as their brother and their friend . . . Their friend who lay there had had a hard life and met with a hard death; and if society had been differently constituted from what it was, that man's life might have been a delightful, a beautiful one, and a happy one to him. It was their business to try and make this earth a very beautiful and happy place. They were engaged in a most holy war, trying to prevent their rulers . . . making this great town of London nothing more than a prison. He could not help thinking the immense procession in which they had walked that day would have the effect of teaching a great lesson. He begged them to do their best to preserve order in getting back to their homes, because their enemies would be only too glad to throw a blot upon that most successful celebration; and they should begin to-morrow to organize for the purpose of seeing that such things should not happen again.

His Socialist League comrade H. A. Barker remembered how 'He threw his whole soul into his speech. There was a fearful earnestness in his voice when referring to the victim he had just laid to rest. He cried out, "Let us feel he *is* our brother". The ring of brotherly love in it was most affecting.' In the gathering gloom of the cemetery the crowd, led by the choir, began to sing the lugubriously stirring words of Morris's 'Death Song', set to Malcolm Lawson's music:

> What cometh from west to east a-wending?
> And who are these, the marchers stern and slow?
> We bear the message that the rich are sending
> Aback to those who bade them wake and know.
> *Not one, not one, nor thousands must they slay,*
> *But one and all if they would dusk the day.*

The Times, the next morning, quoted with some alarm from this ultimate revolutionary hymn.

Morris's role at the Linnell funeral subtly altered his standing in the Socialist movement. He had now become the well-known and the loved figure. There was a sense of awe, almost of 'He who comes among us'. He had gravitated into the movement's grand old man. The day after the funeral he turned to Barker and said he 'loved ceremony' with what was surely a beatific smile.

To Janey it seemed only a matter of time before Morris was arrested: 'My husband is not in prison yet, but I should think it would not be long before he will have an opportunity of writing the longest poem ever penned by man.' She wrote this in November 1887, to Wilfrid Scawen Blunt. Several of the Morrises' friends were now in danger. Blunt himself had been arrested in October 1887 at an anti-eviction meeting in Woodford in Galway and sentenced by magistrates to two months' imprisonment, but subsequently released on bail. He returned to England until the trial in January when he was sentenced to two months' hard labour, which he served in Galway and Kilmainham gaols.

573

Morris was mildly sympathetic about Blunt, but made the comment that at least the Irish prisons were better than the English. He never took Blunt's politics altogether seriously and no doubt he was irritated by Janey's all too evident concern. Of more direct interest to him was the fate awaiting Robert Cunninghame Graham and John Burns after their arrest in Trafalgar Square. Cunninghame Graham, the widely travelled, opinionated and amusing Scottish nationalist, had become a particular friend of his. Morris wrote of him: 'Cunninghame Graham is a very queer creature, and I can't easily make him out: he seems ambitious, and has some decent information.' However, his handwriting made Morris fear the worst: 'such a preposterous illegible scrawl as he does must have a screw loose.' There is a poignant example of 1880s' humour in the invitation sent out around their friends to Cunninghame Graham's appearance at the police court in November 1887 as if it were a social At Home: 'MRS CUNNINGHAME GRAHAM Bow Street Police Court'. Morris liked the joke and he accepted very fulsomely, sending his 'cordial congratulations on the honourable position in which Mr Graham's courage and foresight has placed him'.

Cunninghame Graham and Burns were sentenced to six weeks' imprisonment in Pentonville. Morris's worst fears about the state of British prisons were illustrated by the treatment they received. At the end of their sentences, in 19 February 1888, Morris went to Pentonville to greet them. He missed Cunninghame Graham, who was let out early and whose hand he shook as he was passing in a cab. He described the scene to Jenny:

So then we went on to the prison, and found . . . Burns walking up and down a by street waiting for his wife who hadn't come yet; so I went up to *him* and we had a talk, and he showed me the bit of bread that the poor men have for their breakfast and supper – just two mouthfuls – no more. He looked a good deal pulled down. Well then he went away, and I walked down the street to look at the miserable place and it made my blood boil to think that men should elaborate such a monument of folly, and thought how I should like to live to pull it down or turn it into a floor-cloth factory or something of that sort.

Morris would soon be writing *News from Nowhere* in which the Houses of Parliament have been turned into a Dung Market. The visionary transformation of buildings is already in his mind.

Outside the gates of Pentonville a small crowd had assembled to meet the released prisoners. Some thoughtful people had bought meat pies which they thrust into their hands. Morris noticed with what greed the prisoners 'wolved' them. That evening there was a Socialist League 'tea-drinking' to celebrate the returning heroes. May and Harry shared the serving with 'the big ex-sergeant major' of the Hammersmith Branch. Morris confessed to Jenny: 'As the meeting seemed likely to last until midnight (from 6 o'clock) May and Harry and I came away about 10 and we went and had supper at the Solferino and so home to bed.'

The momentous public events of the winter of 1887–88 in London had distracted attention from the Socialist League problems. But Morris had seen for some time that the League was in decline. Back in the summer of 1887 he had determined to put all his energies into holding it together for at least another year, but he admitted: 'It is a tough job; something like the worst kind of pig-driving I should think; and sometimes I lose my temper over it.' One of the things that most infuriated him about the internal squabbles was that on the whole the quarrellers got on well together personally. He tried to comfort himself with the reflection that this was simply history repeating itself: 'All this is very sickening: but I never heard of a revolutionary movement in which it didn't happen.' He attempted to be philosophical even at the prospect of a personal humiliation when it was suggested that *Commonweal*, in dire financial trouble, should be turned back to a monthly. 'True it would be a defeat', he wrote to Glasier, 'but we must get used to such trifles as defeats, and refuse to be discouraged by them. Indeed I am an old hand at that game, my life having been passed in being defeated; as surely as every man's life must be who finds himself forced into a position of being a little ahead of the average in his aspirations.' Morris faced, without bitterness, the painfulness of challenging the national preference for the second-rate.

By the beginning of 1888 even William Morris was losing his resilience. The Bloomsbury Branch, the most politically formidable of the Socialist League branches, whose membership included Edward and Eleanor Marx Aveling, A. K. Donald, Thomas and Will Binning and the most determined of the parliamentarian faction, started stirring up trouble, making demands for an amalgamation of all Socialist bodies. In fact years later, in the 1890s, Morris himself was to come round to this view. But for the moment he took it, as it was probably intended, as rebellion. He felt depressed and needled. Agitation made him absent-minded: at the end of a propaganda journey he discovered he had left his

575

whole bundle of *Commonweals* in the train. In March he wrote to Georgie:

I cannot shake off the feeling that I might have done much more in these recent matters than I have; though I really don't know what I could have done: but I feel beaten and humbled. Yet one ought not to be down in the mouth about matters; for I certainly never thought that things would have gone on so fast as they have in the last three years; only, again, as opinion spreads, organization does not spread with it.

He could see that if the Bloomsbury Branch pursued what he described as its 'mischievous resolution' at the Socialist League's annual conference, this would have the effect of driving a wedge between the parliamentarians and anti-parliamentarians and would force a break-up of the League.

The Fourth Annual Conference was held on 20 May 1888. Bruce Glasier, Morris's ally from the Glasgow Branch, was staying at Kelmscott House. After breakfast the local of the comrades, including Emery Walker and H. B. Tarleton, an anti-parliamentarian on the League executive, assembled in the library. With Morris and May they travelled by omnibus from Hammersmith Broadway to the meeting at Farringdon Road. It was a long day, with discussions continuing from ten-thirty in the morning to nearly ten at night. The result was not an out-and-out disaster for the League. The Bloomsbury resolution was

42 Political squib aimed at Morris by the anti-parliamentarians in the Bloomsbury Branch of the Socialist League.

rejected. The parliamentarians refused to stand for election to the Council. Morris seconded a resolution recommending the Council 'to take steps to reconciliate or, if necessary, exclude the Bloomsbury Branch' from the League. A week later the Bloomsbury Branch was suspended, on the technical grounds that it had sold 'publicly in the streets' an 'illustrated squib' ridiculing Morris and his adherents. Subsequently an independent Bloomsbury Socialist Society was formed.

The Socialist League was still in existence. Morris had not lost his temper in public, as he boasted to Janey at the dinner table in Hammersmith on the evening of the conference. He sighed with relief that 'the damned business' was over for another year and promised himself a late-night celebration reading from *Huckleberry Finn*. But this is not to say that Morris did not realize the implications. He told Glasier, 'We have got rid of the parliamentarians, and now our anarchist friends will drive the team.'

In a curiously revealing little episode, Morris ended the day in one of his frightening paroxysms of anger. The initial provocation was a small one: Glasier had made a naïve comment about one of Ned's paintings, the 'Sea Nymph', which he had just viewed at the New Gallery. He told Morris that it seemed as if the artist was trying to imitate some very early style of art rather than nature itself. Glasier was astounded as Morris turned upon him: 'Hardly had I completed my sentence than Morris was on his feet, storming words upon me that shook the room. His eyes flamed as with actual fire, his shaggy mane rose like a burning crest, his whiskers and moustache bristled like pine-needles.' There, in Glasier's bedroom, he launched into a hysterical attack on the artistic degradation of the age: the 'damnable architecture, the damnable furniture, and the detestable dress of men and women'. He stormed up and down the room like a caged lion', as Glasier trembled on the edge of his bed.

Morris was now isolated in the League. With the loss of the Avelings and Alexander Donald much of the party's intellectual strength had gone. Bax too deserted Morris and in 1888 rejoined the SDF. Meanwhile the Anarchist wing of the League had gathered confidence from the growth and growing ambitiousness of the Anarchist movement in the country as a whole, following the protests at the execution of the Chicago Anarchists. There was a new Anarchist group within the League, more vocal and extreme than the old 'Chaucerian' leftist triumvirate of Lane, Kitz and Mainwaring. These declared and committed

577

Socialist League Anarchists were led by Charles Mowbray, the East End tailor who had served in the army and was a printer of subversive literature; Fred Slaughter (alias 'Fred Charles'), a clerk who like Mowbray came from Norwich, and had now become secretary to the Council of the League; and David Nicoll, the League's librarian and propaganda secretary, an emotionally unstable Anarchist propagandist still in his mid-twenties, who compiled the 'Revolutionary Calendar' for *Commonweal*. The Anarchists put pressure upon Morris to divert the Socialist League to violent action. At the end of 1888, he was still complaining of 'a sort of curse' of quarrelling: 'The Anarchist element in us seem determined to drive things to extremity and break us up if we do not declare for anarchy: which I for one will not do.'

Through the various turmoils of the Socialist League, Morris had always been able to rely on Philip Webb and Charley Faulkner, much the oldest of his comrades. But in the past two years Webb had been frequently unwell, and in October 1888, three days after giving the Sunday night lecture in the Coach House, Faulkner had the stroke that left him permanently paralysed, in a state of 'living death'. Morris's grief was intense. His friendship with Faulkner, on the surface so jovial and hail-fellow-well-met, had an inner core of deep emotionalism, recognized by Webb: 'The unbreakable courage and clear honesty of Faulkner held Morris as closely as friendship, pure and simple, could bind two men together, regardless of difference in quality of mind. They each did for the other what they could not have done for anyone else; and I had the good luck to be alive to this perfect love.'

Faulkner had never married. He devoted all his energy to Morris and the Socialist League, jeopardizing his academic career. The League files in Amsterdam hold the poignant records of his efforts: his fruitless attempts to get the newsagents in Oxford to distribute *Commonweal*; his donation of his MA gown, now green with age, for a Socialist League performance; his and Webb's subsidy of the League. They were both paying one pound towards salaries and one pound to the *Commonweal* fund every week in 1888. Morris, on his anguished visits to a now barely communicating Charley, felt some of the same guilt that Jenny's illness had induced in him: 'It is such a grievous business altogether that, rightly or wrongly, I try not to think of it too much lest I should give way altogether, and make an end of what small use there may be in my life.' Ned too felt great despair as Charley lingered on so painfully. When Faulkner finally died three years later, he unequivocally and angrily blamed his Socialism: 'Oh yes, it killed him, by the most painful of deaths.'

Disappointment and grief bore in on Morris. On Wilfred Blunt's first visit to Kelmscott in November 1889, a visit on which his 'intimacy was renewed' with Mrs Morris, he found him 'going through a period of disenchantment with regard to public affairs'.

In June 1889 Morris was in Paris for what was in effect his Socialist League swansong. He and Frank Kitz were the League's delegates to the International Socialist Working Men's Congress, which was to be the basis of the Second International. The Congress was attended by delegates from all over Europe and from America. Over plans for this conference Morris was again in contact with Engels, though it seems doubtful if this altered Engels' view of him as 'a settled sentimental socialist'. He was by now scornful of Morris's political impotence as a 'puppet' of the Anarchists.

Morris's last visit to Paris had been in January 1883, when he had accompanied Thomas Armstrong of the South Kensington Museum to bid for a fine collection of historic textiles. They had dined at an excellent though inexpensive restaurant where Morris had ordered goujons of sole. The scene sixteen years later, in the blazing heat of summer, was altogether different. Morris approved of the internationalist purpose of the Congress and he found the 'earnestness and enthusiasm' of the individual delegates impressive. But the administration was chaotic. Edward Carpenter, the delegate from the Sheffield Socialists, described how they sat 'from 10 to 4, regardless of dinner – martyrs to the cause! the noise and excitement at times was terrific. The president ringing his bell half the time – climbing on his chair, on the table – anything to keep order – personal disputes occasionally taking place – several delegates talking at once etc. etc.' Eleanor Marx Aveling, one of the translators, could not make her voice heard above the confusion. Morris became more and more impatient at this Tower of Babel. The tensions were exacerbated by the fact that there was not one but two International Congresses in progress in Paris, simultaneously. One had been convened by the orthodox Marxists or Guesdists, led by Jules Guesde. This was the conference that Morris was attending. At another meeting-hall the Possibilists had gathered. These were also known as the Broussists, supporters of Dr Paul Brousse, in favour of more immediate practical reforms. Two days were spent by the Marxists in discussing

feasibility of fusion with the Possibilist Congress so that many resolutions were left undiscussed.

Morris had been chosen as the English spokesman by the international committee, in which the German Marxists predominated. This
gives us an indication of his international standing at the time. He
provided a fair and reasonably optimistic summary of the state of British
Socialism: 'Altogether though our organization is very bad in England
still we are getting on very well. We are thoroughly International in
spirit and we add a distinct contribution to the Socialist movement in
supporting the aesthetic side.' He pointed out that the Socialist League
itself was not in favour of going into Parliament but he mentioned with
tentative approval 'the new County Councils'. Local government in
Britain was being overhauled and in 1888 elected county councils were
brought in as the replacement of the County magistrates' Quarter Sessions meetings. Morris welcomed what he saw as the step back in the
direction of the populist Althing, the old Parliament of Iceland. He told
the Paris conference the County Councils 'seemed like being the germ of
real local self-government'.

Carpenter listened enthralled to Morris's speech, which he saw as
refreshingly homely:

After the glib oratorical periods of Jules Guesde and others, what a contrast to
see Morris – in navy blue pilot shirt – fighting furiously there on the platform
with his own words (he was not feeling well that day), hacking and hewing the
stubborn English phrases out – his tangled grey mane tossing, his features
reddening with the effort! But the effect was remarkable. Something in the
solid English way of looking at things, the common sense and practical outlook
on the world, the earnestness and tenacity, as of a skipper beating up against
wind and wave on the great deep, made that speech one of the most effective in
the session.

Morris was absent from the last day of the conference, showing Rouen,
his best of all cathedrals, to his Socialist comrades Tarleton and Kitz.

Morris returned from Paris to face a protracted break-up of the League.
By autumn 1889 the branches were declining: Edinburgh amalgamated
with the local SDF to form the Scottish Socialist Federation. Glasgow,
Leicester, Norwich and Yarmouth were now dominated by the Anarchists, while others, including Leeds, Bradford and Manchester, had
gravitated to the parliamentarians. In the great Dock Strike in London

in August, and in the gas workers' and tailoresses' strikes in Leeds that autumn, the Socialist League, with no point of contact with the militant workers, was all too evidently out on a limb. The League now stood apparently deliberately apart from the mass movement towards trades unionism getting under way, particularly in the north. New propaganda papers – Keir Hardie's *Miner*, *Labour Elector*, the *Yorkshire Factory Times* – seemed more directly in touch with current issues than *Commonweal*. The Socialist League made suicidal blunders. When it came to May Day 1890, the Council decided on Thursday 1 May as the day of celebration while the London Trades Council had decided to hold a May Day rally on Sunday 4 May. A few thousands turned up at Clerkenwell Green whereas more than 100,000 were at the trades union rally in Hyde Park. There were only fourteen delegates at the sixth Annual Conference on 25 May.

This was the usual long meeting dragging on from ten a.m. to ten p.m. in the big bare Socialist Hall above the clatter of Farringdon Road. But it was much tenser than any of its predecessors as the Anarchists dominated the proceedings, electing themselves in force on to the executive and isolating Morris with Philip Webb and the two Hammersmith Branch members. Morris, as treasurer, managed on the whole to keep his temper except when cross-examined on a detail of his Financial Report when he retorted, 'Well, Mr. Chairman, I can't see that it matters a damn; for I receive £10 in one hand, and with the other I pay out £50.' In fact at this period Morris was subsidizing the League, including *Commonweal*, at a rate of £500 a year.

At the meeting the Anarchists succeeded in ousting Morris and Sparling from the editorship and replacing them with Kitz and Nicoll. May described the scene as these manoeuvrings continued:

It is four o'clock; the air is heavy with tobacco-smoke, with dust and London dullness; and the person who has the floor is driving us almost to tears of boredom by a long discourse on ill-digested political economy, under cover of speaking to a resolution. On the platform, the Chairman fidgets with his agenda-paper and the Treasurer with raised eyebrows draws flower-patterns all over the margins of his sheet of notes. Suddenly he flings himself back in his chair which creaks under him, and exclaims in a voice which rolls all down the long dull room: 'Mr. Chairman, *can't* we get on with the business? I want my TEA!'

After the conference, the Hammersmith party took the train home and walked down from the High Street to the freshness of the river, standing for a few minutes under the elm trees and looking over the black water in the moonlight. It seemed to May like a scene from *News from Nowhere*. A small tug with a string of laden barges went past, making waves that broke against the stone bastion where they stood. 'This is better than Farringdon Road,' said someone. 'The wind's in the West,' said Morris, breathing deeply. 'I can almost smell the country.'

Morris did not withdraw his support immediately. He resisted the making of an ending although he had seen it coming for so long. But the contents of *Commonweal* became increasingly provocative as well as less literate. Nicoll was calling for immediate barricades. In the No Rent Campaign, H. B. Samuels, a Leeds anarchist, contributed a bloodthirsty account of the attack on the blacklegs in the Leeds gas strike: 'If the people had only had the knowledge the whole cursed lot would have been wiped out. As the horses and men picked themselves up, it was seen that many were bruised and bleeding, but, alas!, no corpses to be seen.' Morris, still *Commonweal*'s proprietor and publisher, would have had to bear the brunt of any public prosecution of a paper he continued to finance. He was forced to write and remonstrate with Nicoll:

I have been looking at this week's *Commonweal*, and I must say that I think you are going too far: at any rate further than I can follow you. You really must put the curb upon Samuels's blatant folly, or you will *force* me to withdraw all support. I never bargained for this sort of thing when I gave up the editorship.

He still attempted to be calming and conciliatory. He told Nicoll, 'I look upon you as a sensible and friendly fellow, and I am sure that you will take this in a friendly spirit as it is meant to you ... Please understand that this is meant to be quite private, and do your best not to drive me off.' But Morris knew in his heart the situation was irreparable. And when Samuels was later revealed to be a police spy the tragedy took on an element of farce.

Morris's indulgence was 'often painful to witness' and was counter-productive since it 'opened the door to all sorts of doubtful characters', as Andreas Scheu was later to point out. Through the late summer the Socialist League was becoming power-crazy through its own impotence. On 3 August a 'Revolutionary Conference' was held at the Autonomie Club in London. Six London and four provincial branches attended, with a dozen or so obscure groups of foreign refugees. 'All red-tapeism and quasi-authoritarianism were banished.' The office of chairman at the meeting was abolished. The conference was set up to plan for United International Action for a European Crisis. Mowbray's proposal in the event of a crisis at home was 'to fire the slums and get the people into the West-end mansions'. Kitz declaimed 'we should preach to the thieves, the paupers and the prostitutes . . . The first act of the Revolution ought to be to open the prison doors.' Morris, wisely, did not attend the meeting. He was at Kelmscott Manor a good deal at the beginning of the autumn and, without publicizing his decision, by November had decided definitely to go. He wrote to Glasier:

I never wait to be *kicked* downstairs . . . we have borne with it all a long time; and *at last* have gone somewhat suddenly . . . Personally, I must tell you I feel twice the man since I have spoken out. I dread a quarrel above all things, and I have had this one on my mind for a year or more. But I am glad it is over at last; for in good truth I would almost as soon join a White Rose Society as an Anarchist one; such nonsense as I deem the latter.

On 21 November 1890 the Hammersmith Branch severed its connection with the Socialist League and Morris retreated to his own home ground. The branch was renamed the Hammersmith Socialist Society with Emery Walker reinstated as its secretary, and a new banner was designed. At that time the Hammersmith Branch consisted of 120 members. This, in Morris's estimation, was as many as the entire membership of the rump Socialist League.

On 9 December, in the black and stormy weather of a bitterly cold winter, Morris settled down to write yet another party manifesto, disclaiming both the parliamentarians and Anarchists: 'it is a troublesome and difficult job, and I had so much rather go on with my Saga work.'

Morris made his official farewell to the League in an article in *Commonweal*, 'Where Are We Now?', a résumé of the past seven years of Socialist activity and what he felt it had achieved in raising public consciousness: 'Few movements surely have made so much progress during this short time.' But his real farewell was the serial that had been appearing in the paper regularly all through this troubled period, from 11 January to 4 October 1890, and which was probably responsible for the small rise in circulation from April of that year. *News from Nowhere* was revised for publication in book form in March 1891. It is Morris's most enduringly popular and most wonderfully disconcerting work. Janey, writing to Blunt, arrives at a very good description of the almost indescribable: she explains that Morris's story gives 'a picture of what he considers likely to take place later on, when Socialism shall have taken root'.

News from Nowhere is in a tradition of the futuristic novel that Morris, long attracted to it, pursued with a new fervour in the years of his Socialist conversion. He was reading Thomas More's *Utopia* aloud at Kelmscott Manor in the autumn of the year he joined the Democratic Federation, and at that same period he read with admiration Samuel Butler's satirical fantasy *Erewhon* (1872) about an imaginary country where morality is equated with health and beauty and where the development of machinery, which had threatened to usurp human supremacy and brought about a civil war, has now been banned. More's *Utopia* appears between George Borrow and John Ruskin in Morris's list of his 100 best books.

The immediate spur to *News from Nowhere* was a contemporary novel, *Looking Backward*, by an American writer, Edward Bellamy. This book was published in 1888 and, like *After London* a few years earlier, it soon became the book that everyone was reading. The plot centres on a young Bostonian, Julian West, who falls into a trance in 1887 to awake in the year 2000 and find himself in a country almost unrecognizably transformed. A new social order has taken over in which capitalism has disappeared and all citizens work for and are members of the State. Bellamy's picture of a rigid and centralized state system in which the machines were virtually masters was anathema to Morris. He wrote to Glasier: 'I suppose you have seen or read, or at least tried to read 'Looking Backward'. I *had* to on Saturday, having promised to lecture on it. Thank you, I wouldn't care to live in such a cockney paradise as he imagines.' It provoked him into saying that, 'if they brigaded *him* into a regiment of workers he would just lie on his back and kick'. In a long review of the book in *Commonweal* he expanded his objections to the aridity of life in Bellamy's state Communist regime serviced by 'a huge standing army, tightly drilled, compelled by some mysterious fate to unceasing anxiety for the production of wares to satisfy every caprice, however wasteful and absurd'. The glitteringly fluid, poetic, open-ended *News from Nowhere* is Morris's riposte.

This is another of Morris's dream narratives, beginning in the present at one of the interminable Socialist meetings with six comrades present and six sections of the party represented, 'four of which had strong but divergent Anarchist opinions'. We can easily read into *News from Nowhere* a subversive, autobiographical sub-text for the Anarchists, appearing as it did in the paper Morris founded, now almost completely under Anarchist control. The discussion was on the future of society on the Morrow of the Revolution. 'If I could but see it! If I could but see it!' mutters the narrator, William Guest, a version of Morris, as he returns to his house by the riverside at Hammersmith . . . When Guest awakes it is in brilliant hot sunshine, to find a world transformed.

The peculiar magic of Morris's *News from Nowhere* is its disorientation. Where are we and when is it? This is and is not England. It is a place of communistic freedom, where men, women and children are equal, beautiful and healthy; money, prisons, formal education and central government have been abolished; the countryside has been reclaimed from industrial squalor and pollution. In this country momentous events are remembered to have taken place in 1952. Guest sets out to get his bearings, arriving at the Guest house in Hammersmith, where the commemorative plaque informs him this was once the lecture room of the Hammersmith Socialists. He acquires a guide, Robert Hammond, and an interpreter of the past, Old Hammond. In the long conversations between Guest and Old Hammond, Guest asking obtuse questions, Hammond answering him patiently, the comic moral dialogues Morris originally wrote for *Commonweal* acquire a new satiric edge.

In the final chapters Guest leaves London with Robert, his wife Clara, and the freckled, windswept and intelligent girl Ellen, Morris's dream combination of Pre-Raphaelite angel and Socialist New Woman, eternally within and out of reach. This is the famous journey by boat up the Thames to the house that so closely resembles Kelmscott Manor, 'the many gabled old house built by the simple country-folk of the long-past times'. Desire can go no further. It is here the dream must end.

Guest comes to with a thud. There is an interlude of darkness, described in terms of the surfacing from a fit or faint, and he is back in 'dingy Hammersmith'. But 'indeed *was* it a dream?' The question is never answered. Morris has out-argued Bellamy and *Looking Backward* in the personal terms of his own Socialist life history. This is the generous vision he has held to, and still holds to in 1890, stubbornly:

Dick brought me at once into the little field which, as I had seen from the garden, was covered with gaily-coloured tents arranged in orderly lanes, about which were sitting and lying on the grass some fifty or sixty men, women and children, all of them in the height of good temper and enjoyment – with their holiday mood on, so to say.

Here are the haymakers, assembled near the river, a group of resplendently well dressed, well adjusted, healthy people, who take work seriously and put no strict boundaries between their work and leisure. It is the attitude to work in *News from Nowhere* that challenges most passionately and surprisingly the prevailing nineteenth-century attitudes.

There is also the immediacy of the response to nature. As Hammond delineates it: 'The spirit of the new days, of our days, has to be delight in the life in the world.' The form this joy takes is physical and sensual, explained in terms of sexual passion, of fondling, pressing, merging. The sexual act is seen as replicating, celebrating the shifting planes and variations of texture of the land itself. With this heightened physical awareness comes awakened interest in 'all the little details of life': the weather, the hay crop, the latest new house, the presence or absence of the birds. In Nowhere almost everyone, even intellectuals and scholars, talks about these things with real interest, 'not in a fatuous or conventional way'. Women know as much about them as men. Guest, the critic, cannot get used to this:

'How strangely you talk', said I, 'of such a constantly returning and consequently commonplace matter as the sequence of the seasons.' And indeed these people were like children about such things . . .

Related to the reawakened interest in life's intimate detail has been the 'recovery' of the domestic arts. Whereas before the revolution bread was sent to the country from London, delivered with the newspapers on the early train, bread in Nowhere is available, as it is again now in England in the middle 1990s, in 'several different kinds, from the big, rather close, dark-coloured, sweeter tasting farmhouse loaf' to 'the thin pipe-stems of wheaten crust', the *grissini* Hammond remembered eating in Turin. There is no more selfconsciousness in dealings between people. People call each other 'neighbour' and they touch each other constantly. There are no inhibitions about the free expression of admiration and sexual desire.

In this transformed England, fluent, beautiful, evocative, there is no dividing line between the country life and town life. In London the soap works Guest used to know had vanished, with their smoke-vomiting chimneys. New vistas of the Thames at Hammersmith revealed a river-edge grown over and rebuilt:

Both shores had a line of very pretty houses, low and not large, standing back a little way from the river; they were mostly built of red brick and roofed with tiles, and looked, above all, comfortable, and as if they were, so to say, alive and sympathetic with the life of the dwellers in them. There was a continuous garden in front of them, going down to the water's edge, in which the flowers were now blooming luxuriantly, and sending delicious waves of summer scent over the eddying stream. Behind the houses, I could see great trees rising, mostly planes, and looking down the water there were the reaches towards Putney almost as if they were a lake with a forest shore, so thick were the big trees.

Morris's visionary landscape is both decorous and lavish, mysterious and homely, an extraordinary and deeply imagined image of urban possibility. We can see its effect as the Garden Cities burgeoned early on in the next century and other writers worked their own transforming visions of the landscape, D. H. Lawrence envisaging his mining village turned into a New Jerusalem.

Many thousands of words have been spent on the interpreting of *News from Nowhere*, with intellectual contortions that would have kept Morris in guffaws. The laborious attacks on Nowhere's economics, its technology, its race relations, are absurd in a book that was never intended as a blueprint from which people could plan a working social system. Glasier got closer to it when he described the book as Morris's *jeu d'esprit*. This is not to say it does not have a deep and influential inner seriousness. Its effect is as a catalyst. Morris releases the imagination by suggesting that another form of society is *possible*. For people suffering political stagnation – then and now – it points to a way out. By 1898 *News from Nowhere* had been translated into French, Italian and German, and this 'slightly constructed and essentially insular romance' was being read in many more countries than his 'more important works of prose and verse', to the disapproval of his first biographer, Mackail. It was widely distributed in Russia in the years just before the Revolution. It was also the Socialist Bible of the supposedly dyspeptic politicians who built the post-war British Welfare State: G. D. H. Cole, Clement Attlee and the rest.

For the late-twentieth-century reader the message we recognize in *News from Nowhere* is 'the personal is political'. Morris shows an almost

587

uncanny prescience of many of the issues addressed by the feminist and gay liberation movements in Europe and the USA from the 1960s on. Nowhere is a place of real sexual equality. Women do work traditionally regarded as men's work and vice versa. Ideas of possessiveness and ownership have vanished. In all sexual liaisons the partners are free to come and go. Old Hammond comments:

We do not deceive ourselves, indeed, or believe that we can get rid of all the trouble that besets the dealings between the sexes. We know that we must face the unhappiness that comes of a man and woman confusing the relations between natural passion, and sentiment, and the friendship which, when things go well, softens the awakening from passing illusions: but we are not so mad as to pile up degradation on that unhappiness by engaging in sordid squabbles about livelihood and position, and the power of tyrannising over the children who have been the result of love or lust.

In Ellen, Morris makes himself a twentieth-century heroine: feminine and boyish, sexual and yet almost asexual, intelligent and animal:

She led me up close to the house, and laid her shapely sun browned hand and arm on the lichened wall as if to embrace it, and cried out, 'O me! O me! How I love the earth, and the seasons, and weather, and all things that deal with it, and all that grows of it – as this has done!'

This must rate as one of the most passionately erotic invitations in any novel of the time.

'Morris's views on sexual entanglements are set out in *News from Nowhere*', wrote Sydney Cockerell primly. When Bruce Glasier told him he had fallen in love with Ellen, Morris replied 'that he had fallen in love with her himself!'

CHAPTER SEVENTEEN

Hammersmith, One: 1890–93

There is a powerfully prophetic passage in *A Dream of John Ball*:

I pondered how men fight and lose the battle, and the thing that they fought for comes about in spite of their defeat, and when it comes turns out to be not what they meant, and other men have to fight for what they meant under another name.

By 1890 Morris's direct political influence was virtually over and the Socialist League in sad disarray. He had retreated back to Hammersmith with his few staunch allies; the activities of the Hammersmith Socialist Society were necessarily low-key. With its battle cry of 'Agitate! Educate! Organise!' Morris's Socialism already seemed part of another era as Fabianism, the trades union movement, the parliamentary Labour party began to gather strength. It might have been expected that Morris's creative energy would dwindle and indeed this last phase in Morris's life is often represented as a period of retrenchment, of withdrawal. The very opposite is true.

The post-Socialist phase, with Morris now in his late fifties, is the period at which much work can be seen to reach fruition. In the 1890s he was writing a whole series of new novels of imaginary landscape and dream sequence, the development of themes suggested earlier in so many of his stories and his poems. Morris & Co. stained glass and tapestries and interiors were all in their culminating phase. In May 1891 the Kelmscott Press was printing the first of the sixty-six volumes to be published in the next seven years. Most important of all was the visible impact of Morris's ideas on art and society and attitudes to making. The Arts and Crafts movement spread through the late-nineteenth- and early twentieth-century Europe and America, spawning a whole series of visionary craft communities, exploring the philosophy of simple life. This was Morris's most tangible and crucial achievement, the ultimate expression of his Socialist beliefs. It was not quite what he meant by the Revolution. And yet this workshop movement has been a revolution in terms of the challenge to conventional views of work and leisure, the things we choose to make and the ways we use our lives.

For over thirty years, since the small beginnings at Red Lion Square, Morris had been evolving radical new ways of working, not in principle but practice. This is what made him a much more effective practical design reformer than John Ruskin: he was involved in the techniques of the workshop. He could demonstrate how the thing was done. In a totally convincing way he showed the wrong-headedness in separating off the design process from making: one was a necessary stage towards the other; the designer and maker could be one and the same person, the person who came to be defined as artist-craftsman. Another false perception he attacked was that the fine artist had no role in industrial production. Morris had designed for many factories and workshops, on varying scales and in different materials, and had proved this to be patently untrue. As May, who worked with him, observed:

He was in direct relation with silk-weavers and carpet-weavers, dyers and blockers, with pattern-makers and block-cutters, with cabinet makers and carvers in wood; with glass painters, kiln-men and labourers and with his wallpaper printers; and it was not as if he sat in an office and received reports from managers of different departments with the technical details of which he was unfamiliar: he had grasped the nature of those he employed – understanding their limitations as well as their capabilities.

Morris's strength, the principle he passed on to another generation of artist-craftsmen, derived from the acquisition of skill. Nothing was embarked on in his workshops that he did not know how to do himself. The sheer range of crafts he covered was also influential: these were mainly crafts to do with furnishing and building, deriving from architecture as the 'mother art'. The ideal of fellowship, the working band of brothers, traceable back to the Pre-Raphaelite Brotherhood, inherent in the founding of Morris, Marshall, Faulkner & Co., was extended by Morris in his Socialist lectures into a more generalized vision of workshops and idyllic small-scale factories, gregarious, productive, joyful places with built-in training schemes and mutual support systems on the lines of the mediaeval guilds. The most radical innovation was of course the social one: the concept of the educated person pursuing what might be known as handwork but in fact was manual labour, traditional occupation of the artisan.

Through the 1880s these ideas had taken root. The first quasi-Morris workshop to be formed was the Century Guild in 1882. This was the partnership of designers led by A. H. Mackmurdo, architect, sociologist and impractical economist, a disciple of Ruskin's with whom he had travelled to Italy in 1874. Mackmurdo's father was a successful manufacturer of chemicals and a member of the Fishmongers' Company in London. His mother was a D'Oyly Carte of the family who first promoted Gilbert and Sullivan. The brilliant and quirky Mackmurdo was no passive admirer of Morris's: 'He had no hope in the world except through Revolution. I had great hope in the world through Evolution and we crossed swords upon this many a time.' But he always left Morris 'impressed with his great vigour'. He followed Morris's example in teaching himself craft techniques before he set up the Century Guild, learning modelling and carving, embroidering, repoussé work in brass, and apprenticing himself to a skilled cabinet maker to acquire the basic knowledge of materials and constructive processes he needed to embark on his own post-Renaissance and highly original furniture design. This was a workshop of the second generation. Mackmurdo was in his early thirties when he founded it. His associates, Selwyn Image, Herbert Horne, Clement Heaton, Benjamin Creswick, were as young as, or younger than, Morris and his partners had been at Red Lion Square. There were striking similarities of atmosphere with Mackmurdo's communistic ménage in Fitzroy Street, in the same shabby part of London. As William Rothenstein remembered it, writing in 1931:

It was an Adam house, with large lofty rooms; Selwyn Image, and his wife, now had rooms there; so had Henry Carte with his son Geoffrey. They all had meals together at an ancient oak table, without a cloth, of course; in the middle stood a plaster figure and four bowls of bay which, I noticed, were covered in dust. Mackmurdo believed in the simple life.

There was an even more direct connection between Morris and T. J. Cobden-Sanderson. In 1883 it had been Janey who had first suggested he should become a bookbinder when, at the age of forty, he had given up the law. Meeting her at dinner with the Richmonds he had told her he was anxious to work with his hands. 'Then why don't you learn

591

bookbinding?' she had said. 'That would add an Art to our little community, and we would work together. I should like to do some little embroideries for books, and I would do so for you.' It is interesting to see Janey in the role of recruiting officer for the Arts and Crafts. Cobden-Sanderson was easily persuaded, taking lessons from Roger de Coverly, then opening his own workshop off the Strand, in Maiden Lane. Morris gave him one of his earliest commissions, to bind his personal copy of the French edition of Marx's *Das Kapital* which, as Cobden-Sanderson noted, 'had been worn to loose sections by his own constant study of it'. He bound the book in a deep turquoise leather with elaborate gilt-tooled decoration of buds and spots and stars. The title in gilt letters 'KARL MARX LE CAPITAL 1867' sits within a garland, and on the back is the inscription 'WILLIAM MORRIS AND FRIENDS 1884'. Philip Webb arrived to see the binding on the day it was finished. He 'pronounced it beautiful'.

By 1884 Morris's views had found such a general level of acceptance that a much larger group, the Art Workers' Guild, was founded. This was a decisive moment in the history of architecture and design and craft. The founder members were a group of five young architects from Norman Shaw's office: W. R. Lethaby, Edward Prior, Ernest Newton, Mervyn Macartney and Gerald C. Horsley. Lethaby was already a devotee of Philip Webb's. Mackmurdo has described how on 15 January a group of architects and craftsmen met together and 'in a serious mood but festive manner they took the oath of allegiance to the Sovereignty of Art, banding themselves together after the fashion of the Guild'. He emphasized how much its inception owed to Morris: 'the central idea dominating this association of architects, painters, sculptors, metal workers, decorators, etchers, lithographers, etc. was an idea identical with that which had led to the banding together of the architect, the artists and craftsmen who worked around William Morris as a brotherhood.' He added, typically but not inaccurately, 'It was also identical with the idea which led to the working association known as the Century Guild of Artists.'

The Art Workers' Guild had been arrived at through a merger of two earlier discussion groups: the St George's Art Society, a gathering of architects, and the Committee of Fifteen, which was mainly made up of decorative artists and craftsmen. Both had elected Morris as an honorary member, showing how they acknowledged his lead in campaigning for the interdependence and the equal status of all forms of visual expression, doing away with misleading and corrupting divisions into the 'lesser' and the 'finer' arts.

In its first few months the guild had elected fifty craftsmen members. Women were not admitted. Attitudes to women amongst Morris's craftsman followers were in general much more conservative than Morris's own. By the end of 1884 the membership consisted of twenty-six painters, fifteen architects, four sculptors and eleven other craftsmen in varied categories. In 1885 the membership totalled sixty-six; in 1886 it was seventy-five; by 1890 it had risen to 150, reflecting growing numbers of practitioners of the Arts and Crafts. At first the guild was relatively inbred and domestic, holding internal lectures, demonstrations of techniques, social evenings, small private exhibitions, but with the formation of the Arts and Crafts Exhibition Society as a separate organization in 1888 it found its public face. The Art Workers' Guild was the mainstay of another new organization, the National Association for the Advancement of Art and its Application to Industry, also founded in 1888. The latter held Art Congresses in Liverpool in 1888 and Edinburgh in 1889. Through all the contemporary reports of these activities the influence of Morris shines out like a small beacon: the idea of the crusade against current aesthetic values; the excitement at the rediscovery of lost craft techniques; the rumbustious masculinity of social events that take one back to Morris at Oxford in the days of the 'jovial campaign'. The guild inherited from Morris that species of male reticence that found its outlet in a ritual conviviality. William Rothenstein defined it so exactly and so bitchily when writing about Lethaby that 'he was inclined, as were others connected with Morris, to say "No" to life'.

Perhaps, among themselves, these men said 'Yes', but they made me feel that we painters were doubtful characters, with second wives hidden away somewhere, and an absinthe bottle in the studio cupboard.

It was a tendency to emotional suppression that, followed through, explains much about the sturdy but curiously sexless character of early twentieth-century British design compared with art nouveau as it developed on the Continent and which the Art Workers viewed with an extreme distrust.

In 1888 the group was founded that acted out most literally Morris's scenario for the small community regenerated through the crafts. This was C. R. Ashbee's Guild and School of Handicraft, originally set up in the East End of London, later moving out to Chipping Campden in the Cotswolds in the most poignant and fascinating episode in the history of

English Arts and Crafts. Ashbee, while still at Cambridge, cast around for hero figures: one was Edward Carpenter; Morris was the other. While training as an architect in G. F. Bodley's office Ashbee went to live at Toynbee Hall, the philanthropic East London settlement founded by the Rev. Samuel Barnett. Ned and Morris, at Oxford, had had similar yearnings for artistic philanthropy in the London slums. Ashbee, the homoerotic worshipper, was eager to acknowledge and even to exaggerate the debt he owed to Morris. He expounds it in his book *An Endeavour towards the Teaching of John Ruskin and William Morris*, printed by the Essex House Press on the Albion hand-press Ashbee had acquired from the Kelmscott Press after William Morris's death. The typeface is Ashbee's own wonderfully cranky 'Endeavour' design. The climax of the text is the intensely solemn chapter, 'Idealism in Industry', in which Ashbee considers the 'deeper Questions' that have a bearing upon communal life:

the question of the influence of the work a man does, upon his life and his value as a citizen; the question of the influence of his surroundings and his education upon his productive power; and the question as to whether the socialistic aspirations – I use the word in the widest sense – that make the backbone of the working class movements, do or do not supply those higher wants which the artist and the educator deem essential to the fuller living of life.

To Ashbee, the young man with ideals but no direction, Morris's blistering critique and captivating certainties provided the focus for his energies. It was a pattern that was to repeat itself over the next decades innumerable times.

It is perhaps surprising that in the early phase of Arts and Crafts activity, between 1884 and 1888, the notable absentee is William Morris. These were the most zealous years of his Socialist involvement. 'I have little life now outside the movement – which is as it should be', as he wrote austerely in February 1888. He had partially withdrawn from his old interests and friendships, even from his own creation, the Society for the Protection of Ancient Buildings. He could still be relied upon to write the necessary letters to the newspapers: the ill-fated campaign against the restoration of Westminster Hall came within this period. He could still arouse himself to attend the successive annual meetings and deliver an effective and emotional tirade in defence of such irreplaceable buildings as the mediaeval Staple Inn in Holborn or

Fairfax House in Putney, a fine example of the London town-house threatened with division into smaller units.

Whatever else happens, whatever glories or happiness befalls the English people in the future, these things, if we once lose them, we can never get back again; and yet they are treated just as if they were so much merchandise or cattle, to be bought and sold for the purpose of accumulating money . . . I say, once for all, it is an absolute disgrace that such buildings as these should be considered to be private property at all.

But though commercial vandalism still provoked a storm of anger, Morris was no longer being punctilious in attending the weekly Anti-Scrape committees, appearing at only nine in 1886 and eleven in 1887. His work for Socialism had altered his perspective. In the context of his hopes for a total revolution, campaigns for the saving of individual buildings could not seem so urgent. It also explains his reservations as the ideas about art and workmanship he had developed began to be accepted as the norm.

In the mid-1880s we see Morris having doubts about the movement he himself had set in motion. He was not one of the original members of the Art Workers' Guild. He did not seek election, and there was apparently some opposition to his eventual election in 1888. Ashbee recollected how someone had dared to blackball the master-craftsman and how another Art Worker 'spying the ball, deftly put his hand in the ballot box and subtracted it. Here was a handling indeed of the *liberum* veto of Democracy by unscrupulous intelligence!' When the organizers of the first exhibition for the Arts and Crafts Exhibition Society had written to ask for his support Morris had written back high-handedly, saying he felt the project was financially not viable:

the general public don't care one damn about the arts and crafts; and our customers can come to our shops to look at our kind of goods; and the other kind of exhibits would be some of Walter Crane's works and one or two of Burne-Jones: those would be the things worth looking at: the rest would tend to be of an amateurish nature, I fear. In short, at the risk of being considered a wet blanket, a Job, or Job's comforter, and all that sort of thing, I must say I rather dread the said exhibition.

The early days of the Arts and Crafts movement show Morris at his most curmudgeonly. Nor was he polite to his disciples. Poor Ashbee, visiting him in December 1887 to discuss the plans for his School of

Handicraft, got 'a great deal of cold water' poured upon a project that Morris considered so far from a solution to the problems of society as to be hardly worth his while.

Even Cobden-Sanderson came under fire. To his astonishment his patron Morris turned on him one day at lunch in Rules and told him he thought his work too costly: 'bookbinding should be "rough"; did not want to multiply the minor arts(!); went so far as to suggest that some machinery should be invented to bind books.'

But within the next few years a change came over Morris. We see him gradually edging inwards, almost irresistibly aligning himself with the groups and the activities of the Arts and Crafts. When the first Arts and Crafts Exhibition opened on 4 October 1888 at the New Gallery in Regent Street, Morris realized that far from the disaster he had predicted the exhibition was proving quite successful. He was forced to admit, 'I believe they are getting on pretty well.' Ned too, who had felt depressed, was now elated, finding at the gallery 'amongst some stuff and nonsense are some beautiful things, delightful to look at, and here for the first time one can measure a bit the change that has happened in the last twenty years'. Morris & Co. were well represented in the exhibition with furniture, fabrics, carpets and embroideries. There were Burne-Jones cartoons for stained glass, including the new 'Nativity' for Birmingham Cathedral. Bessie Burden had contributed three female figures embroidered in silk and worsted: 'Helen of Troy', 'Hippolite' and 'Penelope'. There was a collection of silks from Thomas Wardle and a case of embroideries on tusser by Mrs Wardle's ladies of Leek. May had exhibited her silk-embroidered cover for *Love Is Enough*. A portière, designed by Morris and worked in silks on linen jointly by Janey and Jenny, was on display in the entrance hall. Aglaia Coronio showed a screen and a box, both in mother of pearl with silk embroidery, in the Western Gallery. Georgie had lent a collection of the manuscripts Morris had written out for her many years before: *The Story of the Dwellers of Eyr*, leaves from his *Odes of Horace*, the *Rubaiyat of Omar Khayyam* and the small, perfect and personal *A Book of Verse* emblazoned with its portrait of Morris. The first Arts and Crafts Exhibition contained a first Morris biography in family things.

In the course of the exhibition Morris talked on 'Tapestry' as part of a series of lectures by practitioners. These lectures were open to the public with a substantial reduction in the entrance fee for workers in the arts and crafts. The texts were later published as *Arts and Crafts*

Essays. They were technical and practical in their approach. Morris lectured with a background of actual examples of tapestries, including his own precious Persian carpet borrowed from the dining-room at Kelmscott House. A certain theatricality of staging aimed to bring the craft techniques to life. At a later exhibition Morris the weaver set up his loom and demonstrated on the platform, inspiring the best of all Burne-Jones's cartoons of him. One of the Kelmscott Albion presses was installed, turning out copies of Morris's lecture on 'Gothic Architecture', at the exhibition in 1893, 'under the eyes of an interested and constantly renewed crowd, whose presence imposed a severe strain upon the pressman Collins' Celtic modesty'.

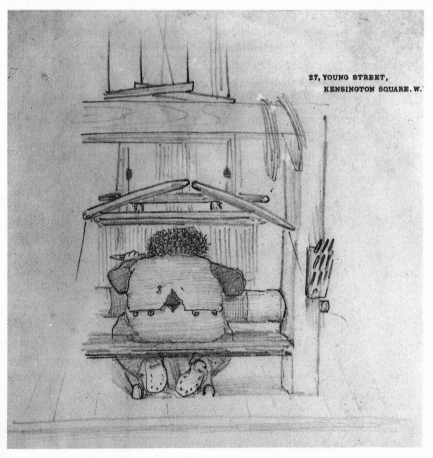

27, YOUNG STREET, KENSINGTON SQUARE. W.

43 *William Morris giving a weaving demonstration.* Caricature by Edward Burne-Jones.

597

In 1888 he had gone, without enthusiasm, to the Liverpool Art Congress, snatching time from a Socialist propaganda tour of Lancashire. The next year he attended the Edinburgh Art Congress with Cobden-Sanderson and Walter Crane. He was still grumbling: he told Jenny, 'I was in the chair at some monumentally dull papers; and you may imagine how I fidgetted, my dear.' He was still reporting cynically: 'Art for the working-classes was talked of by men who chose to ignore the fact that men anxiously facing starvation or wearily bearing it, are not free to receive pleasure from a work of art.' The conference did not impress him. The interesting thing is that he had allowed himself to be persuaded to be there. In 1891 his mood had changed to the extent that he took over from Crane as President of the Arts and Crafts Exhibition Society. In 1892 he was elected Master of the Art Workers' Guild. Soon he was back in his old routine of SPAB committees and assessment meetings. Morris, though by no means reneging on his Socialism, was now back at the centre of the world he had seemed to turn his back on. Why the volte-face?

Morris's life unfolded in cycles. Ned understood this thoroughly, writing in the 1890s:

When I first knew Morris nothing would content him but being a monk, and getting to Rome, and then he must be an architect, and apprenticed himself to Street, and worked for two years, but when I came to London and began to paint he threw it all up, and must paint too, and then he must give it up and make poems, and then he must give it up and make window hangings and pretty things, and when he had achieved that, he must be a poet again, and then after two or three years of Earthly Paradise time, he must learn dyeing, and lived in a vat, and learned weaving, and knew all about looms, and then made more books, and learned tapestry, and then wanted to smash everything up and begin the world anew, and now it is printing he cares for, and to make wonderful rich-looking books – and all things he does splendidly – and if he lives the printing will have an end – but not I hope, before Chaucer and the Morte d'Arthur are done; then he'll do I don't know what, but every minute will be alive.

Morris had a remarkable capacity for absorbing experience and recasting that long accumulation of language, skill, patience and anger into a new form.

When he returned to the handicrafts this can be viewed as the completing of a cycle. It was partly the familiar reflex action: the urge to reach back, after an experience physically or emotionally draining, for the familiar, controllable, the known. But he now seems to approach the handicrafts with new vigour and a new depth of understanding gathered in his Socialist years. His pronouncements on arts and crafts have a different character from his art lectures of the late 1870s and early 1880s. They seem more rounded, more relevant, more urgent. He had found new things to say. In 1891 he wrote an article on 'Art' for the *New Review* series on 'The Socialist Ideal', confronting the results of a widespread loss of skill with a perceptiveness that still seems relevant after another century:

This, then, is the position of art in this epoch. It is helpless and crippled amidst the sea of utilitarian brutality. It cannot perform the most necessary functions: it cannot build a decent house, or ornament a book, or lay out a garden, or prevent the ladies of the time from dressing in a way that caricatures the body and degrades it. On the one hand it is cut off from the traditions of the past, on the other from the life of the present. It is the art of a clique and not of the people. The people are too poor to have any share of it.

Morris's point is that the Socialist ideal of art 'should be common to the whole people'. This is only possible if the 'art' content is recognized as integral to any manufactured product. He argues with new force that art depends on *satisfaction* for the maker: 'the pleasurable exercise of our energies is at once the source of all art and the cause of all happiness: that is to say, it is the end of life.' Morris suggests that in 'the making of wares', whether entirely by hand, entirely by machine or by a combination of the two, there must be 'some of the spirit of the handicraftsman'. The craftsman with his human skill and human judgement as the setter of the standard, almost the arbiter, of machine production: this was a view absorbed into the mainstream theory of twentieth-century industrial design. Morris's final plea was for a *meaning* to the product, a looking forward to a time when 'nothing which is made by man will be ugly, but will have its due form, and its due ornament, and will tell the tale of its making and the tale of its use, even where it tells no other tale.' He continues, in one of those intoxicating passages in which his words seem to take on their own movement:

And this because when people once more take pleasure in their work, when the pleasure rises to a certain point, the expression of it will become irresistible, and that expression of pleasure is art, whatever form it may take.

Morris had the power to influence. It is now we see him emerging as the leader of a new group of much younger architects and designers who were themselves to have great influence on the development of twentieth-century art and design. There were several dozen of these *aficionados*, young men under the spell of Philip Webb as well as Morris, in the interlocking circles of the Art Workers' Guild, the Arts and Crafts Exhibition Society and the Anti-Scrape. The inner group closest of all to Morris consisted of W. R. Lethaby, Ernest Gimson, Sidney Barnsley and Detmar Blow, all architects and versatile designers, and W. A. S. Benson, who had also trained as an architect but now specialized in metalwork. Morris addressed him as 'Mr. Brass Benson'. He had assisted Burne-Jones with his studies of armour and provided King Cophetua with his crown.

These architects were mostly in their thirties, Detmar Blow still in his twenties. They were emphatically middle-class, well read and well travelled, receptive and admiring. Perhaps Morris found himself relaxed by their attentiveness after the quarrelsome rigours of the Socialist League. These men had many of the traits defined in the 1980s as 'young fogey'. They were country lovers, knowledgeable about rural traditions, understanding of vernacular architecture, romantic in their urge to resurrect lost rural skills. They were earnestly Socialist, though far from Anarchist. Morris had first met Gimson when he went to give his lecture on 'Art and Socialism' at the Secular Hall in Leicester in 1884 and had recommended him to J. D. Sedding, the Arts and Crafts architect in London, effectively starting him off on his career. It was after that lecture that Morris was introduced to a local clergyman, the Rev. Page Hopps, who said that the Socialist society Morris was envisaging would need God Almighty himself to manage it. 'All right, man, you catch your God Almighty, we'll have him,' cried Morris, jumping up, ruffling his hair and shaking his fist close to Page Hopps's face. Morris's fault and virtue was his blind eye to original sin.

We know so much about Morris's friendships in this period because he had acquired his Boswell, Sydney Cockerell, the ambitious son of a London coal merchant. Cockerell, like Detmar Blow, was a protégé of Ruskin's who gravitated to the Morris orbit. Unhappy with his prospects in the family firm, he infiltrated himself gradually into the Morris household, first arriving to catalogue Morris's books and manuscripts, staying to become secretary to the Kelmscott Press, exuding the keenness and diplomacy that later made him the ideal director of the Fitzwilliam

Museum in Cambridge. Georgie summed Cockerell up wonderfully: 'You are the most ubiquitous person I ever knew.' His meticulous diaries and the résumés in his later letters of the events and relationships within the Morris household are written in an inimitable style in which self-importance frequently gives way to gossip. In this he was the 'Chips' Channon of his day.

He was twenty-four when he first came to work for Morris. As he so typically and reliably informs us this was five years before he first embraced a woman. Sydney Cockerell belonged to the same generation as William Morris's architect disciples and was the friend of most of them, particularly Lethaby and Blow. His memoirs describe well the ritual weekly suppers held at Gatti's, a convivial Italian restaurant known for providing plenty of good food at a very modest price. The Anti-Scrape meetings ended at seven p.m.:

It was then customary for Morris, Webb, Walker, Lethaby, and one or two other favoured mortals to cross the Strand to Gatti's where, as a relaxation from the two hours of wearisome discussion, they supped frugally but merrily together, looking at medieval manuscripts produced by Morris from his satchel, and indulged in friendly gibes that were often the wonder of the neighbouring tables.

Lethaby would order a carafe of red wine, Webb a half bottle of Graves. Cockerell would sometimes treat himself to chocolate made with milk rather than water. Emery Walker was likely to eat the whole of his fish, including the skin and bones. Webb and Morris, the elders, would behave like boys together. Morris dining at Gatti's surrounded by his cronies looks like the great king-hero of his early Nordic tale, 'Svend and his Brethren', settled and at home.

When the histories of the Arts and Crafts movement started to be written in the 1960s, Lethaby emerged as one of the key figures, the founder of the Central School of Arts and Crafts where Morris's ideas of truth to materials dominated a curriculum devoted to practical crafts. Lethaby was also one of the founder-partners, with Ernest Gimson, Sidney Barnsley, Mervyn Macartney and Reginald Blomfield, of Kenton & Co., a furniture workshop 'with the object of supplying furniture of good design and good workmanship'. Gimson and Barnsley then moved to the Cotswolds where, with Sidney's brother Ernest, they set up rural workshops making superb examples of 'good citizens' furniture. Here too the direct Morris influence is clear. W. A. S. Benson, the metalworker, specialized in designing for mass production: the successful exemplar of Morris's theory of applying craft skills to industrial design. His *Times* obituary described how 'his lamps, vases, entrée dishes, etc., were all the outcome of profound study of the capabilities of heavy stamping plant, spinning lathes and shaping tools which he was able to put down in his Hammersmith works.' Benson eventually became a director of Morris & Co.

Of all these young men so susceptible to Morris, Detmar Blow's history is the least well known. Yet in a way it is the most interesting episode, showing Morris's influence percolating through, even *ad absurdum*, to a later generation in the details of their lives. Blow became one of the leading country-house architects of the pre-First World War period, competing with Lutyens. When he came to build his own house, Hilles in Gloucestershire, it was an idealized version of Kelmscott, a ruralist dream-mansion with stone gables and thatched roof rising steeply above the valley of the Severn. The house was furnished with Morris Sussex chairs and Ernest Gimson settles. It was perhaps the ultimate example of the Simple Life. Experiments were held in eating with the servants: 'everyone', wrote a visitor, 'enjoys the same food and, to a large extent, the same conversation'. The day began with the children assembling in the hall and singing a folksong or a hymn; in the evening there was often country dancing, and again the servants would be invited in. Detmar, on his fiddle, would play old country dances, Sir Roger de Coverley and Sellinger's Round. Hilles was a place of endless hospitality, both for the artistic aristocrats and connections of the Souls, who formed the Blows' chief social circle, and the various country wanderers and tramps whom the wonderfully trusting Blow admitted for the night. The charm of Hilles, vouched for in many memoirs, lay in its unexpectedness and kindness. Morris's great importance is the way that he revealed to so many different people on different social levels such previously unimagined possibilities in life.

'I wish I were well out of it, and living in a tent in a Persian desert, or a turf hut on the Iceland hill side.' This Morris never managed: his way of life had settled into the late Victorian, mildly bohemian, but bourgeois routine. However, a long succession of experimental artistic communities, some out on the edges of conventional society, followed in his wake. A recent study has located 130 separate organizations of the Arts and Crafts movement in Britain, with a peak of activity in the period between 1895 and 1905. By that time there were groups in Surrey and

Somerset, Westmorland and Ireland as well as in the Cotswolds, where the landscape, architecture and the lingering ancient craft traditions made it seem the promised country of the Arts and Crafts.

There were also guilds and workshops in the large industrial cities, Birmingham, Manchester, Liverpool and Glasgow, idealistic in their motivation, challenging accepted commercial practice from within the city itself. Morris's ideas spread over into the New Education movement of the late 1880s: they were keen on handicraft work, and indeed on spadework, at the new schools of Abbotsholme and Bedales, as Lytton Strachey, an Abbotsholme pupil in the 1890s, found to his alarm. There are further echoes in the 1920s. Eric Gill's huge wooden crucifix rising defiantly above the Guild workshops and the chapel of SS. Joseph and Dominic at Ditchling in Sussex is another version of Morris's 'fiery cross'. The agricultural and social experiments of the Elmhirsts at Dartington Hall in Devon express a very similar practical romanticism, down to the banners in the mediaeval hall. Even in the post-1945 period the Morris-inspired movement of workshop as social protest reawakened in the back-to-the-Celts migrations of the 1960s and the more professional official craft revival set in motion by the Crafts Council from 1973.

Morris's views fell on particularly fertile ground in late nineteenth-century America, tilled by the functionalist aesthetic of the early Puritan and visionary religious communities. The Shakers, after all, produced a proto-Morris chair. His urges for 'simplification of life, and the curbing of luxury and the desires for tyranny and mastery' were prefigured by the gentle nineteenth-century New England transcendentalism: there is already something of *News from Nowhere* in Bronson Alcott's Utopian agricultural settlement at Fruitlands and the Emersonian simple-life community at Brook Farm. The Morris movement in America began at a time when the consumer culture was reaching a high peak and the 'labor problem' was a constant source of anguish to the liberal conscience. The founder of the New Clairvaux handicraft community, Edward Pearson Pressey, was not alone in seeing Arts and Crafts as 'a soul reaction from under the feet of corporations and the wheels of machines'. The spiritual element was strong, stronger than in England, in the hundreds of craft communities and workshops formed in America between 1890 and 1910: Boston and New York, Chicago and California were the main areas of activity. The Rose Valley community was established in 1901 in its lush valley fourteen miles from Philadelphia, directly in the Morris tradition, with workshops installed in derelict mill buildings: the parallels with Ashbee's Chipping Campden Guild are striking. The movement in America, as in England, was fuelled by the deeply symbolic idea of the exodus from the alienating city to the human scale of the landscape in the country. There was the belief that the best work could be done close to the rhythms of nature and the cycles of the seasons. The wooded site for the Utopian Byrdcliffe Colony at Woodstock, New York, was chosen for its beauty and its moral 'healthfulness'.

Morris had an ingrained resistance to America. He never went there. But in America, much more than in England, he became a personal hero, partly because of the American attachment to cults, then as now, and partly because distance lent enchantment. Morris was the distant guru. By the end of the century *The Ladies' Home Journal* commented that 'a William Morris craze has been developing, and it is a fad that we cannot push with too much vigour'. Morris's and Ruskin's photographs gazed down from the walls of the Hull House social settlement in Chicago where the inner sanctum of the founder, Ellen Gates Starr, was furnished almost as a Morris shrine. His views were promulgated, often simplified and vulgarized, in the journals of the American communities: the Roycrofters' *The Philistine*, *The Craftsman* of the Stickleys, the Rose Valley *The Artsman*. Gustav Stickley, the Syracuse furniture designer, adopted for his own use Morris's motto 'Als ik kan', with its Red House overtones.

Throughout northern Europe the art colonies multiplied from 1900 onwards. At Hvitträsk near Helsinki in 1903 the architects Herman Gesellius, Armas Lindgren and Eliel Saarinen set themselves up in a working community, a gathering of red-tiled mediaevalist buildings around a garden courtyard rising like a castle in the pinewoods above the Gulf of Finland. At Darmstadt near Frankfurt the much larger-scale Artists' Colony established itself in a small village of hipped-roof houses clustering around Josef Maria Olbrich's fantastical Secessionist exhibition hall with the gold-tipped Wedding Tower reaching for the sky like one of Morris's own fictional buildings in *The House of the Wolfings* or *The Roots of the Mountains*. It is impossible to visit these places without being conscious of Morris's quests, dreams and imaginings, impinging upon European visual culture in a profound and liberating way. When the Bauhaus was set up at Weimar in 1919, Walter Gropius, born in Berlin in 1883, wrote a proclamation of intention that was almost a paraphrase of Morris:

The complete building is the final aim of the visual arts. Their noblest function was once the decoration of buildings. Today they exist in isolation, from which they can be rescued only through the conscious, cooperative effort of all craftsmen. Architects, painters and sculptors must recognize anew the composite character of a building as an entity. Only then will their work be imbued with the architectonic spirit which it has lost as 'salon art'.

Architects, sculptors, painters, we must all turn to the crafts. Art is not a 'profession'. There is no essential difference between the artist and the craftsman. The artist is an exalted craftsman. In rare moments of inspiration, moments beyond the control of his will, the grace of heaven may cause his work to blossom into art. But proficiency in his craft is essential to every artist. Therein lies a source of creative imagination.

Let us create a new guild of craftsmen, without the class distinctions which raise an arrogant barrier between craftsman and artist. Together let us conceive and create the new building of the future, which will embrace architecture and sculpture and painting in one unity and which will rise one day toward heaven from the hands of a million workers like the crystal symbol of a new faith.

Morris's ideas do permeate the Bauhaus in its early years: the emphasis on education through doing; the principle of mastering of one's materials; the structure of the workshops; the purposeful sense of community, united in its critique of society; the pursuit of fellowship. Was Morris then a modernist? There have been almost as many attempts over the years to claim him for the modernists as there have been to claim him for the Marxists. In his closely argued study, *Pioneers of the Modern Movement from William Morris to Walter Gropius* (1936), the dogmatically modernist Nikolaus Pevsner attempted to establish the logical line of descent from William Morris to the Bauhaus, and thence to the trans-European development of twentieth-century functional design. It is certainly an alluringly neat theory, up to a point convincing. But in the years since Pevsner's book was published, Morris, as so often, seems to have slipped away, successfully escaping the attempt to lock him into one straitjacket or another, refusing to be so strictly categorized. He can hardly be described as a modernist because his sense of history made him in other ways so thoroughly Victorian. It was his instinct not to jettison but to incorporate the past. Perhaps in the light of our own mellow postmodernist eclecticism we can accept Morris more easily as the conservative radical he really was.

*

In his final two years in the Socialist League Morris had begun to write 'a novel not socialistic except by inference'. *The House of the Wolfings* is a short epic of the Germanic tribes rambling and rampaging through central Europe in the second or third century A.D. and their first confrontation with the Romans. Crom Price's diary for August 1888 refers to Morris reading 'a large slice of a new Romano-Gothic story from manuscript' at breakfast at The Grange. This book was the first of the eight long tales that Morris wrote continuously, in an obsessive new phase of literary creativity, from then until his death. *The House of the Wolfings* was a departure both in subject and in structure: these distant events are unfolded in a combination of prose and verse. The effect is of grand opera, with pauses for the arias at high peaks of emotion. This is Morris in his most Wagnerian mode. The novel is also notable for the attention Morris paid to its design and its typography: 'the book will be rather peculiar in make-up,' he told Samuel Reeves, its publisher. Later he wrote to Jenny, 'It will be a pretty piece of typography for modern times.' Morris's involvement in the details of production of *The House of the Wolfings* and its successor, *The Roots of the Mountains*, were important stepping-stones to the foundation of the Kelmscott Press in 1890.

Morris had of course always been sensitive to the *look* of a book as the expression of its contents. It was he, the enthusiast as well as client, who had negotiated with Charles Whittingham of the Chiswick Press, the printer of *The Oxford and Cambridge Magazine*, and helped to set the visual style: if the results now appear a little tentative, it has to be remembered that Morris at the time was only twenty-one. His self-schooling in calligraphy and illumination had, by the early 1870s, sharpened his sense of the visual possibilities in page design, the subtleties in balance of text and illustration. If only he had achieved his planned illustrated edition of *Love Is Enough*.

Through the years when F. S. Ellis was his publisher, from 1868 to 1885, a small special edition of each book would be printed on Whatman paper, often with wider margins than the standard trade edition: Morris planned these 'big-paper' copies, his name for what the trade called 'large-paper' editions, in collaboration with Ellis. They show him working for a standard well above the norm. In his Socialist League years Morris's interest in book design and printing, like so many of his old pursuits, was in abeyance, crowded out by the pressure of events and the sense of political urgencies that made such activities seem suddenly irrelevant. *Commonweal* is merely decent, hardly innovative. Harry

Sparling, working alongside Morris in the Farringdon Road offices, was aware of a lack of interest in the layout of the Socialist leaflets and pamphlets that later struck him as surprising. But even at this period there is proof of a lingering perfectionism in the large-size handmade paper and the handsome wine-red binding of the special edition of Morris's collected Socialist Lectures, *Signs of Change*, published by Reeves and Turner in 1888. In that mood of new enthusiasms and reclaimings of abandoned territory in the late 1880s and early 1890s Morris's reawakened interest in book design and lettering is the one that counts the most.

While Morris was writing *The House of the Wolfings*, he had been returning to his old interest in early printed books, with a newly focused concentration on the type itself. He was starting once again to cast covetous eyes on rare books and manuscripts as they came on to the market, pondering his purchases with the agonies of indecision that still amused his friends. His acquisitions in the 1890s are on a new level of discriminating purchases and they influence his practice as typographer and printer: once again Morris is feeding the present with the past. In all this, Emery Walker was confessor and confederate, filling the role Thomas Wardle had occupied when Morris was learning dyeing at Leek. May records him constantly 'talking shop' with Walker. They made a joint decision on the type to be used to print *The House of the Wolfings* at the Chiswick Press. This was one of Charles Whittingham's own types, a reproduction of an old Basel type of Froben's; curiously, this same typeface had been used years earlier for some trial pages for an illustrated edition of *The Earthly Paradise*. Morris designed and pondered over and altered his own title page. Henry Buxton Forman, civil servant and editor who had worked with Morris, came across him by chance at the Chiswick Press and was drawn into discussion over the proof of the title page, where the fourth and fifth lines, 'written in prose and verse by William Morris', struck Morris as visually incorrect:

The line wanted tightening up: there was a three-cornered consultation between the Author, the Manager and myself. The word *in* was to be inserted – written in prose and *in* verse – to gain the necessary fulness of line. I mildly protested that the former reading was the better sense and that it should not be sacrificed to avoid a slight excess of white that no one would notice. 'Ha!' said Morris, 'now what would you say if I told you that the verses on the title-page were written just to fill up the great white lower half?'

The verses in question begin:

> Whiles in the early winter eve
> We pass amid the gathering night
> Some homestead that we had to leave
> Years past; and see its candles bright
> Shine in the room beside the door
> Where we were merry years agone
> But now must never enter more . . .

Hardly Morris's best.

Morris was not entirely satisfied with *The House of the Wolfings* when it was published in December 1888. He felt the type itself lacked character. But it had taught him a good deal about typesetting, and proved to him how much more sensitive the printers of the fifteenth and sixteenth centuries were than modern printers in their typographic practice: they understood the art of word- and letter-spacing. He was more concerned with this kind of visual detail in the preparations for the printing of *The Roots of the Mountains*, a much longer romance of the Gothic tribes in the Italian alps in the early middle ages, published in two volumes in 1889.

The same type was used, with an amended lower-case 'e'; but the proportions of the page are altered, with shoulder notes instead of headlines. The title page is typographically much improved. For the special edition of 250 copies Morris had a paper purpose-made by Whatman and the books were bound in a Merton Abbey printed linen. The completed volume sent Morris into ecstasies: 'I am so pleased with my book, typography, binding, and must I say it, literary matter – that I am any day to be seen huggling it up, and become a spectacle to Gods and men because of it.' A satisfying book evoked from Morris a positively erotic response.

It was after *The Roots of the Mountains* was published that Morris began on serious plans for 'turning printer' himself, 'in a small way'.

On 12 January 1891 Morris rented a cottage at No. 16 Upper Mall, Hammersmith, a few doors east of Kelmscott House. These were the first premises of the press inevitably named the Kelmscott, after Kelmscott Manor, now lodged immovably in Morris's mind as 'the type of the pleasant places upon earth'. Up the curling staircase of the little house were two rooms. One held an iron Albion hand-press, acquired second-hand. The other was equipped with racks, type cases and imposing stones. The ground floor was used for stores. William Bowden, an elderly master printer, who had printed Morris's *News from Nowhere* for Reeves and Turner before he retired, was taken on to act as the entire staff, alternating as compositor and pressman. However, in a week or two this plan proved so impracticable that Bowden was joined by his daughter Mrs Pine. Morris assisted with the installation; Bowden noticed his tendency, through inexperience, to put the founts of type away in the wrong box, muttering to himself, 'There, bother it; in the wrong box again!' But in these early days he was ebulliently busy, with the rush of happiness that always came over him at the start of a new enterprise. Bowden described later how he suddenly ran off and then returned again 'bustling up the path – and in my mind I can see him now – without a hat, and with a bottle of wine under each arm, with which to drink the health of Kelmscott Press'.

Morris was to give an account of his aims at Kelmscott Press in the same succinct style with which he explained 'How I became a Socialist':

I began printing books with the hope of producing some which would have a definite aim of beauty, while at the same time they should be easy to read and should not dazzle the eye, or trouble the intellect of the reader by eccentricity of form in the letters. I have always been a great admirer of the calligraphy of the Middle Ages, and of the earlier printing which took its place. As to the fifteenth century books, I had noticed that they were always beautiful by force of the mere typography, even without the added ornament, with which many of them are lavishly supplied. And it was the essence of my undertaking to produce books which it would be a pleasure to look upon as pieces of printing and arrangement of type.

Before the Press was ready to begin on its first volume, there had been a year of intense preparation. Morris had now set himself to master the techniques yet again of a new and highly complicated craft and started a search for suppliers of materials of another almost unknown trade. Harry Sparling had watched him making, 'as humbly and thoroughly as though he had been a raw beginner', his experiments with materials, methods and tools, starting from scratch with a scientific discipline that reminded Sparling of Charles Darwin, 'in order to know exactly where and in what manner they might be improved upon or set aside'. Morris had acquired much technical knowledge both from Emery Walker and

44 First colophon for the Kelmscott Press.

from C. T. Jacobi, head of the Chiswick Press; with them he spent many hours in comparing historic and contemporary types and papers and inks.

Morris had a clear idea of the quality he wanted to achieve in the publications of the Kelmscott Press. 'It was a matter of course that I should consider it necessary that the paper should be hand-made, both for the sake of durability and appearance.' He was faced with the same problem he had had when he began on his experiments with dyeing: the contemporary tendency to adulterate any product, from flour to ink. Most handmade papers at that period were being made of cotton whereas Morris insisted on unmixed linen rags. Even handmade papers were being hurried through their processes of bleaching and 'making with chemical additions that, it seemed to Morris, removed the life from them: an acceptable quality could be arrived at only by a patient sequence of fermentation, followed by careful boiling and beating, after which the paper would be 'laid' slowly sheet by sheet by a workman using his judgement on a mould in which the wires had not been woven too regularly. Morris was very insistent on this point, especially disliking the monotonous 'ribbed' surface of contemporary papers. He took a sample of his perfect paper, a Bolognese paper made in 1473, when he went with Emery Walker to discuss his requirements with the paper manufacturer Joseph Batchelor of Little Chart in Ashford in Kent. In Batchelor he found an equal enthusiast. Three handmade papers were eventually supplied by Batchelor's for the Kelmscott Press, named after

45 Colophon for the quarto books of the Kelmscott Press.

the watermarks designed for them by Morris: 'Flower', 'Perch' and Apple'. On that first visit Morris could not resist taking his coat off and trying to make a sheet of paper. He succeeded at the second attempt.

A few special copies of most of the Kelmscott books were printed on vellum. This entailed a renewed search for a supplier since the stock Morris had originally laid in for his calligraphy was almost at an end and his Italian source had dried up now that its entire production was reserved by the Vatican: Morris was tempted to intercede directly with the Pope on the grounds that his projected edition of *The Golden Legend*, Jacobus de Voragine's collection of the lives of the saints, originally published in the fifteenth century, deserved the Pope's support. But he found a more local supplier, Henry Band of Brentford in Middlesex, already making vellum for binding as well as parchments, drum-heads and banjo-heads. There was a period of trial and error, but a successful vellum was achieved, produced from the carefully selected skins of calves less than six weeks old. Kelmscott vellum was made especially thin and with the fine natural finishes specified by Morris was not faked with white lead, as was common practice. For the binding of the books, in vellum and half holland, Morris favoured vellum with a brownish rather than a chalk-white tone. Calf skins showing the baby calves' brown hair marks were reserved for the binding of his own copies of the books.

The worst of Morris's technical troubles was with ink: 'as one might have known', he expostulated, 'seeing that those damned chemists have a free hand with it!' He was in search of a pure black ink based on linseed oil, allowed to mature slowly without chemical additives, the only source of pigment being an organic lampblack, ground into the mixture of oil and turpentine until 'absolutely impalpable'. Such an ink was unobtainable on the English and indeed the American market, as he discovered after innumerable trials. He eventually turned to a German manufacturer, Gebrüder Jänecke of Hanover, the owner of which, as he may have known, was a fellow Socialist. Even this ink was not entirely satisfactory, for it was so stiff to use that the pressmen threatened to rebel. Morris counter-threatened that if his employees did not use the German ink he would close the Press. So much for fellowship. He sometimes spoke of his plans for making his own ink; but this was one craft that passed him by.

Central to Morris's plans for the Press was his intention to design his own type. May remembered as the spur to action the lantern-slide lecture on 'Letterpress Printing' that Emery Walker gave at the first of the Arts and Crafts Exhibitions at the New Gallery in 1888. It was Walker's début as a public speaker and he was clearly suffering 'untold agonies of shyness and nervousness'. But the audience was delighted by the ancient printed books he showed them, magically enlarged upon the screen:

One after another the old printers passed before us, one after another their splendid pages shone out in the dark room – such things as Boccaccio's De Claris Mulieribus by John Zainer of Ulm, with its woodcuts which my father thought could not be excelled for romantic and dramatic force, Schoeffer's Psalter of 1457, a Jenson of 1470, a Sweynheim and Pannartz Livy (Rome 1469) – books which moved him to repeat more than once that 'the first printed books were the best ever done – the first and the last of fine printing'.

For Morris these enlargements had the force of revelation, emphasizing the qualities inherent in the typefaces. He felt, in his childlike logic, that what had been done once could be done again. On the way home from the lecture he said to Walker, 'Let's make a new fount of type.'

Morris at this early stage invited Walker to become his partner in the Kelmscott Press. But Walker was the son of a coach builder who had started work at the age of fourteen as a labourer and had a built-in cautiousness. He told Wilfrid Blunt later that he had had 'too good a sense of proportion to accept'. He may well have been influenced by Morris's jovial warning that all the decisions would be his. However,

Walker, Morris's right-hand man in local Socialism, fell naturally into this same role in local printing. Though his work for the Press was unofficial, Walker was Morris's partner in all but name.

The first type to be designed for the Kelmscott Press was 'Golden'. 'What I wanted', Morris wrote, 'was letter pure in form; severe, without needless excrescences; solid, without the thickening and thinning of the line, which is the essential fault of ordinary modern type, and which makes it difficult to read; and not compressed laterally, as all later type has grown to be owing to commercial exigencies.' He found his obvious source for this perfected Roman type in the work of the fifteenth-century Venetian printer Nicolaus Jenson. 'Walker and I both think Jenson's the best model, taking all things into consideration. What do you think? Did you ever have his Pliny? I have a vivid recollection of the vellum copy at the Bodleian,' Morris was writing to F. S. Ellis in November 1889. He studied the Jenson examples very carefully, getting them photographed to a big scale, and drawing them over many times. It is interesting to see Morris, in his pursuit of mediaeval sources, making use of the Victorian new technology.

Walker also had photographed for him some pages from Aretinus's *Historiae Florentini populi*, printed in Venice by Jacobus Rubeus in 1476. He was able to study 'the proportions and peculiarities' of the letters. He started designing his own type on this large scale. As a next stage each letter was reduced photographically to actual size. May watched while Morris and Walker criticized and brooded over them, fascinated to watch 'the very beginnings of this new-old industry taking form and growing more or less under our own roof'. The large-scale and small-scale versions were considered side by side and when the type was cut the impression in the form of a 'smoke proof' was looked at again, and the letter would at this stage sometimes be recut. Morris went around with matchboxes containing these 'smokes' of type stuffed into his pockets. Sometimes, sitting talking at home, he would get one out and thoughtfully examine the little scraps of paper inside.

Morris's 14-point roman-Gothic 'Golden' type was followed by the 18-point 'Troy' type, a semi-Gothic design modelled on the mediaeval typefaces of Peter Schoeffer of Mainz, Günther Zainer of Augsburg and Johann Mentelin at Strassburg. With 'Troy' Morris hoped to 'redeem the Gothic character from the charge of unreadableness which is commonly brought against it'; this was Gothic consciously made more functional. The third Kelmscott Press type is a smaller version of

'Troy', cut to 12 point, brought in for the printing of the Kelmscott *Chaucer*. The punches for all these types were cut by Edward Prince, an experienced craftsman Morris respected, and the type was cast by machine.

I any the more: though it would indeed be hard if there were nothing
else in the world, no wonders, no terrors, no unspeakable beauties. Yet

not see how these can be better spent than in
making life cheerful & honourable for others
and for ourselves; and the gain of good life
to the country at large that would result from
men seriously setting about the bettering

46 Kelmscott Press specimens of 'Troy' and 'Chaucer' type.

The Kelmscott Press was a typically Morris combination of the pragmatic and romantic. 'Its career was a marvel from the beginning', Janey wrote to Sydney Cockerell in 1898; so it was, not least in the way its anti-commercial principles found their own level in the market. Morris followed through his perfectionist urges, but never to a point beyond practicality. Almost from the outset, the Press was intended to be a commercial success. Morris loved it, but he recognized its ambivalence, and his own:

Pleased as I am with my printing, when I saw my two men at work on the press yesterday with their sticky printers' ink I couldn't help lamenting the simplicity of the scribe and his desk, and his black ink, and blue and red ink, and I almost felt ashamed of my press after all.

He wrote this when the Press had been in operation for only a few weeks.

The Golden Legend had been planned as the first title of the Press. But Morris was still having problems with his paper. Only a small consign-ment had arrived and it was decided to change plans and to advance the publication of Morris's own short novel of love and quest in an idealized Germanic society, *The Story of the Glittering Plain*. A trial page was struck off in January 1891. Morris gave it to Walker with the inscription: 'William Morris fuit hic January 31st.' Morris, the next day, was in triumphant mood, comparing his own product with a page of the Saga Library, printed by the Chiswick Press, which looked very poor beside it. Cockerell, meeting him at Emery Walker's, blanched at the vigour with which Morris boasted of getting up at four a.m. in order to get half a day's work finished by breakfast time.

Originally it had been intended that twenty copies only of this first book would be printed, in an edition to be given as presents to Morris's friends. But after the response to pre-publicity in *The Athenaeum* Morris decided to print 200 copies, 180 of which would be for sale at two guineas each, with half a dozen special vellum copies. At the end of March, when Cobden-Sanderson first visited the Kelmscott Press, he saw 'the new type, and sheets, paper and vellum, already printed of *The Glittering Plain*'. Coming out he met, by chance, Morris and Janey opposite Kelmscott House, out walking in the sun. *The Glittering Plain* was published on 8 May 1891 and was distributed by the trade publisher, Reeves and Turner. Until the end of 1892, when the Press took over its own distribution, Morris's books were issued either by Reeves and Turner or Bernard Quaritch. The edition of *The Glittering Plain* sold out so quickly that in July an embarrassed Morris was writing to Aglaia: 'amidst one thing or another I forgot to keep a copy of *The Glittering Plain*, and there is not a copy to be had for less than about £4. However promises must be kept, and I believe I can let you have one of my own.'

Morris claimed that the books he wanted to print were those he most loved to read and to own. In fact, as the books flooded out over the years, the largest number of titles were of Morris's own works. *The Glittering Plain* was followed immediately by his *Poems by the Way*. The Press published twenty-three of Morris's books in all, with a total gross value of £15,945, and almost as many mediaeval texts, with the larger gross value of £22,941, in the context of an overall total of £50,299 for the publications of the Kelmscott Press. The mediaeval texts included *The Recuyell of the Historyes of Troye* (1892), edited by Harry Sparling; *The Order of Chivalry* (1893), edited by F. S. Ellis; *The History of Godefrey of Boloyne and of the Conquest of Iherusalem* (1893), again edited by Sparling; *Laudes Beatae Mariae Virginis* (1896), edited

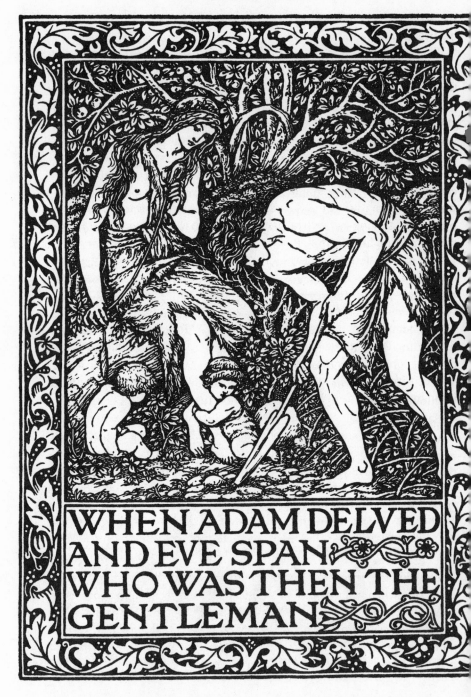

47 Opening page from the Kelmscott Press 1892 edition of *A Dream of John Ball*, with wood engraving from Edward Burne-Jones's illustration, and lettering designed by Morris.

by Sydney Cockerell: as in all his enterprises Morris made much use of his friends and family.

There was a further category of Kelmscott Press titles that appealed to Morris for sentimental reasons: *The Poems of John Keats* (1894); a three-volume *Shelley* (1894, 1895); *Atalanta in Calydon: A Tragedy. By Algernon Charles Swinburne* (1894); *Sidonia the Sorceress* (1893); the enormous *Chaucer*, planned in 1891 and finally completed in 1896: a great compendium from Morris's eclectic literary past. He republished the chapter 'On the Nature of Gothic' from John Ruskin's *The Stones of Venice*, the work that influenced him while still at Oxford, repaying the compliment Ruskin had paid to him: 'Morris is beaten gold'. The Press was also prepared to print a few books on commission or for commercial publishers so long as the text met with Morris's approval. One of these was an edition for Macmillan & Co. of Tennyson's *Maud*.

One of the charms, from the subscriber's point of view, was the sense of exclusivity: of being allowed entry to someone's secret history, to someone's private library. The enterprise in this sense was totally at variance with the normal practice of trade publishing in the late nineteenth century. When Morris wrote to Philip Webb, 'I do the books mainly for you and one or two others', he was, perhaps unconsciously, defining one of the reasons for the Kelmscott Press success. Philip Webb, forever scrupulous, had to have his presentation copies forced upon him. After one of his protests Morris wrote to him in fable form:

My dear Fellow

A traveller once entered a western hotel in America and went up to the clerk in his box (as the custom is in that country) and ordered chicken for his dinner: the clerk, without any trouble in his face, put his hand into his desk, and drew out a derringer, wherewith he covered the newcomer and said in a calm historic voice: Stranger, you will not have chicken; you will have hash.

This story you seem to have forgotten. So I will apply it and say that you will have the Kelmscott books as they come out. In short you will have hash because it would upset me very much if you did not have a share in my larx.

A copy of the letter was included in each volume of Philip Webb's collection when he gave it to Trinity College, Cambridge, in 1903.

Morris was serious in his ideas of reforming typography. In his many discussions with Emery Walker on what constituted 'beautiful books', whether special editions or books printed 'in quite ordinary type', he arrived at two principles that had great influence on twentieth-century typographic practice. The first was that the text should be set with close spacing, forestalling 'ugly rivers' of white, formed by too loose a disposal of letters, running vertically down the page. Morris's other principle concerns what he calls 'the position of the printed matter on the page', which should revert to the mediaeval rule in leaving the inner margin the narrowest, the top 'somewhat wider', the outside edge wider still and the bottom widest of all. In proposing that 'the unit of a book' was not just one page but a pair of pages, what would now be called a double-spread, Morris was consciously challenging contemporary practice. The two opposite pages must be visually balanced; illustration and ornament must be carefully considered in relation to the text. Morris writes, 'It is only natural that I, a decorator by profession, should attempt to ornament my own books suitably: about this matter I will only say that I have always tried to keep in mind the necessity for making my decoration a part of the page of type.'

48 Variations of initial letter designed by William Morris for the Kelmscott Press.

It is of course the decoration that gives the publications of the Kelmscott Press a visual character so particular it sometimes approaches the bizarre. It is not just a matter of the Burne-Jones illustrations, which in fact appear in relatively few of the volumes, although when they do appear they tend to dominate the book. The peculiar visual quality of Kelmscott books lies more in the accumulation of initial words, frames for woodcuts, special lettering for title pages, decorative borders and printers' marks produced at such high speed and with that obsessive fluency that Morris brought to any manual task. He uses visual detail to create an alternative imaginary territory just as, in his late novels, the strange vocabulary holds the reader suspended in an outlandish scene.

Lethaby observed him working on a border for the Press at Kelmscott Manor: 'There were two saucers, one of Indian ink and the other of Chinese white, and two brushes: with one brush he blacked over a length of border, and then with the other began to paint in the stems and leafage of his pattern, solving all the problems of the twists and turns as he came to them'. May Morris expands on the description, making it clear that Morris habitually sketched in a pattern lightly in pencil before going over it carefully with a fine black line, filling in the black background, correcting with white and adding in any small details with white upon black.

Morris's frenetic pursuit of decoration has the effect both of creating a historical perspective by establishing connections with a half-recognized mediaeval landscape, and of drawing the reader into a new world of strange visual juxtapositions. The graphics evolved by Morris for the

Kelmscott Press resemble the heightened quasi-mediaeval language of his novels of this period, both suspending disbelief and sharpening responses. These books are Victorian and yet anti-Victorian. They create another world which is a critique of all that Morris hated in Victorian visual culture: its shams and its stolidity. The more highly wrought of the Kelmscott publications have the edginess of modern experimental film.

But these sixty-six volumes are not at all the same. It is only when you see a whole run of them together that you realize how varied they are in size and mood and detail, and how they express different facets of

Morris's predilections and personality. *News from Nowhere* (1892), fat and welcoming, is a real story book. *Sidonia the Sorceress* (1893) is a galumphing volume, 28 × 20 cm, 456 pages thick. Morris's translation *Of the Friendship of Amis and Amile* (1894) is a delicate confection of 67 pages, 15 × 11 cm. To understand their quality you need to hold and stroke these Kelmscott books in their limp vellum covers just as Morris used to clasp his mediaeval incunabula. Most of them are secured with small silk ties specially woven and dyed in four colours: red, blue, yellow and green. They ask to be unlaced.

Hammersmith now took its place as a productive centre, rivalling Merton Abbey for Morris's attention. Morris's attendance at Merton was in any case less urgent now that George Wardle had retired and the business-like Smith brothers had been elevated to partners in the Firm. The Kelmscott Press, so close to home, was of the two the more domestic and dynastic, standing rather in the same relation to the works at Merton Abbey as the Hammersmith Branch had previously done to the headquarters of the Socialist League. In June 1890 May and Harry Sparling had finally been married, still to Janey's lamentations, at Fulham Register Office. It was Jenny who signed the register as witness with her father and wrote later of the lugubrious proceedings, entailing a long wait in 'a dismal little cell'. At the time of the marriage Sparling was given paid employment by Morris, as secretary of the Kelmscott Press. A photograph of the Press includes May as well as Sparling, in a family group around Morris as proprietor, and she is in evidence at Press dinners, at one of which 'Mrs. Sparling' gave a rendering to guitar accompaniment of 'Snowy-breasted Pearl'.

The 'cottage', although picturesque, soon proved inadequate. Morris felt he needed to get through double the amount of work in the same time. At the end of May 1891 the Kelmscott Press had moved next door into No. 14 Upper Mall, part of a once imposing eighteenth-century brick building known as Sussex House. The house, in its decline, had been put to use as kennels. Morris refers to 'taking the doggeries' and in April was reporting that the evacuation of the dogs was in progress. The adjoining half of Sussex House was occupied, conveniently, by Emery Walker's process-engraving firm. In November 1891 Morris acquired a second Albion to speed up his production as the 1,310 pages of *The Golden Legend* were by no means complete. Within the family this book replaced *The Earthly Paradise* as Morris's 'Interminable': the project without end.

The staff at the Press had also now expanded. The original all-purpose

49 Portrait book-plate designed by Walter Crane as the Hammersmith Branch of the Socialist League's tribute to May Morris on her marriage to Harry Sparling.

William Bowden retired but his son William Henry Bowden had joined the Press, as had his daughter Mrs Pine. Among the new compositors was Thomas Binning, Morris's old comrade from the Socialist League and indeed one of the Bloomsbury Branch seceders: Morris's nature was eternally forgiving. Kelmscott Press employees formed a chapel of their trade union, the London Society of Compositors. Thomas Binning was the Father of the Chapel, a role he was to repeat in later years, working for C. R. Ashbee and the Guild of Handicraft. There was pressure on Mrs Pine to join the union, and she became the first woman member of the LSC.

We have no evidence of Morris's response to the trade union. Certainly his practice in Hammersmith, as at Merton Abbey, was a long way from his Socialist theory. This was not the workshop of the Revolution. It is ironic that the programmes of the Kelmscott Press Annual

Dinners, indigestible menus of fried eels, boiled fowl and ham, roast beef, plum tart, jellies, blancmanges, itemized in execrable typography, inevitably feature 'W. Morris Esq. in the Chair'. When Count Harry Kessler, the German connoisseur later to set up his own Cranach Press, went to visit Morris's Press he was surprised to find that it 'looked like any printing works, just that, since only hand-presses are used, there is neither steam nor smoke, so everything can be kept cleaner'. He commented that Morris gave an impression of being 'thoroughly practical, not in the least *Pinafore*-like'. As they toured the works, he gathered that the relationship betwen Morris and his workmen was 'entirely what one would expect between a master and his well-trained servants'. He seemed friendly and benevolent towards them; they all automatically addressed Morris as 'Sir'.

It is easy to be scathing about this evidently paternalistic set-up, where the pressmen were compensated with an extra five shillings a week for blistered hands. But in the context of its time, and within the limits of what Morris considered commercial feasibility, the Press offered great advantages. The workmen were paid higher than average wages for a forty-six-and-a-half-hour week. According to Bowden the younger men were conscious of Morris's ideal that a man 'should be a workman in the best sense of the word; that he should take a high interest in his work; that he should have good surroundings; the very best materials to use; and should not be harried at his work by the everlasting thought of how the job was to pay him'. Morris had the generosity to give his workmen *time* to do the job to the best of their abilities. The Press had its own life, with internal celebrations and the outings known as Wayzegooses. Morris invited his staff to breakfast on the morning of the Boat Race: they were stiff and shy to start with, but the ice was broken later. Under Morris's aegis the workers at the Press were conscious of connections with the growing Hammersmith Arts and Crafts community beyond.

May and Harry were now living a few minutes' walk westward at No. 8 Hammersmith Terrace, a row of small houses with long gardens stretching down to the river where some of the residents kept boats moored. The Sparlings' house was the main outpost of Morris & Co. embroidery. The small group of needlewomen worked in May's drawing-room, under her direction. Some were recruited from the local schools, others were the wives and friends of Morris's circle: for instance, Mary De Morgan, sister of the potter; Mrs Jack, the wife of the Firm's chief furniture designer; Lily, the sister of W. B. Yeats. Morris paid a daily visit. The embroideresses, who wore uniform white cotton overalls, were allowed into May's dining-room to eat their lunch.

Five doors east, at No. 3, lived Emery Walker, a short distance from his workshops. This was a close dependence. Morris, whenever in London, kept in daily touch. In 1893 Cobden-Sanderson moved into No. 15 Upper Mall, opposite the Kelmscott Press, and established the Doves Bindery. He was no longer physically able to continue his practical work as a craft bookbinder, but was now the designer and director of a small staff which consisted of Douglas Cockerell, apprentice; Bessie Hooley, sewer; Charles Wilkinson, forwarder; and Charles McLeish, finisher. The plan was that the Bindery would work in association with the Kelmscott Press, binding special editions. The Bindery worked a forty-eight-hour week. This too was a small-scale and convivial environment. Cobden-Sanderson wrote: 'We begin at 8.30, and go on to 6.30, with an hour in the middle of the day, and an interval for tea, which they all have on the premises. After tea, the men smoke or play quoits in the garden; Miss Hooley washes up.' For a time Morris himself was a tenant in this building, renting the attic and first-floor room on the south for £15 a year as a further extension of the Kelmscott Press.

At first much of Cobden-Sanderson's work was in mending, rebinding and recovering the early printed books in Morris's library. He welcomed this as 'a means of training Cockerell' to the kind of work wanted. Douglas Cockerell, Sydney's brother, was to become the best-known binder in the country: an example of the Hammersmith mafia at work. The Doves bindings of the Kelmscott books give them a new dimension, adding to their splendour. A gilding of the lily? Robert Herrick in a blue morocco with Japanese vellum endpapers; Swinburne in a dazzling mosaic binding of blue with inlays of morocco in olive and brick red. Caxton's *Reynard the Foxe* was bound by Cobden-Sanderson in a white pigskin for a client who kept this and the Kelmscott Press *Shakespeare* together in a glass-fronted bookcase protected from the light by green silk curtains. He took them out and dusted them each Sunday morning with a silk handkerchief.

Morris's influence endured in this little London enclave. After his death Walker and Cobden-Sanderson joined to form the Doves Press at No. 1 Hammersmith Terrace. Edward Johnston, the calligrapher, came to live in Hammersmith, and here Hilary Pepler first came into contact with Eric Gill. Their joint venture, the ruggedly Roman Catholic

S. Dominic's Press, had a proselytizing fervour Morris might well have recognized: they too were visibly and volubly on the side of the poor. In the twentieth century, Morris's influence spread wider: to the Essex House, the Ashendene, the Vale Press, the Eragny, the Golden Cockerell, the Gregynog, and their counterparts in Germany especially and in the United States. It is not just a matter of a new approach to the meaning of the making of the book. More importantly this was a new concept of a press as a community with a life and a creative volition of its own.

One of the first books to be printed at the Kelmscott Press was Wilfrid Scawen Blunt's *The Love-Lyrics and Songs of Proteus*, an edition including his previous *Love-Sonnets of Proteus* now reprinted with additions and amendments. This was the subject of some anxious correspondence between Janey and Blunt in 1890 and 1891. Blunt was bearing the cost of the edition, estimated by Morris as 'very little above the ordinary cost'. He seems to have made no demur about publishing the poems of his wife's lover, not to mention poems far below the calibre of the others published by the Press. The Kelmscott Press also was to bring out two volumes of Rossetti – *Ballads and Narrative Poems* and *Sonnets and Lyrical Poems* – in the next two years.

It is Janey's correspondence with Blunt that reveals the full horror of events of February 1891 when Jenny had a sudden attack of meningitis. When Janey wrote, distraught, Jenny was 'still very ill, with two nurses attending her night and day . . . It was almost a death blow to me and to May, who was unfortunately in the house at the time.' Blunt, expanding on this episode later in his diary, writes that Jenny 'really went mad', imagining she had murdered her father and attempting to throw herself out of the window. 'She was so violent that she had to be tied down to the bed.'

Morris's illnesses were inevitably linked to Jenny's. He now collapsed as well. Janey wrote to Blunt, 'My husband has been very ill, the shock of Jenny's illness was too much for him, and he broke down entirely a few days afterwards . . . I fear it will be a long time before he is anything like his real self.' Morris was himself now noticeably showing some of the symptoms connected with epilepsy. He told Ellis, 'My hand seems lead and my wrist string.' On top of his recurring complaint of severe gout his kidneys were discovered to be badly affected. He was told by his doctors that he must now consider himself more or less an invalid,

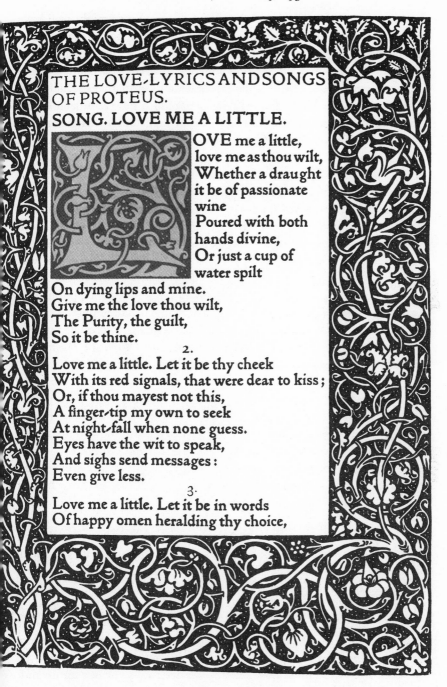

THE LOVE-LYRICS AND SONGS OF PROTEUS.

SONG. LOVE ME A LITTLE.

OVE me a little,
love me as thou wilt,
Whether a draught
it be of passionate
wine
Poured with both
hands divine,
Or just a cup of
water spilt
On dying lips and mine.
Give me the love thou wilt,
The Purity, the guilt,
So it be thine.

2.

Love me a little. Let it be thy cheek
With its red signals, that were dear to kiss;
Or, if thou mayest not this,
A finger-tip my own to seek
At night-fall when none guess.
Eyes have the wit to speak,
And sighs send messages:
Even give less.

3.

Love me a little. Let it be in words
Of happy omen heralding thy choice,

50 Title page from the Kelmscott Press edition of Wilfrid Scawen Blunt's poems, set in
William Morris's 'Golden' type, 1892.

making himself take plenty of rest and keeping to a healthy diet.

In March in Hammersmith Cobden-Sanderson found him slightly improved, eating oysters for his supper. He had just finished when Cobden-Sanderson went into his room where he was sitting in a chair by the fire with his large silk handkerchief spread over his knees. 'He looked – despite his supper! – a little empty, his clothes hanging somewhat loosely upon him.' Four months later, when he had taken Jenny down to Folkestone for a double convalescence, he was writing to Georgie in depression, 'I am ashamed to say that I am not as well as I should like, and am even such a fool as to be rather anxious – about myself this time.' He is wise enough to realize the anxiety may be part of the ailment. Georgie had apparently been unwell too. He wrote her a strange prophetic description:

a sea-fog came on in the afternoon after a bright morning, which gradually invaded the whole land under the downs; but we clomb to the top of them and found them and all the uplands beyond lying under a serene calm sunny sky, the tops of the cliffs towards Dover coming bright and sharp above the fog, and throwing a blue shadow on it; below a mere sea of cloud, not a trace of the sea (proper), wave on wave of it. It looked like Long Jokull (in Iceland), only *that* was glittering white and this was goose-breast colour. I thought it awful to look on, and it made me feel uneasy, as if there were wild goings on preparing for us underneath the veil.

In August 1891, encouraged by the doctors, Morris took Jenny on a tour of northern France, visiting the churches and cathedrals at Abbeville and Amiens, Beauvais, Soissons and Reims. Jenny's current nurse-companion, Miss Lamb, was with them. Some of these were places Morris had not visited since his Oxford vacation trip of 1855. He had not wanted to go, but felt sure he would enjoy it once he started on the journey. So, in a sense, he did. He responded, as always, to the high spots of his travels with great shouts of the superlative. In Reims Cathedral, he tells Webb, 'almost the whole of the original glass (unrestored) is left in the clerestory, and is a miracle of colour.' In the interesting little church of St Rémy, 'the choir has some splendid 12 cent. glass; the East window the finest I ever saw, I think – such a mass of blue!' He reports a good quarrel with the sacristan who tried to sell him photographs of Laon Cathedral, then under restoration, 'telling him I didn't want photos of restored churches'. He describes, in Mark Twain terms, a curious encounter in a farmyard alongside the church at St Riquier:

4 French dogs, big, sitting in the litter of a shed, barked at us no allowance, but we thought they were tied up and went on, but when we came back, out bounced a big one very flamboyant, but did not get so far as the legs of the rear guard (me to wit) chiefly I think because 3 or 4 bloused French men cursed him till *all* was blue.

As a traveller he is still high-spirited and greedy for experience. He tells Walker, 'As for the town of Gournay it is uninteresting, but they make cream cheeses of the very best: *crede mihi experto.*' But the tone of his letters home is noticeably different from those sent from the same places when he was young. There is now a little sign of strain. Morris is with a middle-aged daughter, an invalid appearing more abnormal than she is. He travels at her pace, takes his pleasures in her pleasure. He mentions 'hanging back' on Jenny's account. At her insistence he buys Janey a 'present from Abbeville', a wide-mouthed jug with a 'comic lady and gentleman on it, rude modern, but traditional pottery'. In northern France, Morris was in attendance, in a curious replay of the summer at Bad Ems.

Work followed him abroad. In the weeks before he left, Morris had begun to design the lower-case alphabet of the new Kelmscott Press 'Troy' type. Trials were now sent for him to assess. 'I chuckled over the upside A,' he told Walker, from Beauvais. 'I have written to Prince: he has now done *e i h l n o p r t*. The *t* does not look well: I think I shall have to re-design it. The *e* also looks a little wrong, but might be altered. The rest looks very well indeed.' 'Troy' was Morris's favourite of the Kelmscott types.

In the weeks after his return the printers began on Wilfrid Scawen Blunt's *Love-Lyrics*. This was the only Kelmscott Press book in which the initial letters were printed in red, at Blunt's request. When he saw the first sheet Morris told Janey it looked 'very gay and pretty'. He added, 'but think I prefer my own style of printing', perhaps forgivably.

In September 1891 Morris was back at Kelmscott Manor. He had been there very little in his busiest years of political activity. Now he longed for Kelmscott, in his mood of the retrieval of lost pleasures, of wanting to 'cease being bumbled up and down'. Blunt too was at Kelmscott at the end of September, as he had been in the late summer or the autumn of the past three years. Janey more or less entreated him to come. The constant nervous strain of Jenny's illness seemed to have made her even more dependent on Blunt's affection and attentions. 'I want much to hear what you have written,' she told him; 'you once read me the beginning of the long poem . . . where the hard-hearted little boy did not cry when his mother died but wept bitterly over a pet snail.'

The enduring appeal of Blunt for Janey has its mysteries. How much was it the attraction of the unobtainable? Blunt was endlessly evasive, and very far from tactful. At this period he was also in pursuit of Marie Stillman, another raven-haired Pre-Raphaelite beauty so similar to Janey as to be easily mistaken for her, a former model, possibly a lover of Rossetti's, and now Janey's greatest friend. Blunt wrote in his diary, of Marie Stillman, 'She is like a woman in a dream': almost a repeat of his description of Janey. The previous year Blunt had left Kelmscott in a hurry to follow Marie to Cambridge where together they examined the Morris & Co. windows in Jesus College and Blunt noted, with a trace of the self-mockery that makes his diaries such fascinating reading, that Marie Stillman was 'the most beautiful woman that ever lived or ever will live in the world, though she can't be less than 45.' Janey knew of Blunt's susceptibility to Marie. In her letters there are teasingly indignant references to 'Mrs. S'.

Possibly Janey clung to some small hope of reforming him. But Blunt dates from summer 1888, when his work for Irish nationalism finished, the final collapse of his attempt to lead 'a more or less seriously Catholic life'. Any good intentions were undermined by the added value his imprisonment in Kilmainham Gaol had given him: 'the episode was a title to romantic interest which made it easy for me to resume my place and more than my place in society,' he wrote complacently. Janey had been as susceptible as anyone: 'I think I was never more genuinely pleased in my life than when I got your last note – I am not alarmist by nature, but somehow I feared that you would never leave that dreadful den, it was all like a nightmare,' she had written at the time of his release. By 1891 Blunt had acquired several new mistresses, among them Blanche Hozier and Margaret Talbot. He had made it all too clear that she was one of many. In June 1891, soon after Jenny's illness, he invited Janey to his estate at Crabbet. He had also invited Sibell, widow of the Duke of Westminster's heir, newly married to Blunt's cousin, George Wyndham. He was already in the grip of a new passion: 'Heaven knows I have not sought it . . . yet it tempts me, like looking down a precipice.' The next day, with his usual expertise, he had 'George paired off with Mrs. Morris' while he took Sibell in his boat to the island in the lake and they talked about love and then went for a long drive, stopping at Crawley monastery to say a prayer together, kneeling at a well-placed tomb. Janey does not appear to have made a scene about it. She apparently accepted the role Blunt allotted her as a continuing 'quiet interest' in his life.

For Blunt his Kelmscott visits had hazardous delights:

Kelmscott was a romantic but most uncomfortable house with all the rooms opening into each other and difficult to be alone in. The rooms below were all passage rooms opening on to the garden, so large and so low that they were completely commanded from outside. My room was sometimes one of these, sometimes a room upstairs which was also a passage room connecting the main house with the servants quarters. The upstairs drawing room where we sat in the evenings, the tapestried chamber, was a cul-de-sac approachable only by passing through Morris's own bedroom where he lay at night in a great Elizabethan four-poster. Mrs. Morris slept alone at the end of a short passage at the head of the staircase to the right. All was uncarpeted with floors that creaked. In the daytime with the sun streaming through the windows the old house was full of happy life, but in the darkness of the night it was a ghostly place full of strange noises where every movement was heard plainly from room to room. To me such midnight perils have always been attractive. Rossetti seemed a constant presence there, for it was there that he and Janey had had their time of love some 14 years before – and I came to identify myself with him as his admirer and successor.

We cannot tell exactly how Morris was affected by Janey's infatuation with Blunt or by this repeat invasion of his most-loved house. The only hint of his resentment comes in a letter he sent to F. S. Ellis: 'I wish you had been here instead of the new comer, whose shortcomings I am not used to like I am to yours and mine.' The letter was written at the time of Blunt's first visit to Kelmscott, when he busied himself correcting the proofs of the poems he had written in prison, the turgid sequence later published as *In Vinculis* for which Janey designed a book cover with a shamrock motif. It seems almost certain from the dating of the letter that the uncongenial 'new comer' was Blunt. But Blunt tried hard to win Morris. He liked to be affectionate to the husbands of his lovers. It gave him an extra *frisson*. He and Morris soon appear to be on terms, if not of friendship, at least of eager argument and amiable banter, though Blunt never quite appreciated Morris's subtlety. He saw him as looking like 'a Norwegian sea captain', which had by then become one of the clichés of the time, and he was arrogantly unaware Morris's sexual complexity:

629

'One thing only, I think, he did not know, much as he had written about it, the love of women, and that he never cared to discuss. Here he had no real experience and remained a child.'

Even if he half resented him, Morris evidently found Blunt entertaining, with his reservoir of esoteric information, his combative political views. He operated in a cultured, convivial, *male* world Morris knew. Morris may also have glimpsed Blunt's inner loneliness, the solitariness of the compulsive traveller. He shared some of Blunt's yearnings for the desert spaces: Charles Montagu Doughty's *Travels in Arabia Deserta* (1888) was one of Morris's most treasured books. Besides Blunt was rich, and a good client. He was now commissioning from Morris & Co. at Merton Abbey a version of the tapestry 'The Adoration of the Magi', originally designed by Ned for Exeter College Chapel. With his enormous tastelessness he asked for the addition of a camel and an Arab horse.

In spite of, or perhaps because of, Wilfrid Blunt's incursions at this period one is conscious of a growing dependence and a mutual fondness between Morris and his wife. They visit doctors together, soothing one another. He sends her 'a thousand loves' in his letters when she is away. Late in life they seem to have reached a loving compromise. By 1892 Morris is writing to Glasier, 'at present the absolute *duties* of my life are summed up in the necessity for taking care for my wife and daughter, both of whom in one way or another are in bad health: my *work* of all kinds is really an amusement taken when I can out of my duty time.' Even physically they seem to have come closer. Visitors noted how both now had almost white hair, and they seem a pair of curiously beautiful old people, aged versions of their early selves at Red House. As Cockerell described them at Hammersmith in November 1892:

When I went up into the drawing room to say goodnight Morris and his wife were playing at draughts, with large ivory pieces, red and white. Mrs. M. was dressed in a glorious blue gown, and as she sat on the sofa, she looked like an animated Rossetti picture or page from an old MS of a king and queen.

Janey was in an especially nervous state that winter. Her doctors attributed this to the great strain of being continually in the house with Jenny, frightened by the evidence of her homicidal tendencies, never knowing when to expect a new attack. Janey was showing a form of paranoia, unable to bear being with other people, especially if Jenny was there. She was advised to go away completely for at least three or four months. Otherwise, as she told Blunt, she would almost certainly 'break down entirely, and pass beyond the help of any doctor'. Blunt was sympathetic but bumptious, commenting, 'I fancy that, if I had not been there to console her nine or ten years ago after Rossetti died, she might have been before this in a madhouse. She is a singularly uncomplaining woman, and things must be bad with her if she has spoken about them.' When she lunched with Blunt in London in October, he 'did what he could' to console her, and Janey told him that he had been a great comfort to her. Late in November Morris took Janey by train to Bordighera, becoming so unwell himself *en route* that she was forced to start looking after him. But he recovered in a few days and came home, leaving Janey in the Hotel Belvedere where she found friends, including the MacDonalds, now living in Italy, and a good many people 'of a frivolous and amusing kind'. She stayed through the winter, recovering gently and taking part in the New Year *'tableaux vivants'* in which she was cast as chief lover because she was so much taller than anybody else.

Morris spent Christmas 1892 at Kelmscott. It was the first time he had been there in mid-winter. Jenny was said to be 'extremely happy' at the prospect. Janey, waiting anxiously for news in the Riviera sunshine, hoped she would not hear of any deaths from cold. Assembled at Kelmscott for the freezing holiday were May, Harry and Bernard Shaw, the new Arthurian triangle in embryo. The Mystic Betrothal would be resurrected soon. Morris wrote: 'Shaw is happy because (as he sleeps with his window wide open) his water jug is frozen deeper than anyone else's.' Shaw confirmed this, scrawling 'Frightful cold' in the Kelmscott Manor Visitors' Book.

Tennyson died on 6 October 1892. His funeral was held in Westminster Abbey, with an immensely distinguished troop of pall-bearers, political, literary and scientific. Veterans of the Light Brigade were lined along the aisle. The coffin was draped with the Union Jack. The choir sang 'Crossing the Bar' and 'The Silent Voices', Tennyson's last poem. Edward Burne-Jones wrote to his son Philip, 'Did you see that up to the very end of the end all was perfect about that splendid life?' He was especially excited that the city of Mantua had sent bay from Virgil's birthplace to lay in the tomb. George Meredith and Thomas Hardy were at the Abbey. This was a funeral, like Wellington's, Morris did not attend, expressing his relief that he now no longer had to write an editorial commentary on Tennyson's death in *Commonweal*.

Tennyson had been Poet Laureate since 1850. Morris had sometimes shuddered at the poems of royal commemoration this honorific post entailed. In 1887 he had written to Jenny: 'I am sorry poor old Tennyson thought himself bound to write an ode on our fat Vic's Jubilee: have you seen it? It is like Martin Tupper for all the world.' Tupper was the author of the popular *Proverbial Philosophy*, a collection of banal poetic maxims, the Patience Strong of his day. Morris disliked ceremonial verse as a genre, seeing it as empty rhetoric. In 1888, on the twenty-fifth anniversary of the Prince of Wales and Princess Alexandra of Denmark's marriage, he had been indignant when some newspapers, confusing him with his contemporary poet Lewis Morris, taunted him, the Socialist, for composing a 'Silver Wedding Ode' written by the other Morris. 'Just fancy my writing a poem on the Prince of Wales!' In a paragraph in *Commonweal*, under the heading 'Time Brings Revenge', Morris had written 'If this kind of thing goes on, I shall change my name.'

The serious consideration given to William Morris as Tennyson's possible successor as Poet Laureate tells us a good deal about public perceptions of Morris at this period. It was as if *Chants for Socialists* had not been written. He was still, in official eyes, the author of *The Earthly Paradise*. There were in point of fact few convincing alternatives. Robert Browning too was dead. Morris's friend Dixon had never really surfaced. Morris himself had favoured Swinburne, also apparently Queen Victoria's favourite; but he was ruled out by republicanism and irreligion. The other poets chiefly in the running were those dismissed by Blunt as the 'ridiculous trio Lewis Morris, Edwin Arnold and Alfred Austin'. Blunt, for once the gentleman, gave his vote to Morris.

In 1892 Gladstone was again prime minister, embarking on his fourth, and last, term of office. James Bryce, now a member of the Cabinet, went to see Morris unofficially, to sound him out. Bryce was a particular admirer of Morris's, a colleague from the anti-Turk campaigns of fifteen years before. Morris, with little hesitation, turned down the suggestion that he should be put forward. There is anyway some evidence that Gladstone would have vetoed the appointment of 'an out-and-out Socialist'. The laureateship passed to the undistinguished Austin, soon to make himself ridiculous with his ode, published in *The Times*, in celebration of the Jameson Raid. Robert Bridges, with hindsight the best candidate, had to wait for twenty years. Morris certainly never regretted his decision. Cockerell quotes him saying he could never see himself 'sitting down in crimson plush breeches and white stockings to write birthday odes in honour of all the blooming little Guelfings and Battenbergs that happen to come along'.

Two years later Burne-Jones was made a baronet. Gladstone wrote from Biarritz to ask him to accept the honour 'in recognition of the high position which you have attained by your high achievement in your noble art'. There was some amazement in the circles of the Art Workers. 'Astounding news that Mr. Burne-Jones has been made a baronet. What next!' wrote Helen, William Blake Richmond's daughter, in her diary. Janey too was flabbergasted: 'It is all too funny, and makes one roar with laughing – I have got over the sadness of it now – it seemed to me such an insult to offer the same to a man of genius and a successful publican, and then for him to accept. But I have always taken life too seriously I fancy, and have cared little for what most people value greatly.' Ned joked about the honour to William De Morgan: 'I should like to tell you that I accepted this haughty eminence to gratify Mr. Morris: I hope soon to be able to write the Right Revd. Mr. Morris.' The implications were submerged in a wave of friendly badinage. But Ned had not dared to tell Morris the news personally, in spite of the fact that he had dined with him the previous evening, leaving him to find out from the papers. In the delicate relations between Burne-Jones and Morris, the baronetcy was an added blow.

In the 1890s Morris continued writing poetry. In some of his letters there are little glimpses of poems virtually taking over, interrupting everything, forcing their way out. He tells Jenny in the summer of 1892 'I worked hard at my story on Tuesday: and this morning I have finished one poem that was stopping the way, and begun another: for there are two of them.' He was planning his own poetic version of *Beowulf*, the Old English heroic narrative of monsters and man-monsters, later in that same year. But his main creative energies had veered away from verse and into that extraordinary sequence of fantasy stories which began with *News from Nowhere* and which he was still writing in the weeks before his death. These are *The Story of the Glittering Plain* (1890); *The Wood beyond the World* (1894); *The Well at the World's End* (1894); *The Water of the Wondrous Isles* and *The Sundering Flood*. The last two were published posthumously by the Kelmscott Press in 1897 and 1898.

633

These works are unlike anything else in Morris's *œuvre* or indeed in Victorian fiction as a whole. They come much closer to the twentieth-century fantasies of J. R. R. Tolkien and C. S. Lewis, or some more recent American writers of science fiction, in the way they remove the reader from reality into the curiously convincing detail of their imagined worlds. These are essays in a new country, out of place and out of time, pervaded by an extreme eroticism. They are stories that end in the fulfilment of desire. As far as Morris is concerned, what makes them so surprising is the way that these intensely concentrated books were written in the midst of such a *mélange* of day-to-day activity: the Press; the pattern-making; the residue of Morris's political life; the meetings and the visits of Anti-Scrape and his bourgeoning involvement with the Arts and Crafts. Sydney Cockerell, the eye-witness in residence, described a day at Hammersmith in 1892:

Spent 3 hours alone with William Morris, looking at old books. When I went in he was writing away at the Well at the World's End, which he says will run into at least 700 pages. He showed me trial proofs of the proposed Chaucer which Burne-Jones is to illustrate and a number of capitals and borders. We went into the garden which was full of big hollyhocks.

In his earlier novels *The House of the Wolfings* (1888) and *The Roots of the Mountains* (1889) Morris had developed the ideas of the quest that had fascinated him since he was a child. These books too described long journeys through imaginary landscapes. But they had a basis in a recognizable historic past. The books of the 1890s are different in the way they float away into a world where connections are more arbitrary. In the two-volume *Well at the World's End*, the novel which ran to 228,000 words, at the time the longest fantasy novel ever written, we are in the chancy terrain of fairytale:

And so the four sons of the King drew straws to see which of them would rule the little kingdom after their father, and which would ride to the north or the east or the west in quest of adventure. And so the youngest of the four princes set forth on his destrier, Falcon, and departed from the little kingdom of Upmeads in quest of Utterbol which lieth beyond the Wood Perilous, the Castle of Abundance, the Burg of the Four Friths, and the Vale of the Tower, to the place of the miraculous Well.

Morris's style in these last novels has been ridiculed, often one suspects by those who have never read them. In fact their language is not all that high-flown. Morris's magic stories are told in a fairly straightforward, mainly monosyllabic, prose. Its directness is reminiscent of Old English. We should remember he already had his mind on *Beowulf*. He uses strange plain names, especially for his women. *The Story of the Glittering Plain* is Hallblithe's search for 'the Hostage', the bright-haired grey-eyed woman abducted by the pirates. In *The Wood beyond the World*, Walter is temporarily distracted by 'the Lady', one of Morris's snake-like sadistic seductresses, from his true love, 'the Maid'. The language of these novels has an effect of distancing. Morris draws his readers into these dream worlds by creating his own language, hiving himself off from what he saw as the corrupted English of his day.

When a reviewer in *The Spectator* suggested that *The Wood beyond the World* was an allegory of Capital and Labour, Morris was indignant. 'I had not the least intention of thrusting an allegory into *The Wood beyond the World*; it is made for a tale pure and simple,' he replied. 'On the other hand, I should consider it bad art in anyone writing an allegory not to make it clear from the first that this was his intention, and not to take care throughout that the allegory and the story should interpenetrate, as does the great master of allegory, Bunyan.' All the same, it is difficult not to read contemporary political significance into these fantasies, with their two moral poles of energy and lassitude, and even more difficult not to relate his heroes' resilience to Morris's own remarkable powers of recovery. As Hallblithe of the *Glittering Plain* reminds himself, shaking himself out of the stupor of depression, 'I have an errand in the world.' Nor indeed are these stories so far away from Bunyan, as their heroes toil up craggy passes through the mountains, survive the dismal wastelands, sail over savage seas from one island to another, outwit treacherous companions, fend off insinuating women, empowered by the conviction of their spiritual quest. Morris's last novels are written with a glowing belief in the pursuit of the equal society and – in this quite unlike Bunyan – the sexual happiness with which democracy is merged in Morris's mind.

In *News from Nowhere*, the so-called 'Emancipation of Women question' is dismissed as 'an old story'. In Morris's Utopia 'the women do what they like best, and the men are neither jealous of it or injured by it'. Ellen is put forward as the ideal spontaneous, confident, non-flirtatious woman who looks her suitors straight in the eye. Her radiance springs from the sense of her own value and her self-determination, the 'power of will' that she has over her own life. Morris contrasts this with her inevitable fate in the earlier society before the Revolution: then Ellen's beauty and cleverness and brightness would have been 'sold to rich men'. In the novel Ellen takes the sexual initiative, adding to the narrator's sense of disorientation and delight. Morris's later heroines are all developments of the charming stalwart Ellen, 'manly minded women' who do the kissing first.

The idea of active women always attracted Morris. In *News from Nowhere* the head carver on the new building is a woman, Mistress Philippa, 'a rather little woman' working away busily with her mallet and her chisel. In *The Water of the Wondrous Isles*, Birdalone, like Morris's daughter May, is the professional embroiderer, establishing a workshop and taking on apprentices in the City of the Five Crafts. There is an exquisite description of Birdalone stitching a gown with a design of roses, lilies and a tall tree 'springing up from amidmost the hem of the skirt' with a hart on either side. It is idle women, decorative, parasitic, that provide the nightmare image in this novel when Birdalone arrives at the Isle of the Queens. In the great hall the long tables are set; the hall is crowded with women, some sitting and some serving. There is not a man in sight. These are mostly lovely women 'and none less than comely; their cheeks were bright and their eyes gleamed, and their hair flowed down fair of fashion'. But no one moves and no one speaks. Birdalone swoons to realize that these images of perfect femininity are dead.

In these last novels, Morris creates a new woman who is not simply a worker but a warrior. Ursula in *The Well at the World's End* wears armour over a green-sleeved silken surcoat; she marches with the soldiers. When they enter the city through the gates she goes in first, bearing the hallowed staff, ahead of the 'big men on their big horses' looking like 'very bodyguards of war'. Even Ursula is outdone by Birdalone in *The Water of the Wondrous Isles*, who is 'armed in a light hauberk' and has 'covered up the lovely shapeliness of her legs with long boots of deer leather'. The image here is more of Barbarella or of Diana Rigg in *The Avengers*: the swashbuckling female of the 1960s sexual revolution. Birdalone was 'girt with a good sword' as well as a quiverful of arrows and 'a strong horseman's bow'. It would be interesting to know how much Morris's obvious fascination with warrior women was affected by his contacts in the Socialist movement. He knew Charlotte Wilson, the Anarchist editor of *Freedom*, who lived on the edge of violence. He would have known of Annie Besant's courage in Trafalgar

Square on 'Bloody Sunday', attempting to obstruct a charge of mounted police. It is almost certain Morris had some personal contact with Louise Michel, the veteran woman warrior of the Paris Commune, now in exile in London and the headmistress of an International Socialist School in Fitzroy Square. As she draws her naked sword Birdalone subverts supremely the ideal of the gentle, docile female. In the twentieth century *The Water of the Wondrous Isles* was Barbara Castle's favourite of William Morris's books.

Perhaps it is only within the bounds of fairytale that Morris dares confront the sexually liberated woman. His heroines have the choice of the disposal of their bodies; they love where it pleases them. Birdalone is indoctrinated by the more worldly Viridis into the secrets of mutual desire and female sexuality: 'Sister! sister! even in such wise and no other, as they desire us do we desire them; it is no mere good will toward them from us, but longing and hot love.' Viridis holds out the promise of true love to her, and her response is unreservedly physical:

They were silent now a little, and it was as if some sweet incense had been burned within the chamber. For Birdalone the colour came and went in her cheeks, her flesh quaked, her heart beat quick, and she was oppressed by the sweetness of longing. More daintily she moved her limbs, and laid foot to foot and felt the sleekness of her sides; and tender she was of her body as of that which should one day be so sorely loved.

The Water of the Wondrous Isles is Morris's only completed novel with a woman as protagonist. But May quotes a little fragment of one of the many partly finished tales and plans for tales dating from this period. It was to be a story called 'The Wasted Land'. It opens: 'I have heard say that there was once a fair house built by the side of a forest wherein dwelt a lady, and how in this house there were no men, but a great many damsels.' The beginning of Morris's last feminist novel? One wishes he had managed to go on.

However, Morris cannot quite be regarded as a thoroughgoing feminist, though feminists from time to time attempt to capture him. He felt that women's suffrage was not the urgent issue: 'To speak plainly my *private* view of the suffrage matter is that it is no use until people are determined on Socialism,' he wrote to Jane Cobden in 1884. In his Socialist League policies he supported equality in principle but had practical reservations, as he explained to Glasier in 1886:

you must not forget that child-bearing makes women inferior to men, since a certain time of their lives they must be dependent on them. Of course we must claim absolute equality of condition between men and women, as between other groups, but it would be poor economy setting women to do men's work (as unluckily they often do now) or *vice versa*.

Morris did however stress the importance of influencing working-class *women* as a means to influencing working-class men.

Morris was too hemmed in by his age and class and by his peculiar mix of inhibitions to sustain a feminist critique. His views on the woman question are less radical than his opinions on factory environment or education or old age. Like Walter in his novel, and indeed so many of his male contemporaries, he is forever poised between the lascivious Lady and the steadfast Maid. Even in these novels there are disappointing moments as his female warriors remove their shining armour to wait on the menfolk at the celebration feast. But they are the nearest Morris comes to visions of strong women. They reveal him as at least a semi-feminist.

When Wilfrid Blunt had been staying at Kelmscott in that autumn of 1891 he had many talks with Morris as they walked and fished for gudgeon under the willow trees. He summed up the situation: 'Politically he is in much the same position as I am. He has found Socialism impossible and uncongenial, and has thrown it wholly up for art and poetry, his earlier loves. I fancy I may have influenced him in this.' Blunt was a journalist *manqué*. The entry in his diary demonstrates his talent for the neat analysis at the expense of total accuracy. But, like all his knowing comments and rapid thumbnail sketches, it embodies an element of truth.

In the space of seven years Morris had endured two débâcles: the split within the Social-Democratic Federation, followed by his virtual expulsion from the Socialist League. In public he had put a brave face on it, still claiming he intended to take an active part in Socialist politics. But to closer friends he admitted his depression. In 1891 he wrote to James Joynes, his old SDF colleague, 'How curiously things have changed since the older days of the SDF! I am sometimes rather elated, oftener disappointed at the course of events.' And in a later letter to Georgie he expresses the accumulated suffering of a whole lifetime: 'I was thinking just now, how I have wasted the many times when I have been "hurt"

and (especially of late years) have made no sign, but swallowed down
my sorrow and anger, and nothing done!' He would have been better
taking to his bed and staying there for a month or two like one of his
Icelandic heroes, he suggests.

CHAPTER EIGHTEEN

Hammersmith, Two: 1893–96

In the early 1890s Morris's Socialist engagements were reduced to a mere trickle of Hammersmith activity. He played his part in the Sunday morning preachings, but his more formal speeches and lectures had dwindled to a total of only about twelve in 1891 and seven in 1892. He travelled only twice outside London to lecture in this period, once to Birmingham and once to Manchester. Nor in fact does he appear to have been as energetic in the Hammersmith Socialist Society as he was in the Hammersmith Branch of the Socialist League. Though minutes show him still attending meetings Morris was more rarely in the chair. The *Hammersmith Socialist Record*, a four-page monthly, was published from October 1891, ostensibly to give him a new mouthpiece; but he contributed only intermittently and it only lasted a few issues. It was no substitute for *Commonweal*.

Gradually, however, Morris started drifting back to his old Socialist alliances, recovering his lost stamina and hopes and beginning to appear in a new role as an arbiter, a peacemaker, partyless, ubiquitous. On May Day in London in 1891 he was on the platform of the main inter-party demonstration with Aveling as chairman. Other speakers were Cunninghame Graham, Shaw for the Fabians and Harry Quelch for the SDF. Engels was also on the platform. Morris too was becoming an elder statesman figure, one of English Socialism's saints and heroes.

With his breadth of culture and his international contacts, he was now a focal figure for the *émigrés* in London. He was back in the midst of them by early December 1891 when he attended a meeting of the Friends of Russian Freedom in a tiny crowded room hung with mirrors and heavy, floor-length curtains. The main speaker was the

Russian Felix Volkhovsky who described the iniquities of the repressive government of Tsar Alexander III. Stepniak spoke next.

William Morris then sprang up and dashed into English Socialism, his voice rang out as he said that it was all very well to free Russia but were we not slaves ourselves, if Russia was in a mess we were in a terrible mess, let enlightened people join hands and help each other . . .

There were many interruptions but Morris persisted, crying out that if they were going to free Russia they did not have to make a slave of him.

When he left the Socialist League in 1890 Morris had settled all debts and bequeathed to the Council the type, plant and copyright of *Commonweal*. But it was impossible to sever all connection. Even after the League finally collapsed in February 1891, the inevitable victim of its own anarchic tendencies, its ghosts returned to haunt him through the years. In the chaos of its dying days Frank Kitz, the Anarchist Morris had once employed at Merton, was said to have absconded with 'moneys and books of the League' and, it was argued, was 'unfit to continue as a comrade in the movement'. He died in Leeds, in penury, in 1923.

More seriously for Morris, David Nicoll and Charles Mowbray were arrested in April 1892, after the publication of a particularly reckless article in *Commonweal*. This followed a *cause célèbre* of the period, the Walsall Anarchist Case, in which six men, all with Socialist connections, were accused, on doubtful evidence, of manufacturing a bomb. The bomb was certainly genuine. But it emerged that the case had been set up by Auguste Coulon, one of the many *agents provocateurs* by then at work in London. He had been in the employ of the police for two years.

Coulon was a regular contributor to *Commonweal* where his International Notes gave approving coverage to acts of foreign terrorism; he was a familiar figure at the Hammersmith Branch of the Socialist League, selling copies of *L'Indicateur Anarchiste*, a terrorist do-it-yourself book of instructions on the making of bombs and dynamite. When what then seemed savage sentences were passed on four of the Walsall Anarchists – ten years' penal servitude for Fred Charles, Victor Cailes and Jean Battola, five years for Deakin – David Nicoll wrote his violent article in their defence. It read as an incitement to the murder of the judge in the case and of Chief Inspector Melville. The heading was 'Are these men fit to live?' *Commonweal* was published on 9 April. Nine days later the police raided the offices. In a tone of exasperation Morris wrote to Jenny:

You will be sorry to see that Nicoll and Mowbray, two of our old comrades, have got into trouble with the *Commonweal*. It was very stupid of Nicoll, for it seems that he stuck in his idiotic article while Mowbray was away, so that the latter knew nothing of it. I think Mowbray will get off. I am sorry for him, and even more for the *Commonweal*.

Charles Mowbray's wife had died only days before he was arrested. He was granted permission to attend the funeral only after Morris appeared before the court and entered into surety for him for £500. In 1894 Morris travelled from Kelmscott specially to give evidence on behalf of another old Socialist League comrade, Tom Cantwell, accused of soliciting the murder of members of the royal family. The following year, when a campaign was launched to free the imprisoned Walsall Anarchists Morris wrote an official letter of support, maintaining that they had already been punished enough for 'nothing but a piece of hair-brained [sic] folly'. He singled out Fred Charles, the ringleader, whom, wrote Morris, 'I once saw a good deal of when we were in the Socialist League together. I believe him to be a very honest man, friendly and humane, but very enthusiastic – in fact to rashness . . . I cannot understand such a man being a criminal.'

Morris denounced Anarchist violence repeatedly and strongly. He stated in an interview in *Justice* in 1894: 'The acts themselves are criminal, criminal because inexpedient and stupid, and criminal in as much as they are attacks on people who are personally innocent, and are as destructive and harmful out of all proportion to any possible good they might produce.' Why then did he go to such lengths to defend these Anarchists or quasi-Anarchists, risking his reputation by association with an underworld of terrorists and *agents provocateurs*? First because of his old loyalties: to Morris, Socialist Leaguers remained 'our people', to be supported stubbornly. Also because there was a streak of fantasy in Morris's make-up that prevented him from taking bomb scares altogether seriously. At the height of the Anarchist outrages in London in the early 1890s Walter Crane was in Morris's Hammersmith study, where the papers overflowed on the table and chairs. Richard Grosvenor came in. 'There's no dynamite under the papers', Morris said, offering him a chair.

On 10 March 1893 Morris gave a lecture to the Hammersmith Socialist Society in which he explained his fears and hopes in politics in the light of new developments. He called it 'Communism'. It is an updated 'Where Are We Now?' There is something bizarre in the picture of Morris standing up in his own Coach House like one of his own dream narrators looking back on his own history:

There are doubtless not a few in this room, myself perhaps amongst them (I say *perhaps* for one's old self is apt to grow dim to one) – some of us I say once believed in the inevitableness of a sudden and speedy change.

Instead of almost instant transformation, carried through with the decisiveness of the French Revolution, Morris now forces himself to contemplate a future of gradual and very much less dramatic improvement in social conditions in Britain. What he calls the arrival of 'business-like administration' instead of 'the old Whig muddles of laissez-faire backed up by coercion and smoothed by abundant corruption', has some obvious gains which appeal to Morris's spirit of tidiness:

The London County Council, for instance, is not merely a more useful body for the administration of public business than the Metropolitan Board of Works was: it is instinct with a different spirit; and even its general *intention* to be of use to the citizens and to heed their wishes, has in it a promise of better days, and has already done something to raise the dignity of life in London amongst a certain part of the population, and down to certain classes. Again, who can quarrel with the attempts to relieve the sordidness of civilized town life by the public acquirement of parks and other open spaces, planting of trees, establishment of free libraries and the like? It is sensible and right for the public to push for the attainment of such gains.

Morris had already had his own experience of the benefits of the new regime: the Society for the Protection of Ancient Buildings had sent three separate deputations to the LCC and had been received with what Morris described as 'a human point of view; arguments listened to and weighed, and opinion changed in consequence. This for a public body is certainly wonderful.'

But what worries him is, first, that better environmental standards, better housing, better schooling will inevitably be unevenly distributed, benefiting the middle rather than the working classes. And he also suspects the British are *en route* to a soulless and ultimately enervating future, based on a *machinery* of socialism rather than socialism itself. Morris's comments on 'gas and water Socialism' are uncannily prescient. He marshals the arguments that were to be reassembled after the Second World War in Britain against the Welfare State.

Morris's fear is of a terrible inertia sweeping through the country as a Fabian dream world of efficiency triumphs. 'The world is going your way, Webb, but it is not the right way in the end,' he told Sidney Webb in 1895, with a fear of a future not so far from Aldous Huxley's *Brave New World* (1932). Morris, with his hypersensitivity to his own tendency to dreaminess and lassitude, can see how the new measures with their captivating logical solutions have the power to dull the mind. His hopes, now expressed with fresh surges of conviction, are still for the working people to reach a real understanding of and an '*ardent desire*' for socialism. It is remarkable that Morris, now so visibly ageing, after so much disappointment, can still speak with such visionary fervour of the future:

Since it seems to me necessary that in order to make any due use of socialist machinery one should have some sort of idea as to the life which is to be the result of it, let me now take up the often told tale of what we mean by communism or socialism; for between complete Socialism and Communism there is no difference whatever in my mind. Communism is in fact the completion of Socialism: when that ceases to be militant and becomes triumphant, it will be communism.

What is so ironic is that the Communism Morris was proposing is quite different from, in many ways the obverse of, 'Communism' as it arose in the 1930s in the Soviet Union and in Eastern Europe in the years after the war.

Since addressing the mass meeting in Northumberland in 1877, Morris had felt a special rapport with the miners. He had come to comprehend the true significance of the Dock Strike of 1889. Now he was swept up in the Socialist support for the great strikes in the coalfields of 1892 and 1893. Blunt, lunching at Hammersmith on 16 November 1893, noted 'Morris full of the coal war, and the proposed settlement of it by Rosebery. His view was that the miners had shown political naïveté in putting themselves out of employment and starving. They ought to have refused to work and gone to the workhouse. This would have thrown the whole cost of the strike on the masters, "but", he said, "they have an idea of honour in the matter, which I suppose had to be reckoned with."' A few days earlier Morris had written a letter to *The Daily Chronicle* under the heading, 'The Deeper Meaning of the

Struggle'. This is one of the most eloquent of all his letters to the press, in which he explains his continuing belief in 'a genuine new birth of art, which will be the spontaneous expression of the pleasure of life innate in the whole people'. The change for the better can only be realized by the efforts of the workers. 'That they are finding this out for themselves and acting upon it', Morris writes, 'makes this year a memorable one indeed . . .

what these staunch miners have been doing in the face of such tremendous odds, other workmen can and will do; and when life is easier and fuller of pleasure, people will have time to look round them and find out what they desire in the matter of art, and will also have power to compass their desires. No one can tell now what form that art will take; but . . . it is certain that it will not depend on the whim of a few persons, but on the will of all.

Morris had made his peace with Hyndman. The SDF was now the only serious revolutionary party left. Morris started to appear as a guest speaker on the SDF platforms. He supported the young George Lansbury, fighting a Walworth by-election for the SDF in February 1894. Lansbury, the pacifist, was to be one of the leaders of the Labour party in the coming century. The previous autumn Morris had supported Hyndman's own candidature in Burnley, travelling north to Lancashire and delivering two full-length speeches, one in the afternoon, one on the same evening, in St James's Hall. On that visit Hyndman took him to the top of the Manchester Road to view the town below, 'one hideous Malebolge of carbon laden fog and smoke', with the tall factory chimneys of the weaving mills rising above the masses of thick cloud. The two old revolutionaries stood together looking down upon 'this infernal pit of degradation', and Morris swore.

In his new mood of conciliatory optimism Morris hoped once and for all to end factionalist squabbles. He told Glasier, 'I sometimes have a vision of a real Socialist Party at once united and free.' In 1893 the Hammersmith Socialist Society took the initiative in forming a Joint Committee of Socialist Bodies, with five of its own delegates, five from the Fabians, five from the SDF. Shaw points out that 'The Fabians relied on the support of the amiable and platonic HSS to get a majority over the SDF. The SDF made exactly the same calculation.' Interestingly the Independent Labour party, formed two years earlier, was not considered fully fledged enough to be asked to join. Convivial planning conferences were held at Kelmscott House. Morris drew up a manifesto, submitted for discussion by a committee consisting of Edward Pease for the Fabians, Hyndman, and himself. In a letter to May Morris, Pease later recollected, 'Your father drafted it; and Hyndman and I spoiled it.' Morris's draft struck him as almost a repeat of the prospectus for the Hammersmith Socialist Society. Pease explained succinctly the problems of the enterprise: 'The root difference was that there was no real agreement between us except on purely negative points. We all hated commercial civilisation; but as to the process of getting rid of it there was hardly an immediate step on which the Fabians and the SDF could agree.' Their joint manifesto foundered when the Fabians withdrew their delegate. Shaw, watching these proceedings with the satirist's eye, commented, 'Experience has shown that it is not possible to carry union further than a supper club.'

The next winter in Rottingdean Georgie stood for election to the Parish Council. Morris wrote to congratulate her on beginning her 'agitation'. Ned described her energy with admiration and alarm: 'She is so busy – she is rousing the village – she is marching about – she is going like a flame through the village.' She showed all the moral courage of her Methodist background, writing an 'Open Letter to the Electors' and canvassing around the pubs of Rottingdean. Georgie's views were, for the period, formidably feminist, claiming that women brought a special perceptiveness to subjects that men would automatically dismiss as unimportant. For some years she was the only woman on the Council. Gas-and-water Socialism could not be for her.

Shaw's comparison of Morris with Auguste Rodin is superficially seductive. Morris was indeed like Rodin in physical appearance, in integrity and intensity of work. But there is a whole spiritual (not to mention sexual) difference between them. Morris did not work in solitary grandeur. The masterpieces of his last decade in fact are collaborative work, the logical development of the ideas of communal art that began with Morris, Marshall, Faulkner & Co.

From the late 1880s Burne-Jones's stained-glass windows designed for Morris & Co. reach a new maturity. The quasi-mediaeval sweetness of the early Morris windows has been left behind in these vast compositions with their mosaic-like elongated figures and expanses of iridescent colour, blood red, deep peacock blue, shrimp pink. His new versions of the six 'Angels of Creation' for Manchester College chapel are almost

Symbolist in feeling, holding their blue spheres in their arms like giant beach balls, faintly fearsome angels with ruby red wings. The triumphant example of the stained glass that Morris and Burne-Jones together had arrived at are the windows in St Philip's Cathedral, Birmingham. The 'Nativity' and the 'Crucifixion' were designed in 1887. Ned, as usual, complained bitterly he had been underpaid for them. 'The Last Judgement', dominating the west end of the cathedral, shows Christ, in white, surrounded by a host of fierce red angels. Beneath their feet whole buildings fall cascading into ruins. The dead stand on their graves, in robes of green, blue, white and scarlet. The designs for this window were completed a few weeks after William Morris's death.

From 1892 to 1895 Morris's nine tapestry weavers at Merton were at work on a project as spectacular and as important in its period as the stained-glass windows for Birmingham. These were the six narrative panels of the Quest of the San Graal, the mystical progression beginning with 'The Knights of the Round Table summoned to the Quest by a Strange Damsel', and ending with 'The Attainment'. The panels were commissioned for Stanmore Hall in Middlesex, by the Australian mining engineer William Knox D'Arcy as part of a total redecoration scheme by Morris & Co. Perhaps the choice of subject was seen partly as a reprimand to Knox D'Arcy, another of Morris's despised rich clients. On Morris's first visit the carriage was sent to meet him 'and', he wrote to Jenny, 'I couldn't help laughing to see the men I met touching their hats, clearly not to me, but to *it*.' The tapestries, all eight feet high, were designed to be hung around the upper half of the Stanmore Hall dining-room and viewed from below. Morris co-ordinated the designing and weaving, and provided drawings for the heraldry, perusing the British Museum copy of the heraldic source-book *Gyron le Courtoys, avecques la devise des armes de tous les chevaliers de la table ronde*, published in Paris in 1520. It is the authenticity of mediaeval detailing that gives these tapestries their uncanny other-worldliness, so similar to many of the Kelmscott Press designs.

The last few years of Morris's life were occupied almost constantly with the Kelmscott *Chaucer*, the closest of all his collaborations with Burne-Jones. In summer 1891 Morris had begun speaking of an edition of the work of the writer to whom he felt more attuned than perhaps to any other. Burne-Jones analysed the similarity between them: 'Chaucer is very much the same sort of person as Morris; unless he can begin his tale at the beginning and go steadily on to the end, he's bothered.'

Chaucer entered the Morris's household mythology: 'the pen Chaucer used to write the first line of the *Canterbury Tales*' was the answer to a Kelmscott 'Twenty Questions' game. In December 1892 the Press announced the forthcoming edition, to be printed in Morris's new 'Chaucer' type, the reduced version of the 'Troy' type, 'with about sixty designs by E. Burne-Jones'.

There were eventually eighty-seven illustrations. Their work together on the *Chaucer* brought Morris and Ned back almost on to their old terms of exhilaration and intimacy. As a preparation they sat down to re-read Chaucer together, Morris sometimes pretending that he could not understand it. Ned had his own misgivings: 'I wonder, if Chaucer were alive now, or is aware of what is going on, whether he'd be satisfied with my pictures to his book or whether he'd prefer impressionist ones. I don't trust him. And if he and Morris were to meet in heaven, I wonder if they'd quarrel.' Morris egged on Ned to provide graphic equivalents of Chaucer's bawdy: 'especially', Ned wrote to Swinburne, 'he had hopes of my treatment of the Miller's Tale'. But Burne-Jones was adamant in resisting these entreaties, maintaining that Morris 'ever had more robust and daring parts' than he did, an assessment far from accurate, as Ned well knew.

It was very slow progress. There were technical problems with the transfer of Burne-Jones's designs on to wood for the engraving. But as the *magnum opus* gradually took shape you can sense Morris's spirits rising. In March 1893 he had finished his design for the initial page: 'My eyes! how good it is!' On 10 August 1894 the first page of the *Chaucer* was printed on vellum and Morris told Jenny that this had been successful after a little trouble: 'I have done a big O for the Man of Law's tale, and am now doing the title page to the Book of Wisdom and Lies.' On 22 August he wrote to her, 'They are printing the Chaucer very well. Item it is all sold except 3 vellum copies and people are quarrelling over the privilege of buying it.' On 8 January 1895, a second Albion press began operation in additional premises at No. 21 Upper Mall, and two presses were occupied almost exclusively by the Kelmscott *Chaucer* from then on.

From 1893, simultaneously with *Chaucer*, Morris was working on his *Beowulf* translation. He was not in any sense an Anglo-Saxon scholar. He worked from the original but with a prose paraphrase supplied by the more expert A. J. Wyatt of Christ's College, Cambridge, which he used as a safety net. When the first batch of Wyatt's translation reached him he responded immediately, 'I have rhymed up the lines of Beowulf which you sent me.' He was finding it 'the most delightful work'. Morris suggested reading through the original with Wyatt to help him to get the feel of the real language, as he had done with Magnússon in his early Saga days. On 25 February he made a note in his rough diary, 'Finished the first lot of Beo: about 700 lines.' As he worked through the 3,182 lines of the original he took it week by week to read to Ned and Georgie at the Sunday breakfasts at The Grange. Few people have had a good word to say for Morris's *Beowulf* (least of all in Oxford). I will not attempt one. It is Morris at his most garrulous and loose. The translation is an unexpected failure since Morris, with his taste for the heroic, might have been expected to respond to the starkness of the setting and the embattlement of giants.

Morris was still capable of wild outbursts of excitement. When he heard that Ruskin, now in his seventies, had called him 'the ablest man of his time' he ordered up a bottle of his favourite Imperial Tokay from the cellar at Kelmscott House to celebrate. The old spasms of anger still occasionally seized him. He was showing his manuscripts, in Hammersmith in 1895, to five earnest teenage girls when one of them dared to put a finger delicately on the gilding. Morris immediately flared up. Helen Thomas remembered, 'Our horror at what one of us had in ignorance done and the humiliation we felt at his anger, I can feel to this day.' Once he had recovered he was, as always, eager to make amends, bustling up and down stairs and in and out of rooms, bringing in more books and manuscripts and pictures by Rossetti and Burne-Jones.

But Morris was becoming gradually more muted. His biographer-to-be, Mackail, who knew him at this period, observed how 'his whole personality ripened and softened'. He was kinder and more patient. At Hammersmith the life of the river seemed to soothe him. He was not so irritated by the raucous local children. 'Yesterday', he wrote one summer, 'I dined with May and Harry; and after dinner we sat out of doors and watched the tide coming up and the boats going about . . . but presently I felt sleepy, and lay back in a garden chair, and so did May, and we meditated for a minute and then went to sleep.'

The 1890s were a time of consolidation for Morris. They were also years of severance and change. May's short-lived Socialist marriage ended, as Janey predicted. In the weeks before the legendary ice-cold Christmas at Kelmscott in 1892 Bernard Shaw had moved into No. 8

Hammersmith Terrace, the place he described as May's 'quiet little house, with an embroidery factory cumbering the drawing room from nine to five'. It had been intended as a temporary arrangement, while Shaw recovered from nervous exhaustion. But he stayed on and, as he recalled later, in his usual tone of self-satisfaction, 'everything went well for a time in that *ménage à trois*', with May enthusiastic in her welcome and Sparling pleased because Shaw kept May 'in good humour' and producing a cuisine that no mere husband could elicit. 'It was probably the happiest passage in our three lives.' Although there is no evidence in family correspondence, it is still maintained in Morris circles that the Sparlings had had a still-born child. If so, this could explain the alacrity with which they welcomed Shaw, as entertainer and distraction. But the idyll could not last. Shaw blamed the Mystic Betrothal: 'It made me from the first the centre of the household.' By the time he had clearly recovered from his illness and there was no longer any excuse for staying in May's house unless he proposed to do so permanently, 'her legal marriage had dissolved as all illusions do'. It was a theme Shaw pursued with a devastating candour in his play *The Philanderer*, which was being written through the spring and summer while he was residing in the Sparlings' house. (The last act was finally unearthed and produced in 1991. It had been considered too 'advanced' to stage.) In August May and Shaw travelled to Zürich together, with the British delegation, to the International Socialist Workers' Congress. Eleanor Marx Aveling was in the party, too.

Sparling was indignant about the situation, feeling himself betrayed both by his Socialist colleague and his wife. May was all too obviously hoping that the Mystic Betrothal would at last bear fruit. Shaw, as so often, made his exit from what was now becoming a scene of alarming emotional entanglement. Sparling told Holbrook Jackson that 'after completely captivating his wife Shaw suddenly disappeared, leaving behind him a desolated female who might have been an iceberg so far as her future relations with her husband went'. Shaw, taxed with this, commented, 'Sparling was wrong about the captivation. Nothing of the kind occurred. We had been captivated long before.' He explained further: 'As I had enough sexual satisfaction available elsewhere I was perfectly content to leave all that to Sparling and go on platonically; but May was not. The catastrophe followed.'

What Shaw spoke of with such self-serving flippancy had long reverberations within the Morris household. In May 1894 Janey wrote to

Blunt, 'May's married life has come to an end, and although we always expected some catastrophe or other in that direction, the blow is no less heavy now it has come. We have not yet spoken of it outside the family.' She felt she would never be able to pay visits or to see friends again. Two days later she sent Blunt a few more words of explanation: 'May's position is this, she has been seeing a good deal of a former lover, and made her husband's life a burden to him, he refuses to bear it any longer – she is still abroad but when she comes back they will go their separate ways.' In June 1894 Sparling left to live in Paris. Perhaps May was in any case better off without him: there is a cryptic reference in Cockerell's diary to Sparling offering to sell him Morris manuscripts. May stayed alone in Hammersmith Terrace. It is curious that Janey never seemed to correlate May's *ménage à trois* with her own.

Morris's response to May's disaster is equivocal. This was after all a situation he had not only lived through, but described over and over in his poems and his novels. *The Roots of the Mountains* contains Morris's most poignant and sympathetic narrative of the end of married love. There is no doubt that faced with the choice between Sparling and Shaw as a son-in-law he would still have preferred Shaw. In purely practical terms he now had to replace Sparling in his role in his own business, and in May 1894 Sydney Cockerell was appointed the new secretary to the Kelmscott Press. May brought a case against Sparling for the restitution of conjugal rights and was granted a divorce in 1899. Perhaps she clung to her hopes that Shaw would return to her. Shaw's sister Lucy, seeing May at an Arnold Dolmetsch concert, commented 'There goes Mrs. Sparling (daughter of William Morris). She has just divorced her husband, because she wants to marry George.' But the immediate effect was to make May more than ever concentrated on her father. In 1896 she wrote to Morris's old comrade Andreas Scheu: 'I fear it is the cry of an uncourageous heart to say that the thought of him and his work and his love has been for a good many years my only comfort and pleasure in life; but so it is.'

Janey's last affair was coming to an end, in its physical sense, as May's marriage foundered. Blunt had commented on Janey's physical deterioration in the summer of 1893, when he had stayed at Kelmscott with his wife and daughter: 'Mrs. Morris is much aged this year, being my own age 53.' The following August, he returned to Kelmscott Manor, complaining as Rossetti had about the dreary landscape, as he tramped through the rain-drenched meadows by the river. Janey was accustomed to leave a pansy in Blunt's bedroom to suggest he should advance along the creaking corridors to claim her. Blunt recorded in his diary: 'I found a pansy on the floor of my room when I went to bed. But it is too late alas, and I slept soundly.' Blunt later analysed the situation as he saw it: 'We never had the smallest quarrel, but drifted apart with advancing age, retaining a strong affection though we rarely met. In this way love dies very easily and without strong pain.'

A few days after Blunt left Kelmscott a meteor appeared. With her interest in signs and portents Janey watched it from the window of the Tapestry Room: 'The moon was distinctly seen from the other window at the time – altogether the effect was very weird.'

The last disorientating event of this strange year was the death of Morris's mother. She had had a fine old age. Five years earlier Janey, calling her the 'liveliest old lady possible', who read and talked incessantly, had predicted she would live until 1919 at least. Although Morris had been worried by her growing deafness, and then her advancing illness, her death, when it came, was an unexpectedly deep grief to him. He told Georgie, 'Altogether my old and callous heart was touched by the absence of what had been so kind to me and fond of me.' Perhaps he thought back to his lugubrious early poem 'My Mother Under the Mould'. Shaw, lecturing at Kelmscott House one Sunday evening soon after her burial, found Morris 'in extreme trouble and low spirits' and unable to face the usual tableful of guests. They had a little supper on their own and Shaw was able to rouse him from despondency only by suggesting the Kelmscott Press should bring out a *Pilgrim's Progress*. Philip Webb had the job of designing Mrs Morris's tombstone. The inscription was to read 'In memory of Emma, widow of William Morris, who fell asleep in Jesus on 7 December 1894 in the 90th year of her age. Thine eyes shall see the King in his beauty.'

By the end of 1894, now in his seventh decade, Morris's physical energy was waning. He was no longer able to go out for whole days' fishing at Kelmscott. Country walks were getting shorter. Mackail was out walking with him on an autumn day. When his companions perched on a gate to rest, Morris sat down on the roadside with his legs stretched out in front of him saying, 'I shall sit on the world'. Mackail wrote, 'It would be difficult to convey to anyone who did not know him well the sense of mingled oddness and pathos that the words gave.'

As Morris became weaker he gazed at the world around him with a

51 William Morris sketched by Walter Crane speaking at a May Day rally
in Hyde Park two years before his death.

new intensity, defending his familiar landscapes and loved buildings
with a fierceness arising from the sense of his impending loss. The
twelve mediaeval statues on the spire of St Mary's Church in Oxford;
the fifteenth-century church built in flint on the marshland at Blythburgh in Suffolk; the interior of Peterborough Cathedral; the north-
west tower of Chichester; Rouen, the superb cathedral where attempts
at restoration would be 'much on a level with a fifth form boy's Latin
verses set against a passage of the *Aeneid*': these were all campaigns of
Morris's last three years. He entered into a vituperative correspondence
with the Thames Conservancy Board over the re-roofing of the lock-
keeper's cottage at Eaton Weir by Kelmscott, and was especially protective of the buildings of his immediate neighbourhood. He described to
Georgie his dismay at the crudeness of rebuilding of a small barn he had

653

known well near Black Bourton: 'I saw all my worst fears realised; for there was the little barn we saw being mended, the wall cut down and finished with a zinked iron roof. It quite sickened me when I saw it.' The sight still produces a physical response. In his old age all Morris's senses appear heightened. In summer 1895, after going with his printers on their 'Wayzegoose' in the meadows around Cookham, the pungent scent of violets lingered on for hours.

That summer Morris's condition was beginning to alarm his close circle. Ned wrote, 'It is sad to see his enormous vitality diminishing.' He could only just summon up energy to clip the yew dragon at Kelmscott. Perhaps it was a measure of his frustration that he threatened to re-cut it as a peacock. He did, however, manage to make his annual visit to the ancestral White Horse. Georgie, staying at Kelmscott for the first time for nine years, was with him. She sensed a new serenity in Morris: 'Topsy looks very happy,' she wrote, 'and is so sweet down here. The garden is enchanting with flowers, one mass of them, and all kept in beautiful order.' But there was a strangeness in the scene: 'I feel the added years in Janey and Topsy and me, so that it seems like visiting something that is not quite real.'

The bed that Morris slept in at Kelmscott Manor was a huge seventeenth-century carved oak four-poster. In the 1890s it was adorned with hangings that were in themselves a culmination of Morris & Co. embroidery. May designed the two curtains, a trellis and bird pattern in bright coloured silks and wools on a plain linen backing, a reworking of the original 'Trellis' wallpaper of 1864 that May had had on the walls of her own nursery. The curtains were stitched under her supervision in the drawing-room at Hammersmith Terrace. The valance was embroidered with Morris's verses composed especially 'For the Bed at Kelmscott':

> The Wind's on the wold and the night is a-cold
> And Thames runs chill twixt mead and hill
> But kind and dear is the old house here
> And my heart is warm midst winter's harm.
> Rest then and rest and think of the best
> Twixt summer and spring when all birds sing
> In the town of the tree and ye lie in me
> And scarce dare move lest earth and its love
> Should fade away ere the full of the day.

I am old and have seen many things that have been
Both grief and peace and wane and increase.
No tale I tell of ill or well
But this I say: night treadeth on day
And for worst and best right good is rest.

A year or two later a coverlet was added, a floral pattern including sprigs of daisies. Mary De Morgan helped Janey to embroider it. The bed cover was signed, 'Si je puis. Jane Morris. Kelmscott'.

On 23 December 1895 Sergius Stepniak was struck down by a train on a level-crossing near his home in Bedford Park. He was killed almost instantly. Stepniak was only forty-three. His death was officially declared 'accidental', but there were rumours of suicide. Kropotkin wrote to tell Morris of the funeral arrangements, and five days later he was one of the speakers at what *The Times* described as an 'assemblage of Socialists, Nihilists, Anarchists, and outlaws of every European country' outside Waterloo Station in the drizzling rain. A long procession of Russian Jewish exiles had arrived from Whitechapel, marching to the Dead March, carrying the black and crimson flag. The German Communistic Club carried a magnificent wreath 'In Namen des Communistischen'. The hearse, carrying Stepniak's coffin, with his widow in attendance, was followed by two mourning carriages and greeted by a funeral band. The mourners included the Russian Volkhovsky who spoke in broken English 'under much emotion'; Malatesta, who spoke briefly in Italian; an East End tailor, Kahn, who spoke in Yiddish; Verjbitsky of the Polish Political Club, who addressed the crowd in Polish; Eleanor Marx, who delivered an impassioned feminist oration, saying she spoke for women 'because Stepniak understood there could be no emancipation for men except it went alongside of emancipation for women'. John Burns spoke; also Keir Hardie in his burring Scottish accent. In comparison Linnell's funeral in 1887 seemed a homespun affair.

But now, as then, Morris rose to the occasion, delivering an address of great dignity and feeling. According to *The Times* reporter, Morris said:

he was one of the speakers, at all events, who were there to represent the feelings of the English Socialists on the death of their lost comrade. His message was, first, simply to express their deep sorrow and regret at the loss they had sustained in Stepniak's death, and their appreciation of his noble qualities.

Next, he wished to express the feelings of love and brotherhood entertained by all their party for the great Russian people.

When one of the speakers suggested that Stepniak had latterly abandoned his revolutionary outlook and veered towards Fabianism, Morris interrupted him fervently and startlingly, crying out above the crowd: 'That is a lie – to suggest that Stepniak had ceased to be a revolutionary!' His words bore the conviction of someone who had weathered similar unjust accusations. The train bore Stepniak's body off to Woking Crematorium. Morris did not go with it. It was his last speech in the open air.

Over the next few weeks there were many last appearances. His final political speech was given at the SDF's New Year Meeting on 3 January 1896 at Holborn Town Hall. George Lansbury moved a resolution of international greetings, a message of fellowship that Morris seconded in a heartfelt speech against imperialism. Hyndman wrote: 'He was ill at the time, and I fear that even coming to this meeting was an overtasking of his strength. None who were present will ever forget the touching appeal that he then made or the words of counsel and good cheer he then spoke.' A few days later he was writing in a letter to America, 'I have *not* changed my mind about Socialism'.

On 31 January Morris was at a meeting at the Society of Arts. This was called by a new body, the Society for Checking the Abuses of Public Advertising. Morris made a brief speech, his very last in public. He hated the sight of the large advertising posters that were beginning to pollute the countryside.

'The best way of lengthening out the rest of our days, old chap, is to finish off our old things', was Ned's advice. That Christmas Morris had begun his final novel, *The Sundering Flood*, the tale of two lovers cut off by a colossal river. It was based on a contemporary Icelandic story with a recognizably Icelandic setting of mountains and gorges and great wastes of tumbled stones. May forever associated its beginnings with this sombre period in her father's life. On Sunday 5 January, unable to sleep, he entered in the diary he was now once again keeping: 'got up and worked from 1 – 4 at Sundering.'

He was also writing poetry. On Tuesday 7 January he sent verses to Georgie with a pencilled note: 'This may be called "a poem by the way". A stanza got into my head on Friday last, and so I thought I would go on

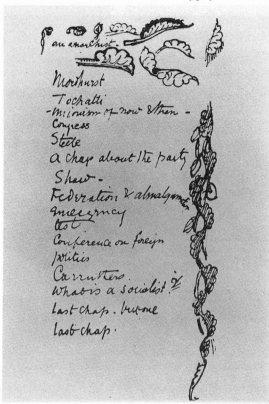

52 The notes for Morris's last political paper, 'One Socialist Party', delivered
to the Hammersmith Socialist Society on 5 January 1896.

with it. I send it on so that it may not interrupt tomorrow [Wednesday's
reading] as that is *business* and is like to take time.' This is the poem
known as 'She and He':

> She. The blossom's white upon the thorn,
>   The lily's on the lea,
>   The beaded dew is bright to morn;
>   Come forth and o'er to me!
>
>   And when thou farest from the ford
>   My hand thine hand shall take;
>   For this young day about my board
>   Men sing the feast awake.

And I am lady of the land,
My hall is wide and side,
And therein would I have thee stand
Midst the blooming of my pride.

Since oft a days forth wandered we
O'er mead and dale and down,
Till on the edges of the sea
Aloof we saw the town.

Since oft a days we turned and went
And left the wind-worn shore,
And there below the sheep-fed bent
Stood by the little door.

Twas oft from glooming of the lea
Into the house we turned
And I by thee, and thou by me
Watched how the oak-log burned.

Wherefore while yet the day is young,
And the feast awoke with morn,
Come o'er and hear my praises sung
And the day when I was born.

With 'She and He' Morris suggests that he and Georgie still stand on opposite sides of a great river of their own.

By early 1896 he was noticeably feebler. Though still only sixty-two he was appearing almost ancient. To the Mackails' small daughter Angela he was 'the old man (or so I thought him) with the aggressive mop of white hair who was talking, between fits of coughing, to my grandmother.' One Sunday at The Grange, in the middle of breakfast, he had begun leaning his forehead on his hand. Ned had not seen him do this before, in all the years he had known him. This was in fact to be the final Sunday morning at The Grange.

It was Ned who took matters into his own hands, telegraphing to Sir William Broadbent for an appointment for Morris and, in February, accompanying him for the initial consultation. Broadbent was one of the most famous physicians of the period, created a baronet three years before. His enormously successful private practice was in Brook Street in Mayfair; it provided an income of over £13,000 a year. Broadbent was already 'physician in ordinary' to the Prince of Wales, later Edward VII, and was appointed Queen Victoria's 'physician extraordinary' in 1896. Morris sent on his detailed report to Philip Webb: the 'great doctor', he wrote, was

a pleasant looking man, not given to long words and circumlocutions. He examined me, partly bare, for about 3 quarters of an hour. And said that sugar there *was* in my water, but not so much as to be serious and expected to get rid of it by rigid diet, eggs, milk, purée of meat, at first, and when my stomach can stand it un-fat flesh meat. Thought he would soon get rid of it. The other thing is that my stomach is swollen immensely, and even when it has digested the stuff, is too lazy to get rid of it. He is giving something of a knitting up character for that and expects to get it right soon. But you see he may be wrong, and it may go worse with me.

It is notable how Morris finds it easier to confide the details of his physical condition to Webb than to any other male or female friend. This letter ends with a sad attempt at jauntiness, quoting Surtees: 'Hopes you'll brick your neck you old thief! says the gipsy to Mr. Jorrocks. Hopes I shan't says Mr. J.'

Janey had been aware for years of his diabetic problems, but had been unable to get Morris either to see the danger or to 'seek advice from a competent doctor'. She felt relieved he was now in Broadbent's hands.

Morris's diary for this period is sad reading. Almost every day in February he describes himself as 'seedy'. Emery Walker administered an enema the night after Morris's visit to Broadbent. The devoted Walker became Morris's medical attendant. Shaw perceptively analysed the worst of it as the enforced change of rhythm: 'From being a man who was never idle or listless, he suddenly, to his own dismay, found himself sitting about doing nothing and quite at a loss, his voice weakened and his energy scattered.' He was carrying on with *The Sundering Flood* as well as with the writing of *The Well at the World's End* and the decorations for the Kelmscott *Chaucer*, but his diary reveals painfully the depth of his frustration: 'Began a new ABC (open work) also did a p or 2 of Sundering almost nothing to either'; 'did an A also 6 pp of Sundering but feeling seedy'; 'I don't feel any better – so weak.'

Janey too had been especially unwell, feeling the strain of Morris's illness. The previous autumn she had been, as Morris put it, 'bothered with boils and blains like Job', and in a bizarre episode a telegram with news of Janey's illness had been misinterpreted by Philip Webb as the announcement of her death. After the 'weary dark winter' she had been 'in bed with rheumatism and worry', she told Blunt. In April Morris was considered just enough improved to make the journey to Kelmscott Manor and the two of them were there from 22 April to 5 May. Morris was very weak, hardly able to walk beyond the garden. But the cronies gathered: first Walker and then Ellis. He was able to do some drawing and a very little writing. It was a beautiful spring, with 'the grass well grown and well coloured' and more blossom on the apple trees than he had ever seen. The raspberry canes had been trellised up so neatly by Giles, the gardener, that Kelmscott was looking 'like a mediaeval garden'. Morris listened to the rooks and blackbirds in the garden and noted in his diary that at seven a.m. three mornings running a cuckoo sang. Some major improvements were in train at Kelmscott Manor. Webb was in charge of a scheme for the replacement of the old stone flags with wooden flooring in many of the ground-floor rooms. This involved a thorough overhaul of the foundations, 'to get rid of the congestion of rottenness underfoot'.

On the final evening of what turned out to be Morris's last visit to Kelmscott Sydney Cockerell arrived, bearing the twelfth-century English manuscript, a Bestiary, he had just bought in Stuttgart on Morris's behalf. Manuscripts could still unfailingly rouse Morris from his apathy. At the prospect of new purchases his old acquisitive instincts would resurface and his eyes would glimmer with the greed of the small child. In March he had purchased from his friend 'Brass' Benson a fine folio Testament of the twelfth century which he found had emanated from the same religious house near Dijon as a Josephus manuscript he had acquired earlier: his joy in such esoteric details, bibliophiles' mania, was a feature of Morris's advancing age. The resplendent Bestiary, with its 106 miniatures, was his greatest treasure yet, finer than any of the Bestiaries in the British Museum. Morris had trusted Cockerell to pay £900 for it. 'There the murder is out', he confessed to Webb shamefacedly. 'But you see it will certainly fetch something when my sale comes off.'

Morris returned to London no better. His cough had improved and he was sleeping better. But he was feeling generally weaker, complaining of being 'bothered with belly ache and pains in the limbs'. He was still very listless, struggling to get himself to work on his Kelmscott Press border, when he and Janey went to stay with the Blunts at Newbuildings at the end of May. Blunt was shocked by the change in him, but found that his spirits were still 'fairly good' and that at times he talked as brilliantly as ever. They discussed the new piece of tapestry that had been made at Merton, the Burne-Jones version of Botticelli's 'Spring', now hanging in Blunt's drawing-room. It had turned out better than Morris had expected. 'We think the three figures with the flowers are March, April and May,' Blunt wrote. He and Morris had 'many interesting talks on art, politics and religion. As to the last he does not believe in any God the Creator of the World, or any Providence, or, I think, any future life. But he is not a pessimist, and thinks mankind "the crown of things", in spite of man's destructive action and his modern craze of ugliness. His illness does not make him gloomy; only it troubles him in his work.'

Morris on this visit was quiet, endearing, reminiscent. Blunt seems to have concentrated on him wholly: there is no mention of Janey whatsoever in his diary account. Janey's former lover drove her husband gently around the Sussex countryside. Blunt wrote: 'He is, I think, happy here. The oak woods are new to him, though he was born in Epping Forest, and he likes the multitude of birds. He creeps about a little among them in the sun.' The only time he was aroused to his old levels of vehemence was when Blunt took him to look at Shipley church, with a once fine Norman tower Morris considered 'quite spoiled by restoration regardless of expense'. Here it was the old irascible Morris, marching down the aisle and swearing at the parsons who allowed such an atrocity: 'Beasts! Pigs! Damn their souls!'

Morris's doctors were puzzled by his lack of improvement. His weight loss continued. In early June he had lost two pounds within a fortnight: he now weighed under ten and a half stone. A new consultant, Dr Pavy, a diabetic specialist, was brought in by Broadbent. Pavy felt Morris's 'belly-parts' all over, but could find nothing seriously wrong. However, they decided to recommend the seaside and Morris and Janey spent the next few weeks stranded in the Norfolk Hotel, Folkestone. Here he managed to write a little more of *The Sundering Flood*. But it was largely an invalid's routine of daily drives down to the harbour where, Morris told Webb, 'I toddle about, and sit down, lean over the chairs, and rather enjoy it, especially if there are any craft about.' There were visits from Georgie and Ned, Ellis and Walker, Cockerell and Robert Catterson-Smith, Blunt and his new *innamorata* Lady Elcho, the society beauty. Georgie offended Janey by suggesting that Morris needed a professional nurse and by saying that 'his food was not always as carefully selected as it ought to be'. Morris still felt isolated and complained of lack of books.

He had been very depressed by the death, at the age of only fifty, of his old colleague John Henry Middleton, the exuberant and brilliant director of the South Kensington Museum, whom Morris had first met on board the *Diana* on his second Iceland voyage. The news had been kept from Morris until he was actually in the train to Folkestone. Like Rossetti, Middleton had been a chloral addict, as Janey had discovered soon after they first knew him. He had married her friend Marie Stillman's daughter Bella. When she heard of his death Janey expressed surprise that Bella ever left the bottle within his reach.

Only two events enlivened the despondent Folkestone visit. One was the expedition Morris made to Hythe with Walker where they found Lympne Court, 'a most exceedingly lovely house knocked about as a farm-house but quite unrestored'. The other was Douglas Cockerell's arrival on 24 June, with the first sample bound copy of the Kelmscott *Chaucer* for Morris's approval. Morris had designed the special binding, carried out at Cobden-Sanderson's Doves Bindery, in white pigskin with silver clasps. The five-year project was now nearing its completion. Ned wrote later: 'When Morris and I were little chaps at Oxford, if such a book had come out then we should have just gone off our heads, but we have made at the end of our days the very thing we would have made then if we could.'

At the beginning of July Morris returned to London. He was still full of plans for producing a great volume of Froissart, a companion to the *Chaucer*; he was already working on the borders of the folio edition of *Sigurd the Volsung* that loomed large in his mind. After his return he completed negotiations with Lord Aldenham, paying him £1,000 for a magnificent illuminated Psalter of *c.*1270. The Psalter had several pages missing. Morris already owned four of these pages, which he had exchanged with Fairfax Murray for five sheets of drawings on vellum by an Italian master of the fifteenth century. It was a bibliophile's dream coup, the last of his 'wot larx!' Morris had had his mind on an even finer Psalter belonging to the Duke of Rutland. He wrote droolingly about it: '*such* a book! *my* eyes! and I am beating my brains about to see if I can find any thread of an intrigue to begin upon so as to creep and crawl toward possession of it.' But even he could not.

Morris's doctors, in despair, had now prescribed a cruise to Norway. Hyndman paid a farewell visit to Hammersmith and found him pinched and wasted but still flaring up from time to time with his old enthusiasm. They took a turn around the garden. 'This has been a jolly world to me and I find plenty to do in it,' Morris said.

CHAPTER NINETEEN

Norway
1896

The doomed ship drives on helpless through the sea,
All that the mariners may do is done
And death is left for men to gaze upon,
While side by side two friends sit silently;
Friends once, foes once, and now by death made free
Of Love and Hate, of all things lost or won;
Yet still the wonder of that strife bygone
Clouds all the hope or horror that may be.

Thus, Sorrow, are we sitting side by side
Amid this welter of the grey despair,
Nor have we images of foul or fair
To vex, save of thy kissed face of a bride,
Thy scornful face of tears when I was tried,
And failed neath pain I was not made to bear.

'The Doomed Ship' is one of the poems of *The Earthly Paradise* period
not published until the 1930s, when it appeared in May's final collection
of her father's work. It could have been written after his Icelandic
voyages. The journey it most resembles is in fact the cruise to Norway
taken by the dying Morris and his friend John Carruthers in July 1896.

The four-week voyage had been put over as a hopeful one. Early in
July, on their return from Folkestone, Morris and Janey went together
to see Broadbent, who suggested that Morris was a little better. He had
already survived a trial day trip, accompanied by Cockerell, from Folkestone to Boulogne. It was arranged that Morris would travel to Norway
with a friend and with a 'medical man' supplied by Broadbent. Cockerell
booked the berths for Morris and Carruthers on the Orient Line steamer

SS *Garonne* sailing from Tilbury to the very northernmost coast of Norway on 22 July. It later emerged that Broadbent had no real hope of Morris's recovery. Dr Dodgson, Broadbent's nominee to care for Morris on the cruise, realized that any improvement would be temporary. Only Morris and Carruthers were unaware that 'the voyage had been recommended as a forlorn hope that it might postpone the inevitable end'.

John Carruthers, who had offered gladly to be Morris's companion, was one of the stalwart companions he always attracted, another of the gentleman-Socialist henchmen who, like Charley Faulkner, absorbed Morris's charisma while sharing very little of his aesthetic sense. But Carruthers had a romantic streak. He had travelled widely in his work as a constructional engineer, building railways in New Zealand, Venezuela, Argentina, then going to Australia to advise on the design and construction of the Coolgardie water supply. He had been a useful member of the SPAB with his practical knowledge of building structure and had been called in as the specialist adviser on the conservation of Stonehenge. Morris liked to see Carruthers as a fellow-Norseman, an adventurer. Carruthers' daughter wrote of him, 'he roamed at night, watching the stars and thinking'. Strong, generous and calm, he could not have been a more ideal companion for the journey. But even so Morris resisted the idea of leaving England. At Tilbury he showed unusual signs of panic. Cockerell and Walker had come to see him off and Morris had implored them not to go.

The SS *Garonne* was a large cruise ship, carrying about a hundred passengers, many of them young and in holiday mood. There was a more purposeful contingent of British astronomers, headed by Sir Norman Lockyer, travelling to Norway to observe the sun's eclipse which was due to take place on 8 August. Life on board, dedicated as it was to health and pleasure, must have reminded Morris of Bad Ems. To begin with all went reasonably well. After a little turbulence crossing the North Sea, which made Morris slightly queasy, there were calm seas and fine weather. Morris, clearly an invalid, needed assistance in moving around the ship, or shifting position. Carruthers noted with amusement how he asked to be positioned with a good view of 'the younger and prettier women'. A woman with red gold hair, 'of the colour the Italian painters loved', especially impressed him. Morris was still in pursuit of stunners in 1896. On 27 July, Carruthers began sending optimistic telegrams home. Off Bergen, as the ship was heading up the western coast of Norway, Morris wrote to Philip Webb quite cheerfully. He told him that although the food on board was abominable, the eggs and milk having 'a strong scientific flavour', the wine was 'rather good'.

In May, when he was staying at Newbuildings with the Blunts, Morris had talked a good deal about his Icelandic journey, still vivid in his mind after twenty years. He had what Blunt called 'a sick man's fancy' for repeating the experience. 'I am a man of the North,' he had insisted, surprising Blunt by castigating the fine weather, longing for a tempest so that he could stay indoors 'and watch it beating on the windows'. As the ship arrived at Bergen, 'a dramatic entry', Morris was conscious that he was re-entering the northern landscape of his travels and his fantasies. He told Webb, 'This is a pleasant place with a good deal left of the old town and all of the old hills, which the eyes of the old men looked on when they did their best against the Wends.'

When they reached Vadsö near the North Cape Morris seemed well enough for Carruthers to leave him on shore with Dr Dodgson while the steamer went on to Spitsbergen. Carruthers came back a week later to find him out walking with Dr Dodgson in the village. He said he had enjoyed his quiet days there staying in clean and comfortable rooms and eating simple food the reverse of 'scientific'. On the return journey through the fjords there were some additional passengers. One was a Mr Taylor, an Oxford man to whom Morris took a liking and with whom he had 'many animated discussions on literary subjects', and Dr Brodrick, to whom he also enjoyed talking, 'although the super-Oxonian superiority of the Master of Merton was the subject of a few quiet jokes'.

But Carruthers was by now aware that Morris was declining. Soon after they left Trondheim, where Morris had been greatly impressed by the cathedral, he was gathering depression: '"All these hills and fjords are", he said, "classic ground but I cannot take interest in them as I should once have done".' On the return journey Morris managed to go ashore at Hammerfest and again at Bergen; but from then on Carruthers could sense his withdrawal which he blamed on the gloom of the north Norwegian scenery, 'depressing in its barrenness', followed by the lurching of the ship as it crossed the North Sea. Morris began having sinister hallucinations, like Evelyn Waugh in *The Ordeal of Gilbert Pinfold*. The ropes, curled up on the deck, seemed like coiled snakes.

They landed at Tilbury on 18 August. Cockerell and Walker arrived at 10 a.m. to find the *Garonne* there before them and the passengers making their way into the tender. Morris, in the optimism of arrival,

666

said he felt 'better in spite of the voyage'. He said nothing would induce him to take another cruise. He ate his lunch with gusto, saying how nice it was to have cutlets that tasted of *meat* again, 'instead of having the flavour of deal boards'. Janey wrote that day to May, who was travelling in France, 'Papa has arrived and is certainly much better for the voyage – but still the cough remains.' They planned to go back to Kelmscott Manor the following week to join Jenny. She did not like the thought of Morris spending time in town.

No one knew that at the time of the arrival Dr Dodgson had taken Cockerell aside and warned him that Morris's condition was critical. There were signs that congestion of the lung had now set in. Morris, still in the euphoria of homecoming, set off the next morning to The Grange. Ned had just arrived from Rottingdean to attend the funeral of Sir John Everett Millais in St Paul's Cathedral the following day. A mood of depression gradually took over as Morris realized he was weaker than he imagined. He was clearly not well enough to go to Kelmscott and on 20 August wrote in great grief to Jenny:

Dearest own child
I am so distressed that I cannot get down to Kelmscott on Saturday; but I am not well, and the doctors will not let me; please my own dear forgive me, for I long to see you with all my heart.

Now Kelmscott House began to be turned into a nursing home. The knocker was muffled. Morris ordered it to be unwrapped: 'folks would think he was having a baby'. Cockerell took to staying at Kelmscott House on a couch in the library, in case he was needed in the night. Through August and early September Morris's condition fluctuated. On some days he was able to work a little, designing a few ornaments for the Kelmscott Press and answering some letters. On 27 August he dictated to Cockerell the last four and a half pages of *The Sundering Flood*. But on his worst days he was too ill to undress himself. He replied to Thomas Wardle, who had invited him to stay at his grandiose new mansion in Staffordshire, 'at present I cannot walk over the threshold, being so intensely weak'.

By the end of August Dodgson wrote to tell Cockerell in confidence that the lung trouble had proved to be tubercular. Janey, who had been so brave at the beginning, was now feeling the strain of it. W. Graham Robertson, visiting Kelmscott House, remembered the histrionic gesture with which, when asked for news of Morris, she had turned to the wall and fallen against it, 'her bowed head hidden in her hands'.

On 9 September Morris made a new will in the presence of Janey, Crom Price and the garrulous and competent Mary De Morgan, now installed at Kelmscott House as companion and nurse. Ellis and Cockerell were to be executors in addition to Janey. Provision was made to finance Jenny's nursing care for the rest of her lifetime. Cockerell felt that the making of the will had been a great relief to Morris. Last things were now concerning him. He had, a few days earlier, asked Cockerell whether he and Walker would be willing to continue with the Kelmscott Press after his death. When Cockerell told him he preferred to think of the Press closing in its glory rather than begin producing inferior volumes Morris seemed inclined to agree. He was now failing mentally, suffering from loss of memory and disturbed with wild hallucinations, which he called 'the screaming horrors', and nocturnal fantasies. One of these, in mid-September, was that he was composing Dean Farrar's *Life of Christ*.

By 12 September Cobden-Sanderson wrote in his eerie Gothic style:

Morris is dying, slowly. It is an astonishing spectacle. He sits speechless, waiting for the end to come.

Every night, darkness destroys the world of light; every day, the night of death which shall destroy for ever the light of life is before his imagination in the distance. It comes nearer and nearer. He waits. Soon it will envelop all the familiar scene, the sweet river, England green and grey, Kelmscott, Kelmscott House, the trees which tremble with little noises in their leaves, the Press, the passage, the Bindery, the light coming in through the windows, the green paint within, the old books on the shelves, the dining-room, the long table, the big chair at the head, the long garden, all, all, all. The darkness of death will destroy all and for ever. 'But,' he said to Mary de Morgan, 'but I cannot believe that I shall be annihilated.'

His friends tried desperately to divert him. F. S. Ellis read out Border ballads for him, and encouraged him to imagine he was making his selection for a new volume for the Kelmscott Press. R. H. Benson brought a whole succession of rare manuscripts from the Dorchester House library for Morris to admire and fondle. One was a Psalter from Amiens, another was a *Bible Historiée et Vies des Saints* with 1,034 illustrations beginning with the Creation and extending to the coming of the Anti-Christ and the world's end. On 21 September Arnold Dolmetsch came after tea and played the virginals for Morris. He performed several pieces by English sixteenth-century composers, including a pavane and galliard by William Byrd. Cockerell noted, 'WM enjoyed it extremely, but was a good deal affected.' He was now becoming tremendously emotional. He had wept on one of Georgie's visits when they talked about the hard life of the poor. Nevertheless, apart from Webb and Carruthers, it does not appear that Morris's old Socialist colleagues came to see him. The proletarian Socialists are notably absent from Cockerell's detailed records of attendance at the sick bed. Morris, dying, was more or less successfully reclaimed by his class.

It appears that Wilfrid Blunt was kept at arm's length. On 4 September he had visited Kelmscott House. His published diary gives an account of this visit: 'Mrs. de Morgan [sic] was there and Cockerell, and while I was sitting with them in came Madeline Wyndham, beautiful in her old age.' Typically, he omits the further comment in his 'secret' diary that Morris would not see him 'as he had a number of people with him and was tired'. However, three weeks later Blunt dined at Kelmscott House and on that occasion Morris 'came in like a man from the grave, and sat a few minutes at the table, but seemed dazed and unable to follow the conversation'. To Blunt he appeared sunk in his own gloom.

The following day he was suddenly feeling much better. It was a bright morning and Cockerell, Mary De Morgan, Ellis and Georgie wheeled him out into Ravenscourt Park in his bath chair. This invalid chair was a feature, almost the symbol, of those last few weeks in Hammersmith: Morris, huddled into it, resembled his old self, acting the aged gentleman in the Socialist play *The Duchess of Bayswater*. In the park they were met by a small girl, Ellis's granddaughter, who gazed in wonder. It was one of those mysterious encounters with children that Morris, in Iceland, had so vividly described. Morris was cheerful on that outing. It was the furthest he had yet been in the wheelchair. He said he felt strong enough to do a little walking. After lunch Carruthers came. He left Kelmscott House at a quarter to five. Cockerell went out for a few minutes to the post-box. When he got back he found Morris upstairs with blood streaming from his mouth. Ellis was with him. They helped him downstairs and put him to bed. The doctor, Dr Hogg, was summoned. Lethaby came in the evening. Mary De Morgan sat up with him all night.

He was breathing very heavily when Cockerell arrived on Wednesday 3 October. Georgie came to visit in the morning and Ned in the afternoon. Morris was wandering in his mind a good deal but he still recognized them. He depended especially on Georgie's visits: 'Come soon,' he would entreat her, 'I want a sight of your dear face'. Detmar Blow, Emery Walker and Cockerell stayed up that night with him. He imagined he was back on board the *Garonne*, heaving through the Nordic seas.

On Thursday he was still wandering and restless. His deaconess sister Isabella came to see him in the morning. He was given a linseed poultice. Mary De Morgan and Detmar Blow sat through another night. By Friday he was 'very quiet'. He was clearly receding and was failing to recognize even Georgie, who came again that morning, followed by Ned in the afternoon. Ned did not think Morris was ever in much pain but 'the weakness was pitiful'. He knew that he was seeing him for the last time. Philip Webb arrived at six p.m. A professional nurse came who, said Cockerell, was 'a great comfort'. Nurse Gillespie and Emery Walker watched together through the night. But Morris's temperature was rising.

He died at eleven-fifteen the next morning. Janey, May, Detmar Blow, Mary De Morgan and Georgie were in the room. Georgie said he had died 'as gently, as quietly as a babe who is satisfied drops from its mother's breast'.

Mary De Morgan and Emery Walker set off straight away to Kelmscott Manor to break the news to Jenny. She bore the news 'bravely'. Later in the day Carruthers, Crom Price and Philip Webb arrived. Fairfax Murray made two drawings from the corpse. Cockerell, who had never seen a dead man before, was startled to see the change in Morris. 'The face was singularly beautiful,' wrote Cockerell; the expression of repose made it look quite unlike the Morris that he knew.

Cockerell sent out telegrams. Georgie wrote to Wilfrid Blunt. The day after Morris's death he wrote in his diary, not quite accurately, 'He is the most wonderful man I have known, unique in this, that he had no thought for anything or person, including himself, but only for the work he had in hand.' The next day Blunt came to London to see if he could 'be of any use at Kelmscott House', first lunching with Burne-Jones who told him that his interest in life had come to an end with Morris's death, 'as all their ideas and plans and work had been together all their lives'. At Hammersmith he found Morris in his coffin, ' a very plain box', lying in his little bedroom downstairs. On the coffin was an antique embroidered cloth 'and a small wreath of leaves and sad-coloured flowers'. In his secret diary Blunt gave his account of how he went to commiserate with Janey:

I found Mrs. Morris lying on the sofa upstairs just as usual, she was not in black and wore her usual blue shawl, her hair was now quite white. I kissed her which I had not done for long and comforted her as well as I could. 'I am not unhappy' she said, 'though it is a terrible thing, for I have been with him since I first knew anything.'

It was difficult for those close to Morris to accept the absence of someone who had seemed to them so solid. Cockerell felt it was 'as though some great mountain that I had been seeing daily had sunk into the earth'. Philip Webb complained of how his coat felt thinner and of how – using their shared architectural image – there was now a buttress gone. Crom Price, the old headmaster, missed Morris's subversiveness: 'He led us all a dance – not for the first or last time – would he could lead us some more.' Even Henrietta, perhaps the least compatible of Morris's four sisters, expressed great desolation: 'the world is different in every way now to me and I feel lost and utterly alone'.

As a sign of respect to its late president, the Arts and Crafts Exhibition Society postponed the fifth exhibition at the New Gallery in Regent Street. The private view was to have been held on the day of Morris's death. When the exhibition opened four days later a wreath of bay and a memorial poem by Walter Crane had been placed in the showcase containing the Kelmscott Press exhibits, including the new *Chaucer*. During the course of the exhibition these tributes disappeared.

Out in the wider world the news spread fast. A STOP PRESS TELEGRAM appeared in the fourth edition of *The Globe and Traveller*, 'The Oldest Evening Paper', announcing 'William Morris, the poet, died today'.

It is striking that in most of the obituaries of the next few days Morris was remembered primarily as a writer. 'A poet, and one of our half dozen best poets, even when Tennyson and Browning were still alive,' maintained *The Times*; 'the most genuine master of poetry who remained amongst us,' wrote *The Daily News*. There was some attempt to cover his contribution to the visual arts in the sense of 'awakening aesthetic sympathies in the minds of the British middle classes'. The same obituarist commented perceptively that the wallpapers and furniture produced 'first in the little shop in Bloomsbury and subsequently in the larger establishment at Merton' succeeded in bringing an artistic awareness to people unreceptive to poems or to pictures.

The daily papers on the whole were dismissive of his politics. *The Times* poured scorn on 'the force that drew him, without much regard for logic, or for the facts of life, into a sentimental Socialism'. At least, the writer added, 'Mr. Morris's Socialistic doctrines are not likely to have worked much harm. They were addressed to the working man in a poetic dialect, which, for all its elaborate simplicity, was strange to them.' This leading article began a whole tradition of supercilious belittlement of Morris that, a century later, still persists. Only *The Daily Telegraph* obituary writer suggested the strength of his underlying anger and his lasting ability to spring surprises. If William Morris was essentially lion-like in appearance his personality was more that of the bear; 'a little uncouth in his manners and movements, good tempered till he was crossed, a difficult man to tackle, and with the possibility of giving you a most unpleasant hug'.

The Socialist press was united in its grief. Robert Blatchford wrote, 'I cannot help thinking that it does not matter what goes into the *Clarion* this week, because William Morris is dead . . . he was our best man, and he is dead. How can we think of the movement today but as a thing struck motionless?' Socialist memorial meetings were held over the next weeks. The SDF, the London Anarchists and ex-members of Morris's old Socialist League came together at Holborn Town Hall for a stunned and emotional evening of speeches in which the resolution of thanksgiving for Morris was carried not by the usual show of hands 'but the complete and almost painful silence of the meeting'. John Burns, speaking at the close of a mass meeting of cab drivers in Trafalgar Square, asked for a vote of condolence to show 'how the heart of London Labour has been touched by the death of one of its truest friends'.

Some of the most moving tributes appeared in Icelandic papers. The first was in the travellers' newspaper *Bjarki*, published in the east coast fishing port of Seyðisfjörður.

William Morris, one of the most famous poets of England, is reported to have died on the 3rd of this month. He travelled around Iceland, loved everything Icelandic, and chose material for his poetry from several of our sagas, such as Laxdaela, Völsunga etc. He was a great freedom lover, a dedicated socialist and a most outstanding man.

CHAPTER TWENTY

Return to Kelmscott
1896 and after

Since the early 1880s Burne-Jones had been working on his masterpiece, 'Arthur in Avalon'. This stupendous canvas, now in Puerto Rico, shows the king lying outstretched on his bier in the Celtic 'Isle of the Blest' to which he was carried after his death. Above him is a canopy with scenes from the Quest of the Holy Grail sculpted in relief. Avalon had been Ned's 'own cherished design', an emotional investment; he painted and repainted it obsessively in a large-scale studio he took especially for this one painting in Campden Hill Road. But during the terrible months of Morris's illness Ned had not had the spirit to continue with King Arthur. 'Avalon gets to look vile,' he wrote.

William Morris's funeral took place on Tuesday 6 October, on what began as a cold wet morning and worked up into a storm of Saga-like ferocity as the day progressed. By eight a.m. a little crowd had gathered in Hammersmith to watch the coffin being borne out of Kelmscott House *en route* for St George's church at the other Kelmscott, its final resting place. Some of the Socialists, including John Burns and H. M. Hyndman, were amongst these mourners. There were also Morris's work people from the Kelmscott Press, conspicuous among them a big broad-shouldered press man, probably Stephen Mowlem. The small procession followed the hearse slowly along Rivercourt Road towards the station. With a final irony Morris's body was to travel from Paddington to Lechlade by the 'abhominable' train.

At Paddington another crowd was waiting, a more cosmopolitan assembly of the deputations of the Russian and Polish and Jewish Socialist societies, bearing their wreaths and their garlands of bright flowers. According to the *Daily Chronicle* reporter many of these people were 'obviously very poor and very downcast'. Prince Kropotkin the

Anarchist was on the platform. There were none of the conventional trappings of the funeral: no undertakers and very few black funereal top hats. Morris in his coffin was loaded into a section of the guard's van, with his feet towards the platform in what seemed like a little mobile private chapel. The coffin was now surrounded by the wreaths. Morris's mourners collected in a reserved section of the train. Janey and May were supported on the journey by Ned, Emery Walker and the avuncular Crom Price.

There was a halt at Oxford. It was by now late morning. Rain was pouring down in torrents. No representatives of the University met Morris's coffin: he had become as ambivalent to Oxford as Oxford was to him. The special portion of the train travelled on another twenty-five miles to Lechlade. As the passengers stepped out on to the wet and windswept platform local carts on the bridge halted and the drivers gazed inquisitively over the parapet. The station road was absolutely empty except for one solitary policeman. There was a long pause. Then several single-horse carriages, sent to transport the mourners back to Kelmscott Manor, could be seen filing down slowly to the station. With them was a traditional harvest-cart painted yellow with red wheels. Poles attached to all four corners were intertwined with willow boughs. Twine strung across the poles was festooned with vine leaves. The roan mare pulling the cart had vine leaves in its blinkers. The bottom of the cart was lined with moss. This funeral cart struck Arthur Hughes, the painter, as looking like a page out of a Morris magic story. It was the creation of Detmar Blow, who had gone ahead from London the previous day to organize the décor of the funeral. Blow himself drove this hearse, dressed in a wagoner's smock which made him 'look coeval with the Saxon Chronicle'. Four countrymen in moleskin conveyed the coffin gently to its place on the moss carpet. Over it was laid the precious fragment of Broussa brocade from Morris's hoard of textiles, and a laurel wreath.

Janey, looking 'sadly white and shaken', leaning on Ned's arm, entered the first of the carriages. She was followed by Jenny, weeping piteously. May, in a new relation towards an ailing mother and invalid sister, was appearing relatively calm. Harry Sparling had returned from France for Morris's funeral and was staying with the family at Kelmscott Manor. Morris's sisters Henrietta and Isabella, the latter in her deaconess's bonnet, were installed in another of the carriages, with 'two brothers' of Morris, presumably Edgar and either Stanley, the southern counties farmer, or Arthur, the Colonel, who had retired from the Army six years before. In all there were about forty mourners from London: F. S. Ellis; Morris's neighbours in Hammersmith, the Richmonds; Walter Crane; poor John Carruthers, exhausted by his vigilance in Norway, with his daughter; Janey's sister Bessie Burden. Philip Webb does not appear to have made the journey, nor is there any record that Aglaia was there. The local carter, in his mackintosh cape, took the mare by the rein and the funeral procession started off, winding its way through Lechlade, a *News from Nowhere* village of ancient grey stone houses with their stone slate roofs. Villagers, with their children, stood in doorways watching as the horses splashed along the road and past the now saturated meadows. Rain-drenched hedges on either side of the three-mile route to Kelmscott still glowed with hips and haws.

Arthur Hughes, who had never been to Kelmscott church before, called it 'the simplest barn form with a tiny open arch belfry at one end very very rural on a flat damp land'. Morris had loved the primitive beauty of this miniature twelfth-century church and defended it even more fiercely than most other ancient buildings because he felt it a part of his own countryside and history. He had financed the releading of the roof of the chancel, and provided a new stone roof for the nave. When the cortège reached Kelmscott church a group of villagers were waiting with the Rev. William Fulford Adams, vicar of the neighbouring village of Little Faringdon. All those years before, Adams had been at Marlborough and then at Exeter with Morris, another potent connection with the past. The church bell was ringing quietly. Rain was still falling hard. Local labourers heaved the coffin up on to their shoulders and carried it through the double file of mourners and the lime-trees lining the stone-flagged churchyard path.

The church was decorated for the harvest festival, with pumpkins, marrows, carrots, enormous shiny apples and sheaves of corn heaped up around the font. Deep red autumn leaves cascaded from the pillars of the nave. The lamps in the church were wreathed with ears of oats and barley. Morris's country funeral was the absolute antithesis of Tennyson's burial in Westminster Abbey in 1892. Almost uncannily the service at Kelmscott was fulfilling to the letter one of Morris's last recorded sentences: 'I want to get Mumbo Jumbo out of the world.' In the simple village pews, intermingled with the family, were old Socialist Leaguers, workmen from Merton Abbey, salesmen and clerks from Morris & Co. in Oxford Street, Arts and Crafts colleagues, and people from Kelmscott village in their normal working clothes. Parson Adams's sermon was low-key and deeply felt, a gentle rural eulogy, taking as its text the words from 2 Corinthians, 'As unknown, and yet well known'. He did not venture into the controversial territory of Morris's religion of the Cause. But Adams reached a truth about Morris, emphasizing his twenty-five years of Kelmscott associations and his unknown and unpublicized acts of kindness to his country neighbours. In St Paul's words he approached the central paradox: 'as having nothing, and yet possessing all things'; 'as dying, and, behold, we live'.

The rain stopped temporarily as the coffin was carried out from the church to the grave, although the winds were still rushing through the branches of the elm trees, blowing up towards the storm. Morris's grave had been dug at the south-east side of the churchyard. As the coffin was lowered a small group of red-cheeked villagers, men and boys like John Ball's peasants, gaped across the churchyard wall. The grave was filled almost to the brim with wreaths and garlands, composed of so many of the flowers Morris had used as a basis for his textiles and his wallpapers. At the foot of the grave stood a curious tribute from the workers at Merton, a Welsh harp with a frame of purple flowers.

His family and friends stood dankly round the grave in a long silence that, according to Georgie, 'could be heard'.

Philip Webb designed the tomb for Morris. He observed sadly, beginning this commission: 'It seems to me that I've been designing nothing but tombs all my life.' Morris had always had mixed feelings about monuments. The memorials in Westminster Abbey had appalled him as 'the most hideous specimens of false art that can be found in the whole world; mere Cockney nightmares and aberrations of the human intellect'. The wonderfully quirky tomb that Philip Webb designed him would, we can assume, have pleased Morris rather more. The tomb has a coped roof like a small house or a large dog kennel. The design was inspired by a piece of fourteenth-century stonework found lying around the churchyard. It was typical of Webb, with his love of paradox, to base his monument on an *objet trouvé*. The foundations were dug by Giles, the Kelmscott Manor gardener. The WILLIAM MORRIS inscription has an idiosyncratic looped letter-form. The tomb is carved with trees sprouting along its big flat sides. Morris's tomb is like an early Frank Lloyd Wright organic building, pushing up out of the soil in its English churchyard setting. It is also peculiarly, startlingly Icelandic, a tomb that would encourage one of those Nordic heroes to rise singing from his grave.

Three days after the funeral Janey went to stay with Wilfrid Blunt at Newbuildings. She took May with her. In the middle of November Blunt invited them both to El Hashish, Blunt's joke name for El Kheysheh, the romantic Pink House he had built in the desert at Sheykh Obeyd in Egypt for Mary Elcho. After a few days he was writing in his diary, 'Mrs. Morris's visit has been rather a disappointment – her daughter May is an obstinately silent woman . . . Neither of them ride, not even donkeys, though Mrs. Morris has made an attempt, and life here without riding is impossible. One cannot walk on account of the heavy sand, so they sit indoors all day. I go to see them twice a day but with May it is impossible to keep up any conversation and I am at my wits end how to amuse them for I cannot make love to either of them and what else is to be done.' This problematic holiday ended in April and Janey installed herself at Kelmscott for the summer. Blunt advised her to set up a dairy farm 'as old age without a hobby is sad'. Janey, like Blunt himself, was now fifty-six.

After May's divorce in 1899 she reverted to the name May Morris and entries under her married name were expunged from Kelmscott Manor Visitors' Book. Her emotional life became a little gloomy. 'The pain touched woman in a dark dress', as Philip Webb described her anxiously, noting how she had inherited some of her father's shyness. 'Majestic . . . Mournful . . . Morose', wrote Janet Ashbee after Mary's performance as St Helena in 1899 in the Art Workers' Guild Masque. May became more than ever fixated on her father, commemorating each anniversary of his funeral by laying a wreath of laurel on his tomb. A short play she wrote in 1903, *White Lies*, centres on the figure of the absconding father: it is full of images of resentment and of loss. But May's own design work flourished. Her embroideries of the early 1900s are perhaps the most original and certainly the most technically accomplished of their period. May developed Morris's range of visual reference, flowers, vines, birds, heraldry, mediaeval detailing, with a richness and fluency that was her own. She became the virtual leader of the craftswomen in England, showing some of her deaconess aunt Isabella's proselytizing vigour, and in 1907 she founded the Women's Guild of Art.

Accounts of Jenny's later life make painful reading. She felt lost at

Morris's death. He had been not just her father but her main companion and in a sense her last real link with the outside world. She hated the idea of a biography of Morris: 'Oh Sydney, what wretched thing a biography is for those who knew the subject,' she wrote to Sydney Cockerell. Cockerell, who was brotherly and kind to her, described her after Morris's death as 'infinitely pathetic and brave and frank'. For the rest of her life she was in and out of nursing homes or attended at home by nurses and companions, one of whom proved so 'incapable and brutal' she had to be dismissed. Her condition was a ceaseless source of worry to her mother. By 1909 her epileptic attacks had increased in violence and her sedation had to be increased. In 1914, when her mother died in Bath, after a quiet but surprisingly resilient old age, Jenny was present at her funeral at Kelmscott, a tragic sobbing figure clutching Sydney Cockerell's arm. Jenny herself lived on till 1935. May found it heartbreaking to see her at that period with just occasional 'flashes of her old self' coming back. Jenny still came to stay at Kelmscott sometimes and would be found wandering around the garden: 'I often walk here in the evening hoping to meet my dear father, he was such a sweet companion,' she said.

Ned survived Morris by only two years. After Morris's death he had slowly tried to gather his life together and recover his old energy. But the blow had been so heavy that he never quite got over it. Sundays without Topsy were particularly hard.

In 1906 Aglaia Coronio, in a condition of acute depression on the day after the death of her daughter Calliope, committed suicide at home in Kensington, using embroidery scissors to stab herself repeatedly in the abdomen and throat.

Philip Webb died in 1915, after a sad old age in which the 'baffling clouds' descended. He had had a whim for his ashes to be scattered in the cloisters of New College Chapel in Oxford, but when the college authorities refused permission Emery Walker took them up on top of the White Horse Hill in Berkshire that he and Morris used to visit and flung them to the winds.

Georgie lived on until 1920, increasingly strong-minded and formidable, a 'little, very upright figure', still in her sweeping Pre-Raphaelite skirts. Her young granddaughter went with her on some of her uplifting visits to the poor, watching in embarrassment as Lady Burne-Jones sat in some small cottage 'with her large blue eyes fixed on some gnarled unlettered old woman, telling her tidings of comfort from *Fors*

Clavigera.' Mackail, in his beautiful and almost reckless *Times* obituary, stressed the great importance to her of her rapport with Morris and identified her similar 'clear flame-like spirit – *lucerna ardens et luceus.*'

Wilfrid Blunt died in 1922, with little diminution of self-congratulation or the habit of pursuit. In 1898 Janey had given him the scrubbed oak dining-table used first at Red House, then for the Socialist suppers at Kelmscott House in Hammersmith. Blunt wrote an execrable poem for it:

> At this fair oak table sat . . .
> William Morris, whose art's plan
> Laid its lives in ample span.

Morris's table is at Newbuildings still. In 1911 Mary Elcho brought her daughter, also Mary, to meet Wilfrid Blunt, her father, for the first time. Blunt gave the girl of seventeen, 'a miracle of beauty', the 'barbaric ornament' he had purchased years before for her. This ornament contained a lock of William Morris's hair.

In the year before her death Janey had finally purchased Kelmscott Manor and 9¾ acres around it, for £4,000. May lived on at Kelmscott through the years between the wars. She completed the great task of editing the twenty-four volumes of her father's works in 1915, and in the 1930s assembled two final volumes of his writings with biographical commentary. These were published in 1936. In 1924 and 1931 she made journeys to Iceland, retracing his steps.

After another abortive affair, this time with John Quinn the New York lawyer and literary patron, May had finally found love and devoted companionship with the former land-girl Mary Frances Vivian Lobb, who had come to work at Kelmscott in the First World War. May was by now looking tall and rather haggard, 'moving with dignity, and clad in garments of a rich design and stately in a fashion that was all her own'. The observant noticed that the Socialist daughter and Pre-Raphaelite beauty had grown a faint moustache. Miss Lobb, as she was known, was 'large, hearty, cropheaded and always dressed in an old knickerbocker suit'. They settled down together like the two lesbian ladies of Llangollen, the source of speculation and just a little ridicule, especially from the bright young aesthetes of the 1930s.

Evelyn Waugh, John Betjeman and Osbert Lancaster rediscovered Kelmscott Manor with a shriek of joy and created around it their own fantastical version of a Pre-Raphaelite soap opera. Waugh wrote the biography of Rossetti. Osbert Lancaster drew a lewd cartoon of Morris, Janey and Rossetti sitting in a line on the antique triple lavatory they found in the farm buildings. Betjeman even installed himself at Kelmscott for a while.

In October 1934, the centenary of Morris's birth, Kelmscott became once again a place of pilgrimage. After years of begging letters around the Morris circles, May's dream of a village Memorial Hall with meeting-room, reading-room and recreation room, a *News from Nowhere* concept, was realized at last. The Hall, a simple Cotswold building, had been designed by Ernest Gimson, one of Morris's young Art Workers' Guild henchmen, before his own death in 1919. With distant echoes of the Mystic Betrothal the Hall was opened by Bernard Shaw who said that Morris was a saint and 'in a more sensible age' would perhaps have come to be called St William of Kelmscott. 'Oxford can do many wonderful things,' said Shaw, with a Socialist swipe at quite a lot of the people who had helped support the building, 'but it cannot turn out a man like Morris, except in the sense of turning him out of the door.' They sang 'Onward Christian Soldiers', which Shaw claimed to have led with 'stentorian vigour', while Morris 'turned in his grave around the corner'. There was a surprise appearance of Ramsay Mac-Donald, the Labour prime minister, at that time the leader of the National Coalition government. He was hardly able to push his way through the crowded Memorial Hall to reach the platform. MacDonald, as a young recruit to the SDF, knew Morris in days of Red Flag Socialism and regaled the audience with Farringdon Road memories before they adjourned for country cakes and tea.

May died in October 1938, followed only a few months later by Miss Lobb. May's funeral was said to have been a repeat of her father's, also in St George's church. Mackail, Morris's biographer, ageing himself, was too tired to attend. Kelmscott was left in trust to Oxford University. In July 1939, two months before the outbreak of the Second World War, a sale was held at Kelmscott Manor of final remaining 'Furnishings and Effects'. Final sales are always poignant. This one, held on a damp morning with desultory bidding in the garden of the manor, was more desolate than most.

There were dresses, brocades, embroidery, catalogued as 'made by or worn by the late Mrs. Morris or late Miss Mary Morris'. Three peasant aprons. A green silk dress, embroidered by Miss Morris. A blue eastern

Djibbah. A cashmere bodice, worn by Mrs William Morris. An Italian bolero and an Eastern vest. A white embroidered cot quilt, embroidered by Mrs Morris. Two hanks of wool, labelled 'dyed by William Morris'. Morris's French working blouse, and his silk handkerchief with worked initials 'WM'.

Sources and Reference Notes

with abbreviations used in reference notes

Place of publication is London unless otherwise stated

1. Works by William Morris

Works
ed. May Morris, *The Collected Works of William Morris*, 24 vols., Longmans, Green & Co., 1910–15. These volumes assemble the majority of the principal published writings of William Morris, which are as follows:

Contributions to the *Oxford and Cambridge Magazine*, Bell and Daldy, 1856

The Defence of Guenevere and Other Poems, Bell and Daldy, 1858

The Life and Death of Jason, Bell and Daldy, 1867

The Earthly Paradise, F. S. Ellis, parts I and II, 1868; parts III and IV, 1870

Grettis Saga, The Story of Grettir the Strong, prose translation with Eiríkr Magnússon, F. S. Ellis, 1869

Völsunga Saga, The Story of the Volsungs and Niblungs, prose translation with Eiríkr Magnússon, F. S. Ellis, 1870

Love is Enough or the Freeing of Pharamond, A Morality, Ellis and White, 1873

Three Northern Love Stories and Other Tales, prose translation with Eiríkr Magnússon, Ellis and White, 1873

The Aeneids of Vergil, verse translation, Ellis and White, 1876

The Story of Sigurd the Volsung and the Fall of the Niblungs, Ellis and White, 1877

Hopes and Fears for Art, collected lectures 1878–1881, Ellis and White, 1882

A Summary of the Principles of Socialism, written with H. M. Hyndman for the Democratic Federation, The Modern Press, 1884

Contributions to *Justice*, Democratic Federation publication, 1884

Contributions to *The Commonweal*, Socialist League publication, 1885–90

The Manifesto of the Socialist League, Socialist League publication, 1885

Chants for Socialists, Socialist League, 1885

The Pilgrims of Hope, originally published in *The Commonweal*, April 1885–July 1886

The Odyssey of Homer, verse translation, Reeves and Turner, 1887

The Tables Turned; or Nupkins Awakened, A Socialist Interlude, Socialist League, 1887

Signs of Change, collected lectures, Reeves and Turner, 1888

A Dream of John Ball and *A King's Lesson*, reprinted from *The Commonweal*, Reeves and Turner, 1888

The House of the Wolfings, Reeves and Turner, 1888

The Roots of the Mountains, Reeves and Turner, 1889

News from Nowhere; or, An Epoch of Rest, originally published in *The Commonweal*, January–October 1890; reprinted by Roberts Brothers, Boston, 1890; first English edition Reeves and Turner, 1891

Statement of Principles of the Hammersmith Socialist Society, Hammersmith Socialist Society, 1890

The Story of the Glittering Plain, Kelmscott Press, 1891

Poems by the Way, Kelmscott Press, 1891

The Saga Library, prose translations with Eiríkr Magnússon. Vol. I, *The Story of Howard the Halt*, *The Story of the Banded Men*, *The Story of Hen Thorir*, Bernard Quaritch, 1891; Vol. II, *The Story of the Ere-Dwellers* and *The Story of the Heath Slayings*, 1892; Vols. III to VI, *The Stories of the Kings of Norway (Heimskringla)* by Snorri Sturluson, 1893, 1894, 1895 and 1905

Manifesto of English Socialists, with H. M. Hyndman and George Bernard Shaw, The Twentieth Century Press, 1893

Socialism, Its Growth and Outcome, with E. Belfort Bax, Swan Sonnenschein, 1893

Contributions and preface to *Arts and Crafts Essays*, Rivington, Percival, 1893

King Florus and the Fair Jehane, translation, Kelmscott Press, 1893; *Of the Friendship of Amis and Amile*, translation, Kelmscott Press, 1894; *The Tale of the Emperor Coustans and of Over Sea*, translation, Kelmscott Press, 1894. These were published as a collection, *Old French Romances*, George Allen, 1896

The Wood beyond the World, Kelmscott Press, 1894

The Story of Beowulf, translation with A. J. Wyatt, Kelmscott Press, 1895

Child Christopher and Goldilond the Fair, Kelmscott Press, 1895

The Well at the World's End, Kelmscott Press, 1896

The Water of the Wondrous Isles, Kelmscott Press, 1897

The Sundering Flood, Kelmscott Press, 1897

Introductions May Morris's introductions to these volumes have been published in a separate edition, *The Introductions to the Collected Works of William Morris*, 2 vols., Oriole Editions, New York, 1973

Journals Morris's diaries of his journeys to Iceland in 1871 and 1873 have been published in a separate edition, intro. James Morris, *Icelandic Journals by William Morris*, Centaur Press, Fontwell, 1969

WMAWS ed. May Morris, *William Morris, Artist, Writer, Socialist*, 2 vols., Basil Blackwell, Oxford, 1936

Socialist Diary ed. Florence Boos, *William Morris's Socialist Diary, January to April 1887*, Journeyman Press, 1985

LeMire ed. Eugene D. LeMire, *The Unpublished Lectures of William Morris*, Wayne State University Press, Detroit, 1969

Letters ed. Norman Kelvin, *The Collected Letters of William Morris*, vol. 1, 1848–1880, Princeton University Press, 1984; vol. 2, 1881–1888, 1987; vol. 3, 1889–1896 in preparation

Political Writings ed. Nicholas Salmon, a selection of Morris's unpublished political journalism and polemic from *Justice* and *The Commonweal* 1883–1890, Thoemmes Press, Bristol, 1994

Henderson ed. Philip Henderson, *The Letters of William Morris to his Family and Friends*, Longmans, Green & Co., 1950

The Novel ed. Penelope Fitzgerald, *The Novel on Blue Paper*, unfinished novel, *c.*1871, published for The William Morris Society, Journeyman Press, 1982

Unless otherwise indicated quotations from Morris's letters are from Norman Kelvin's edition of the *Collected Letters* and follow his interpretation and dating; quotations from Morris's writings are taken from the *Collected Works*. Apart from William Morris's own diaries, kept intermittently and listed in the relevant chapter sources, there is little formal autobiographical material. However, Morris's letters and lectures are full of autobiographical flashbacks, and the brief account of his life he gave to Andreas Scheu in 1883 is published in Kelvin's *Collected Letters*, vol. 2.

2. Manuscript Sources

British Library British Library, London
  Ashley Library Papers
  May Morris Bequest
  William Morris Papers (the Robert Steele Gift)
  Hammersmith Socialist Society Papers
  Bernard Shaw Papers
  The Cockerell Papers

Bodleian Bodleian Library, Oxford
  May Morris Bequest

Castle Howard Castle Howard Archive, York
  Correspondence with George and Rosalind Howard (later Earl and Countess of Carlisle)

Cheltenham Cheltenham Art Gallery and Museum
  Emery Walker Library

Fitzwilliam Fitzwilliam Museum, Cambridge
  Blunt and Lytton Papers
  Burne-Jones Papers

IISH International Institute of Socialist History, Amsterdam
Socialist League Archives
Andreas Scheu Papers

NAL National Art Library, Victoria and Albert Museum
The Cockerell Letters
G. Warington Taylor correspondence
Philip Webb correspondence

NAL Archive National Art Library, Archive of Art and Design
Arts and Crafts Exhibition Society minutes

Price Price family collection
Cormell Price letters and diaries

Reykjavík National Library of Iceland, Reykjavík
Eiríkr Magnússon Papers

John Rylands John Rylands Library, University of Manchester
Fairfax Murray Papers

SPAB Society for the Protection of Ancient Buildings
Minutes, correspondence and case histories

WMG William Morris Gallery, Walthamstow
May Morris correspondence
J. Bruce Glasier correspondence
J. W. Mackail notebooks used for his biography of Morris

3. Secondary Sources

Blunt Wilfrid Scawen Blunt, *My Diaries*, Martin Secker, 1919
Bryson ed. John Bryson, *Dante Gabriel Rossetti and Jane Morris, Their Correspondence*, Clarendon Press, Oxford, 1976
Burne-Jones Georgiana Burne-Jones, *Memorials of Edward Burne-Jones*, 2 vols., Macmillan & Co., 1904
Cockerell *Friends* ed. Viola Meynell, *Friends of a Lifetime*, *Letters to Sydney Carlyle Cockerell*, Jonathan Cape, 1940
Cockerell *Best of Friends* ed. Viola Meynell, *The Best of Friends, Further Letters to Sydney Carlyle Cockerell*, Rupert Hart-Davies, 1956
Doughty and Wahl ed. O. Doughty and J. R. Wahl, *Letters of Dante Gabriel Rossetti*, 4 vols., Oxford University Press, 1965-7
Faulkner ed. Peter Faulkner, *Jane Morris to Wilfrid Scawen Blunt*, University of Exeter, 1968
Fredeman William E. Fredeman, 'Prelude to the Last Decade: Dante Gabriel Rossetti in the summer of 1872', *Bulletin of the John Rylands Library*, Manchester, vol. 53, 1971
Horner Frances Horner, *Time Remembered*, William Heinemann, 1933
JWMS The Journal of the William Morris Society, 1961-
Lago ed. Mary Lago, *Burne-Jones Talking*, John Murray, 1981
Lang ed. C. Y. Lang, *The Swinburne Letters*, 6 vols., Yale University Press, 1959-62
Laurence ed. Dan H. Laurence, *Bernard Shaw Collected Letters 1874-1950*, 4 vols., Max Reinhardt, 1965-88

Lethaby *W. R. Lethaby, Philip Webb and his Work*, Oxford University Press, 1935
Mackail J. W. Mackail, *The Life of William Morris*, 2 vols., Longmans, Green & Co., 1899

4. Published Works on Morris and His Circle

There have been several dozen biographies of Morris over the century since his death, none perhaps as illuminating as the first biography by Edward Burne-Jones's son-in-law, J. W. Mackail. What follows is a personal selection of the books and essays I have found most valuable in offering a new interpretation of Morris or for their vividness of recall.

J. Bruce Glasier, *William Morris and the Early Days of the Socialist Movement*, Longmans, Green & Co., 1921

R. Page Arnot, *William Morris: A Vindication*, Martin Lawrence, 1934; revised ed. *William Morris, the Man and the Myth*, Lawrence & Wishart, 1964

George Bernard Shaw, 'Morris as I knew him', essay in *WMAWS*, vol. 2, 1936; separate ed. William Morris Society, 1966

E. P. Thompson, *William Morris, Romantic to Revolutionary*, Lawrence & Wishart, 1955; reprinted with new introduction, Merlin Press, 1976

Philip Henderson, *William Morris, His Life, Work and Friends*, Thames & Hudson, 1967

Paul Meier, *La Pensée Utopique de William Morris*, Editions Sociales, Paris, 1972; trs. Frank Gubb, *William Morris: the Marxist Dreamer*, Harvester Press, Sussex, 1978

Penelope Fitzgerald, *Edward Burne-Jones, A Biography*, Michael Joseph, 1975

Jack Lindsay, *William Morris*, Constable, 1975

Roderick Marshall, *William Morris and his Earthly Paradise*, Compton Press, Tisbury, 1979

Jan Marsh, *Jane and May Morris*, Pandora, 1986

The most comprehensive surveys of Morris's work have been:

Aymer Vallance, *William Morris: His Art, his Writings and his Public Life*, George Bell and Sons, 1898

Ray Watkinson, *William Morris as Designer*, Studio Vista, 1967

Paul Thompson, *The Work of William Morris*, Heinemann, 1967

Charles Harvey and Jon Press, *William Morris, Design and Enterprise in Victorian Britain*, Manchester University Press, 1991

The most useful short introductions to Morris's life and work are:

Peter Faulkner, *Against the Age: An Introduction to William Morris*, George Allen & Unwin, 1980

Peter Stansky, *William Morris*, Oxford University Press Past Masters series, Oxford, 1983

ed. Asa Briggs, *William Morris: Selected Writings and Designs*, Penguin Books, 1962

ed. Clive Wilmer, *William Morris: 'News from Nowhere' and Other Writings*, Penguin Books, 1993

Other books on more specific aspects of Morris's works are included in the chapter sources lists which follow.

INTRODUCTION

viii 'rum and indescribable' quoted Mackail
'tempestuous and exacting' *ibid.*
'pacing up and down' Henry Holiday, *Reminiscences of My Life*, Heinemann, 1914
'Beg Pardon, Sir' Mackail notebooks, WMG
'the nerves of the flaccid' Edward Burne-Jones to William De Morgan, 1879?, Fitzwilliam

xi 'My view about these volumes' Sydney Cockerell to May Morris, 25 August 1913, British Library

xii 'How extraordinarily interesting' J. W. Mackail to Sydney Cockerell, 7 December 1897, British Library

xiii 'worse than beastly' WM to Charles Faulkner, 16 October 1886
'the same as he professes' F. S. Ellis to William Bell Scott, 17 May 1887
'The fluctuations of illness' J. W. Mackail to Sydney Cockerell, 16 June 1897

xv 'if they led him' 'Death of Mr. William Morris', obituary in *The Times*, 5 October 1896

xvi 'he is one of those' E. P. Thompson, *William Morris, Romantic to Revolutionary*, Lawrence & Wishart, 1955
'I became a Socialist' G. D. H. Cole, 'William Morris as a Socialist', William Morris Society lecture, 16 January 1957

xvii 'You can be very' Harold Laski to May Morris, 27 July 1932, British Library
'I argued that a body' Graham Wallas to May Morris, 4 November 1930, British Library
'The Message of the March Wind' WM, *The Pilgrims of Hope*, 1886, quoted Barbara Castle, 'A Book that Changed Me', article in *The Independent on Sunday Review*, 18 March 1990

xviii 'Forsooth, brothers' WM, *A Dream of John Ball*, 1888
'I was telling' Clement Attlee to Sydney Cockerell, 23 November 1953, British Library
'Well, you know' Clement Attlee/Kenneth Harris BBC TV interview, 1954, quoted Kenneth Harris, *Attlee*, Weidenfeld & Nicolson, 1954

xix 'If you are' Raymond Williams in discussion at Institute of Contemporary Arts, London, quoted *Crafts* magazine, July/August 1984

CHAPTER ONE: Walthamstow 1834–48

For this chapter I have drawn on the accounts of Morris's childhood in May Morris's *William Morris, Artist, Writer, Socialist* and in Mackail's *Life*, augmented by Janet Grierson, *Isabella Gilmore, Sister to William Morris*, SPCK, 1962, and more recent research on Morris's family background undertaken by the William Morris Gallery for the exhibition *A Morris Family Album*, 1992.

For the Morris's family finances: Charles Harvey and Jon Press, 'The City and Mining Enterprise: The Making of the Morris Family Fortune', *JWMS*, Spring 1990, and the early chapters of their book *William Morris, Design and Enterprise in Victorian Britain*, Manchester University Press, 1991.

For Morris's early family relationships: Linda Richardson, 'William Morris's Childhood and Schooling', *JWMS*, Autumn 1990, and her unpublished Oxford University dissertation 'William Morris and Women: Experience and Representation', deposited at the Bodleian Library, Oxford.

Additional local background in Sir William Addison, *Portrait of Epping Forest*, Robert Hale, 1977, and H. V. Miles, *William Morris in Walthamstow*, The Walthamstow Press, 1951. Visits to Epping Forest and Queen Elizabeth's Hunting Lodge, and to Woodford Churchyard, where the tomb of William Morris's father still stands. A plaque on the local fire station marks the site of Morris's birthplace, Elm House; and near by a rather cheerless double terrace of early post-war housing is named William Morris Close.

CHAPTER ONE
1 'To this day' Mackail
'and the large blue plums' WM, *News from Nowhere*, 1890
'bruising scent' WM, *The Novel*, c.1871
'the ordinary bourgeois' WM to Andreas Scheu, 15 September 1883

2 'sucked at a bottle' WM to Jenny Morris, 18 August 1888
3 'I am a boor' Lawrence Pearsall Jacks, *Life and Letters of Stopford Brooke*, John Murray, 1917
  'a *very* good boy' WM to Georgiana Burne-Jones, 26 March 1876
  'lovely ancient literature' WM to Henry Richard, 11 March 1882
  'All my literary life' WM to Jón Sigurðsson, 18 March 1873
3 'little queer grey' WM to Aglaia Coronio, 7 April 1875
4 'a plain roomy building' Mackail
5 'by making a clean sweep' Cormell Price to Jenny Morris, 24 July 1897, British Library
  'Ever since I could remember' WM to Andreas Scheu, 15 September 1883
6 'the clang of the scourge' Sir Walter Scott, *The Talisman*, 1825
  'And it is good' WM, 'Gertha's Lovers', 1856
  'noticed their devices' WM to Eiríkr Magnússon, *WMAWS*
  'what a comfortable life' WM to Edward Carpenter, 2 May 1885
  'an administration of *things*' WM to George Bainton, 10 April 1888
7 'the good luck only' WM, 'Art and the Beauty of the Earth', lecture 1881
  'nicer than anything' *WMAWS*
8 'a greedy fisher' Wilfrid Scawen Blunt, ms. diaries, 21 August 1890, Fitzwilliam
  Morris's gardens Cormell Price diary, 15 August 1885, Price
  'the beautiful *hepatica*' WM to Jenny Morris, 2 April 1895, British Library
9 'in after days' WM, *The Novel*, c.1871
  'the happy child' WM, *News from Nowhere*, 1890
10 'beside them stood the *Cage*' WM to Jenny Morris, 23 December 1888
  Emma Morris picture *WMAWS*
11 'the babe 'neath thy girdle' WM, *The Pilgrims of Hope*, 1885–6
  'whose sweet and kindly' WM, *The Novel*, c.1871
  'and yet 'twixt thee and me' WM, *The Pilgrims of Hope*, 1885–6
  'I used to dread Sunday' WM to Louisa Baldwin, 15 November 1874
  'rich establishment puritanism' WM to Andreas Scheu, 15 September 1883
12 'though it did fill' Lago, 28 February 1896
13 'Past the Docks' WM, *News from Nowhere*, 1890
  'that delightful quickening' WM to Georgiana Burne-Jones, September 1887
14 'in its present position' WM to the Metropolitan Board of Works, April 1879
  Morris on the river Blunt, summer 1889
  'the dark green deeps' WM, *The Sundering Flood*, 1897
  'save the crown of them' WM, *The House of the Wolfings*, 1889
15 'I don't care much' WM to Georgiana Burne-Jones, Easter Monday 1889, Mackail
  'certainly the biggest' WM to the *Daily Chronicle*, 23 April 1895, Henderson
  'I have a sudden vision' *Intros*
16 'go on for hours' Cormell Price diary, 22 February 1883, Price
  'a light blue green colour' WM to Rosalind Howard, 13 December 1879
17 'hung with faded greenery' WM, 'The Lesser Arts of Life', lecture 1882
  'a carved ivory junk' Mackail
  'half way between painting' Lago, 11 June 1896
18 'that exhilarating sense' WM, *News from Nowhere*, 1890
  'clad in albes of white' 'Kilian of the Closes', unfinished story, 1896
  'the angel painted' WM, *The Well at the World's End*, 1896
  'all is measured, mingled' WM, 'The Lesser Arts of Life', lecture 1882
  account of Canterbury visit WM to *The Times*, 7 June 1877
  'the gates of heaven' Blunt, 31 May 1896
19 'I, who have seen' WM, Intro. to 'The Proud King', *The Earthly Paradise*, part I, 1868

19 'Is Monreale the nearest' Sydney Cockerell to W. R. Lethaby, 2 August 1915, British
  Library
  'kind of careful delicacy' WM to Georgiana Burne-Jones, 10 June 1890
21 'my parents did' WM to William Sharman, April 1886
23 'Hark, the wind' WM, *The Pilgrims of Hope*, 1885–6
  'a crowd that swept o'er' *ibid.*
24 'Come, Pa, turn to' WM, 'The Boy Farms at Fault', *Commonweal*, 30 July 1887
  'I wonder if any' WM to the *Manchester Guardian*, 4 October 1884
25 'rich men' WM to Eiríkr Magnússon, 3 June 1875
  'I've never known a man' Luke Ionides, *Memories*, Herbert Clarke, Paris, 1925
  'We advise the far-famed' undated local newssheet, WMG
26 'amiable people' *WMAWS*
  'the strongest will' 'Frank's Sealed Letter', *Oxford and Cambridge Magazine*, April 1856
  'My father died' WM to Andreas Scheu, 15 September 1883
28 'how often it consoles me' WM to Georgiana Burne-Jones, 13 May 1885
  'sheer faith' *Intros*
  'and it was this picture' WM, 'Kilian of the Closes', unfinished story, 1896

CHAPTER TWO: Marlborough 1848–52

Background to the early years at Marlborough College is taken chiefly from the Archive at
Marlborough; the Marlborough College Records in the Bodleian Library, Oxford; A. G.
Bradley, A. C. Champneys and J. W. Baines, *A History of Marlborough College*, John Murray,
1893; Edward Lockwood, *Early Days of Marlborough College*, Simpkin, Marshall, Hamilton,
Kent & Co., 1893; and the early chapters of Thomas Hinde's *Paths of Progress: A History of
Marlborough College*, James & James, 1992.

The anthology *Marlborough Town and Countryside*, Whittington Press, Andoversford,
1978, includes *The Ecclesiologist* article, illuminating on the High Church bias at
Marlborough. There is a good account of Blore's original chapel in Niall Hamilton's *A History
of the Chapel of St Michael and All Angels*, produced for Marlborough College by Alan Sutton
Publishing, Gloucester, 1968.

At Marlborough, Morris's old house, A-house, remains in use: it has been renamed Morris
House and is currently a girls' residential block. It is still easy to retrace the routes of his
schoolboy expeditions to Silbury Hill, to Avebury, the Kennet barrow and White Horse Hill
near Lambourn on the Berkshire Downs.

Water House in Walthamstow is now the William Morris Gallery, open to the public and
containing the best collection of Morris memorabilia anywhere. J. W. Mackail, Morris's first
biographer, had been in contact with the son of F. B. Guy, William Morris's private tutor, and
his research notebooks, kept at Walthamstow, are informative on this otherwise rather hidden
phase.

CHAPTER TWO
29 Morris's nickname A. L. Irvine, *JWMS*, Winter 1968 and *The Diary of R. A. L. Nunns*,
  Supplement to *The Marlburian*, August 1931
  'in reply to which' Rev. G. H. Mullins, quoted Mackail
30 'Morris, William, son of Mrs. Morris' Marlborough College Records, Bodleian
  'gloomiest' period at Marlborough A. G. Bradley, A. C. Champneys and J. W. Baines,
  A History of Marlborough College, 1893
31 'architects of the "ignorance"' Mackail
  'like an Italian town palace' undated architectural article in Marlborough College Archive
  'such a dismal place' WM to Philip Burne-Jones, December 1874

32 'Hughes and Glennie' *The Diary of R. A. L. Nunns* 26 and 27 April 1852
blacksmiths hammering on an anvil Edward Lockwood, *Early Days of Marlborough College*, 1893
'the crushing repressions' *A History of Marlborough College*
'for the rest' WM to Philip Burne-Jones, December 1874
33 'children bring each other up' *Intros*
'I am sure' WM to Emma Morris, 1 November 1848
34 'Today being a Saints day' WM to Emma Morris, *ibid.*
'We have begun' Tom aged 12, letter to his sister, 1846, quoted *Marlborough Town and Countryside*, 1978
William Morris's school record Marlborough College Records, Bodleian
'I was educated' WM, *The Review of Reviews*, 14 March 1891
35 'the strongest intellect' Wilfrid Scawen Blunt, 'A Few Words about William Morris', typescript 15 January 1913, British Library
'rich men's sons' WM, *News from Nowhere*, 1890
'sturdy figure' H. E. Luxmoore to Sydney Cockerell, Epiphany 1924, Cockerell *Friends*
'politics and Socialism' Sydney Cockerell diary, 2 August 1891, British Library
36 'in the teeth of' W. B. Yeats, *Autobiographies*, Macmillan, 1956
'with knobbed sticks' *A History of Marlborough College*
37 'in a very beautiful country' WM to Andreas Scheu, 15 September 1883
'prettier than Twickenham' Lady Hertford quoted Nikolaus Pevsner, *The Buildings of England, Wiltshire*, Penguin Books, 1963
'an artificial hill' WM to Emma Morris, 13 April 1849
38 'the tower was very pretty' *ibid.*
'So for your edification' WM to Emma Morris, 13 April 1849
39 'a little scrubby town' WM to Jenny Morris, 23 August 1879
'no end to them almost' WM to May Morris, 31 August 1882
'intense and overweening love' WM, *News from Nowhere*, 1890
40 'Not seldom I please myself' Mackail
'In afternoon went with Tomkins' *The Diary of R. A. L. Nunns*, 18 October 1852
42 'with good oak fittings' Marlborough College article in *The Ecclesiologist*, April 1849
'taking them up' H. M. Hyndman, *Record of an Adventurous Life*, Macmillan, 1911
'Even then he mooned' D. R. Fearon, Mackail
'warm blue' *The Marlburian*, 3 December 1896
43 'She was most beautifully' *The Marlborough Magazine*, 24 April 1848, Bodleian
'When tidings came' *The Marlburian*, *loc. cit.*
44 'just that amount' *The Ecclesiologist*, April 1849
'We have had the same anthem' WM to Emma Morris, 13 April 1849
46 'Punctually at that hour' *A History of Marlborough College*
'I always did' WM to Rosalind Howard, 28 November 1881
'Tramp, tramp, tramp' Edward Lockwood, *Early Days of Marlborough College*
48 'Deep green water' WM, 'Golden Wings', 1858
49 'I don't like the boy' quoted J. M. S. Tompkins, *William Morris: an Approach to the Poetry*, Cecil Woolf, 1988
'"classical, poetic" temperament' R. W. Dixon account, Mackail notebooks, WMG
'the queer ante-dated' WM to Morgan George Watkins, 21 August 1867
'Morris has sat' Blunt, 30 June 1893
'an organic connection' Oliver Sacks, 'Tourette's Syndrome and Creativity', *British Medical Journal*, 19–26 December 1992
50 'You know, one has fits' WM, *The Novel*, c.1871
'his favourite sister or chum' WMAWS

50 'I see a little girl' WM, 'Frank's Sealed Letter', *Oxford and Cambridge Magazine*, 1856

CHAPTERS THREE, FOUR AND FIVE: Oxford 1853–55, Northern France 1855–56, Red Lion Square 1856–59

These chapters are drawn chiefly from William Morris's letters, J. W. Mackail's *Life*, Georgiana Burne-Jones's *Memorials*; W. R. Lethaby, *Philip Webb and his Work*, Oxford University Press, 1935; Cormell Price family correspondence and diaries; R. W. Dixon reminiscences in Mackail notebooks; ed. O. Doughty and J. R. Wahl, *Letters of Dante Gabriel Rossetti*, Oxford, 1965–7; ed. Virginia Surtees, *The Diaries of George Price Boyce*, Real World, Norwich, 1980.

On Oxford in general: Rev. W. Tuckwell, *Reminiscences of Oxford*, Cassell, 1901; three mid-Victorian Oxford novels: John Henry Newman, *Loss and Gain*, James Burns, 1848; Cuthbert Bede, *The Adventures of Mr. Verdant Green*, Nathaniel Cooke, 1853; Thomas Hughes, *Tom Brown at Oxford*, Macmillan, 1864.

On Morris at Oxford: Val Prinsep, 'A Chapter from a Painter's Reminiscences: the Oxford Circle: Rossetti, Burne-Jones and William Morris', article in *The Magazine of Art*, No. 2, 1904; J. D. Renton, *The Oxford Union Murals*, pamphlet published by the Oxford Union, 1983; K. L. Goodwin, 'William Morris's New and Lighter Design', *JWMS*, Winter 1968; Eugene D. LeMire, 'The "First" William Morris and the 39 Articles', *JWMS*, Spring 1987; Jon Whiteley, 'Morris's Oxford', *Oxford Today*, Trinity 1989.

On Morris and chivalry: Carolyn P. Collette, 'William Morris and Young England', *JWMS*, Winter 1983; Elizabeth Brewer, 'Morris and the "Kingsley" Movement', *JWMS*, Summer 1980; Mark Girouard, *The Return to Camelot: Chivalry and the English Gentleman*, Yale University Press, 1981.

On Morris's early writing: Florence S. Boos, *The Juvenilia of William Morris*, William Morris Society, New York and London, 1983; J. M. Baissus, 'Morris and the Oxford and Cambridge Magazine', *JWMS*, Winter 1983; Helen Timo, 'A Church without God: William Morris's "A Night in a Cathedral"', *JWMS*, Summer 1980; chapters on the early romances and *The Defence of Guenevere* in J. M. S. Tompkins, *William Morris, An Approach to the Poetry*, Cecil Woolf, 1988, and Amanda Hodgson, *The Romances of William Morris*, Cambridge University Press, 1987; Isobel Armstrong's chapter on 'The Grotesque as cultural critique: Morris' in *Victorian Poetry*, Routledge, 1993; Amanda Hodgson, 'Riding Together: William Morris and Robert Browning', *JWMS*, Spring 1992.

On Jane Morris's Oxford background: Jan Marsh, *Jane and May Morris*, Pandora, 1986; Margaret Fleming, 'Nothing but landscape and sentiment', *JWMS*, Summer 1984.

On Morris's tour of northern France: John Purkis, *Check-list of the Cathedrals and Churches visited by William Morris and Edward Burne-Jones*, William Morris Society, 1987.

On G. E. Street's office: A. E. Street, *Memoir of George Edmund Street*, John Murray, 1888; J. P. Cooper, 'The Work of John Sedding', *Architectural Review*, vol. 3, 1897–8; C. M. Smart, *Muscular Churches*, University of Arkansas Press, Fayetteville, 1989; Andrew Saint, *Richard Norman Shaw*, Yale University Press, 1976.

On Morris and painting: Jan Marsh, 'William Morris's Painting and Drawing', *The Burlington Magazine*, August 1986.

On Red Lion Square furniture: Pat Kirkham, 'William Morris's Early Furniture', *JWMS*, Summer 1981; Annette Carruthers, 'Like incubi and succubi', *Craft History Two*, April 1989; chapter on 'Morris & Co' in Jeremy Cooper, *Victorian and Edwardian Furniture and Interiors*, Thames & Hudson, 1987; J. Mordaunt Crook, *William Burges and the High Victorian Dream*, John Murray, 1981.

Morris's Oxford survives, in the interstices of late-twentieth-century development of a crassness even Morris could not have conceived. Research for this chapter was sustained by many visits to Morris's favourite buildings in Oxford, including Merton Chapel and the cloister at New College; to his own college, Exeter; and to the Oxford Union, where the murals were last restored, not wholly successfully, in 1987.

Most of the great churches and cathedrals of Morris's intensive tour of Northern France in 1855 are standing, and it is still feasible to follow that inspiring if exhausting route.

Bloomsbury, although much changed, is still evocative. 8 Red Lion Square has been demolished. Morris's and Burne-Jones's old lodgings at No. 17 Red Lion Square still exist, although the façade has now been rebuilt.

CHAPTER THREE

52 'He was slight in figure' Edward Burne-Jones, quoted Mackail
'the most important town' WM to *The Pall Mall Gazette*, 16 July 1881
'a place, a second home' draft for SPAB committee, Huntington Library, San Marino, California
'A vision of grey-roofed houses' WM, *A Dream of John Ball*, 1888
'"jewel" city' WM, 'Art under Plutocracy', lecture, 1883
'a kind of terror' WM to Georgiana Burne-Jones, 16 August 1881
53 'gloomy disappointment' Burne-Jones
'It was clear' *ibid.*
'I took very ill' WM to Andreas Scheu, 15 September 1883
'the headquarters of Anglo-Catholicism' John Betjeman, chapter in *My Oxford*, ed. Ann Thwaite, Robson Books, 1977
'a huge upper public school' WM to the *Daily News*, 20 November 1885
'the Brasenose' Edward Burne-Jones to Cormell Price, Burne-Jones
54 'a rather rough' Mackail
'My life is going' WM to Cormell Price, 29 September 1855
'A University education' WM to Emma Shelton Morris, 11 October 1855
'and its less interesting sister' WM, *News from Nowhere*, 1890
55 'fell to very vigorously' WM to Andreas Scheu, 15 September 1883
'the unfolding of medieval thought' WM address to SPAB AGM, 18 July 1893
'the newly invented study' WM to *The Athenaeum*, 5 March 1877
'monster beauty of a keep' Philip Webb, quoted Lethaby
'the best men could do' John Ruskin, quoted Lethaby
56 'essentially part of the street' WM to *The Pall Mall Gazette*, 16 July 1881
'all friends living' Horner
57 'which was nice' *ibid.*
'In an age of sofas' *ibid.*
58 'Nothing was ever' *ibid.*
'Saturday wet' *ibid.*
59 'how flat' *ibid.*
'star' Burne-Jones
'one of the cleverest' Edward Burne-Jones to Cormell Price, Burne-Jones
'No glimpse' *WMAWS*
60 'How Morris seems to know' R. W. Dixon, quoted Mackail
61 'another a brass' WM to Cormell Price, 3 April 1855
'all the host' Edward Burne-Jones to Cormell Price, Summer 1853, quoted Burne-Jones
'His countenance' R. W. Dixon, quoted Mackail
'All reading men' *ibid.*
62 'He suddenly raised' *ibid.*
64 'a good deal influenced' WM to Andreas Scheu, 15 September 1883
'for the Christian Socialists' Edward Burne-Jones to Henry Macdonald, Burne-Jones

64 'welcomed gladly' Burne-Jones

65 'unquestionably one' Mackail

66 'so that to look upon' Friedrich de la Motte Fouqué, *Sintram and his Companions*, London, 1820

67 'a half college' John Henry Newman to Maria Giberne, quoted *Cardinal Newman*, National Portrait Gallery, 1990
'nothing to be seen' Brian Martin, *John Henry Newman: His Life and Work*, Chatto & Windus, 1982
'I have set my heart' Edward Burne-Jones to Cormell Price, 1 May 1853, Burne-Jones

68 'under certain religious ordinances' Arthur Edmund Street, *Memoir of George Edmund Street*, 1888
'the mystery' Burne-Jones

69 'I won't make' WM to Cormell Price, 3 April 1855
'sort of revelation' WM to Andreas Scheu, 15 September 1883
'in future days' WM, intro. to Kelmscott Press edition 'On the Nature of Gothic', 1892
'we soon saw' Mackail

70 'marvellous inspiration' WM, 'The Revival of Architecture', article in *Fortnightly Review*, May 1888

71 'We are always' John Ruskin, *The Stones of Venice*, Vol. 2, 1853
'ferocity of Carlyle's gloom' WM to Georgiana Burne-Jones, 6 July 1881

72 'The Museum rose' Rev. W. Tuckwell, *Reminiscences of Oxford*, 1901
'the first building' Jennifer Sherwood and Nikolaus Pevsner, *The Buildings of England, Oxfordshire*, Penguin Books, Harmondsworth, 1974

73 'I was working' Burne-Jones

74 'Here, one morning' Mackail
'We sat down' *ibid.*
'While still an undergraduate' WM to Andreas Scheu, 15 September 1883

75 'exceedingly seedy' WM to Cormell Price, 3 April 1855

76 'there are no facts' WM to Cormell Price, *ibid.*
'boundless admiration' WM to Charles Cowden-Clarke, 17 September 1868

77 '"The Skylark" was one' WM to Cormell Price, April 1855
'ingenuous callowness' WM to Charles Fairfax Murray, quoted Florence Boos, *The Juvenilia of William Morris*, 1983
'A little more *piano*' Mackail notebooks, WMG
'dealing himself vigorous blows' Mackail

78 'When he was to go' Mackail notebooks, WMG
'as men are shaken' George Bernard Shaw, 'More about Morris', review in *The Observer*, 6 November 1949

79 'He is mad' Lethaby
'He would imitate' Mackail
'There must have been' George Bernard Shaw to Sydney Cockerell, 10 April 1950, Cockerell, *Best of Friends*

80 'Morris has become' Burne-Jones
'Mrs. Ned' Dante Gabriel Rossetti to William Allingham, 31 July 1860, Doughty and Wahl
'spiritual affinity' Sydney Cockerell to George Bernard Shaw, 17 April 1950, British Library
'That's Morris' Burne-Jones

CHAPTER FOUR

82 'a very great country' Emery Walker, quoted Neville Lytton, 'A Discussion about William Morris', *The Nation & Athenaeum*, undated article, Cheltenham

82 'so thick' WM to Jenny Morris, 30 January 1883
railways as 'ABOMINATIONS' WM to Cormell Price, 10 August 1855
'yet to me' WM to Cormell Price, 6 July 1855

83 'the French poplar meadows' WM to Georgiana Burne-Jones, 3 May 1881
'all splendid churches' WM to Cormell Price, 10 August 1855
'We were all' WM to Emma Shelton Morris, 29 July 1855
'bit of a hill' WM to Cormell Price, 6 July 1855
'surveyed it' William Fulford, quoted Burne-Jones

84 'stern knights' WM, 'A Night in the Cathedral', *Oxford and Cambridge Magazine*, May 1856
'go forth again' John Ruskin, 'On the Nature of Gothic', *The Stones of Venice*, 1851–3

85 'We came out' WM, 'The Churches of Northern France: Shadows of Amiens', *Oxford and Cambridge Magazine*, February 1856
'poached eggs' WM to Charles Fairfax Murray, 27 May 1875
'filling the streets' Edward Burne-Jones, quoted Mackail
'seen by twilight' WM to Emery Walker, 13 August 1891
'to this day' WM, 'Gertha's Lovers', *Oxford and Cambridge Magazine*, July and August 1856

86 'What a day' Burne-Jones
'and for nothing else' WM to Emma Shelton Morris, 29 July 1855
'Morris seemed' William Fulford, quoted Burne-Jones

87 'he has been dying' *ibid.*
'through the boughs' WM, 'The Story of the Unknown Church', *Oxford and Cambridge Magazine*, January 1856
'quaint streets' WM to Emma Shelton Morris, 29 July 1855
'beautiful statues' WM to Cormell Price, 10 August 1855

88 'more than six hundred' WM, 'The Story of the Unknown Church', *op. cit.*
'great spires' *ibid.*
'The windows' WM, 'Stained Glass' entry in *Chambers' Encyclopaedia*, WMAWS

89 'till a sound' 'A Dream', *Oxford and Cambridge Magazine*, March 1856
'quaint nondescript' WM to Emma Shelton Morris, 29 July 1855

90 'looking as if' WM to Cormell Price, 10 August 1855
'very quaint old town' WM to Emma Shelton Morris, 29 July 1855
'very forlorn' WM to Cormell Price, 10 August 1855

91 'far-off clinching' D. H. Lawrence, *The Rainbow*, 1915
'huge free space' WM, 'The Beauty of Life', lecture, 1880
'O! the trees!' WM to Cormell Price, 10 August 1855

92 'Well here we are' WM to Emma Shelton Morris, 29 July 1855
'what a wonder' WM to Georgiana Burne-Jones, 15 May 1878
'swarming like an ant-hill' John Murray, *Handbook for Travellers in France*, John Murray, 1854
'the two great architectural' WM to *The Daily Chronicle*, 4 October 1895, Henderson

93 'And weren't they sung' WM to Cormell Price, 18 August 1855
'wildness of thought' John Ruskin, *The Stones of Venice*, 1853
'and its steeples' WM, *The Well at the World's End*, 1896

94 'a glorious walk' WM to Emma Shelton Morris, 7 August 1855

95 'a life of art' Burne-Jones
'I wanted to go' Horner
'I MUST make haste' WM to Cormell Price, 6 October 1855

96 'somewhat roughly' WM to Emma Shelton Morris, 11 November 1855
'a kind of tea gardens' WM to Cormell Price, 29 September 1855

97 'F says Morris' Margaret Price diary, quoted Mackail
98 'I don't think' WM to Cormell Price, 6 October 1855
   'mainly Tales' Cormell Price quoted Burne-Jones
   'We have such a deal' Edward Burne-Jones to Maria Choyce, quoted Burne-Jones
99 'for it cannot be published' *ibid.*
   'truthfulness and earnestness' Alfred Tennyson, quoted Mackail
   'Topsy has surrendered' Edward Burne-Jones to Cormell Price, quoted Burne-Jones
   'grindelays' background R. W. Dixon account, Mackail notebooks, WMG
   'I am to have a grind' WM to Cormell Price, 11 January 1856
100 'We were both' R. W. Dixon account, Mackail notebooks, WMG
   'You men at Oxford' William Fulford to Cormell Price, Mackail notebooks, WMG
   'Topsy has got' Mackail
   'To think of a beggar' *ibid.*
   'it does not often' WM, review of *Men and Woman*, *Oxford and Cambridge Magazine*,
   March 1856
102 'I shall ignore' Cormell Price to Samuel Price, 23 January 1856, Price
   'a slim boy' Lethaby
103 'Radley, Cumnor, and Littlemore' *ibid.*
   'I propose asking' WM to Emma Shelton Morris, 11 November 1855
   'it would be glorious' WM to Cormell Price, 6 October 1855
104 Street family tree Mary Comino, *Gimson and the Barnsleys*, Evans Brothers, London,
   1980
105 'What is this rattles' Lethaby
   'in the chase' Philip Webb to May Morris, 7 July 1898, British Library
   'country saw-bones' Lethaby
   'I explored' *ibid.*
106 'Ships sailing' WM, 'The Hollow Land', *Oxford and Cambridge Magazine*, September
   1856
107 'as if they were' Sir Edmund Birkett, *A Book of Building*, 1876
   'the moulding and altering' WM, 'The Prospects of Architecture in Civilisation', lecture,
   1881
108 'I really think' A. E. Street, *Memoir of George Edmund Street*, 1888
   'except in the negative' Philip Webb to J. W. Mackail, 8 December 1898, Cheltenham
   'sat with Georgie' Hannah Macdonald diary, 31 July 1856, quoted Sue Mooney, 'Self
   Revelation in Morris's Unfinished Novel', *JWMS*, Spring 1993
109 'One won't get' WM to Cormell Price, July 1856
   'Oh how I long' WM to Aglaia Coronio, 25 November 1872
   'has always slightly' Max Beerbohm to Sam Behrman, February 1956, ed. Rupert Hart-
   Davis, *Letters of Max Beerbohm 1892–1956*, John Murray, 1988

CHAPTER FIVE
110 'Topsy and I' Burne-Jones
   'the richest city' WM, 'The Prospects of Architecture in Civilisation', lecture, 1881
111 London population figures Geoffrey Best, *Mid-Victorian Britain*, Weidenfeld &
   Nicolson, 1971
112 'the spreading sore' 'Art and Socialism', lecture, 1884
   'this world-without-end' WM to William De Morgan, 17 March 1881
   'all pasty' WM to Jenny Morris, 15 April 1884
   'London in the older' WM to Georgiana Burne-Jones, 10 May 1891, quoted Mackail
   'well-remembered days' WM to Louisa Macdonald Baldwin, 25 March 1875
   'it is much *greater*' Margaret Price 1875, quoted Burne-Jones

113 'whenever Topsy' *ibid.*
 'Will you do me' WM to Edward Burne-Jones, 17 May 1856
114 'tensity rather than' Derek Patmore, *The Life and Times of Coventry Patmore*, Constable,
 1949
 'Ah Gabriel' Horner
 'the mind and soul' Edward Burne-Jones to F. G. Stephens, 24 August 1894, Fitzwilliam
115 'one of the nicest' Dante Gabriel Rossetti to William Allingham, 6 March 1856, Doughty
 and Wahl
 'Rossetti says' WM to Cormell Price, July 1856
 'it needs a person' WM to (?) Manson, 23 January 1883
 'I can't enter' WM to Cormell Price, July 1856
116 'a tallish, slim' WM to Cormell Price, July 1856
 'I could soon' WM, 'Frank's Sealed Letter', *Oxford and Cambridge Magazine*, April 1856
 'the greatest poet' Edward Burne-Jones, quoted Mackail
 'the Mag. is going' *ibid.*
117 'Poor boys!' Lago
 'books, boxes' Edward Burne-Jones, quoted Burne-Jones
118 'rather doing the magnificent' Dante Gabriel Rossetti to William Allingham, 18
 December 1856, Doughty and Wahl
 'A gentleman who' Henry Price quoted Pat Kirkham, 'William Morris's Early
 Furniture', *JWMS*, Summer 1981
120 'all the passages' Edward Burne-Jones, quoted Mackail
 'noble confusion' Frederic W. Macdonald, *As a Tale that is Told*, Cassell, 1919
 'when we have painted' Edward Burne-Jones to Miss Sampson, Burne-Jones
 'interesting drawings' ed. Virginia Surtees, *The Diaries of George Price Boyce*, 4 May
 1858, 1980
122 'He Alma Redemptoris' Frederic W. Macdonald, *As a Tale that is Told*
 'the art that is life' W. M. Price, subtitle for *The Artsman*, Journal of the Rose Valley
 community, Pennsylvania, 1903–07
 'If you want' Holbrook Jackson, *The Eighteen Nineties*, Grant Richards, 1913
 'both are men' Dante Gabriel Rossetti to William Bell Scott, February 1857, Doughty
 and Wahl
123 'It is all' Dante Gabriel Rossetti to William Bell Scott, June 1857, Doughy and Wahl
 'knocking about' Lethaby
 'You know' Dante Gabriel Rossetti to William Allingham, 18 December 1856, Doughty
 and Wahl
124 'He who tells' Frederic W. Macdonald, *As a Tale that is Told*
 'In all illumination' Mackail
125 'the most unequivocal' Burne-Jones
 Red Lion Mary Horner
 'I seemed so necessary' Burne-Jones
 'Mary, this egg' Horner
126 'She liked Gabriel' *ibid.*
 'horrid eggs' *ibid.*
127 'This play is a curse' *ibid.*
 'like a good woman' Burne-Jones
 'a poor miserable' ed. Virginia Surtees, *The Diary of Ford Madox Brown*, 27 January
 1858, Yale University Press, 1981
 'closely followed' Burne-Jones
128 'bore an iron ring' WM, *The Well at the World's End*, 1896
 'who liked it' Burne-Jones

128 'At these times' Dante Gabriel Rossetti to William Allingham, November 1854, Doughty and Wahl
    'a domestic Wild Bull' Lethaby
129 'He was very kind' WM to William Bell Scott, 27 April 1882
    'jovial campaign' Dante Gabriel Rossetti to Alexander Gilchrist, June 1861, Doughty and Wahl
130 'there's one' Val Prinsep, 'A Chapter from a Painter's Reminiscences', *The Magazine of Art*, No. 2, 1904
131 'Charley comes out' Mackail
    'Spent afternoon' Cormell Price diary, October 1857, Price
    'their laughter' Rev. W. Tuckwell, *Reminiscences of Oxford*, Cassell, 1901
    'This is mine' Arthur Hughes, Mackail notebooks, WMG
    'He had a way' Mackail
    'Morte d'Arthur' Val Prinsep, 'A Chapter', *op. cit.*
132 'Poor Topsy' *ibid.*
    'extremely ludicrous' WM to James Richard Thursfield, 1869
    'new and lighter' First Report of the Oxford Union Fresco Committee, 12 November 1874
133 'By God' Mackail notebooks, WMG
    'great spirit' Arthur Hughes, J. W. Mackail notebooks, WMG
    'embedded in iron' Mackail
    'voluptuous radiance' Coventry Patmore, 'Walls and Wall Paintings in Oxford', *The Saturday Review*, 26 December 1857
134 'What fun!' Val Prinsep, 'A Chapter', *op. cit.*
    'those wonderful seething' Burne-Jones
    'the whole affair' WM to James Richard Thursfield, 1869
    'When dinner' Val Prinsep, 'A Chapter', *op. cit.*
135 'very, very Topsian' Burne-Jones
    'swears awfully' A. C. Swinburne to Edwin Hatch, 26 April 1858, Lang
    'the forcible' Burne-Jones
    'He was the essence' Val Prinsep, 'A Chapter', *op. cit.*
    'out of the run' Horner
    'Topsy raves' Cormell Price to Samuel Price, 10 December 1857, Price
136 Janey as a girl Rev. W. Tuckwell, *Reminiscences of Oxford*
137 'to be beautiful' George Bernard Shaw, *The Observer*, 6 November 1949
138 'And yet, again' WM, 'Pygmalion and the Image', *The Earthly Paradise*, part 2, 1868
139 'absurdly prejudiced' R. W. Dixon, Mackail notebooks, WMG
    'I cannot paint' Gerald H. Crow, *William Morris Designer*, The Studio, 1934
    'Her great eyes' WM, 'In Praise of My Lady', *The Defence of Guenevere*, 1858
140 'content with that' A. C. Swinburne to Edwin Hatch, 17 February 1859, Lang
141 'to take his' Lago
    'He made one' ed. Virginia Surtees, *The Diaries of George Price Boyce*, 2 June 1858
    'A most beautiful' *ibid.*, 15 December 1858
    'we have unearthed' R. W. Dixon, Mackail notebooks, WMG
    'dear little Carrots' Burne-Jones
142 'Having a volume' WM to Alexander Macmillan, 25 October 1857
    'Sir Guy of the Doleful Damn' Helena M. Sickert Swanwick, *I Have Been Young*, Gollancz, 1935
    'More like Browning' Mackail
143 'Midways of a walled garden' WM, 'Golden Wings', *The Defence of Guenevere*, 1858
144 'not gone to powder' WM, 'Concerning Geffray Teste Noire', *ibid.*

144 'To find her' WM, 'Sir Peter Harpdon's End', *ibid.*
'I see her' *Intros*
145 'like a curved sword' WM, 'Concerning Geffray Teste Noire', *The Defence of Guenevere*, 1858
'with empty hands' WM, 'The Haystack in the Floods', *ibid.*
'Alas! alas!' WM, 'The Wind', *ibid.*
146 'With camel's hair' R. W. Dixon, 'Dream', *Poems from Christ's Company*, 1861
'Through the floor' WM, 'The Blue Closet', *The Defence of Guenevere*, 1858
'Enter Two Angels' WM, 'Sir Galahad, A Christmas Mystery', *ibid.*
'That party' A. C. Swinburne to Edwin Hatch, 26 April 1858, Lang
'all cold' unsigned review, *Saturday Review*, 20 November, 1858
147 'Poetry is concerned' *ibid.*
Mrs Browning WM in conversation with Sydney Cockerell, 28 November 1892, Mackail notebooks, WMG
'he could sling' George Bernard Shaw to Mrs Patrick Campbell, 7 February 1913, Laurence
148 'made for quiet places' Dante Gabriel Rossetti to Elizabeth Gaskell, 18 July 1859, Doughty and Wahl
'literally shouted' Hilda Doolittle, quoted Humphrey Carpenter, *A Serious Character: The Life of Ezra Pound*, Faber & Faber, 1988
'with great wonder' W. B. Yeats to Olivia Shakespear, 2 March 1929, ed. Allan Wade, *The Letters of W. B. Yeats*, Rupert Hart-Davis, 1954
'Looking down' Lethaby
149 'You fellows' *ibid.*
'with their total change' *ibid.*
150 'I'll show you' *ibid.*
'The upper part' *ibid.*
'the very strawberries' Burne-Jones
151 'Jones is going' ed. Virginia Surtees, *The Diary of Ford Madox Brown*, January 1858, 1981
'the Stunner' ed. Virginia Surtees, *The Diary of George Price Boyce*, 6 March 1859
'taken a strong fancy' Mackail
152 'William and Mary' Burne-Jones
'This place' Philip Webb to Charles Canning Winmill, quoted Joyce M. Winmill, *Charles Canning Winmill*, J. M. Dent, 1946
'You can walk' WM to Emma Shelton Morris, 24 July 1874
153 'It was now' WM, *The Well at the World's End*, 1896

CHAPTERS SIX, SEVEN AND EIGHT: Red House 1859–65, Queen Square 1865–69, Bad Ems 1869–71

Apart from William Morris's letters, Georgiana Burne-Jones's *Memorials* and May Morris's childhood memories, these chapters rely mainly on W. R. Lethaby, *Philip Webb and his Work*, Oxford University Press, 1935; ed. O. Doughty and J. R. Wahl, *Letters of Dante Gabriel Rossetti*, Oxford University Press, 1965–7; ed. John Bryson, *Dante Gabriel Rossetti and Jane Morris, their Correspondence*, Clarendon Press, Oxford, 1976; ed. Virginia Surtees, *The Diaries of George Price Boyce*, Real World, Norwich, 1980; ed. H. Allingham and D. Radford, *William Allingham, A Diary 1824–1889*, Centaur Press, Fontwell, 1967; ed. Virginia Surtees, *The Diary of Ford Madox Brown*, Yale University Press, 1981; Warington Taylor memoirs and correspondence in Fitzwilliam Museum, Cambridge, and at National Art Library; George Wardle memoir in British Library; information from the town archive at Bad Ems.
On Red House: Edward Hollamby, *Red House*, Architecture, Design and Technology Press,

1991; Ray Watkinson and Edward Hollamby, *Red House, A Guide*, William Morris Society, 1993; Mark Girouard, 'Red House, Bexleyheath, Kent', *Country Life*, 16 June 1960; Peter Blundell Jones, 'Red House', *Architects' Journal*, January 1986.

On Morris, Marshall, Faulkner & Co. (later Morris & Co.): Minutes book in Berger Collection, Carmel, California (copy in Hammersmith Libraries Archive); Paul Thompson, *The Work of William Morris*, Heinemann, 1967; Charles Harvey and Jon Press, *William Morris, Design and Enterprise in Victorian Britain*, Manchester University Press, 1991; Peter Stansky, *Morris & Co.*, catalogue of exhibition at Stanford Art Gallery, Stanford University, 1975; Charlotte Gere, *Morris and Company*, catalogue of exhibition at The Fine Art Society, London, 1979.

On Morris interiors and furniture: Mark Girouard, 'The Origins of "Queen Anne"', chapter in *Sweetness and Light: the Queen Anne Movement, 1860–1900*, Clarendon Press, Oxford, 1977; Jeremy Cooper, 'Morris and Company', chapter in *Victorian and Edwardian Furniture and Interiors*, Thames & Hudson, 1987; Charles Mitchell, 'William Morris at St. James's Palace', *Architectural Review*, January 1947; John Y. Le Bourgeois, 'William Morris at St. James's Palace, a sequel', *JWMS*, Spring 1974; Barbara Morris, 'William Morris and the South Kensington Museum', William Morris Society, 1987; Barbara Morris, *Inspiration for Design: The Influence of the Victoria & Albert Museum*, Victoria and Albert Museum, 1986; Edward Burne-Jones account books at Fitzwilliam Museum; Philip Webb account books in collection of John Brandon-Jones (copy at Birmingham Art Gallery). Major surviving examples: Red House, Upton; Green Dining-Room, Victoria and Albert Museum; St James's Palace; Peterhouse Hall, Cambridge; Jesus College Chapel, Cambridge; All Saints, Cambridge.

On Morris embroidery and textiles: Linda Parry, *William Morris Textiles*, Weidenfeld & Nicolson, 1983; Norah Gillow, *William Morris Designs and Patterns*, Bracken Books, 1988; Oliver Fairclough and Emmeline Leary, 'Textiles by William Morris and Morris & Co., 1861–1940', catalogue of exhibition at Birmingham Museum and Art Gallery, 1981; J. Anne George and Susie Campbell, 'The Role of Embroidery in Victorian Culture and the Pre-Raphaelite Circle', *The Journal of Pre-Raphaelite Studies*, vol. 7, May 1987. Collections at Victoria and Albert Museum; William Morris Gallery, Walthamstow; Birmingham Museums and Art Gallery; Whitworth Gallery, Manchester.

On Morris wallpapers: Fiona Clark, *William Morris, Wallpapers and Chintzes*, Academy Editions, 1973; Peggy Vance, *William Morris Wallpapers*, Bracken Books, 1989. Collections as for embroidery and textiles.

On Morris table glass: Judy Rudoe and Howard Coutts, 'The Table Glass Designs of Philip Webb and T. G. Jackson for James Powell and Sons, Whitefriars Glassworks', *Decorative Arts Society Journal*, No. 16, 1992. Examples in the Victoria and Albert Museum and Birmingham Museums and Art Gallery.

On Morris stained glass: A. Charles Sewter, *The Stained Glass of William Morris and his Circle*, 2 volumes, Yale University Press, 1974–5; Martin Harrison, 'The Secular Reaction: Morris, Burne-Jones and their Followers', chapter in *Victorian Stained Glass*, Barrie & Jenkins, 1980; David O'Connor, 'Morris Stained Glass: "an Art of the Middle Ages"', essay in catalogue of exhibition *William Morris and the Middle Ages*, Whitworth Gallery, Manchester University Press, 1984. Major stained glass of this period at All Saints, Selsley; St Martin's, Scarborough; St Michael's, Brighton; St Oswald's, Durham; St John's, Tue Brook, Liverpool; St Michael's, Lyndhurst; St Helen's, Darley Dale; All Saints, Catton, Yorks.; Bradford City Art Gallery; Victoria and Albert Museum.

On Morris's illuminated manuscripts: Alfred Fairbank, 'A Note on the manuscript work of William Morris', survey in William Morris and Eiríkr Magnússon, *The Story of Kormak*, William Morris Society, 1970; Graily Hewitt, 'The Illuminated Manuscripts of William Morris', paper read to Double Crown Club, 2 May 1934, printed by Shenval Press; A. S. Osley, 'The Kelmscott Manor Volume of Italian Writing-Books', *The Antiquaries Journal*, vol. LXIV, part 2, 1984. Collections: Bodleian Library, Oxford; Victoria and Albert Museum; Fitzwilliam Museum, Cambridge.

On Dante Gabriel Rossetti and the image of Janey: Alicia Craig Faxon, *Dante Gabriel Rossetti*, Phaidon Press, Oxford, 1989; Michael Bateman, *The Pre-Raphaelite Camera: Aspects of Victorian Photography*, Weidenfeld & Nicolson, 1985; Andrea Rose, *Pre-Raphaelite Portraits*, Oxford Illustrated Press, Sparkford, 1981.

On *Jason* and *The Earthly Paradise*: Peter Faulkner, introduction to *William Morris Selected Poems*, Carcanet Press, Manchester, 1992; J. M. S. Tompkins, *William Morris, an Approach to the Poetry*, Cecil Woolf, 1988; Paul Thompson, *The Work of William Morris*, Heinemann, 1967; David Latham, '"A Matter of Craftsmanship": William Morris's manuscripts', *JWMS*, Summer 1985; ed. Peter Faulkner, *William Morris, The Critical Heritage*, Routledge & Kegan Paul, 1973; Florence Boos, 'Victorian response to *Earthly Paradise* tales', *JWMS*, Winter 1983; Joseph R. Dunlap, *The Book That Never Was*, Oriole Editions, New York, 1971.

On Aglaia Coronio and the Greeks in London: Luke Ionides, *Memories*, Herbert Clarke, Paris, 1925; Alexander C. Ionides, *Ion: a Grandfather's Tale*, privately printed, Cuala Press, Dublin, 1927; Julia Atkins (Ionides), 'The Ionides Family', *Antique Collector*, June 1987; Julia Ionides, 'Aglaia Coronio', unpublished typescript of talk given at Modern Languages Association Convention, Washington, 30 December 1989.

Red House still stands, in remarkable condition, having been well tended by its architect-owner Edward Hollamby, who has lived there since 1952. It is occasionally open to the public. The Firm's premises, and Morris's home, at No. 26 Queen Square, were demolished soon after the National Hospital for Nervous Diseases acquired the freehold in 1882, paying Morris out at £3,000 for a lease that still had eight years to run.

Bad Ems is still a prospering spa town, catering to the modern craze for health and fitness, with much of its nineteenth-century centre intact. But it has lost the social and political cachet it had in 1869.

CHAPTER SIX

154 'The Towers of Topsy' Dante Gabriel Rossetti to Ford Madox Brown, 23 May 1860, Doughty and Wahl
  'an immense red-tiled' ed. W. Minto, *Autobiographical Notes on the Life of William Bell Scott*, James R. Osgood, McIlvaine & Co., 1892
  'very mediaeval' WM to Andreas Scheu, 15 September 1883
156 'The keep is' Lethaby
  'a most noble' Dante Gabriel Rossetti to Charles Eliot Norton, 9 January 1862, Doughty and Wahl
  'never shall I' Burne-Jones
  'was surprised' ed. Virginia Surtees, *The Diaries of George Price Boyce*, 31 January 1860, 1980
157 'I can't think' ed. W. Minto, *Autobiographical Notes on the Life of William Bell Scott*
  'where a thin' Burne-Jones
158 'Like all the' Dante Gabriel Rossetti to Mrs Gabriele Rossetti, 13 April 1860, Doughty and Wahl
  'the beautifullest place' Edward Burne-Jones, quoted Mackail
  'painting the inner walls' Dante Gabriel Rossetti to William Allingham, autumn 1960, Doughty and Wahl
159 'Don't be a damned fool' Dr Furnivall, in discussion following lecture on Morris by F. S. Ellis, *Journal of the Society of Arts*, 27 May 1898
  'Top has taken' Mackail
160 'material such as' Jane Morris to May Morris, c.1912, British Library

160 'Morris was a pleased man' Burne-Jones
'the first principle' Jane Morris to May Morris, *op. cit.*
'could not be improved' Burne-Jones
161 'I had some hand' Jane Morris to Dante Gabriel Rossetti, undated letter, Bryson
'exceedingly young' WM to Andreas Scheu, 15 September 1883
'the hideousness of' F. S. Ellis, 'The Life Work of William Morris', address to the Society
of Arts, *Journal of the Society of Arts*, 27 May 1898
162 'gave me' unidentified visitor quoted Aymer Vallance, *The Life and Work of William
Morris*, George Bell, 1897
'painted coarsely' ed. W. Minto, *Autobiographical Notes on the Life of William Bell Scott*
'You fellows' Lethaby
'I see her' Burne-Jones
163 'noble communal hall' WM, 'How We Live and How We Might Live', lecture, 1885
164 'delicate and distinguished' J. W. Mackail, obituary note, February 1920, NAL
'a real artist' Virginia Surtees, *Rossetti's Portraits of Elizabeth Siddal*, Scolar Press,
Aldershot, 1991
'It is pathetic' Burne-Jones
165 'Do you know' Burne-Jones
'square-plot and trained-hedge' Lethaby
'large and small' WM, 'Making the Best of It', lecture, c.1879
'a kind of younger-brother' Burne-Jones
166 'a strange garment' *ibid.*
'he and Morris' ed. Virginia Surtees, *The Diaries of George Price Boyce*, 26 January 1861
167 'you will see' WM to F. B. Guy, 19 April 1861
'and accordingly in 1861' WM to Andreas Scheu, 15 September 1883
168 'dear boys' Burne-Jones
169 'How deadly dull' WM, 'How I Became a Socialist', article in *Justice*, 16 June 1894
'We are not intending' Dante Gabriel Rossetti to William Allingham, January 1861,
Doughty and Wahl
'like a picnic' Lethaby
'the character' Charles Faulkner to Cormell Price, April 1862, Mackail
170 'supremely comical' A. M. W. Stirling, *The Richmond Papers*, Heinemann, 1926
Tooley Street fire account Burne-Jones
171 'both wicked and mad' Wilfrid Scawen Blunt, ms. diaries, 31 May 1896
172 'Morris, Marshall' prospectus Mackail
'rather despaired' Arthur Hughes, Mackail notebooks, WMG
174 'Big Peter Paul' Burne-Jones
'the Topsaic Laboratory' Dante Gabriel Rossetti to Mrs John Dalrymple, 1861, Doughty
and Wahl
176 'You see we are' WM to F. B. Guy, 19 April 1861
'What's this?' Charles Faulkner, Mackail notebooks, WMG
'throwing fair colours' WM, 'A Dream', *Oxford and Cambridge Magazine*, 1856
177 'He could do' Lethaby
'the worth of stained' WM, 'Stained Glass', article for *Chambers' Encyclopaedia*,
WMAWS
'the highest point' *ibid.*
178 'and the men' WM to Henry Holiday, ?1877
'tell stories' 'Stained Glass', *op. cit.*
179 'to illustrate points' Mackail
180 'Our stained glass' Dante Gabriel Rossetti to Charles Eliot Norton, 9 January 1862,
Doughty and Wahl

180 'We are looking' *WMAWS*
'The getting ready' Mackail
'we were naturally' WM to Andreas Scheu, 15 September 1883
181 'As we strolled' *London Society*, vol. I, August 1862
'studied the art' WM to Andreas Scheu, 15 September 1883
'I should have painted' Sydney Cockerell, Mackail notebooks, WMG
182 'on common brown' Dante Gabriel Rossetti to William Allingham, January 1861, Doughty and Wahl
'disliked *flowers*' Warington Taylor to Edward Robert Robson, *c.*1863, Fitzwilliam
'in which the leaves' *ibid.*
183 'allowed nothing to pass' Metford Warner, quoted *Journal of the Society of Arts*, 27 May 1898
'a shop like Giotto' Dante Gabriel Rossetti to Charles Eliot Norton, 9 January 1862, Doughty and Wahl
184 'we came into' Mackail
'we'll let you have' Lawrence Danson, *Max Beerbohm and 'The Mirror of the Past'*, Princeton University Press, New Jersey, 1982
185 'the Great Shop' Dante Gabriel Rossetti to Alexander Gilchrist, 2 September 1861, Doughty and Wahl
'old manuscripts' WM to unidentified recipient, October 1858
'Have nothing in your houses' WM, 'The Beauty of Life', lecture, 1880
'Kid having appeared' WM to Ford Madox Brown, 18 January 1861
186 'little accident' Dante Gabriel Rossetti to William Allingham, January 1861, Doughty and Wahl
'went together' Burne-Jones
'Hush, Ned!' *ibid.*
'quite cowed' Peter Paul Marshall, quoted Mackail notebooks, WMG
187 'Mrs. Morris being the statue' Burne-Jones
'I ought to have had' *ibid.*
'a very handsome' *ibid.*
'what a man's love was' M. K. Trevelyan diary, 1904, quoted Pat Jalland, *Women, Marriage and Politics*, Oxford University Press, 1986
188 'speaking indeed' WM to Emma Shelton Morris, 5 November 1855
'Shy and reserved in life' Mackail
189 'For who, indeed' WM, 'The Ring given to Venus', *The Earthly Paradise*, part 4, 1870
'Upon the gilded door' WM, 'The Love of Alcestis', *The Earthly Paradise*, part 2, 1868
190 'we talked hard' Mackail
191 'I am the Menelaus' WM, 'Scenes from the Fall of Troy', *Collected Works*, vol. 24, 1915
192 'By steamer' William Allingham, *A Diary, 1824–1889*, 18 July 1864, 1967
'The Red House' *ibid.*, 19 July 1864
'Have you ever' Georgiana Burne-Jones to Sydney Cockerell, 26 October 1917, NAL
'certain dream-pictures' *Intros.*
193 'He struck me' George Wardle, 'Reminiscences of William Morris', Christmas 1897, British Library
194 'the evenings were always' Burne-Jones
'he had borne' ed. Daphne du Maurier, *The Young George du Maurier, A Selection of his Letters 1860–67*, Peter Davies, 1951
'Jones poor fellow' *ibid.*
195 'Who does not know' *ibid.*
'As to our palace' WM to Edward Burne-Jones, November 1864
196 'he could not bear' Burne-Jones
'some of us saw' *ibid.*

CHAPTER SEVEN

197 'to Cabmen' Fitzwilliam
198 'an antiquated ex-fashionable' Henry James to Alice James, 10 March 1869, ed. Percy
   Lubbock, *Letters of Henry James*, Macmillan, 1920
   'in his unflinching way' Burne-Jones
   'the jewel-like colours' *Intros*
199 'made to shine' Burne-Jones
   'a huge lump' *Intros*
200 'brooding over' Burne-Jones
201 'Monday July 30' William Allingham, *A Diary*, 30 July 1866, 1967
202 'in deadly sleep' WM, 'The Story of Cupid and Psyche', *The Earthly Paradise*, part 2,
   1868
   'Ned only makes' William Allingham, *A Diary*, 18 August 1866
203 'Mr. Morris came possessed' George Wardle, 'Reminiscences of William Morris',
   Christmas 1897, British Library
   'a gloriously' *Intros*, vol. 3
204 'true poetry' Octavia Hill to a friend, 4 October 1868, ed. C. Edmund Maurice, *The Life
   of Octavia Hill*, Macmillan, 1913
   'Naturally I am' WM to Edward Burne-Jones, 20 June 1867
   'hit the bird' George Saintsbury, 'Mr. William Morris', chapter in *Corrected Impressions.
   Essays on Victorian Writers*, Heinemann, 1895
205 'so broad and sad' A. C. Swinburne, *Fortnightly Review*, July 1867
   'You cannot find' Burne-Jones
   'the endless hithering' C. S. Lewis, unsigned review in *The Times Literary Supplement*,
   29 May 1937
206 'and once more' WM, *The Life and Death of Jason*, 1867
   'patent, ubiquitous' C. S. Lewis, 'William Morris', chapter in *Rehabilitations and Other
   Essays*, Oxford University Press, 1939
   'a journey' George Bernard Shaw, 'Morris as I knew him', 1936, *WMAWS*
   'As for my archaeology' WM to Morgan George Watkins, 21 August 1867
   'in the position' WM to F. B. Guy, 25 November 1867
207 'Advances of Intellectual' Edward Burne-Jones to George Howard, undated, Castle
   Howard
   'M..rr..s of Emperor's Square' William De Morgan to Edward Burne-Jones, A. M. W.
   Stirling, *William De Morgan and his Wife*, Henry Holt, New York, 1922
   'though not much like' WM to Morgan George Watkins, 21 August 1867
208 'had not yet found' Burne-Jones
   '*intense honest* desire' Warington Taylor to Edward Robert Robson, undated,
   Fitzwilliam
   'that he was keeping' Burne-Jones
209 'What about moveable' Warington Taylor to Edward Robert Robson, 1865, Fitzwilliam
   'I don't understand' *ibid.*, October 1866
   'Just remember' Warington Taylor to Philip Webb, 27 December 1866, NAL
210 'like a wild animal' W. R. Lethaby, *William Morris as Work-Master*, 1901
   'Sandwiches are often' Warington Taylor to Philip Webb, undated, NAL
   'very nervous' Warington Taylor to Dante Gabriel Rossetti, autumn 1867, NAL
   'work of this sort' WM to Edmund Henry Morgan, 27 November 1866
   'The escapades' WM to George Campfield, 11 March 1867
211 'when some rooms' Georgina Cowper-Temple, *Memorials*, privately printed, 1890,
   British Library
213 'I know something' WM to George Howard, 25 July 1867

214 'a glorious haul' Burne-Jones
'Morris is simple' ed. Derek Hudson, *Munby, Man of Two Worlds*, John Murray, London, 1972
'bored a good deal' William Allingham, *A Diary*, 2 July 1867
'There's a louse' *ibid.*, 16 October 1867
215 'a fine, square, spacious' *Intros*
216 'I remember his swinging' Burne-Jones
'copiously and interestingly' William Allingham, *A Diary*, 30 August 1866
217 'What better place' *The Earthly Paradise*, part 2, 1868
'Naturally he chose' Burne-Jones
'a mournful place' WM to Georgiana Burne-Jones?, 19 July 1895, Henderson
218 'a deadly-lively place' Dante Gabriel Rossetti to William Allingham, 25 August 1868, Doughty and Wahl
'O love, turn' WM, *The Earthly Paradise*, part 3, 1870
'a strange, quaint' George Meredith to Captain Maxse, 13 June 1862, Doughty and Wahl
219 'a sort of dressing gown' Horner
'Then when someone passes' *ibid.*
'cordial stunner' ed. Virginia Surtees, *The Diaries of George Price Boyce*
220 'F. sometimes says' William Allingham, *A Diary*, 14 October 1867
'Joined Rossetti' *The Diaries of George Price Boyce*, 16 August 1862
'I had rather' Luke Ionides, *Memories*, Herbert Clarke, Paris, 1925
'Mrs. Morris for beginners' W. Graham Robertson, *Time Was*, Hamish Hamilton, 1931
221 'I am something' WM to Philip Webb, 20 August 1869
'Morris and his wife' *The Diaries of George Price Boyce*, 30 July 1860
'gently caustic' Burne-Jones
222 'sitting side by side' J. A. McN. Whistler, journal entry 1863, quoted Philip Henderson, *Swinburne*, Routledge & Kegan Paul, 1973
223 'I don't think the frame' WM to Janey Morris, 5 December 1870
'How are you Morris?' Dante Gabriel Rossetti to Ford Madox Brown, 13 October 1868, Doughty and Wahl
224 'who was howling' Dante Gabriel Rossetti to Miss Losh, 9 November 1868, *ibid.*
'a huge party of Greeks' Dante Gabriel Rossetti to Alice Boyd, 17 November 1868, *ibid.*
'Gabriel had not tried' William Bell Scott to Alice Boyd, 9 November 1868, Fredeman
'a host of himself' William Bell Scott to Alice Boyd, 26 November 1868, *ibid.*
225 'time and again' WM, 'The Hill of Venus', *The Earthly Paradise*, part 4, 1870
226 'I never quite gave' Wilfrid Scawen Blunt, ms. diary, 11 August 1892, Fitzwilliam
227 'He knew that' George Bernard Shaw, 'William Morris as I knew him', 1936, *WMAWS*
'Copulation is worse' WM to Charles Faulkner, 16 October 1886
'just alighting' William Allingham, *A Diary*, 27 May 1868
228 'Mary proceeded' Alexander Constantine Ionides Junior, *Ion: A Grandfather's Tale*, 1927
'beauty and misfortune' Burne-Jones
'Poor Ned's affairs' Dante Gabriel Rossetti to Ford Madox Brown, 23 January 1869, Doughty and Wahl
'I would go' Luke Ionides, *Memories*, Herbert Clarke, Paris, 1925
229 'Janey has stopped' Dante Gabriel Rossetti to Charles Augustus Howell(?), 25 January 1869, Doughty and Wahl
'who combines' Charles Eliot Norton to John Ruskin, 19 September 1868, Charles Eliot Norton, *Letters*, Constable, London, 1913
'crowning day' Henry James to Alice James, 10 March 1869, ed. Percy Lubbock, *Letters of Henry James*
230 'like a hedghog' WM to Edward Burne-Jones, 25 May 1869

CHAPTER EIGHT

231 'That is really' WM to Philip Webb, 31 July 1869
'a mutilated body' Philip Webb to WM and Jane Morris, 23 July 1869, British Library
'it will be' WM to Philip Webb, 22 July 1869
'they were literally' *Intros*
232 details of Ems stay Bad Ems City Archive
'rum old 17th century' WM to Philip Webb, 31 July 1869
233 'the *gem* of the German' Edward Gutmann, *The Watering Places and Mineral Springs of Germany, Austria and Switzerland*, Sampson Low, Marston, Searle & Rimington, 1869
234 'noisy and uninteresting' WM to Charles Eliot Norton, 5 August 1869
'As you may imagine' WM to Philip Webb, 31 July 1869
'J. has seen' *ibid.*
235 'in roaring and offensive' WM to F. S. Ellis, 18 August 1869
'without the sour' *ibid.*
'The level ground' WM, 'The Death of Paris', *The Earthly Paradise*, part 3, 1870
'one is so boxed in' WM to Philip Webb, 31 July 1869
'very jolly' WM to Philip Webb, 9 August 1869
236 'O Lord' *ibid.*
'a brilliant red-lead' WM to Philip Webb, 15 August 1869
'I am not sanguine' WM to Philip Webb, 31 July 1869
'why then' WM, 'Acontius and Cydippe', *The Earthly Paradise*, part 3, 1870
237 'Acontius I know' WM to A. C. Swinburne, 21 December 1869
'Why dost thou' WM, 'Why dost thou struggle', *c.* 1865–70
239 'Like waking' WM, 'The Land East of the Sun and West of the Moon', *The Earthly Paradise*, part 3, 1870
240 'rather put a spoke' WM to Philip Webb, 27 August 1869
'There's a publishing' quoted Lona Mosk Packer, *Christina Rossetti*, Cambridge University Press, 1963
241 'a mild florin' WM to Philip Webb, 27 August 1869
'I want to make' WM to Philip Webb, 15 August 1869
'He will be onto' Warington Taylor to Philip Webb, July 1869, NAL
242 'what does an extra' Warington Taylor, memo to Firm, July 1869, NAL
'there is a great deal' WM to Philip Webb, 20 August 1869
'the dear old thing' Dante Gabriel Rossetti to Jane Morris, 30 August 1869, Bryson
'Pray take my love' *ibid.*, 23 August 1869
243 'I think they will come' *ibid.*, 30 July 1869
'It seems quite' *ibid.*, 14 August 1869
'I suppose Topsy' *ibid.*
244 'He is a round' Dante Gabriel Rossetti to Miss Losh, 21 September 1869, Doughty and Wahl
'A Joy, A Triumph' Dante Gabriel Rossetti to William Rossetti, 21 September 1869, *ibid.*
'All that concerns' Dante Gabriel Rossetti to Jane Morris, 30 July 1869, Bryson
246 'I drank' WM to Philip Webb, 29 August 1869
'a tin box' *ibid.*
'If Janey' Philip Webb to WM and Jane Morris, 1 September 1869, British Library
'two or three' WM to Philip Webb, 3 September 1869
247 'part of it hither' WM, 'Architecture and History', lecture, 1884
'Art will utterly perish' WM, 'The Aims of Art', lecture, 1886
248 'sufficient to this time' Georgiana Burne-Jones to Rosalind Howard, undated, Castle Howard
249 'those stormy years' J. W. Mackail to Aglaia Coronio, 12 May 1899, quoted *The Times Literary Supplement*, 7 September 1951

249 'I turned to' Georgiana Burne-Jones to May Morris, 6 September 1910, British Library
'We meet, we laugh' WM, ms. poem, British Library
250 'She wavered' WM, ms. poem, British Library
'sympathy was' J. W. Mackail, *The Times*, 4 February 1920
251 'If I were but' WM to Edward Burne-Jones, 16 February 1886
252 'almost certain' Dante Gabriel Rossetti to Charles Howell, 18 September 1869, Doughty and Wahl
'perfect' Dante Gabriel Rossetti to A. C. Swinburne, 29 October 1869, *ibid.*
'soaked through' Dante Gabriel Rossetti to William Michael Rossetti, 13 October 1869, *ibid.*
'with a little' Dante Gabriel Rossetti to Ford Madox Brown, 14 October 1869, *ibid.*
'the truth must' Dante Gabriel Rossetti to William Michael Rossetti, 13 October 1869, *ibid.*
'about him' WM to Georgiana Burne-Jones, October 1869
253 'stiff and laboured' Mackail
'that a master' WM, 'Poems by Dante Gabriel Rossetti', *The Academy*, 14 May 1870
'in her ripest' Edmund Gosse to A. C. Swinburne, early 1871, quoted the Hon. Evan Charteris, *The Life and Letters of Sir Edmund Gosse*, Heinemann, 1931
254 'I think she has' Dante Gabriel Rossetti to Jane Morris, 4 March 1870, Bryson
'more than all' Dante Gabriel Rossetti to Jane Morris, 4 February 1870, Bryson
'For the last' *ibid.*, 30 January 1870
'a broken state' Dante Gabriel Rossetti to Mrs Alexander Gilchrist, 4 December 1869, Doughty and Wahl
256 'a noble girl' Dante Gabriel Rossetti to Charles Eliot Norton, 11 April 1870, *ibid.*
'Top and Janey' Dante Gabriel Rossetti to F. S. Ellis, 27 March 1870, *ibid.*
'Janey Morris is here' Dante Gabriel Rossetti to Mrs Gabriele Rossetti, 18 April 1870, *ibid.*
'blessed with large' Dante Gabriel Rossetti to Christina Rossetti, 8 November 1853, *ibid.*
'Barbara does not' Dante Gabriel Rossetti to William Allingham, 17 March 1870, *ibid.*
'about the best' Dante Gabriel Rossetti to Barbara Bodichon, 14 April 1870, *ibid.*
'at least Bessy' WM to Jane Morris, 15 April 1870
257 'I shall certainly' *ibid.*, 26 April 1870
'like anybody else' Dante Gabriel Rossetti to Barbara Bodichon, 14 April 1870, Doughty and Wahl
'On this sweet bank' Dante Gabriel Rossetti, 'The House of Life' sonnet sequence, ed. William M. Rossetti, *The Works of Dante Gabriel Rossetti*, London, 1911
'perhaps he could not' William Bell Scott to Alice Boyd, 28 September 1870, Fredeman
258 'Such a rumpus' WM to Jane Morris, 25 November 1870
'a suit of Clothes' *ibid.*, 29 November 1870
'As for living' *ibid.*, December 1870
'a sudden revelation' *Intros*
259 'subtle and exhaustive' unsigned review in *The Spectator*, March 1870, xliii
260 'Morris may build' C. S. Lewis, 'Morris, Mr. Yeats and the Originals', unsigned review, *The Times Literary Supplement*, 29 May 1937
'Ah, my dears' WM, *Collected Works*, vol. 24, 1915
'In the verses' Mackail
'All thought' WM, 'The Hill of Venus', *The Earthly Paradise*, part 4, 1870
261 'Apart from the desire' WM, 'How I became a Socialist', *Justice*, 16 June 1894
262 'His faculty for work' George Wardle, 'Reminiscences of William Morris', Christmas 1897, British Library
'if a chap' Mackail

262 'Topsy goes on' Dante Gabriel Rossetti to Miss Losh, 8 October 1869, Doughty and Wahl
'they are all' WM to A. C. Swinburne, 21 December 1869
264 'We take Morris's poem' George Eliot to John Blackwood, June 1868, *The George Eliot Letters*, vol. 4, New Haven, 1954–5
'I find now' WM to Jane Morris, 25 November 1870
'pleasure work' WM to Louisa Baldwin, 25 March 1875
265 'let us try' Reverse page of Morris's ms. *The Aeneids of Vergil*, 1874–5, reproduced in catalogue of Sotheby's sale of Sir Sydney Cockerell's collection, 10 December 1956
266 'the dash' Graily Hewitt, 'The Illuminated Manuscripts of William Morris', paper given at Double Crown Club meeting, 2 May 1934
'Was more impressed' Priscilla Johnston, *Edward Johnston*, Faber & Faber, 1959
'his forest' *Intros*
267 orders for vellum WM to Charles Fairfax Murray, 18 February 1874
'Let us study' WM, 'The Lesser Arts', lecture, 1878
'and the thing' WM, 'Some Thoughts on the Ornamented Manuscripts of the Middle Ages', unfinished essay, 1894
268 'Mother and Love' WM, 'To the muse of the North', ms. poems, c. 1870, facsimile Scolar Press, 1980
'with things' *Intros*
269 'firm broad hand' *ibid.*
'blooming letters' WM to Charles Fairfax Murray, 1870
'youthful zest' Elaine Quigley to the author, April 1992
270 'a devil of a cold' WM to Jane Morris, 15 April 1870
'handsome in his youth' description in contemporary Greek magazine quoted Julia Ionides, MLA Convention, Washington, 30 December 1989
271 'a stunner' ed. Daphne du Maurier, *The Young George du Maurier, A Selection of his Letters 1860–67*, Peter Davies, 1951
'poetical appearance' Emma von Niendorf, quoted Julia Ionides, *op. cit.*
'his friend' Burne-Jones
'grins and guffaws' Dante Gabriel Rossetti to Jane Morris, 6 October 1879, Bryson
'My dear Mrs. Coronio' WM to Aglaia Coronio, 25 April 1870
272 'The conversational star' Alexander C. Ionides, *Ion: A Grandfather's Tale*, 1927
'I am going' WM to Jane Morris, 26 April 1870
273 'I am going' *ibid.*, 3? December 1870
'women did not' Luke Ionides, *Memories*, 1925
'the friendship' Mackail
'in low spirits' Edward Burne-Jones, 31 October 1896, Horner
'to see if' WM to Louisa Baldwin, 22 June 1872
274 Mooney theory Sue Mooney, 'Self-Revelation in Morris's Unfinished Novel', *JWMS*, Spring 1992
'the expectant longing' *The Novel*, c. 1871
'all spoilt' *ibid.*
275 'cleverer than clever' Georgiana Burne-Jones to Rosalind Howard, 13 February 1876, Castle Howard
'with much approbation' WM to Georgiana Burne-Jones, March 1888
''tis nothing' WM to Louisa Baldwin, 22 June 1872
'because it was written' Penelope Fitzgerald, intro. to *The Novel*, 1982
'a little house' WM to Edith Marion Story, 10 May 1871
276 'whither do you' WM to Charles Faulkner, 17 May 1871
'How beautiful' WM to Jane Morris, 6 July 1871
'With Rossetti' Edward Burne-Jones to George Howard, undated, Castle Howard

CHAPTER NINE: Iceland 1871

The main sources for this chapter, and for the account of Morris's second journey to Iceland in Chapter Ten, have been his own daily journals of which the original draft, in a series of black limp leather notebooks, is now in the British Library. The fair copy of the journal written out for Georgiana Burne-Jones with additional notes and explanations, inscribed 'Georgie from WM, July 8, 1873', is in the Library of the Fitzwilliam Museum, Cambridge.

Besides Morris's letters his views on Iceland come across most vividly in his Preface to the 1869 edition of *The Story of Grettir the Strong* and in his lectures, in particular 'The Early Literature of the North – Iceland', first delivered in the lecture hall at Kelmscott House in 1887. I have also drawn on Eiríkr Magnússon's introduction to his and Morris's translation of the *Heimskringla*, vol. IV, which incorporates the obituary of Morris written by Magnússon for the *Cambridge Review*, 26 November 1896. The Magnússon papers in the National Library at Reykjavík throw much light on the detail of their collaboration and its tragic aftermath. J. W. Mackail was unsympathetic to Morris's long involvement with the Sagas and his treatment of Morris's Icelandic travels is merely dutiful. May Morris is more understanding of this central obsession of her father's life. Other sources:

On Iceland and the Sagas in general: Lord Dufferin, *Letters from High Latitudes*, John Murray, 1857; C. W. Shepherd, *The North-West Peninsula of Iceland*, Longmans, Green & Co., 1867; W. G. Collingwood and Jón Stefánsson, *A Pilgrimage to the Saga-Steads of Iceland*, W. Holmes, Ulverston, 1899; W. H. Auden and Louis MacNeice, *Letters from Iceland*, Faber & Faber, 1937; Magnus Magnusson, *Iceland Saga*, Bodley Head, 1987.

On Morris and the Sagas: J. N. Swannell, 'William Morris and Old Norse Literature', lecture given in 1958, printed version for William Morris Society, 1961; Dorothy M. Hoare, *The Works of Morris and Yeats in relation to Early Saga Literature*, Cambridge, 1937; Grace J. Calder, introduction to *The Story of Kormak, the Son of Ogmund*, William Morris Society, 1970; Dudley L. Hascall, '"Volsungasaga" and Two Transformations', *JWMS*, Winter 1968.

On Morris in Iceland: John Purkis, *The Icelandic Jaunt: A Study of the Expeditions made by Morris to Iceland in 1871 and 1873*, William Morris Society, 1962; Hugh Bushell, 'News from Iceland', *JWMS*, Winter 1961; Jane W. Stedman, 'A Victorian in Iceland', *Opera News*, New York, 20 February 1960; James Morris, intro. to William Morris's *Icelandic Journals*, Centaur Press, Fontwell, 1969; Ruth Ellison, 'The Saga of Jón Jónsson Saddlesmith of Lithend-cot', *JWMS*, Autumn 1992; Gary L. Aho, 'William Morris and Iceland', *Kairos*, vol. 1, no. 2, 1982; Florence Boos, 'With William Morris in Iceland', account of journey in 1986, William Morris Society in the US Newsletter, April 1987; Jane S. Cooper, 'The Iceland journeys and the late Romances', *JWMS*, Winter 1983; Amanda Hodgson, *The Romances of William Morris*, Cambridge University Press, 1987; Lesley A. Baker, 'Iceland and Kelmscott', *JWMS*, Winter 1984–5; Richard L. Harris, 'William Morris, Eiríkr Magnússon and the Icelandic Famine Relief Efforts of 1882', *Saga-Book* 20, 1978–9; Ruth Ellison, 'Icelandic Obituaries of William Morris', *JWMS*, Autumn 1988. It is still possible to retrace the main routes of Morris's Icelandic travels, as I did in the summer of 1991, expertly and generously guided by Magnus Magnusson whose translations of the Sagas both contrast with and amplify William Morris's own.

Modern urban redevelopment in Iceland has taken a direction Morris would have much resented. In particular Reykjavík is a sad mixture of ramshackle incompetence and superficial glitz. But the landscape still 'gapes' for us, as it did for Morris, and to follow in his footsteps takes one close to his responses to functional artefacts (farm implements, *skyr* tubs), basic rural architecture and the dramatic extremes of fire and ice.

Njál country, especially, remains much as he described it and at Keldur you can still find the farmhouse where, watched by twelve men, women and children, Morris cooked a piece of half salt ling 'with great care' on 29 July 1873.

CHAPTER NINE
278 'If you look' 'The Early Literature of the North – Iceland', lecture, 1887, LeMire
     'that the most grinding' WM to Andreas Scheu, 15 September 1883
     'romantic desert' *ibid.*
     'Toothed rocks' WM, *Poems by the Way*, 1891
279 'the man of the South' Evelyn Waugh, *Rossetti, his Life and Works*, Duckworth, 1928
     'a good corrective' WM to Andreas Scheu, 15 September 1883
     'ruddy-complexioned' Eiríkr Magnússon, obituary of William Morris, *Cambridge Review*, 26 November 1896
     'up and down' May Morris to Stefán Einarsson, 1925, quoted Stefán Einarsson, 'Eiríkr Magnússon and his Saga Translations', *Scandinavian Studies and Notes*, vol. XIII, 1933–5
280 'a quiet well conducted' WM to Charles Faulkner, 12 June 1871
     'By Gum the great' WM to Charles Faulkner, May 1871
     Iceland equipment list loose page in *A Journal of Travel in Iceland* ms., 1873, Fitzwilliam
     Morris's barbecue Mackail
     'one of those landscapes' *Journals*, 6 July 1871
281 'impatient to an absurd' *ibid.*, 8 July 1871
     'frowsy' *ibid.*, 7 July 1871
282 'I felt happy' *ibid.*, 8 July 1871
     'Morris has gone away' Edward Burne-Jones to George Howard, undated, Castle Howard
     'We were soon' *Journals*, 9 July 1871
283 'it was all' *ibid.*, 10 July 1871
     'I confess' *ibid.*, 11 July 1871
285 'After that' *ibid.*, 11 July 1871
286 'nothing out of' WM to Jane Morris, 16 July 1871
     'oiled pigs' WM to Jenny and May Morris, 16 July 1871
     'a dark brown ragged' *Journals*, 13 July 1871
     'Ah! what came we' *Poems by the Way*, 1891
     'the end of the world' WM to Louisa Baldwin, 16 July 1871
287 'an ice-tract' *Journals*, 13 July 1871
     'a collection of wooden' Lord Dufferin and Ava, *Letters from High Latitudes*, 1887
     'There are but two' Sabine Baring-Gould, *Iceland*, quoted 'Views of Reykjavík', *JWMS*, Summer 1985
288 'not a very attractive' *Journals*, 14 July 1871
     'Such jolly little fellows' WM to Jane Morris, 16 July 1871
289 'all my fears' *Journals*, 15 July 1871
     'I hope you are' WM to Jenny and May Morris, 16 July 1871
290 'From the very first' Eiríkr Magnússon obituary, *op. cit.*
     'that most glorious' WM to Georgiana Burne-Jones, 27 January 1877
     'This is the Great Story' WM, Preface to *The Story of the Niblings and Volsungs*, 1870
291 'No, I can't be bothered' Eiríkr Magnússon obituary, *op. cit.*
     'The dialect' Eiríkr Magnússon, Preface to the *Heimskringla*, vol. 4, Bernard Quaritch, 1905
     'there is nothing' WM to Charles Eliot Norton, 21 December 1869
     'In fact he found' Eiríkr Magnússon obituary, *op. cit.*
292 'If Iceland was once' quoted G. T. McDowell, 'The Treatment of the Völsunga Saga by William Morris', *Scandinavian Studies and Notes*, vol. VII, 1921–3
     'too homely' WM to Georgiana Burne-Jones, 27 January 1877
     'the dealings between' WM, 'The Early Literature of the North – Iceland', *op. cit.*

292 'a queer, ugly-looking' *Journals*, 17 July 1871
293 'a huge waste' *ibid.*, 18 July 1871
'Stones, More Stones' W. H. Auden and Louis MacNeice, *Letters from Iceland*, 1937
'which made such' *Journals*, 18 July 1871
'a great chest-shaped' *ibid.*, 19 July 1871
294 'And Hekla' James Thomson, 'Winter', *The Seasons*, 1726–30
'just the shape' *Journals*, 13 August 1871
295 'something the shape' *ibid.*, 21 July 1871
296 'Ye who have come' WM, *Poems by the Way*, 1891
297 'their twist isn't' Mackail
'I dealt summarily' *Journals*, 21 July 1871
'just like the hell-mouths' *ibid.*, 22 July 1871
299 'the ugly seared white' *ibid.*, 25 July 1871
'a joyful meeting' *ibid.*, 27 July 1871
'as though a spring' *ibid.*, 28 July 1871
300 'and there we are' *ibid.*, 29 July 1871
'a sentiment' WM to Charles Eliot Norton, 13 May 1869
'it gave quite' *Journals*, 18 August 1871
'a dismal place' *ibid.*, 30 July 1871
301 'bitterest morning' *ibid.*, 1 August 1871
302 'The snow-filled' *ibid.*, note to entry 30 July 1871
'Three months ago' WM, *The Well at the World's End*, 1896
303 'Certainly this is' *Journals*, 29 July 1871
'grumbling life' WM to Charles Eliot Norton, 19 October 1871
'with that inexpressibly' Eiríkr Magnússon obituary, *op. cit.*
'Dead and gone' undated MS, British Library
'in huge excitement' *Journals*, 11 August 1871
304 'I am tremendous' WM to Jane Morris, 11 August 1871
305 'a black head' *Journals*, 14 August 1871
'the open-work' *ibid.*, 4 August 1871
'a queer little den' *ibid.*, 13 August 1871
'defensive bootjack' Dante Gabriel Rossetti to William Bell Scott, 15 September 1871
306 'My heart beats' *Journals*, 25 August 1871
307 'And first below' *Poems by the Way*, 1871
'Grim Goatshoe' *Journals*, 26 August 1871
308 'the greatest men' WM, 'The Early Literature of the North – Iceland', *op. cit.*
'thence away' *Journals*, 28 August 1871
309 'wondrous dull' *ibid.*, 7 September 1871
'Holy Land' WM, 'The Early Literature of the North – Iceland', *op. cit.*
310 'something in its way' WM to Louisa Baldwin, 21 September 1871
'I know clearer' WM to Aglaia Coronio, 25 November 1872
on Journal publication Jane Morris to Sydney Cockerell, 1897, British Library

CHAPTERS TEN, ELEVEN, TWELVE AND THIRTEEN: Kelmscott Manor
1871–75, Leek 1875–78, Kelmscott House 1878–81, Merton Abbey 1881–83

From the 1870s Morris's own letters, particularly those to his wife and daughters and to
Georgiana Burne-Jones, are the essential source of information on his day-to-day activities and
developing political views. A diary of his work on the 'Cabbage and Vine' tapestry in 1879 is in
the National Art Library, a more general journal for the year 1881 is in the British Library,
together with the log-book of the journey down the Thames from Kelmscott to Kelmscott in

1880. In addition these chapters depend mainly on May Morris's memoirs; *Dante Gabriel Rossetti and Jane Morris, their Correspondence*, edited by John Bryson, Clarendon Press, Oxford, 1976; Morris family correspondence in the British Library; Burne-Jones correspondence at the Fitzwilliam Museum, Cambridge; Burne-Jones and Howard correspondence at Castle Howard; Philip Webb correspondence at the National Art Library and British Library; George Wardle memoir in the British Library; the Richmond/Meyrick family papers.

On Kelmscott Manor and environs: A. R. Dufty, *Kelmscott, An Illustrated Guide*, The Society of Antiquaries, 1984; *William Morris and Kelmscott*, Design Council in association with West Surrey College of Art and Design, Farnham, 1981; William Morris 'Gossip about an Old House on the Upper Thames', article originally published in *The Quest*, Nov. 1894, reprinted in May Morris, *WMAWS*, vol. I; Geoffrey Grigson, 'The River-land of William Morris', *Country Life*, 29 May 1958; Lorraine Price, 'Cormell Price Esq.', *JWMS*, Winter 1983/4.

On Rossetti at Kelmscott: ed. O. Doughty and J. R. Wahl, *Letters of Dante Gabriel Rossetti*, Oxford University Press, 1965–7; William E. Fredeman, 'Prelude to the Last Decade: Dante Gabriel Rossetti in the Summer of 1872', *Bulletin of the John Rylands Library*, Manchester, vol. 53, 1971; S. C. Dyke, 'Some Medical Aspects of the Life of Dante Gabriel Rossetti, *Proceedings of the Royal Society of Medicine*, December 1963; Theodore Watts-Dunton, obit. of William Morris, *The Athenaeum*, 10 October 1896; Alicia Craig Faxon, *Dante Gabriel Rossetti*, Phaidon Press, Oxford, 1989; Julia Atkins, 'Rossetti's "The Day Dream"', *V & A Album*, Spring 1989, Victoria and Albert Museum.

On George and Rosalind Howard: Dorothy Henley, *Rosalind Howard, Countess of Carlisle*, Hogarth Press, 1958; Charles Roberts, *The Radical Countess*, Steel Brothers, Carlisle, 1962; Virginia Surtees, *The Artist and the Autocrat, George and Rosalind Howard*, Michael Russell, Wilton, 1988; E. V. Lucas, *The Colvins and their Friends*, Methuen, London, 1928; Christopher Newall, *The Etruscans, Painters of the Italian Landscape*, 1850–1900, catalogue of exhibition at Stoke-on-Trent Museum and Art Gallery, 1989; Bill Waters, 'Painter and Patron: the Palace Green Murals', *Apollo*, Nov. 1975.

On Leek and the Wardles: J. W. Mackail, 'The Parting of the Ways', address given in William Morris Labour Church, Leek, 1902, published Hammersmith Publishing Co., 1903; Wardle archive in Leek Library, Nicholson Institute, Leek; Anne Jacques, 'The Wardle–Morris Connection', *Staffordshire History*, vol. 8, autumn 1988; Anne Jacques, *Leek Embroidery*, Staffordshire Libraries, Arts and Archives, 1990; Philip Clayton, 'Larner Sugden and the William Morris Labour Church', unpublished paper *c*. 1990.

On the Eastern Question Association: Henry Broadhurst, *The Story of his Life from a Stonemason's Bench to the Treasury Bench*, Hutchinson, 1901; Richard Millman, *Britain and the Eastern Question 1875–1878*, Clarendon Press, Oxford, 1979; R. W. Seton-Watson, *Disraeli, Gladstone and the Eastern Question*, Macmillan, London, 1935; W. H. G. Armytage, *A. J. Mundella: The Liberal Background to the Labour Movement*, Ernest Benn, 1951; George Howard papers at Castle Howard.

On Kelmscott House: *The Survey of London*, Hammersmith volume, 1915; R. C. H. Briggs, *A Guide to Kelmscott House*, William Morris Society, 1962; A. M. W. Stirling, *The Richmond Papers*, William Heinemann, 1926; Helena M. Sickert Swanwick, *I Have Been Young*, Gollancz, 1935; Greville MacDonald, *George MacDonald and his Wife*, Allen & Unwin, 1924; J. M. Baissus, 'The Expedition of the Ark', *JWMS*, Spring 1977; Violet Hunt, ed. Lady Mander, 'Kelmscott to Kelmscott', *JWMS*, Winter 1968.

On Morris and the SPAB: archive of Society for the Protection of Ancient Buildings, London; W. R. Lethaby, *Philip Webb and his Work*, Oxford University Press, 1935; 'William Morris's SPAB: "A School of Rational Builders"', catalogue of exhibition at RIBA Library, 1982; Frank C. Sharp, 'A Lesson in International Relations: Morris and the SPAB', *JWMS*, Spring 1993.

On Merton Abbey: 'Morris at Merton Abbey' chapter in Charles Harvey and Jon Press,

William Morris: Design and Enterprise in Victorian Britain, Manchester University Press, 1991; Ray Watkinson, 'Merton before Morris', *JWMS*, Spring 1992; 'On the Wandle', article in *The Spectator*, 23 November 1883; Emma Lazarus, 'A Day in Surrey with William Morris', *The Century Illustrated Magazine*, July 1886; Edward Payne, 'Memories of Morris & Co.', *JWMS*, Summer 1981; ed. Denis Smith, recorded interview with Douglas Griffiths, 'Morris and Company: Merton Abbey Works', 17 December 1975, WMG.

On William De Morgan: A. M. W. Stirling, *William De Morgan and his Wife*, Henry Holt & Co., New York, 1922; May Morris, 'William De Morgan', *The Burlington Magazine*, vol. 31, 1917; William Gaunt and M. D. E. Clayton-Stamm, *William De Morgan*, Studio Vista, 1971; Martin Greenwood, Richard Dennis and William E. Wiltshire III, *The Designs of William De Morgan: A Catalogue*, Shepton Beauchamp, Somerset, 1989. Collections: Leighton House, London; Victoria and Albert Museum; William Morris Gallery, Walthamstow. Old Battersea House in London contains a large collection of De Morgan and some Morris work.

On Morris textiles and interiors: Linda Parry, *William Morris Textiles*, Weidenfeld & Nicolson, 1983; Norah Gillow, *William Morris Design and Patterns*, Bracken Books, 1988; Oliver Fairclough and Emmeline Leary, *Textiles by William Morris and Morris & Co.*, *1861–1940*, catalogue of exhibition at Birmingham Museum and Art Gallery, 1981; H. C. Marillier, *History of the Merton Abbey Tapestry Works*, Constable, 1927; Linda Parry, 'The revival of the Merton Abbey Tapestry Works', *JWMS*, Summer 1983; Peter Fuller, 'William Morris Textiles', chapter in *Images of God: the Consolations of Lost Illusions*, Chatto & Windus, 1985. Collections: Victoria and Albert Museum; William Morris Gallery, Walthamstow; Birmingham Museum and Art Gallery; Whitworth Gallery, Manchester. The 'Cabbage and Vine' tapestry is in the collection at Kelmscott Manor. Interiors at Queen's College Hall, Cambridge; Peterhouse Hall and Combination Room, Cambridge; St James's Palace. There are no complete surviving domestic interiors but Linley Sambourne House, No. 18 Stafford Terrace, London W8, is an excellent example of a house furnished in 1870s aesthetic style with Morris elements.

On Morris stained glass: A. Charles Sewter, *The Stained Glass of William Morris and his Circle*, 2 vols., Yale University Press, 1974–5. Magnificent glass of this period at All Hallows, Allerton; All Saints, Middleton Cheney; Jesus College, Cambridge; All Saints, Putney; St Michael and St Mary Magdalene, Easthampstead; Christ Church Cathedral, Oxford; St Martin's, Brampton; St Mary's, Nun Monkton; St Mary's, Tadcaster.

On *Love Is Enough* and *Sigurd the Volsung*: J. M. S. Tomkins, *William Morris, an Approach to the Poetry*, Cecil Woolf, 1988; Paul Thompson, *The Work of William Morris*, Heinemann, 1967; Amanda Hodgson, *The Romances of William Morris*, Cambridge University Press, 1987; ed. Peter Faulkner, *William Morris, The Critical Heritage*, Routledge & Kegan Paul, 1973.

On *The Novel on Blue Paper*: Penelope Fitzgerald's introduction to William Morris Society edition, 1982; Sue Mooney, 'Self-Revelation in Morris's Unfinished Novel', *JWMS*, Spring 1993; Linda Richardson, 'William Morris and Women: Experience and Representation', Ph.D. for University of Oxford, 1989.

On Morris, Janey and Wilfrid Scawen Blunt: Wilfrid Scawen Blunt, *My Diaries*, 2 vols., Martin Secker, 1919 and 1920: Wilfrid Scawen Blunt, manuscript diaries at the Fitzwilliam Museum, Cambridge; Peter Faulkner, 'Wilfrid Scawen Blunt and the Morrises', lecture, William Morris Society, 1981; ed. Peter Faulkner, *Jane Morris to Wilfred Scawen Blunt*, University of Exeter, 1986; Geoffrey Syer, 'Morris and the Blunts', *JWMS*, Winter 1981; Lady Wentworth, intr. to *The Authentic Arab Horse and his Descendants*, George Allen & Unwin, 1945; Neville Lytton, chapter on Blunt in *The English Country Gentleman*, Hurst & Blackett, 1925; Elizabeth Longford, *A Pilgrimage of Passion*, Weidenfeld & Nicolson, 1979; Jane Morris correspondence with Judith Blunt (Lady Wentworth) in British Library.

Kelmscott Manor remains the most evocative of William Morris's houses. On May's death in 1938 it was left in trust to the University of Oxford which, embarrassed by the acquisition, eventually brought a case before the High Court of Justice to declare the trust invalid. The house passed to the Society of Antiquaries as the residuary legatee of the Morris estate in 1962. It was restored, according to SPAB principles, in the 1960s and is now open to the public. The original furnishings have been supplemented by furniture and memorabilia brought later from the Morris homes in Hammersmith. The small churches around Kelmscott and the barn at Great Coxwell remain more or less as Morris knew them.

Leek has suffered less than many English towns from the ruthless redevelopments of the 1960s and much of its Victorian centre, including the resplendently enlightened Nicholson Institute, is still intact. This is the work of Larner Sugden, a Socialist disciple of Morris's. The Morris influence is also obvious in the many superb embroideries dispersed through the churches of the town.

Kelmscott House in Hammersmith is in private ownership and in excellent condition, on its beautiful and faintly melancholy riverside site. This small area of Hammersmith remains an unexpected oasis in West London and has many associations with the Arts and Crafts movement of the late nineteenth and early twentieth century. The William Morris Society has its headquarters on the lower floor of Kelmscott House.

The Morris & Co. shop in Oxford Street is recognisable, in its original red brick building. At the time of writing the ground floor was occupied by Jean Jeannie and the first floor by Laura Ashley's Home Furnishings department, selling fabrics not uninfluenced by William Morris. A narrow staircase with double wooden handrail, which seems to be original, leads up to the second floor and Passports-While-U-Wait.

At Merton Abbey there is a lingering sense of the old community of small industries along the river. The Liberty site has been refurbished, though Morris would have found it sickeningly 'heritagized'. Morden Hall Park (now National Trust) and the footpaths through the watermeads give a suggestion of the pleasant semi-rural area it must once have been. But the Morris & Co. site has sunk without trace in an area now massively redeveloped for a Sainsbury Savacentre. With a peculiar irony Morris is enshrined in a mural above the escalator which leads up to the supermarket. Shopping trolleys lie abandoned in the Wandle in a scene of commercial devastation that is a *News from Nowhere* in reverse.

CHAPTER TEN
311 'beautiful and strangely naif' WM to Charles Eliot Norton, 19 October 1871
    'an E' WM, 'Gossip about an Old House on the Upper Thames', 1894, *WMAWS*
312 'buttered over' *ibid.*
    'lies at the very end' *ibid.*
313 'There is work' WM, 'The Half of Life Gone', *The Pilgrims of Hope*, 1885
    'within a stone's throw' WM to Charles Eliot Norton, 19 October 1871
    'small but interesting' WM, 'Gossip about an Old House on the Upper Thames', *op. cit.*
314 'its best ornament' *News from Nowhere*, 1890
    'some half-dozen' WM, 'Art and the Beauty of the Earth', lecture, 1881
    'infinitely curious' WM, 'Gossip about an Old House on the Upper Thames', *op. cit.*
    'These are the works' WM, 'Art and the Beauty of the Earth', *op. cit.*
    'surely the most beautiful' Mackail
    'must have run it' *Intros*
315 'but look, suppose' WM to Louisa Baldwin, 26 March 1874
    'Midsummer in the country' WM, 'Under an Elm-Tree; or Thoughts in the
      Countryside', *The Commonweal*, 6 July 1889
    'with the complexion' WM to Emma Oldham, 1871
    'with all that burden' *Intros*
316 'loveliest "haunt"' Dante Gabriel Rossetti to Mrs Gabriele Rossetti, 17 July 1871,
      Doughty and Wahl

316 'full of fat' Dante Gabriel Rossetti to William Bell Scott, 17 July 1871, *ibid.*
'look settled down' Dante Gabriel Rossetti to Mrs Gabriele Rossetti, 17 July 1871, *ibid.*
'most triumphant' Dante Gabriel Rossetti to William Bell Scott, 1871, *ibid.*
'Between Holmscote' ed. William Rossetti, *The Poetical Works of Dante Gabriel Rossetti*, Ellis and Elvey, 1905
317 'carried through' Dante Gabriel Rossetti to William Bell Scott, 17 July 1871, Doughty and Wahl
'the rather broad' *Intros*
'I saw coming' Theodore Watts-Dunton, obituary of William Morris, *The Athenaeum*, 10 October 1896
318 'I asked Gabriel' William Bell Scott to Alice Boyd, 23 October 1871, Fredeman
319 'The year 1872' Burne-Jones
Rossetti's breakdown S. C. Dyke, 'Some Medical Aspects of the Life of Dante Gabriel Rossetti', *Proceedings of the Royal Society of Medicine*, December 1963
320 'and not discomposed' William Bell Scott to Alice Boyd, 17 June 1872, Fredeman
'dreadful dreams' Jane Morris to Ford Madox Brown, undated, Bryson
321 'on Friday afternoon' William Bell Scott to Alice Boyd, June 1872, Fredeman
'Topsy is DG's alias' William Bell Scott ms., Fredeman
'indeed we thought' WM to Emma Shelton Morris, 11 June 1872
'Come by all means' WM to Ford Madox Brown, June 1872
'All the birds' William Bell Scott to Alice Boyd, July 1872, Fredeman
'all, I now find' Dante Gabriel Rossetti to William Rossetti, 17 September 1875, *ibid.*
'That Gabriel was *mad*' Jane Morris to Theodore Watts-Dunton, *c.*1884, British Library
'I have always' Philip Webb to Jane Morris, 12 September 1872, British Library
322 Brother dragon story Mackail notebooks, WMG
'rambling and most egotistical' WM to Aglaia Coronio, 25 November 1872
323 'a fantastic little book' WM to Andreas Scheu, 15 September 1883
'The poem is' Dante Gabriel Rossetti to William Bell Scott, 2 October 1871, Doughty and Wahl
'long swinging lines' *Intros*
'whom nothing but love' WM, *Love Is Enough*, 1872
324 'out of the maze' WM to Louisa Baldwin, 13 February 1872
'lofty and delicate' Basil Champneys, *Memoirs and Correspondence of Coventry Patmore*, G. Bell & Sons, 1908
'The Songs are' George Meredith to Frederick Greenwood, 1 January 1873, ed. C. L. Cline, *The Letters of George Meredith*, Oxford, 1970
325 'It was part' Edward Burne-Jones, 7 January 1898, Lago
'though the translating' WM to Aglaia Coronio, 23 January 1873
'almost a desecration' George Wardle, 'Reminiscences of William Morris', Christmas 1897, British Library
'for this long time' WM to Aglaia Coronio, 11 February 1873
326 'a *very* little' WM to Aglaia Coronio, 23 January 1873
'the little shed' Philip Webb to Jane Morris, 8 November 1878, British Library
'very good' Jane Morris, Mackail notebooks, WMG
'a beastly tin-kettle' quoted A. M. W. Stirling, *William De Morgan and his Wife*, Henry Holt, New York, 1922
'quantities of crumpets' Margaret Burne-Jones, Mackail notebooks, WMG
'I can always' WM to Aglaia Coronio, 23 January 1873
'pretty room' WM to Louisa Baldwin, 22 October 1873
327 'very interesting' ed. Virginia Surtees, *The Diaries of George Price Boyce*, 22 March 1874, Real World, Norwich, 1980

327 'very little pots' Margaret Burne-Jones, Mackail notebooks, WMG
'the bare light room' *Intros*
'Do you suppose' Mackail
'He really was' Edward Burne-Jones, 7 January 1898, Lago
'marvels' WM to Jane Morris, 6 April 1873

328 'not to form' WM to Philip Webb, 10 April 1873
'with the leaves' WM to Jane Morris, 6 April 1873
'merchandising for the firm' WM to Philip Webb, 10 April 1873

329 'your most glorious' WM to the Prefect of Florence, 26 January 1881?
'certainly the most' WM to Jane Morris, 6 April 1873
'as a pig is' WM to Philip Webb, 10 April 1873

330 'We sighted Iceland' *Journals*, 24 July 1873
'I fancy' WM to Aglaia Coronio, 23 January 1873
'Iceland gapes' WM to Aglaia Coronio, 11 February 1873
'Lord, how strange' *Journal*, 24 July 1873

331 'Morris, the greatest gun' Edmund Gosse to Philip Gosse, 24 October 1871, quoted Hon.
Evan Charteris, *The Life and Letters of Sir Edmund Gosse*, Heinemann, 1931
'very vivid and amusing' Edmund Gosse to Philip Gosse, 1872, *ibid.*
'round and burly' quoted Ann Thwaite, *Edmund Gosse: A Literary Landscape*, Oxford
University Press, 1984
'all in a heap' *Journals*, 24 July 1873
'It is all like' WM to Jane Morris, 18 July 1873

332 'a little fellow' *Journals*, 24 July 1873
'extremely or not' Jane Morris to Wilfrid Scawen Blunt, 28 May 1889, Faulkner
'he had no comforts' *Intros*
'in a thymy valley' *Journals*, 19 July 1873

333 'all looked somewhat' *ibid.*, 29 July 1873
'The raven flies' *ibid.*, 4 August 1873
'It is not a flat' *ibid.*, 6 August 1873

334 'So to Einarsstaðir' *ibid.*, 14 August 1873
'a most lovely morning' *ibid.*, 9 August 1873
'surely I have gained' WM to Aglaia Coronio, 14 September 1873

335 'romping and skirmishing' *Intros*
'As to the future' WM to Dante Gabriel Rossetti, 16 April 1874

336 'It would take' *Intros*
'the country people' WM to Emma Shelton Morris, 24 July 1874

337 'puffing and blowing' WM to Jane Morris, 23 February 1881
'certainly one' WM to Aglaia Coronio, 13 August 1874

338 'the most captivatingly' E. V. Lucas, *The Colvins and their Friends*, Methuen, 1928
'like a flow' Dorothy Henley, *Rosalind Howard, Countess of Carlisle*, Hogarth Press, 1958
'desire to be' Virginia Surtees, *The Artist and the Autocrat*, Michael Russell, Wilton, 1988
'the imaginary part' May Morris quoted E. V. Lucas, *The Colvins and their Friends*, *op. cit.*

339 'bright presence' Jane Morris to Rosalind Howard, 1878, Castle Howard
'such a diminutive' Rosalind Howard quoted E. V. Lucas, *The Colvins and their Friends*, *op. cit.*
'yesterday morning' Edward Burne-Jones to George Howard, undated, Castle Howard
'breathe in fresh' Georgiana Burne-Jones to Rosalind Howard, 31 July 1874, Castle
Howard
'sniffed the smell' WM to Aglaia Coronio, 13 August 1874
'the abode' R. W. Dixon to Cormell Price, quoted Mackail

340 'do you know' WM to Rosalind Howard, 20 August 1874
341 'perhaps rather a "fad"' WM to Emma Shelton Morris, 27 May 1875
     'and a Welsh poney' WM to Jenny and May Morris, 5 April 1875
     'I should very much' WM to Aglaia Coronio, 11 February 1873
342 'I will do' WM to Eiríkr Magnússon, 18 March 1873
344 'My dear Gabriel' WM to Dante Gabriel Rossetti, October 1874
     The Death of Topsy Dante Gabriel Rossetti, ms. dated *c.*1878, British Library
347 'Once I went' Burne-Jones
     'recalcitrant partners' WM to Emma Shelton Morris, 25 March 1875
     'I have got' WM to Charles Fairfax Murray, 27 May 1875

CHAPTER ELEVEN
348 'taking in dyeing' WM to Georgiana Burne-Jones, 26 March 1876
     'I have been learning' WM to Rosalind Howard, 30 July 1875
349 'a woeful cold' WM to Jane Morris, 20 July 1875
     'the ruffians' WM to Thomas Wardle, 11 December 1876
350 'My days are' WM to Georgiana Burne-Jones, 26 March 1876
351 'I never met' Thomas Wardle, address at Bradford Municipal Technical College, 9
     December 1903, Leek Library
     'Of these dyes' WM, 'Of Dyeing as an Art', *Arts and Crafts Essays*, 1893
352 'The air at home' *Intros*
     'There are more difficulties' WM to Aglaia Coronio, 28 July 1875
     'This morning I assisted' WM to Aglaia Coronio, 28 March 1876
353 'gim-crack palace' WM to Georgiana Burne-Jones, 26 March 1876
     'such a dull town' WM to Georgiana Burne-Jones, 4 February 1877
     'the most beautiful' WM to Jenny Morris, 13 June 1877
     'Mr. Morris is' Georgiana Burne-Jones to Rosalind Howard, 6 October 1877, Castle
     Howard
     'I am now prepared' Georgiana Burne-Jones to Rosalind Howard, 28 March 1876, Castle
     Howard
     'Your old Proosian' WM to Jenny Morris, 21 July 1883
354 'We have got' WM to Aglaia Coronio, 21 October 1875
     'I shall make' WM to Thomas Wardle, 31 October 1876
     'a very good yellow' WM to Thomas Wardle, 17 November 1876
     '1018 yellow marigold' WM to Thomas Wardle, 3 September 1875
     '1112 Indian diaper' WM to Thomas Wardle, 24 December 1875
355 'I am sure' WM to Thomas Wardle, 3 September 1875
     'I mean that' WM to Thomas Wardle, 17–30 November 1876
     'they have been' WM to Georgiana Burne-Jones, 4 February 1877
     'I don't suggest' WM to Thomas Wardle, 28 October 1875
356 'He must be' WM, 'Making the Best of It', lecture, 1880
     'temples of over-crowding' WM, 'A Factory as It Might Be', *Justice* article, *WMAWS*
     'weaving sheds' WM, 'Why not?' article, *WMAWS*
357 'I am drawing' WM to Aglaia Coronio, March 1876
     'rational growth' WM, 'Some Hints on Pattern Designing', lecture, 1881
358 'the strawberry bed' WM to Jane Morris, 9 July 1876
     'they are depths' W. R. Lethaby, reply to an address, 18 January 1922, Oxford University
     Press, Cheltenham collection
359 'Do you think' *WMAWS*
     'a past-Mistress' *WMAWS*
     'There was a peculiar' Mackail

360 'but I must' WM to May Morris, 21 March 1878
'to restore' Linda Parry, *William Morris Textiles*, 1983
'washed to death' WM to Thomas Wardle, 13 April 1876
361 'simple feasts' William Morris Labour Church, *The Reformers' Year Book*, 1901
'When I lust' Luke Ionides, *Memories*, Herbert Clarke, Paris, 1925
'Morris came over' Edward Burne-Jones to George Howard, undated, Castle Howard
'bright swift writing' Edward Burne-Jones to George Howard, undated, Castle Howard
362 'in the thick of poetry' WM to Jane Morris, 8 March 1876
'I set myself' WM to Jane Morris, 7 February 1877
'a poet' WM to Eiríkr Magnússon, November 1875?
'to a national' Henry Nettleship, review, *The Academy*, vol. X, November 1875
'long lolloping lines' George Bernard Shaw to Henry Salt, quoted Stephen Winsten, *Salt and his Circle*, Hutchinson, 1951
'I sing of arms' WM, *The Aeneids of Vergil*, 1875
363 'Wherein you are' WM to unknown recipient, 22 March–8 April 1876
364 'violent and indignant' Dante Gabriel Rossetti to Henry Treffry Dunn, 24 October 1875, Doughty and Wahl
'wonders gathered' Dante Gabriel Rossetti to Charlotte Polidori, December? 1875, *ibid.*
'arduous in her delicate' Dante Gabriel Rossetti to Christina Rossetti, 3 December 1875, *ibid.*
'rather short of victuals' WM to Jane Morris, 9 November 1875
'dreary' Jane Morris quoted Wilfrid Scawen Blunt, ms. diaries, 1 October 1892, Fitzwilliam
365 'Mrs. M. and her daughter' Dante Gabriel Rossetti to Thomas Gordon Hake, 26 March 1876, Doughty and Wahl
'Mystery: lo!' Dante Gabriel Rossetti, 'Astarte Syriaca', 1876
'staying with Mr. Rossetti' *Intros*
'not always portraying' William Michael Rossetti, *Some Reminiscences*, Brown Langham & Co., 1906
366 'making fun' Wilfrid Scawen Blunt, ms. diaries, 1 October 1892, Fitzwilliam
'the Scalands one' Dante Gabriel Rossetti to Jane Morris, 18 March 1878, Bryson
'a feeling far deeper' Dante Gabriel Rossetti to Jane Morris, 31 May 1878, Bryson
'to be left' WM to Jane Morris, 18 March 1876
367 Morris's children Jane Morris quoted Wilfrid Scawen Blunt, ms. diaries, 11 September 1887, Fitzwilliam
'formidable proportions' Helena M. Sickert Swanwick, *I Have Been Young*
368 'book box' *Intros*
'tall, stoutish, hefty' Violet Hunt, ed. Lady Mander, 'Kelmscott to Kelmscott', *JWMS*, Winter 1968
Jenny's first fit Joan Larkin in conversation with the author, 9 February 1994
'there came a note' Georgiana Burne-Jones to Sydney Cockerell, 20 October 1917, British Library
369 'her head' Wilfrid Scawen Blunt, ms. diaries, intro. 1889, Fitzwilliam
'I am so glad' WM to Jane Morris, 18 July 1876
370 'I am today' WM to Aglaia Coronio, 4 September 1876
Visitors' Book reproduced Lorraine Price, 'Cormell Price Esq.', *JWMS*, Winter 1983/4
'We had no' Georgiana Burne-Jones to Charles Fairfax Murray, 9 January 1877, Fitzwilliam
'it is as if' Jane Morris to Wilfrid Scawen Blunt, 9 August 1888, Faulkner
'I do verily' WM to Louisa Baldwin, 25 March 1875
'From this distress' Mackail

370 'It was touching' Wilfrid Blunt, ms. diaries, intro. 1889, Fitzwilliam
371 'meet to forget' WM, 'Making the Best of It', lecture, 1880
'another love-saga' WM to Henry Buxton Forman, Nov.–Dec. 1870
372 'as an artist' WM to Henry Buxton Forman, 12 November 1873
'puffing steam' *Intros*
373 'there rose up' *Sigurd the Volsung*, Book II, 1876
'could hardly read' W. B. Yeats to Olivia Shakespear, 24 October 1933
374 'I found it hard' WM to James Richard Thursfield, 16 February 1877
375 'of unimpeachable' Mackail
'for which no one' *Intros*
'I was born' WM to Eiríkr Magnússon, 24 January 1876
'We are on' W. B. Richmond to Thomas Richmond, c.1879, A. M. W. Stirling, *The Richmond Papers*, Heinemann, 1926
'By the way' WM letter c. May 1877, Mackail
376 'Take proper care of' edited from John Ruskin, *The Seven Lamps of Architecture*, 1849
Burford account *Intros*
'Why, I could carve' W. R. Lethaby, 'William Morris as Work-Master', lecture given at Birmingham School of Art, 1901
377 'to the best time' SPAB Manifesto, *WMAWS*
'it seems to me' WM to William De Morgan, 3 April 1877
378 'I suppose that' WM to *The Times*, 4 June 1877
'would restore' WM to Henry Wallis, 29 August 1880
'convicted out of' WM to Thomas Wardle, 13 April 1877
'the (happily) dead' WM to Georgiana Burne-Jones, 13 May 1889, Henderson
'monuments of ancient art' Morris & Co. circular, 9 April 1877, WMG
379 'We take the Times' Georgiana Burne-Jones to Rosalind Howard, 22 August 1876, Castle Howard
'About the time' WM to Andreas Scheu, 15 September 1883
380 'Sir, I cannot' WM to the *Daily News*, 24 October 1876
'the Bishops, the Parsons' W. H. G. Armytage, *A. J. Mundella*, Ernest Benn, 1951
381 'The hall' Burne-Jones
'a very solemn' WM to Thomas Wardle, 11 December 1876
'and he turned' *WMAWS*
'great stew' WM to Jane Morris, 2 May 1877
'They seem to have' WM to Georgiana Burne-Jones, 4 May 1877
383 'after the example' WM to Jane Morris, 29 October 1877
'penny lecture' Edward Burne-Jones to George Howard, undated, Castle Howard
'full of truths' Philip Webb to Jane Morris, Jenny and May, 5 December 1877, British Library
'crazy for war' WM to George Howard, 27 December 1877
'a glorious victory' WM to Jenny Morris, 4 January 1878
'magnificent' WM to Jane Morris, 19 January 1878
384 'an inspiriting song' Henry Broadhurst, *The Story of his Life*, Hutchinson, 1901
'When we took' Burne-Jones
'a Nonconformist' Henry Broadhurst, *op. cit.*
'cheered lustily' WM to Jane Morris, 19 January 1878
'Mr. W. Morris' *The Times*, 17 January 1878
385 'a bad beating' WM to George Howard, 1 February 1878
'they had 400 roughs' WM to Jane Morris, 1 February 1878
'I am full of' WM to Charles Faulkner, 5 February 1878
'We were received' WM to Jenny Morris, 11 February 1878

385 'was quite hot' WM to Jane Morris, 20 February 1878
386 'for the boat race' WM to Jane Morris, 11 April 1878
'I should not' WM to Jane Morris, 2 April 1878
'There will certainly' WM to Charles Faulkner, 5 February 1878
'which I fancy' Jane Morris to Rosalind Howard, 6 September 1877, Castle Howard
'It will be' WM to Emma Shelton Morris, 28 October 1877
'Wouldn't it' WM to Jane Morris, 23 November 1877
'celebrated thrift' WM to Jane Morris, 29 November 1877
'which is expensive' WM to Jane Morris, 4 February 1878
'Mouse looks' WM to Jenny Morris, 6 March 1878
387 'kinswomen' WM to Jane Morris, 26 March 1878
'very best love' WM to Jenny Morris, 14 January 1878
'The Ms are not' Rosalind Howard to Lady Stanley, quoted Virginia Surtees, *The Artist and the Autocrat*, 1988
'haggard and wistful-eyed' Lady Frederick Cavendish, quoted Virginia Surtees, *ibid.*
'poor Lizzie's' Dante Gabriel Rossetti to Jane Morris, 27 February 1878, Bryson
'dreadful' Rosalind Howard to Lady Stanley, quoted Virginia Surtees, *The Artist and the Autocrat*
388 'hashish or bhang' WM to Jane Morris, 12 March 1878
'Can't you imagine' WM to Georgiana Burne-Jones, 27 April 1878
'signs of the toe-devil' WM to Jane Morris, 28 December 1877
'being lame' WM to Jenny Morris, 6 March 1878
'things began' WM to Georgiana Burne-Jones, 27 April 1878
389 'the hobbler's Paradise' *ibid.*
'crawl across' WM to Charles Fairfax Murray, 29 April 1878
'small cots' *Intros*
'What a beautiful' WM to Georgiana Burne-Jones, 15 May 1878
'beyond all praise' WM to George Howard, 18 May 1878
390 'Let me confess' WM to Georgiana Burne-Jones, 15 May 1878
'gouty old fogy' WM to Aglaia Coronio, 7 March 1878
'and was dreaming' WM to Georgiana Burne-Jones, 29 April 1878
'through the emotion' *Intros*
'I am still' WM to Georgiana Burne-Jones?, 25 May 1878

CHAPTER TWELVE
391 'a convenient' *Intros*
'charms for others' *The Westminster Review*, No. 41, 1872
392 'a ceiling of' A. W. M. Stirling, *William De Morgan and his Wife*, Henry Holt & Co., New York, 1922
'a nice one' Dante Gabriel Rossetti to Jane Morris, *ibid.*
393 'the house could' WM to Jane Morris, 18 March 1878
'I don't think' WM to Jane Morris, *ibid.*
394 'we should only' WM to Jane Morris, 12 March 1878
'if only for' WM to Jane Morris, 2 April 1878
'several inches' Jane Morris to Dante Gabriel Rossetti, May 1878, Bryson
'I thought it' Jane Morris to Rosalind Howard, undated, Castle Howard
395 'between the yells' Philip Webb to Jane Morris, 8 November 1878, British Library
'one of the prettiest' WM to Jane Morris, 18 March 1878
'Eastern carpets' *Intros*
'The Macs have' WM to Jane Morris, March 1878
'The dining room' Dante Gabriel Rossetti to Jane Morris, 1 April 1878, Bryson

396 'enchanted interior' Cockerell, *Friends*
'Above this table' *Intros*
'it is all' WM to May Morris, 21 March 1878
397 'Some people' George Bernard Shaw, 'William Morris as I Knew Him', 1936,
WMAWS
'almost frugally' *Intros*
'1st, a walnut' WM to Jane Morris, March 1878
398 'poor old Matthews' WM to Jane Morris, 19 March 1881
'as a pleasure ground' WM to Emma Morris, 23 May 1889, WMG
'old shoes' Burne-Jones
'there is a dreadful' Jane Morris to Wilfrid Scawen Blunt, 20 March 1885, Faulkner
'Mrs. Morris reclining' Helena M. Sickert Swanwick, *I Have Been Young*
399 'bright chatty little woman' W. Graham Robertson, *Time Was*, Hamish Hamilton, 1931
'delicious chuckling' Helena M. Sickert Swanwick, *op. cit.*
'We settled ourselves' Rudyard Kipling, *Something of Myself*, Macmillan, 1937
400 'a labyrinth' Dante Gabriel Rossetti to Jane Morris, 1 April 1878, Bryson
'ragged mites' *Intros*
'Have a ride' WM to Jenny Morris, 30 March 1887
'Look you' WM, 'Art and the Beauty of the Earth', lecture, 13 October 1881
401 'bright dream' WM to Thomas Wardle, 13 April 1877
'I am writing' WM to Georgiana Burne-Jones, March 1879
'I very much want' WM to Thomas Wardle, 25 March 1877
'Our Froggy weaver' WM to George Howard, 29 June 1877
'did not feel' F. G. Guy, 21 September 1877, quoted Mackail
402 'many a time' WM to George Howard, 29 June 1877
'the [willow] pattern' F. G. Guy, *op. cit.*
'queer old sheds' *Intros*
'various dates from' Diary of work on 'Cabbage and Vine' tapestry, 10 May–17 September
1879, NAL
'I am studying' WM to Thomas Wardle, 25 March 1877
403 'And while he thought' 'The Watching of the Falcon', *The Earthly Paradise*, part 2, 1868
'fit only' *Intros*
'to make England' Circular for Morris & Co. exhibition of rugs, May 1880, Mackail
404 'I saw yesterday' WM to Thomas Wardle, 13 April 1877
'*grande poeta*' *Intros*
'we had but' Jane Morris to Rosalind Howard, undated, Castle Howard
405 'He took us' Octavia Hill to Mrs Shaen, 3 June 1881, ed. C. Edmund Maurice, *The Life of
Octavia Hill*, Macmillan, 1913
'designs in little' *Intros*
406 'Breakfast is over' WM to Jane Morris, 24 August 1880
'a mosaic' WM, 'Textiles', *Arts and Crafts Essays*, 1893
407 'The *Widow Guelph*' WM to Thomas Wardle, 24 October 1877
'Let's clear off' WM to Thomas Wardle, 14 November 1877
Morris on Windsor Aymer Vallance, 'The Revival of Tapestry Weaving', *The Studio*,
July 1894
'General feeling' WM to Thomas Wardle, 14 November 1877
408 'a month' Diary of work on 'Cabbage and Vine' tapestry, 10 May–17 September 1879,
NAL
'under the nervous' *Intros*
'I have taught' WM to William Bell Scott, 13 October 1879
'Lord bless us' WM to Georgiana Burne-Jones?, autumn 1879

408 'The Empress Brown' WM to Jenny Morris, 6 March 1878
409 'a shed' WM to Thomas Wardle, 10 April 1877
'both Mr. Morris' Georgiana Burne-Jones to Rosalind Howard, 28 March 1876, Castle Howard
'You are very welcome' WM to Lucy Faulkner Orrinsmith, 20 July 1877
'I wish to goodness' A. W. M. Stirling, *William De Morgan and his Wife*, Henry Holt & Co., New York, 1922
'Painted Glass' Morris & Co. entry in catalogue of Boston Foreign Fair, 1883
410 'the spirit' *Building News*, 11 June 1880
'a simple little glass' *Intros*
'Item, I can do' WM to Rosalind Howard, 24 November 1881
411 'recommended' WM to Rosalind Howard, 4 November 1881
'Everything was' Luke Ionides, *Memories*
'the cotters' houses' WM to Georgiana Burne-Jones, 18 October 1877
'Work at St. James' WM to Jane Morris, February 1881
'the great man' Mrs Russell Barrington, *The Life of Walter Bagehot*, Longmans, Green & Co., 1914
412 'ministering to the' Lethaby
'sadly stupid' WM to Jenny Morris, 21 July 1883
'really when one' WM to Jenny Morris, 24 March 1885
'that a branch' Moncure Conway, *Travels in South Kensington*, Trübner & Co., 1882
'We were to see' W. B. Yeats, *Autobiographies*, Macmillan, 1956
'full of cranks' Richard Norman Shaw to Canon Irton Smith, 27 July 1898, quoted Andrew Saint, *Richard Norman Shaw*, Yale University Press, 1976
'Morris was impetuous' Reginald Blomfield, *Richard Norman Shaw RA*, Batsford, 1940
413 'when married tutors' *Daily Telegraph* obituary, 5 October 1896
'green serge gowns' Penelope Fitzgerald, *Edward Burne-Jones*, Michael Joseph, 1975
'when you poked it' Vyvyan Holland, *Son of Oscar Wilde*, Rupert Hart-Davis, 1954
'strangely designed wallpapers' Hubert Bland, 'The Faith I Hold', Fabian Society paper, 1907
'limited cash' Beatrice Webb, February 1890, ed. Norman and Jeanne MacKenzie, *The Diary of Beatrice Webb*, Virago, 1986
'dark and jungly' Frances Partridge, *Memories*, Victor Gollancz, London, 1981
'chintzy rooms' Helen Witt, quoted Sybille Bedford, *Aldous Huxley*, Paladin Books, 1987
'the rather dark' Geoffrey Keynes, *The Gates of Memory*, Clarendon Press, Oxford, 1981
'the perfect Morris' Richard Aldington, *Lawrence of Arabia*, Collins, 1955
414 'irredeemable' Kenneth Clark, *Another Part of the Wood*, John Murray, 1974
'ingeniously enlivened' Osbert Lancaster, *With an Eye to the Future*, John Murray, 1967
'the greatest' W. R. Lethaby, quoted *WMAWS*
'to some people' *WMAWS*
415 'deep satisfaction' WM to Georgiana Burne-Jones, 16 May 1878
'a marvel of art' WM to *The Daily News*, 31 October 1879
'headlong rashness' *ibid.*
416 'to me' WM to Robert Browning, 7 November 1879
'Have you had' Charles Keane to Joseph Crawhall, 23 November 1879, quoted A. H. Layard, *Autobiography and Letters*, John Murray, 1903
'real and living' speech at AGM of SPAB, 28 June 1879, *WMAWS*
418 'As to poetry' WM to Georgiana Burne-Jones, 13 October 1879
'I even tried' WM to Jane Morris, 20 December 1877
'I have been' WM to Jane Morris, 13 February 1880
'Our country' WM, 'Socialism up to date', ms., British Library

418 'polite and attentive' WM to Jane Morris, 19 March 1881
419 'feeling the ground' *Intros*
'in his early addresses' Burne-Jones
'after all' *Intros*
'for 'tis no' WM to Georgiana Burne-Jones, 10 August 1880
420 'I am among' WM, 'The Art of the People', lecture, 1879
421 'I am sitting' WM to Georgiana Burne-Jones, late autumn 1879
422 'though but in' WM to *The Daily News*, 17 October 1879
'I wonder sometimes' WM to Anthony John Mundella, 21 May 1880
'new sphere' WM to Henry Broadhurst, 4 April 1880
'When a man' *WMAWS*
'I left Sandringham' Henry Broadhurst, *The Story of his Life from a Stonemason's Bench to the Treasury Bench*, Hutchinson, 1901
'one might further' WM to Charles Edmund Maurice, 22 June 1883
423 'I am in hopes' WM to Jane Morris, 3 March 1881
'everything vague' Mackail
'Set agoing' WM, ms. diary, 15 January 1881
'a strong political' George Wardle, 'Reminiscences of William Morris', Christmas 1897, British Library
424 'Little things' WM to Georgiana Burne-Jones, 10 August 1880
'a sort of insane' *Intros*
'what a joy' WM to Georgiana Burne-Jones, 10 August 1880
'One is made' Jane Morris to Dante Gabriel Rossetti, August 1879, Bryson
'lying down' WM to Georgiana Burne-Jones, 19 August 1880
425 'What a stink' 'Description of an expedition by boat', manuscript August 1880, British Library
'Note by' ed. A. M. W. Stirling, *William De Morgan and his Wife*, Holt & Co., New York, 1922
'Cockney Waters' WM to Georgiana Burne-Jones, 19 August 1880
'boteler by acclamation' 'Description of an expedition', *op. cit.*
'like the high priest' WM to Georgiana Burne-Jones, 19 August 1880
426 'very beautiful' *ibid.*
'who retired' 'Description of an expedition', *op. cit.*
427 'I recognised' Violet Hunt, ed. Lady Mander, 'Kelmscott to Kelmscott', *JWMS*, Winter 1968
'in spite of' ed. A. M. W. Stirling, *William De Morgan and his Wife*, *op. cit.*
428 'they were haymaking' WM to Georgiana Burne-Jones, 19 August 1880
'Night fell' *ibid.*
'for stately is' WM, *News from Nowhere*, 1890

CHAPTER THIRTEEN
429 'The fictionary' WM to William De Morgan, 16 April 1881
'but very ill-demorganized' A. M. W. Stirling, *William De Morgan and his Wife*
430 'I know' WM to George Howard, 3 November 1881
'big and solid' WM to Jane Morris, 10 March 1881
'Drury Lane' *Intros*
431 'first, it would' WM to Jane Morris, 19 March 1881
'one can scarcely' *Intros*
432 'the hand-looms' 'On the Wandle', article in *The Spectator*, 23 November 1883
'into the peaceful' Emma Lazarus, 'A Day in Surrey with William Morris', *The Century Illustrated Magazine*, July 1886

433 'a large, low room' 'On the Wandle', *op. cit.*
'each full waged' WM, ms. diary, 26 May 1881, British Library
'I laboured hard' WM to Thomas Wardle, 9 February 1881
'Tom Wardle called' WM, ms. diary, 23 February 1881, British Library
'Tom Wardle there' WM, *ibid.*, 4 April 1881

434 'the bleaching ground' *Intros*
'a beautiful almond' WM to Emma Lazarus, 5 March 1884?
'certain of the workmen' George Wardle, 'Reminiscences of William Morris', Christmas 1897, British Library
'no vice' Effie Morris family reminiscences, WMG
'Edgar and his missis' WM to Jenny and May Morris, 25 December 1877

435 'port in a storm' WM to Jane Morris, 29 November 1877
'Edgar taking stock' WM, ms. diary, 4 January 1881, British Library
'Edgar says' WM to Jenny Morris, 19 May 1883
'a dreamy man' Blunt, 5 July 1892
'where there are' Jane Morris to Dante Gabriel Rossetti, 2 February 1881, Bryson
'I can't go owing' WM to Jane Morris, February 1881
'I didn't fall' Henry James to Fanny Kemble, March 1881, ed. Leon Edel, *Letters of Henry James*, Harvard University Press, Cambridge, Mass., 1974

436 'I think it does' Jane Morris to Dante Gabriel Rossetti, 2 February 1881, Bryson
'though May is' WM to Jane Morris, February 1881
'drag through' Jane Morris to Dante Gabriel Rossetti, December 1879, *ibid.*
'when we cracked' Philip Webb to Jane Morris, 10 April 1881, British Library
'looked very old' WM to Jane Morris, 19 April 1881
'Not but what' *ibid.*, 31 March 1881

437 'to see the last' *ibid.*, 3 March 1881
'grey and hazy' WM to Georgiana Burne-Jones, 20 September 1881
'in military dangers' petition in *The Nineteenth Century*, April/May 1882
'turned up' WM, ms. diary, 1 May 1881, British Library

438 'to us country' WM to Georgiana Burne-Jones, 20 September 1881

439 'mansion' Dante Gabriel Rossetti to Jane Morris, February 1881, Bryson
'the sea-air' Jane Morris to Dante Gabriel Rossetti, 5 March 1881, *ibid.*
'lying like a box' WM to Georgiana Burne-Jones, 10 January 1882
'If you read' Dante Gabriel Rossetti to Jane Morris, 16 August 1881, Bryson
'Your letter' Dante Gabriel Rossetti to Jane Morris, 18 August 1881, *ibid.*

440 'A dozen copies' Dante Gabriel Rossetti to Jane Morris, 1 October 1881, *ibid.*
'I don't think' WM to Dante Gabriel Rossetti, 28 October 1881
'The lady' Hall Caine, *Recollections of Rossetti*, Cassell & Co., 1928
'She was especially' Hall Caine to Bernard Shaw, 24 September 1928, British Library

441 'He was in' Wilfrid Scawen Blunt, ms. diaries, 13 May 1890, Fitzwilliam
'lay down' Dante Gabriel Rossetti to Theodore Watts-Dunton, 28 September 1881, Doughty and Wahl
'decisively, instantly' account of Rossetti's last illness in S. C. Dyke, 'Some Medical Aspects of the Life of Dante Gabriel Rossetti', *Proceedings of the Royal Society of Medicine*, December 1963
'anything of his' Hall Caine to Bernard Shaw, 24 September 1928, British Library

442 'love letters' Wilfrid Scawen Blunt, ms. diaries, 13 May 1890, Fitzwilliam
'What can I say' WM to William Bell Scott, 27 April 1882
'found D.G.R. out' Bernard Shaw to Sydney Cockerell, 10 April 1950, Cockerell, *Best of Friends*
'This household' Mackail

442 'extraordinarily late' WM to the *The Daily News*, 27 September 1882
443 'indeed I am' WM to Georgiana Burne-Jones, 30 August 1882?
'To Merton Abbey' WM, ms. diary, 22, 27 and 30 December 1881, British Library
'reduce it to' WM to George Howard, 16 March 1882
'I think you will' WM to James Bryce, 16 March 1882
444 'the printing seems' WM to May Morris, 6 January 1883
'the colour mixer' WM to Jenny Morris, 14 March 1883
445 'the cheapest chair' WM to James Mavor, 16 April [1887?]
'a great number' Morris & Co. brochure, 1882, NAL
'there is a new' WM to May Morris, 6 January 1883
446 'he was at once' George Wardle, 'Reminiscences of William Morris', *op. cit.*
'I thought' WM to Jenny Morris, 14 April 1883
447 'I am the ancient' 'Pomona', *Poems by the Way*, 1891
'and we had made friends' Blunt, 1889
'She must' Wilfrid Scawen Blunt, ms. diaries, 17 January 1914, Fitzwilliam
448 'cynically regarded' Lady Wentworth, intro. to *The Authentic Arab Horse and his Descendants*, George Allen & Unwin, 1945
'Love is to me' Wilfrid Scawen Blunt, ms. diaries, 24 November 1889, *ibid.*
449 'I found her' Wilfrid Scawen Blunt, ms. diaries, 1872, *ibid.*
450 'Blanche Hozier' Rosalind Howard to Wilfrid Scawen Blunt, ms. diaries, July 1888, *ibid.*
'He always seemed' Wilfrid Scawen Blunt, ms. diaries, 27 January 1914, *ibid.*
'We talkled about' Wilfrid Scawen Blunt, ms. diaries, 5 May 1892, *ibid.*
451 'ours is a very curious' Wilfrid Scawen Blunt, ms. diaries, 7 May 1891, *ibid.*
'Please believe' Jane Morris to Wilfrid Scawen Blunt, July 1884, Faulkner
'She was a loveable' Wilfrid Scawen Blunt, ms. diaries, 1889, Fitzwilliam
452 'I'm afraid' May Morris to Emery Walker, 1918?, WMG
'I am much encouraged' WM to Georgiana Burne-Jones, 23 August 1882
'I believe that' WM to Andreas Scheu, 1883
453 'with happy joyous' Gabriel Mourey, *Passé le Detroit*, quoted Aymer Vallance, *The Life and Work of William Morris*, 1897
'Mr. Morris believes' quoted Isabella Gilmore, A. M. W. Stirling, *The Merry Wives of Battersea*, Robert Hale, 1956
'The work of weaving' quoted Linda Parry, *William Morris Textiles*, 1983
'a certain weekly' George Wardle, 'Reminiscences of William Morris', *op. cit.*
454 'work light in duration' WM, 'A Factory as It Might Be', 1884, WMAWS
'the highest' George Wardle, 'Reminiscences of William Morris', *op. cit.*
455 Top and the beggar Mackail
456 'except with a small' WM to Emma Lazarus, 21 April 1884
'they would all' Thomas Cobden-Sanderson, *The Journals, 1879–1922*, 16 January 1884, Richard Cobden-Sanderson, 1926
457 'I am the poet' Edward Carpenter, *Towards Democracy*, 1883
'that there was his wife' Thomas Cobden-Sanderson, *op. cit.*, 16 January 1884
'Household expenses' WM 'Cabbage and Vine' diary, 1879, NAL
458 'those other partners' WM to Georgiana Burne-Jones, 1 June 1884
'not all pure' WM to Jenny Morris, 19 May 1883
'The latter part' George Wardle, 'Reminiscences of William Morris', *op. cit.*
460 'it sometimes seems' WM to Georgiana Burne-Jones, 19 January 1882?
'my mind is very full' WM to Georgiana Burne-Jones, 1 January 1882
'advanced political' Democratic Federation announcement in *The Radical*, 28 May 1881
461 'some kind of culture' WM to Georgiana Burne-Jones, 2 July 1881

461 'These are' *ibid.*
'it is good' *ibid.*, 16 September 1881
'for between us' 'The Prospects of Architecture', lecture, 1881

CHAPTERS FOURTEEN, FIFTEEN AND SIXTEEN: Westminster Palace
Chambers 1883–84, Farringdon Road, One: 1885–87, Farringdon Road, Two:
1887–90

In the Socialist years Morris's correspondence was voluminous. It is only now, in Norman
Kelvin's edition of the *Collected Letters*, that we are able to read it through in sequence in a
way that sheds new light not just on the complex events themselves but on Morris's response to
them. In these chapters the letters have been an invaluable source.

May Morris's own commentaries on these years, when she was so much at her father's side,
are vivid and have, I think, been greatly underestimated. Besides her official account in the
Introductions to the *Collected Works* (1910–15) and in the much fuller second volume of
William Morris, Artist, Writer, Socialist (Basil Blackwell, Oxford 1936), there is her
illuminating correspondence with Andreas Scheu at the International Institute of Socialist
History in Amsterdam, and with Bernard Shaw at the British Library.

Morris kept a diary, briefly, in his Socialist period. The original is in the British Library,
and there is an edition, *William Morris's Socialist Diary*, edited and annotated by Florence
Boos, Journeyman Press, London, 1985. I have also drawn especially on the Hammersmith
Socialist Society archive in the British Library; the Emery Walker papers at Cheltenham
Museum and Art Gallery; Philip Webb correspondence at the National Art Library, Victoria
and Albert Museum; the unpublished diaries and letters of Wilfrid Scawen Blunt at the
Fitzwilliam Museum in Cambridge, as well as the correspondence *Jane Morris to Wilfrid
Scawen Blunt* in Peter Faulkner's edition, University of Essex, 1986.

Any writer about Morris in the second half of the twentieth century must express a debt to
E. P. Thompson whose massive reassessment, *William Morris: Romantic to Revolutionary*,
first published in 1955, overturned the accepted view of Morris's politics. In these chapters,
and the one that follows, my debt to E. P. Thompson is considerable. Paul Meier's two-volume
exploration of the Marxism of Morris, *La Pensée utopique* (1972), published in its English
translation as *William Morris the Marxist Dreamer* (1978), has also been a source of
inspiration, not least useful for those points on which I find myself in disagreement with it.

Morris's own best accounts of his 'conversion' are given in his letter to Andreas Scheu, 15
September 1883, and 'How I Became a Socialist, the essay first published in *Justice*, 16 June
1894.

Other sources:

On May Morris: Jan Marsh, *Jane and May Morris*, Pandora, London, 1976; Anthea Callen,
The Angel in the Studio: women of the arts and crafts movement 1870–1914, Astragal, 1978:
May Morris, catalogue of exhibition at William Morris Gallery, Walthamstow, 1989.

On Deaconess Gilmore: Janet Grierson, *Isabella Gilmore, Sister to William Morris*, SPCK,
1962.

On Morris's politics in general: records in Labour History Library, Manchester, and Marx
Memorial Library, London; ed. George Edward Roebuck, *Some Appreciations of William
Morris*, centenary publication, Walthamstow Antiquarian Society, 1934; G. D. H. Cole,
'William Morris as a Socialist', lecture, William Morris Society, 1960; Edward Thompson,
'The Communism of William Morris', lecture, William Morris Society, 1965; R. Page Arnot,
William Morris, the Man and the Myth, Lawrence and Wishart, 1964; A. L. Morton, 'Morris,
Marx and Engels', *JWMS*, Autumn 1986; Paul Thompson, 'Liberals, Radicals and Labour in
London, 1880–1900', *Past and Present*, April 1964; Gareth Stedman-Jones, *Outcast London*,
Oxford University Press, 1971; Michael Dibb and Peter Fuller, 'William Morris, Questions of

Work and Democracy: interview with Raymond Williams', *William Morris Today* catalogue, ICA, 1984; Peter Fuller, 'Conserving "Joy in Labour"', chapter in *Images of God: The Consolations of Lost Illusions*, Chatto & Windus, 1985; Mervyn Jones, 'Humane Socialist', *New Statesman*, 23 March 1984; Ray Watkinson, 'The Vindicator Vindicated: William Morris and Robin Page Arnot', *William Morris Today* catalogue, ICA, 1984; Linda Richardson, 'William Morris and Women: Experience and Representation', Ph.D. thesis, University of Oxford; Paul Thompson, 'Why William Morris Matters Today: Human Creativity and the Future World Environment', lecture, William Morris Society, 1991.

On Morris and the Democratic Federation (later SDF): H. W. Lee and E. Archbold, *Social Democracy in Britain*, Social-Democratic Federation, 1935; early chapters of Henry Pelling, *The Origins of the Labour Party*, Clarendon Press, Oxford, 1965; J. Burgess, *John Burns*, Glasgow, 1911; W. Kent, *John Burns: Labour's Lost Leader*, Williams & Norgate, 1950; Henry Mayers Hyndman, *The Record of an Adventurous Life*, Macmillan, 1911, and *Further Reminiscences*, 1912; Chushichi Tsuzuki, *H. M. Hyndman and British Socialism*, Oxford University Press, 1961; Raymond Postgate, *George Lansbury*, Longmans, Green & Co., 1951; Tom Mann, *Memoirs*, Labour Publishing Co., 1912; Dona Torr, *Tom Mann and his Times*, Lawrence & Wishart, 1956; Henry Salt, *Seventy Years among Savages*, George Allen & Unwin, 1921; Stephen Winsten, *Salt and his Circle*, Hutchinson & Co., 1951; ed. George and Willene Hendrich, *The Savour of Salt*, Centaur Press, Fontwell, 1989.

On Morris and the Socialist League: records and correspondence in Socialist League and Andreas Scheu archives, International Institute of Socialist History, Amsterdam; Hammersmith Branch records in British Library and Emery Walker collection, Cheltenham Art Gallery and Museum; Alf Mattison archive, Brotherton Library, University of Leeds; James Alfred Wickes, 'Memories of Kelmscott House', *JWMS*, Summer 1968; Tom Barclay, *Memoirs and Medleys: the Autobiography of a Bottle Washer*, Edgar Backus, 1934; John Cowley, *The Victorian Encounter with Marx: A Study of Ernest Belfort Bax*, British Academic Press, 1992; Edward Carpenter, *My Days and Dreams*, George Allen & Unwin, 1916; ed. Gilbert Beith, *Edward Carpenter, In Appreciation*, memorial volume, George Allen & Unwin, 1931; Chushichi Tsuzuki, *Edward Carpenter*, Cambridge University Press, 1980; Sheila Rowbotham and Jeffrey Weeks, *Socialism and the New Life: The Personal and Sexual Politics of Edward Carpenter and Havelock Ellis*, Pluto Press, 1977; J. Bruce Glasier, *William Morris and the Early Days of the Socialist Movement*, Longmans, Green & Co., 1921; John Carruthers, *Economic Studies*, Chiswick Press, 1915; James Leatham, *William Morris, Master of Many Crafts*, Turrif, 1899; Chushichi Tsuzuki, *The Life of Eleanor Marx*, Oxford, 1967; Yvonne Kapp, *Eleanor Marx*, vol. 2: *The Crowded Years*, Lawrence & Wishart, 1976; Andreas Scheu, *Umsturzkeime*, Vienna, 1923; W. B. Yeats, *Autobiographies*, Macmillan, 1956; Peter Faulkner, *William Morris and W. B. Yeats*, Dolmen Press, Dublin, 1962.

On Morris and the Fabians: Norman and Jeanne MacKenzie, *The First Fabians*, Weidenfeld & Nicolson, 1977; Ian Britain, *Fabianism and Culture: A Study in British Socialism and the Arts, 1884–1918*, Cambridge University Press, 1982; Annie Besant, *An Autobiography*, Theosophical Publishing House, 1908; Anne Taylor, *Annie Besant*, Oxford University Press, 1992; Bernard Shaw, 'William Morris as I Knew Him', *WMAWS*, vol. 2, 1936; Michael Holroyd, *Bernard Shaw, vol. 1: The Search for Love*, Chatto & Windus, 1988.

On Morris and the Anarchists in London: James W. Hulse, *Revolutionists in London*, Clarendon Press, Oxford, 1970; Peter Marshall, *Demanding the Impossible. A History of Anarchism*, Harper Collins, London, 1992; George Woodcock, *Anarchism: a history of Libertarian ideas and movements*, Meridian Books, Cleveland, 1962; Peter Kropotkin, *Memoirs of a Revolutionist*, Century Hutchinson, 1988; Sergius Stepniak, *Underground Russia*, Smith Elder & Co., 1883; ed. Barry Johnson, *Tea and Anarchy! The Bloomsbury Diary of Olive Garnett, 1890–1893* and second volume *1893–1895*, Bartlett's Press, Birmingham, 1989 and 1993; Richard Garnett, *Constance Garnett, A Heroic Life*, Sinclair-Stevenson, 1991; Colin

Ward, 'Morris as Anarchist Educator', essay in *William Morris Today* catalogue, ICA, 1984.

On Morris's Socialist lectures and journalism: ed. Eugene D. LeMire, *The Unpublished Lectures of William Morris*, Wayne State University Press, 1969; A. L. Morton, intro. to *Political Writings of William Morris*, Lawrence & Wishart, 1973; Helen Irving, 'William Morris and the contemporary Socialist press', *JWMS*, Winter 1984–5; Nicholas Salmon, Ph.D. thesis on 'William Morris as a Propagandist', University of Reading; ed. Nicholas Salmon, *Political Writings*, selection in the William Morris Library, Thoemmes Press, Bristol, 1994; texts in *Justice*, 1884–94; *The Commonweal*, 1885–90; *Hammersmith Socialist Record*, 1891–3.

On Morris's Socialist dramas: Pamela Bracken Wiens, 'The Reviews Are In: Reclaiming the Success of Morris's "Socialist Interlude"', *JWMS*, Spring 1991; Nicholas Salmon, 'Mr. Olaf Entertains; or William Morris's Forgotten Dialogues', *JWMS*, Spring 1992.

On *News from Nowhere*: ed. Stephen Coleman and Paddy O'Sullivan, *William Morris and News from Nowhere*, Green Books, Bideford, 1990; Jan Marsh, '*News from Nowhere* as Erotic Dream', *JWMS*, Spring 1990; Michael Fellman, 'Bloody Sunday and *News from Nowhere*', *JWMS*, Spring 1990; J. Alex Macdonald, 'The Revision of News from Nowhere', *JWMS*, Summer 1976; Peter Faulkner, '*News from Nowhere*, in Recent Criticism', *JWMS*, Summer 1983; Ady Mineo, 'Eros Unbound: Sexual Identities in *News from Nowhere*', *JWMS*, Spring 1992.

Morris's Socialist sites have not fared well. The Socialist League offices in Farringdon Street and Farringdon Road, just to the west of Smithfield, have been replaced by long rows of architecturally undistinguished offices, though it might have interested Morris to see that one of these houses the Social Security and Child Support Commission.

Westminster Palace Chambers, once the offices of the Democratic Federation, lasted longer. But by 1994 they were in the process of demolition to make way for the New Parliamentary Building by the Michael Hopkins Partnership, a confident edifice in stone and bronze.

CHAPTER FOURTEEN
462 'some disturbance' *Intros*
463 'In the early winter' Mackail
   Palace Chambers Hubert Bland, *Sunday Chronicle*, 26 May 1895
   'on the look out' WM to Andreas Scheu, 15 September 1883
   'I'm going in' F. S. Ellis to J. W. Mackail, 16 October 1896, Mackail notebooks, WMG
464 'If you ask me' WM, 'How I Became a Socialist', *Justice*, 16 June 1894
   'O! for the Wings' Thomas Okey, *A Basketful of Memories*, J. M. Dent, 1930
   'an *assuming* man' review in the *Nation*, 1911, reprinted in G. Bernard Shaw, *Pen Portraits and Reviews*, Constable, 1932
465 'an arch-Conservative' Friedrich Engels to Friedrich Adolph Sorge, 13 December 1881, *Selected Correspondence of Marx and Engels*, Lawrence & Wishart, 1936
   'weak vessel' Karl Marx to August Bebel, 30 August 1883, *ibid.*
   'a definite text' Edward Carpenter, *My Days and Dreams*, George Allen & Unwin, 1916
   'well worth reading' WM to unknown correspondent, 8 January 1884
466 'the oddest little' Edward Pease family correspondence, quoted Norman and Jeanne MacKenzie, *The First Fabians*, Weidenfeld & Nicolson, 1977
   'the only active' WM to William James Linton, 26 October 1883
467 'He spoke like' WM, *The Pilgrims of Hope*, 1885–6
   'the joy of strife' WM, 'The Beauty of Life', lecture, 1880
   'put the finishing touch' WM, 'How I Became a Socialist', *op. cit.*
   'Top to breakfast' Cormell Price diary, 11 April 1882, Price
468 'agonies of confusion' WM, 'How I Became a Socialist', *op. cit.*
   'to delve' *WMAWS*

468 'I feel myself' WM to Andreas Scheu, 20 August 1884
'Could you lay' WM to Ellis & White, 14 August 1883
'such queer things' WM to Jenny Morris, 4 September 1883
469 'Read Underground Russia' WM to F. S. Ellis, mid-May 1883
'it sounds perfectly' WM to Jenny Morris, 19 May 1883
'inciting causes' Edward Burne-Jones, Mackail notebooks, WMG
'incurably vicious' WM to C. E. Maurice, 1 July 1883
470 'will you say' WM, 'Art and Socialism', lecture, 1884
'a man of strong intellect' Isabel Meredith, A Girl among the Anarchists, Duckworth,
London, 1903
471 'a group of conspirators' Edward Carpenter, My Days and Dreams, op. cit.
'our acknowledged Great' Bernard Shaw, 'Morris as I Knew Him', 1936, WMAWS
'Here, obviously' H. M. Hyndman, The Record of an Adventurous Life, Macmillan, 1911
472 'the unpleasant part' ibid.
'I smiled grimly' Bernard Shaw, 'Morris as I Knew Him', op. cit.
'so I am in' WM to Jenny Morris, 19 May 1883
473 'a fiery' WMAWS
'Socialism!' Henry Salt, Seventy Years among Savages, George Allen & Unwin, 1921
'If our whole system' Stephen Winsten, Salt and his Circle, Hutchinson & Co., 1951
'her lofty air' WMAWS
474 'a big gun' WM to George Bernard Shaw, 8 July 1884
'since those who suffer' WM to Jenny Morris, early 1883?
'conducting what most' Bernard Shaw, 'Morris as I Knew Him', op. cit.
'the dear father' WMAWS
475 'I came across' Georgina Sime and Frank Nicholson, Brave Spirits, privately printed,
1952
476 'studied socialism' WM to John Lincoln Mahon, 20 May 1884
''tis to be' WM to Jenny Morris, 9 January 1883
'a letter from' WM to Jenny Morris, 14 March 1883
'It was the purpose' WM to Editor of The Manchester Guardian, 14 March 1883
'only I intend' WM to Jenny Morris, 14 March 1883
'As to Hyndman' WM to Charles Faulkner, 23 October 1883
477 'It is better' John Ruskin to William Morris, 24 April 1882, British Library
'here in Oxford' WM, 'Art under Plutocracy' (originally 'Art and Democracy'), lecture,
1884
479 'unusually well acquainted' Mackail
'sympathetic report' WM to W. T. Stead, 16 November 1883
'I have been living' WM to Georgiana Burne-Jones, 27 November 1883
'Your Correspondent' WM to The Standard, 21 November 1882
480 'startled and flustered' Walter Crane, An Artist's Reminiscences, Methuen & Co., 1907
'like Aaron's rod' ibid.
'Chat with Top' Cormell Price diary, 3 January 1884, Price
'argued with Mrs Howard' unacknowledged entry in Mackail notebooks, 2 April 1884,
WMG
'I was rather' William De Morgan, Mackail notebooks, WMG
'for singing at meetings' WM to Algernon Charles Swinburne, 17 November 1883
'as a single' Algernon Charles Swinburne to WM, 21 November 1883, Lang
481 'the little rift' Cormell Price diary, 6 January 1884, Price
'before all things' Burne-Jones
482 'little Supper-Clubs' H. M. Hyndman, The Record of an Adventurous Life, op. cit.
'favourite rendezvous' Walter Crane, An Artist's Reminiscences, op. cit.

482 'Consider what' Burne-Jones
'Poetry goes' WM to Georgiana Burne-Jones, 21 August 1883
483 'The one thing' WM to Georgiana Burne-Jones, September 1883
'I have never' WM to Thomas Coglan Horsfall, 25 October 1883
'At the last' WM to Clara Richmond, 29 December 1883?
484 'Item I have' WM to Jenny Morris, 4 September 1883
'Come hither lads' *Chants for Socialists*, 1885
485 'a large sum' *WMAWS*
'He was not overburdened' F. S. Ellis, 'The Life-Work of William Morris', lecture, 10
May 1898, *Journal of the Society of Arts*, 27 May 1898
'a certain gaunt' *WMAWS*
486 'the all-important' *Justice*, 19 January 1884
'There was Hyndman' Jack Williams, *Justice*, 15 January 1914
487 'Morris's *Justice*' William Allingham, *A Diary*, 26 July 1884, ed. H. Allingham and D.
Radford, Centaur Press, Fontwell, 1967
'I fear the element' WM to Jenny Morris, 16 January 1884
'They waited patiently' James Macdonald, 'How I Became a Socialist', *Justice*, 11 July
1896
'it will be' WM to Jane Morris, 18 March 1884
488 'On Sunday' WM to Jane Morris, *ibid.*
489 'claptrap style' WM to Andreas Scheu, 17 December 1884
'Morris fought' Sam Mainwaring, *Freedom*, January 1897
'*an old man*' WM to Andreas Scheu, 26 July 1884
'rose-water' WM to Thomas Wardle, 8 March 1878
490 'When they have' WM to William Allingham, 26 November 1884
'seizing' WM to Robert Thomson, 24 July 1884
'the books were' Emma Lazarus, 'A Day in Surrey with William Morris', *The Century
Illustrated Magazine*, July 1886
491 'came off successfully' WM to Jenny Morris, 5 November 1883
'the men are' WM to Jenny Morris, 26 January 1884
'our Merton folk' WM to Jenny Morris, 16 January 1884
'the condition of' Hammersmith Branch minutes, 14 June 1884, British Library
'Craig had been' *WMAWS*
492 'rag-tag-and-bobtail' Bernard Shaw, 'Morris as I Knew Him', *op. cit.*
'like going to Persia' Margaret McMillan, *The Life of Rachel McMillan*, J. M. Dent, 1927
'a beautiful address' Dollie Radford, ms. diary, 30 November 1884, William Andrews
Clark Memorial Library, University of California at Los Angeles
493 'All State churches' Hammersmith Branch minutes, 3 September 1884, British Library
'should be self-supporting' *ibid.*, 18 August 1884
'There was always' Hubert Bland, *Sunday Chronicle*, 26 May 1895
494 'was better than' WM to Andreas Scheu, 13 August 1884
'under the pretence' *Justice*, 26 January 1884
'tendency towards' Socialist League Manifesto, *The Commonweal*, February 1885
'Hyndman is thinking' Friedrich Engels to Karl Kautsky, 22 June 1884, *The
Correspondence of Marx and Engels 1846–1895*, Lawrence & Wishart, 1934
495 'As you know' WM to Georgiana Burne-Jones, 26 August 1883
'all hollow' WM to Jane Morris, 18 March 1884
'to desert' WM to Georgiana Burne-Jones, 1 June 1884
'to be more "politic"' WM to Andreas Scheu, 9 July 1884
496 'if I have' WM to Andreas Scheu, 18 July 1884
'What do you' WM to Andreas Scheu, 28 August 1884

496 'I am afraid' WM to Andreas Scheu, 13 August 1884
497 'What we have' George Bernard Shaw to Andreas Scheu, 26 October 1884, Laurence
'my flesh creeps' WM to Andreas Scheu, 8 October 1884
'I really begin' WM to Andreas Scheu, 6 December 1884
'Some people' *WMAWS*
Falstaff letter WM to unknown recipient, December 1884?
'were not beautiful' WM to Jenny Morris, 14 December 1884
498 'I don't know' WM to Andreas Scheu, 8 October 1884
'was decorated' J. Bruce Glasier, *William Morris and the Early Days of the Socialist Movement*, Longmans, Green & Co., 1921
499 'cram full' WM to Jenny Morris, 14 December 1884
'eager, intelligent' J. Bruce Glasier, *William Morris and the Early Days of the Socialist Movement, op. cit.*
500 'Does Comrade Morris' *ibid.*
'when I got up' WM to Jane Morris, 18 December 1884
'I found Aveling' WM to Andreas Scheu, 17 December 1884
501 'what a pleasure' WM to Andreas Scheu, 18 December 1884
'Last night came off' WM to Georgiana Burne-Jones, 24 December 1884
'I listened' *ibid.*
502 'I was angry' WM to James Joynes, Christmas Day 1884
'I have had' WM to Emma Shelton Morris, 26 December 1884
'There was a good' WM to Georgiana Burne-Jones, 28 December 1884
503 'It was as clear' Bernard Shaw, 'Morris as I Knew Him', *op. cit*
'WM uncomfortable' Cormell Price diary, January 1885, Price
'work for Merton' Philip Webb to WM, 3 February 1885, NAL
'the winter garden' WM to Georgiana Burne-Jones, 28 December 1884

CHAPTER FIFTEEN
504 'This morning' WM to Georgiana Burne-Jones, 28 (or 29?) December 1884
'in hot discussion' Cormell Price diary, 1 January 1885, Price
505 'Fellow Citizens' Socialist League Manifesto, *The Commonweal*, February 1885
506 'entirely dependent' ed. Stanley Weintraub, *Bernard Shaw, An Autobiography 1898–1950*, Max Reinhardt, 1971
'the learned' *WMAWS*
507 'or rather' *Socialist Diary*, 15 February 1887
508 'like a euphonium' *WMAWS*
'that gifted' *WMAWS*
'Our modern bourgeois' Socialist League Manifesto, *op. cit.*
509 'in a friendly' Henry Havelock Ellis, 'Eleanor Marx', *The Adelphi*, October 1935
'weak in *political*' WM to Andreas Scheu, 28 December 1884
'the only honest' Friedrich Engels to Edouard Bernstein, 29 December 1884, *Labour Monthly*, October 1933
'Chaucerian' Bernard Shaw to Harold Laski, 27 July 1945, Laurence
'After attending' Tom Mann, *Memoirs*, Labour Publishing Co., 1912
510 'like most of' WM to James Joynes, 3 February 1885
'primitive simplicity' Bernard Shaw to Harold Laski, *op. cit.*
'out of work' Georgiana Burne-Jones to Margaret Burne-Jones, 30 January 1885, Mackail notebooks, WMG
'a turnip bogie' WM to James Joynes, 25 December 1884
'when the crisis' Socialist League Manifesto, *op. cit.*
511 'it does seem' WM to J. Bruce Glasier, 27 July 1887

512 'not bad' WM to Jane Morris, 10 February 1885
'Dull and dirty' WM, *The Pilgrims of Hope*, 1885–6
513 'the deeper matters' *WMAWS*
'we were born' WM to James Frederick Henderson, 19 October 1885
'Too long' Herbert Burrows, 'To the People', *The Commonweal*, March 1886
514 'It speaks out' Socialist League Archives, IISH
515 'We do not' Catherine Holiday to Socialist League, 3 October 1885, *ibid.*
'please address' Georgiana Burne-Jones to Editor of *The Commonweal*, 30 September
1885, *ibid.*
'as a Socialist' WM to Wilfrid Scawen Blunt, 3 March 1885
'up to the eyes' *Intros*
'It makes me' Charles Faulkner to J. L. Mahon, 1 February 1885, IISH
'a great many' WM to Georgiana Burne-Jones, 28 February 1885
516 'a wretched Commercial' WM, 'Commercial War', lecture, 1885
'some very good' WM to Jenny Morris, 28 April 1885
'I was really' *ibid.*
517 'a queer book' WM to Georgiana Burne-Jones, 28 April 1885
'frugal meeting place' *WMAWS*
519 'At Hammersmith' Elizabeth Robins Pennell, *The Life and Letters of Joseph Pennell*,
Ernest Benn, 1930
'Positively I felt' George Gissing to Algernon Gissing, 24 November 1885, *The Collected
Letters of George Gissing*, Ohio University Press, 1991
'I shall be' WM to May Morris, 14 April 1885
'early days' May Morris to Andreas Scheu, 15 August 1889, IISH
520 'the little group' *WMAWS*
'It is a beautiful' WM to Georgiana Burne-Jones, summer 1887
522 'an institution' *WMAWS*
'a basket' Georgina Sime and Frank Nicholson, *Brave Spirits*, privately published, 1952
'He used to' H. G. Wells, *Experiment in Autobiography*, Victor Gollancz, London, 1934
523 'more or less' W. B. Yeats, *Autobiographies*, Macmillan, 1956
'Old Morris' C. R. Ashbee, ms. journals, 4 January 1886, King's College, Cambridge
'Why do people' W. B. Yeats, *Autobiographies, op. cit.*
'I looked' Bernard Shaw, 'Morris as I Knew Him', *WMAWS*, 1936
524 'rather a disloyal' May Morris to Bernard Shaw, 14 February 1886, British Library
525 'like a romantic' Elizabeth Robins Pennell, *The Life and Letters of Joseph Pennell, op. cit.*
'very rough jostles' Bernard Shaw, 'Morris as I Knew Him', *op. cit.*
'On Sunday' WM to Georgiana Burne-Jones, 27 May 1885
526 'one side' WM Socialist League survey for 1885, British Library
527 'commenced an assault' Edward Aveling, *The Commonweal*, October 1885
MR. SAUNDERS *The Daily News*, 22 September 1885
528 'the behaviour of' WM to Jane Morris, 22 September 1885
'Do you see' George Gissing to Algernon Gissing, 22 September 1885, *The Collected
Letters of George Gissing, op. cit.*
'I shall probably' 'The Poet and the Police, An interview with Mr. William Morris', *The
Pall Mall Gazette*, 23 September 1885
530 'leg-tied completely' WM to Jenny Morris, 26 October 1885
'much like this' WM to Georgiana Burne-Jones, 31 October 1885
'I go to' May Morris to Bernard Shaw, 10 November 1885, British Library
531 'I have had' WM to Oswald Birchall, 10 November 1885
'a funny twangling' WM to Emma Shelton Morris, 27 December 1885
'When some people' May Morris to Andreas Scheu, 25 December 1885, IISH

531 'As to the British' WM to F. S. Ellis, 26 December 1885
532 'I do not love' WM to Georgiana Burne-Jones, May 1886
'And I cling' *The Pilgrims of Hope*, 1885–6
'DO NOT VOTE' Socialist League pamphlet, IISH
533 'You will not' Friedrich Engels to Frederick Adolf Sorge, 29 April 1886, *Labour Monthly*, November 1933
'make running' WM to John Carruthers, 25 March 1886
'The Hyndman' WM to J. L. Mahon, 26 December 1885
'a mere faction' WM to John Carruthers, 25 March 1886
'immense mass' *WMAWS*
534 'As to Monday's' WM to John Glasse, 10 February 1886
535 'contemptible as' WM to John Carruthers, 25 March 1886
'a violent set' Secret memo: Mr Munro, Assistant Commandant, to Sir Edmund Henderson, 18 February 1886, Public Record Office
'Many thanks' WM to Edward Burne-Jones, 16 February 1886
'I had a brisk' WM to Jenny Morris, 9 August 1886
536 'I went to' Sam Mainwaring, *Freedom*, January 1897
'white-haired fool' *The Pilgrims of Hope*, 1885–6
'desperately uncomfortable' Bernard Shaw, *The Observer*, 6 November 1949
'did wilfully obstruct' Marylebone Police Court Summons, 18 July 1886, British Library
537 'He was impelled' H. G. Arnold, 'The War in Bell Street', *The Commonweal*, 24 July 1886
'many other known' Report of Hearing at Marylebone Police Court, 24 July 1886, Home Office files, Public Record Office
538 'May and I' WM to Jenny Morris, 14 August 1886
539 'Keep 1/11 to 13' Home Office file 144/166/A42480, Public Record Office
'as likely a place' Socialist League Archive, IISH
'in the form' WM to May Morris, May 1886
540 'all I could' WM to Jenny Morris, 26 September 1886
'a gross form' WM Socialist League survey for 1886, British Library
'looking like' Wilfrid Scawen Blunt, ms. diaries, 11 April 1887, Fitzwilliam
'On the whole' *WMAWS*
'deep green' WM to Jenny Morris, 9 April 1886
541 'sort of cosy' WM to Jane Morris, 15 April 1886
'a peculiar calm' Owen Carroll, 'William Morris among the Reds', 23 September 1933, Alf Mattison Archive, Brotherton Library, University of Leeds
543 'shooting stars' WM to Jenny Morris, 21 May 1886
'original Socialist' E. P. Thompson, 1976 postscript to *William Morris, Romantic to Revolutionary*, Merlin Press, 1977
'an air' *WMAWS*
544 'the sun should' George Wardle, 'Reminiscences of William Morris', Christmas 1897, British Library
'I am almost' WM to J. L. Mahon, 25 March 1886
'You would like' Jane Morris to Wilfrid Scawen Blunt, 16 January 1889, Faulkner
'the good man' WM to Jenny Morris, 16 January 1889, British Library
545 'There was a little' WM to Jenny Morris, 21 January 1889, Henderson
'I cannot for the life' WM to James Tocchati, 21 December 1893, WMG
'I demand' WM, 'The Society of the Future', lecture 1887
546 'It really would' WM to Jenny Morris, October 1886
548 'much admired' WM to Jane Morris, 25 November 1886

733

548 'we all felt' J. Bruce Glasier, *William Morris and the Early Days of the Socialist Movement, op. cit.*
'John Ball's Dream' *The Diary of Beatrice Webb*, 7 September 1890, ed. Norman and Jeanne MacKenzie, Virago, 1986
'in house after house' quoted Paul Thompson, *The Work of William Morris*, Heinemann, 1967
549 'a merrymaking' May Morris to Andreas Scheu, 23 November 1885, IISH
'We are among' May Morris to Andreas Scheu, 23 April 1886, *ibid.*
'extreme terror' May Morris to Andreas Scheu, 6 May 1886, *ibid.*
'my future son-in-law' WM to Theodore Watts-Dunton, 16 December 1886
'May is away' Jane Morris to Rosalind Howard, 23 August 1887, Castle Howard
550 'Mrs. Morris's daughter' Wilfrid Scawen Blunt, ms. diaries, 11 September 1887, Fitzwilliam
'I thought' Emma Shelton Morris to Jenny Morris, 19 April 1887, WMG

CHAPTER SIXTEEN

551 'positive genius' *WMAWS*
'unwarranted and extravagant' J. L. Mahon to Socialist League, 19 October 1885, IISH
'loose and disorderly' Thomas Binning to Socialist League, 3 June 1886, *ibid.*
'I should like' Will Binning to Socialist League, 29 June 1887, *ibid.*
'large barn-like' Hubert Bland, *Sunday Chronicle*, 26 May 1895
552 'It will be' Frank Kitz, *The Commonweal*, 5 February 1887
553 'a small circle' Frank Kitz obituary, *Justice*, 20 January 1923
'The study of' Joseph Lane, *An Anti-Statist Communist Manifesto*, quoted Florence Boos, *William Morris's Socialist Diary*, 1982
'a regular intriguer' WM to Henry F. Charles, 16 June 1887
'I wish he would' WM to J. L. Mahon, 15 January 1886
'that disreputable dog' WM to John Glasse, 23 September 1887
554 'Harry and I' May Morris to Andreas Scheu, 6 November 1886, IISH
'As for Socialism' WM to John Carruthers, 25 March 1886
'as a kind' WM to Jenny Morris, 9 March 1887
555 'I went down' *Socialist Diary*, 25 January 1887
'had clearly' *ibid.*, 26 January 1887
556 'the room' *ibid.*, 7 February 1887
'a wretched place' *ibid.*, 12 February 1887
'a tumble down' *ibid.*, 23 February 1887
557 'a scanty audience' *ibid.*, 21 March 1887
'no use grumbling' *ibid.*, 24 March 1887
'a big club' *ibid.*, 30 March 1887
'underfoot misery' *ibid.*, 21 March 1887
'I spoke last' *ibid.*, 21 March 1887
558 'I got my brother' Janet Grierson, *Isabella Gilmore*, SPCK, 1962
559 'I preach Socialism' quoted *ibid.*
'wretched looking country' WM to Jenny Morris, 23 April 1887
'the goodman' *Socialist Diary*, 27 April 1887
560 'a swell but ugly' WM to Jenny Morris, 23 April 1887
'soon swelled' *Socialist Diary*, 27 March 1887
561 'It was very' WM to Jenny Morris, 23 April 1887
'a blind, unguided' *The Newcastle Chronicle*, 12 April 1887
'in time' *Socialist Diary*, 27 March 1887
562 'all Classical art' *ibid.*, 27 January 1887

562 'the kind of book' WM to *The Pall Mall Gazette*, 2 February 1886
'great simplicity' WM to F. S. Ellis, 18 February 1886
'He would be' H. Halliday Sparling, *The Kelmscott Press and William Morris Master-Craftsman*, Macmillan, 1924

563 'I have now' WM to Georgiana Burne-Jones?, 25 August 1887
'a few pounds' WM to Jane Morris, 16 April 1887
'Tell me' WM, *The Odyssey*, 1887
'far more Norse' Oscar Wilde, *Pall Mall Magazine*, 5 November 1888

564 'a sort of fairy' WM to William Bell Scott, 5 December 1887
'interlude' WM to Georgiana Burne-Jones?, 24 September 1887
'A pair of' Bernard Shaw, 'Morris as Actor and Dramatist', *The Saturday Review*, 10 October 1896

565 'My lord' WM, *The Tables Turned; or Nupkins Awakened*, 1887, WMAWS
'happened to combine' Bernard Shaw, 'Morris as Actor and Dramatist', *op. cit.*
'capering forward' H. A. Barker, 'Notes on Morris and Socialism', 1897, Mackail notebooks, WMG

566 'a kind of artist' 'Honesty is The Best Policy', *The Commonweal*, 12 November 1887
'Owen Marx' 'Wings Astray', *The Commonweal*, 19 January 1889
'It is written' May Morris to John Drinkwater, 9 March 1912, Beinecke Rare Book and Manuscript Library, Yale University
'You probably' WM to Robert Browning, 7 November 1887

567 'Sir – Apropos' WM to *The Daily News*, 10 November 1887, 'Morris and Trafalgar Square' *JWMS*, Winter 1961

568 'Into the net' *The Commonweal*, 19 November 1887
'the police' *The Times*, 14 November 1887

569 'a sort of' *The Commonweal*, 19 November 1887
'A strange sensation' WM, *News from Nowhere*, 1890

570 'As to the Trafalgar' WM to William Bell Scott, 5 November 1887
'from an angry' WMAWS

572 'poor attempt' *The Times*, 19 December 1887
'There was to me' Mackail
'There lay' *The Commonweal*, 24 December 1887

573 'He threw' H. A. Barker, 'Notes on Morris and Socialism', *op. cit.*
'My husband' Jane Morris to Wilfrid Scawen Blunt, 30 November 1887, Faulkner

574 'Cunninghame Graham' WM to Bruce Glasier, 18 March 1887
Mrs Cunninghame Graham's At Home Walter Crane, *An Artist's Reminiscences*, Methuen 1907
'cordial congratulations' WM to Gabriela Cunninghame Graham, 26 November 1887
'So then we went' WM to Jenny Morris, 19 February 1888

575 'It is a tough' WM to Georgiana Burne-Jones?, 1887
'All this is' WM to J. Bruce Glasier, 19 May 1887
'True it would be' WM to J. Bruce Glasier, 15 August 1887

576 'I cannot shake off' WM to Georgiana Burne-Jones, March 1888

577 'to take steps' Socialist League minutes, IISH
'the damned business' J. Bruce Glasier, *William Morris and the Early Days of the Socialist Movement*, Longmans, Green & Co., 1921

578 'a sort of curse' WM to J. Bruce Glasier, 15 December 1888
'living death' Mackail
'The unbreakable' Philip Webb to J. W. Mackail, 4 June 1898, Mackail notebooks, WMG
'It is such' WM to Georgiana Burne-Jones, Easter Monday 1889

579 'Oh yes, it killed' Edward Burne-Jones, 12 February 1896, Lago

579 'going through' Wilfrid Scawen Blunt, ms. diaries, November 1888, Fitzwilliam
'a settled sentimental' Friedrich Engels to Laura Lafargue, 13 September 1886, *Frederich Engels, Paul and Laura Lafargue Correspondence*, Foreign Languages Publishing House, Moscow, 1959
'from 10 to 4' Edward Carpenter, conference report to the Sheffield Socialists, 17 July 1889, Sheffield City Archives
580 'Altogether though' quoted Edward Carpenter, *ibid.*
'After the glib' Edward Carpenter, *Freedom*, December 1896
581 'Well, Mr. Chairman' *WMAWS*
582 'I have been' WM to D. J. Nicoll, July 1890, Henderson
'often painful' Andreas Scheu, *Umsturzkeime*, Vienna, 1923
583 'All red-tapeism' *The Commonweal*, 16 August 1890
'I never wait' WM to J. Bruce Glasier, 5 December 1890, Henderson
'it is a troublesome' WM to Georgiana Burne-Jones, 9 December 1890, Mackail
'Few movements' *The Commonweal*, 15 November 1890
584 'a picture' Jane Morris to Wilfrid Scawen Blunt, 11 February 1890, Faulkner
'I suppose' WM to J. Bruce Glasier, 13 May 1889, Henderson
'if they brigaded' *WMAWS*
'a huge standing' WM, 'Looking Backward', *The Commonweal*, 22 June 1889
'four of which' *News from Nowhere*, 1890
587 'slightly constructed' Mackail
588 'Morris's views' Sydney Cockerell to Bernard Shaw, 17 April 1950, British Library
'that he had fallen' J. Bruce Glasier, *William Morris and the Early Days of the Socialist Movement*, *op. cit.*

CHAPTERS SEVENTEEN, EIGHTEEN, NINETEEN AND TWENTY:
Hammersmith, One: 1890–93, Hammersmith, Two: 1893–96, Norway 1896, Return to Kelmscott 1896 and after

For these final years the main source of information, besides Morris's family letters and May Morris's accounts, are Morris's brief day-to-day diaries for 1893, 1895 and 1896 in the British Library, and the interchange of letters with Philip Webb, now in the National Art Library. There is a particularly full and sensitive account of Morris in the 1890s in the last three chapters of the 1899 biography of Morris by J. W. Mackail, a period at which he was already observing Morris from within the circle of the Burne-Jones family. The important new source of information is the young Sydney Cockerell who was Morris's personal assistant in the 1890s, later becoming secretary to the Kelmscott Press. Cockerell's meticulous diaries are invaluable for their record of the tenor of Morris's last days.

On the Kelmscott Press: H. Halliday Sparling, *The Kelmscott Press and William Morris Master-Craftsman*, Macmillan, 1924; William S. Peterson, *The Kelmscott Press, A History of William Morris's Typographical Adventures*, Clarendon Press, Oxford, 1991; Paul Needham, Joseph Dunlap and John Dreyfus, *William Morris and the Art of the Book*, Pierpont Morgan Library, New York, and Oxford University Press, 1976; Duncan Robinson, *William Morris, Edward Burne-Jones and the Kelmscott Chaucer*, Gordon Fraser, 1982; Colin Franklin, *Printing and the Mind of Morris*, The Rampant Lions Press, Cambridge, 1986; Colin Franklin, *The Private Presses*, Studio Vista, 1969; Sir Basil Blackwell, Ray Watkinson and Anthony Eyre, *William Morris's Printing Press*, William Morris Society, 1983; John Dreyfus, 'Morris and the printed book', lecture, 1986, William Morris Society, 1989; Holbrook Jackson and James Shand, lectures on 'The Typography of William Morris', Double Crown Club, 2 May 1934; chapter on William Morris in Robin Kinross, *Modern Typography*, Hyphen Press, 1992; L. M. Newman, 'Harry Gage-Cole, Pressman', MATRIX 12, Winter 1992; Susan Otis

Thompson, *American Book Design and William Morris*, R. R. Bowker, New York, 1977.
On Morris's magic novels: chapter on 'The Later Romances' in J. M. S. Tompkins, *William Morris, an Approach to the Poetry*, Cecil Woolf, 1988; *The Romances of William Morris*, Cambridge University Press, 1987; Nancy J. Tyson, 'Art and Society in the Late Prose Narratives of William Morris', *Journal of Pre-Raphaelite Studies*, May 1978; John David Moore, 'The Vision of the Feminine in William Morris's *The Water of the Wondrous Isles*', *Journal of Pre-Raphaelite Studies*, May 1980; John R. Wilson, 'The Eve and the Madonna in Morris's *The Wood Beyond the World*', *Journal of Pre-Raphaelite Studies*, November 1983; Florence Boos, 'Gender Division and Political Allegory in the last Romances of William Morris', *Journal of Pre-Raphaelite Studies*, vol. 1, no. 2, 1992.
On Morris and the Arts and Crafts: records at Art Workers' Guild, London, and in Arts and Crafts Exhibition Society archive at National Art and Design Library; H. J. L. Massé, *The Art Workers' Guild*, Shakespeare Head Press, Oxford, 1935; Peter Stansky, *Redesigning the World: William Morris, the 1880s and the Arts and Crafts*, Princeton University Press, 1985; *Arts and Crafts Essays* by members of the Arts and Crafts Exhibition Society, Scribners, New York, 1893.
On Arts and Crafts generally: Gillian Naylor, *The Arts and Crafts Movement*, Studio Vista, 1971; Peter Davey, *Arts and Crafts Architecture*, Architectural Press, 1980; Margaret Richardson, *Architects of the Arts and Crafts Movement*, Trefoil Books, 1983; Isabelle Anscombe and Charlotte Gere, *Arts and Crafts in Britain and America*, Academy Editions, 1978; Lionel Lambourne, *Utopian Craftsmen*, Astragal, 1980; Elizabeth Cumming and Wendy Kaplan, *The Arts and Crafts Movement*, Thames & Hudson, 1991; Wendy Kaplan, *'The Art that is Life'*, catalogue of exhibition, Museum of Fine Arts, Boston; Leslie Greene Bowman, *American Arts and Crafts; Virtue in Design*, catalogue of collection at Los Angeles County Museum of Art.
On Art Communities and Simple Life: W. H. G. Armytage, *Heavens Below: Utopian Experiments in England, 1560–1960*, Routledge and Kegan Paul, 1961; Michael Jacobs, *The Good and Simple Life, Artists' Colonies in Europe and America*, Phaidon, 1985; David E. Shi, *The Simple Life, Plain Living and High Thinking in American Culture*, Oxford University Press, 1985.
On individual Arts and Crafts designers:
C. R. Ashbee: C. R. Ashbee, *An Endeavour towards the Teaching of John Ruskin and William Morris*, Essex House Press, 1901; Peter Stansky, *William Morris, C. R. Ashbee and the Arts and Crafts*, Nine Elms Press, 1984; Alan Crawford, *C. R. Ashbee, Architect, Designer and Romantic Socialist*, Yale University Press, 1985; Fiona MacCarthy, *The Simple Life, C. R. Ashbee in the Cotswolds*, Lund Humphries, 1981.
W. A. S. Benson: Peter Rose, 'W. A. S. Benson', *Journal of the Decorative Arts Society*, 1985.
Detmar Blow: Christopher Hussey, 'Hilles, Stroud, Gloucestershire – the home of Detmar Blow', articles in *Country Life*, 7 and 14 September 1940; Neville Lytton, portrait of Blow in *The English Country Gentleman*, Hurst & Blackett, 1915.
T. J. Cobden-Sanderson: *The Journals of Thomas Cobden-Sanderson, 1897–1922*, R. Cobden-Sanderson, 1926: T. J. Cobden-Sanderson, *The Arts and Crafts Movement*, Hammersmith Publishing Co., 1905; Marianne Tidcombe, *The Doves Bindery*, British Library, 1991.
Walter Crane: Walter Crane, *An Artist's Reminiscences*, Methuen, 1907; *William Morris to Whistler*, G. Bell, 1911; Isobel Spencer, *Walter Crane*, Studio Vista, 1975; eds. Greg Smith and Sarah Hyde, *Walter Crane, Artist, Designer and Socialist*, catalogue of exhibition, Whitworth Art Gallery, University of Manchester, 1989.
Lewis F. Day: Lewis F. Day, *Everyday Art: short essays on the arts not-fine*, Batsford, 1882; 'William Morris and his Art', *Art Journal* Annual, Easter 1899.

Eric Gill: Peter Faulkner, 'William Morris and Eric Gill', William Morris Society, 1975; Fiona MacCarthy, *Eric Gill*, Faber & Faber, 1989.

Ernest Gimson, and Sidney and Ernest Barnsley: Mary Comino, *Gimson and the Barnsleys*, Evans Brothers, 1980; Norman Jewson, *By Chance I Did Rove*, Roundwood Press, Kiveton, 1973; Mary Greensted, *The Arts and Crafts Movement in the Cotswolds*, Alan Sutton, Stroud, 1993; Annette Carruthers, *Edward Barnsley and his Workshop*, White Cockade, Wendlebury, 1982; David Pendery, 'Ernest Gimson's Work in Kelmscott', *JWMS*, Autumn 1993; W. R. Lethaby and others, *Ernest Gimson: His Life and Work*, Shakespeare Head Press, Stratford-upon-Avon, 1924.

Henry and Catherine Holiday: Henry Holiday, *Reminiscences of My Life*, Heinemann, 1914.

W. R. Lethaby: Godfrey Rubens, *William Richard Lethaby: His Life and Work, 1857–1931*, Architectural Press, 1986; *Architecture, Mysticism and Myth*, Perceval, 1891; *Form in Civilisation*, Oxford University Press, 1922; *Home and Country Arts*, 'Home and Country' Publications, 1923; ed. Sylvia Backemeyer and Theresa Gronberg, *W. R. Lethaby: Architect, Designer and Educator*, catalogue of exhibition at the Central School, London, Lund Humphries, 1984.

A. H. Mackmurdo: A. H. Mackmurdo, manuscript account of Arts and Crafts movement, William Morris Gallery.

Thomas Okey: Thomas Okey, *A Basketful of Memories*, J. M. Dent, 1930.

John Sedding: John Sedding, *Art and Handicraft*, Kegan Paul, Trench, Trübner, 1883.

C. F. A. Voysey: *Individuality*, Chapman & Hall, 1915; David Gebhard, *Charles F. A. Voysey, Architect*, Hennessy and Ingalls, Los Angeles, 1975; Duncan Simpson, *C. F. A. Voysey: an architect of individuality*, Lund Humphries, 1979; Stuart Durant, *C. F. A. Voysey*, Academy Editions, 1992.

Emery Walker: Dorothy Harrop, *Sir Emery Walker 1851–1933*, Nine Elms Press, 1986; John Brandon-Jones, 'Memories of William Morris in London: 7 Hammersmith Terrace', *Country Life*, 13 May 1964.

Philip Webb: W. R. Lethaby, *Philip Webb and his Work*, Oxford University Press, 1935; Mark Swenarton, 'Philip Webb: Architecture and Socialism in the 1880s', chapter in *Artisans and Architects: The Ruskinian Tradition in Architectural Thought*, Macmillan, 1989.

CHAPTER SEVENTEEN

589 'I pondered' WM, *A Dream of John Ball*, 1888

590 'He was in' *WMAWS*

591 'He had no hope' A. H. Mackmurdo, 'History of the Arts and Crafts Movement', unpublished ms., WMG
'It was an Adam' Sir William Rothenstein, *Men and Memories*, Faber & Faber, 1931
'then why don't' T. J. Cobden-Sanderson, *Journals 1879–1922*, 24 June 1883

592 'had been worn' Cobden-Sanderson autograph note on flyleaf of Morris's copy of *Das Kapital*

592 'pronounced it' T. J. Cobden-Sanderson, *Journals 1879–1922*, 13 October 1884
'in a serious' A. H. Mackmurdo, 'History of the Arts and Crafts Movement', *op. cit.*

593 'he was inclined' Sir William Rothenstein, *Men and Memories*, *op. cit.*

594 'the question of' C. R. Ashbee, *An Endeavour towards the Teaching of John Ruskin and William Morris*, Essex House Press, 1901
'I have little' WM to John Glasse, 10 February 1888

595 'Whatever else' WM report at AGM 1885, SPAB Archive
'spying the ball' C. R. Ashbee, 'William Morris', in series of portraits of masters of the AWG, ms. journals, King's College, Cambridge
'the general public' WM to W. A. S. Benson?, 31 December 1887

596 'a great deal of' C. R. Ashbee, ms. journals, 5 December 1887, King's College, Cambridge

'bookbinding should be' T. J. Cobden-Sanderson, *Journals 1879–1922*, 21 March 1885

'I believe they' WM to Jenny Morris, 17 October 1888

'amongst some stuff' Burne-Jones

597 'under the eyes' H. Halliday Sparling, *The Kelmscott Press and William Morris Master-Craftsman*, Macmillan, 1924

598 'I was in' WM to Jenny Morris, 2 November 1889, Henderson

'Art for the working' *WMAWS*

'When I first' Horner

599 'This, then,' 'The Socialist Ideal. Art', article for *The New Review*, January 1891

600 'All right, man' Sydney Gimson, *Random Recollections of the Leicester Secular Society*, Part 1, 1932, Leicestershire Records Office

601 'You are the most' Georgiana Burne-Jones to Sydney Cockerell, 13 May 1913, NAL

'It was then' Sydney Cockerell, *Friends*

602 'his lamps' W. A. S. Benson obituary, *The Times*, 9 July 1924

'everyone enjoys' Neville Lytton, *The English Country Gentleman*, 1925

'I wish I were' WM, 'The Beauty of Life', lecture, 1880

organisations in the Arts and Crafts movement Alan Crawford and Lynne Walker, paper to Victorian Society conference in Birmingham, 1978

603 'a soul reaction' Edward Pearson Pressey, editorial in *Country Time and Tide 4*, September 1903

604 'William Morris craze' Edward Bok in *The Ladies' Home Journal*, quoted David E. Shi, *The Simple Life*, 1985

605 'The complete building' First Proclamation of the Weimar Bauhaus, 1919

606 'a novel not' WM to J. Bruce Glasier, 18 September 1888

'a large slice' Cormell Price diary, 19 August 1888, Price

'the book will' WM to Samuel Reeves, 12 September 1888

'It will be' WM to Jenny Morris, 4 December 1888

607 'talking shop' *Intros*

'The line wanted' *ibid.*

608 'Whiles in the early' title page poem, *The House of the Wolfings*, 1888

'I am so pleased' Mackail

'turning printer' WM to F. S. Ellis, 21 November 1889

'the type of' Mackail

609 'bustling up' H. Halliday Sparling, *The Kelmscott Press*, *op. cit.*

'I began printing' 'A note by William Morris on his aims in founding the Kelmscott Press' 11 November 1895, *ibid.*

'as humbly' H. Halliday Sparling, *ibid.*

610 'It was a matter' 'A note by William Morris', *ibid.*

611 'as one might' H. Halliday Sparling, *ibid.*

612 'untold agonies' *Intros*

'too good a sense' Blunt, 31 December 1911

613 'What I wanted' 'A note by William Morris', *op. cit.*

'Walker and I' WM to F. S. Ellis, 21 November 1889, Mackail

614 'Its career' Jane Morris to Sydney Cockerell, 17 March 1898, NAL

'Pleased as I am' WM to Georgiana Burne-Jones?, 20 May 1891, Henderson

615 'the new type' T. J. Cobden-Sanderson, *Journals 1879–1922*, 4 April 1891

'amidst one thing' WM to Aglaia Coronio, 29 July 1891, Henderson

Kelmscott Press stock value Charles Harvey and Jon Press, *William Morris, Design and enterprise in Victorian Britain*, Manchester University Press, 1991

617 'Morris is beaten gold' John Ruskin to Sydney Cockerell, 1887, quoted H. Halliday
Sparling, *op. cit.*
'I do the books' WM to Philip Webb, 27 August 1894, Henderson
'beautiful books' 'A note by William Morris', *op. cit.*
619 'There were two' *WMAWS*
620 'a dismal little' Jenny Morris to Sydney Cockerell, 16 August 1898, British Library
'taking the doggeries' WM to Jane Morris, 10 May 1891, Mackail notebooks, WMG
622 'W. Morris Esq.' programme for 2nd Annual Dinner of the Kelmscott Press, 8
September 1893, Cheltenham
'looked like' Count Harry Kessler, diary for 20 June 1895, quoted MATRIX 12, Winter
1992
'should be a workman' H. Halliday Sparling, *op. cit.*
623 'We begin at' T. J. Cobden-Sanderson, *Journals 1879–1922*, 1894
624 'very little above' Jane Morris to Wilfrid Scawen Blunt, 29 December 1890, Faulkner
'still very ill' Jane Morris to Wilfrid Scawen Blunt, 28 February 1890, *ibid.*
'really went mad' Wilfrid Scawen Blunt, ms. diaries, 18 May 1893, Fitzwilliam
'My husband has' Jane Morris to Wilfrid Scawen Blunt, 13 April 1891, Faulkner
'My hand seems' WM to F. S. Ellis, February 1891, Henderson
626 'He looked' T. J. Cobden-Sanderson, *Journals 1879–1922*, 28 March 1891
'I am ashamed' WM to Georgiana Burne-Jones, 29 July 1891, Henderson
'almost the whole' WM to Philip Webb, 19 August 1891, *ibid.*
627 '4 French dogs' WM to Philip Webb, 11 August 1891, *ibid.*
'As for the town' WM to Emery Walker, 13 August 1891, *ibid.*
'hanging back' WM to Georgiana Burne-Jones, 27 August 1891, Mackail notebooks, WMG
'present from Abbeville' WM to Jane Morris, 8 August 1891, Henderson
'I chuckled over' WM to Emery Walker, 13 August 1891, *ibid.*
'very gay' WM to Jane Morris, 22 October 1891, *ibid.*
'cease being' WM to Georgiana Burne-Jones, 16 October 1890, Mackail
628 'I want much' Jane Morris to Wilfrid Scawen Blunt, 29 July 1891, Faulkner
'She is like' Wilfrid Scawen Blunt, ms. diaries, 18 November 1889, Fitzwilliam
'the most beautiful' *ibid.*, 7 September 1890
'Mrs. S.' Jane Morris to Wilfrid Scawen Blunt, 12 December 1889, Faulkner
'a more or less' Wilfrid Scawen Blunt, ms. diaries, summer 1888, Fitzwilliam
'the episode was' *ibid.*, summer 1889
'I think I was' Jane Morris to Wilfrid Scawen Blunt, 15 March 1888, Faulkner
'Heaven knows' Wilfrid Scawen Blunt, ms. diaries, 24 June 1891, Fitzwilliam
'George paired off' *ibid.*, 25 June 1891
629 'quiet interest' *ibid.*, November 1888
'Kelmscott was' *ibid.*, survey of 1889
'I wish you' WM to F. S. Ellis, 8 October 1888
'a Norwegian' Wilfrid Scawen Blunt, ms. diaries, 1889, Fitzwilliam
630 'at present' WM to J. Bruce Glasier, 14 October 1892, WMG
'When I went' Sydney Cockerell, ms. diary, 7 November 1892, British Library
631 'break down' Wilfrid Scawen Blunt, ms. diaries, 14 October 1892, Fitzwilliam
'of a frivolous' Jane Morris to Wilfrid Scawen Blunt, 22 November 1892, Faulkner
'extremely happy' Jane Morris to Wilfrid Scawen Blunt, 21 December 1892, *ibid.*
'Shaw is happy' WM to James Joynes, 27 December 1892, British Library
'Frightful cold' Kelmscott Visitors' Book, Christmas 1892, British Library
'Did you see' Burne-Jones
632 'I am sorry' WM to Jenny Morris, 30 March 1887
'Just fancy' WM to Jenny Morris, 4 March 1888

632 'If this' *The Commonweal*, 31 March 1888
   'ridiculous trio' Wilfrid Scawen Blunt, ms. diaries, 6 October 1892, Fitzwilliam
   'an out-and-out' M. P. Pariser, 'The Poet Laureateship, 1892', *Manchester Review*,
   Winter 1958–9
633 'sitting down' Sydney Cockerell, intro. to reissue of J. W. Mackail's *The Life of William
   Morris*, World's Classics, 1950
   'in recognition' Burne-Jones
   'Astounding news' Helen Richmond, ms. diary, 5 February 1894, Richmond-Meyrick
   family papers
   'It is all' Jane Morris to Wilfrid Scawen Blunt, 12 March 1894, Faulkner
   'I should like' Edward Burne-Jones to William De Morgan, A. M. W. Stirling, *William
   De Morgan and his Wife*, Henry Holt, New York, 1922
   'I worked hard' WM to Jenny Morris, 14 July 1892, British Library
634 'Spent 3 hours' Sydney Cockerell, ms. diary, 31 July 1892, British Library
   'And so' WM, *The Well at the World's End*, 1896
635 'I had not' WM to *The Spectator*, 20 July 1895, Henderson
   'I have' WM, *The Story of the Glittering Plain*, 1890
   'an old story' WM, *News from Nowhere*, 1890
636 'manly minded' WM, *The Well at the World's End*, 1896
   'a rather little' WM, *News from Nowhere*, 1890
   'springing up' WM, *The Water of the Wondrous Isles*, 1897
637 'I have heard' WM, 'The Wasted Land', incomplete ms. quoted *Intros*
   'To speak plainly' WM to Jane Cobden, 12 January 1884
638 'you must not' WM to J. Bruce Glasier, 24 April 1886
   'Politically he is' Blunt, 30 September 1891
   'How curiously' WM to James Joynes, 4 August 1891, British Library
   'I was thinking' WM to Georgiana Burne-Jones, August 1895, Henderson

CHAPTER EIGHTEEN
641 'William Morris' Olive Garnett diary, 2 December 1891, *Tea and Anarchy!*, ed. Barry C.
   Johnson, Bartlett's Press, Birmingham, 1989
   'moneys and books' Hammersmith Socialist Society minutes, 13 March 1891, British
   Library
642 'You will be' WM to Jenny Morris, 21 April 1892, British Library
   'nothing but' WM to Henry J. Wilson, 26 May 1895, Sheffield City Archive
   'The acts' 'A Socialist Poet on Bombs and Anarchism', interview in *Justice*, 27 January 1894
   'There's no dynamite' Walter Crane, *An Artist's Reminiscences*, Methuen, 1907
643 'There are doubtless' WM, 'Communism', lecture, 1893
   'a human point' WM to J. Bruce Glasier, 9 March 1892, Henderson
644 'The world is going' quoted Charles Harvey and Jon Press, *William Morris, Design and
   enterprise in Victorian Britain*, Manchester University Press, 1981
   'Since it seems' WM, 'Communism', lecture, 1893
   'Morris full of' Blunt, 16 November 1893
645 'a genuine new' WM to *The Daily Chronicle*, 10 November 1893, Henderson
   'one hideous Malebolge' H. M. Hyndman, *Further Reminiscences*, Macmillan, 1912
   'I sometimes have' WM to J. Bruce Glasier, 9 March 1892, Henderson
   'the Fabians relied' Bernard Shaw to Walter Crane, 15 December 1895, Laurence
646 'Your father' Edward Pease to May Morris, 24 April 1913, British Library
   'Experience has shown' Bernard Shaw to Walter Crane, 15 December 1895, Laurence
   'agitation' WM to Georgiana Burne-Jones, 7 December 1894, Mackail notebooks, WMG
   'She is so busy' Edward Burne-Jones to Mrs Watts, 17 December 1894, Fitzwilliam

647 'and I couldn't' WM to Jenny Morris, 23 December 1888
'Chaucer is' Burne-Jones
648 'with about sixty' Sydney Cockerell account in H. Halliday Sparling, *The Kelmscott Press*, Macmillan, 1924
'I wonder' Burne-Jones
'My eyes!' Mackail
'I have done' WM to Jenny Morris, 11 August 1894, British Library
'They are printing' WM to Jenny Morris, 22 August 1894, Henderson
649 'I have rhymed' WM to A. J. Wyatt, 26 February 1893, Henderson
'Finished the first' WM, ms. diary for 1893, British Library
'the ablest man' Sydney Cockerell, diary, 18 April 1892, *Friends*
'Our horror' Helen Thomas, *A Visit to William Morris*, The Whittington Press, Andoversford, 1963
'Yesterday I dined' WM to Jenny Morris, 25 June 1892, British Library
650 'quiet little house' Bernard Shaw to Janet Achurch, 7 July 1893, *Collected Letters 1874–97*, Laurence
'everything went well' Bernard Shaw, 'Morris as I Knew Him', 1936, *WMAWS*
May's stillborn child Joan Larkin in conversation with the author, 9 February 1994
'after completely' Hesketh Pearson, *Bernard Shaw*, Collins, 1942
'Sparling was' Hesketh Pearson, *GBS: A Postscript*, Collins, 1951
651 'May's married life' Jane Morris to Wilfrid Scawen Blunt, 24 May 1894, Faulkner
'May's position' Jane Morris to Wilfrid Scawen Blunt, 16 May 1896, *ibid.*
'There goes' Mabel Dolmetsch to H. G. Farmer, 27 November 1947, H. G. Farmer, *Bernard Shaw's Sister and her Friends*, E. J. Brill, Leiden, 1959
'I fear' May Morris to Andreas Scheu, 17 October 1896, IISH
'Mrs. Morris is' Wilfrid Scawen Blunt, ms. diaries, 6 October 1893, Fitzwilliam
652 'I found' *ibid.*, 15 August 1894
'We never had' *ibid.*, 27 January 1914
'The moon was' Jane Morris to Wilfrid Scawen Blunt, 28 August 1894, Faulkner
'liveliest old' Jane Morris to Wilfrid Scawen Blunt, 12 February 1889, *ibid.*
'Altogether my old' Mackail
'in extreme trouble' Bernard Shaw, 'Morris as I Knew Him', *op. cit.*
'In memory of' Philip Webb to WM, 20 August 1895, NAL
653 'much on a level' WM to *The Daily Chronicle*, 4 October 1895, Henderson
654 'I saw all' Mackail
'It is sad' Mackail
'The Wind's on' WM, 'For the Bed at Kelmscott', *Poems by the way*, 1891
655 'assemblage of' *The Times*, 30 December 1895
656 'That is a lie' R. Page Arnot, *William Morris: A Vindication*, Martin Lawrence, 1934
'He was ill' H. L. Hyndman, *Justice*, 10 October 1896
'I have *not*' quoted E. P. Thompson, *William Morris: Romantic to Revolutionary*, 1955
'The best way' Burne-Jones
'got up and worked' WM, ms. diary, 5 January 1896, British Library
657 'The blossom's white' 'She and He', 1896
658 'the old man' Angela Thirkell, *Three Houses*, Oxford University Press, 1931
659 'great doctor' WM to Philip Webb, 23 February 1896, NAL
'seek advice' Jane Morris to Lucy Orrinsmith, undated letter, WMG
'From being' Bernard Shaw to Robert Ross, 13 September 1916, Laurence
'Began a new' WM, ms. diary, 4 February 1896, British Library
'did an A' *ibid.*, 11 February 1896
'I don't feel' *ibid.*, 26 February 1896

659 'bothered with boils' WM to Philip Webb, 11 September 1885, NAL
660 'weary dark' Jane Morris to Wilfrid Scawen Blunt, 20 April 1896, Faulkner
'the grass well grown' WM to Georgiana Burne-Jones, 27 April 1896, Henderson
'to get rid' Philip Webb to WM, 28 April 1896, NAL
'There the murder' WM to Philip Webb, 4 May 1896, Henderson
661 'fairly good' Blunt, 19 May 1896
'quite spoiled' WM, ms. diary, 19 May 1896, British Library
'Beasts! Pigs!' Blunt, 31 May 1896
'belly-parts' WM to Philip Webb, 6 June 1896, NAL
'I toddle about' ibid., 14 June 1896, NAL
'his food' Jane Morris to Wilfrid Scawen Blunt, 27 June 1896, Faulkner
662 'a most exceedingly' WM to Philip Webb, 1 July 1896, NAL
'When Morris' Burne-Jones
'such a book!' Mackail
663 'This has been' H. M. Hyndman, Justice, 10 October 1896

CHAPTER NINETEEN
664 'The doomed ship' WMAWS
665 'the voyage' John Carruthers to May Morris, 23 February 1913, British Library
'he roamed' WMAWS
666 'a strong scientific' WM to Philip Webb, 27 July 1896, NAL
'a sick man's' Blunt, 31 May 1896
'a dramatic entry' WM to Philip Webb, 27 July 1896, NAL
'many animated' John Carruthers to May Morris, 23 February 1913, British Library
667 'better in spite' Sydney Cockerell, ms. diary, 18 August 1896, British Library
'Papa has arrived' Jane Morris to May Morris, 18 August 1896, Mackail notebooks, WMG
'Dearest own child' WM to Jenny Morris, 20 August 1896, Henderson
'folks would think' Cormell Price diary, 6 September 1896, Price
'at present' WM to Thomas Wardle, 26 August 1896, Mackail
'her bowed head' W. Graham Robertson, Time Was, Hamish Hamilton, 1931
668 'the screaming horrors' Sydney Cockerell, ms. diary, 11 September 1896, British Library
'Morris is dying' T. J. Cobden-Sanderson, Journals 1879–1922, 12 September 1896
669 'WM enjoyed' Sydney Cockerell, ms. diary, 21 September 1896, British Library
'Mrs. de Morgan' Blunt, 3 September 1896
'as he had' Wilfrid Scawen Blunt, ms. diaries, 3 September 1896, Fitzwilliam
'came in like' Blunt, 28 September 1896
670 'Come soon' Mackrail
'very quiet' Sydney Cockerell, ms. diary, 4 October 1896, British Library
'the weakness was' Edward Burne-Jones to George Howard, 5 October 1896, Castle Howard
'a great comfort' Sydney Cockerell, ms. diary, 2 October 1896, British Library
'as gently' Burne-Jones
'bravely' Sydney Cockerell ms. diary, 4 October 1896, British Library
'The face was' ibid., 3 October 1896
'He is the most' Blunt, 4 October 1896
'be of any use' ibid., 5 October 1896
671 'I found Mrs. Morris' Wilfrid Scawen Blunt, ms. diaries, 6 October 1896, Fitzwilliam
'as though' Sydney Cockerell to Georgiana Burne-Jones, 9 October 1896, British Library
'He led us' Cormell Price, quoted Mackail notebooks, WMG
'the world is' Henrietta Morris to Sydney Cockerell, 9 October 1896, British Library

671 'A poet' *The Times*, 5 October 1896
'the most genuine' *The Daily News*, 5 October 1896
'awakening aesthetic' *The Times*, 5 October 1896
672 'the force that drew' *ibid.*
'a little uncouth' *The Daily Telegraph*, 5 October 1896
'I cannot help' Robert Blatchford, *The Clarion*, 10 October 1896
'but the complete' *Justice*, 17 October 1896
'how the heart of' *Labour Leader*, 17 October 1896
'William Morris' *Bjarki*, 24 October, quoted Ruth Ellison, 'Icelandic Obituaries of William Morris', *JWMS*, Autumn 1988

CHAPTER TWENTY
673 'own cherished design' Burne-Jones
'Avalon gets to' Edward Burne-Jones to Dr Evans, 29 June 1896, Fitzwilliam
'obviously very poor' *The Daily Chronicle*, 7 October 1896
674 'look coeval with' Bernard Shaw to Frances Dillon, 21 November 1908, Laurence
'sadly white' *ibid.*
675 'the simplest barn' William E. Fredeman, 'William Morris' Funeral', *JWMS*, Spring 1966
'I want to get' Mackail
676 'As unknown' Morris's funeral sermon, recorded 11 October 1896, Mackail notebooks, WMG
'could be heard' Burne-Jones
'It seems to me' Lethaby
'the most hideous' WM to *The Daily News*, 30 January 1889, Henderson
677 'Mrs. Morris's visit' Wilfrid Scawen Blunt, ms. diaries, 29 November 1896, Fitzwilliam
'The pain touched woman' Philip Webb to Jane Morris, 18 January 1899, British Library
'Majestic . . . Mournful' Janet Ashbee, Ashbee journals, summer 1899, King's College, Cambridge
678 'Oh Sydney' Jenny Morris to Sydney Cockerell, 23 September 1897, British Library
'infinitely pathetic' Sydney Cockerell to W. R. Lethaby, 28 December 1896, British Library
'incapable and brutal' Jane Morris to Sydney Cockerell, 6 June 1910, NAL
'flashes of her old self' May Morris to Sydney Cockerell, 13 March 1934, NAL
'I often walk here' quoted Katharine Adams to Sydney Cockerell, 4 November 1934, *Best of Friends*
'baffling clouds' Sydney Cockerell to Georgiana Burne-Jones, 9 August 1915, NAL
'little, very upright' Angela Thirkell, *Three Houses*, Oxford University Press, 1931
679 'clear flame-like' J. W. Mackail, Georgiana Burne-Jones obituary, *The Times*, 4 February 1920
'At this fair oak' Faulkner
'a miracle of beauty' Wilfrid Scawen Blunt, ms. diaries, 26 September 1911, Fitzwilliam
'moving with dignity' Basil Blackwell, 'More about Miss Lobb', *The Bookseller*, 27 October 1962
680 'in a more sensible' Bernard Shaw, quoted *The Times*, 22 October 1934
'stentorian vigour' Bernard Shaw to Henry Salt, 7 December 1934, Laurence
'made by' Catalogue of Sale at Kelmscott Manor, 19 and 20 July 1939, WMG

Acknowledgements

I am grateful for facilities and information from the following institutions, and for the relevant permissions to quote:

Bad Ems Town Archive; the Bancroft Library, University of California at Berkeley; the Beinecke Rare Book and Manuscript Library, Yale University; the Bodleian Library, Oxford; Boston Public Library Rare Books Collection; the British Library Manuscripts Room; the British Library Newspaper Library; the Brotherton Library, University of Leeds; Duke University, Durham, North Carolina; Exeter College, Oxford; the Syndics of the Fitzwilliam Museum, Cambridge; the National Library of Iceland; the International Institute of Socialist History, Amsterdam; Leek Library, Nicholson Institute; Morden Library Local Collection; the Oxford Union; the Public Record Office, Home Office papers; the Royal Society of Arts Library; the John Rylands Library, University of Manchester; Worcester College, Oxford. Also to Felicity Ashbee for permission to quote from her father C. R. Ashbee's journals in King's College Library, Cambridge; Lorraine Price for her help in making accessible the Price family papers; Christopher Walker for his assistance with the Richmond-Meyrick family papers; and the Howard family for permission to quote from the Castle Howard archives, York.

For assistance well beyond the bounds of duty I need to thank:

Alan Powers at the Art Workers' Guild; Stephen Wildman at Birmingham Museums and Art Gallery; Christine Hopper at Bradford City Art Gallery, Cartwright Hall; Christopher Sheppard at the Brotherton Collection, University of Leeds; Eeyan Hartley, Keeper of Archives at Castle Howard; George Breeze, Helen Brown and Sophia Wilson at Cheltenham Museum and Art Gallery; Jeffrey Seddon at Epping Forest Museum; Simon Jervis, Paul Woudhuysen and Elizabeth Orton at the Fitzwilliam Museum, Cambridge; Anna Manthorpe at Hammersmith and Fulham Archives; Dóra Ásgeirdóttir at the Embassy of Iceland; Donald and Pat Chapman at Kelmscott Manor; Douglas Matthews at the London Library; D. C. R. West at Marlborough College

Archive; Tish Newland at the Marx Memorial Library; Meg Sweet at the National Art and Design Library Archive; Terence Pepper at the National Portrait Gallery Archive; Bernard Nurse at the Society of Antiquaries of London; Cecily Greenhill at the Society for the Protection of Ancient Buildings; Anders Clason of the Swedish Embassy; Stephen Astley and Lionel Lambourne at the Victoria and Albert Museum; Jennifer Harris at the Whitworth Art Gallery, University of Manchester; Norah Gillow, Peter Cormack and Liz Wood at the William Morris Gallery, Walthamstow; David Rodgers at the William Morris Society, Hammersmith.

Dr Winston Leigh gave a very helpful professional opinion on the history of epilepsy in the Morris family. I am grateful for his time and patience. I am also indebted to Elaine Quigley for her expert assessment of William Morris's handwriting.

In my travels in pursuit of Morris & Co. stained glass I would like to thank the following for opening their churches to me specially and supplying useful background information:
Rev. Peter Atkinson at All Saints, Dedworth; Rev. Roy Davis at All Saints', Selsley; Rev. R. I. Davison at Christ Church, Bishopswearmouth, Sunderland; Rev. Edward Farley at St Edward the Confessor, Cheddleton; Adrian Gunning at St Mary Magdalene, Paddington; Rev. Canon C. J. Hawthorn at St Martin's-on-the-Hill, Scarborough; Fr Frederick Jackson at St Michael and All Angels, Brighton; Rev. Ben de la Mare at St Oswald's, Durham; Ernest Paulson, St Helen's, Darley Dale; Prebendary Eric Rastall at All Saints, Denstone; Rev. Oliver Simon, St Michael and St Mary Magdalen, Easthampstead; Rev. G. C. Thomas, All Saints, Middleton Cheney; Rev. Keith Yates, Holy Trinity Church, Sloane Street.

My special thanks for help, information, hospitality and the flood of conversation and discussion that has made the research for this biography so pleasurable:
Floss Adkins; Gary L. Aho; Dr Ian Allan; Philip Athill; Colin Banks; James E. Benjamin; Sanford Berger; Detmar and Isabella Blow; Professor Florence Boos; Marilyn Carter; Eileen Cassavetti; Philip Clayton; Alan Crawford; Brooke Crutchley; Jane Darke; John Dreyfus; Penelope Fitzgerald; Richard Garnett; Mr and Mrs C. Gazely; David Gentleman; Candida Lycett Green; Laura and Christopher Hampton; Thomas Hinde; Julia Ionides; James Joll; Joan Larkin; Magnus Magnusson; Jan Marsh; Margaret Marshall; Christopher Miele; Dorothy W. Morgan; Dawn Morris; Linda Parry; Adam Pollock; David Puttnam; John Randle; Dr Bernard Richards; Andrew Saint; Nicholas Salmon; Douglas E. Schoenherr; Lionel Selwyn; Fr Brocard Sewell; Peyton Skipwith; Frances Spalding; the late Heather Tanner; Ina Taylor; Kate Thirkell; Anthony Thwaite; Ray Watkinson; Allan Wilkinson.

During my research I have much appreciated the friendship and generous encouragement of Professor Norman Kelvin, nearing the end of his own thirty years' labour on the *Collected Letters of William Morris*. His meticulous approach has been a constant inspiration.

My successive literary editors, Philip Howard of *The Times* and Michael Ratcliffe of *The Observer*, deserve thanks for their patience with and interest in this project. An unknown facet of the literary editors' task is their nurturing of their own reviewers' books in progress. My colleague Nicci Gerrard has also been warm in her support. Christopher Driver read the first draft of my typescript and his comments have, as always, been invaluable.

Betty Wilson transferred this book from manuscript on to word processor with great attentiveness and skill.

Giles de la Mare, my editor at Faber and Faber, has given much good advice over my five years' work on William Morris. Both he and Charles Elliott, my editor at Knopf, have been unstinting in their enthusiasm for what turned into an epic enterprise. I was glad of Elfreda Powell's and Anthony Turner's careful copy-editing, and Stephen Stuart-Smith's sympathetic co-ordination of the final text. Working with Ron Costley on the design for *William Morris* has been as pleasureable as it was for *Eric Gill*.

List of Illustrations and Acknowledgements

BLACK AND WHITE

749

28 Dante Gabriel Rossetti, *carte de visite*. Price family collection.

29 *Ford Madox Brown*, pencil drawing. National Portrait Gallery, London.

30 *Lizzie Siddal*, pencil drawing, present whereabouts unknown. Photograph, Fitzwilliam Museum, Cambridge.

31 *Jane Burden*, pencil drawing. William Morris Gallery, Walthamstow.

32 *Study of Janey as Guinevere*, pencil drawing. Manchester City Art Galleries.

33 Georgiana Macdonald, photograph. Georgiana Burne-Jones, *Memorials*, 1904.

34 Edward Burne-Jones, photograph. Jeremy Maas collection.

35 Design for Red House, pen and ink. Victoria & Albert Museum, London.

36 Red House interior. *Country Life*.

37 Philip Webb portrait, watercolour. National Portrait Gallery, London.

38 *Study of Mrs Morris*, pencil and Indian ink. Victoria & Albert Museum, London.

39 Jane Morris *carte de visite*. Price family collection.

40 May Morris, photograph. William Morris Gallery, Walthamstow.

41 Cartoon for 'Artemis', Indian ink, chalk and wash. Carlisle Museums and Art Gallery.

42 *Knights*, sketch from Morris notebook. British Library, London.

43 *Flowers*, sketch from Morris notebook. British Library, London.

44 'The Legend of St George' design, pen and wash. Victoria & Albert Museum, London.

45 William Morris, photograph. William Morris Gallery, Walthamstow.

46 John Ruskin and Dante Gabriel Rossetti, photograph. Jeremy Maas collection.

47 No. 26 Queen Square. Victoria & Albert Museum, London.

48 No. 16 Cheyne Walk. Photograph by Emery Walker. National Portrait Gallery, London.

49 Group photograph at No. 16 Cheyne Walk. Photograph by William Downey. Virginia Surtees.

50 Jane Morris seated, photograph. St Bride Printing Library, London.

51 Jane Morris reclining, photograph. St Bride Printing Library, London.

52 *Mrs William Morris reading*, pencil drawing. Ashmolean Museum, Oxford.

53 *Aglaia Coronio*, pastel drawing. Victoria & Albert Museum, London.

54 Aglaia Coronio, *carte de visite*. Hastings Museum and Art Gallery.

55 *Marie Spartali*, pastel drawing. Fogg Art Museum, Harvard University.

56 *Maria Zambaco*, pencil drawing. Private collection. Photograph, Jeremy Maas.

57 View of Bad Ems. Bad Ems town archive.

58 The Kesselbrunnen at Bad Ems. Bad Ems town archive.

59 Landscape near Reykjavík. Hulton Deutsch Collection.

60 Eiríkr Magnússon photograph. National Library of Iceland.

61 Kelmscott Manor, the east front. RCHME Crown Copyright.

62 *Jenny Morris*, pastel drawing. The Society of Antiquaries, Kelmscott Manor.

63 *May Morris*, pastel drawing. The Society of Antiquaries, Kelmscott Manor.

64 The attics at Kelmscott Manor. William Morris Gallery, Walthamstow.

65 *Mrs William Morris sewing*, pencil drawing. Christie's, London.

66 William Morris, photograph. William Morris Gallery, Walthamstow.

67 The Morris & Co. showrooms. William Morris Gallery, Walthamstow.

68 Thomas Wardle, photograph. Christine Woods.

69 Elizabeth Wardle and pupils, photograph. Staffordshire County Council Archives.

70 The Morris and Burne-Jones families, photograph. National Portrait Gallery, London.

71 The Morris and Burne-Jones children, photograph. By courtesy of the Director and University Librarian, the John Rylands Library, University of Manchester.

72 Emma Shelton Morris, photograph. William Morris Gallery, Walthamstow.

73 Kelmscott House. Hammersmith and Fulham Archives, London.

74 The Boat Race at Hammersmith. Hammersmith and Fulham Archives, London.

75 Jenny Morris, photograph. William Morris Gallery, Walthamstow.

ILLUSTRATIONS IN TEXT

Index

755

214, 266, 358, 424, 565, 649

ferocity 3, 26, 29, 43, 59, 90, 113, 128, 133, 151,
159, 176, 209–10, 355, 382, 412, 415, 421, 478,
497, 542, 565, 577, 581, 649, 652–3, 661

feuds, propensity for 108, 129, 341–7, 378, 433,
495, 501, 533, 553

fluency, creative 74, 100, 142, 147, 262, 357–9,
403, 444–5, 460, 562

generosity 65, 109, 214, 371, 442, 552

geniality 157, 523, 601, 609, 649

greed 134–5, 151, 388

handwriting 269, figs. 20, 32, 34, 51, plates 14,
38, 90

humour, sense of 150, 219, 425, 430, 477, 528,
566, 574, 617, 626–7

imagination, quality of 36, 39–40, 43, 267–8,
463–4, 542–3, 627

hyper energy 49–50, 134, 230, 234–5, 246, 331,
419, 458, 499, 522, 615

innovation, urge for 350–4, 360, 400–1, 403–4,
406–7, 444, 609–10

insularity 86, 90, 234, 327, 372, 402

knowledge, breadth of 5, 8, 35, 42, 60, 91, 216,
305

male badinage, dependence on 97, 150, 162,
170–1, 280–1, 593

masochistic streak 118, 130–1, 375, 525–6,
539–40, 557–8

mood, swings of 29, 49–50, 95, 139, 295, 458

productivity 262, 357, 361, 372, 458–9, 486, 513,
562, 633–4

purism 260, 378, 397, 452, 480, 493–4, 532–3,
552, 594–6

recall, precision of 2, 10, 18–19, 20, 36, 38

resilience 148, 198, 358, 388–9, 578, 626–7,
662–3

reticence 59, 139, 188, 221, 226, 258

ruthlessness 116, 340, 347, 387, 480, 490, 497

skill, manual 29, 133, 203, 265, 268–9, 408,
590–1

smell, sense of 1, 82, 397, 654

speech, manner of 58, 60, 69, 419, 475, 499, 520,
542, 560–1, 573, 580

stoicism 32–3, 291–2, 302–3, 371–2, 545, 575,
638–9

versatility i, 133, 262, 562–3

victimization, collusion in 79, 134–5, 162, 169,
216, 226

see also health; sexual orientation; views

Charles, Fred (also Slaughter) 578, 641

Charles, Henry 505, 552

Charleston, Firle 161

Charleville, Countess of 411

Chartists, see political connections

Chartres, Morris in 82, 87–9

Chaucer, Geoffrey 77, 91, 271, 647
Canterbury Tales, The 154, 199
Legend of Good Women, The 160
Romaunt of the Rose, The 360
Troilus and Criseyde 190

Chaucer, Kelmscott, see Kelmscott Press

Chesterfield, Morris in 96, 517

Chicago Anarchists case 566, 577

Chichester Cathedral 653

Children of the New Forest, The (Captain Frederick
Maryatt) 41

chintzes, see textiles, printed

Chipping Campden, see Ashbee, C. R.

Chiswick, Morris in 9, 326–7, 556, 577

Chiswick Press 203, 606, 607, 615

Christian Socialism, see religious affiliations

Christian Socialist, The 484

Christie Johnstone (Charles Reade) 497–8

church furnishings, see embroideries; interiors;
stained glass

Churchill, Lord Randolph 486

Cirencester, Morris in 438

Clark, Kenneth, Baron Clark 414

Clarion, The 672

Clarke, William J. 500–1, 505

Clarkson, Thomas of Preston 357

Clay Cross, Morris in 96

clay modelling, Morris's 108, 133

Clayton & Bell 176

clients, Morris's: see Bagehot, Walter; Bell, Sir
Isaac Lowthian; Blunt, Wilfrid Scawen;
Bodley, G. F.; Cowper-Temple, William;
D'Arcy, William Knox; Dilke, Sir Charles;
Dunlop, Walter; Foster, Birket; Howard,
Rosalind; Ionides, Alexander; Lorillard,
Catherine; Prinsep, Valentine; Westminster,
the Duke of

Clouds, East Knoyle 248, 406

Clutton and Burges 108

Cobbett, William 336, 468

Cobden, Jane 637, plate 76

Cobden-Sanderson, Anne (*née* Cobden) 526, plate
76

Cobden-Sanderson, Thomas James (formerly
Sanderson) 456, 526, 591–2, 596, 623, 626,
668, plate 76 see also Doves Bindery; Doves
Press

Cockerell, Douglas 623, 662

Cockerell, Sir Sydney plate 111
early history 600–1
relations with Morris and family 19, 396, 522,
600, 660, 661, 664, 667–71, 678
at Kelmscott Press 601–2, 615–6, 634, 651
as Morris's executor x–xii, 413, 668
as Director of Fitzwilliam Museum 600

Cole, G. D. H. xvi, 414, 548, 587

Cole, Sir Henry 167–8, 212

Cole, Dame Margaret 414

collections, Morris's:
of metalwork 396; of paintings 113, 123, 195; of
pottery 396
of rare books and manuscripts 202, 204, 216, 240,
485, 592, 607, 660, 662
of textiles 317, 396, 402, 403, 445, 674

Collectivists, the 512, 556

Collins, Charles 73, 86

Collins, W. 597, plate 110

Colvin, Sidney 338

Combe, Thomas 73

Comely, Philip, and Mrs. 316

Committee of Fifteen, The 592